Series Editors:
Steven F. Warren, Ph.D.
Joe Reichle, Ph.D.

**Communication
and Language
Intervention
Series**

Volume 2

Enhancing Children's Communication

Also available in the Communication
and Language Intervention Series:

Volume 1
*Causes and Effects in Communication
and Language Intervention*
edited by Steven F. Warren, Ph.D.
and Joe Reichle, Ph.D.

Communication
and Language
Intervention
Series

Volume 2

Enhancing Children's Communication
Research Foundations for Intervention

Edited by

Ann P. Kaiser, Ph.D.
Professor of Special Education
and Psychology and Human Development
Peabody College of Vanderbilt University
Nashville, Tennessee

and

David B. Gray, Ph.D.
National Center for Medical Rehabilitation Research
National Institute of Child Health and
Human Development
Rockville, Maryland

·P·A·U·L·H·
BROOKES
PUBLISHING Cº

Baltimore· London· Toronto· Sydney

Paul H. Brookes Publishing Co.
P.O.Box 10624
Baltimore, Maryland 21285-0624

(This work may be reproduced in whole or part for the official use of the
United States Government or any authorized agency thereof.)
This book is based on the conference, "The Social Uses of Language:
Pathways to Success," June, 1990, sponsored by The National Institute of
Child Health and Human Development and the John F. Kennedy Center for
Research on Education and Human Development, held at Vanderbilt
University.

Typeset by The Composing Room of Michigan, Inc., Grand Rapids, Michigan.
Manufactured in the United States of America by
The Maple Press Company, York, Pennsylvania.

This book is printed on recycled paper.

Library of Congress Cataloging-in-Publication Data

Enhancing children's communication : research foundations for
   intervention / edited by Ann P. Kaiser and David B. Gray.
         p.   cm.—(Communication and language intervention series :
2)
   Includes bibliographical references and index.
   ISBN 1-55766-076-X
   1. Learning disabled children—Language.   2. Language disorders in
children—Treatment.   3. Speech therapy.   4. Social interaction in
children.   I. Kaiser, Ann P.   II. Gray, David B.   III. Series.
LC4704.85.E54   1993
371.91′4—dc20   92-21039
                                                                      CIP

(British Library Cataloguing-in-Publication data are available from the British
Library.)

Contents

Series Preface   ix
Editorial Advisory Board   xi
Volume Preface   xiii
Contributors   xv
Acknowledgments   xix

PART I   Perspectives on Intervention

Chapter 1   Introduction: Enhancing Children's Social
             Communication
                   Ann P. Kaiser   3

Chapter 2   Then, Now, and the Path Between:
             A Brief History of Language Intervention
                   Diane Bricker   11

PART II   Effective Intervention in the Social
          Use of Language

Chapter 3   Can Developmentally Delayed Children's
             Language Development Be Enhanced
             Through Prelinguistic Intervention?
                   Paul J. Yoder and Steven F. Warren   35

Chapter 4   Parent-Implemented Language Intervention:
             An Environmental System Perspective
                   Ann P. Kaiser   63

Chapter 5   Language Learning Through Augmented
             Means: The Process and its Products
                   Mary Ann Romski and Rose A. Sevcik   85

Chapter 6   Developing an Initial Communicative
             Repertoire: Applications and Issues
             for Persons with Severe Disabilities
                   Joe Reichle, James Halle,
                   and Susan Johnston   105

PART III   Shared Meanings and Important Partnerships
in Communication

Chapter 7   "Don't Talk to Him; He's Weird:" A Social
Consequences Account of Language
and Social Interactions
Mabel L. Rice 139

Chapter 8   Facilitating Children's Social-Communicative
Interactions Through the Use of Peer-Mediated
Interventions
Michaelene M. Ostrosky, Ann P. Kaiser,
and Samuel L. Odom 159

Chapter 9   Communicating the Meaning of Events
Through Social Referencing
Tedra A. Walden 187

Chapter 10 Affective Development and Communication
in Young Children with Autism
Connie Kasari, Marian Sigman, Nurit
Yirmiya, and Peter Mundy 201

Chapter 11 Speech Intelligibility and Communicative
Competence in Children
Raymond D. Kent 223

PART IV   Foundations for Enhancing the Effectiveness
of Intervention

Chapter 12 Programming Conceptual and Communication
Skill Development: A Methodological
Stimulus-Class Analysis
William J. McIlvane, William V. Dube,
Gina Green, and Richard W. Serna 243

Chapter 13 Acquisition of Early Object Labels: The Roles
of Operating Principles and Input
Carolyn B. Mervis and Jacquelyn Bertrand 287

Chapter 14 Structuring Environmental Input To Facilitate
Generalized Language Learning by Children
with Mental Retardation
Howard Goldstein 317

Chapter 15 Speech and Language Abilities of Children
with Down Syndrome: A Parent's Perspective
Siegfried M. Pueschel and
Marita R. Hopmann 335

PART V   Perspectives on the Future

Chapter 16 Parent Perspectives: Best Practice and
Recommendations for Research
Diane M. Crutcher 365

Chapter 17   Early Communication and Language
Intervention: Challenges for the 1990s
and Beyond
        Steven F. Warren 375

Author Index 397
Subject Index 409

Series Preface

THE PURPOSE OF THE *Communication and Language Intervention Series* is to provide meaningful foundations for the application of sound intervention designs to enhance the development of communication skills across the life span. We are endeavoring to achieve this purpose by providing readers with presentations of state-of-the-art theory, research, and practice.

In selecting topics, editors, and authors, we are not attempting to limit the contents of this series to those viewpoints with which we agree or which we find most promising. We are assisted in our efforts to develop the series by an editorial advisory board consisting of prominent scholars representative of the range of issues and perspectives to be incorporated in the series.

We trust that the careful reader will find much that is provocative and controversial in this and other volumes. This will be necessarily so to the extent that the work reported is truly on the so-called cutting edge, a mythical place where no sacred cows exist. This point is demonstrated time and again throughout this volume as the conventional wisdom is challenged (and occasionally confirmed) by various authors.

Readers of this and other volumes are encouraged to proceed with healthy skepticism. In order to achieve our purpose, we take on some difficult and controversial issues. Errors and misinterpretations are inevitably made. This is normal in the development of any field, and should be welcomed as evidence that the field is moving forward and tackling difficult and weighty issues.

Well-conceived theory and research on development of both children with and children without disabilities is vitally important for researchers, educators, and clinicians committed to the development of optimal approaches to communication and language intervention. For this reason, each volume in this series includes chapters pertaining to both development and intervention.

The content of each volume reflects our view of the symbiotic relationship between intervention and research: Demonstrations of what may work in intervention should lead to analyses of promising discoveries and insights from developmental work that may in turn fuel further refinement and development by intervention researchers.

An inherent goal of this series is to enhance the long-term development of the field by systematically furthering the dissemination of theoretically and empirically based scholarship and research. We promise the reader an opportunity to participate in the development of this field through the debates and discussions that occur throughout the pages of the *Communication and Language Intervention Series*.

Editorial Advisory Board

Volume Preface

THIS BOOK REFLECTS PRESENTATIONS MADE at the 1990 Conference in Early Language Development and Language Intervention. The conference was sponsored by the Mental Retardation and Developmental Disabilities Branch of the National Institute on Child Health and Human Development and the John F. Kennedy Center for Research on Education and Human Development at Peabody College of Vanderbilt University. The purpose of this conference was to bring together a group of active researchers who were currently addressing issues relevant to understanding early language development and intervention from the perspective of the social use of language. As a result of preliminary discussions among the conference planners exploring early language from a social perspective, the content of the conference and of the current volume was broadened to showcase the empirical and conceptual work of researchers in mental retardation with primary interests in aspects of language development and use. Although the final set of papers extended beyond the period of early language learning and beyond the social use of language, these two themes were central to the conference.

The goal of improving communication skills of people with mental retardation has been an area of research that has received support from NICHD since the 1960s. At NICHD, David Gray developed a plan for a conference that would review the current scientific knowledge on the development of communication skills and their use in social interactions by people with mental retardation and other developmental disabilities. The conference plan was reviewed and approved by Felix de la Cruz, Chief, Mental Retardation and Developmental Disabilities Branch, and Duane Alexander, Director of NICHD. This conference was the first in a series planned to emphasize the Mental Retardation Research Centers (MRRC) program of the NICHD. This program has provided core support (equipment development and repair, subject recruitment and testing, data collection and analysis, animal care, and publication preparation services) for scientists conducting research in the fields of mental retardation and developmental disabilities at 14 major universities. Al Baumeister, then director of the Kennedy Center, agreed to co-host the conference. Under his able leadership a committee of Kennedy Center researchers including Tom Klee, Paul Yoder, Bill Brown, Cathy Alpert, Ann Kaiser, and Steve Warren drafted a working proposal for the conference and met numerous times to discuss the conceptual issues in early language intervention that formed the basis for the final conference proposal. Steve Warren, Mabel Rice, Jon Miller, Sig Pueschel, Ann Kaiser, and David Gray were responsible for the planning of the final conference agenda and selection of participants. The staff of the Kennedy Center, particularly Jan Rosemergy, provided extensive support for local arrangements and ensured that the conference ran smoothly. Throughout the planning process, the NICHD staff were enormously helpful.

The conference was held in June of 1990 at Peabody College of Vanderbilt

University. Participants included: Cathy Alpert, Al Baumeister, Diane Bricker, Diane Crutcher, Rebecca Eilers, Howard Goldstein, Ann Kaiser, Ray Kent, William McIlvane, Carolyn Mervis, Jon Miller, Sam Odom, Kim Oller, Lesley Olswang, Siegfried Pueschel, Joe Reichle, Mabel Rice, Mary Ann Romski, Richard Schiefel-busch, Marian Sigman, Lee Synder-McLean, Alan Vanbiervleit, Tedra Walden, Steve Warren, and Paul Yoder.

Although not every participant contributed to this volume, the content of nearly every chapter was shaped by the stimulating discussions and insightful comments of the conference participants. Certainly, the range of interests and skills of the conference participants provided a context in which individual papers were enriched and enlarged.

Contributors

The Editors

Ann P. Kaiser, Ph.D., Professor of Special Education and Psychology and Human Development, Peabody College of Vanderbilt University, Nashville, TN 37203. Dr. Kaiser's research has focused on early language intervention, parents as facilitators of their children's language development, and the ecological analysis of language-learning environments. In conjunction with the Milieu Teaching Group at Vanderbilt, she has completed a series of studies comparing the effects of alternative language interventions on the language development of young children with disabilities.

David B. Gray, Ph.D., Acting Director, National Center for Medical Rehabilitation Research, National Institute of Child Health and Human Development, National Institutes of Health, Rockville, MD 20852. Dr. Gray has worked as a scientist in the field of behavior genetics and behavior modification and as a health science administrator in the areas of human learning and behavior. After serving as the Director of the National Institute on Disability and Rehabilitation Research, he returned to the NIH. Improving communicative skills of people with disabilities through better research and best practice remains an area of great interest to Dr. Gray.

The Chapter Authors

Jacquelyn Bertrand, Ph.D., Research Associate, Department of Psychology, Emory University, Atlanta, GA 30322. Dr. Bertrand's research interests include acquisition of language-learning strategies by children who are developing normally and by children with mental retardation.

Diane Bricker, Ph.D., Professor of Special Education and Director, Center on Human Development, University of Oregon, Eugene, OR 97403-1211. Dr. Bricker's professional career has focused on the development of effective intervention approaches for infants and young children who are at risk and who have disabilities, and on the development of language intervention programs that emphasize critical communicative functions.

Diane M. Crutcher, M.S., Parent Advocate, 1310 Heritage Road East, Normal, IL 61761. Currently the Director of Human Resource Development of BroMenn Healthcare, Ms. Crutcher has been active in the disability community—federally, statewide, and locally—since her 18-year-old daughter, Mindie, was diagnosed as having Down syndrome. She is co-founder of the Central Illinois Down Syndrome Organization, a member of the Governor's Council on Rehabilitation, a federal consultant to the Departments of Education and Health and Human Services, and the former Executive Director of the National Down Syndrome Congress.

William V. Dube, Ph.D., Associate Scientist, Behavioral Sciences Division, Eunice Kennedy Shriver Center for Mental Retardation, 200 Trapelo Road, Waltham, MA 02254. Dr. Dube also holds an appointment in the Psychology Department at Northeastern University. His research examines discrimination learning in individuals with mental retardation. His current areas of emphasis include rapid discrimination acquisition and computer-mediated programmed instruction.

Gina Green, Ph.D., Associate Scientist, Behavioral Sciences Division, Eunice Kennedy Shriver Center for Mental Retardation, 200 Trapelo Road, Waltham, MA 02254. Dr. Green is also Director of Research at the New England Center for Autism, Southborough, MA. Her research investigates basic questions in stimulus equivalence and the application of stimulus-control procedures for the remedial training of people with mental retardation, autism, and head injuries.

Howard Goldstein, Ph.D., Director of Communication and Psychiatry, University of Pittsburgh, Pittsburgh, PA 15260. Dr. Goldstein's research has examined various aspects of language development in children with developmental disabilities. In particular, he has sought to identify conditions that facilitate generalized language learning. He is currently studying classroom-based interventions for enhancing the communication skills of young children with disabilities.

James Halle, Ph.D., Professor of Special Education, University of Illinois, Champaign, IL 61820. Dr. Halle's primary area of research focuses on the efficacy of communication intervention strategies to establish initial communicative repertoires among individuals with moderate and severe developmental disabilities. Dr. Halle is currently Editor of the *Journal of The Association for Persons with Severe Handicaps*.

Marita R. Hopmann, Ph.D., Director, Down Syndrome Language Development Program, Child Development Center, Rhode Island Hospital, 593 Eddy Street, Providence, RI 02903. Dr. Hopmann has been the Director of the Down Syndrome Language Development Center since 1985, combining basic research projects with outreach services to families with a family member with Down syndrome. She also holds an appointment as Clinical Assistant Professor of Pediatrics at Brown University.

Susan Johnston, B.A., Doctoral Student, Department of Communication Disorders, University of Minnesota, Minneapolis, MN 55455.

Connie Kasari, Ph.D., Assistant Professor, Graduate School of Education, University of California–Los Angeles, 405 North Hilgard, Los Angeles, CA 99024. Dr. Kasari is Assistant Professor of Educational Psychology, and her research has focused on the development of emotion and social cognition in typical and atypical children.

Raymond D. Kent, Ph.D., Professor of Communicative Disorders, Waisman Center, University of Wisconsin–Madison, 1500 Highland Avenue, Madison, WI 53705-2280. Dr. Kent's research has been primarily in the areas of speech production in normal and impaired speakers (particularly those with neurologic disorders), vocal development in typically and atypically developing infants, methods for the acoustic and physiologic study of speech, and theories of speech production and its disorders. A major focus of his current research is the measurement of intelligibility in individuals with speech motor disorders and in children with developmental disabilities.

William J. McIlvane, Ph.D., Associate Director, Behavioral Sciences Division, Eunice Kennedy Shriver Center for Mental Retardation, 200 Trapelo Road, Waltham, MA 02254. Dr. McIlvane also holds an appointment in the Psychology Department of Northeastern University. His research focuses on discrimination learning in individuals with mental retardation, emphasizing frequency analysis of stimulus control relations and the study of stimulus classes.

Carolyn B. Mervis, Ph.D., Professor of Psychology, Emory University, Atlanta, GA 30322. Dr. Mervis's research has focused on early language and cognitive development by children who are developing normally and by children with mental retardation.

Peter Mundy, Ph.D., Assistant Professor, Department of Psychology, University of Miami, Miami, FL 33155. Dr. Mundy is also Director of the Psychological Services Center at the University of Miami. His research has focused on social and cognitive skills as they contribute to developmental delays and early psychopathology.

Samuel L. Odom, Ph.D., Associate Professor of Special Education, Peabody College of Vanderbilt University, Nashville, TN 37203. Dr. Odom is the former Editor of the *Journal of Early Intervention,* currently serves on the editorial boards of four journals, and, with colleagues Scott McConnell and Mary McEvoy, recently co-edited a text on the social competence of young children with disabilities. His research interests are in the areas of the social skills acquisition of preschool children with disabilities, observational methodology for assessing children's social competence, and early intervention.

Michaelene M. Ostrosky, Ph.D., Assistant Professor of Special Education, University of Illinois, Champaign, IL 61820. Dr. Ostrosky's research has focused on social interaction, parent-implemented language interventions, and the use of nondisabled peers as facilitators of social and communicative interactions between children with and without special needs. Dr. Ostrosky is on the editorial board of the *Journal of The Association for Persons with Severe Handicaps.*

Siegfried M. Pueschel, M.D., Ph.D., M.P.H., Director, Child Development Center, Rhode Island Hospital, 593 Eddy Street, Providence, RI 02903. Dr. Pueschel also holds an appointment as Professor of Pediatrics at Brown University. Director of the Child Development Center since 1975, Dr. Pueschel has continued to pursue his interests in clinical activities, research, and teaching in the fields of developmental disabilities, biochemical genetics, and chromosome abnormalities, and he has published extensively.

Joe Reichle, Ph.D., Professor of Communication Disorders and Educational Psychology, University of Minnesota, Minneapolis, MN 55455. Dr. Reichle has published extensively in the area of communication and language intervention and is actively involved in the training of speech-language pathologists and special educators. He currently serves as Chair of the Publications Board of The Association for Persons with Severe Handicaps.

Mabel L. Rice, Ph.D., Professor of Speech-Language-Hearing, University of Kansas, Lawrence, KS 66045. Dr. Rice is also Director of the Child Language Program and the Kansas Early Childhood Research Institute, and has extensive research and clinical experience with children with specific language impairment (SLI). Her current research addresses several aspects of children with SLI: social and academic consequences, lexical learning, morphology, and preschool language intervention.

Mary Ann Romski, Ph.D., Associate Professor of Communication and Psychology, Georgia State University, Atlanta, GA 30303. Dr. Romski is also affiliated with the Language Research Center of Georgia State University. Her research has focused on studying the language acquisition process of nonspeaking children with mental retardation via the use of assistive technology.

Richard W. Serna, Ph.D., Assistant Scientist, Behavioral Sciences Division, Eunice Kennedy Shriver Center for Mental Retardation, 200 Trapelo Road, Waltham, MA 02254. Dr. Serna has been a faculty member of the Psychology Department at Illinois Wesleyan University and an adjunct faculty member of the Department of Educational Psychology and Special Education at Northern Illinois University. His current research interests include auditory discrimination learning and prerequisites for rudimentary reading.

Rose A. Sevcik, Ph.D., Assistant Research Professor, Language Research Center, Georgia State University, Atlanta, GA 30303. Dr. Sevcik's research interests include language and communication acquisition and impairments, mental retardation, neuropsychology, and nonhuman primate behavior. Currently, she is examining the language comprehension skills of children with mental retardation.

Marian Sigman, Ph.D., Professor, Neuropsychiatric Institute, University of California–Los Angeles, Los Angeles, CA 99024. Dr. Sigman has published widely in the areas of applied developmental psychology and clinical child psychology. Her research interests have focused on longitudinal studies of infants and children with autism and developmental delays, as well as preterm and malnourished infants and children.

Tedra A. Walden, Ph.D., Associate Professor of Psychology, Peabody College of Vanderbilt University, Nashville, TN 37203. Dr. Walden's research interests are in the area of early parent–child interactions and early peer relationships. She is particularly interested in early emotional development, its relation to early interactions with caregivers and peers, and risk for aberrant or maladaptive development in both normally developing children and children with delayed intellectual development.

Steven F. Warren, Ph.D., Professor of Special Education and Psychology and Human Development, Peabody College of Vanderbilt University, Nashville, TN 37203. Dr. Warren is also Associate Director of the John F. Kennedy Center for Research on Education and Human Development at Vanderbilt University and Co-director of the Center's Mental Retardation Research Training Program. He has conducted extensive research on language generalization and milieu intervention approaches.

Nurit Yirmiya, Ph.D., Assistant Professor, Department of Psychology, Hebrew University of Jerusalem, Mount Scopus, Jerusalem, ISRAEL. Dr. Yirmiya also holds an appointment in the School of Education at the Hebrew University of Jerusalem. Her research has focused on identifying the cognitive and affective deficits involved in autism.

Paul J. Yoder, Ph.D., Assistant Professor of Special Education, Peabody College of Vanderbilt University, Nashville, TN 37203. Dr. Yoder is also an investigator at the John F. Kennedy Center for Research on Education and Human Development at Vanderbilt University. His research has focused on the social influences of language use and development in children with and children without disabilities. He is currently working on developing and testing the efficacy of language and prelinguistic communication interventions toddlers with mental retardation.

Acknowledgments

THIS VOLUME WAS PREPARED as a result of the conference on the social use of language sponsored by the Mental Retardation and Developmental Disabilities Branch of the National Institute on Child Health and Human Development and the John F. Kennedy Center for Research on Education and Human Development. The conference was held at Peabody College of Vanderbilt University in June, 1990. We are extremely grateful for the support of the Kennedy Center staff, particularly Dr. Jan Rosemergy, in making this conference possible.

We are very grateful to Carole Douglas for her careful word processing of this manuscript and for coordinating communication with authors throughout the process of developing this book. We also thank Carol R. Hollander for her excellent technical editing and continuing insightful advice about the format of this manuscript.

*"No one sleeps in this room without
the dream of a common language. . . ."*
—Origins and History of Consciousness
Adrienne Rich

*One day when I was 7 years old, I stood watching my 5-year-old brother
who could not yet talk or walk. I was overwhelmed with the sadness of not
being able to connect with him and to understand him. For years afterward,
I had a recurring dream of him talking to me.*

*The dream of a common language shared by children with disabilities
and the people who care about them has been nourished in my
professional life by Don Baer, Dick Schiefelbusch, Joe Spradlin, and Betty
Hart. This book is dedicated to them with greatest gratitude and affection.*

—A.P.K.

Volume 2

Enhancing Children's Communication

PART I

Perspectives on Intervention

1

Introduction
Enhancing Children's
Social Communication

Ann P. Kaiser

O NE OF THE MOST REMARKABLE and important developments in language intervention in the 1980s and 1990s has been a gradual shift from teaching specific speech and language skills to an emphasis on enhancing children's social communication. The shift from the formal aspects of language to social functions as they are expressed by linguistic forms increases both the purview and the significance of early language intervention. To a considerable extent, that shift reflects our growing understanding of the interrelated aspects of children's social, cognitive, and linguistic development and improvements in our technology for teaching generalized language skills in naturally occurring contexts.

Implicit in the changes in emphasis during these years is the view that is emerging of the child with language disabilities as a child living everyday at home, in the classroom, on the playground, and with friends and family. The child with language disabilities needs social interaction and meaningful, close personal relationships; communication skills are the primary tool humans use in meeting those needs. Thus, intervention to teach communication skills is critical in supporting the social relationships that are essential in the child's life.

Communication skills are a *means* for personal social interaction, not just the desired *outcome* of an intervention or development. Communication in social interaction is the fabric of children's lives. Children use whatever communication skills they have at the moment as the foundation for social communication. To communicate in a socially effective way, children require more than skill in vocabulary use, articulation, semantic relationships, and simple grammar. They require a functional, socially effective communication system to carry on essential everyday transactions. And, until they have that fully functioning system, they make do with the set of skills they currently possess. Children's social and academic lives do not wait until their communication skills develop. Lives go on regardless of children's skill levels; however, the quality and richness of those lives may vary greatly depending on their skills.

Social communication skills, perhaps more than any other single domain of children's skills, are integrative in their development and fully integrative as used in everyday life. Social communication skills integrate the contributions of specific speech and language skills, social interaction skills, and cognitive development. The remarkable complexity of social communication—the requirements of flexible use, contextual adaptation, and correspondence with the general rules of a culture and the specific constraints of the communication exchange—makes the mastery of social communication skills both essential and difficult for children with disabilities. Without some mastery of social communication skills, children are limited in academic learning and in the development of complex, ongoing relationships with peers and family members. For many children, limitations in social communication skills contribute to the development of patterns of antisocial or challenging behavior that further limit their learning and their productive social interactions.

Nowhere are children and interventionists, researchers, and parents more challenged than in attempting to enhance children's social communication. As our understanding of the complexity of social communication grows, the need for research and for empirically validated intervention practices becomes more pressing.

This volume provides an overview of many aspects of communication that require understanding if we are to intervene successfully with children who have limited social communication skills. The volume is unique in its particular attention to the social uses of language and to the fundamental connection between language and social behavior. Across the chapters, there is systematic consideration of the range of systems and processes that contribute to functional social communication. While neither the emphasis on social language use nor the attention to the many systems and processes involved in language learning are new in the study of child language, the perspectives in this book are distinctive for the field of language intervention in several ways.

First, both social processes and learning processes (from behavioral and cognitive information processing perspectives) are acknowledged as influencing the acquisition and appropriate use of the child's communication system. Parts II and III of the book focus on early intervention in the social use of language and on the importance of shared meaning and partnerships in communication. In Part II, the four chapters examine the design and application of naturalistic teaching strategies. The chapters vary in the specifics of the intervention model, the mode of communication, and the population for whom the intervention was designed. They share a common emphasis on building social communication in natural settings. Each chapter addresses a different population of children; in responding to the social communication needs of that population and the opportunities for teaching functional language, each author builds a slightly different intervention model while still adhering to basic designs of naturalistic teaching. Yoder and Warren (Chapter 3) describe a prelinguistic intervention intended to assist young children in forming the interactive foundation for language use and learning. A critical assumption underlying this model is that both cognitive processes, such as attention and memory, and social processes, such as responsiveness, influence children's acquisition of early communication skills. Interventions that target aspects of both systems are predicted to be relatively more facilitative of development than those addressing only one system. Kaiser (Chapter 4) reports on a model for parent-implemented language intervention that incorporates the building of a context for communication, a responsive interactional environment, and the use of milieu teaching in interventions with children in the early stages of language use. Chapter 5, by Romski and Sevcik, describes an augmented intervention using synthesized speech provided by a computer. The results of this intervention are described in terms of changes in the participants' social language use with adults and peers. Their results are particularly important because they highlight how participation in social-communicative interactions further enhances learning and communication. In Chapter 6, Reichle, Halle, and Johnston discuss specific issues in naturalistic intervention that arise for learners with severe disabilities. In this chapter in particular, the importance of learners' social motivation and related cognitive and social skills to the development of a social language repertoire is emphasized.

Part III examines aspects of children's development that affect the social use of language. These five chapters take widely varied theoretical perspectives. In doing so, they underscore the range of factors that affect language use. In no instance does the argument made in any single chapter appear to conflict fundamentally with the arguments made in other chapters. As a result, the emergent view from this section is one that emphasizes the extent to which social communication rests on a range of child skills and experience. Rice's chapter provides a rich examination of the social consequences of language delay and how these consequences might contribute to the child's social language use. Ostrosky, Kaiser, and Odom review the relatively modest literature on interventions designed to address both social interaction and language use in interactions with peers. In combination, these two chapters underscore the potential challenges of increasing children's social interaction with peers and the importance of continued attempts to do so.

The next three chapters each examine an aspect of the complex interrelated array of skills that contribute to appropriate use of language in social contexts. Walden reports on the development of social referencing in parent–

child interactions and suggests ways that referencing may contribute to shared social meanings and communication. Kasari and her colleagues describe findings from their work on the development of affect in children with autism. These findings underscore the particular relationship between nonverbal communication and the mapping of social meaning using linguistic means. The chapters by Walden and by Kasari and colleagues provide somewhat divergent theoretical perspectives of how basic social development may specifically affect children's communication. Yet both views are reasonably included in the complex picture of social communication. In the last chapter in this section, Kent examines speech intelligibility as it contributes to the overall communicative competence of children in social interactions. Although the study of speech intelligibility and efforts to intervene in order to improve intelligibility have a long history, this chapter represents a uniquely social approach to speech and contributes a new perspective to the range of factors included in the social use of language.

Part IV focuses on learning processes that influence language development and use. Three chapters contribute empirical evidence that may enhance the effectiveness of our intervention efforts. These chapters provide theoretical and empirical evidence of how learning, as well as social processes, influence children's communication use and development. Three chapters (Goldstein; McIlvane, Dube, Green, & Serna; Mervis & Bertrand) address learning processes that directly influence children's acquisition of early language skills. Notably, these chapters provide quite different, yet not incompatible, analyses of underlying learning from behavioral and information process perspectives. McIlvane and colleagues report evidence that stimulus equivalence models might account for the complex generalization required in language use. Mervis and Bertrand present a set of principles that may guide children in rapidly acquiring the meaning of specific words. While Mervis and Bertrand do not discuss their rules as actual guidelines for class formation using principles of discrimination and generalization, the rules appear potentially to function as a description of these processes. The third chapter in this section, by Goldstein, also discusses generalization as a foundation for learning and for intervention. Thus, the chapters by McIlvane and colleagues, Mervis and Bertrand, and Goldstein together draw our attention to the particular power of concept and class formation via rule-governed principles. Regardless of which theoretical perspective is adopted, the need to consider the rule-based nature of language use is well-established by these chapters.

The final chapter in this section draws attention to the functional needs for communication and the types of intervention children with Down syndrome are currently receiving. This chapter is an important counterpoint to the theoretical perspectives of the preceding three chapters and to the optimistic designs for new interventions in Part II. Clearly, there is a gap between what we know and what we are able to deliver to young children with communication limitations. This chapter is an important foundation for future intervention because it grounds theory, models, and data firmly in the need to deliver services to children and families.

The final section of the book speaks to the future and places the preceding chapters in the context of the progress in early language intervention that we have witnessed since the 1970s. The chapter by Warren offers an historical perspective that complements the personal retrospective by Bricker. His review of the history of the field is an optimistic one emphasizing the benefits of the patterns of change we have observed. Warren is optimistic about the possibilities of intervention in the context of increased understanding of the contributions of biologic systems to children's learning. Crutcher, like Pueschel and Hopmann in the previous section, writes from the perspective of a parent who has experienced the actual delivery of services to children with language disabilities. Crutcher directs researchers to address questions that affect the everyday lives of children and families, and she asks for a level of accountability that can be measured by real changes in children's abilities to communicate. Her perception of what is needed is an important balance to Warren's optimistic view of what is possible, and to Bricker's view of progress in intervention research.

In addition to the actual content offered by individual chapters, the combined efforts of these authors make two important points about early social communication: First, communication is based in both learning processes specific to linguistic forms and in social interaction. Second, the construction of social meanings occurs primarily in social interactions between the child and significant others.

The view that communication is based in *both* learning and social processes is evident in the chapters discussing current language interventions, as well as in the chapters specifically addressing the social processes that contribute to communication. In the chapters describing contemporary models of early language intervention, learning and social use are viewed as necessary, dependable targets for language intervention. Conjoint intervention into both the formal and social aspects of communication is evident in the four naturalistic models of intervention, as well in the review of peer-mediated interventions by Ostrosky and her colleagues. The critical relationship between social and learning processes is also evident in the description of the successes and limitations of interventions designed to enhance children's communication that is provided by Rice. Throughout the book, there is evidence supporting the importance of building the linkage among learning and social processes as essential to enhancing the functional and social use of language.

The third important point made in this volume is that social communication is effective when meanings are shared between conversational partners. Shared meanings are affected by the child's skills in all aspects of the social-communicative system and by the quality of the conversational partner's participation in the interaction. Simply put, meaning is negotiated and jointly constructed in conversations. In addition to presuming that there is a linkage between learning and social processes, the chapters in this volume presume that successful functioning of the communication system in everyday use depends on the successful negotiation of meanings between conversational partners. Again, chapters by Walden, Kasari and colleagues, and Rice speak directly to the role of the partner in successful social transactions. Kent's discussion of research on speech intelligibility places intelligibility in the context of social language use, as Kent addresses the impact of this aspect on everyday social exchanges. Kaiser presents a parent-implemented language intervention model that relies on arranging the environment to clarify meanings for both the child and the parent, on laying a responsive interaction foundation for learning, and on teaching in contexts where the child's intended meaning is clear to the parent. The prelinguistic intervention model of Yoder and Warren presents a related strategy for earlier intervention. Ostrosky, Kaiser, and Odom address the specific role of peers in social-communicative interactions. Ostrosky and her colleagues suggest ways that peer conversation partners might be taught to increase their responsiveness to children with limited language, with the result of more meaningful and friendship-like interactions. Reichle, Halle, and Johnston describe the particular challenges in social-communicative interventions for persons with severe disabilities and for whom conversational interactions are especially difficult.

This volume is unique in its presentation of multiple perspectives on the complex challenge of facilitating children's communicative use. Rarely does a single volume contain theoretical, empirical, historical, and consumer perspectives on issues, and there is a great deal to be learned when these perspectives can be brought together.

This volume is formidable in its breadth and in the careful consideration of individual topics and shared interests; it is also remarkable for what it does not contain. Missing from this book are a comprehensive conceptualization of the child's development of social language use, a model of intervention that fully addresses the development of socially competent communication, and empirical data that demonstrate that any intervention can have a long-lasting and meaningful impact on the lives of children with disabilities. Intelligent discussion of theoretically divergent views, much less the integration of these views into a cohesive perspective that might inform intervention or raise important research questions, are notably absent from this volume, as they were from the conference that formed the basis for this volume. Even recognizing that books are rarely the forum for the presentation of powerful data, there is little here to suggest that as a field we have data demonstrating that our interventions are powerful enough to have meaningful impact on the lives of children. The modest changes in children's specific skills, which typically have limited generalization to actual communication with untrained partners as we have reported systematically for 20 years, do not support our notions that we have an effective technology of language intervention. Furthermore, even if we had produced convincing evidence of a powerful technology in our research studies, there is no indication that we have changed the delivery of services to young children with disabilities in such a way that we can honestly report that there is a powerful technology for language intervention in practice. Four chapters in this book provide a dramatic contrast: the two chapters on professional perspectives on the field of language intervention and the two chapters describing the experiences of parents of children with language disabilities. It is essential that we pay attention to the contrast that is presented. Across these four chapters, and implicitly throughout the rest of the book, we see the professional advances in understanding the processes related to language learning and intervention juxtaposed against the slower progress in meeting the needs of children with language disabilities.

Here, as in many aspects of education and developmental disabilities, the translation of knowledge into accessible services moves slowly. And here again, the distinction between knowledge in the general academic sense and in the pragmatic sense that informs best practice is readily apparent.

To point out what is missing from this volume does not diminish its contributions; the book balances this with an appreciation of the depth and importance of the problem that it seeks to address. The glass is half full and half empty. As a field, we have made progress; yet, we have not reached the goal of enhancing children's communication in the ways we have always intended. It is essential that we remain clearly focused on our goal and that we weigh our empirical and conceptual work against that goal. Facilitating children's social communication is an absolutely worthwhile endeavor. It will take all our talents and collaborative thinking to achieve it. Our success should be measured not only by our growing empirical knowledge base, but by meaningful changes in the lives of children with language disabilities.

2

Then, Now, and the Path Between
A Brief History of Language Intervention

Diane Bricker

THIS ACCOUNT OF THE HISTORY of language intervention is driven primarily by my observations and knowledge of the field, which span the entirety of language intervention efforts with young children with moderate to profound disabilities. For the most part, this chapter does not address the historical development of language intervention programs for children who are at risk for or who have specific communication problems such as aphasia.

According to my calendar, the preliminary or foundational work in language intervention was initiated during the late 1960s when a variety of single subject studies examining specific forms of verbal behavior appeared in the literature (e.g., Guess, Sailor, Rutherford, & Baer, 1968; Kerr, Meyerson, & Michael, 1965). I believe that it is fair to set 1970 as the point when formal language programs first appeared, so the field currently has a history of a little more than 20 years. Although such a time frame is less than a nanosecond when compared to the history of humankind, the conceptual and clinical changes in language intervention that have occurred since 1970 are remarkable.

The use of the word "remarkable" clearly tips my hand and indicates my unbridled enthusiasm for what we have learned about language intervention during this brief span. Rather than save the conclusion for the final section of this chapter, I will offer my analysis of this 20-year endeavor first and then present the information that has led me to this conclusion.

One could draw a number of conclusions from the 20-year span of language intervention work. It might be fair to say that considerable time and energy were wasted following unproductive avenues. Large investments of

Support for the preparation of this chapter has come in part from Grant Nos. H029D90110, H029B0254, and H029Q90086 from the U.S. Office of Special Education Programs to the Center on Human Development, University of Oregon.

resources still have not yielded strategies that produce desired changes in children with language delays or disorders. This conclusion, while accurate, is overridden by a more potent observation: Great progress has been made—considering the complexity of human learning, the complexity of language acquisition and usage, and the short time that investigators and practitioners have been attempting to develop and implement programs of language intervention.

THEN

1960s

The "then" portion of this retrospective analysis of language intervention refers to the late 1960s and early 1970s. Discussing a few of the conceptual positions held by many professionals and laypersons at this time may assist in understanding the type of intervention then offered to persons with disabilities.

During this period, many professionals believed in the constancy of the IQ. At least two interrelated assumptions supported this belief. First, intellectual ability (e.g., language and thought) was viewed as largely genetically and biologically determined and, therefore, little subject to change. Second, environmental change or rearrangement was assumed to have a limited effect on changing severely deviant or deficient repertoires. These assumptions offered little hope that intervention efforts with persons having low IQs would produce significant changes. In fact, during this time, most persons identified as moderately to profoundly disabled were placed in residential facilities that offered few therapeutic or educational programs (Sarason & Doris, 1969).

The second assumption more specific to the topic was that children needed a variety of prerequisite behaviors before clinicians or therapists could or, perhaps more accurately, would include them in language intervention programs. These prerequisites were not directed at precursors to speech or language but rather dealt with children's self-help skills (e.g., would take care of their toilet needs independently), social skills (e.g., would not aggress toward other children or adults), cognitive skills (e.g., would attend to an activity for 15–20 minutes), and motor skills (e.g., would sit in a chair for extended periods of time). I have a vivid recollection of an episode in the early 1960s in which a young school-age child with mental retardation was excluded from speech therapy because she was not toilet trained and might have had an accident in the therapy room.

Despite these prevalent views about the teachability, or even trainability, of specific children and adults, a group of researchers and clinicians using principles derived from the experimental analysis of behavior began working on improving the speech production skills in populations with severe disabilities (e.g., McLean, 1976). In addition to an array of studies that focused on teaching discrete response forms such as plural morphemes, a few preliminary attempts were introduced to foster more comprehensive approaches to assisting children with severe disabilities develop speech and language processes.

MacAulay (1968) described a program for teaching speech and reading to "nonverbal retardates." Lovaas (1968) in the same volume contributed a chapter entitled "A Program for the Establishment of Speech in Psychotic Children." Although these program descriptions provided broad intervention content and guidelines, they were directed primarily to the development of speech production. One of the few to use the term "language training" during the 1960s was Richardson (1967). She proposed a comprehensive approach to language intervention that included training in motor and sensory areas. Gray and Fygetakis (1968) also wrote about the development of language as opposed to speech.

With the few exceptions noted, during the 1960s and well into the 1970s, the focus of most training was on speech production. Little mention was made of language or communication. Fundamental components of communication such as semantics and the social use of language were at that time, for most of us, beyond the pale.

1970s

A backward look into the early 1970s reveals two important events. First, the early 1970s saw the advent of broad-based formal training programs focused on teaching aspects of language, as opposed to concentrating on speech production. Second, the Chula Vista Conference was held on language intervention and the elaborated conference proceedings were published.

Formal language programs that included written descriptions that specified in some detail the content, the sequence in which it should be taught, and strategies for teaching it first appeared in the early 1970s. Bricker and Bricker (1970) described an operant approach designed in a hierarchical fashion. Although features other than speech were targeted, this program was dependent upon children being able to produce imitative responses. Kent and her colleagues (1972) described a similar program built on operant shaping of imitative responses.

Another important change during this period was the advent of programs that broadened their intervention focus to include teaching syntactic structures. Some of the more notable of these programs were developed by Gray and Ryan (1973), Miller and Yoder (1972), and Stremel (1972).

One obvious index of the change occurring during this period was the appearance of the words "language" and "program" in describing these intervention approaches. These terms reflected the change in intervention approaches to more broad-based content (e.g., syntax, imitation, as well as speech) and to more organized, cohesive approaches (e.g., content and training sequences specified).

In 1973, NICHD sponsored a conference on language intervention at the Chula Vista Lodge located in the Wisconsin Dells. According to Schiefelbusch and Lloyd (1974): "The primary purpose of the Chula Vista Conference was to formulate a valid basis for teaching language to the mentally retarded and others with language retardation (or disability)" (p. 11). In addition to addressing this general purpose, participants at this conference formally recognized that the development and implementation of effective language training programs required input from a broad array of disciplines and fields, such as the experimental analysis of behavior, psycholinguistics, special education, and speech pathology.

Subsequent to the Chula Vista Conference, a volume entitled *Language Perspectives: Acquisition, Retardation, and Intervention* was published (Schiefelbusch & Lloyd, 1974). This volume contained several chapters (e.g., Bowerman, 1974; Bricker & Bricker, 1974; Schlesinger, 1974) emphasizing the need to develop language intervention approaches that included attention to cognitive factors as well as to major elements of language, including syntax, expressive and receptive skills. In addition, other authors (e.g., Cromer, 1974; Menyuk, 1974) suggested the need to use information from psycholinguistics to formulate intervention content. Finally, Horton (1974) remarked in this volume that, "Review of recent writings on mental retardation . . . reveals that no major consideration is given intervention in the 0- to 2- or 3-year period" (p. 480). This volume was a landmark for the field of language intervention because it helped launch the serious study of language acquisition and intervention for young children with communication delays and disorders.

Beginning in 1974–1975, a more comprehensive approach to designing intervention programs appeared. Many of the earlier programs were broadened to reflect important developmental and psycholinguistic content and were expanded to include younger children. Graham (1978) reviewed a number of these programs (e.g., Bricker & Bricker, 1974; MacDonald & Blott, 1974; Miller & Yoder, 1974; Stremel & Waryas, 1974) and discussed the ways in which these programs synthesized psycholinguistic and developmental content with behavioral approaches.

Nondevelopmental approaches were also expanded during this period. Two of the more notable approaches were completed by Guess, Sailor, and Baer (1978) and Kent (1974). These programs derived their content of instruction through task analysis of needed behaviors. Instructional sequences were to be taught using carefully structured operant procedures.

During this period, nonvocal symbol-system language programs were developed for individuals with severe language impairments. Carrier (1978) and his colleagues developed an approach that they termed "a nonspeech language system." Interestingly, this nonvocal system was based on earlier work conducted with chimpanzees in which small abstract symbols were used in place of words (Premack & Premack, 1974). In addition, nonvocal systems for children with severe motor impairments were developed. These systems were based largely on the use of augmentative equipment (e.g., iconic symbols, communication boards) that provided the child a nonvocal vehicle for communication (Vanderheiden & Harris-Vanderheiden, 1978).

The advent of augmentative systems for nonspeaking children required that the field of language intervention reconceptualize its major goals and purposes. The need for a reconceptualization was further emphasized by reliable findings that infants and their caregivers developed communication systems long before the onset of language (Schaffer, 1977). The shift in focus from the formal aspects of language to communication was a highlight of language intervention in the 1970s.

It was also during the 1970s that parents and caregivers were first included in language intervention programs. In most cases, as pointed out by Baker (1976), the role of the parent/caregiver had been seen as an extension of the role of clinician or interventionist. That is, parents were expected to conduct systematic training in their homes and collect data on the success of their efforts. The programs developed by MacDonald and his colleagues (e.g., MacDonald & Horstmeier, 1978) were designed specifically to include family members in intervention efforts.

Although important changes occurred during the 1970s, programs continued to be highly structured, conducted in individual and small group sessions, adult directed, and used massed-trial training formats that frequently employed contrived materials and events. Language continued to be taught as an artificial system rather than as a vehicle for children to convey their needs and control their environment. In addition, the social use of language had yet to be addressed by developers of language intervention programs. Although the social use or social context of language had been discussed by Mahoney (1975) and McLean and Snyder-McLean (1978), the translation of these discussions into intervention programs did not begin until the 1980s.

1980s

In a small volume, *Language Intervention with Children* (Bricker, 1980), Schiefelbusch (1980) projected a series of trends for the decade of the 1980s. (A review of these projected trends reinforces the judgment that Richard Schiefelbusch's understanding of the field is second to none. Further, his influence has spanned the life of the field and, to our good fortune, that influence has been continually positive and constructive.) The more important trends that Schiefelbusch described were:

1. Interdisciplinary models and theories will be employed to broaden and strengthen language intervention approaches.

2. The importance of encouraging social competence in the language-disabled child will be reflected in the development of functionally based language intervention programs.
3. Language intervention programs will be developed for infants and young children who need communicative assistance.
4. Researchers and clinicians will study and develop a variety of alternative communication strategies for individuals who appear likely to be unable to use verbal systems effectively.
5. Language intervention programs will increasingly attend to the ecological context in which language is developed and used.

A review of these trends reflects the historical development of language intervention during the 1980s.

Interdisciplinary Approaches

A review of the language intervention programs introduced during the 1980s finds professionals from a variety of disciplines involved in these efforts. Speech pathologists, psycholinguists, psychologists, and special educators made substantial contributions during the decade of the 1980s. Not only were contributions made by professionals from a variety of disciplines, but program developers increasingly constructed intervention approaches that reflected a multidisciplinary approach. An excellent example is the program developed by Dunst (1981). This program, described as "Infant Learning: A Cognitive-Linguistic Intervention Strategy," was based on a three-dimensional model that included behavioral, developmental, and ecological principles in teaching language to infants. Dunst's intent was to integrate important principles from these areas into a unified training approach. The evolution of the programs developed by Bricker and her colleagues (Bricker & Schiefelbusch, 1984) shows a similar multidisciplinary expansion, first to include attention to cognitive factors and then to address social influences on language.

Interestingly, the trend was also reflected in the Education of the Handicapped Act Amendments of 1986. PL 99-457 specifies that intervention efforts for infants and young children must be multidisciplinary, because the nature of the problems facing these children cannot be adequately addressed by a single discipline. This legal mandate seemed to confirm Schiefelbusch's argument for an interdisciplinary perspective as a basis for language intervention programs.

Social Competence

The second projected trend was that of increased attention to developing the social competence of the individual with a language disability. Schiefelbusch predicted that to improve children's social competence program developers would shift to developing strategies that were functional and retreat from approaches designed to teach specific forms apart from functional use. This would require, according to Schiefelbusch, "knowledge of the ways infants and small children socialize, process information, learn skills, perceive the world, and seek affection" (1980, p. 8). A flurry of research on these topics emerged during the 1980s. Studies that examined the development of early pragmatics or social competence in infants were conducted (cf. Stark, 1981).

Several important language intervention strategies that either directly or indirectly addressed the need for functional approaches emerged or were expanded during this decade. One of the more important, the milieu language training model (Hart & Rogers-Warren, 1978), appears to have evolved, in part, from the original work of Hart and Risley (1975) on "incidental teaching." Preliminary investigations suggested that naturalistic training strategies (Hart, 1985) might enhance language acquisition and generalization. Fey (1986) used the term "hybrid" to refer to approaches that retained an underlying teaching structure and sequence but that employed "intervention activities that are highly natural."

The development of naturalistic or hybrid approaches clearly recognized the need to shift communication and language intervention into modes that are functional for children and their families. The benefits of this trend have been language training procedures that capitalize on daily activities and routine events of children and families and that stress the need for communication that meets the needs of the communicator.

Language Intervention for Infants

During the 1960s and 1970s, little formal or informal training was conducted for infants and young children. Only with the institution of PL 99-457 in 1986 has the field of early intervention gained the recognition and legitimacy that had eluded it for the previous 15 years. Although there were a few language intervention programs developed in the 1970s for young children, there has been increasing concern for and attention to the capacities of infants and young children. A consensus of research outcomes has provided evidence that infants communicate long before the onset of formal language skills (Stark, 1981). This evidence has spurred the development of programs for infants and young children who demonstrate serious delays or have not yet developed critical communicative behaviors. Programs developed by Bricker and Schiefelbusch (1984, 1990), Dunst (1981), MacDonald (1985, 1989), Mahoney and Powell (1986), and Manolson (1984) targeted infants or very young children and included attention to early social-communicative behaviors such as establishing joint attention, eye contact, and turn-taking.

The concept of play has also taken on considerable importance in the development of early social-communication skills in infants and young children. MacDonald (1989) discusses the importance of play to the development of social and communicative interactions. Fey (1986) suggests that play is the mode of choice for interventionists and caregivers who wish to follow less structured, child-oriented approaches. The Mahoney and Powell (1986) approach, although not directed totally to language, stresses the importance of interaction between caregiver and infant/child. The authors suggest that, "Play is the ideal form of adult–child interaction." Mahoney and Powell (1986) go on to propose that play is one of the primary vehicles through which children gain cognitive, language, social, and motor skills. A number of authorities on young children share this perspective (Sachs, 1984).

In the 1980s, the field of language intervention became increasingly concerned about infants and young children whose communicative or language behaviors are impaired and who have developed strategies to counter these problems. This concern extends beyond those infants who are hearing impaired and for whom programs have long been in place (Horton, 1974) to all infants and young children who demonstrate problems in the area of communicative functioning.

Alternative Modes of Communication

The fourth trend proposed by Schiefelbusch was expanded work on the development of alternative approaches to communication. Since the early work in augmentative communication, there has been an explosion of different approaches and modes particularly directed to the individual with more serious disabilities. Two shifts, one legislative-legalistic and the other attitudinal, help account for the great progress in developing and implementing augmentative and alternative communication approaches.

The legislative-legalistic shift occurred with the passage of PL 94-142. Although signed into law in 1975, it was well into the 1980s before many of the children with severe handicaps entered public schools. As these children joined public school programs, the need to develop appropriate intervention programs became apparent. Most often, these needs were addressed in the children's individualized education programs (IEPs). An IEP priority for most children with severe disabilities was communication training, as well as a communication specialist to help design and implement a program. These specialists faced the daunting task of helping "difficult-to-teach children" (Keogh & Reichle, 1985).

During this same period, the second shift in the field focused on changing teacher, interventionist, and caregiver attitudes about the form of language to be taught. This shift was from teaching formal *language* skills to teaching *communication* skills and was required because of the behavioral repertoires presented by children with severe disabilities. Generally, children with severe disabilities have substantial problems such as poor motor control and limited cognitive functioning that may interfere or completely preclude learning a representational system such as speech. Learning skills (e.g., labeling pictures out of context) that are not immediately rewarded as communicative attempts is a slow and unproductive process for children with severe disabilities. Increasingly, interventionists found the need for functional systems that could compensate for the child's problems and could be used across a range of environments and settings in order for the child's response to become an effective form of communication. The empirical and philosophical work of the 1970s laid the foundation for service delivery personnel to shift from attempting to teach representational systems (e.g., words) to children with severe impairments to assisting them in developing a communication system that would permit greater control of their environments and more personal satisfaction. These two important shifts in the field greatly enhanced efforts to discover and evaluate a broad range of nonvocal communication systems for difficult-to-teach children.

Some of the alternative and augmentative communication training work of the 1980s was designed to assist interventionists in selecting children who would profit from the use of nonvocal systems (McCormick & Shane, 1990; Yoder, 1980). Another consistent theme was selecting the appropriate system for a child from the array of available approaches (Musslewhite & St. Louis, 1982).

In addition to work that offered general intervention strategies (Keogh & Reichle, 1985; Noonan & Siegel-Causey, 1990), formal programs for individuals with severe disabilities were developed (Peck, Schuler, Tomlinson, Theimer, & Haring, n.d.; Stremel-Campbell, Guida, Johnson-Dorn, & Udell, 1984). Interestingly, these newer programs moved away from the carefully structured training paradigms of the 1970s (e.g., Guess, Sailor, & Baer, 1978) to more naturalistic approaches that attempted to embed communication training in ongoing, meaningful, daily activities.

Ecological Perspective

In discussing this projected trend, Schiefelbusch (1980) placed a particular emphasis on the inclusion of parents as members of the intervention team. The need to include parents reflected a growing recognition that language skills acquired by children in training settings did not generalize. Researchers reported the acquisition of target communicative responses but often did not examine the transfer of these responses to other settings and conditions (Guess, Keogh, & Sailor, 1978; Snyder-McLean & McLean, 1987). Investigators who did examine the generalization of skills often reported disappointing outcomes in that children failed to maintain the response over time. Increasingly, program developers began designing interventions that included caregivers as important partners in children's learning of communication skills (MacDonald, 1989).

The inclusion of caregivers as intervention partners was tied closely to the move to make language intervention programs more functional. The use of natural settings and daily activities as intervention vehicles made the inclusion of parents and other caregivers considerably more straightforward than integrating them into specific instructional regimes that demand careful delivery of cues and shaping of specific responses using massed-trial formats. A number of the programs developed or expanded during this time proposed using a dialogic framework. MacDonald (1985) suggested developing scripts to help direct conversations between adults and children with language impairments. Snyder-McLean, Solomonson, McLean, and Sack (1984) described an intervention strategy that relied on structuring joint action routines between children and adults.

One of the earliest approaches built on a dialogue format was developed by Blank (1983). She proposed that through thoughtfully directed verbal exchanges, adults could not only assist children in expanding their language skills but also could enhance their problem-solving abilities. The dialogue or exchange format has also been proposed as useful with children who have more serious disabilities. Koegel and Johnson (1989) devised what they termed a natural teaching approach for children with autism. One of the important features of this approach is the development of turn-taking.

The Mahoney and Powell (1986) and Manolson (1984) programs also recognized the importance of caregiver–child communicative exchanges and direct intervention efforts to the improvement or enhancement of these exchanges. This same philosophy appeared in programs developed for the infant with hearing impairments, such as Parent-Infant Communication (Schuyler et al., 1985).

A logical expansion to including caregivers in intervention efforts is the inclusion of children's peers. I am unaware of a comprehensive, formal language intervention program that specifically targets the use of peers; however, there is a body of literature that suggests it is a promising approach (Goldstein & Kaczmarek, 1992). It seems likely that the later part of the 1990s will see increased clinical and empirical work addressing how to make communicative intervention appropriate to children's ecological contexts.

During the 1980s, progress in the area of language intervention was effectively captured in the trends discussed above. What we learned during this decade provides the foundation for now and the future.

NOW AND THE FUTURE

Three important perspectives that emerged from the work and findings of the 1980s are affecting current language intervention content and strategies and will continue to be influential in future developments. These perspectives include attention to the social uses of language, the needs and characteristics of the learner, and the learner's environment. None of these perspectives is new; however, the growing relevance and application of each to language intervention programming is of major importance.

The Social Uses of Language

Without doubt, the need for focusing training efforts on the social aspects of communication was recognized during the 1980s, and, as noted above, many of the programs developed in this era reflect this perspective. Currently and in the future, the social uses of language will gain more attention and the field will discover more effective ways to translate the theory surrounding social communication into formal intervention procedures and approaches. We will seek a more clear and precise understanding of young children's communication problems and will develop strategies to remediate those problems within their social milieu.

Three aspects of the social use of language have particular relevance for language intervention programming today and in the future: the social context in which intervention occurs, the embedding of communicative goals and objectives in daily activities, and the inclusion of caregivers in intervention efforts.

The language intervention programs that have most seriously addressed training on communication targets in children's usual social environment or context are those called naturalistic approaches (Duchan & Weitzner-Linn, 1987). In general, these programs are designed to enhance children's communicative competence through daily and typical interactions with salient objects, events, and people in their environments. One of the well-known and better studied approaches is milieu language training. "Milieu language teaching is a naturalistic language intervention strategy that uses everyday instances of social-communicative exchanges as opportunities to teach elaborated language" (Kaiser, Hendrickson, & Alpert, 1991).

A second approach that is particularly directed to encouraging the primary intervention to occur in children's daily and routine interactions is activity-based intervention.

> Activity-based intervention is a child-directed, transactional approach that embeds intervention on children's individual goals and objectives in routine, planned, or child-directed activities and uses logically occurring antecedents and consequences to develop functional and generalizable skills. (Bricker & Cripe, 1992, p. 40)

Although there are differences in these two approaches, they have similarities with each other and with other naturalistic approaches (Bricker & Cripe, 1992). Such approaches are designed to encourage following the children's leads in conversation, to superimpose training on daily activities that children find rewarding and meaningful, and to assist children in acquiring communicative behavior that will enhance their lives.

When language intervention programs focus training on the social use of language, they address not only the social context of training, but they also address the mapping of training objectives onto the child's daily, meaningful activities. For example, joint attention can be targeted as an objective during snack time when the infant can be helped to focus on the bowl of food in front of him or her or on a ball retrieved during a play session. Names of objects can be learned as the child manipulates them during self-directed play activities. Request functions can be "naturally" introduced as children require objects or assistance throughout the day. Syntax improvement can occur with use of a puppet to model appropriate grammatical constructions. Using play and routine activities as training vehicles is likely to be more appealing to children, to enhance generalization, and, therefore, to enhance children's functional use of language (Giumento, 1990).

Language intervention programs directed to improving children's social use of language must acknowledge and incorporate procedures for including parents, family members, and other caregivers in intervention efforts. The need to include caregivers as intervention partners has long been recognized; however, recently there has been interest in the use of nondisabled peers as language intervention partners, particularly as the pressures to mainstream children increase. Goldstein and Kaczmarek (1992) discuss the potential for using communicative interactions between children with language impairments and their nondisabled peers as an effective intervention approach. These authors report that verbal interaction between preschoolers who are disabled and nondisabled preschoolers can be increased, and the use of peer-mediated learning may help both disabled and nondisabled children acquire important skills. Currently there is "little published curricular support available to implement peer-mediated communicative interventions" (Goldstein & Kaczmarek, 1992). Building on the important work of Goldstein and Ferrell (1987), Guralnick (1976), Strain (1977), and their colleagues, significant future efforts will develop a variety of peer-mediated strategies that interventionists will be able to employ to enhance the communicative development of children with language impairments.

The use of naturalistic approaches to enhance social communication skills with populations of children with serious disabilities is also increasing. Romski and Sevcik's work (chap. 5, this volume) with populations of children with severe mental retardation suggests that augmented language learning can occur during natural communicative interaction between children and their partners. These authors indicate that the learning of communication skills may be significantly greater if the use of augmentative systems is integrated into naturally occurring daily interactions of children's lives, as opposed to using artificially derived training routines. Klinger and Dawson (1992) express a similar position for developing communicative skills in populations of children diagnosed as autistic. They propose that social interaction can be facilitated, in part, by mapping training efforts on "naturally occurring patterns of early social interactions" (Klinger & Dawson, 1992). These are exciting training directions for children with serious disabilities because these strategies may enhance caregiver and teacher opportunities to support the children's communication efforts. The use of daily interactions may also enhance the children's acquisition of communication because the content is more relevant and useful.

In the 1990s, language intervention researchers are directing their efforts toward studying the effectiveness of procedures that focus on the social use of language (Cole, Dale, & Mills, 1991; Giumento, 1990; Kaiser, Yoder, & Keetz, 1992). Based on the outcomes of this body of work, advances in content and strategies will emerge. My guess is that outcomes will continue to support the need for and effectiveness of approaches that map training on children's daily interactions.

Learner-Oriented Approaches

Language training efforts, for the most part, should occur within children's daily environmental interactions; however, following this regimen may not be sufficient. By definition, communication requires a message sender and a message receiver. Intervention programs that teach children only to respond to the initiations and cues of others are teaching only half of the behavioral repertoire necessary for effective communication. Children should be able to send messages as well as respond to messages. Communication is not taking place if the individual is unable to direct and control at least some portion of his or her environment. Toward the end of the 1980s, program developers began recognizing the necessity of helping children become communicative initiators rather than merely communicative responders (Carlson & Bricker, 1982).

There are some powerful reasons why the field of language intervention is shifting to learner-oriented training in which work on goals and objectives is embedded in activities of interest to the learner. First, training focused on targets removed from learners' experiences and interests is likely to lack meaning for them (Brown, Collins, & Duguid, 1989). Second, the use of artificial contingencies in teaching has not been shown to produce behavior that is maintained once those contingencies are removed. Designing interventions that use artificial contingencies to maintain children's responses does not enable the learner to communicate in a social environment that does not provide artificial feedback. For example, if children's communicative requests are rewarded by receiving stickers, they may not use the learned requests in settings (e.g., home and store) where stickers are not available.

Following the learner's lead and teaching in response to his or her initiations does much to counter these two problems. As mentioned, children are likely to engage in activities that are of interest and meaning to them. Thus, they may be motivated to acquire skills and information that enable them to accomplish or enjoy chosen activities. Second, teaching in response to child initiations and self-engagement does not require the delivery of artificial contingencies. What *is* required is that interventionists and caregivers find ways to use these initiations and self-engagement to promote language learning and usage. An array of useful techniques is available to encourage child initiations and self-engagement. Interventionists and caregivers may find many opportunities to enhance communication if they follow the response initiations of children as well as use child-selected activities to shape targeted communicative responses.

During the 1990s, language intervention is increasingly focusing on approaches that recognize the importance of shaping and encouraging child initiations (Bricker & Cripe, 1992). Rather than providing interventionists and caregivers a discrete set of steps to follow or specific content to be taught, programs instead are formulated to offer broad guidelines for using children's initiations and self-directed activities as vehicles for training content that is specific to children's interests and needs.

Learner's Environment

The third important perspective affecting language intervention now and in the future is that of attention to the learner's environment. Again, this perspective is not new, but our orientation to it has changed. Increasingly, developers of language intervention programs include guidelines that assist interventionists in examining the communicative environment of the learner. Detailed analysis of the learner's environments and attempts to relate aspects of these environments to outcomes are being conducted (Carta, Sainato, & Greenwood, 1988). Outcomes from such investigations will change the current tendency of interventionists to pay little heed to the physical and social surroundings of the learner to one of directing their attention to aspects of children's milieus that affect their communicative outcomes.

Particularly important components of most children's social environments are their peers. Yet, as indicated above, few language intervention programs have included procedures for incorporating peers into training efforts. As Goldstein and Kaczmarek (1992) argue, peer-mediated learning is a likely rich and available source to use for language training efforts. Study of learners' environments and of interactions between children with and without disabilities should provide some important insights for stimulating functional communication in both groups of children.

Adult caregivers are also important elements of children's social environments. Although mother–child interactions have long been scrutinized, more serious attention is being given to the development of pragmatic methods that caregivers can incorporate into their daily interactions. More detailed study of the communicative interactions between caregivers and children may uncover intervention procedures that are simple to integrate into daily interactions (Yoder, Davies, & Bishop, 1992). Tannock and Girolametto (1992) further suggest the need for better designed and executed studies to help determine effective parent intervention strategies. They indicate that studies that examine aptitude by treatment effects and longitudinal effects are needed to assist in designing intervention strategies that will be appropriate to families and to children. Future challenges include identifying intervention strategies that caregivers are willing and able to use on a regular basis and determining which strategies are effective with which families and children.

Prior to the development or selection of a language intervention program, careful consideration should be given to the child's environment. Where does the child spend time, with whom does he or she exchange communicative messages, and what teaching resources are available are a few of the essential pieces of information that should be obtained in order to select an intervention program. According to Peck (1989), improvement in social communication requires:

> direct observation in classroom and home environments, design of interventions that can be implemented within these environments, and consideration of child needs and goals in the context of personal and professional needs, as well as priorities in the broader family and educational "systems." (p. 12)

In this same vein, Reichle, York, and Sigafoos (1991) point out the need to select or adopt augmentative systems that complement the learner's communicative opportunities and existing repertoire. To accomplish this goal, the interventionist must spend time observing and coming to understand the individual's communicative environment. This element will become an important addition to effective language intervention programs.

The decade of the 1990s will see the advent of language intervention programs that focus on the development of social-communicative behaviors and increasing sensitivity to the orientation of the learner. Accompanying these important shifts will be increased attention to assessment of the learner's environment that, in turn, will help direct the selection of the language intervention approach.

SUMMARY

This chapter began with the conclusion that "remarkable" progress has been made in the field of language intervention during its brief 20-year history. It seems to me that the reader could not be convinced otherwise; however, our feelings about the past are much less important than our approaches to the future.

Significant challenges remain for those researchers, clinicians, administrators, and caregivers who know that we can do better than we have done. It is important to build future efforts on the best the past has to offer, but clearly we must expand our knowledge if we are to provide more assistance to children with communicative impairments.

The interface between research and application in the field of language intervention needs to be enhanced. That enhancement should take several forms. First, better relationships between those conducting research and those applying the outcomes are needed. Indeed, investigators who are able to conduct studies using true experimental procedures frequently make clear their superiority to the applied researcher, who is often unable to attain such control. The elimination of the research–practitioner dichotomy and the introduction of a continuum on which all of us are necessary might be helpful in recognizing that we each have contributions to make to the field of language intervention. These contributions differ but are equally important.

Second, improved dialogue between research and practitioner communities is needed. Researchers tend to speak and write for other researchers and practitioners tend to do likewise (Bricker, 1982). The research community needs a better grasp of the problems and barriers that face interventionists and caregivers. Investigators need to understand the daily demands and the lack of resources that confront the practitioner for two reasons. First, many of the problems and barriers practitioners experience require study to devise useful solutions. Some extremely important breakthroughs might occur if practitioners were given more direct assistance in solving the problems that interfere with their efforts. Second, recognition of the realities facing practitioners might help the research community to provide information in formats that make the findings understandable and usable. Equally important is that practitioners understand the requirements of the research community. Both groups need to expand their accommodation of the other. A potential solution might be conducting empirical investigations within applied settings. Such undertakings would require both researchers and practitioners who understand the other's demands and who are willing to adjust as necessary. Joint projects could do much to educate the wide variety of professionals associated with language intervention programs.

By most standards, the history of language intervention has been short, although it has certainly not been uneventful. As I have indicated, the progress that has occurred during this brief history has been remarkable. Remarkable, because we have broadened approaches to include children with severe disabilities. Remarkable, because we now consider early communicative intervention with infants who are at risk and disabled to be best practice. Remarkable, because we are genuinely committed to including caregivers in intervention efforts. Remarkable, because we have dramatically changed the content of intervention as well as the procedures used to present the content. And perhaps most remarkable because we have come to recognize that communicative intervention is not successful unless individuals with impairments are able to develop systems that enhance their independence, problem-solving capacities, and interactions with their social environments.

REFERENCES

Baker, B. (1976). Parent involvement in programming for developmentally disabled children. In L. Lloyd (Ed.), *Communication assessment and intervention strategies* (pp. 691–733). Baltimore: University Park Press.

Blank, M. (1983). *Teaching learning in the preschool.* Cambridge, MA: Brookline Books.

Bowerman, M. (1974). Discussion summary: Development of concepts underlying language. In R. Schiefelbusch & L. Lloyd (Eds.), *Language perspectives: Acquisition, retardation, and intervention* (pp. 191–209). Baltimore: University Park Press.

Bricker, D. (Ed.). (1980). *Language intervention with children.* San Francisco: Jossey-Bass.

Bricker, D. (1982). From research to application. In D. Bricker (Ed.), *Intervention with at-risk and handicapped infants* (pp. 1–9). Baltimore: University Park Press.

Bricker, D., & Cripe, J. (1989). Activity-based intervention. In D. Bricker (Ed.), *Early intervention for at-risk and handicapped infants, toddlers, and preschool children* (pp. 251–274). Palo Alto, CA: Vort.

Bricker, D., & Cripe, J. (1992). *An activity-based approach to early intervention.* Baltimore: Paul H. Brookes Publishing Co.

Bricker, D., & Schiefelbusch, R. (1984). Infants at risk. In L. McCormick & R. Schiefelbusch (Eds.), *Early language intervention* (pp. 243–246). Columbus, OH: Charles E. Merrill.

Bricker, D., & Schiefelbusch, R. (1990). Infants at risk. In L. McCormick & R. Schiefelbusch (Eds.), *Early language intervention* (2nd ed., pp. 333–354). Columbus, OH: Charles E. Merrill.

Bricker, W., & Bricker, D. (1970). A program of language training for the severely language handicapped child. *Exceptional Children, 37,* 101–111.

Bricker, W., & Bricker, D. (1974). An early language training strategy. In R. Schiefelbusch & L. Lloyd (Eds.), *Language perspectives: Acquisition, retardation, and intervention* (pp. 431–468). Baltimore: University Park Press.

Brown, J., Collins, A., & Duguid, P. (1989). Situated cognition and the culture of learning. *Educational Researcher, 17,* 32–42.

Carlson, L., & Bricker, D. (1982). Dyadic and contingent aspects of early communicative intervention. In D. Bricker (Ed.), *Intervention with at-risk and handicapped infants* (pp. 291–308). Baltimore: University Park Press.

Carrier, J. (1978). Application of a nonspeech language system with the severely language handicapped. In L. Lloyd (Ed.), *Communication assessment and intervention strategies* (pp. 523–547). Baltimore: University Park Press.

Carta, J., Sainato, D., & Greenwood, C. (1988). Advances in the ecological assessment of classroom instruction for young children with handicaps. In S.L. Odom & M.B. Karnes (Eds.), *Early intervention for infants and children with handicaps: An empirical base* (pp. 217–239). Baltimore: Paul H. Brookes Publishing Co.

Cole, K., Dale, P., & Mills, P. (1991). Individual differences in language delayed children's responses to direct and interactive preschool instruction. *Topics in Early Childhood Special Education, 11,* 99–124.

Cromer, R. (1974). Receptive language in the mentally retarded: Processes and diagnostic distinctions. In R. Schiefelbusch & L. Lloyd (Eds.), *Language perspectives: Acquisition, retardation, and intervention* (pp. 237–267). Baltimore: University Park Press.

Duchan, J., & Weitzner-Linn, B. (1987). Nurturant-naturalistic intervention for language-impaired children. *Asha, 29,* 45–49.

Dunst, C. (1981). *Infant learning: A cognitive-linguistic intervention strategy.* Hingham, MA: Teaching Resources Corp.

Fey, M. (1986). *Language intervention with young children.* San Diego, CA: College-Hill Press.

Giumento, A. (1990). *The effectiveness of two intervention procedures on the acquisition and generalization of object labels by young children who are at-risk or who have developmental delays.* Unpublished doctoral dissertation, University of Oregon, Eugene.

Goldstein, H., & Ferrell, D. (1987). Augmenting communicative interaction between handicapped and nonhandicapped preschoolers. *Journal of Speech and Hearing Disorders, 19,* 200–211.

Goldstein, H., & Kaczmarek, L. (1992). Promoting communicative interaction among children in integrated intervention settings. In S. Warren & J. Reichle (Eds.), *Communication and language intervention: Vol. 1. Causes and effects in communication and language intervention* (pp. 81–111). Baltimore: Paul H. Brookes Publishing Co.

Graham, L. (1978). Language programming and intervention. In L. Lloyd (Ed.), *Communication assessment and intervention strategies* (pp. 371–422). Baltimore: University Park Press.

Gray, B., & Fygetakis, L. (1968). The development of language as a function of programmed conditioning. *Behavior Research and Therapy, 6,* 455–460.

Gray, B., & Ryan, B. (1973). *Programmed conditioning for language (Monterey Language Program).* Palo Alto, CA: Monterey Learning Systems.

Guess, D., Keogh, W., & Sailor, W. (1978). Generalization of speech and language behavior: Measurement and training tactics. In R. Schiefelbusch (Ed.), *Bases for language intervention* (pp. 373–395). Baltimore: University Park Press.

Guess, D., Sailor, W., & Baer, D. (1978). *Functional speech and language training.* Lawrence, KS: H & H Enterprises.

Guess, D., Sailor, W., Rutherford, G., & Baer, D. (1968). An experimental analysis of linguistic development: The productive use of the plural morpheme. *Journal of Applied Behavioral Analysis, 1,* 297–306.

Guralnick, M. (1976). The value of integrating handicapped and nonhandicapped preschool children. *American Journal of Orthopsychiatry, 42,* 236–245.

Hart, B. (1985). Naturalistic language training techniques. In S. Warren & A. Rogers-Warren (Eds.), *Teaching functional language* (pp. 63–88). Baltimore: University Park Press.

Hart, B., & Risley, T. (1975). Incidental teaching of language in the preschool. *Journal of Applied Behavioral Analysis, 8,* 411–420.

Hart, B., & Rogers-Warren, A. (1978). A milieu approach to teaching language. In R. Schiefelbusch (Ed.), *Language intervention strategies.* Baltimore: University Park Press.

Horton, K. (1974). Infant intervention and language learning. In R. Schiefelbusch & L. Lloyd (Eds.), *Language perspectives: Acquisition, retardation, and intervention* (pp. 469–491). Baltimore: University Park Press.

Kaiser, A., Hendrickson, J., & Alpert, K. (1991). Milieu language teaching: A second look. In R. Gable (Ed.), *Advances in mental retardation and developmental disabilities* (Vol. IV, pp. 63–92). London: Jessica Kingsley Publishers.

Kaiser, A., Yoder, P., & Keetz, A. (1992). Evaluating milieu teaching. In S. Warren & J. Reichle (Eds.), *Communication and language intervention: Vol. 1. Causes and effects in communication and language intervention* (pp. 9–47). Baltimore: Paul H. Brookes Publishing Co.

Kent, L. (1974). *Language acquisition program for the retarded or multiply impaired.* Champaign, IL: Research Press.

Kent, L., Klein, D., Falk, A., & Guenther, H. (1972). A language acquisition program for the retarded. In J. McLean, D. Yoder, & R. Schiefelbusch (Eds.), *Language intervention with the retarded* (pp. 151–190). Baltimore: University Park Press.

Keogh, W., & Reichle, J. (1985). Communication intervention for the "difficult-to-teach" severely handicapped. In S. Warren & A. Rogers-Warren (Eds.), *Teaching functional language* (pp. 157–194). Baltimore: University Park Press.

Kerr, N., Meyerson, L., & Michael, J. (1965). A procedure for shaping vocalizations in a mute child. In L. Ullman & L. Krasner (Eds.), *Case studies in behavior modification.* New York: Holt, Rinehart & Winston.

Klinger, L., & Dawson, G. (1992). Facilitating early social and communicative development in children with autism. In S. Warren & J. Reichle (Eds.), *Communication and language intervention: Vol. 1. Causes and effects in communication and language intervention* (pp. 157–186). Baltimore: Paul H. Brookes Publishing Co.

Koegel, R., & Johnson, J. (1989). Motivating language use in autistic children. In G. Dawson (Ed.), *Autism.* New York: The Guilford Press.

Lovaas, O. (1968). A program for the establishment of speech in psychotic children. In H. Sloane & B. MacAulay (Eds.), *Operant procedures in remedial speech and language training* (pp. 125–154). Boston: Houghton-Mifflin.

MacAulay, B. (1968). A program for teaching speech and beginning reading to nonverbal retardates. In H. Sloane & B. MacAulay (Eds.), *Operant procedures in remedial speech and language training* (pp. 102–124). Boston: Houghton-Mifflin.

MacDonald, J. (1985). Language through conversation: A model for intervention with language-delayed persons. In S. Warren & A. Rogers-Warren (Eds.), *Teaching functional language* (pp. 89–122). Baltimore: University Park Press.

MacDonald, J. (1989). *Becoming partners with children.* San Antonio, TX: Special Press.

MacDonald, J., & Blott, J. (1974). Environmental language intervention: The rationale for a diagnostic and training strategy through rules, context, and generalization. *Journal of Speech and Hearing Disorders, 39,* 244–256.

MacDonald, J., & Horstmeier, D. (1978). *Environmental language intervention program.* Columbus, OH: Charles E. Merrill.

Mahoney, G. (1975). Ethological approach to delayed language acquisition. *American Journal of Mental Deficiency, 80,* 139–148.

Mahoney, G., & Powell, A. (1986). *Transactional intervention program.* Farmington, CT: Pediatric Research and Training Center, University of Connecticut Health Center.

Manolson, A. (1984). *Hanen early language program.* Toronto: Hanen Early Language Resource Center.

McCormick, L., & Shane, H. (1990). Communication system options for students who are nonspeaking. In L. McCormick & R. Schiefelbusch (Eds.), *Early language intervention* (pp. 427–471). Columbus, OH: Charles E. Merrill.

McLean, J. (1976). Articulation. In L. Lloyd (Ed.), *Communication assessment and intervention strategies* (pp. 325–370). Baltimore: University Park Press.

McLean, J., & Snyder-McLean, L. (1978). *A transactional approach to early language training.* Columbus, OH: Charles E. Merrill.

Menyuk, P. (1974). Early development of receptive language from babbling to words. In R. Schiefelbusch & L. Lloyd (Eds.), *Language perspectives: Acquisition, retardation, and intervention* (pp. 213–235). Baltimore: University Park Press.

Miller, J., & Yoder, D. (1972). A syntax training program. In J. McLean, D. Yoder, & R. Schiefelbusch (Eds.), *Language intervention with the retarded* (pp. 191–211). Baltimore: University Park Press.

Miller, J., & Yoder, D. (1974). An ontogenetic language teaching strategy for retarded children. In R. Schiefelbusch & L. Lloyd (Eds.), *Language perspectives: Acquisition, retardation, and intervention* (pp. 505–528). Baltimore: University Park Press.

Musslewhite, C., & St. Louis, K. (1982). *Communication programming for the severely handicapped: Vocal and non-vocal strategies*. San Diego, CA: College-Hill Press.

Noonan, M., & Siegel-Causey, E. (1990). Special needs of students with severe handicaps. In L. McCormick & R. Schiefelbusch (Eds.), *Early language intervention* (pp. 383–425). Columbus, OH: Charles E. Merrill.

Peck, C. (1989). Assessment of social communicative competence: Evaluating environments. *Seminars in Speech and Language, 10*, 1–15.

Peck, C., Schuler, A., Tomlinson, C., Theimer, R., & Haring, T. (n.d.). *The social competence curriculum project*. Santa Barbara, CA: Special Education Program, University of California.

Premack, D., & Premack, A. (1974). Teaching visual language to apes and language-deficient persons. In R. Schiefelbusch & L. Lloyd (Eds.), *Language perspectives: Acquisition, retardation, and intervention* (pp. 347–376). Baltimore: University Park Press.

Reichle, J., York, J., & Sigafoos, J. (1991). *Implementing augmentative and alternate communication: Strategies for learners with severe disabilities*. Baltimore: Paul H. Brookes Publishing Co.

Richardson, S. (1967). Language training for mentally retarded children. In R. Schiefelbusch, R. Copeland, & J. Smith (Eds.), *Language and mental retardation*. New York: Holt, Rinehart & Winston.

Romski, M., & Sevcik, R. (1992). Developing augmented language in children with severe mental retardation. In S. Warren & J. Reichle (Eds.), *Communication and language intervention: Vol. 1. Causes and effects in communication and language intervention* (pp. 113–130). Baltimore: Paul H. Brookes Publishing Co.

Sachs, J. (1984). Children's play and communicative development. In R. Schiefelbusch & J. Pickar (Eds.), *The acquisition of communicative competence*. Baltimore: University Park Press.

Sarason, S., & Doris, J. (1969). *Psychological problems in mental deficiency* (4th ed.). New York: Harper & Row.

Schaffer, H. (Ed.). (1977). *Studies in mother–infant interactions*. London: Academic Press.

Schiefelbusch, R. (1980). Synthesis of trends in language intervention. In D. Bricker (Ed.), *Language intervention with children* (pp. 1–15). San Francisco: Jossey-Bass.

Schiefelbusch, R., & Lloyd, L. (1974). Introduction. In R. Schiefelbusch & L. Lloyd (Eds.), *Language perspectives: Acquisition, retardation, and intervention* (pp. 1–15). Baltimore: University Park Press.

Schlesinger, I. (1974). Relational concepts underlying language. In R. Schiefelbusch & L. Lloyd (Eds.), *Language perspectives: Acquisition, retardation, and intervention* (pp. 129–151). Baltimore: University Park Press.

Schuyler, V., Rushmer, N., Arpan, R., Melum, A., Sowers, J., & Kennedy, N. (1985). *Parent-infant communication* (3rd ed.). Portland, OR: Infant Hearing Resources, Good Samaritan Hospital and Medical Center.

Snyder-McLean, L., & McLean, J. (1987). Effectiveness of early intervention for children with language and communication disorders. In M. Guralnick & F. Bennett (Eds.), *The effectiveness of early intervention for at-risk and handicapped children* (pp. 213–274). New York: Academic Press.

Snyder-McLean, L., Solomonson, B., McLean, J., & Sack, S. (1984). Structuring joint action routines. *Seminars in Speech and Language, 5,* 213–228.

Stark, R. (Ed.). (1981). *Language behavior in infancy and early childhood.* New York: Elsevier/North Holland.

Strain, P. (1977). Effects of peer social initiation on withdrawn preschool children: Some training and generalization effects. *Journal of Abnormal Child Psychology, 5,* 445–455.

Stremel, K. (1972). Language training: A program for retarded children. *Mental Retardation, 10,* 47–49.

Stremel, K., & Waryas, C. (1974). A behavioral–psycholinguistic approach to language training. In L. McReynolds (Ed.), *Developing systematic procedures for training children's language* (ASHA Monograph No. 18). Danville, IL: Interstate Press.

Stremel-Campbell, K., Guida, J., Johnson-Dorn, N., & Udell, T. (1984). *Communication curriculum.* Monmouth, OR: Teaching Research Integration Project.

Tannock, R., & Girolametto, L. (1992). Reassessing parent-focused language intervention programs. In S. Warren & J. Reichle (Eds.), *Communication and language intervention: Vol. 1. Causes and effects in communication and language intervention* (pp. 49–79). Baltimore: Paul H. Brookes Publishing Co.

Vanderheiden, G., & Harris-Vanderheiden, D. (1978). Communication techniques and aids for the nonvocal severely handicapped. In L. Lloyd (Ed.), *Communication assessment and intervention strategies* (pp. 607–652). Baltimore: University Park Press.

Yoder, D. (1980). Communication systems for non-speech children. In D. Bricker (Ed.), *Language intervention with children* (pp. 63–78). San Francisco: Jossey-Bass.

Yoder, P., Davies, B., & Bishop, K. (1992). Getting children with developmental disabilities to talk to adults. In S. Warren & J. Reichle (Eds.), *Communication and language intervention: Vol. 1. Causes and effects in communication and language intervention* (pp. 255–275). Baltimore: Paul H. Brookes Publishing Co.

PART II

Effective Intervention
in the
Social Use of Language

3

Can Developmentally Delayed Children's Language Development Be Enhanced Through Prelinguistic Intervention?

Paul J. Yoder and Steven F. Warren

Part h of pl 99-457 has created incentives for states to provide services to children with disabilities who are 3 years of age and younger. One effect of this legislation has been to dramatically increase interest in direct intervention efforts with these children and their families. However, existing empirical support for educational interventions with very young children with disabilities is minimal. In particular, little research has focused on the development and evaluation of intervention strategies designed to facilitate prelinguistic communication, despite the importance of such communication and its possible relationship to later language development.

"Prelinguistic communication" refers to children's intentional communication behaviors. We exclude from our definition of prelinguistic communication those child behaviors to which adults attribute communicative value when there is no compelling evidence that the child intended to communicate with the adult. For example, few researchers would consider a newborn's hunger cry an indication of purposeful communication in order to get an adult to feed him or her. However, the cry certainly communicates the child's distress and thus warrants a response. We regard such cries as unintentional communication. For the purposes of this chapter, intentional communication is a behavior that conveys information or has some pragmatic function directed to an adult (Wetherby, Cain, Yonclas, & Walker, 1988). An example of intentional communication occurs when a child gives the mother an empty

Preparation of this chapter was supported in part by Grant Nos. HD22812 and HD15051 from the National Institute of Child Health and Human Development and Grant Nos. G008730528 and HD023A10009 from the U. S. Department of Education.

bottle, conveying that he or she wants some milk. Unintentional communication is important but is not the focus of this chapter.

This chapter discusses the bases for investigating the relationship between prelinguistic and linguistic communication development in young children with developmental delays. We first discuss the importance of the relationship between prelinguistic and linguistic communication development, then we discuss why one might expect this relationship to be causal. Next, we focus on what is presently known about this relationship. We discuss the necessity of prelinguistic intervention to determine whether this relationship is, in fact, causal. Our focus then shifts to a brief review of the current state of prelinguistic communication intervention. In the context of intervention, we describe a modification of the milieu language teaching model that we believe is an appropriate prelinguistic intervention approach. We then discuss our proposal for how prelinguistic communication intervention should be evaluated and review the current efficacy data. Finally, we highlight some of the research and educational implications and needs relative to the development of effective prelinguistic intervention. Because prelinguistic intervention research is in its early stages, our intent is to help the reader appreciate both the complexities of this topic and the potential benefits to be attained through systematic research efforts.

THE RELATIONSHIP BETWEEN
PRELINGUISTIC AND LINGUISTIC COMMUNICATION

The Importance of this Relationship

There are two primary reasons for studying the relationship between prelinguistic and linguistic communication. First, doing so may help us better understand how all children learn to talk. Second, studying this relationship may improve our ability to intervene effectively with children with communication delays.

The transition from prelinguistic to linguistic communication is important to the study of language development. Understanding how communication gradually develops may help us understand how children learn to talk. Evidence that intervening on prelinguistic communication skills has an effect on both prelinguistic and linguistic communication would support the notion that the environment may be important in determining why some children learn language before others. As in many fields of human development, there is an ongoing debate among language scholars concerning the primacy of nature versus nurture in explaining major developmental transitions. On one hand, nativists have used the rapid and seemingly abrupt acquisition of language to argue that language acquisition must be due to an inborn "language acquisition device" located somewhere in the brain (Chomsky, 1965). The nativist position assumes then that prelinguistic communication intervention will not affect language development directly, because delays in language acquisition are primarily attributed to irreparable neurologic deficits (Lenneberg, 1967, p. 169). On the other hand, the interactionist position (e.g., Bates, O'Connell, & Shore, 1987) views language acquisition as developing gradually out of prelinguistic communication and as dependent on perception, cognition, and motor development as well as on environmental factors (e.g., the ways that adults talk to children). Interactionists posit that the role of social interaction in language development is important. This view allows the possibility that early intervention may be effective. Demonstrations that early intervention on prelinguistic communication skills can produce changes in prelinguistic communication that subsequently affect linguistic communication would support the interactionist view of language development.

The second reason for studying the relationship between prelinguistic and linguistic communication is that such knowledge may improve our ability to intervene effectively with prelinguistic children who are developmentally delayed. Many children who have mental retardation are delayed in their prelinguistic communication skills beyond the level expected for their mental age (Miller, 1988; Mundy, Sigman, Kasari, & Yirmiya, 1988; Smith & von Tetzchner, 1986). These early communication delays have been reported consistently in children with Down syndrome (Miller, 1988), but delays have also been reported in children with other etiologies of developmental disabilities (Miller, Chapman, & Bedrosian, 1978). Miller (1988) and others (Mundy et al., 1988; Smith & von Tetzchner, 1986) have suggested that these unexpected delays in linguistic development may be partly due to delays in prelinguistic development. If so, directly targeting prelinguistic development may increase the benefit of subsequent linguistic intervention. In fact, this hypothesis is the underlying basis for many current early intervention efforts. As is explicated in the next section, prelinguistic intervention may indirectly affect later linguistic communication for two main reasons. First, facilitating vocalizations and the breadth of pragmatic functions for which intentional communication is used may lay the groundwork for the child to better utilize adult input in learning to talk. Additionally, increasing the frequency and clarity of child communication may elicit the types of adult–child interactions that facilitate language development.

Alternative Explanations for the Relationship

There are two main categories of approaches to explaining the relationship between prelinguistic and linguistic communication: approaches emphasizing only within-child factors and approaches emphasizing both within-child and environmental factors.

Child-Driven Models

Approaches emphasizing only within-child factors point out that prelinguistic and linguistic communication share many components. We discuss two forms of the child-driven model. They are organized according to the shared components of linguistic and prelinguistic communication that they emphasize: 1) similar forms and 2) shared communicative functions.

In one child-driven model, a relationship between prelinguistic and linguistic communication is posited because babbling and many first words sound alike. Many early words and advanced forms of babbling share the CV or CVCV form. In fact, many of the same sounds are used in both babbling and some early words (e.g., "b" in baba for bottle, "m" in mama). One reason for these similarities may be a motoric constraint equally applied to babbling and speech. Another reason may be that adults adapt their speech to children's phonological capabilities (e.g., greater use of reduplicatives such as "choo choo" or "dada" [Locke, 1990]). If the prelinguistic–linguistic relationship can be accounted for by shared phonetic forms, then the words the child first learns should be composed of the sounds the child used during the last stage of babbling (i.e., canonical babbling stage). Looking only at the words the child produces, there is a relationship between the sounds in the child's vocalizations and the words he or she learns during the first stage of language learning (Schwartz, 1988). However, there is no relationship between sounds in babbling and the words the child comprehends during this first stage of language learning (Schwartz, 1988). Therefore, the second child-driven model is more widely cited than this first one.

This second child-driven model posits that prelinguistic and linguistic communication may be related because they are used for the same purposes. Gestures and intentional vocalizations often serve the same early functions as first words (i.e., requests, comments, and protests) (Bruner, 1978). Some interactionists suggest that early words are those that encode the objects and events about which the child communicated in prelinguistic ways earlier in his or her development (e.g., Bates et al., 1987; Bruner, 1978; Snow, Perlmann, & Nathan, 1987). Looking at the first 50 words used by typically developing children, Benedict (1979) reported that almost all of the words were those commonly used in routines or for objects common in the child's environment. Implicit in this model is the notion that both prelinguistic and linguistic communication are manifestations of the same cognitive achievements. For example, both may rely on the understanding that desired objects can be acquired via indirect means (i.e., means–end) and that this means is often a person (i.e., social agency [Bates, Benigni, Bretherton, Camaioni, & Volterra, 1979; Golinkoff, 1981]). Teaching a child to communicate prelinguistically may also implicitly teach the child these two lessons. The child who has mastered means–end and social agency may be better able to deploy his or her attention to learning the words for what he or she is requesting prelinguistically than is the child who is still struggling with these cognitive foundations of requesting. The empirical support for the primacy of cognitive achievements before language acquisition is quite equivocal and conflicting

(Rice & Kemper, 1984). Nevertheless, for the purpose of understanding why prelinguistic intervention may enhance linguistic communication, it is enough to know that facilitating cognitive achievements enhances later linguistic communication. Kahn (1984) found that directly training means–end relations facilitated language learning in subsequent language intervention in children with mental retardation.

In summary, the child-driven models posit that children with advanced skills in the prelinguistic period are better able to utilize adult input, which in turn helps them learn to talk. In the phonetic model, advanced babblers are better able to produce their first words than are less mature babblers. In the shared communicative function model, children who frequently communicate a wide range of functions are better able to attend to and thus learn the words for what they have been communicating prelinguistically for months.

If either of the child-driven models is found to best explain the prelinguistic–linguistic relationship, it should be possible to predict specific prelinguistic communication behaviors that are related to and/or cause specific linguistic communication behaviors. For example, facilitating the production of early CVCV combinations should be related to the production of words that use the same consonant–vowel combinations. Similarly, if the relationship is explained via the shared pragmatic function of requesting, then object labels for the objects most frequently requested using prelinguistic means should be in the child's earliest vocabulary.

Transactional Model of Parent–Child Interaction

One aspect of the transactional model is that children affect the environment. Additionally, the environment, now changed, affects the children. In this way, both child and environment change over time and affect each other in a reciprocal fashion.

Figure 1 illustrates the transactional model of parent–child interaction as it applies to the relationship between prelinguistic communication and linguistic communication. As with the child-driven models, the transactional model of parent–child interaction (Sameroff, 1983) acknowledges that early achievements may pave the way for subsequent ones. In the figure, this effect is represented by the arrows between child prelinguistic communication and child language development. The additional factor that the transactional model posits is that clear and frequent communication elicits more frequent parental use of certain types of facilitating input (Goldberg, 1977; Sameroff, 1983). In the figure, this reciprocal effect is represented by alternating arrows between child prelinguistic communication, parent linguistic input, and, finally, child language development. The social-cognitive perspective of language development (Snow & Gilbreath, 1983) and the conversational model of language intervention (MacDonald, 1985) suggest that enhancing prelinguistic communication may indirectly affect later linguistic communica-

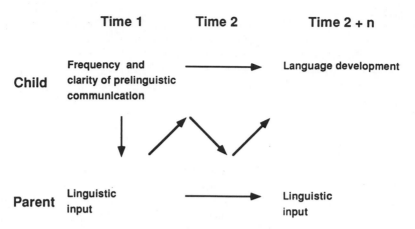

Figure 1. The transactional model of parent–child interaction applied to the relation of prelinguistic communication to linguistic communication.

tion, because frequent communicators may participate in facilitating dialogues more often than infrequent or unclear communicators.

Three types of parental linguistic input to children have theoretical and empirical support as facilitative of language development: 1) maternal responsiveness to child communication; 2) a specific type of responsiveness, that is, linguistic mapping of the child's nonverbal message (i.e., saying the child's communicative message in a more grammatical or lexically precise manner); and 3) the use of relatively short sentences when addressing the child. Theoretically, responsiveness to the child's communicative behavior is facilitative of communication development because it may enhance the child's belief that his or her communicative acts have an effect on the world, and because it may shape more conventional communicative behavior (Goldberg, 1977). Children are said to attend to linguistic mapping more than to other speech directed to them because the contrast between the child's way of communicating a message and the adult's way of communicating the same immediately preceding message makes the adult's input salient to the child (Nelson, 1989). Additionally, since the meaning in the adult's linguistic mapping is presumably identical to the child's immediately preceding message, the probability that the child will understand the adult's input is increased. Relatively short parental utterances may facilitate language learning because children may be more likely to attend to and analyze the input in short sentences than in longer ones (Furrow, Nelson, & Benedict, 1979; Murray, Johnson, & Peters, 1990). Empirically, all three types of linguistic input have been correlated with later child language development (Furrow et al., 1979; Murray et al., 1990; Nelson, 1989; Snow et al., 1987; Yoder, 1990).

Empirical support for the child's effect on parents' use of potentially facilitating behaviors is primarily correlational evidence. Yoder and Munson (in preparation) found that the frequency that mothers of 11-month-old children interpreted their babies' behavior as communicative was positively related to the amount of coordinated attention to an object and person that occurred during parent–child free play. Infant cues that contained coordinated attention were responded to more often than were other infant cues (Yoder & Munson, in preparation). In another correlational study, the length of mothers' utterances to their babies tends to decrease during the first year of life (Sherrod, Friedman, Crawley, Drake, & Devieux, 1977; Stern, Spiker, Barnett, & MacKain, 1983), particularly in families that maintain generally stimulating and responsive homes (Murray et al., 1990). Mothers may "fine-tune" their speech to children at about 10 months, possibly because the qualitative changes in the child's prelinguistic communication prompt some mothers to respond as if words had been spoken or in anticipation of the child's first words (Murray et al., 1990). Finally, Lojkasek, Goldberg, Marcovitch, and MacGregor (1990) found that child responsiveness was the strongest child predictor of maternal responsiveness in dyads with babies with handicaps. Although these correlational studies are suggestive, there is no direct experimental evidence to support the view that frequent and clear communicators elicit these types of facilitative parental linguistic input.

As with all concurrent correlational studies, determining the direction of effect is problematic in the studies just described. For example, in Yoder and Munson's study (in preparation), it is not clear whether the parents who interpreted and responded more to coordinated attention caused their children to develop and use this behavior or whether the children's use of coordinated attention elicited greater parental interpretation and responsiveness. An experimental study is the only way to determine who affects whom. If one wants to know if clear and frequent communicators elicit facilitative input, one must experimentally induce children to communicate more often using clear cues and determine if doing so influences parental use of facilitating input.

If the transactional model of parent–child interaction accounts for the prelinguistic–linguistic relationship, it should be possible to specify particular prelinguistic behaviors that are most likely to affect facilitating parental input and, thus, most likely to affect later linguistic development. However, it would not be possible to predict specific vocabulary items or particular pragmatic functions that would be facilitated by earlier prelinguistic communication skill, because the elicited parental input may not be specific to a particular pragmatic function or phonetic pattern.

In summary, the transactional model posits that prelinguistic communication intervention may influence later linguistic communication for two reasons. Like the child-driven models, the transactional model posits that getting children to communicate more clearly and frequently may prepare them to learn better from adults' linguistic input. Unlike the child-driven models, the transactional model of parent–child interaction applied to the prelinguistic–linguistic communication relationship posits that clear and frequent prelinguistic communicators should elicit from adults more frequent facilitating input. Current support for this application of the transactional model is correlational and thus ambiguous.

Empirical Support for the Prelinguistic–Linguistic Communication Relationship

Empirical support for the relationship between prelinguistic communication and linguistic development is restricted to four correlational studies at present. In an exploratory study with normally developing children, Bates et al. (1979) found a positive relationship between the frequency of pointing, showing, giving, and ritualized requesting at 9–10 months and later expressive and receptive vocabulary measures.

Three correlational studies support the prelinguistic–linguistic relationship in children with mental retardation. Mundy et al. (1988) have shown a concurrent relationship between the frequency of prelinguistic requesting and general expressive and receptive language level. In a follow-up study, Mundy and Kasari (1989) found that the frequency of nonverbal commenting predicted receptive language age 13 months later. Smith and von Tetzchner (1986) found a positive relationship between the frequency of nonverbal commenting and requesting of children studied at age 24 months and expressive and receptive language level at age 36 months.

In summary, we do have replicated evidence that there is a positive relationship between prelinguistic and linguistic communication in one sample of normally developing children (Bates et al., 1979) and in two samples of children with mental retardation (Mundy & Kasari, 1989; Mundy et al., 1988; Smith & von Tetzchner, 1986). (It should be noted that the Mundy and Kasari [1989] and Mundy et al. [1988] studies are of the same sample of children.) These four studies show only an association between the amount of certain types of prelinguistic communication and later linguistic level. No causal connection has been established.

Evidence that children who communicate relatively frequently prelinguistically also tend to communicate early linguistically does not tell language interventionists and interactionist language theorists what they want to know. Early language interventionists want to know whether an interaction that helps a child learn to communicate intentionally eventually helps him or her learn to talk earlier than he or she would without such prelinguistic intervention. Interactionists want to know whether learning to communicate prelinguistically somehow facilitates the child in learning to communicate linguistically.

Shatz (1983) has pointed out that the topography or form of prelinguistic and linguistic communication can be similar without indicating that prelinguistic communication facilitates linguistic communication. Bates et al.

(1979) also pointed out that many behaviors precede later ones without facilitating them, even if the two behaviors are similar in some way. For example, using gestures to get an adult to obtain a desired object may resemble using words to get an adult to obtain an object because the two tasks require structurally similar solutions (i.e., using an adult to acquire an object). However, learning to do one may not affect a child's ability to learn to do the other, because the child may not generalize prelinguistic requesting ability to linguistic requesting ability. Shatz (1983) argues that it is premature to conclude that much of the knowledge about communication is acquired before language and that such knowledge forms a solid basis for language acquisition itself.

In summary, the most convincing answer to the question of whether prelinguistic communication abilities facilitate later language development would be obtained in the form of a well-controlled experiment in which prelinguistic communication was manipulated using a successful intervention that later resulted in advanced linguistic skills. Such an experiment is necessary because an association between prelinguistic and linguistic communication can occur for many reasons that have little to do with any facilitative effect of prelinguistic communication on linguistic communication.

PRELINGUISTIC COMMUNICATION INTERVENTION

In this section, we attempt to address four points. First, we briefly describe recently published or in-press studies on prelinguistic intervention to demonstrate the need for more research in this area. Second, we review the specific intervention techniques that have been used to facilitate various aspects of prelinguistic communication and the available evidence of the effects of these strategies. Third, we introduce a new intervention method, which we call prelinguistic milieu teaching. Fourth, we discuss methodological issues for evaluating prelinguistic communication intervention and review the empirical support for existing intervention packages.

Current Prelinguistic Communication Intervention Studies

It has been shown that prelinguistic requesting and commenting can be facilitated by educational experience in low socioeconomic status (SES) children (O'Connell & Farran, 1982). Additionally, treatment techniques and approaches explicitly designed to facilitate prelinguistic communication in children with developmental disabilities are beginning to be developed and tested (cf. Mahoney & Powell, 1988; McCollum & Stayton, 1985; Rosenberg & Robinson, 1985; Wilcox, in press). However, none of the published intervention studies with children who are developmentally delayed has used randomly assigned control groups or within-subject design controls, which are necessary to infer intervention effects on generalized prelinguistic communication variables.

The strongest of the published or in-press studies, Wilcox (in press), used a matched-sample control group and showed dramatic group differences in the frequency of posttreatment child intentional communication in parent–child interaction sessions. However, parents were among the interventionists, so increases in generalized prelinguistic communication were not measured. It is also difficult to determine if the responsive interaction treatment in this (Wilcox, in press) study actually caused the group differences, because the use of matching as a method of producing pretreatment group equivalence may be even less effective in prelinguistic intervention studies than it is in many other intervention studies. First, we do not have precise measures of individual differences between children at the prelinguistic period, so samples that appear matched may actually be quite different in their abilities to learn to intentionally communicate. Second, we have not identified many variables that covary with intentional communication, so we do not know the variables that we need to match on. Therefore, there is a need for further investigation of the efficacy of prelinguistic communication intervention.

Specific Intervention Techniques

One of the simplest prelinguistic intervention strategies is the adult's contingent imitation of the child's behavior. Contingent imitation may benefit the child because it allows him or her to regulate the amount of social stimulation received, increases the probability that adult input will be easily processed and understood (Dawson & Lewy, 1989), and may encourage the child to imitate adult behavior (Snow, 1989). Empirically, contingent imitation has been shown to result in greater child attention to the adult social partner (Dawson & Adams, 1984; Dawson & Lewy, 1989; Field, 1977), correlate with child vocal and verbal imitation (Snow, 1989), result in greater exploratory play (Tiegerman & Primavera, 1981), and result in more differentiated play schemes (Dawson & Adams, 1984). All of these child outcomes have empirical and theoretical links to communication development (Bates et al., 1979; Harding, 1983; Snow, 1989).

The second strategy used in prelinguistic intervention is that adults respond contingently to the child's current communication behaviors about an activity or material that the child selects and shows interest in. Such adult behavior is termed contingent responsivity. As mentioned earlier, responsiveness to the child's communicative behavior is said to be facilitative of communication development because it may enhance communicative efficacy (i.e., believing that one's communicative acts have an effect) and shape more conventional communicative behavior (Goldberg, 1977). There are two reasons why teaching to the child's attentional lead is probably superior to directly recruiting the child's attention and then teaching. First, young children have difficulty deploying their attention on command for more than very short periods (Goldberg, 1977). Second, the quality of the young child's attention is probably greater to objects or events of the child's choosing than to objects or events of the adult's choosing (Bruner, Roy, & Ratner, 1980).

Responsiveness to child communicative behaviors appears to facilitate the development of at least some correlates of prelinguistic communication. For example, interventions based on these two principles have facilitated exploratory behavior and cause–effect learning (Riksen-Walraven, 1978) and vocabulary acquisition (Tomasello & Farrar, 1986; Valdez-Menchaca & Whitehurst, 1988) in children who are typically developing. In samples of children who have language delays and mental retardation, such interventions have facilitated vocabulary and semantic development (see Warren & Kaiser, 1986, for a review).

The third and fourth strategies that have been used in prelinguistic communication interventions are linguistic mapping and scaffolded modeling. Linguistic mapping is using slightly more mature ways to communicate the child's immediately preceding communicative message. Imitation of the adult model is not elicited. Scaffolded modeling is giving the child an explicit prompt to imitate a model of a more mature way to communicate his or her immediately preceding communicative message. These strategies take advantage of the child's propensity to attend most closely to a new stimulus when it is embedded in the context of familiar stimuli. For example, children probably attend more readily to new words or new word endings tagged onto a familiar utterance (Nelson, 1989). The literature on expansions, recasts, and incidental teaching supports the effectiveness of linguistic mapping and scaffolded models in facilitating linguistic development in normally developing children (see Snow et al., 1987, for review) and in children with language impairments (see Nelson, 1989, and Warren & Kaiser, 1986, for reviews).

A fifth intervention technique, using social routines as an intervention context, appears to elicit children's early communicative behaviors and may facilitate the acquisition of new communicative skills in children who are typically developing and in children with mental retardation. Routines are defined as repetitive, predictable, turn-taking games and rituals such as peek-a-boo, pat-a-cake, and feeding. The predictable structure of these games and rituals may help children learn and remember an appropriate interactive role. Theoretically, once the child learns a predictable role in a routine, he or she can devote greater attention to analyzing adult models of new ways to communicate (Conti-Ramsden & Friel-Patti, 1987; Nelson, 1989). Additionally, the salience of adult models may be enhanced because slight variations in the routine may create a "moderately novel" situation that is particularly salient to young children (Piaget & Inhelder, 1969). Research with children who are developing normally and with children who have mental retardation has shown that social routines are particularly powerful elicitors of children's linguistic (Snow et al., 1987; Yoder & Davies, in press) and prelinguistic (Bakeman & Adamson, 1986) communication.

Designing intervention strategies gleaned exclusively from the literature of mother–normal child interaction may not result in optimally effective interventions for children with developmental disabilities. The learning strategies and characteristics of children with developmental disabilities typically require additional procedures to enhance the effectiveness of parental behaviors that may facilitate communication in children who are normally developing. For example, as degree of mental retardation increases, the frequency (Brooks-Gunn & Lewis, 1984; Yoder & Feagans, 1988) and clarity (Yoder, 1987) of naturally occurring prelinguistic communication tends to decrease. Thus, children with mental retardation may not spontaneously use many of the clear cues that can serve as stimuli for teaching episodes using scaffolded models and linguistic mapping. Therefore, the frequency of learning opportunities may be too low for these children to learn efficiently. Furthermore, it may be necessary to enhance the salience of communication models for efficient learning to occur. For example, it is possible that the need for routines and scaffolded verbal models is even greater in children with disabilities than in children who are developing normally. Finally, there is evidence that children with mental retardation have difficulty spontaneously generalizing newly acquired communication skills (Warren, Baxter, Anderson, Marshall, & Baer, 1981), suggesting the need for intervention techniques that are also known to facilitate generalization.

In summary, an approach that includes aspects of mother–child interaction that appear to facilitate prelinguistic communication in normally developing children and that addresses the special learning characteristics of children with developmental delays is needed for effective prelinguistic intervention with children with such developmental disabilities. The conceptual foundations of the milieu teaching model may provide much guidance in formulating such an approach.

Prelinguistic Milieu Teaching Method

Milieu teaching utilizes several behavioral principles or techniques that have been shown to contribute to the facilitation of communication development. Milieu teaching increases the number of opportunities for responsively teaching new skills by eliciting child communication through the use of environmental arrangement, the mand-model, and time-delay procedures. Milieu teaching increases the child's attention to the model of the new communication behavior by encouraging spontaneous and prompted imitations (Warren & Bambara, 1989). By embedding teaching in typical, developmentally appropriate activities, milieu teaching enhances the probability of generalization by minimizing differences between training and generalization contexts (Stokes & Baer, 1977; Warren & Kaiser, 1986).

From a developmental perspective, several elements assumed to facilitate communication and language learning are implicit in the milieu teaching approach. In light of the empirically supported assumption that children are better able to attend to and learn from adult communicative models presented when a child is already attending to the referent (Bruner et al., 1980; Snow & Ferguson, 1977; Tomasello & Farrar, 1986), the milieu teacher follows the child's attentional lead and teaches to his or her interests and communicative intentions. To increase the probability that an easy-to-difficult sequence of skills is followed, the normal developmental sequence of skill acquisition is used as a guide for target skill selection and sequencing. Selection of appropriate targets slightly in advance of the child's productive competence and the explicit use of scaffolded models contingent on the child's communicative behavior ensure that there is a communicative match between the child and the adult (see Snow et al., 1987, for a review).

Both developmentally and behaviorally oriented researchers assume that learning can be enhanced by increasing a child's rate of appropriate engagement with people and objects (see McWilliams, 1991, for a review). Milieu teaching explicitly attempts to increase a child's engagement with people by using three prompting techniques: mand-model, time delay, and incidental teaching. Engagement with objects is targeted with teaching that involves objects and activities that are of interest to the child.

The milieu model differs from several other naturalistic intervention models (MacDonald, 1985; Manolson, 1985; Weiss, 1981; Wilcox, in press) in the use of explicit prompts for specific communicative behaviors. Explicit prompts for child communication are likely to be effective because many children with mental retardation do not communicate as clearly or as frequently as children of the same mental age who are normally developing (Brooks-Gunn & Lewis, 1984). Correlational evidence (Yoder & Munson, in preparation) and theory (Goldberg, 1977) suggest that clear cues may be interpreted and responded to more often than less clear cues. Responding and linguistically mapping children's communicative intent may be an important method of facilitating children's linguistic communication (Snow & Gilbreath, 1983). Without explicit prompts to communicate, children with disabilities, many of whom are infrequent communicators, are likely to have less frequent exposure to these facilitative parental behaviors than are their developmentally matched peers. Finally, research with children who are mentally retarded indicates that teaching facilitates productive communicative skills more efficiently if elicited production is a component of the teaching method (Ezell & Goldstein, 1989). Therefore, prompting more frequent and clear communication may be particularly important for facilitating communicative development in children who are developmentally delayed.

Intervention models that exclude explicit prompts for communication (MacDonald, 1985; Mahoney & Powell, 1988; Manolson, 1985; Weiss, 1981; Wilcox, in press) do so because their authors assume that such prompts interrupt social interaction or inhibit development (MacDonald, 1985; Mahoney & Powell, 1988). Many consider explicit prompts to communicate a type of directive, because the child is directed to behave in a specific way (Mahoney & Powell, 1988; Mahoney & Robenalt, 1988). Those who assume that prompts are negative point to literature that shows a negative relationship between adult directives to children and children's later language development (Furrow et al., 1979; Newport, Gleitman, & Gleitman, 1977). It should be noted, however, that directives have also been positively correlated with later language development (Barnes, Gutfreund, Satterly, & Wells, 1983). More recent data indicates that directives that follow the child's attentional lead are positively correlated with later vocabulary development, while directives that intrude upon the child's attentional focus are not related to later vocabulary development (Akhtar, Dunham, & Dunham, 1991). Similarly, Yoder and Davies (1990) found that questions that continue the child's topic were more likely to elicit child replies than were questions that initiated a new topic. Our position is that prompts to communicate that are about the child's attentional focus, particularly prompts for more advanced ways to communicate the message that the child has just tried to communicate, are likely to enhance the prelinguistic child's development, not inhibit it.

Because prelinguistic children may not understand some mands, some forms of time delay, or some violations of routines, prompts other than those used in milieu interventions to target linguistic skills are necessary. For example, physical prompting and explicit verbal prompting of a specific component of the target behavior (e.g., "Look at me") may be necessary to communicate to the child what to do to fulfill his or her interactive role in the routine. This more directive form of prompting is not typically used in teaching linguistic target skills, but it fits easily into milieu teaching's well-developed hierarchy of prompting. Additionally, we recommend a greater use of interactive routines as an eliciting context for child communication (Halle, Chadsey-Rusch, & Collet-Klingenberg, in press), because it has been shown that interactive routines elicit communication in children with mental retardation (Yoder, Davies, & Bishop, 1992) and without mental retardation (Bakeman & Adamson, 1984). Such routines may be critical in eliciting and teaching developmentally advanced forms of commenting.

A final modification of the milieu teaching model for prelinguistic children is the addition of contingent imitation as a means for initially building routines and encouraging vocal imitation. Contingent imitation is used in response to a child's vocal or nonvocal behavior. In either case, the adult exactly imitates or slightly modifies the behavior exhibited by the child immediately after it occurs. Contingent vocal imitation typically is used to stimulate additional instances of or modifications in child vocalizations. For example, the child may say "ba." The adult immediately responds "ba ba ba." If the child says "bo bo," the adult might respond "bo do" to introduce variation and stimulation for what may be a developmentally more advanced form of babbling (Stoel-Gammon, 1989). Contingent motor imitation is used to begin teaching a social routine. For example, if the child pushed a toy car near the adult, an instance of contingent motor imitation would be the adult immediately pushing the car back at the child. If the child hits a pot with his or her spoon, the adult might then hit the table with a spoon. Although the efficacy of contingent imitation on modifications in child action and turn-taking has not been documented, our clinical experience suggests that further investigation is warranted.

We do not yet know whether such a prelinguistic milieu teaching method or any other prelinguistic communication intervention will result in changes in parental interaction style or child linguistic communication. Investigating such long-term changes is important to understand the relationship between prelinguistic and linguistic communication in children with developmental delays. We have preliminary information that the prelinguistic milieu model facilitates the development of generalized prelinguistic communication skills. We review this support in the next section.

Evaluating Prelinguistic Intervention

The models that have been previously described provide guides for evaluating prelinguistic intervention. The transactional model suggests that prelinguistic communication intervention may influence later linguistic development, in part because frequent and clear communicators elicit more frequent parental use of behaviors that facilitate child linguistic development. Therefore, enhancing prelinguistic communication through intervention should affect parent interaction style and linguistic input to the child, as well as subsequent language development.

Child Prelinguistic Communication

Intervention may most profitably target four prelinguistic variables, because of their importance to early communication development. Two of the variables are communicative functions, requesting and commenting, and two are means by which conventional forms may be learned to express these functions, imitation and participation in social routines.

Requesting and commenting are the two most frequent communicative functions expressed during the prelinguistic period (Wetherby et al., 1988). Together, requesting and commenting provide communicative contexts in which three important developmental achievements are demonstrated: intentionality, conventionality, and referencing (Bates et al., 1987).

Request episodes provide one of the earliest contexts in which intentionality and conventionality are demonstrated (Bates et al., 1987). Requesting, or instrumental communication, has been defined as behavior that: 1) clearly indicates the child wants something; 2) is sustained until the "goal" is reached or becomes unreachable; and 3) excludes reflexive activities, cyclical variations in the child's state, or simple indications of interest in an object (Rogoff, Mistry, Radziszewska, & Germond, 1988). Before the age of 6 months, mothers usually interpret crying as indicating internal needs, such as hunger. After 6 months, maternal interpretations of crying include indications of wanting an object or social interaction (Bruner, 1983). By 9 months, babies can coordinate their attention between objects and adult, offering what many researchers consider the first sign of intentional communication (Bakeman & Adamson, 1984; Harding & Golinkoff, 1979; Yoder & Feagans, 1988). Rogoff et al. (1988) found that by 11–15.5 months, 77% of requesting episodes contained stylized gestures, such as pointing, touching an object to request it, or offering an object to request help in operating it. As children mature, vocalizations and stylized gestures are frequently coordinated (Bakeman & Adamson, 1984; Harding & Golinkoff, 1979). By 11–15.5 months, 36% of requesting episodes contained conventional communicative forms, such as words or head nods (Rogoff et al., 1988). Early requests are almost exclusively interpreted as regulating social interaction. As children approach 20 months, they request objects or assistance in operating objects with increasing frequency (Bakeman & Adamson, 1984; Rogoff et al., 1988).

Requesting was taught to four children with mental retardation in a recent study (Warren, Yoder, Gazdag, & Kim, in press). The prelinguistic milieu teaching model was introduced in a multiple-baseline design across children. The results indicated abrupt increases in the frequency of requesting in all four children during the treatment sessions. Three of the four children showed strong generalization to adults in nontraining settings using nontraining materials and not using the milieu procedures. Generalization effects with the fourth subject were more modest.

Commenting episodes provide one of the earliest contexts in which referencing is demonstrated (Bates et al., 1987). Referencing is the act of drawing another's attention to a single object of interest (Werner & Kaplan, 1963). Because communication before 9 months rarely indicates coordinated attention to an object and a person, early commenting is restricted to indications of child interest or enjoyment in an object or game and is not considered "referential." In the same way, noncommunicative pointing (i.e., extending the index finger to touch an object that is within reach) shows interest, without signaling a listener. However, by 9 months, babies show and give objects to adults to gain adult attention, providing one of the earliest indications of "referencing." By 11 months, children begin to use communicative pointing (extending the index finger on the dominant hand toward an object or interest that is out of reach). Finally, by 15 months, early functional words (e.g., "look" or "that") are used to draw adults' attention to objects.

In children who are normally developing, O'Connell and Farran (1982) found more frequent commenting (giving or showing an object to an adult to gain attention) in low SES children who had been randomly assigned to and experienced daily daycare for at least 17 months, in comparison to a control group of similar children who did not experience daycare. These data indicate that commenting can be affected by educational experience; however, we do not know which aspect of the daycare experience facilitated the commenting. With children who have mental retardation, Warren et al. (in press) found that the one child with commenting as a goal increased the frequency of intentional commenting in both treatment sessions and in generalization sessions after prelinguistic milieu teaching. These data are consonant with the interpretation that the prelinguistic milieu teaching procedure facilitates commenting. However, because only one child in the study had commenting as a goal, there was no opportunity for replication of these effects, and they should be viewed conservatively.

Vocal imitation is the third goal of prelinguistic communication interventions because of its assumed relationship with speech. There is consensus that children learn the conventional communication behaviors specific to their culture through imitation (see Snow, 1989, for a review). Although controversy exists over the more complex roles imitation may play in facilitating language development, vocal and gestural imitation have been positively correlated with language level in samples of children who are normally developing (Snow, 1989). Vocal imitation has been correlated with language level in children with autism (Yoder & Layton, 1988). In addition to these suggestions of a direct effect on language learning, imitation of communicative forms may serve the immediate purpose of taking an interactive turn when the child does not fully understand his or her role in the interaction (Clarke, 1977; Snow, 1981). Currently, there is no strong experimental support that we can facilitate exact or modified vocal imitation in nontraining interactions in prelinguistic children with disabilities.

Social routines (i.e., predictable, turn-taking interactions) may enable children to learn and use new communicative forms earlier than they would from nonroutines. This enabling effect is probably most apparent when the child is taking an active role in the routine (Snow et al., 1987). Gustafson, Green, and West (1979) found that infants become increasingly more active in routines and initiate games more often with increasing age. Eventually, children take the adult's role in the routines (Bruner, 1983). Therefore, active participation is a goal of prelinguistic communication intervention because such participation may increase the probability that intervention techniques will have an effect on communication development.

The Warren et al. (in preparation) study with children with mental retardation indicated that two of the four children increased their turn-taking concurrently with adults' increased use of turn-taking. We cannot be sure that the intervention was the cause of these changes; there was no baseline information on participation in routines that provide the supportive context for turn-taking, because these activities simply were not established as routines (i.e.,

predictable and familiar games) for the children until after baselining. Therefore, there is no experimental evidence that we can facilitate children's abilities to engage in social routines through intervention. Nevertheless, clinical
experience suggests that we can. Future experimental research is needed to
confirm clinical experience.

In summary, evidence that intervention can have generalized effects on
the child's prelinguistic communication skills is limited because this is a new
area of study. We still do not know if these changes are long lasting or
widespread. We certainly do not know what effect these changes have on the
interactors with whom the child engages. Nor do we know whether these
changes in prelinguistic communication will affect later linguistic development. However, in the following sections, we suggest specific variables that
bear further investigation.

Parent Interaction Style

In our discussion of the transactional model of parent–child interaction and
why prelinguistic intervention may affect linguistic communication, we noted
that the social-cognitive perspective of language development (Snow &
Gilbreath, 1983) and the conversational model of language intervention (Mac-
Donald, 1985) suggest that enhancing prelinguistic communication may indirectly affect later linguistic communication, because frequent communicators
probably participate in facilitating dialogues more often than infrequent and
unclear communicators. Even when intervention is carried out by adults other
than the child's parents, changes in the child may positively affect the type of
linguistic input the child receives from his or her parents.

Theory allows us to posit changes in three parent behaviors as possible
outcomes of prelinguistic communication intervention: 1) parental responsiveness to child communication; 2) a specific type of responsiveness, linguistic mapping of the child's nonverbal message; and 3) using relatively
short utterances. There has not yet been any empirical demonstration that
facilitated changes in children's prelinguistic communication elicit greater
parental use of these behaviors. However, one experiment provides evidence
that changes in children's communication skills do affect untrained adults' use
of other possibly facilitative behaviors directed to the children. In generalization sessions, Warren et al. (in preparation) found that classroom teachers
used substantially more prompts to communicate to children during the treatment phase than they used during baseline phases. The classroom teachers
were not trained to use the milieu procedures, and the generalization sessions
were conducted in a nontraining setting with nontraining materials. Presumably, these increases occurred because the children's prelinguistic communication skills were increasing, thus providing the adults with more reason to
expect that the children would respond to their prompts. Because only the
children's, not the adults', behavior was trained directly, these data are conso-

nant with the notion that the changes in the children's behavior elicited these changes in the adults' behavior. Theoretically, the increased adult prompts might, in turn, facilitate immediate child use and, perhaps, later development of communicative skills.

Child Linguistic Communication

Changes in two aspects of linguistic communication are the most likely outcomes of prelinguistic communication intervention: increases in early vocabulary and increases in the extent to which intentional communication is verbal. Increased vocabulary is predicted because past research has demonstrated a relationship between prelinguistic communication and expressive and receptive vocabulary size (Bates et al., 1979; Mundy & Kasari, 1989; Smith & von Tetzchner, 1986). Additionally, early aspects of language are more likely to be related to prelinguistic intervention than later aspects because less time transpires between intervention and follow-up testing in the former case. Intervention effects tend to become less evident as time passes between the end of the intervention and the proposed outcome (Cook & Campbell, 1979). Second, responsiveness and linguistic mapping are two of the parental behaviors that are most likely to be elicited by the changes in children's prelinguistic communication. Parental responsiveness may work together with linguistic mapping to teach children how to communicate their messages linguistically. If so, then the extent to which children's communication is verbal would also be a logical long-term outcome of intervention. Although there are theoretical reasons to expect long-term effects of prelinguistic communication intervention, we have no empirical evidence that prelinguistic intervention results in later benefits in the form of facilitated linguistic communication or vocabulary development.

Research Implications

Prelinguistic communication intervention research is still in its early stages. Fortunately, its development may be accelerated by applying some of what we have learned in over two decades of language intervention research. For instance, it seems obvious that effective approaches to prelinguistic intervention will employ activities and objects in which the child shows a current interest. Additionally, target behaviors that are components of intentional communication behaviors (e.g., eye contact) should not be taught separately from genuine communicative intent; otherwise, generalization to communicative use is unlikely. These principles derived from early language intervention research should be equally applicable to the prelinguistic period, when development is even less differentiated than in the early stages of language learning. The Warren et al. study (in press) suggests that the prelinguistic milieu teaching approach shows considerable promise. Future research should investigate which children benefit most from this intervention approach and compare the efficacy of this approach with other prelinguistic communication intervention strategies (e.g., the responsive interaction approach [Wilcox, in press]).

The transactional model of development (Sameroff & Chandler, 1975) and the family-systems approach to early intervention (Dunst, Trivette, & Deal, 1988) posit that a change in any member of the family affects other members of the family. These effects on the family are thought to have future effects on the child. In fact, this general notion is at the heart of family-focused intervention models. Applied to prelinguistic intervention, enhanced prelinguistic skills should stimulate parents to interact with children in facilitative ways. If this proves to be the case, the efficiency of subsequent language intervention should be increased. It is estimated that by the time typical children are 4 years old, they have spoken 10–20 million words and had 20–40 million words directed at them (Chapman, in press). Children swim in an ocean of language 12 hours per day, while professionals can only provide direct intervention a few minutes a day. Therefore, if children are taught to communicate more frequently and more clearly, they may seek linguistic input at those times they are most likely to benefit from it (e.g., immediately after they speak).

Practical Implications

Given that research on prelinguistic intervention is in the early stages of development, our notions of best practices are truly preliminary. In the area of identifying communication delays, our present level of knowledge provides a good start for an empirical basis for predicting which children are at risk for later language delays. We have replicated evidence that the frequency of prelinguistic commenting and requesting predicts language level several months to 1 year later. Such evidence only helps us identify which aspects of prelinguistic and linguistic communication are related. We do not yet know how frequently a typically developing 18-month-old communicates. To use such normative information for the purposes of identifying children at risk for language delays, we also need standardized formats for assessing prelinguistic communication, because the context affects the frequency and incidence of prelinguistic communication (Coggins, Olswang, & Guthrie, 1987). Wetherby and her colleagues (Wetherby et al., 1988; Wetherby, Yonclas, & Bryan, 1989) are developing such an instrument, the Communication and Symbolic Behavior Scales (Wetherby & Prizant, 1990). Norming of this instrument is currently underway (A.K. Wetherby, personal communication, November, 1991).

As for intervention, our knowledge that children with advanced prelinguistic skills typically exhibit advanced language skills argues in favor of intervening with children as soon as we have evidence of a problem. While researchers are working on testing whether prelinguistic communication intervention influences later language development, clinicians are well advised to directly address the current communicative needs of prelinguistic children. However, we do not yet know the best prelinguistic communication intervention methods. In fact, most comparisons between communication intervention methods have indicated that one teaching method works best for one group of children, while another works best for another group of children (e.g., Cole, Mills, & Dale, 1989; Friedman & Friedman, 1980; Yoder, Kaiser, & Alpert, 1990). One alternative to the prelinguistic milieu teaching method is Wilcox's responsive interaction method (in press). Wilcox's model teaches significant others to be very consistent and contingently responsive to the child behaviors that have been identified as meaningful. It strikes us that this model should be particularly useful for children before they intentionally communicate. The primary task of pre-intentional children is to learn that their behavior has an effect on the world. Research with children who are normally developing has demonstrated that responsiveness facilitates children's generalized cause-and-effect learning (Riksen-Walraven, 1978). Explicit prompts for particular behaviors may have little place in facilitating intentional action and this generalized notion of cause and effect. However, as children begin to direct communication to adults by using coordinated attention between objects and adults (e.g., showing objects to adults), prelinguistic milieu teaching may be more efficient than the responsive interaction approach. Explicitly eliciting more conventional and intentional communication behaviors at appropriate times, as is done in prelinguistic milieu teaching, may prove to be more efficient than waiting for such behavior and differentially reinforcing it, as is done in the responsive interaction model. It should be noted that this view is not yet supported by research. Above all, practitioners should monitor the literature in the next 5–10 years for evidence of the differential effectiveness of various prelinguistic intervention approaches.

CONCLUSIONS

Does prelinguistic communication intervention facilitate linguistic communication in children with developmental delays? We suspect, based on theory and correlational evidence, that the final answer to this question will be a qualified "yes." The qualifications of this affirmative answer will probably concern the developmental levels or types of disabilities of the children before intervention, the type of intervention, the nature of the children's family systems, and the aspects of linguistic development that are measured. Because of the field's related experiences with language intervention and the expanded interest in very early intervention, we predict that the research needed to answer this question may be completed by the end of the century.

The world is becoming increasingly dependent on the rapid exchange of information. The critical nature of communication and language development to the future functioning of human beings has never been more obvious. Additionally, many learning disabilities, reading problems (Feagans & Farran, 1979), and behavior disorders (Goetz & Sailor, 1985) may have their origins in early communication and language problems. For these and many other reasons, it is difficult to overstate the importance of establishing effective methods of enhancing the communicative abilities of young children with disabilities.

REFERENCES

Akhtar, N., Dunham, F., & Dunham, P. (1991). Directive interactions and early vocabulary development: The role of joint attentional focus. *Journal of Child Language, 18,* 41–50.

Bakeman, R., & Adamson, L. (1984). Coordinating to people and objects in mother–infant and peer–infant interaction. *Child Development, 55,* 1278–1289.

Bakeman, R., & Adamson, L. (1986). Infants' conventionalized acts: Gestures and words with mothers and peers. *Infant Behavior and Development, 9,* 215–230.

Barnes, S., Gutfreund, M., Satterly, D., & Wells, G. (1983). Characteristics of adult speech which predict children's language development. *Journal of Child Language, 10,* 65–84.

Bates, E., Benigni, L., Bretherton, I., Camaioni, L., & Volterra, V. (1979). *The emergence of symbols: Cognition and communication in infancy.* New York: Academic Press.

Bates, E., O'Connell, B., & Shore, C. (1987). Language and communication in infancy. In J. Osofsky (Ed.), *Handbook of infant development* (pp. 149–203). New York: John Wiley & Sons.

Benedict, H. (1979). Early lexical development: Comprehension and production. *Journal of Child Language, 6,* 183–200.

Brooks-Gunn, J., & Lewis, M. (1984). Maternal responsivity in interactions with handicapped infants. *Child Development, 55,* 782–793.

Bruner, J.S. (1978). Berlyne memorial lecture: Acquiring the use of languages. *Canadian Journal of Psychology, 32*(4), 204–218.

Bruner, J.S. (1983). *Child's talk: Learning to use language.* New York: Norton.

Bruner, J., Roy, C., & Ratner, N. (1980). The beginnings of request. In K.E. Nelson (Ed.), *Children's language* (Vol. 3, pp. 91–138). New York: Gardner Press.

Chapman, R. (in press). Child talk: Assumptions of a developmental process model for early language learning. In R.S. Chapman (Ed.), *Child talk: Process for language acquisition and disorders.* Chicago: Mosby-Year Book.

Chomsky, N. (1965). *Aspects of the theory of syntax.* Cambridge, MA: MIT Press.

Clarke, R. (1977). What's the use of imitation? *Journal of Child Language, 4,* 341–359.

Coggins, T., Olswang, L.B., & Guthrie, J. (1987). Assessing communicative intents in young children: Low structured observations or elicitation tasks? *Journal of Speech and Hearing Disorders, 52,* 44–49.

Cole, K., Mills, & Dale, P. (1989). A comparison of the effects of academic and cognitive curricula for young handicapped children one and two years postprogram. *Topics in Early Childhood Special Education, 9*(3), 110–127.

Conti-Ramsden, G., & Friel-Patti, S. (1987). Situational variability in mother–child conversations. In K.E. Nelson & A. van Kleeck (Eds.), *Children's language* (Vol. 6, pp. 43–64). Hillsdale, NJ: Lawrence Erlbaum Associates.

Cook, T.D., & Campbell, D.T. (1979). *Quasi-experimentation: Design and analysis issues for field settings*. Boston: Houghton-Mifflin.

Dawson, G., & Adams, A. (1984). Imitation and social responsiveness in autistic children. *Journal of Abnormal Child Psychology, 12,* 209–225.

Dawson, G., & Lewy, A. (1989). In G. Dawson (Ed.), *Autism: Nature, diagnosis, and treatment*. New York: Guilford Press.

Dunst, C., Trivette, C.M., & Deal, A.G. (1988). *Enabling and empowering families.* Cambridge: MA: Brookline Books.

Ezell, H.K., & Goldstein, H. (1989). Effects of imitation on language comprehension and transfer to production in children with mental retardation. *Journal of Speech and Hearing, 54*(1), 49–56.

Feagans, L., & Farran, D. (1979). *The language of children reared in poverty: Implications for evaluation and intervention*. New York: Academic Press.

Field, T. (1977). Effects of early separation, interactive deficits, and experimental manipulations on infant–mother face-to-face interaction. *Child Development, 48,* 763–771.

Friedman, P., & Friedman, K.A. (1980). Accounting for individual differences when comparing the effectiveness of remedial language teaching methods. *Applied Psycholinguistics, 1,* 151–170.

Furrow, D., Nelson, K., & Benedict, H. (1979). Mothers' speech to children and syntactic relationships: Some simple relationships. *Journal of Child Language, 6* (3), 423–442.

Goetz, L.G., & Sailor, W. (1985). Using a behavior chain interruption strategy to teach communication skills to students with severe disabilities. *Journal of The Association for Persons with Severe Handicaps, 10,* 21–30.

Goldberg, S. (1977). Social competence in infancy: A model of parent–infant interaction. *Merrill-Palmer Quarterly, 23*(3), 163–177.

Golinkoff, R.M. (1981). The influence of Piagetian theory on the study of the development of communication. In I. Sigel, D. Brodzinsky, & R.M. Golinkoff (Eds.), *New directions in Piagetian theory and practice* (pp. 127–142). Hillsdale, NJ: Lawrence Erlbaum Associates.

Gustafson, G.E., Green, J.A., & West, M. (1979). The infant's changing role in mother–infant games: The growth of social skills. *Infant Behavior and Development, 2,* 301–308.

Halle, J.W., Chadsey-Rusch, J., & Collet-Klingenberg, L. (in press). Applying contextual features of general-case instruction and interactive routines to enhance communication skills. In R.A. Gable & S.F. Warren (Eds.), *Strategies for teaching students with mild to severe mental retardation*. London: Jessica Kingsley Publishers.

Harding, C.G. (1983). Setting the stage for language acquisition: Communication development in the first year. In R.M. Golinkoff (Ed.), *The transition from prelinguistic to linguistic communication* (pp. 93–111). Hillsdale, NJ: Lawrence Erlbaum Associates.

Harding, C.G., & Golinkoff, R.M. (1979). The origins of intentional vocalizations in prelinguistic infants. *Child Development, 50,* 33–40.

Kahn, J. (1984). Cognitive training and initial use of referential speech. *Topics in Language Disorders, 6*(1), 14–28.

Lenneberg, E.H. (1967). *Biological foundations of language*. New York: John Wiley & Sons.

Locke, J. (1990). Babbling and early speech. *First Language, 9*(6), 191–206.

Lojkasek, M., Goldberg, S., Marcovitch, S., & MacGregor, D. (1990). Influences on maternal responsiveness to developmentally delayed preschoolers [Special issue: Families]. *Journal of Early Intervention, 14*(3), 260–273.

MacDonald, J.D. (1985). Language through conversation. In S. Warren & A. Rogers-Warren (Eds.), *Teaching functional language* (pp. 89–122). Baltimore: University Park Press.

Mahoney, G., & Powell, A. (1988). Modifying parent–child interaction: Enhancing the development of handicapped children [Special Issue: Early intervention for infants with handicaps and their families]. *Journal of Special Education, 22*, 82–96.

Mahoney, G., & Robenalt, K. (1985). A comparison of conversational patterns between mothers and their Down syndrome and normal infants. *Journal of the Division of Early Childhood, 10*, 172–180.

Manolson, A. (1985). *It takes two to talk: A Hanan early language parent guidebook*. (Available from the Hanan Resource Centre, Suite 4-126, 252 Bloor St. West, Toronto, Ontario, M5S 1V6, Canada.)

McCollum, J., & Stayton, V. (1985). Infant/parent interaction: Studies and intervention guidelines based on the SIAI model. *Journal of the Division of Early Childhood, 9*, 125–135.

McWilliams, R.A. (1991). Targeting teaching at the children's use of time: Perspectives on preschoolers' engagement. *Teaching Exceptional Children*, summer, 42–43.

Miller, J.F. (1988). Language and communication characteristics of children with Down syndrome. In S.M. Pueschel, C. Tingey, J.E. Rynders, A.C. Crocker, & D.M. Crutcher (Eds.), *New perspectives on Down syndrome* (pp. 233–262). Baltimore: Paul H. Brookes Publishing Co.

Miller, J., Chapman, R., & Bedrosian, J. (1978). The relationship between etiology, cognitive development and language and communicative performance. *New Zealand Speech Therapist's Journal, 33*, 2–17.

Mundy, P., & Kasari, C. (1989, April). *Predictors of language development in atypical children*. Paper presented at the Society for Research in Child Development, Kansas City, MO.

Mundy, P., Sigman, M., Kasari, C., & Yirmiya, N. (1988). Nonverbal communication skills in Down syndrome children. *Child Development, 59*(1), 235–249.

Murray, A.D., Johnson, J., & Peters, J. (1990). Fine-tuning of utterance length to preverbal infants: Effects on later language development. *Journal of Child Language, 17*(3), 511–526.

Nelson, K.E. (1989). Strategies for first language teaching. In M.L. Rice & R.L. Schiefelbusch (Eds.), *The teachability of language* (pp. 263–310). Baltimore: Paul H. Brookes Publishing Co.

Newport, E., Gleitman, L., & Gleitman, H. (1977). Mother, I'd rather do it myself. In C. Snow & C. Ferguson (Eds.), *The acquisition of communicative competence* (pp. 121–148). Baltimore: University Park Press.

O'Connell, J.C., & Farran, D.C. (1982). Effects of day-care experience on the use of intentional communicative behaviors in a sample of socioeconomically depressed infants. *Developmental Psychology, 18*(1), 22–29.

Piaget, J., & Inhelder, I. (1969). *The psychology of the child*. New York: Basic Books.

Rice, M.L., & Kemper, S. (1984). *Child language and cognition*. Baltimore: University Park Press.

Riksen-Walraven, J.M. (1978). Effects of caregiver behavior on habituation rate and self-efficacy in infants. *International Journal of Behavioral Development, 1,* 105–130.

Rogoff, B., Mistry, J., Radziszewska, B., & Germond, J. (1988). Infants' instrumental social interaction with adults. In S. Feinman (Ed.), *Social referencing and the social construction of reality in infancy.* New York: Plenum.

Rosenberg, S., & Robinson, C. (1985). Enhancement of mothers' interactional skills in an infant education program. *Education and Training of the Mentally Retarded, 20*(2), 163–169.

Sameroff, A.J. (1983). Developmental systems: Contexts and evolution. In P.H. Mussen (Ed.), *Handbook of child psychology* (Vol. 1, pp. 237–294). New York: John Wiley & Sons.

Sameroff, A.J., & Chandler, M.J. (1975). Reproductive risk and the continuum of caretaking casualty. In F.D. Horowitz, M. Hetherington, S. Scarr-Salapatek, & G. Siegel (Eds.), *Review of child development research* (Vol. 4, pp. 209–240). Chicago: University of Chicago Press.

Schwartz, R. (1988). Phonological factors in early lexical acquisition. In M.D. Smith & J.L. Locke (Eds.), *The emergent lexicon: The child's development of a linguistic vocabulary* (pp. 185–222). Orlando: Academic Press.

Shatz, M. (1983). On transition, continuity, and coupling: An alternative approach to communicative development. In R.M. Golinkoff (Ed.), *The transition from prelinguistic to linguistic communication* (pp. 43–55). Hillsdale, NJ: Lawrence Erlbaum Associates.

Sherrod, K., Friedman, S., Crawley, S., Drake, D., & Devieux, J. (1977). Maternal language to prelinguistic infants: Semantic aspects. *Infant Behavior and Development, 48,* 1662–1665.

Smith, L., & von Tetzchner, S. (1986). Communicative, sensorimotor, and language skills of young children with Down syndrome. *American Journal of Mental Deficiency, 91,* 57–66.

Snow, C.E. (1981). The uses of imitation. *Journal of Child Language, 8,* 205–212.

Snow, C.E. (1989). The uses of imitation. In G.E. Speidel & K.E. Nelson (Eds.), *The many faces of imitation in language learning* (pp. 103–129). New York: Springer-Verlag.

Snow, C.E., & Ferguson, C. (Eds.). (1977). *Talking to children: Language input and acquisition.* Cambridge: Cambridge University Press.

Snow, C.E., & Gilbreath, B.J. (1983). Explaining transitions. In R.M. Golinkoff (Ed.), *The transition from prelinguistic to linguistic communication.* Hillsdale, NJ: Lawrence Erlbaum Associates.

Snow, C.E., Perlmann, R., & Nathan, D.C. (1987). Why routines are different. In K. Nelson & A. van Kleeck (Eds.), *Children's language* (Vol. 6, pp. 281–296). Hillsdale, NJ: Lawrence Erlbaum Associates.

Stern, D., Spiker, S., Barnett, J.R., & MacKain, K. (1983). The prosody of maternal speech: Infant age and context related changes. *Journal of Child Language, 10,* 1–15.

Stoel-Gammon, C. (1989). Prespeech and early speech development of two late talkers. *First Language, 9,* 207–223.

Stokes, T.F., & Baer, D. (1977). An implicit technology of generalization. *Journal of Applied Behavior Analysis, 10,* 349–367.

Tiegerman, E., & Primavera, L. (1981). Object manipulation: An interactional strategy with autistic children. *Journal of Autism and Developmental Disorders, 1,* 427–438.

Tomasello, M., & Farrar, M.F. (1986). Joint attention and early language. *Child Development, 57,* 1454–1463.

Valdez-Menchaca, M.C., & Whitehurst, G.J. (1988). The effects of incidental teaching on vocabulary acquisition by young children. *Child Development, 59*(6), 1451–1459.

Warren, S.F., & Bambara, L.M. (1989). An experimental analysis of milieu language intervention: Teaching the action–object form. *Journal of Speech and Hearing Disorders, 54,* 448–461.

Warren, S.F., Baxter, D., Anderson, S., Marshall, A., & Baer, D.M. (1981). Generalization and maintenance of question-asking by severely retarded individuals. *Journal of The Association of the Severely Handicapped, 6,* 15–22.

Warren, S.F., & Kaiser, A.P. (1986). Incidental language teaching: A critical review. *Journal of Speech and Hearing Disorders, 51,* 291–299.

Warren, S.F., Yoder, P.J., Gazdag, G., & Kim, K. (in press). The effect of a prelinguistic milieu teaching procedure on generalized intentional prelinguistic communication in children with mental retardation. *Journal of Speech and Hearing Research.*

Weiss, R. (1981). INREAL intervention for language handicapped and bilingual children. *Journal of the Division of Early Childhood, 4,* 40–51.

Werner, H., & Kaplan, B. (1963). *Symbol formation.* New York: John Wiley & Sons.

Wetherby, A.K., Cain, D.H., Yonclas, D.G., & Walker, V.G. (1988). Analysis of intentional communication of normal children from the prelinguistic to the multiword stage. *Journal of Speech and Hearing Research, 31,* 240–252.

Wetherby, A.K., & Prizant, B. (1990). *Communication and Symbolic Behavior Scales-Research Edition.* Chicago: Riverside Publishing.

Wetherby, A.K., Yonclas, D.G., & Bryan, A.A. (1989). Communication profiles of preschool children with handicaps: Implications for early identification. *Journal of Speech and Hearing Disorders, 54,* 148–158.

Wilcox, J. (in press). Enhancing initial communication skills in young children with developmental disabilities through partner programming. *Seminars in Speech and Hearing.*

Yoder, P.J. (1987). The relationship between degree of infant handicap and the clarity of infant cues. *American Journal of Mental Deficiency, 91*(1), 639–641.

Yoder, P.J. (1990). The theoretical and empirical basis of early amelioration of developmental disabilities: Implications for future research. *Journal of Early Intervention, 14*(1), 27–42.

Yoder, P.J., & Munson, L. (in preparation). *Social consequences of coordinated attention to adults and objects in parent–infant interactions.* Unpublished manuscript, Vanderbilt University, Nashville.

Yoder, P.J., & Davies, B. (1990). Do parental questions and topic continuations elicit replies from developmentally delayed children?: A sequential analysis. *Journal of Speech and Hearing Research, 33,* 563–573.

Yoder, P.J., & Davies, B. (in press). Do children with developmental delays use more frequent and diverse language in verbal routines? *American Journal of Mental Retardation.*

Yoder, P.J., Davies, B., & Bishop, K. (1992). Getting children with developmental disabilities to talk to adults. In S. Warren & J. Reichle (Eds.), *Communication and language intervention: Vol. 1. Causes and effects in communication and language intervention* (pp. 255–275). Baltimore: Paul H. Brookes Publishing Co.

Yoder, P.J., & Feagans, L. (1988). Mothers' attributions of communication to prelinguistic behavior of infants with developmental delays and mental retardation. *American Journal on Mental Retardation, 93*(1), 36–43.

Yoder, P.J., Kaiser, A.P., & Alpert, C. (1990). An exploratory study of the interaction between language teaching methods and child characteristics. *Journal of Speech and Hearing Research, 34,* 155–167.

Yoder, P.J., & Layton, T. (1988). Speech following sign language training in nonverbal autistic children. *Journal of Autism and Developmental Disorders, 18,* 217–229.

4

Parent-Implemented
Language Intervention
An Environmental System Perspective

Ann P. Kaiser

THE NOTION OF PARENT-IMPLEMENTED language intervention is not new. Since 1965, more than 30 studies have demonstrated that parents can be trained to implement a variety of language teaching procedures with their children with mental retardation or language delays. Yet the potential of parent-implemented interventions has not been fully realized. This chapter addresses issues of importance if we are to expand this model for early language intervention. The arguments for parent-implemented interventions are briefly reviewed, and the methodology of studies in this area is critiqued. Then a model of the environment as it influences children's language learning and an intervention strategy deriving from that model is presented. Finally, a research agenda for the future is discussed.

Two primary arguments for parents as interventionists have been posited. First, parents are typically the first teachers of early language skills (Table 1). Second, parent involvement in language remediation may be a means of obtaining generalized outcomes of training that are not realized through more traditional forms of intervention (cf. Cooke, Cooke, & Appolloni, 1976; Daurelle, Fox, MacLean, & Kaiser, 1987). A third argument for parent-implemented intervention derives from observations of normal mother–child interactions. In order to successfully facilitate the early social-communicative aspects of language, it may be necessary that the interventionist be an invested caregiver. These caregivers are particularly able to match and respond to the child's changing communicative development, because they are invested in the child's developmental outcomes and have frequent, affectively positive

Preparation of this chapter was supported by Grant No. G008730528 from the U.S. Department of Education and Grant No. HD15051 from the National Institute of Child Health and Human Development.

Table 1.   Rationale for parent involvement in language intervention

Parents are children's first teachers.

Parent-implemented intervention promotes child generalization of newly learned language.

Interactions with an invested caregiver may be critical to facilitating the child's social communication.

There are benefits to the parent and child beyond those resulting from the targeted improvements in the child's language skills.

interactions with the child in a variety of contexts. An important feature of parent–child interaction may be that the parent who has extensive experience with his or her child is better able to read the child's communicative intent than are less familiar adults. This, in turn, suggests that the parent may be able to provide feedback, expansions, and scaffolding that are more precisely semantically contingent. In addition, we propose a fourth argument: Involving the parent in the intervention process may have benefits to the parent and child beyond those resulting from the targeted improvements in the child's language skills. By facilitating immediate and early communication, different and more positive social-communicative interaction patterns may be established that could have long-term benefits for the child's behavioral development and the parent–child relationship.

Although these four arguments favoring parent-implemented intervention appear reasonable, empirical support for the efficacy of parent-implemented intervention as a means of facilitating children's language development is not extensive.

PARENT-IMPLEMENTED LANGUAGE INTERVENTION RESEARCH

Research on parent-implemented language intervention has derived largely from two theoretical perspectives, following many of the same trends as other language intervention research. Early work, in the 1960s and 1970s, was conducted in the tradition of behavior analysis, but more recent work draws from social-interactionist models of language development, using conversation as the basis for intervention.

Many of the first parent-implemented language interventions were based on the didactic language intervention models following from the behaviorist tradition (cf. Goldstein & Lanyon, 1971; Harris, Wolchick, & Milch, 1983; Miller & Sloane, 1976; Risley & Wolf, 1967). Parents were taught to apply operant procedures during highly structured training sessions for the purpose of increasing children's production of linguistic forms. Although these studies successfully demonstrated that parents could teach isolated sets of linguistic forms, such studies did not always target functional communication responses that could be used by the child in a variety of natural contexts. Furthermore, the impact of intervention on the child's general communication development was rarely assessed. Most studies did not assess child generalization; however, those that did (cf. Salzberg & Viallani, 1983) reported little evidence of child generalization, unless parents continued to use the teaching procedures in the settings in which child generalization was assessed. In addition, there was little evidence that parents were able to transfer the use of prompting and reinforcement-based training procedures from training to nontraining settings without specific instruction and coaching.

Research on conversationally based language intervention began with evidence from normally developing children's interactions with their parents and the need to directly intervene to enhance children's social use of language because of the limited evidence of generalization from more structured intervention settings. The resulting models of parent-implemented language intervention focused on increasing parental responsiveness and decreasing directiveness (Cheseldine & McConkey, 1979; Mahoney & Powell, 1986; Price, 1984; Seitz, 1975; Weistuch & Lewis, 1985), increasing the parent's ability to follow the child's lead in conversations (McConkey & O'Connor, 1982; Seitz, 1975), and establishing more balanced or less complex parent turns (Mahoney & Powell, 1986) and shorter utterances by the parent (Cheseldine & McConkey, 1979). Results of these studies indicated that parents were able to change their behavior in these ways. The evidence supporting causal changes in child behavior is limited, in part because the typical pre–posttest designs used in these studies do not rule out maturation as a factor in child change (exceptions are Girolametto, 1988; Girolametto & Tannock, 1992; Weistuch & Lewis, 1985). Interpreting the reported changes in child behavior, which include increased complexity of utterances as measured by use of specific more complex structures or by changes in MLU, increased numbers of utterances, increased vocabulary and improved scores on standardized tests of language development, is greatly constrained by the experimental designs of these studies. In the two most carefully controlled studies of the effects of parent-based conversational intervention to date, by Girolametto (1988) and Tannock, Girolametto, and Siegel (1989), no significant differences in child language outcomes were found between the treatment and randomly assigned control groups.

Current Research

Since the late 1980s, we have researched a model of parent-implemented intervention, milieu teaching, which derives from the behavior analysis tradition but uses naturally occurring conversations in order to teach language.

We have extended the classroom-based applications of milieu teaching to include applications by family members in a series of studies designed to demonstrate that parents and siblings can be trained as language interventionists. Alpert and Kaiser (1992) trained six parents of preschool children with disabilities to use four milieu teaching strategies. All six parents acquired the milieu teaching skills, and they demonstrated generalization across household settings and maintenance of the skills 3 months after training was completed. Increases in child MLU beyond those predicted from their preintervention levels and increases in intelligibility and vocabulary were observed for some subjects. Hemmeter and Kaiser (1990) examined the effects of training a parent in a single aspect of milieu teaching, that of environmental arrangement. The effects for the dyad were clear and immediate: Environmental arrangement was related to an increase in father attempts to teach, in child initiations, and improvement in balance of father–child turns. The magnitude of effects on adult–child interaction did not replicate in a subsequent study with adults in classrooms (Kaiser & Alpert, 1988), suggesting that the parent–child context may be uniquely influenced by the availability of objects and activities that interest the child.

Kaiser and Alpert (in preparation) analyzed home and classroom teaching environments in terms of the structure that specific activities provide to support milieu teaching. Observations of parents and teachers confirmed that activities involving turn-taking are highly facilitative of teaching interactions. For teachers, milieu teaching is most likely to occur when only one or two children are present, and it is highly unlikely to occur when four or more children are present. This analysis (Kaiser & Alpert, in preparation) suggested that one-on-one adult–child interactions involving mutually engaging activities are optimal occasions for milieu teaching. Based on findings describing supportive environmental contexts, Hancock (1988) designed and experimentally analyzed the effects of a home intervention with three siblings serving as milieu teachers for their younger brothers with disabilities. The younger brothers each learned the target utterances and demonstrated changes in responsiveness and initiations within and outside the training setting. Kaiser and Alpert (1988) compared two strategies for teaching parents to use milieu teaching with their children with disabilities. Group instruction was sufficient for parents to acquire the environmental arrangement strategies and some aspects of the four milieu teaching procedures. For seven of eight parents in the study, direct training including coaching and feedback was necessary before they mastered the teaching procedures and applied them accurately and frequently. Twelve monthly follow-up observations were conducted with six of the families. In each case, parents continued to use milieu teaching. While there were some decreases in parent frequency and accuracy in using the techniques, child responsiveness to parent teaching and the use of trained linguistic skills were maintained at high levels.

These studies offer consistent evidence that parents can be trained to use milieu teaching and that the effects of their training will maintain, but they do not provide data regarding the impact of this training on the interaction of the dyad outside the milieu teaching episodes. Our analyses of child outcomes have been limited primarily to acquisition of targets and responsiveness to the teaching techniques. These studies are of value in demonstrating the extension of milieu teaching to applications by parents and the effects of the nonsocial environment on the implementation of milieu teaching, but they do not present complete analyses of the potential effects of parent-implemented milieu teaching.

Empirical Limitations

While the existing studies support the notion that parents can change their behaviors in a variety of ways that will support children's language learning, the empirical evidence for the *effectiveness* of parent-implemented language intervention is mixed. In part, the limited empirical evidence results from the methodological constraints imposed by designs used to measure the effects of parent-implemented intervention (Table 2). There is evidence from research using behavior modification strategies and milieu teaching approaches that short-term changes in child use of targeted language skills can be consistently achieved (Kaiser, Yoder, & Keetz, 1992, provides a comprehensive review of the effects of milieu teaching). Evidence of child generalization and maintenance of these skills is, however, modest and comes largely from recent studies using the milieu intervention. Because most studies assessed children's use of target utterances in situations where the parent was teaching, it is not clear that children generalize newly learned skills to other interactional contexts. There is little consistent evidence from the behavior analysis studies of changes in children's global language development, since often no measures of this type of outcome were taken.

Those studies in which parents were trained to use conversational facilitation strategies, such as responsive interaction (Mahoney, 1988; Tannock & Giralametto, 1992), report generally positive, but varied, findings. However, findings relating to both immediate and more global language changes are difficult to interpret because of the designs used in the studies. A number of studies show gains from pre- to posttest but do not adequately control for maturation. The three studies that used a control group for maturation report mixed results in terms of parent and child change. While group-design studies

Table 2. Methodological limitations

Experimental designs have not controlled for maturation.

Evaluations have focused on short-term assessments of changes in child language and interaction style during interactions with parent.

Generalization of child change has not been measured independently of changes in dyad; no assessments of child learning, changes in strategy, or maintenance of specific child gains have been reported.

Fidelity of parent implementations of the treatment has not been analyzed as it affects child outcomes.

have more typically employed standardized tests for outcome measures, these studies have not assessed changes in children's use of language outside the parent–child dyad.

Other Methodological Limitations

In addition to the methodological limitations discussed above, resulting from the design chosen to evaluate treatment effects, interpretations of the research findings on parent-implemented intervention have been limited by the types of measures of child language outcomes selected, the settings in which treatment effects were evaluated, the potential limitations in fidelity of treatment, the period of treatment, and assessment of parent and child outcomes.

Accurate evaluation of the impact of parent intervention on child language development requires that measures of the child's language development be taken outside the parent–child dyad. At least two strategies might be employed. First, in both group and single-subject designs, assessment should include analyses of generalization to a responsive but nontraining interactor to determine if either the child's newly acquired social responses or specific language forms generalize outside the dyadic training context. A further assessment of the child's conceptual learning (i.e., generalization across members within a class of language stimuli and assessment of changes in comprehension and production of newly learned grammatical or lexical skills) is needed to gauge the extent of new learning of specific grammatical or lexical skills. Second, group designs are better suited for comparing children receiving treatment with those not receiving treatment on measures of global language development (e.g., standardized tests, MLU). Such measures, while an interesting addition to single-subject studies, are not easily interpreted. When no control group is available for comparison because maturation is likely to occur across the period of the intervention, it is difficult to evaluate changes on developmental measures.

There are several issues related to fidelity of treatment in research on parent-implemented interventions. First, studies must demonstrate that parents mastered the targeted behaviors before any reasonable assessment of change in child behavior can be undertaken. Not only is it important to know *that* parents acquired the target behaviors, it is important to know *when* they did so in order to ascertain the duration and intensity of treatment provided for the child. For example, in an 11-week training course (cf. Girolametto, 1988), parents may not demonstrate sufficiently high levels of the behaviors targeted for change until late in the program; thus, the children may receive as little as 2 or 3 weeks of effective intervention. In addition, measurement of parent generalization to the settings in which child generalization will be measured is important in interpreting those child effects. The fidelity of treatment implementation outside the training sessions is usually unknown. Finally, even when parent generalization is demonstrated, accurate estimates of the amount of intervention that a child receives across time are almost impossible to make. The techniques for collecting parent generalization data (e.g., video- or audiotaping in the home by a research assistant) are sufficiently reactive for the generalization analysis to produce the "best" example of what parents can do rather than representing what they typically do.

The length of time across which changes in parent and child behavior are evaluated is also important. Without long-term assessments using appropriate control groups, the impact of parent-implemented intervention on children's language development cannot be determined. No studies to date have provided such assessments.

Conceptual Limitations

Although most parent-implemented interventions draw directly from behavioral or social-interactionist models of language development, clearly articulated conceptual frameworks for parent-implemented intervention, which relate parent behavior to specific expected outcomes for the child, are lacking. Researchers typically have cited findings from other contexts (i.e., teacher- or therapist-implemented behavioral interventions or normal parent–child interactions) to support general approaches to parent-implemented intervention. Researchers in neither tradition have fully considered the environmental context of interactions involving a child with disabilities. There has been almost no consideration of the adaptations in parent-implemented interventions that might be necessary to fit children's behavior and developmental characteristics, which might also require that the intervention differ from the ideal profile of parent–child interaction. Proponents of parent-implemented interventions tend to argue for a general intervention approach without consideration of the child's language level and social behavior. While different conversational skills may be targeted for children at varying developmental levels, within a specific theoretical orientation, the basic approach to intervention tends to be quite similar for all children. Evidence from therapist-implemented intervention research increasingly suggests that different types of interventions may be optimal for children exhibiting different levels of language skills (cf. Yoder, Kaiser, & Alpert, 1991).

Further, research on parent-implemented interventions has typically considered changes in parent behavior in isolation rather than as a part of the environmental system that supports the child's communication and language development. Conceptualization of the environmental system includes recognition of the child's language skills as a critical condition for the selection of an intervention, but such a conceptualization also includes the role of the physical context, the child's engagement with that context, other parental behaviors relating environmental context and language, and the child's changing linguistic and behavioral repertoire over time.

Summary

Although there has been considerable research on parent-implemented language interventions, much remains to be done before there is conclusive empirical evidence indicating the effectiveness of this type of intervention for improving the language skills of children with developmental disabilities. While improvements in measurement and design would increase the credibility of the database, I propose that two fundamental changes in the approach to parent-implemented interventions must occur. First, a more accurate and complete conceptualization is needed of the environmental system in which the parent is expected to intervene. Second, this conceptualization should be accompanied by the design of more comprehensive intervention strategies that respond to the characteristics of the child and to language-learning environments as a system.

THE ENVIRONMENTAL SYSTEM:
IMPLICATIONS FOR PARENT-IMPLEMENTED INTERVENTIONS

Figure 1 presents a schematic representation of the child's language-learning environment. There are three central components to the environment: 1) the physical setting, 2) the caregiver (representing the social component of the environment), and 3) the child. In addition, there are three *relational* or interactive aspects of the environment: 1) the child's engagement with the physical environment, 2) the child–caregiver contingencies of interaction (that are presumed to be bidirectional and represent both the caregiver's direct response to the child and the caregiver's responsive mediation of the social environment), and 3) the caregiver's mediation of the physical environment.

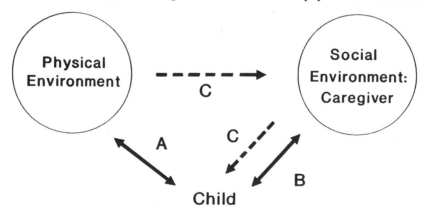

Figure 1. A model of the child's language-learning environment. A = child engagement with physical environment, B = caregiver–child contingencies, C = caregiver mediation of physical environment.

Most settings for young children contain physical and social components that are essential to providing a context for language learning. The extent to which a particular setting is an *effective* language-learning environment depends on the presence of the three critical relational aspects of the environment shown in Figure 1. For language learning to occur *efficiently:* 1) the child must engage with the environment; 2) the child and the caregiver must interact contingently with each other; and 3) the caregiver must mediate the physical and social environment for the child, thus linking the child's communication to the environment. These three relational aspects of the environment are indicative of the processes by which the environment influences child communication development and use. The three processes interact, and each influences the other processes so that the aspects of the environment function as a system, not simply as individual components.

Child engagement functionally defines the aspects of the physical and social environment that influence the child's language learning and use. Engagement includes focused visual attention, physical manipulation, and other forms of nonverbal or verbal interaction with physical and social stimuli. Attention is *necessary* but not always *sufficient* to indicate child engagement. Child engagement with the physical and social aspects of the environment may be self-initiated or prompted by another person in the setting.

Only those aspects of the environment with which the child engages directly affect language learning. That is, such engagement defines the relevance of the physical environment to the child's learning, not a particular aspect of the object itself. Proximity, salience, and function of objects may contribute to the child's engagement with an aspect of the environment. For example, very young children engage with a subset of objects (their preferred foods, toys) and people (caregivers or other familiar family members) present in their homes at any given time. Some physical objects and events are irrelevant to their language learning because they do not engage with them. Objects, events, and other aspects of the environment may be of little interest to the child at one time, but highly interesting at another.

Mediation of the environment refers to the adult's establishment of a functional relationship between the child's communication attempts and the physical and social aspects of an environment. Caregiver mediation of the child's language-learning environment occurs in several ways. First, the adult responds socially and verbally to the child's attempts to communicate and, in doing so, creates the specific social context for language. Second, the adult promotes the child's engagement with the physical environment. Third, the adult provides access to the physical environment as a specific consequence of the child's interest in and communication about that aspect of the environment. By directing the child's attention, by giving an object to the child, or by inviting the child to participate in an activity, the adult mediates the physical environment so that an occasion for communication is created, and a mutual topic for conversation is established.

When the adult is a responsive communicator, he or she mediates the social aspects of the environment and is specifically and contingently responsive to the child's communicative attempts. In this role, the adult may also provide critical models of language in context, opportunities for the child to elaborate communication, and feedback for the content and form of the child's communication attempt. The adult further mediates the physical aspects of the environment by facilitating the child's access to and control over these aspects of the environment. For example, when the adult responds to a child's request for an object by giving the out-of-reach object to the child, the adult mediates the child's functional relationship with the physical environment. From a behavioral perspective, mediation of the social and physical environment provides reinforcing consequences for child language (see Hart & Rogers-Warren, 1978). The consequences the adult provides might easily be seen as reinforcing the child's behavior. While the reinforcing aspects of mediation are important, the process of mediation itself is of particular interest in our efforts to understand how specific environmental contexts become an influence on the child's language learning.

Contingencies represent a third relational aspect of environments. Contingencies, as considered here, include not only specific reinforcement contingencies but also the temporal contingencies in turn-taking interactions and in overall caregiver–child responses. Topic maintenance, semantic matching in conversations, and expansions of child utterances are special cases of contingency, because the adult's response to the child is related in both timing and meaning. The language development literature that describes the important aspects of caregiver–child interaction contributing to language development is consistent in reporting that this aspect of intervention is particularly influential (Cross, 1978; Olson, Bayles, & Bates, 1986).

Contributions of Child and Caregiver

The *child* him- or herself is a critical component of this environmental system, because his or her social and communicative behavior affects the behavior of the caregiver. Figure 2 suggests three ways that the child influences his or her language-learning environment. First, as a stimulus for caregiver communication, the child's communicative competence influences the linguistic complexity and the topical content of the adult's language input. Adults simplify their syntax and make their speech more intelligible in response to particular characteristics of children's communication in order to facilitate child comprehension (Snow, 1977). Second, child engagement with the environment indicates the child's interest and, thus, establishes an occasion for joint attention, defines a shared topic of conversation between child and caregiver, and supports semantically related, meaningful responses by the caregiver. Joint

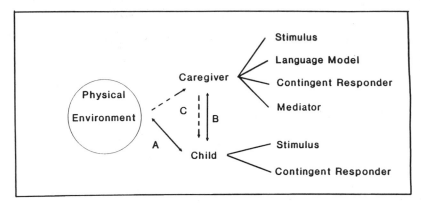

Figure 2. A model of the child's environment for language learning. A = child engagement with physical environment, B = caregiver–child interaction, C = caregiver mediation of physical environment.

caregiver–child attention to an object has been observed to positively affect child learning in dyadic interactions (Bruner, Roy, & Ratner, 1980). Establishing joint attention allows the adult to model or prompt language that closely follows the child's topic of interest. Contiguity between child interest and adult models of language has been suggested as a critical condition for the acquisition of new vocabulary (Whitehurst & Zimmerman, 1979). Third, child engagement may also influence the allocation of parent talk to language modeling and behavioral directives. When children are not engaged with the environment, adults more frequently prompt them to engage, and, thus, the adult style becomes more directive (Maurer & Sherrod, 1987).

Finally, child responsiveness *may* influence the choices adults make about how to facilitate children's language use. Kaiser and Blair (1987) observed mothers of children with disabilities and mothers of normally developing children at similar language levels and found that mother behavior was differentially related to patterns of responsiveness in the two groups of children. Mothers consistently used the language-eliciting strategies to which their children responded best. Children with disabilities were highly responsive to modeling and less responsive to other maternal attempts to elicit verbalizations, while children who were normally developing responded well to a wide range of mother behavior. Other studies have not consistently demonstrated this effect *within* groups of children with disabilities or groups of children who were normally developing.

The role of the *caregiver* in the child's language-learning environment is a complex one, as indicated by the previous discussion. As shown in Figure 3, the caregiver (or person) may be a general stimulus for social interaction or a specific stimulus for language. In addition, the caregiver models general use of language, specific language forms that map ongoing events, and appropri-

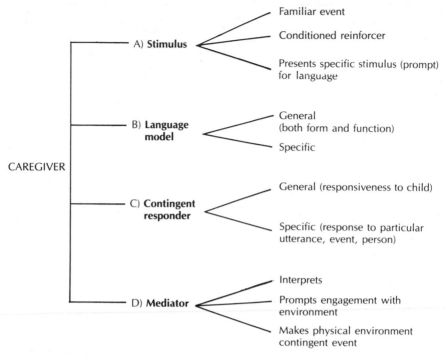

Figure 3. Multiple functions of a caregiver in the child's language-learning environment.

ate uses of language in social interactions. The caregiver is also the mediator of the physical and social environment. He or she provides broad contingencies (e.g., being generally positive and responsive to the child) and specific contingencies for child language and other child behavior. The caregiver, in fulfilling these four functions, is a critical influence on the child and the child's language-learning environment. In the model presented in Figure 3, the caregiver contributes to both the essential social context of language learning and the relational processes that support learning.

The Learning Environment as a System

The six aspects of the environment discussed previously (see Figure 1) function together as a system that provides support for language learning. The aspects are interrelated so that changes in any single aspect of the environment may affect other aspects, as well as change the overall quality of the learning context. Each aspect represents a potential point of an intervention to enhance the child's language learning. For example, enhancing the physical setting to include more objects of interest to the child may increase child engagement with the physical environment. Increased engagement provides new opportunities for the adult to model language, as well as additional opportunities for the adult to mediate the environment for the child. While interventions have traditionally focused on directly changing caregiver (or teacher) behavior directed toward the child, the environmental systems model suggests that there are multiple points of intervention and that intervention at any single point may affect other aspects of the environment, which in turn might further enhance language-learning opportunities.

A HYBRID MODEL FOR PARENT-IMPLEMENTED LANGUAGE INTERVENTION

In the following section, a hybrid model of parent-implemented language intervention is described. This model derives from research on milieu teaching, from research on responsive interaction models for parent-implemented interventions, and from consideration of the environmental system that supports children's language learning. To date, no single theoretical model of intervention has proven fully effective in remediating the social, linguistic, and learning deficits of young children with developmental disabilities, and alternative models of intervention strategies are needed. An optimal model appears to be one in which social communication is built through interactions with an invested caregiver, and salient, but limited, episodes of incidental teaching are focused slightly in advance of the child's current language level. An optimal model of intervention also includes strategies for arranging the environment and the interactional context to be fully supportive of the targeted language intervention.

Components of the Hybrid Model

The hybrid model is composed of three components: environmental arrangement, responsive interaction strategies, and milieu teaching strategies. These components are summarized in Figure 4.

The component of *environmental arrangement* is designed to increase the child's engagement with the physical setting and with the parent or caregiver and to provide frequent opportunities for the caregiver or parent to communicate with the child, to elicit communicative responses, to model appropriate language forms and functions, and to respond contingently to the child's verbal and nonverbal communication attempts.

Parents are taught to select toys and materials that are of interest to the child, to engage in play with the child with these toys and materials, and to match and elaborate the child's play schemes as a means of promoting and enhancing the child's engagement with the environment. Effective toy selection and play also provide the parent with more opportunities to elicit and model language while following the child's attentional lead and addressing the nonverbal topics of interest to the child as indicated by his or her play. By joining the child in play and engaging with the child, the parent has increased

```
                              III. Milieu Teaching Strategies
                                   Provide prompts for production
                                   in highly functional contexts

              II. Responsive Interaction Strategies
                  Provide conversational base for language learning

  I. Environmental Arrangement
     Provide physical context for language facilitation
```

Figure 4. Hybrid model of intervention and its effects.

the opportunities to mediate the environment for the child. That is, the parent can provide access to aspects of the environment that are not readily available to the child independently. This mediation forms the basis for incidental teaching and functional reinforcement of the child's communication attempts.

In addition to the arrangement of the physical setting and increased engagement with the child in a play context, parents are taught to provide a more optimal affective environment for the child. Positive affective response to the child's verbal and nonverbal behavior is basic to responsive interaction strategies for language teaching. For some parents, simply increasing play engagement with the child is sufficient to create a positive affective context for language teaching. Other parents require specific support in learning to match their affective style to the needs of the child. For example, a very withdrawn child, who is slow to respond, may be more easily engaged if the parent increases his or her animation, using greater prosody and emphasis in the verbal interchanges with the child. Other children may respond more frequently if their parents are instructed to be somewhat quieter and slower paced in interactions so that the children can easily initiate turns in conversation.

In the *responsive interaction* component of the intervention, emphasis is placed on developing a conversational style of interaction that promotes balanced communication between parent and child as well as models of appropriate language. Parents learn basic principles of interaction (responsiveness following the child's lead, facilitating turn-taking, matching and extending the child's topic) and basic language modeling strategies (matching the child's linguistic level, imitating or mirroring the child, expansions of child utterances, descriptive talk). To a considerable extent, these strategies extend the basic principles learned in the environmental arrangement component and apply them in ways that enrich the child's language-learning environment and provide a basis for conversational interaction.

Since responsive interaction includes both enhancement of the conversational interaction and enrichment of the linguistic environment, it may work well for children at different levels of language learning. For very young children or for children at the earliest stages of language learning, the responsive interaction component introduces the conversational format and supports turn-taking and increased responsiveness to parent verbalizations. For children who have acquired these basic interaction skills, enrichment of the linguistic environment through modeling, expansions, and topic continuance provides multiple opportunities to acquire new forms and functions of language through observational learning.

Milieu teaching is a naturalistic, conversation-based teaching procedure in which the child's interest in the environment is used as a basis for eliciting elaborated child communicative responses (Kaiser, Hendrickson, & Alpert, 1991). There are four milieu teaching strategies that have been demonstrated to be effective in teaching new language skills to children with developmental disabilities. Incidental teaching (teaching elaborated language in response to child requests) is the primary strategy emphasized in this component of the intervention. Parents are taught to use child-cued modeling, mand-modeling, and time-delay techniques in response to child initiations. Milieu teaching in this hybrid model is embedded in the arranged environment and the conversational style taught in the first and second components of the model. Thus, the milieu teaching episodes are relatively few and carefully matched to the child's interest and intended language functions.

The hybrid model as a multicomponent intervention has three particular strengths. First, it is a model that is consistent with the parenting role and the context of family systems in which parents normally interact with their language-learning children. Second, by including the arrangement of the environment as a primary component of the intervention, support for parent teaching and for child responsiveness to this teaching are built into the model. The intervention includes procedures to enhance all six aspects of the environmental system thought to be critical to the child's language learning (as discussed in the previous section). Third, the multicomponent nature of the model allows the intervention to be tailored to the child's communication skills by emphasizing those aspects of the intervention that most immediately fit the child's learning style and skills. Over time, using the same basic model of intervention, greater emphasis can be placed on the components that fit the child's developing skills.

In addition to these strengths, I believe the combination of components is more likely to address the four central tasks of effective language intervention than any of the components alone. Effective language intervention should: 1) provide conditions for learning the linguistic forms of language, 2) facilitate the development of social communication, 3) link newly acquired forms to contexts for social use, and 4) ultimately facilitate the child's continued acquisition of new aspects of the language system. Both responsive interaction and milieu teaching potentially affect all four criteria. Responsive interaction teaches social communication, but does not teach specific new linguistic forms. Milieu teaching has been demonstrated to teach specific language skills and facilitate the development of specific social communication skills such as responsiveness and requesting, but its impact on general social communication is limited. Both milieu teaching and responsive interaction can potentially affect the child's continued acquisition of new skills, but neither has been researched in terms of the effects on the continued acquisition of new language.

Determining the extent to which this hybrid model is able to accomplish effective language intervention is, of course, an empirical question. We have just begun to conduct research on this model (Hemmeter & Kaiser, 1990).

In our first investigation of the hybrid model with four preschool-age children with significant developmental delays, we found that parents could rapidly learn, apply, and generalize the three-component intervention model. All four children learned their targeted linguistic forms within 20 intervention sessions, and three of the four showed general positive changes in their language skills (increased frequency of speaking, increased responsiveness, increased diversity in vocabulary). Three of the four children showed generalization of their newly learned language skills across two different generalization settings (to the home while interacting with their parents and to an interaction with a nonteaching adult in a setting similar to that of the clinic). Two of the four children showed significant changes on at least one global measure of language development. The two children who showed the clearest changes across the three types of outcome measures were moderately delayed in their language development; the child showing the least change was one of two who were more than 2 years delayed in language development. These results are encouraging, but do not provide conclusive evidence about the range of effects on language development and language use that might be obtained from the hybrid model of intervention. We are beginning a larger study that compares the effects of the hybrid intervention with those of a responsive interaction intervention and of traditional therapist-implemented didactic training.

FUTURE DIRECTIONS IN RESEARCH ON
PARENT-IMPLEMENTED LANGUAGE INTERVENTION

Four types of research questions related to parent-implemented interventions are readily suggested from the preceding discussion: 1) questions related to the longitudinal changes in child language development and learning strategy; 2) questions related to the effect of changes in parent behavior on the language-learning environment of the young child; 3) questions about the role of parent-implemented interventions in enhancing the outcome of other types of primary language interventions; and 4) questions about correlated, non-language outcomes of parent-implemented communication interventions. The potential contributions from answers to these types of questions are both theoretical and practical. From a theoretical perspective, intervention research provides an opportunity to investigate the role of parental input on children's language development in an experimental paradigm not readily available in the study of normal development. Although it has usually been the case that theory is extended from research on normally developing children to applications with children with disabilities, it is not necessary that this always be the direction in which building a knowledge base about language must proceed. In addition to providing a test of social-interactional influences on children's language development, research in this area also provides the opportunity for theoretical questions regarding the modifiability of children's learning processes that bear on acquisition of language in natural environments. Of course, asking questions in each of these areas presumes that the basic methodological issues related to assessment of outcomes outside the dyad, measurement of global as well as immediate changes in child learning, and selecting appropriate nontreatment controls can be addressed adequately.

Longitudinal Assessments of Impact of Intervention on Language Development and Learning Strategies

The central question of the long-term impact of parent-implemented interventions on children's language development is as yet unanswered. In large part, research studies to date have focused on documenting changes in parent behavior and associated short-term analyses of changes in child behavior. Three types of evaluations are closely related to determining the impact of intervention over the longer course of children's language development. Asking these questions assumes that changes in child behavior are fundamentally dependent on establishing and maintaining changes in parent behavior. First, the extent to which parent-implemented language intervention can influence child outcomes under two conditions must be determined: 1) when the parent intervention is relatively short-term and has minimal residual effects on parent–child interactions, and 2) when the parent intervention is ongoing over a considerable period of time and is reasonably presumed to represent a fundamental and continuing change in the pattern of parent–child interactions. Second, there is a need to examine the extent of changes in the child's social use of language and in child mastery of the linguistic system *outside* the context of parent–child interactions. This assessment of generalized and global changes requires a multiple-measures approach consistent with a complex model of child sociolinguistic development. Third, in order to fully understand the processes by which either a short- or long-term parent-implemented intervention might produce positive changes in child language development, it is important to begin to examine the child's behavior before, during, and after intervention for evidence of changes in learning strategies that might promote development of new language skills above and beyond the content that is taught in the intervention. One framework for doing this might be to examine children's interactions for evidence of the emergence or increased use of Shatz's (1987) bootstrapping operations. These operations are proposed to be indicative of the ways in which children practice language, elicit additional linguistic/semantic information, expand their linguistic knowledge, and enter newly acquired information into long-term memory.

Impact on the Environmental System

The model of the environmental system introduced earlier in this chapter prompts a set of research questions related to determining how individual aspects of a setting affect other aspects of a setting and how these components together support the teaching and learning of language. Examining the changes that occur when a simple intervention (increasing child engagement with the environment) or a complex intervention (milieu teaching) is introduced allows a test of the systemic characteristics of the environment and provides a basis for determining the types of interventions that are likely to be durable because they result in changes in other aspects of the system. For example, our current research on the hybrid model of intervention introduces the three components (environmental arrangement, responsive interaction, and milieu teaching) sequentially. We have tentative evidence to suggest that this particular sequence of intervention components supports ease of implementation and effectiveness of the component that follows. The result is a strengthened supportive environment that is somewhat resistant to returning to baseline conditions after the conclusion of the primary intervention. Since it is typically the case that children with disabilities require therapeutic environments for relatively long periods of time in order to make significant progress in language learning (Warren & Rogers-Warren, 1985), constructing durable supportive environmental systems should be a primary concern in intervention research.

Enhancing the Effects of Primary Interventions

Although a main argument for promoting parent-implemented intervention has been the potential facilitation of children's generalization, very little research to date has examined this premise. Rarely are children above the age of 2 provided only with parent-implemented language intervention as the primary language therapy. Most children concurrently or sequentially receive direct therapy in an educational setting. The potential role of preceding or concurrent parent-implemented intervention in promoting generalization, maximizing the rapid acquisition of new linguistic forms, or furthering social pragmatic development is unknown. Researching the enhancement or generalization facilitating effects of parent-implemented interventions is important for several reasons. Generalization and maintenance of treatment gains continues to be an issue in effective language intervention, and the experimental evidence supporting advances that intervention technology have made in this area is still quite limited. It is also possible that parent-implemented interventions, particularly those in the responsive interaction and milieu traditions, teach a different set of social pragmatic skills than are typically targeted in therapist-

or school-based interventions. Determining the extent to which parent-implemented intervention can teach critical social pragmatic skills, and the effects of this teaching on children's continued development of communicative competence, is a particularly challenging area for future research.

Corollary Changes in Family Relationships and Child Behavior

Most research in early language intervention focuses exclusively on changes in children's language skills. There are two important areas for inquiry that go beyond the examination of these changes and consider the impact that parent-implemented intervention may have on the functioning of the parent–child dyad and the child's development of appropriate and inappropriate social behavior.

Recent research on families, including mothers who are abusive (Salzinger, Wondolowski, Kaplan, Kaplan, & Kristal, 1985) and mothers who are insular (Savalle-Boyajian, Wahler, & Kaiser, in preparation), suggests that communicative interactions are a powerful indicator of family dysfunction. No studies to date have provided communication training as intervention to improve family functioning; however, the investigation of these potential effects is intriguing on several grounds. First, children with communication disorders are among the populations most at risk for abuse (Embry, 1981) and for failure to bond in a parent–child relationship. Second, although the stresses associated with parenting a child with a disability are well documented, very little empirical research has examined how stress is related to parent–child communication or how some aspects of that stress might be mediated by improvements in parent–child interaction. Further investigation of linkages between parent–child communication and family functioning are in order.

A second area of corollary research addresses the prevention of behavioral excesses and acting out behavior as a potential positive outcome resulting from early communication intervention. During the last several years, the inverse reciprocal relationship between inappropriate social behavior and functional communication skills has been well documented in individuals with severe disabilities (Goetz & Sailor, 1988). Carr and Durand (1985), Horner and Budd (1985), and Hunt, Alwell, and Goetz (1988), among others, have demonstrated that specific communication skills taught to students with severe disabilities were functionally equivalent to specific inappropriate behaviors identified prior to intervention. Extending this line of research to the context of analyzing long-term effects of parent-implemented intervention is both timely and extremely important to children with disabilities and their families.

Summary

Research in the area of parent-implemented intervention is methodologically challenging and logistically difficult, yet it represents one of the most theoretically rich and practically significant areas for inquiry. The questions proposed here are intended not only to provide more systematic analyses of the effects of parent-implemented interventions, but also to place inquiry into these effects in a broader environmental, sociobehavioral, and family systems context.

CONCLUSIONS

Research on the outcomes of parent-implemented language interventions is in its early stages, despite nearly 20 years of investigations in this area. This chapter has addressed some of the critical research issues related to parent-implemented intervention, has provided a comprehensive model of language-learning environments, and described a multicomponent intervention model as steps toward enriching both research and practice. These models provide a beginning point for discussion about the critical characteristics of effective parent-implemented intervention. I offer our own list of research questions as an initial proposal for expanded inquiry into this important area.

REFERENCES

Alpert, C.L., & Kaiser, A.P. (1992). Training parents as milieu language teachers. *Journal of Early Intervention, 16*(1), 31–52.

Bruner, J., Roy, C., & Ratner, N. (1980). The beginnings of requests. In K.E. Nelson (Ed.), *Children's language* (Vol. 3, pp. 91–138.). New York: Gardner Press.

Carr, E.G., & Durand, V.M. (1985). The social-communicative basis of severe behavior problems in children. In S. Reiss & R. Bootzin (Eds.), *Theoretical issues in behavior therapy* (pp. 219–254). New York: Academic Press.

Cheseldine, S., & McConkey, R. (1979). Parental speech to young Down's syndrome children: An intervention study. *American Journal of Mental Deficiency, 83*(6), 612–620.

Cooke, S.K., Cooke, T.B., & Appolloni, T. (1976). Generalization of language training with the mentally retarded. *Journal of Special Education, 10,* 299–304.

Cross, T. (1978). Motherese: Its association with the rate of syntactic acquisition in young children. In N. Waterson & C. Snow (Eds.), *The development of communication* (pp. 199–216). London: John Wiley & Sons.

Daurelle, L.A., Fox, J.J., MacLean, W.M., & Kaiser, A.P. (1987). An interbehavioral perspective on parent training for families of developmentally delayed children. In D.H. Ruben & D.J. Delprato (Eds.), *New ideas in therapy: Introduction to an interdisciplinary approach* (pp. 159–177). New York: Greenwood Press.

Embry, L. H. (1981, February). *Two emerging models of parent training: General and problem-specific.* Paper presented at the International Symposium of Applied Behavior Analysis in Education, Mexico City.

Girolametto, L. (1988). Improving the social-conversational skills of developmentally delayed children: An intervention study. *Journal of Speech and Hearing Disorders, 53,* 156–157.

Goetz, L., & Sailor, W. (1988). New directions: Communication development in persons with severe disabilities. *Topics in Language Disorders, 8,* 41–54.

Goldstein, S.B., & Lanyon, R.I. (1971). Parent-clinicians in the language training of an autistic child. *Journal of Speech and Hearing Disorders, 36*(4), 522–560.

Hancock, T.B. (1988). *The effects of training siblings as incidental language teachers.* Unpublished doctoral dissertation, Vanderbilt University, Nashville.

Harris, S.L., Wolchick, S.A., & Milch, R.E. (1983). Changing the speech of autistic children and their parents. *Child and Family Behavior Therapy, 4,* 151–173.

Hart, B., & Rogers-Warren, A. (1978). A milieu approach to teaching language. In R.L. Schiefelbusch (Ed), *Language intervention strategies* (Vol. 2, pp. 192–235). Baltimore: University Park Press.

Hemmeter, M.L., & Kaiser, A.P. (1990). Environmental influences on children's language: A model and case study. *Education and Treatment of Children, 13*(4), 331–346.

Horner, R., & Budd, C. (1985). Acquisition of manual sign use: Collateral reduction of maladaptive behavior and factors limiting generalization. *Education and Training of the Mentally Retarded, 20*(1), 39–47.

Hunt, P., Alwell, M., & Goetz, L. (1988). Acquisition of conversation skills in the reduction of inappropriate social interaction behaviors. *Journal of The Association for Persons with Severe Handicaps, 13*(1), 20–27.

Kaiser, A.P., & Alpert, C.L. (1988, August). *Using environmental arrangement and milieu language teaching as interventions for improving the communication skills of nonvocal preschool children.* Invited paper presented at the annual meeting of the International Association for the Scientific Study of Mental Deficiency, Dublin.

Kaiser, A.P., & Alpert, C.L. (in preparation) *Milieu teaching: Strategies for functional language intervention.*

Kaiser, A.P., & Blair, G. (1987). Mother–child transactions in families with normal and handicapped children. *Upsala Journal of Medical Sciences, 44,* 204–207.

Kaiser, A.P., Hendrickson, J.M., & Alpert, C.L. (1991). Milieu language teaching: A second look. In R. Gable (Ed), *Advances in mental retardation and developmental disabilities* (Vol. 4, pp. 63–92). London: Jessica Kingsley Publishers.

Kaiser, A.P., Yoder, P.J., & Keetz, A. (1992). Evaluating milieu teaching. In S.F. Warren & J. Reichle (Eds.), *Communication and language intervention: Vol. 1. Causes and effects in communication and language intervention* (pp. 9–47). Baltimore: Paul H. Brookes Publishing Co.

Mahoney, G. (1988). Maternal communication style with mentally retarded children. *American Journal of Mental Deficiency, 92*(4), 352–359.

Mahoney, G., & Powell, A. (1986). *The transactional intervention program teachers guide.* Farmington, CT: Pediatric Research and Training Center, University of Connecticut Health Center.

Maurer, H., & Sherrod, K.B. (1987). Context of directives given to young children with Down syndrome and non-retarded children: Development over two years. *American Journal of Mental Deficiency, 91,* 579–590.

McConkey, R., & O'Connor, M. (1982). A new approach to parental involvement in language intervention programmes. *CHILD: Care, Health and Development, 8,* 163–176.

Miller, S.J., & Sloane, H.N. (1976). The generalization effects of parent training across stimulus settings. *Journal of Applied Behavior Analysis, 9*(3), 355–370.

Olson, S.L., Bayles, K., & Bates, J.E. (1986). Mother–child interaction and children's speech progress: A longitudinal study of the first two years. *Merrill-Palmer Quarterly, 32*(1), 1–20.

Price, P. (1984). A study of mother–child interaction strategies with mothers of young developmentally delayed children. In J. Berg (Ed.), *Perspectives and progress in mental retardation: Sixth congress of the International Association for the Scientific Study of Mental Deficiency* (pp. 189–199). Baltimore: University Park Press.

Risley, T.R., & Wolf, M.M. (1967). Establishing functional speech in echolalic children. *Behavioral Research Therapy, 5,* 74–88.

Salzberg, C.C., & Viallani, T.V. (1983). Speech training by parents of Down syndrome toddlers: Generalization across settings and instruction contexts. *American Journal of Mental Deficiency, 4,* 403–413.

Salzinger, S., Wondolowski, K., Kaplan, T., Kaplan, S., & Kristal, J. (1985, April). *A discourse analysis of the conversations between maltreated children and their mothers.* Paper presented at the biennial meeting of the Society for Research in Child Development, Toronto.

Savalle-Boyajian, S., Wahler, R., & Kaiser, A.P. (in preparation). *A discourse analysis of insular families: A further examination of the insular mother inconsistency hypothesis.*

Seitz, S. (1975). Language intervention: Changing the language environment of the retarded child. In R. Koch & F. de la Cruz (Eds.), *Down syndrome* (pp. 157–179). New York: Brunner/Mazel.

Shatz, M. (1987). Bootstrapping operations in child language. In K.E. Nelson & A. Van Leek (Eds.), *Children's language* (Vol. 6, pp. 1–22). Hillsdale, NJ: Lawrence Erlbaum Associates.

Snow, C.E. (1977). The development of conversation between mothers and babies. *Journal of Child Language, 4,* 1–22.

Tannock, R., & Girolametto, L. (1992). Reassessing parent-focused language intervention programs. In S. Warren & J. Reichle (Eds.), *Communication and language intervention: Vol. 1. Causes and effects in communication and language intervention* (pp. 49–79). Baltimore: Paul H. Brookes Publishing Co.

Tannock, R., Girolametto, L., & Siegel, L. (1989, March). *Efficacy of a conversational model of language intervention.* Paper presented at the American Speech and Hearing Foundation Treatment Efficacy Conference, San Antonio, TX.

Warren, S.F., & Rogers-Warren, A. (1985, July). *Language remediation with young developmentally delayed children.* Paper presented at the Interamerican Congress of Psychology, Caracas.

Weistuch, L., & Lewis, M. (1985). The language interaction project. *Analysis and Intervention in Developmental Disabilities, 5,* 97–106.

Whitehurst, G.J., & Zimmerman, B.J. (1979). *The functions of language and cognition.* New York: Academic Press.

Yoder, P.J., Kaiser, A.P., & Alpert, C. (1991). An exploratory study of the interaction between language teaching methods and child characteristics. *Journal of Speech and Hearing Research, 34,* 155–167.

5

Language Learning Through Augmented Means

The Process and its Products

Mary Ann Romski and Rose A. Sevcik

LANGUAGE SKILLS PLAY A CRITICAL role in an individual's ability to function in society. From the time a child utters his or her first words, language is used to meet wants and needs, to maintain social contact with others, and to gain knowledge about the world (Berko Gleason, 1988; Berko Gleason, Hay, & Cain, 1989; Bruner, 1983; Tomasello, 1992). There is no question that a language impairment, regardless of the degree or specific type of disability, can affect children's development, especially their base of knowledge and their social interactional skills.

As a result of their language disabilities, speaking children with specific language impairments (SLI) encounter developmental difficulties. Rice and her colleagues (Hadley & Rice, 1991; Rice, 1991; chap. 7, this volume; Rice, Sell, & Hadley, 1991) reported that the social interactions of speaking children with specific language impairments were influenced heavily by the children's language skills. These children typically spoke in short phrases or communicated nonverbally and were more likely to interact with adults than their peers. Adults also tended to characterize them as socially immature.

This chapter is dedicated to the memory of Lois A. Lyle. Her concern for and insights into the communication skills of her son taught us much about augmented language learning by individuals with severe cognitive disabilities.

This chapter and the research described within was funded by Grant No. NICHD-06016, which sustains the Language Research Center cooperatively operated by Georgia State University and the Yerkes Regional Primate Research Center of Emory University. Additional support is provided by the College of Arts and Sciences, Georgia State University and by Grant No. RR-00165 to the Yerkes Center. The authors gratefully acknowledge the youths who participated in this study, their families, and the Clayton County Public School personnel for their enthusiastic cooperation during the longitudinal study. We thank Krista Wilkinson for her comments on drafts of this chapter.

Young children with cognitive disabilities who speak also experience problems interacting socially. Guralnick (1986) suggested that the peer-directed interactions of young speaking children with developmental disabilities may have been influenced by their language and communication skills. Recently, Knopp, Baker, and Brown (1992) found that the social play of young children with mild mental retardation was related not only to their developmental age but also to their communication abilities. Language and communication skills, then, seem to play a role in mediating or advancing the interactive skills of speaking children with disabilities.

The influence of language skill on development is no more striking, however, than in the case of the child who does not learn to talk during the course of his or her early experience, even after considerable attention has been directed toward that goal (Bonvillian & Nelson, 1982; Romski & Sevcik, 1992). Pervasive spoken language impairments, coupled with cognitive disabilities, have significant long-term consequences for development (Schiefelbusch, 1980; Zigler & Hodapp, 1986). Among the many difficulties resulting from the failure to develop spoken language are the specific challenges that these children face in obtaining knowledge, conveying information to, and interacting with adults and other children in a variety of daily educational and social contexts (Knopp & Recchia, 1990). Their interactions with others in socially appropriate ways are often limited significantly because their attempts at communication are extremely difficult for partners to interpret. Although the lack of a conventional language system definitely restricts an individual's educational achievement and social development, there are, however, few studies measuring these inhibiting effects. Augmenting the language skills of children with severe disabilities may serve as a route toward remediating their language deficits, thus also modifying subsequent or accompanying developmental difficulties.

LANGUAGE INSTRUCTIONAL APPROACHES

Research and practice have centered largely on developing instructional approaches that replace or augment the existing receptive and expressive communication skills of children and youths with severe cognitive disabilities (see Mirenda & Iacono, 1990; Romski & Sevcik, 1988, for reviews). These individuals bring a range of receptive language skills and primitive, nonconventional expressive communication skills to the language-learning task (Cirrin & Rowland, 1985; Romski, Sevcik, Reumann, & Pate, 1989) that have substantially affected their development of standard communication.

Teaching approaches for individuals with severe cognitive disabilities have ranged from manual signs to using visual-graphic symbols on communication boards. Despite descriptive reports of positive language outcomes (e.g., development and increases in vocabulary size, production of multisymbol utterances), the long-term process of learning language through augmented means, as well as the broader educational and social implications of this process, have received little empirical or descriptive examination. It is important, then, to determine how the process of language learning through augmented means unfolds, the conditions that best facilitate it, and its broader impact on the course of development.

Our chapter draws on findings from a 2-year longitudinal study of symbol acquisition and use in order to characterize the developmental process through which youths with severe cognitive disabilities and little or no functional speech progress as they learn language through augmented means. We discuss the products of this process and factors that may affect success. Implications for clinical practice and an agenda for future research are presented as well.

LANGUAGE LEARNING THROUGH AUGMENTED MEANS

The language development of 13 ambulatory male youths (mean chronological age = 12 years, 4 months) was examined across a 2-year period. The participants in this study were primary and secondary school-age youngsters with moderate or severe mental retardation and concomitant severe oral language impairments. These youths resided at home and attended the special education program within the Clayton County, Georgia, public schools. At the beginning of the study, each youth had at most 10 intelligible spoken words. Measured speech comprehension skills ranged from an inability to obtain a basal score on the Peabody Picture Vocabulary Test—Revised (Dunn & Dunn, 1981) to an age-equivalent score of 3 years, 5 months.

Because these youths had not acquired language via speech or other modes (e.g., manual signs, visual-graphic symbols on communication boards) prior to the onset of this study, studying their language development required that we provide them with the necessary communicative supports and experiences for them to acquire language. The System for Augmenting Language (SAL) was implemented to facilitate the youths' abilities to communicate in a conventional manner in everyday environments, including school, home, and the community. The five key components that comprise the SAL are listed in Table 1.

The first component of the SAL is a microcomputer-based speech output communication device. For this study, individuals accessed the portable, battery-operated Words+ Personal Voice II System via a Unicorn touch-sensitive expanded keyboard. To communicate, the individual activated a symbol on the keyboard and the synthesized word equivalent was produced by the system's Votrax voice synthesizer. (Personal Voice IIs are no longer produced. All participants in this study readily transferred their skills to the computer-based SuperWolf.)

Table 1.   The System for Augmenting Language

1. Speech output communication devices are available for use in natural communicative environments.
2. Relevant visual-graphic symbol vocabulary with the printed English word equivalent above each symbol are provided.
3. Individuals are encouraged, although not required, to use the device.
4. Communication partners are taught to use the device to augment their speech input to the individual with symbol input.
5. Ongoing resource and feedback mechanisms are provided to support the individuals and their partners' communication efforts.

The second component of the SAL is a relevant vocabulary of visual-graphic symbols. For this study, lexigrams (Rumbaugh, 1977), which are arbitrary visual-graphic symbols, were used to ensure that none of the individuals had any previous experience with the symbol set. Each symbol functioned as the equivalent of a spoken word. The printed English word for each symbol appeared above the symbol to facilitate partner interpretation and use. Original vocabularies were individualized from the category of food-related words (e.g., ice cream, cheese, plate). After initial implementation, vocabulary items representing social regulative words (e.g., thank you, help), leisure words (e.g., magazine, records), location words (e.g., home, school), and work-related words (e.g., time card, breaktime) were incorporated into the vocabularies.

The third component of the SAL involved the individual's use of the device. Loosely structured naturalistic communicative experiences were provided to encourage, but not require, the youths to use symbols in natural communicative opportunities during daily activities. General guidelines on how to manipulate environments so that communication could be facilitated were adapted from research with bonobos or pygmy chimpanzees (*Pan paniscus*), who also communicated via lexigrams on communication devices (Savage-Rumbaugh, McDonald, Sevcik, Hopkins, & Rubert, 1986).

The partner's active role in communicative interactions was the fourth component of the SAL. Prior to the individual's introduction to the device, the primary communication partners (parents and teachers) attended a series of three 1-hour instructional meetings. These sessions served several functions for the partners. They received instruction in the physical operation of the computer-based communication device, viewed videotapes depicting interactions using the devices to illustrate examples of communicative use, and provided input to the investigators about the choice of specific vocabulary items to be placed on the Unicorn board. Communication partners were encouraged to integrate the use of the devices into their own spoken communications by employing what we have characterized as augmented input. In the example "Johnny, let's go OUTSIDE and ride your BIKE," "outside" and "bike" are symbols touched on the board and produced by the synthesizer as well as spoken by the partner. This communicative model permitted each family member or teacher to incorporate use of the device more easily into their communicative interactions.

The fifth and final component of the SAL was a resource and feedback mechanism, the Teacher/Parent Questionnaire (QUEST). Because the successful completion of the study depended heavily on the partners' participation and cooperation, QUEST was devised and implemented to monitor and support their participation in the study. The instrument consisted of a series of 10 questions that provided information about each week's pattern of communication and the accomplishments and/or difficulties that might have been experienced. The investigators administered the questionnaire to the communication partners on a regular basis in conjunction with the collection of the communicative use probes (CUPs) described below.

These five components of the SAL, then, provided an inclusive package for facilitating the youths' ability to communicate in a conventional manner in everyday environments. During the first year of the study, 6 of the 13 individuals were given the SAL to use at home, while the remaining 7 used the SAL at school. All participants used the SAL in both primary locations, home and school, during the second year of the study.

MEASURING SAL ACHIEVEMENT

Measuring the language and communication outcomes of the SAL experience required specific information both about the individual's pattern of SAL use and his knowledge of the symbols he was learning. To gain this information, two forms of data collection were employed: communicative use probes (CUPs) and vocabulary assessment measures (VAMs).

CUPs consisted of 37 live observations and audiotapes of communicative interactions by nonparticipant observers, which were collected in the natural environments (home and school) across the 2 years of the study. Each communicative event within an interaction was coded using a 4-digit, cross-classified code, the Communication Coding Scheme (CCS, Romski & Sevcik, 1992). Each code included information about the *role* of the participant in the communication (initiator, responder), how the participant was communicating (i.e., *modes:* gesture, symbol, vocalization, physical manipulation), what *functions* the participant's communications served, and the *successfulness* (successful, unsuccessful) of the communications. Language transcripts, using the SALT (Systematic Analysis of Language Transcripts) format (Miller & Chapman, 1985), were created from the communicative use probes. These transcripts incorporated the communications of the participants and their partners and included the cross-classified event codes. Using the transcripts as a base, successful events were also coded for effectiveness, in terms of the partner's subsequent communication, and for vocabulary focus. From the 37 transcripts per youth created over the 2-year period, more than 31,000 (mean per youth = 2,432) communicative events were coded and analyzed.

Across the 2-year period, symbol knowledge was measured via 10 tasks, or VAMs. Each vocabulary assessment measure was administered by an investigator in a structured one-on-one format outside of the communication setting. These 10 tasks served to measure what the participants had learned about the meanings of the symbols they were using, for example, in comprehension and production, apart from the supporting contextual framework in which the symbols were used. Together, these two databases (CUPs and VAMs) provided the basis for a longitudinal profile of the youths' symbol learning and use.

LEARNING FIRST SYMBOLS: SAL ACHIEVEMENT

Given naturalistic communicative experience with symbols on speech-output communication devices, what language achievements did these youths exhibit? Regardless of the initial location of instruction, home or school, SAL experience offered a viable learning opportunity for these youths with moderate or severe cognitive disabilities and little or no functional speech.

All 13 youths used the SAL to communicate in conjunction with their existing natural communicative repertoires. Most of their natural communications were unintelligible vocalizations that were primarily used to gain the attention of their partners or to answer yes/no questions. The SAL encoded the broad range of communication functions, from requesting items and information to answering questions.

The majority of communicative events were judged to be successful, that is, they obtained a response from the partner. The youths were more successful when initiating communications with the SAL than without it. When responding to their partners' communications, they were more successful using natural modes than the SAL.

Successful SAL communications were more effective, in terms of how the partners responded to the youths' communications, than communications without it. The youths were also more effective communicators when initiating than when responding to communications initiated by others (Romski, Sevcik, Robinson, & Bakeman, 1991).

In general, then, the SAL permitted the youths to convey specific information that their partners could respond to, thus promoting the initiation as well as the continuation of conversations and the addition of new information. The result was a rich multimodal language system, integrating both natural and symbolic modes, that enhanced communication, as illustrated in the example in Table 2.

Table 2. Example of SAL communicative use

Youth (S) eating lunch at home with his mother (M).
S: [1L4S] {I'M FINISHED} [SS] [E10].
M: No, you need to eat your bread and chicken.
S: [1V4S] XX [VX] [E07].
M: What?
(S burped.)
M: Uhuh.
S: [3L3S] {EXCUSE ME} [SP] [E09].
M: Ok.
(after eating his bread and chicken)
S: [1L4S] {I'M FINISHED} [SS] [E10].
(S gets up from the table and moves toward the door.)
S: [4L3S2L] {PLEASE} {I WANT} {TV} [SSRL].
M: Ok, but don't turn it up too loud.

All transcripts are presented in SALT format. Lexigrams = { }; XX = unintelligible vocalization; [ ] = codes from the Communication Coding Scheme (CCS), effectiveness coding scheme, and social focus coding scheme.

While all of the youths readily employed symbols during communicative exchanges, there was individual variability in the quantity of different symbols they used, as well as in the extent to which they comprehended and produced symbols during the VAMs outside of the context of use. Two distinct learning patterns, characterized as beginning and advanced, were identified (Romski & Sevcik, 1992).

Four youths (31%) evidenced a *beginning learning pattern,* which consisted of the slow acquisition, in both comprehension and production, of a small set of single lexigrams (20–30).These individuals learned to comprehend individual symbols before they produced them. Symbol production skills emerged later in the learning process after the comprehension of a symbol was in place. In contrast, the remaining nine individuals (69%) showed an *advanced learning pattern.* These learners rapidly acquired lexigrams, simultaneously in comprehension and production. The emergence of lexigram combinations and other symbolic skills, such as printed English word recognition and categorization skills, followed.

To account for these two learning patterns, we examined the participants' performances on a battery of language and cognitive tests administered prior to their participation in the study. The salient factor that distinguished the two groups was the speech comprehension skills they demonstrated at the onset of the study. We suggest, then, that individuals who comprehended speech prior to the onset of the study readily extracted the critical visual information from the environment, paired it with their spoken language knowledge, processed it, and produced symbolic communications. Individuals with limited comprehension abilities apparently were confronted with a different task. They had to segment the visual component of the signal, develop a set of visually based symbol experiences, process the visual information, and then first comprehend and later produce symbolic communications.

Participants with each learning pattern exhibited SAL achievements, although their respective accomplishments were strikingly different. The different SAL achievement patterns are consistent with the distinct bases of language knowledge that members of these two groups brought to the learning task. Thus, SAL achievement may take more than one form, depending on where one begins the learning process (see Romski & Sevcik, 1991, 1992, for discussion).

PRODUCTS OF SAL ACHIEVEMENT

In addition to obtaining and using a symbol lexicon, the learning process provided the basis for the development of additional skills by the youths. Four products of SAL achievement are worthy of discussion here.

Emergence of Symbol Combinations

Examination of the language transcript database revealed that meaningful and functional symbol combinations *spontaneously emerged* in the repertoires of 10 participants (combiners). For example, after one individual's mother asked him, "Do you want a piece of chicken?" he used lexigrams to reply, "WANT HOTDOG." The symbol combinations these youths used resembled the forms of young typical children who are developing spoken language use. Of particular interest is that the emergence of symbol combinations appeared after the addition of symbols for social regulative terms. Consistent lexigram ordering rules were employed by five of the combiners, indicating that at least some of the youths were capable of producing rule-governed combinations.

The comprehension of spoken combinations as measured on standardized assessments was found to be related to the production of symbol combinations. These data are consistent with our finding that extant comprehension skills are related to subsequent symbol acquisition, and to the development of symbol combinations as well. An analysis of the composition of the partners' lexigram combinations revealed that the partners of combiners modeled a variety of combinations for them. They did not, however, consistently repeat phrases as models nor did their combinations differ from the partners of the noncombiners. This suggests that individuals' patterns of multisymbol production were not based on rote imitation of their partners' language. Instead, these findings suggest that experience with symbols, coupled with the specific symbol vocabulary available to the individual and his receptive language skills, allowed him to convey increasingly more complex messages (Wilkinson, Romski, & Sevcik, 1992).

Recognition of Printed English Words

Individuals recognized an increased proportion of the printed English words that appeared above the symbols when presented in vocabulary assessment measures (VAMs) independent of the symbols. The printed words were placed above the symbols to facilitate the partners' recognition of the symbols, not in order for the youths to learn. Many of the participants had not evidenced success in school-based pre-reading programs. In comparison to chance-level performance at baseline measurement, across the course of the study they recognized at minimum 60% of the printed words displayed on their communication devices. The printed words they recognized corresponded to the symbols for which the participants had demonstrated appropriate communicative use and for which understanding had been confirmed via VAMs. Most importantly, the participants had not received any known explicit instruction concerning the relationships between the symbols and their printed word equivalents. This finding suggests that the youths' experiences with symbols and print may facilitate the development of early literacy skills (Sevcik, Romski, & Robinson, 1992).

Increases in Intelligible Speech

Another important product of the SAL experience was a general increase in the quantity and quality of the participants' intelligible spoken word productions. Using the VAMs as a database, we found changes in the intelligibility and phonetic structure of the participants' vocalizations. For example, one youth's production of the word "salad" changed from a CV syllable (/sa/) to CVCV syllables (/sa la/), which more closely approximated the adult word form. The phonetic composition of some of the word productions suggested that the youths were not necessarily following the pattern of phonological development evident in young, normally developing children. Instead, they were learning to produce specific words that were in their symbol vocabulary regardless of the word's phonetic complexity. Practitioners have reported the emergence of intelligible speech in nonspeaking individuals when they use augmented means (Romski, Lloyd, & Sevcik, 1988). Our findings offer empirical support for such clinical statements and suggest that the SAL provided these children with a consistent model of the spoken word (albeit in a synthesized form) immediately following each lexigram usage. The findings further suggest that synthetic speech output may play a role in improvements in speech intelligibility (Romski, Sevcik, Robinson, & Wilkinson, 1990).

Interacting with Familiar and Unfamiliar Partners

Finally, and perhaps most importantly, generalization to a range of communication partners and interactional settings was evident for all of the participants. With respect to communication partners, we observed SAL interactions with other youths with disabilities as well as with normally developing peers. The facility to interact socially with peers relies heavily on an individual's ability to communicate. When individuals with cognitive disabilities also have severe spoken language impairments, attempts at communication are frequently difficult for peers to interpret. We found that SAL utterances were significantly more likely to be effective with peers than unintelligible vocalizations or gestures. The SAL appeared to serve as a focus for social interaction as the following example illustrates. Tim and his normally developing peer tutor, John, were talking using the SAL. A friend of John's approached them and began to talk to John, ignoring Tim. John told his friend that he and Tim used the SAL to communicate and that he would have to use the SAL if he wanted to join the conversation. The friend used the SAL, a bit hesitantly at first, with verbal direction from John. He said "Let's go OUTSIDE to the playground." Tim responded, "YES," and the three of them went out to the school playground. The friend was immediately able to communicate with Tim, and Tim with him. These findings highlight the role the SAL may play in mediating or advancing interactive skills between peers. Speech output communication devices may be one important means of enhancing social interactions with nondisabled as well as disabled peer communication partners (Romski, Sevcik, & Wilkinson, 1992).

We also observed increased communicative interactions with unfamiliar partners. The use of the SAL afforded the youths the opportunity to independently participate in community-based activities. Unfamiliar partners, for example, the clerk at a fast-food restaurant, could understand an individual's SAL communication and take his food order without needing interpretation by a more experienced partner. Thus, the individuals could communicate with unfamiliar partners more independently with the SAL than without it.

As the participants in this study have continued to develop within their educational programs, their SAL use has been extended to additional settings, specifically, supported employment programs. Their communicative abilities using the SAL have permitted them to make their wants and needs known during job training activities. David, for example, approached his job coach and used his communication device to say, "I'M FINISHED." Indeed, he was finished with his task, and his job coach asked him if he would like to take his break, to which David replied, "YES." The use of the device also facilitated the individual's ability to socially interact with other employees at the job site, particularly during breaks. The SAL fosters interaction with other employees because it allows them to engage in an interpretable conversation.

Summary

These examples suggest that experience with the SAL can promote a range of language-related achievements. The SAL provides a way to convey information and interact with adults and peers in a variety of daily educational and social contexts. The ability to communicate effectively through the SAL provides a pathway by which youths who have not learned to speak can enter into the social world of symbolic communication and master early language skills. SAL achievement of this magnitude raises questions about the mechanisms involved in its success.

INFLUENCES ON LEARNING
LANGUAGE THROUGH AUGMENTED MEANS

Given these individuals' histories of unsuccessful language learning, what factors might have influenced the patterns of SAL achievement we observed? We propose that five factors may have affected the development of early language skills through SAL experience in this particular group of youths. Two are internal factors that the individuals brought to the augmented language-learning task: receptive language skills and extant communication skills. Three are external instructional factors: use of a speech output communication device, naturalistic learning opportunities, and available vocabulary.

Receptive Language Skills

The participants in this study came to the language-learning task with a wide range of speech comprehension skills (Peabody Picture Vocabulary Test— Revised [Dunn & Dunn, 1981] raw scores from 9 [with no basal score] to 53). While the majority of the participants comprehended single words, with which they could then bootstrap their way into the linguistic world, a few demonstrated no comprehension of speech (Romski & Sevcik, 1992).

Spoken language comprehension skills play an extremely important role in early language learning for typical children (Golinkoff & Hirsh-Pasek, 1990; Huttenlocher, 1974). If a child does not talk, one pathway for a child's referential symbol development is via the comprehension of language (Nelson, 1973). Savage-Rumbaugh (1988) and Sevcik (1989) have reported that bonobos used speech comprehension as a way to acquire productive use of visual-graphic symbols. Language comprehension, then, is an essential foundation upon which individuals, human and nonhuman, can build productive language competence.

The extent of individual SAL achievement may be influenced by receptive language skills. Some individuals have established a relationship between a spoken word and its referent. When a viable productive route, such as the SAL, becomes accessible to them, these receptive skills may serve as a basis for expressive symbol development. In using the SAL, such individuals learned that each symbol represents one real-world item by pairing the symbol with the synthetic spoken word that was produced when the symbol was activated. The individual can build a relationship between the SAL's visual-graphic symbols and already understood spoken words. For individuals who evidence little comprehension of speech at the onset of their SAL experience, there is no existing base of understood words with which to link these new symbol meanings. Thus, they must begin the acquisition process by first establishing the relationship between a visual symbol and its referent. Since they did not understand the meaning of the spoken word, they relied on the cues inherent in the communicative context to extract the meaning of the visual symbol.

Extant Nonsymbolic Communication Skills

Another factor that may influence SAL achievement is extant nonsymbolic communication skills. Typical and atypical youths who learn to speak produce their first words in the context of pointing, gestures, and vocalizations. Quickly, however, words become the primary form of communication and supplant other forms. For the youths whom we studied, vocalizations were a robust form, and vocalizations continued to constitute a high proportion of their communications even after SAL experience. Individuals who vocalized, even unintelligibly, produced forms that marked communicative turns and that were interpreted as serving a communicative function. Symbol use emerged and was maintained in the context of these extant vocal communication skills. Vocal forms apparently provided a familiar context within which symbol usage was placed. Neither the vocal form nor the visual symbol became dominant. Instead, function and experience were equally important in determining how symbols and vocalizations interfaced in communication exchanges.

Use of Speech Output Communication Devices

One very important component of the SAL is the use of the speech output communication device as the medium for language learning. With the exception of a few early studies (Locke & Mirenda, 1988; Romski, Sevcik, & Pate, 1988; Romski, White, Millen, & Rumbaugh, 1984), computer-based communication devices have been usually reserved for individuals with severe physical disabilities and intact cognitive abilities. Manual sign systems and cardboard communication boards have been the traditional choice for able-bodied youths with severe cognitive disabilities for a number of reasons. Turner (1986) suggested that economics were a major reason for this distinction. He argued that professionals typically did not think that these individuals would benefit from technology because of the degree of their cognitive disabilities. With the increase in speech output communication systems targeted specifically to this population (e.g., SuperWolf, IntroTalker), this clinical impression is slowly beginning to change.

The visual modality, a well-established strength of manual signs and communication boards (Fristoe & Lloyd, 1979), may have served to place the youths at a communicative disadvantage. This disadvantage occurs because the modality requires a partner to visually monitor and then visually attend to an individual as the communication is produced. The speech output feature permits an individual to compensate for the use of a visual communication system by automatically linking an individual's visual communication with a familiar auditory/spoken modality. The speech output device provides the youth with a multimodal system of communication including a voice, albeit artificial, yet retains the visual modality that may also be helpful.

Fundamentally, these devices afford opportunities for distal communication exchanges by easing the visual demands on communication partners as well. The synthetic output permits partners to hear the speech feedback that is produced when a symbol is activated and to immediately comprehend the message. This feature is particularly important when individuals are integrated in the general community and interact with unfamiliar communication partners. Clearly, the addition of speech output communication devices can permit youths with little or no functional speech to follow a course of language development that is more similar to that of youths who speak, because synthetic speech technology empowers them to speak through computerized means.

Naturalistic Learning Opportunities

Perhaps the most essential component of the SAL is the teaching method by which learning is facilitated. Until fairly recently, the overarching theme in the literature has been that youths with severe cognitive disabilities require continual prompting and structured practice in order to learn language (Reichle, York, & Sigafoos, 1991). A study of manual sign use by children with mental retardation who did not speak suggested that incidental teaching strategies may function as well as structured teaching approaches (Oliver & Halle, 1982). Yoder, Kaiser, and Alpert (1991) clearly indicated that speaking children acquiring early vocabulary learn better from an incidental teaching approach than from a direct instruction approach. Recent research with the bonobo indicates that observational experience with symbols may be superior to drill and practice in promoting abstract symbol learning (Savage-Rumbaugh, Sevcik, Brakke, Rumbaugh, & Greenfield, 1990). Our results support these findings and lead us to argue that a naturalistic teaching method is a viable alternative to structured approaches for youths with severe disabilities.

When the SAL is employed as input by the youth's communication partners, pairing the visual symbol with the synthetic speech output may permit the youth to extract previously unobtainable spoken words from the language-learning environment. The specific way in which the symbols were produced and paired with synthetic speech served to emphasize the critical word/symbol in the natural stream of speech (e.g., "Let's see your BIKE") and may have facilitated the matching of the symbol/word with its physical referent.

Available Vocabulary

Another important instructional factor in learning language by way of a speech output device is the available lexicon. Although individuals with little or no functional speech are often exposed to a spoken vocabulary comparable to that of a speaking child, their output is likely to be externally constrained by the number of visual-graphic symbol vocabulary items available on their communication boards. One of the features that has been proposed to facilitate their learning via augmented means, use of recognition rather than recall memory (Fristoe & Lloyd, 1979), may also serve to limit their symbol use capabilities because of the number of vocabulary items available at any one time. A wide range of vocabulary items, which are updated or changed as needed by environmental transitions (e.g., school to work, preschool to elementary school), can facilitate vocabulary learning. Although the SAL addresses this issue by updating vocabulary, there are some basic limits on vocabulary access that must be acknowledged.

The symbols that children use are based on the lexicon that is available to them (Beukelman, McGinnis, & Morrow, 1991). Often, referential, easily depicted lexical items have been chosen for youths with severe disabilities. The rationale is that referential words are concrete and more easily learned than abstract words. Social regulative words, however, may be important in facilitating the interactive dimension of communication development and serve an important role in a symbol lexicon. If youths with severe disabilities can master social regulative terms (e.g., please, more, help), their abilities to regulate interpersonal exchanges using culturally appropriate ways of communicating may be greatly enhanced.

We found that when social regulative symbols were available for use along with referential symbols, individuals acquired them rapidly and employed them in over half of the communicative turns with a social focus. Moreover, the availability of social regulative symbols immediately and continually shifted the focus of the participants' conversational turns from referential to social (Adamson, Romski, Deffebach, & Sevcik, in press). When social regulative symbols were available, participants often combined them with other symbols to form more semantically complex utterances ("MORE MILK PLEASE") (Wilkinson et al., 1992).

The lexicon available to the individual who uses the SAL may shape the learner's social interactions as well as the content of communications. The use of a broad range of symbols may influence the youths' abilities to engage in communication with multiple partners in varied social contexts, as well as influence partners' perceptions of the youths' social competence.

Summary

Two intrinsic factors, receptive language and extant communication skills, and three extrinsic factors, the use of a speech output device, naturalistic learning opportunities, and available vocabulary, appear to be factors in the success of the SAL. While these five factors are certainly not exhaustive, evidence of their importance highlights the complexity of the augmented language-learning process and indicates that many factors may interact to influence SAL achievement.

Integrating Youths with Severe Disabilities into Society: The Role of SAL Experience

A fundamental reason for providing SAL experience to a youth with little or no functional speech is to facilitate flexible communication in a variety of social contexts with a range of partners. As such, the use of the SAL serves as an illustration of one way the development of functional communication can promote the inclusion of youths with severe disabilities into the mainstream of society. The SAL permitted users to interact in an auditory world in a way that helped youths with severe disabilities to engage with a range of adult and peer communication partners and to exchange a variety of messages that met the demands of specific environmental contexts.

One potential result of SAL achievement is positive changes in partners' perceptions of the social competence of the youths. The empirical literature suggests that speech and language impairments negatively affect how others perceive children and adults with such disabilities. Alexander (1989) reported that kindergarten teachers rated speaking children with speech and language impairments less favorably then children without such impairments. Gorenflo and Gorenflo (1991) found that the use of computer-based communication devices, coupled with additional information about the individual, increased favorable attitudes of observers toward individuals using augmented communication systems. Although we did not measure partner perception as part of our study, we did obtain information about community perceptions across the course of the study. A manager at a local fast-food restaurant informed the second author that, "If these children can use computers, they must be pretty smart." He went on to say that *now* he would seriously consider hiring them to work at his restaurant.

The use of the SAL may enhance not only the youths' ongoing communication with partners, as we have found, but also judgments of competence by familiar as well as unfamiliar observers. The SAL has the potential to raise expectations of competency that, in turn, influence how the youths are viewed as potential communication partners, thus supporting more varied and complex communication patterns. By extension, changes in partner attitudes should facilitate the inclusion of such individuals with severe disabilities into society as well.

IMPLICATIONS FOR PRACTICE

While the translation of research to practice is often challenging (Landesman & Ramey, 1990), applied research, such as ours, has a responsibility to inform clinical and educational practices. To do so, we have developed Project FACTT (Facilitating Augmentative Communication Through Technology), a cooperative effort between our university research program and the local school system where our research takes place. To facilitate the translation of research to practice, FACTT provides augmented language services to school-age youths with severe disabilities within the school programs through implementation of practices that are based on adaptation of our research findings.

The findings from our research on the use of the SAL and its naturalistic teaching approach have many specific implications for practice. We address only a few of them here.

First and foremost, *youths with severe disabilities can indeed demonstrate language-learning achievements beyond our traditional expectations.* Children with little or no speech comprehension have learned to communicate via the SAL. These and other findings from our study challenge the historically pessimistic clinical expectations for youths with severe disabilities. Best practices are continuing to develop, and the future is finally optimistic for youths with severe disabilities.

An equally important implication for practice is a shift in philosophy about the potential of communications technology and naturalistic teaching strategies for youths with severe levels of disability. *Together,* naturalistic teaching strategies and the use of speech output communication technology can play an important role in facilitating the inclusion of youths with severe disabilities into society. Some caution is advised about the use of technology alone for youths with severe disabilities. When coupled with naturalistic teaching approaches, technology is only *one,* albeit important, component of an overall shift in educational advances. As part of naturalistic teaching approaches, practitioners must also begin to place a greater emphasis on speech comprehension and its importance in augmented language learning.

Clinical and parental concerns regarding augmentation and its effects on speech development are still present. We found, however, that use of the SAL did not inhibit or prevent speech development or use in older children; in fact, it facilitated speech production. These data provide empirical support for the clinical reports of such outcomes and suggest that we should seriously consider providing speech output communication devices to younger children with severe disabilities. To date, we have studied children of primary- and secondary-school age. What long-term effects would SAL experiences and achievements promote if the SAL were initiated during infant, toddler, or preschool years? With the early intervention focus of today, future research and practice must aggressively address this issue.

A FUTURE RESEARCH AGENDA

A research agenda on language learning through augmented means includes a broad range of topics. Some of the most promising findings from our longitudinal research are the long-term effects of communication on facilitating greater inclusion for individuals with severe disabilities. As augmented language learners are integrated into society, studies are needed to examine the effects of SAL achievement on how familiar and unfamiliar partners perceive the social and communicative competence of these individuals.

Research methodologies must also be refined, particularly with respect to treatment efficacy research. Given the severity of the disabilities these youths exhibit, we need to develop innovative approaches to measuring outcomes. The traditional concept of control groups who receive no treatment presents many ethical challenges. As an alternative to control groups, we have begun to examine the use of contrast groups to examine the effects of SAL achievement. We also need to develop research strategies for defining which young children are at high risk for later speech and language development, as well as devising long-term social and educational follow-up of young children who receive SAL experience during their early childhood.

Finally, a critical component of augmented language learning is that the environment must be configured to permit the youths to extract language-relevant information. We have only begun to address questions about the range of both intrinsic and extrinsic factors that influence the youths' abilities to do so. Each of these factors deserves serious investigative attention.

CONCLUSIONS

Severe spoken language impairment, coupled with severe cognitive disability, has specific long-term consequences for an individual's development across the lifespan. Our findings demonstrate that youths with severe cognitive disabilities and little or no functional speech have significant potential for language learning. Through a process that couples extant skills with a unique configuration of technology and naturalistic language-learning opportunities and experiences, the SAL permits these youths to reveal their heretofore untapped conceptualizations of the world, as well as their capacities for symbolic exchange within social interactions. It is hoped that this research will serve as a basis for challenging the traditional assumptions about language development and youths with severe cognitive disabilities and, most importantly, facilitate their meaningful integration into society.

REFERENCES

Adamson, L.B., Romski, M.A., Deffebach, K., & Sevcik, R.A. (in press). Symbol vocabulary and the focus of conversations: Augmenting language development for youth with mental retardation. *Journal of Speech and Hearing Research.*

Alexander, A. (1989). *Kindergarten teachers' impressions of children with communication handicaps.* Unpublished master's thesis, University of Kansas, Lawrence.

Berko Gleason, J. (1988). Language and socialization. In F. Kessel (Ed.), *The development of language and language researchers* (pp. 269–280). Hillsdale, NJ: Lawrence Erlbaum Associates.

Berko Gleason, J., Hay, D., & Cain, L. (1989). Social and affective determinants of language acquisition. In M. Rice & R.L. Schiefelbusch (Eds.), *The teachability of language* (pp. 171–186). Baltimore: Paul H. Brookes Publishing Co.

Beukelman, D., McGinnis, J., & Morrow. D. (1991). Vocabulary selection in augmentative and alternative communication. *Augmentative and Alternative Communication, 7,* 171–185.

Bonvillian, J.D., & Nelson, K. (1982). Exceptional cases of language acquisition. In K. Nelson (Ed.), *Children's language* (Vol. 3, pp. 322–391). Hillsdale, NJ: Lawrence Erlbaum Associates.

Bruner, J. (1983). *Child's talk.* New York: Norton.

Cirrin, F., & Rowland, C. (1985). Communicative assessment of nonverbal youths with severe/profound mental retardation. *Mental Retardation, 23,* 52–62.

Dunn, L.M., & Dunn, L.M. (1981). *Peabody Picture Vocabulary Test—Revised.* Circle Pines, MN: American Guidance Service.

Fristoe, M., & Lloyd, L. (1979). Nonspeech communication. In N.R. Ellis (Ed.), *Handbook of mental deficiency: Psychological theory and research* (pp. 401–430). Hillsdale, NJ: Lawrence Erlbaum Associates.

Golinkoff, R., & Hirsh-Pasek, K. (1990). Let the mute speak: What infants can tell us about language acquisition. *Merrill-Palmer Quarterly, 36,* 67–91.

Gorenflo, C., & Gorenflo, D. (1991). The effects of information and augmentative communication technique on attitudes towards nonspeaking individuals. *Journal of Speech and Hearing Research, 34,* 19–26.

Guralnick, M. (1986). The peer relations of young handicapped and nonhandicapped children. In P.S. Strain, M. J. Guralnick, & H. M. Walker (Eds.), *Children's social behavior: Development, assessment, and modification.* (pp. 93–140). New York: Academic Press.

Hadley, P., & Rice, M. (1991). Conversational responsiveness of speech- and language-impaired preschoolers. *Journal of Speech and Hearing Research, 34,* 1308–1317.

Huttenlocher, J. (1974). The origins of language comprehension. In R.L. Solso (Ed.), *Theories in cognitive psychology: The Loyola symposium.* Hillsdale, NJ: Lawrence Erlbaum Associates.

Knopp, C., Baker, B., & Brown, K. (1992). Social skills and their correlates: Preschoolers with developmental delays. *American Journal on Mental Retardation, 96,* 357–366.

Knopp, C.B., & Recchia, S.L. (1990). The issues of multiple pathways in the development of handicapped children. In R.M. Hodapp, J.A. Burack, & E. Zigler (Eds.), *Issues in the developmental approach to mental retardation* (pp. 272–293). New York: Cambridge University Press.

Landesman, S., & Ramey, C. (1989). Developmental psychology and mental retardation: Integrating scientific principles with treatment practices. *American Psychologist, 44,* 409–415.

Locke, P., & Mirenda, P. (1988). A computer-supported communication approach for a child with severe communication, visual, and cognitive impairments: A case study. *Augmentative and Alternative Communication, 4,* 15–22.

Miller, J., & Chapman, R. (1985). *Systematic analysis of language transcripts.* Madison: University of Wisconsin.

Mirenda, P., & Iacono, T. (1990). Communication options for persons with severe and profound disabilities: State of the art and future directions. *Journal of The Association for Persons with Severe Handicaps, 15,* 3–21.

Nelson, K. (1973). Structure and strategy in learning to talk. *Monographs of the Society for Research in Child Development, 38* (1–2, Serial No. 139).

Oliver, C., & Halle, J. (1982). Language training in the everyday environment: Teaching functional sign use to a retarded child. *Journal of The Association for Persons with Severe Handicaps, 8,* 50–62.

Reichle, J., York, J., & Sigafoos, J. (1991). *Implementing augmentative and alternative communication: Strategies for learners with severe disabilities.* Baltimore: Paul H. Brookes Publishing Co.

Rice, M. (1991). Children with specific language impairment: Toward a model of teachability. In N. Krasnegor, D. Rumbaugh, R. Schiefelbusch, & M. Studdert-Kennedy (Eds.), *Biological and behavioral determinants of language development* (pp. 447–480). Hillsdale, NJ: Lawrence Erlbaum Associates.

Rice, M., Sell, M., & Hadley, P. (1991). Social interactions of speech- and language-impaired children. *Journal of Speech and Hearing Research, 34,* 1299–1307.

Romski, M.A., Lloyd, L.L., & Sevcik, R.A. (1988). Augmentative and alternative communication issues. In R.L. Schiefelbusch & L.L. Lloyd (Eds.), *Language perspectives: Acquisition, retardation and intervention* (2nd ed., pp. 343–366). Austin, TX: PRO-ED.

Romski, M.A., & Sevcik, R.A. (1988). Augmentative and alternative communication systems: Considerations for individuals with severe intellectual disabilities. *Augmentative and Alternative Communication, 4,* 83–93.

Romski, M.A., & Sevcik, R.A. (1991). Patterns of language learning by instruction: Evidence from nonspeaking persons with mental retardation. In N. Krasnegor, D. Rumbaugh, R. Schiefelbusch, & M. Studdert-Kennedy (Eds.), *Biological and behavioral determinants of language development* (pp. 429–445). Hillsdale, NJ: Lawrence Erlbaum Associates.

Romski, M.A., & Sevcik, R.A. (1992). Developing augmented language in children with severe mental retardation. In S. Warren & J. Reichle (Eds.), *Communication and language intervention: Vol. 1. Causes and effects in communication and language intervention* (pp. 113–130). Baltimore: Paul H. Brookes Publishing Co.

Romski, M.A., Sevcik, R.A., & Pate, J.L. (1988). The establishment of symbolic communication in persons with severe retardation. *Journal of Speech and Hearing Disorders, 53,* 94–107.

Romski, M.A., Sevcik, R.A., Reumann, R., & Pate, J.L. (1989). Youngsters with moderate or severe retardation and severe spoken language impairments: I. Extant communicative patterns. *Journal of Speech and Hearing Disorders, 54,* 366–373.

Romski, M.A., Sevcik, R.A., Robinson, B., & Bakeman, R. (1991, April). *Effect of augmented language use by children with mental retardation on their communicative success and effectiveness.* Poster presented at the biennial meeting of the Society for Research in Child Development, Seattle.

Romski, M.A., Sevcik, R.A., Robinson, B., & Wilkinson, K. (1990, November). *Intelligibility and form changes of the vocalizations of augmented communications.* Paper presented at the annual meeting of the American Speech-Language-Hearing Association, Seattle.

Romski, M.A., Sevcik, R.A., & Wilkinson, K. (1992). *Peer-directed communicative interactions of augmented language learners with mental retardation.* Manuscript submitted for publication.

Romski, M.A., White, R., Millen, C., & Rumbaugh, D.M. (1984). Effects of computer keyboard teaching on the symbolic communication of severely retarded persons: Five case studies. *Psychological Record, 34,* 39–54.

Rumbaugh, D.M. (1977). *Language learning in a chimpanzee: The LANA Project.* New York: Academic Press.

Savage-Rumbaugh, E.S. (1988). A new look at ape language: Comprehension of vocal speech and syntax. In D. Leger (Ed.), *Nebraska symposium on motivation* (Vol. 35, pp. 201–255). Lincoln: University of Nebraska Press.

Savage-Rumbaugh, E.S., McDonald, K., Sevcik, R.A., Hopkins, W., & Rubert, E. (1986). Spontaneous symbol acquisition and communicative use by a pygmy chimpanzee *(Pan paniscus)*. *Journal of Experimental Psychology: General, 112,* 211–235.

Savage-Rumbaugh, E.S., Sevcik, R.A., Brakke, K., Rumbaugh, D.M., & Greenfield, P. (1990). Symbols: Their communicative use, comprehension, and combination by bonobos *(Pan paniscus)*. In L.P. Lipsitt & C. Rovee-Collier (Eds.), *Advances in infancy research: Vol. 6.* Norwood, NJ: Ablex.

Schiefelbusch, R.L. (1980). *Nonspeech language and communication.* Baltimore: University Park Press.

Sevcik, R.A. (1989). *A comprehensive analysis of graphic symbol acquisition and use: Evidence from an infant bonobo (Pan paniscus).* Unpublished doctoral dissertation, Georgia State University, Atlanta.

Sevcik, R.A., Romski, M.A., & Robinson, B. (1992). *Printed English word recognition by nonspeaking children with mental retardation.* Unpublished manuscript.

Tomasello, M. (1992). The social bases of language acquisition. *Social Development. 1,* 67–87.

Turner, G. (1986). Funding VOCAs for the lower cognitive functioning population. *Closing the Gap, 5,* 26.

Wilkinson, K., Romski, M.A., & Sevcik, R.A. (1992). *Emergence of augmented symbol combinations in children with mental retardation.* Unpublished manuscript.

Yoder, P., Kaiser, A., & Alpert, K. (1991). An exploratory study of the interaction between language teaching methods and child characteristics. *Journal of Speech and Hearing Research, 34,* 155–167.

Zigler, E., & Hodapp, R. (1986). *Understanding mental retardation.* New York: Cambridge University Press.

6

Developing an Initial Communicative Repertoire

Applications and Issues for Persons with Severe Disabilities

Joe Reichle, James Halle, and Susan Johnston

Rᴇsᴇᴀʀᴄʜᴇʀs ᴀɴᴅ ᴘʀᴀᴄᴛɪᴛɪᴏɴᴇʀs ᴀʀᴇ ɪɴᴄʀᴇᴀsɪɴɢʟʏ aware of the extent of communicative relationships very early in development. Advances in understanding how communication develops and how it can be taught have made earlier communication intervention a viable undertaking for infants and toddlers who experience developmental disabilities. Advances in our ability to establish functional communication skills in the absence of verbal communicative behavior have created new options for intervention for children who have insufficient structure or function of their speech mechanisms to permit spoken communication. As instructional technology has advanced, the acquisition and generalization of new communicative behavior have come to be viewed as part of the same instructional objective, rather than as a sequence of different related objectives. Most recently, interventionists have begun developing intervention strategies that allow effective intervention to be conducted in the learner's regular, natural environments (Kaiser, chap. 4, this volume; Tannock & Girolametto, 1992). Developing such strategies is a particularly critical undertaking, because most intervention opportunities with infants and toddlers occur in the milieu of daily routines in home environments.

The development of this chapter was supported in part by Grant No. H133B80048 from the National Institute on Disability and Rehabilitation Research, U.S. Department of Education to the Research and Training Center on Community Living. Support also was provided by Grant No. H086P90024 awarded by the U.S. Department of Education, Anne Smith, Project Officer to the University of Illinois. Finally, the chapter was completed while the second author received support from a U.S. Department of Education Leadership Training Grant No. H029D90107 awarded to the University of California at Santa Barbara. Points of view or opinions expressed in this chapter do not necessarily represent official positions of the U.S. Department of Education and no official endorsement should be inferred.

Traditionally, most communication intervention strategies were designed to establish an initial repertoire of specific vocabulary to express identified pragmatic functions in interactive exchanges (i.e., Guess, Sailor, & Baer, 1974; Kent, 1974). To the communication interventionist, this is a particularly challenging task, because a number of separable, yet integrally related, aspects of communication can be addressed concurrently. Recently, attention has focused on concurrent intervention to teach communicative forms and functions in the milieu of daily activities (Alpert & Kaiser, in preparation; MacDonald, 1989; Mahoney & Powell, 1986; Weistuch & Lewis, 1986; Yoder & Davies, 1990).

The purpose of this chapter is to characterize major issues that communication interventionists face in selecting and implementing strategies for establishing an initial communicative repertoire in individuals with severe and multiple developmental disabilities. The majority of issues discussed here are most applicable to individuals with severe mental retardation who also have other handicapping conditions, although many issues raised are applicable to individuals with less severe disabilities. We assume that all learners, regardless of their developmental status or chronological age, are candidates for communication intervention. Furthermore, we believe that to the greatest extent possible, intervention should be implemented in the milieu of the learner's natural environments using the least intrusive intervention strategies that have been carefully validated. In this chapter, we explore decision points that must be addressed in order to select what to teach and how to teach it. We begin by tackling the issue of whether initial communicative behavior must be taught in the context of a conversation. Next, we focus on decisions that ensure that initial pragmatic forms selected for intervention actually correspond to the social function that the learner's informal means to convey wants and needs fulfill. Ensuring the best match between pragmatic and social functions may require careful sequencing of intervention procedures. Our discussion next focuses on gestural and graphic options to supplement vocal production for individuals who have severe structural or functional impairments of the speech mechanism. We then discuss issues that arise as a result of the learner's current informal communicative behavior (including challenging behavior). Finally, we discuss variables that influence the extent to which a learner utilizes his or her established communicative repertoire to take advantage of a wide range of conversational opportunities afforded by the natural environment.

IDENTIFYING LEARNERS WHO MAY BENEFIT
FROM A CONVERSATIONAL INTERVENTION CONTEXT

A number of investigators have suggested that communicative behavior must be established in the context of conversations and interactive routines (e.g.,

MacDonald, 1989). Goldstein and Kaczmarek (1992) state that "central to preschool experience of all children is learning to interact with a variety of other children. . ." (p. 81). Yoder, Davies, and Bishop (1992) suggest that engaging in conversational behavior actually serves to facilitate language acquisition in several distinct ways. First, conversational exchanges provide opportunities for adults to expand children's utterances in accordance with milieu approaches to intervention (Warren & Rogers-Warren, 1985). Second, continuing a child's topic appears to increase the likelihood that the child will be more motivated to provide an utterance related to the speaking partner's utterance (Miller, MacKenzie, & Chapman, 1981). Establishing communicative behavior in a conversational framework affords the greatest opportunity for generalized conversational use; however, for some learners it is more straightforward to begin with establishing instrumental communicative functions, with limited emphasis on the conversational aspects of language. For example, referring to the use of a focus on natural episodes of conversation as the exclusive medium for communication intervention, Tannock and Girolametto (1992) stated that, "The extent of the child's disability may constrain what can be achieved by this model of intervention: children who are unable to organize information in a normal manner may benefit from more direct instructional approaches. . ." (p. 72). Although we believe that the most progressive intervention program focuses on intervention in the context of conversational flow, there may be special instances that require consideration of pragmatic functions outside the flow of a conversation.

Reichle (1990a) described a group of persons with moderate and severe developmental disabilities who had not yet learned to enjoy the company of others. Individuals who do not appear to enjoy interactions have been the focus of a number of empirical investigations (see Reichle, York, & Eynon, 1989). In many instances, these individuals invest significant energy to escape from or avoid interactions with others. For these individuals, establishing conversational exchanges would represent an unusually difficult initial communicative objective. In some instances, escape from social interaction represents an important desire, and there are few other readily identifiable environmental circumstances that are of equal importance or interest to the individual. In this case, establishing a "rejecting" or "leavetaking" utterance may be very important in teaching the learner that communicative behavior provides powerful control over one's environment.

Reichle (1991) conducted an investigation in which two learners with severe handicaps were taught to obtain desired items by seeking out adults and producing requests. By establishing a series of conditional discriminations, learners were successful in using an adult as a mediator when desired items could not be reached and in obtaining items independently when they were within reach. However, unless a desired item was the focus, the learners displayed little interest in social interaction. For the most part, when confronted with a prospective communicative partner, these learners attempted to withdraw to the privacy of their rooms rather than remain in close physical proximity to other individuals. Interactive exchanges may indeed be a viable intervention objective for all individuals. At the same time, however, the interventionist's *initial* objective should be to teach learners that they can exert significant control over important aspects of their environment. Sometimes this may be demonstrated through brief and somewhat one-sided exchanges.

For some learners, we believe that early pragmatic intervention strategies should target instrumental communicative intent through relatively abrupt exchanges in which conversation per se is not the primary short-term objective. Alternatively, with learners who are highly motivated to seek and maintain contact with others, interactional aspects of a conversation may receive greater emphasis. With both groups of learners, describing the reason for the learner's production of a communicative behavior is at the heart of determining the appropriate intervention contexts. Consequently, it is very important that the interventionist scrutinize the learner's communicative obligations and opportunities in a wide range of functional environments to ensure that the utterances taught closely match the social functions of the learner's existing communicative behaviors.

DISTINGUISHING BETWEEN
PRAGMATIC FORM AND SOCIAL FUNCTION

Traditionally, communication interventionists have focused on syntactic, morphological, and semantic topographies as targets for beginning communication intervention. As late as the mid- to late 1970s, interventionists focused on teaching grammatical relationships among subjects, verbs, and objects. The operating assumption was that once these forms were taught, the learner would be able to generalize them to the appropriate social contexts.

Unfortunately, once a vocabulary item had been taught in the context of one particular communicative function (i.e., a request), learners (including normally developing children) often appeared to fail to generalize the use of the item to express other communicative functions (Lamarre & Holland, 1985; Reichle, Schermer, & Anderson, 1990). Limited generalization prompted interventionists to focus more on communicative functions and to design taxonomies describing the range of communicative functions that specific vocabulary must address in order for an individual to establish a functional communicative repertoire. Interventionists have increased their emphasis on the communicative function of vocabulary as a result of the growing interest in identifying beginning, proactive communicative repertoires with individuals who communicate using socially unacceptable behavior. Finally, an increasing emphasis on intervening at the earliest possible point in a learner's educational career continues to generate interest in pragmatically referenced intervention strategies.

Carr (1977) hypothesized that many individuals who engage in repertoires of highly idiosyncratic and challenging behavior may do so in order to express a variety of pragmatic functions, which include to obtain attention, desired items, or events, or to escape or avoid interactions with persons or activities. The communicative hypothesis suggests that interventionists should teach communicative forms that are functionally equivalent to the highly idiosyncratic or socially unacceptable forms. Inherent in the communicative hypothesis is the notion of *functional equivalence*. Replacing repertoires of challenging behavior requires that the interventionist precisely match the learner's social intent with the communicative form or function selected for intervention (Carr & Durand 1985). Matching communicative form to social function has focused the communication assessment process for those learners who engage in challenging behavior on incorporating a functional analysis of the learners' current behavior (both vocal and nonvocal).

For those who work with infants and toddlers, the 1980s and early 1990s have resulted in an increasing awareness of the importance of establishing beginning communicative repertoires at increasingly early ages. It is apparent that, initially, very young children engage in natural gestures and vocal behaviors that express a range of social-communicative functions. Because of their limited vocabularies, children who are developing normally often rely on relatively generalized vocabulary associated with an entire response class (e.g., "more" → request, "no" → reject, "done" → leavetake). Given the limited vocal and verbal imitative abilities of very young children, interventionists have become increasingly interested in the range of vocal and gestural behaviors produced by infants and toddlers that can be shaped into acceptable expressions of social-communicative functions. This interest, in turn, has generated interest in systems that can be used to characterize the early social-communicative functions that are expressed by children who are developing normally, as well as children with developmental disabilities.

DESCRIBING COMMUNICATIVE FUNCTIONS

A number of investigators have devised taxonomies to describe instrumental communicative intents (Cirrin & Rowland, 1985; Dore, 1975; Wetherby & Prizant, 1992). Instrumental intents describe why the learner produced a particular utterance, regardless of where it occurred in the flow of an interaction. For example, an individual could "request an object," "comment," or "protest" at any point in an interaction. Five taxonomies are compared in Table 1, which illustrates the similarities and differences among current strategies used to describe communicative functions.

Table 1. Taxonomies designed to describe instrumental communicative intents

Wetherby and Prizant (1989)	Cirrin and Rowland (1985)	McLean and Snyder-McLean (1991)	Coggins and Carpenter (1978)	Dore (1975)
Comment on object: Acts used to direct another's attention to an entity.	**Direct attention to object:** Direction of listener's attention to an external, observable referent, or some object identified by the child. This includes the speaker taking notice of an object, or labeling an object in absence of a request.	**Request attention to other:** Behavior used to direct the communicative partner's attention to some object, person (other than self), event, or state of affairs.		
			Transferring: Gestures intended to place an object in another person's possession.	
Comment on action: Acts used to direct another's attention to an event.	**Direct attention to action:** Direction of listener's attention to an ongoing action or event in the environment. The focus may be the movement or action of an object rather than the object itself. A	(Refer to **Request attention to other**)		**Labeling:** Uses word while attending to object or event. Does not address adult or wait for a response.

"comment" on some ongoing activity.			
Show-off: Acts used to attract another's attention to oneself.	**Request attention to self:** Behavior used to attract attention to oneself. No other referent is indicated.	**Showing off:** Gestures or utterances that appear to be used to attract attention.	
Direct attention to self: Direction of listener's attention to the child as a general attention-getter for some unspecified social purpose.	(Refer to **Request attention to self**)	(Refer to **Showing off**)	
Direct attention for communication: Direction of listener's attention to self as a preface to another communicative behavior that follows immediately.			**Calling:** Calls adult's name loudly and awaits response.
Call: Acts used to gain the attention of others, usually to indicate that a communicative act is to follow.			
Acknowledgment: Acts used to indicate notice of another person's previous statement or utterance.		**Acknowledging:** Gestures or utterances that provide notice that the listener's previous utterances were received.	
Answer: A communicative response from a child to a request for information from the adult listener. This typically takes the form of indicating a choice		**Answering:** Gestures or utterances from the child in response to a request for information from the listener.	**Answering:** Answers adult's question. Addresses adult.

(continued)

Table 1. (continued)

Wetherby and Prizant (1989)	Cirrin and Rowland (1985)	McLean and Snyder-McLean (1991)	Coggins and Carpenter (1978)	Dore (1975)
	Answer (continued) or answering a question.			
Clarification: Acts used to clarify the previous utterance.				
Request object: Acts used to demand a desired tangible object.	Request object: Seeks the receipt of a specific object from the listener where the child awaits a response. The object may be out of reach due to some physical barrier.	Request object: Behavior used to request an object. Interest is on the object desired.	Requesting object: Gestures or utterances that direct the listener to provide some object for the child.	Requesting: Asks question with a word, sometimes with accompanying gesture. Addresses adult and awaits response.
Request action: Acts used to command another to carry out an action.	Request action: Seeks the performance of an action by the listener where the child awaits a response. The child may specify the action (e.g., "sit") or the child's immediately preceding behavior gives evidence that he or she realizes that some action is a necessary step to obtaining some object (e.g., signaling "help" to open a jar).	Request instrumental action: Behavior used to direct a communicative partner to carry out action facilitating access to an object or attainment of a desired effect.	Requesting action: Gestures or utterances that direct the listener to act upon some object in order to make it move. The action, rather than the object, is the focus of the child's interest.	Requesting action: Word or vocalization often accompanied by gesture signaling demand. Addresses adult and awaits response.

Request information: Acts used to seek information, explanation, or clarification about an object, event, or previous utterance. Includes *wh*-question and other utterances having the intonation contour of an interrogative.	**Request information:** Seeks information, approval, or permission from the listener where the child awaits a response. This includes directing the listener to provide specific information about an object, action, or location.	**Request information/feedback:** Behavior used to direct the communicative partner to provide information about an object, action, or location; to request approval/nonapproval, permission, or affirmation.	**Requesting information:** Gestures or utterances that direct the listener to provide information about an object, action, or location.
Request permission: Acts used to seek another's consent or carry out an action; involves the child carrying out or wishing to carry out the action.	(Refer to **Request information**)	(Refer to **Request information/feedback**)	
Request social routine: Acts used to command another to commence or continue carrying out a game-like social interaction.	(Refer to **Request action**)	**Request noninstrumental action:** Behavior used to direct a communicative partner's actions. Goal is to instigate other's actions rather than obtain an object or effect.	

(continued)

113

Table 1. (continued)

Wetherby and Prizant (1989)	Cirrin and Rowland (1985)	McLean and Snyder-McLean (1991)	Coggins and Carpenter (1978)	Dore (1975)
Protest: Acts used to refuse an undesired object or to command another to cease an undesired action.		**Request cessation Reject/avoid:** Behavior used to request a communicative partner to cease an undesired action or activity or to reject an offered object or anticipated event.		**Protesting:** Resists adult's action with word or cry. Addresses adult.
Greet: Acts used to gain another's attention to indicate notice of presence, or to indicate notice of the initiation or termination of an interaction.			**Greeting:** Gestures or utterances subsequent to a person's entrance that express recognition.	**Greeting:** Greets adult or objects upon appearance.
				Repeating: Repeats part or all of prior adult utterance. Does not wait for a response.
				Practicing: Use of word or prosodic pattern in absence of any specific object or event. Does not address adult. Does not await response.

Lack of an entry indicates that a similar intent did not exist in that particular taxonomy.

Given the numerous descriptive taxonomies available to the interventionist, describing the reason for the production of any given utterance would seem to be a relatively straightforward proposition. However, we believe it is easy to misuse pragmatic taxonomies, and to describe communicative *forms* rather than *functions*. For example, consider a learner who is grudgingly engaged in homework. Approximately 1 minute into the task he says, "Mom, can you help me?" His mother dutifully assists him with his first problem. Several minutes later, the learner is again requesting assistance with his assignment. After 10 requests, his assignment has been completed, but the learner has not solved a single problem without his mother's assistance. Most pragmatic taxonomies would have described the learner's behavior as a series of "requests for assistance" or "requests for action," based on the form of utterances and the context. A functional assessment of the situation, however, might suggest that the learner's communicative behavior functioned to avoid or escape engagement in the activity. A request for assistance, in some instances, may serve as a strategy to obtain a highly preferred item (e.g., obtaining assistance to unwrap a piece of candy). On other occasions, requests for assistance may be attempts to escape from an unpleasant task (e.g., homework). Unless the full range of relevant stimulus conditions are addressed during intervention, the interventionist cannot conclude that the learner will generalize across the complete range of environmental circumstances in which the pragmatic functions being taught can be used. Reichle (1990b) reported instances in which a learner, taught to "request assistance" exclusively in the presence of opportunities to escape or avoid highly nonpreferred activities, failed to generalize the use of "request assistance" vocabulary to obtain desired objects and events (e.g., candy that the learner needed help unwrapping). Reichle (1990b) also reported an instance in which a learner with severe developmental disabilities was taught a general rejecting gesture ("no"). All of the identified teaching opportunities occurred when the learner was offered a highly *nonpreferred* object or event. Over time, the learner used a rejecting utterance whenever an offer of an undesired item was made. One of this individual's preferred activities was to go to a coffee shop on Saturday morning for coffee and sweet rolls. Generalization probes conducted in this setting demonstrated that the reject gesture had generalized to previously untrained and undesired breakfast items. For example, when offered bacon or sausage (highly nonpreferred items), the individual gave his rejecting response. However, when offered refills of coffee (a highly preferred item) when he did not wish more, he failed to produce his newly established rejecting utterance. As the intervention process proceeded, it became increasingly clear that, inadvertently, the interventionists had taught the learner to use a rejecting gesture for only a subset of the full range of important functional opportunities.

Our concern is that researchers and interventionists may sometimes fail to match the pragmatic form being taught with the full *range* of social functions that the new utterance is expected to serve. Just as insufficient teaching examples resulted in the problem just described, the same problem may result in the interventionist's attempts to ensure that any given communicative function will be used across a range of different conversational opportunities. For example, Table 2 provides a matrix referenced on the vertical axis by communicative functions (request, reject, and comment). The horizontal axis is referenced by the conversational functions of initiate, maintain, and terminate. For example, it seems reasonable to hypothesize that communicative functions taught primarily as conversation-maintaining strategies may not necessarily generalize to conversational functions that involve initiating or terminating social interactions.

In summary, generalization represents a significant challenge to the communication interventionist. First, it is important that the interventionist separate pragmatic forms from the social functions that communicative behaviors may serve. Second, it is important that the examples used to establish initial

Table 2. Interaction between communicative intents and stages of communicative exchanges

		Initiate	Maintain	Terminate
Request	context	A 6-year-old sees a peer on the playground.	A preschool child is watching his mother blow bubbles.	A learner has lost interest in playing with his younger sibling.
	utterance	He approaches the peer and says, "Wanna play?"	He says, "Do it again."	He says, "Wouldn't you like to watch cartoons now?"
Reject	context	Two children are sitting together. Adult asks one child if he wants to go to a movie.	A preschool child is playing a game with her dad.	A learner and his friend are working on a jigsaw puzzle.
	utterance	The other child says, "I don't want to go to a movie."	The child says, "It's not your turn!"	He says, "I'm not doing this anymore."
Comment	context	A child and an adult are walking at the zoo.	A learner and her friend are talking about a television show.	Two children are waiting to be picked up from school.
	utterance	The child says, "A bear!"	The learner says, "I thought that it was funny."	One child says, "Oh, there's my ride."

Adapted from Reichle, York, and Sigafoos (1991).

communication reflect the total range of situations in which a form is appropriate for the learner to use. Consequently, clearly understanding this could be very important to initial establishment of a functional communicative repertoire.

SEQUENCING INTERVENTION PROCEDURES USED TO ESTABLISH A REPERTOIRE OF COMMUNICATIVE FUNCTIONS

Guess et al. (1974) eloquently articulated the logic for selecting particular communicative topographies for instruction. They suggested that it was important to demonstrate to learners that they could exert significant control over their environment with their communicative behavior. In the communication intervention programs of the 1970s, although specific vocabulary representing highly preferred items were included (Bricker & Bricker, 1974; Guess et al., 1974; Kent, 1974), the initial pragmatic function selected for intervention was often "providing information." This somewhat arbitrary selection of pragmatic class created a potential mismatch between the learner's actual intent and the social function being taught by the interventionist. That is, sometimes primary reinforcers that had no direct correspondence to the vocabulary being taught were provided contingent on the production of a correct utterance. It seems reasonable to hypothesize that some learners may have produced the desired vocabulary item as a *request* when, in fact, the interventionist treated the response as if it were a *provision of information*. This mismatch may have influenced subsequent establishment of other social uses of the same vocabulary item.

In fairness, however, early systematic approaches reflected the knowledge base of the time. For the most part, systematic approaches to communication intervention in the 1970s focused on semantic and syntactic structure rather than on pragmatic function. In spite of this orientation, most initial communication intervention programs attempted to address general classes of pragmatic functions, such as requesting objects and providing information. The prescriptiveness in a program such as that offered by Guess et al. (1974) was reflected in the treatment of what have become commonly referred to as pragmatic or communicative functions. For example, Guess et al. (1974) first taught learners to *provide information* in response to a "What's this" question. Subsequently, learners were taught to *request objects. Protesting* was introduced only as a troubleshooting option in a program designed to teach a learner to respond to yes/no questions. Options to sequence the introduction of pragmatic functions were not a prominent feature of most early intervention programs.

The primary individualization in the early communication intervention programs was in the selection of reinforcers to be used in implementing the program, rather than in the individualization of the specific communicative functions to be taught. Interventionists now recognize that there is a wide range of communicative functions that can be established with a beginning communicator. There appears to be a growing consensus that allowing learners to gain a measure of control over their environments should represent an important criterion for the selection of an initial communicative repertoire (Reichle, York, & Sigafoos, 1991). Today, we recognize that, depending on an individual's preferences, he or she can be taught to exert control over aspects of his or her environment by learning to express a wide variety of communicative functions. In teaching communicative functions, it is very important that the consequences provided by the interventionist match the communicative functions being taught.

Of course, teaching learners to discriminatingly use communicative functions would be easiest if the function could always be associated with the same narrow range of contexts. Unfortunately, this is not the case. For example, convention would suggest that when teaching a general rejecting response, "No, thanks," the interventionist should select items and events that would be maximally discriminable. This logic would result in the interventionist selecting opportunities in which the learner encountered items or events that were strongly disliked. Unfortunately, as we discussed earlier, if the interventionist does not move to less discriminable instances, the rejecting response may not necessarily generalize. Often, intervention procedures to establish a rejecting repertoire focus on teaching examples in which expressing a rejection allows the learner to escape or avoid a highly nonpreferred event. In such a case, a less discriminable event calling for the rejecting response "No, thanks" should occur along with the offer of a desired item in a state of satisfaction. Although it is tempting to focus on only the most salient items or events as discriminative stimuli during intervention, doing so may create overwhelming challenges to generalization.

A related issue involves our tendency as interventionists to view communicative functions as clearly separate and discontinuous classes. To the contrary, in many instances, the distinction between two communicative functions may be somewhat hazy. For example, when asked if he wants a soda, a learner may respond, "Do you have any orange juice?" The function of this utterance is both to reject the soda and to request an alternative. The form of the utterance is a request, but the function of the utterance is also a rejection. We believe that a blurring between pragmatic form and function occur quite often. The interventionist must ensure that careful attention is given to both the form and function of the pragmatic classes being taught so that consistent rules of use are being modeled for the learner.

Available data do not suggest a "best" sequence for introducing a beginning repertoire of communicative functions. For some learners, the strengths of preferred and nonpreferred items may assist in determining which communicative functions might provide the greatest social empowerment. However, for many learners, we believe that a variety of different communicative functions can be implemented concurrently. For example, at mealtime, an individual may strain to reach for a second dessert item that is out of reach. This event represents a potential opportunity to teach a more conventional requesting strategy. Just a few minutes earlier, the same learner may have pulled away from the offer of more green vegetables (a potential opportunity to teach a more conventional rejecting strategy). In each instance, the learner was highly motivated to engage in two distinctively different communicative functions (request in the former, and reject/protest in the latter).

All of the examples presented clearly show that the interventionist must become sufficiently familiar with the range of situations in which an individual is highly motivated. In practice, the interventionist must match a communicative form with the communicative function that corresponds to the individual's social motivation. If the learner is to have a complete grasp of the communicative forms and functions being taught, it is important to select teaching examples that allow the learner to discriminate functions and when each is used, but at the same time display sufficient variety to ensure the generalized use of each targeted communicative function. Finally, specific pragmatic forms and functions must be well coordinated with other aspects of an individual's communicative repertoire.

To be a competent communicator, it is not enough to know how to use requests to maintain interactions. It is equally important to know that requests can be used to initiate and to terminate interactions. The discriminability and generalizability of initial communicative function depend on the interventionist's skill in: 1) identifying the range of opportunities across which each of the communicative functions can be used, and 2) generating sufficient teaching examples in the early phases of intervention that maximize the discriminability of the communicative functions and at the same time demonstrate the range of situations across which a given communicative function can be used.

IDENTIFYING THE FORMS OF BEHAVIOR
USED TO EXPRESS INITIAL COMMUNICATIVE FUNCTIONS

McLean and Snyder-McLean (1988) identified classes of intentional communicative forms that reflect an individual's ability to communicate. The three classes in their taxonomy are primitive, conventional, and referential acts. Primitive acts include gestures that consist of direct motor acts on objects and people. Some common primitive acts include pulling away from an undesired object, gesturing with an object, and leading a person to a desired item or activity. Conventional acts include gestures that do not necessarily involve direct contact with an object or a person (e.g., pointing, motioning for an object to be removed). Referential acts involve the use of symbolic forms and linguistic structures. Examples of referential acts are speaking, signing, or using graphic symbols to express communicative intents. Traditionally, intervention usually began at the referential level (Bricker & Bricker, 1974; Guess et al., 1974; Kent, 1974). Only recently have interventionists begun to address more primitive and conventional forms of communication (McLean & Snyder-McLean, 1988).

Conventional acts are part of most individuals' permanent communicative repertoires. For example, using the index finger to point is quick and socially acceptable. Pointing has the distinct advantage of allowing interaction with a partner without vocally interrupting an ongoing activity. Some primitive forms of communication also serve very useful functions. For example, if one has a mouth full of food as the host approaches to refill a wine glass, simply proferring one's empty glass is efficient, socially acceptable, and highly communicative. On a cold day when a friend drives by in a car with the windows up, a hand wave is a more acceptable and appropriate form of social greeting than screaming "Hello." From these examples, it is clear that sophisticated communicators possess a repertoire of responses that represent a wide continuum of sophistication.

Unfortunately, not all primitive and conventional forms of communication are socially acceptable. For example, holding one's crotch is highly communicative (i.e., "I need a bathroom, now!") but not very socially acceptable. Other more primitive or conventional forms may be socially acceptable but not very communicative. For example, an individual may point to food placed in the center of the table. However, without additional context, it is unclear whether he or she is "requesting" or "commenting." Furthermore, the specific referent for the communicative production may be unclear.

There are a variety of acceptable forms of behavior that can convey communicative functions. Frequently, the modes selected represent a careful mix of vocalizations (or verbalizations), gestures (natural gestures and/or formal signs), and graphic symbols. We do not believe that the interventionist's task in establishing communicative forms is to move from primitive to more conventional gestures without regard to the learner's existing repertoire. Instead, the task is to use the learner's existing repertoire and determine which aspects of it can be blended or shaped into a well-planned system. This blending requires the thoughtful application of the instructional technologies that have emerged since the 1970s.

DESIGNING INSTRUCTIONAL STRATEGIES
THAT CONSIDER EXISTING COMMUNICATIVE REPERTOIRES

To a great extent, the communication intervention literature presumes that individuals with developmental disabilities come to the task of learning communication skills as blank slates. Many intervention procedures marginally address strategies for incorporating portions of an individual's existing communicative repertoire into intervention activities. A variety of instructional strategies may be chosen, depending on the social acceptability and communicative efficiency of the learner's existing repertoire. Two strategies, shaping and chaining, warrant discussion. In shaping, the interventionist identifies an existing communicative form that is qualitatively unacceptable and, by reinforcing successively better approximations of a more acceptable form, makes the original form more communicatively effective. In chaining, the interventionist takes the learner's existing communicative form and teaches him or her to add a new form to it to enhance communicative efficiency and effectiveness. For example, an individual may produce the manual sign for "hamburger." At McDonald's, however, the sign will not be intelligible to the clerk, but at home, using the sign is far faster and thus more efficient than using a communication board. A chaining procedure might teach the learner to continue to produce the sign. However, if his listener does not respond immediately, the learner would select a graphic symbol that represents "hamburger." In this instance, chaining addresses possible limitations of a single communicative mode. Alternatively, chaining techniques can be implemented to enhance a pragmatic clarity. For example, when a child using a communication board produces single-word utterances, the listener must use significant context to decipher the child's intent. If a child says "milk," only the context in which the utterance is produced allows the interventionist to judge if the utterance was a request or a comment. With some learners, it may be helpful to teach chaining a request descriptor with an object vocabulary item to signify a request (e.g., want + milk = request; milk = comment/provision of information [Reichle & Keogh, 1986]).

In some instances, an individual's communicative expressions are so socially unacceptable that they cannot continue to be a part of his or her communicative repertoire. For example, engaging in aggression to communicate protests is unacceptable. In such instances, it is important that new communicative behavior replace an existing communicative repertoire. Consequently, a socially acceptable form that can become functionally equivalent to the learner's aggression is to eliminate reinforcing contingencies for the aggression and to create numerous opportunities in which a newly identified protesting utterance is reinforced (before it is necessary for the learner to engage in aggression). In this example, unless the interventionist carefully considers the learner's existing communicative repertoire in the design of intervention techniques, it may be virtually impossible to establish generalized use of the new communicative repertoire that is being taught.

It is beyond the scope of this chapter to address comprehensively current best practices aimed at replacing challenging behavior with socially acceptable communicative alternatives. However, there has recently been a growing body of empirical work in this area (see Doss & Reichle, 1989; Reichle & Wacker, in preparation, for comprehensive reviews).

In summary, interventionists must ensure that the design of instructional strategies to establish socially acceptable repertoires of communicative behavior consider an individual's existing repertoire. Once the range of useful social functions has been established, communication intervention strategies must determine whether learners are able to produce sequences of communicative functions in the give-and-take of conversations. Conversely, intervention strategies that begin by emphasizing interpersonal exchanges must also provide strategies to facilitate actual conversational exchanges. Although teaching conversational behavior is not particularly easy, it is a critical skill that allows an individual to be increasingly involved in a full range of community activities.

USING COMMUNICATIVE BEHAVIOR
IN ALL PHASES OF SOCIAL INTERACTION

Tannock and Girolametto (1992) observed that, "The precise mechanisms by which early social interaction facilitates language development are not known. . ." (p. 53). Although the precise mechanisms may not be known, current research suggests that there are a number of aspects of listener input that appear to be associated with the acquisition of communicative production. Included among these aspects are: 1) the maintenance of joint attention (e.g., the participants in the interaction are attending to the same aspect of the environment); 2) contingent response to the child's communication (e.g., the partner's response occurs immediately following and is related to the child's communicative attempt); 3) the use of social routines (e.g., interactions that involve joint attention are repetitive, predictable, and provide structure for turn-taking); 4) the use of models and/or expansions (e.g., provision of examples of communicative responses that may or may not build on the content and form of the child's previous communicative response); and 5) the modification of speech to match the complexity of the child's communicative production (Hemmeter, 1991). Given the potential importance and facilitating influence of communicative intervention in the context of conversational exchanges, there is increasing need to identify practical and empirically sound intervention techniques that maximize participation in social exchanges.

Delineating the Components of an Interaction

As we discussed earlier in this chapter, a simple view of social-communicative interactions suggests that there are three broad classes of behavior that may occur in the context of social exchange: social exchanges may be initiated, maintained, or terminated. Most intervention research has focused on teaching individuals to maintain simple interactions. However, the majority of the individual communicative functions discussed in this chapter can be classified as any one of these three conversational classes of behavior. As mentioned previously, Table 2 illustrates the interaction between communicative intents (request, reject, comment) and communicative exchanges (initiate, maintain, terminate).

Initiating Communicative Interactions

There are many instances when an individual may wish to initiate an interaction with others. Table 3 summarizes some of the circumstances that appear to increase the potential for an initiation to occur. Rarely has initiating communicative interactions been the focus of early intervention efforts for persons who have developmental disabilities. More often, initiation has been addressed once the individual has acquired new vocabulary but has failed to use it spontaneously (Carr & Kologinsky, 1983; Charlop, Schreibman, & Thibodeau, 1985; Gobbi, Cipani, Hudson, & Lapenta-Neudeck, 1986; Simic & Bucher, 1980).

Some promising intervention strategies that can be used to establish communicative initiation have been described. Carr and Kologinsky (1983) explored initiated requests among three learners with autism and who were nonverbal. At the outset of intervention, the learners had repertoires that ranged between 25–50 signs. The authors noted that the learners' requests occurred only in the presence of specific objects. Therefore, the intervention was conducted when objects would be available but not visible. This intervention resulted in an increase in the learners' rates and varieties of initiated requests (Carr & Kologinsky, 1983).

Table 3. Circumstances that may promote initiation of interactions

Circumstance	Example
Joining activities that are already in progress	Tom Sawyer instilling an interest among his peers in painting a fence.
Beginning well-established routines	A learner (taught that you can't eat your snack unless all the children in the group have some), upon receiving several cookies turns to a peer who doesn't have any, offers a cookie, and says, "Here."
Calling attention to novel events	At snacktime when a child spills his milk, a learner obtains the teacher's attention to point out what has happened.
Protesting the undesirable actions of another	A waitress, assuming that a customer has finished his meal, attempts to remove a plate that still contains a small amount of food. When this happens, the customer says, "I'm not done."

From Reichle, J., York, J., and Sigafoos, J. (1991). *Implementing augmentative and alternative communication: Strategies for learners with severe disabilities* (p. 150). Baltimore: Paul H. Brookes Publishing Co.; reprinted by permission.

Halle, Baer, and Spradlin (1981) introduced a time-delay prompt fading procedure to establish initiated requesting by six preschoolers with moderate mental retardation. Teachers were taught to delay 5 seconds before offering assistance or providing materials during activities including free play, snack time, and lunch. A child's failure to respond during a time delay resulted in the interventionist's modeling of a correct response. The child received assistance contingent on a self-initiated utterance or utterance resulting from the interventionist's model. Results demonstrated that the constant time delay was efficient in establishing initiated requests for assistance. Other investigators, including Charlop et al. (1985) and Gobbi et al. (1986), reported the successful use of procedures that incorporated the use of time-delay prompt fading strategies.

Maintaining Communicative Interactions

Conversational maintenance involves a number of interrelated skills that include adding to and introducing new topics to the ongoing conversation, as well as identifying and repairing breakdowns in the communicative flow. Breakdowns occur when one participant in a communicative interaction fails to respond to a partner's utterance that requires a response. For example, suppose that an individual directs the utterance "Do you want to play ball?" to a friend. If the friend fails to say anything, a breakdown has occurred. Similarly, if the friend's response appears to share too little relevant information, a breakdown may occur (e.g., "Do you want to play ball?" to which the partner responds "red one"). Communicative breakdowns may be attributable to sensory impairment, memory deficits, or a number of delayed or disordered aspects of language. Repairing communicative breakdowns is a particularly important area for communication interventionists who work with people who are acquiring an initial communicative repertoire. A growing body of literature suggests that beginning communicators readily identify a subset of their own utterances that have not resulted in efficient communicative exchanges with adult partners. For example, Yoder et al. (1992), based on a study conducted by Gallagher (1981), suggested that children with fewer than 70 words in their repertoire tended to repeat their original utterance when presented with a general query "What," while children with over 90 words in their repertoire tended to revise their original utterance. Other investigators have suggested that children's increasing linguistic competence corresponds to more sophisticated conversational repair strategies (Anselmi, Tomasello, & Acunzo, 1986; Brinton & Fujiki, 1982; Brinton, Fujiki, & Sonnenberg, 1988; Gallagher & Darnton, 1978; Wilcox & Webster, 1980).

In addition to the tendency for a child's repair strategy to vary as a function of communicative ability, there is some evidence to suggest that a listener's request for clarification may also be related to the child's repair strategy (Gallagher, 1981). Gallagher found that parents tend to query

Brown's Stage I children's unclear utterances by asking yes/no questions or general "What" queries. As children's mean length of utterance increases so that they are regularly combining words, adults begin to more explicitly query by specifying particular aspects of messages that they did not understand. Although the assumption appears to be that children's production skills contribute to these modifications in requests for clarification, this is an area that warrants attention in future investigations of conversational repair.

Information regarding the participation of persons with developmental disabilities in repairing communicative breakdowns is quite limited. Coggins and Stoel-Gammon (1982) have reported that 5- and 6-year-old children with Down syndrome responded to nearly all requests for repairs to their communicative responses. Interestingly, the majority of these repairs were revised utterances rather than repetitions of their original utterances. These findings were similar to the results of an earlier study conducted by Gallagher (1977), in which subjects were 18 intellectually normal children, 6 each of Brown's Stage I, II, and III.

To date, there is limited research to suggest that a learner's repair varies as a function of the communicative intent of the utterance for which the repair is requested. Shalz and O'Reilly (1990) found that children were more likely to repair their original utterance when it functioned as a request than when it functioned as a comment. In addition, Wilcox and Webster (1980) found that children would repeat their original utterance when a listener interpreted the utterance as a request and revise their utterance when a listener interpreted the utterance as a comment. Based on this information, it appears that a learner's repair may be affected by: 1) his or her motivation to repair the utterance (e.g., the motivation to repair a request for a desired item may be greater than the motivation to repair a comment regarding the weather), and 2) the listener's inference regarding the communicative intent of the original utterance.

Conversational repair presents a particularly difficult challenge for learners with severe developmental disabilities. Repair persistence involves repeated attempts to repair the same message and may be important for several reasons. First, when a learner has an extremely limited communicative repertoire, the listener may require several opportunities to decipher the message. By being persistent and continuing to respond, the listener has enhanced opportunities to request relevant information. Persistence also affords the listener opportunities to implement mand-model intervention strategies that teach the learner to produce more complete responses to queries for information. Currently, with notable exceptions (Brinton & Fujiki, 1988), there is a lack of empirical information addressing this particularly critical area of repair persistence.

In summary, an individual's ability to maintain an interaction is a critical component of any conversational exchange. Two facets involved in maintaining an interaction are the ability of a speaker to repair breakdowns in communication and the ability to communicate to a partner that repair is needed. Although empirical research is limited, there appear to be a number of variables that may affect the success of a communicative repair. Among these variables are: the speaker's motivation to repair a misunderstood utterance, the sophistication of the speaker's repertoire, the clarity of the listener's request for repair, and the clarity of the speaker's repair.

Terminating Communicative Interactions

Typically, interventionists have addressed terminating communicative interactions by using situations in which the learner is highly motivated to escape an interaction because it has become uninteresting. Although this motivation may account for a substantial proportion of the termination of interactions, there are a number of other possible circumstances. Table 4 displays circumstances for terminating a conversation, which may have little to do with undesirable aspects of the ongoing interaction. For example, two children may be playing pleasantly during recess. Suddenly, the school bell rings, signaling that recess is over. One child may turn to the other and say, "Oh oh, I've got to go. See you later." In this instance, the communicative interaction ended to accommodate another planned event, not because the interaction had become undesirable. Interventionists must identify a wide array of situations in which to teach a socially acceptable terminating strategy, otherwise it cannot be assumed that the learner will generalize the use of the strategy across the applicable range of situations.

Table 4. Circumstances that may promote termination of interactions

Circumstance	Example
Ending undesired interactions	A learner becomes bored participating in a game of cards and says, "Let's stop."
Concluding desirable interactions in order to accommodate a schedule	When the bell rings in the school cafeteria, a learner may have to terminate his lunchtime interaction with a peer in order to avoid being late to his next class.
Finishing pleasant interactions to take advantage of a more attractive alternative	A 7-year-old child may be content to play with a 3-year-old child provided no other playmates are available. However, the appearance of another 7-year-old may result in the interaction with the 3-year-old being abruptly terminated.
Discontinuing pleasant interactions due to environmental disruptions	A learner who sees his little brother fall off his bike may need to terminate a play activity, in order to render assistance.

From Reichle, J., York, J., and Sigafoos, J. (1991). *Implementing augmentative and alternative communication: Strategies for learners with severe disabilities* (p. 147). Baltimore: Paul H. Brookes Publishing Co.; reprinted by permission.

Few data exist that directly address the issue of best practice in establishing interactive use of communicative behavior. Persons with moderate and severe developmental disabilities are at a potential disadvantage for interactional competence with communicative behavior for several reasons. First, individuals may have a limited interest in other individuals in their environment. Second, people who interact with these individuals may have reduced expectations for communication, and this discourages competent performance (Mittler & Berry, 1977). Third, due to the societal practice of segregation, the number of competent communication partners is drastically limited. Fourth, restricted communicative repertoires are typically associated with individuals with moderate and severe intellectual disabilities. With these disadvantages, interventionists have much to overcome in order to produce successful outcomes.

In many instances, interventionists may impose an instructional rigor that successfully establishes rudimentary conversational behavior, but which is somewhat unsatisfying, because the learner continues to be dependent on the presence of certain discriminative stimuli before he or she engages in conversational exchanges. As a result, the learner's communicative exchanges may lack spontaneity. Consequently, we believe that it is important for interventionists to consider the role of spontaneity in all aspects of establishing conversational sequences.

THE ROLE OF SPONTANEITY IN INITIATING, MAINTAINING, AND TERMINATING CONVERSATIONS

Much of the communivation intervention literature uses the terms intiation and spontaneity interchangeably. We propose that the two are separate phenomena and that each must be addressed if an individual is to fully generalize his or her communicative repertoire. Spontaneous is defined as "arising from internal forces or causes" (*Random House*, p. 844) and initiate as "to begin or set going. . ." (*Random House*, p. 454). Given these definitions, spontaneity can refer to any aspect of a conversation. For example, internal states such as satiation or habituation may motivate an individual to terminate an event. Similarly, internal states such as thirst or hunger may prompt an individual to initiate a trip to a grocery store. Both of these examples constitute spontaneous events. Consider the distinction between spontaneity and initiation in the following example. A child visiting the local playground for the first time looks at a group of children who are about the same age. First, the child's parent says, "Look, kids to play with!" However, the child fails to act on the opportunity. The parent follows up with, "Why don't you walk over?" The reluctant child continues to ignore the parent's prompts. Finally, the parent says, "Go on over." The child responds, "No." As a last resort the parent says, "If you don't walk over, we're going home and you can do your homework." The threat of negative reinforcement prompts the child to walk over and awkwardly say, "Hi." Although the child's utterance was a conversational initiation, because it was heavily prompted by the parent, it is not considered spontaneous. If initiation and spontaneity are treated as the same skill, learners may fail to receive intervention directed to their conversational needs.

Although it clearly applies, interventionists rarely consider instructional objectives that focus on the extension of spontaneity to maintain or terminate conversational flow. For example, consider an elementary-school student who is conversing with a classmate in the lunch room of an elementary school. Midway through the conversation, a bell signals the end of the lunch period in 2 minutes. Learners who lack spontaneity may fail to conclude the interaction (e.g., "Well, I guess we better go") until the communicative partner asks, "Do you have to go?" At this point, both participants in the interaction rise and depart without actually concluding the interaction.

While we have provided examples of spontaneous and prompted initiations and terminations, spontaneity in maintaining conversations is not easily delineated. Topic changes might be interpreted as an example of spontaneity in conversation maintenance. If, however, the topic change is unrelated to prior content, the listener may not follow the flow or understand the transition. This outcome might indicate the speaker was, in effect, "too spontaneous." The lack of spontaneity in the communicative behaviors of persons with developmental disabilities represents a critical area for further empirical scrutiny. Too often, instructional opportunities focus on opportunities for learners to maintain communicative interaction rather than on opportunities to initiate or terminate interactions. When there are opportunities across the three components of an interaction, it is often instructionally convenient to select a narrow range of teaching examples (i.e., teaching termination of interactions only when the interaction becomes a nonpreferred activity). Care must be taken to focus on the full range of opportunities available for communicative interaction so that persons with developmental disabilities are not at an extreme disadvantage when participating in classroom and community environments.

ENSURING CORRESPONDENCE BETWEEN THE LEARNER'S COMMUNICATIVE UTTERANCES AND ACTIONS

Toddlers' initial utterances usually have referents that are both present and visible. As children mature, they begin to talk about referents that are not present in space and time. To have a wide range of potential conversational topics, an individual should be able to refer to referents and actions that have occurred in the past and that may occur in the future. A number of investigations have examined the correspondence between an individual's communicative productions and actions (Baer, 1990; Baer, Blount, Detrich, & Stokes, 1987; Baer & Detrich, 1990; Baer, Detrich, & Weninger, 1988; Baer, Osnes, & Stokes, 1983; Baer, Williams, Osnes, & Stokes, 1985; Crouch, Rusch, & Karlan, 1984; Deacon & Konarski, 1987; de Freitas Ribiero, 1989; Guevremont, Osnes, & Stokes, 1986a, 1986b; Guevremont, Osnes, & Stokes, 1988a, 1988b; Israel, 1978; Israel & Brown, 1977; Israel & O'Leary, 1973; Karlan & Rusch, 1982; Paniagua, 1989; Paniagua & Baer, 1988; Risley & Hart, 1968; Rogers-Warren & Baer, 1976; and numerous others).

Risley and Hart (1968) attempted to increase the correspondence between disadvantaged preschoolers' self-reports and actual behaviors in two separate situations. In the first situation, a "say-do" pattern, the child first gave a verbal description of what he or she planned to do (e.g., named the toy that he or she was going to play with), and then had the opportunity to engage in a range of activities that included the activity that was the focus of the child's preceding utterance. In the second situation, the "do-say" pattern, the child first engaged in an activity (e.g., played with a particular toy), and then had the opportunity to verbally describe what he or she did. Baseline data revealed that correspondence between the verbal self-report of actions and the actual actions was low regardless of the situation (e.g., "do-say" or "say-do"). However, delivery of a reinforcer contingent on correspondence resulted in an increase in correspondence between verbal self-reports and actual behaviors in both situations. A number of investigations have corroborated the findings of Risley and Hart (1968) in the say-do situation (Baer et al., 1987; Baer et al., 1988; Guevremont, Osnes, & Stokes, 1986a, 1986b; Israel & Brown, 1977), as well as the do-say situation (Israel, 1973; Karoly & Dirks, 1977; Rogers-Warren & Baer, 1976). These results suggest that although individuals may have sufficient vocabulary to produce verbal self-reports about the activities in which they engage, a correspondence between the two may not necessarily occur unless their relationship is consistently reinforced.

In many instances, there may be limited natural contingencies that reinforce children for matching their communicative behaviors with their actions (Tetlie & Reichle, 1986). For example, when a child comes home from preschool and a parent asks, "What did you do today?", it is quite probable that the adult cannot accurately ascertain if the child's report corresponds with the child's actions. It is unlikely that the adult actually knows what the child did. If the adult producing the query is not able to discriminate a correct response from an incorrect response, any plausible answer must be treated as a corresponding utterance. For a learner with a limited communicative repertoire who is engaged in a reinforcing activity when queried, a vague response using well-rehearsed vocabulary is often given. For example, when asked, "What did you do today?", a learner may respond, "We played." If the learner's communicative partner follows with, "What did you play?", the learner may respond by saying "stuff" or "toys." Using well-rehearsed and easy-to-produce vocabulary that marginally match the query may be viewed by the learner as the most efficient method of satisfying the communication partner without having to divert attention from an ongoing activity.

Little research has focused on reasons for a lack of correspondence between communicative behavior and actions in children with developmental disabilities. One obvious explanation is that the learner may not have sufficient vocabulary to describe activities. If a learner is asked, "What did you do today?", but he or she does not have the vocabulary to adequately respond, specific correspondence between behavior and report is unlikely. The smaller the child's vocabulary, the more challenging it will be for the child to produce an utterance that directly matches his or her actions. Learners may resort to one of several strategies to accommodate an insufficient vocabulary, including offering a very general or vague response.

Some learners may fail to correspond their actions with spoken utterances in an effort to maintain an interaction. Learners may acquire routinized stories that they use as a script (e.g., I went fishing today → caught a big one → 15 pounds). Over time, the individual may have learned that a particular utterance or sequence of utterances probably yields not only a listener response, but also continued interaction. Because the learner uses the utterances or sequences of utterances so often, production of these has become a relatively effortless strategy to maintain an interaction.

Another plausible explanation for failure to produce verbal behavior that corresponds to actions is the possibility of a memory deficit. For some learners, correspondence may be jeopardized if significant time passes between engagement in an action and a communicative utterance. Although it is beyond the scope of this chapter, the relationship between memory and language use represents a critical area for investigation with individuals who have developmental disabilities.

In summary, one of the basic conditions of an efficient communicative exchange is that both participants produce truthful and relevant utterances. The available literature suggests that correspondence between learners' actions and communicative utterances does not always occur. There appear to be a number of plausible explanations for this lack of correspondence. Communication interventionists need to consider the extent to which a learner's communicative behavior accurately represents the displaced events to which the learner is referring. There is a critical need for development and systematic evaluation of intervention strategies that focus on ensuring correspondence between actions and communicative utterances. Unless such correspondence exists, it is difficult to improve the quality of social exchanges in which an individual participates.

SUMMARY

In this chapter, we have reviewed a number of factors to consider when establishing an initial repertoire of communication skills with learners who have moderate and severe developmental disabilities. The complexity and magnitude of the task is striking. Communication is among the most complex elements of human behavior. Consequently, it represents a significant challenge to interventionists who are attempting to establish an initial communicative repertoire with individuals who are not acquiring an initial repertoire at a satisfactory rate.

Communicative functions (e.g., request, protest, provide information) are produced under varying stimulus conditions. Interventionists cannot assume that newly acquired forms expressing specific communicative functions will be used across a large array of occasions unless the range of these occasions is reflected in the intervention procedures. Establishing generalized use of a variety of communicative functions is further complicated by potential confusion in their discriminability. It is quite easy to define instances of requesting that are maximally discriminable from rejecting. In other instances, the distinction between these two functions may be quite unclear. The difference in discriminative stimuli that call for a request for an alternative versus a rejection may be very subtle. Consequently, the interventionist must carefully select examples to teach discrimination between, and generalization across, communicative functions.

A particular confusion regarding examples for teaching communicative functions occurs when interventionists do not differentiate the pragmatic form of an utterance from its pragmatic function. That is, if "requesting assistance" has been targeted for intervention, selection of teaching examples could focus on using this behavior to hasten completion of less desirable activities (i.e., "Help me sweep the floor") or to more quickly access desired items or events (i.e., "Help me unwrap this candy"). The interventionist must be cognizant of the exact function that the communicative behavior being taught is serving.

Inherent in the interventionist's establishment of communicative production is the goal of placing the most sophisticated forms within the learner's grasp. That is, moving from one-word to two-word utterances as quickly as possible has been a component of most early communication intervention programs. Although, in general, the more sophisticated the communicative form, the more appealing it is to the listener, there may be important exceptions. Efficient and socially acceptable utterances may be very simple. For example, natural gestures such as pointing in the presence of referents may be highly communicative and socially acceptable. The existence of rudimentary but very engaging forms may cause the interventionist to reconsider the priority of some of the communicative forms targeted for intervention.

Once a beginning repertoire of social-communicative functions and a corresponding vocabulary has been established, interventionists must address the use of those skills across sequences of interactive exchanges with others. Variables directly influencing the range of conversational options, from either the speaker's or listener's perspective, have yet to be elaborated exhaustively.

Although tremendous progress has been made in the delineation of viable communication intervention strategies for individuals with developmental disabilities, much work remains. As our understanding of the variables that influence the acquisition of communicative behavior increases, the sophistication of intervention strategies also increases. The field of communication intervention has advanced rapidly and we are confident that it will continue. For this reason, it is very important to validate empirically the strategies that emerge. If we fail to do so, we run the risk that we will speed in directions that, in the final analysis, will be counterproductive to the advancement of communication intervention expertise. Consequently, good collaborative relationships between researchers and practitioners are more important than ever.

REFERENCES

Anselmi, D., Tomasello, M., & Acunzo, M. (1986). Young children's responses to neutral and specific contingent queries. *Journal of Child Language, 13*, 135–144.

Baer, R. (1990). Correspondence training: Review in current issues. *Research in Development, 11*, 379–393.

Baer, R., Blount, R., Detrich, R., & Stokes, T. (1987). Using intermittent reinforcement to program maintenance of verbal/nonverbal correspondence. *Journal of Applied Behavior Analysis, 20*, 179–184.

Baer, R., & Detrich, R. (1990). Tacting and manding in correspondence training: Effects of child selection of verbalization. *Journal of Applied Behavior Analysis, 54*, 23–30.

Baer, R., Detrich, R., & Weninger, J. (1988). On the functional role of the verbalization in correspondence training procedures. *Journal of Applied Behavior Analysis, 21*, 345–356.

Baer, R., Osnes, P., & Stokes, T. (1983). Training generalized correspondence between verbal behavior at school and nonverbal behavior at home. *Education and Treatment of Children, 6*, 379–388.

Baer, R., Williams, J., Osnes, P., & Stokes, T. (1985). Generalized verbal control and correspondence training. *Behavior Modification, 9*, 477–489.

Bricker, W., & Bricker, D. (1974). An early language training strategy. In R.L. Schiefelbusch & L.L. Lloyd (Eds.), *Language perspectives: Acquisition, retardation, and intervention*. Baltimore: University Park Press.

Brinton, B., & Fujiki, M. (1982). A comparison of request-response sequences in the discourse of normal and language-disordered children. *Journal of Speech and Hearing Disorders, 47*, 57–62.

Brinton, B., & Fujiki, M. (1988). *Conversational management with language-impaired children*. Rockville, MD: Aspen Systems.

Brinton, B., Fujiki, M., & Sonnenberg, E. (1988). Responses to requests for clarification by linguistically normal and language-impaired children in conversation. *Journal of Speech and Hearing Disorders, 53*, 383–391.

Carr, E.G. (1977). The motivation of self-injurious behavior: A review of some hypotheses. *Psychological Bulletin, 84,* 800–816.

Carr, E.G., & Durand, V.M. (1985). Reducing behavior problems through functional communication training. *Journal of Applied Behavior Analysis, 18,* 111–126.

Carr, E., & Kologinsky, E. (1983). Acquisition of sign language by autistic children II: Spontaneity and generalization effects. *Journal of Applied Behavior Analysis, 16,* 297–314.

Charlop, M., Schreibman, L., & Thibodeau, M. (1985). Increasing spontaneous verbal responding in autistic children using a time delay procedure. *Journal of Applied Behavior Analysis, 18,* 155–166.

Cirrin, F., & Rowland, C. (1985). Communicative assessment of nonverbal youths with severe, profound mental retardation. *Mental Retardation, 3,* 52–62.

Coggins, T., & Carpenter, R. (1978). *Categories for coding pre-speech intentional communication.* Unpublished manuscript. University of Washington, Seattle.

Coggins, T.E., & Stoel-Gammon, C. (1982). Clarification strategies used by four Down's syndrome children for maintaining normal conversational interaction. *Education and Training of the Mentally Retarded, 17,* 65–67.

Crouch, K., Rusch, F., & Karlan, G. (1984). Competitive employment: Utilizing the correspondence training paradigm to enhance productivity. *Education and Training of the Mentally Retarded, 19,* 268–275.

Deacon, J., & Konarski, E., Jr. (1987). Correspondence training: An example of rule-governed behavior. *Journal of Applied Behavior Analysis, 20,* 391–400.

de Freitas Ribiero, A. (1989). Correspondence in children's self-report: Tacting and manding aspects. *Journal of the Experimental Analysis of Behavior, 51,* 361–367.

Dore, J. (1975). Holophrases, speech acts, and language universals. *Journal of Child Language, 2,* 21–40.

Doss, L.S., & Reichle, J. (1989). Establishing communicative alternatives to the emission of socially motivated excess behavior: A review. *Journal of The Association for Persons with Severe Handicaps, 14,* 101–112.

Gallagher, T. (1977). Revision behaviors in the speech of normal children developing language. *Journal of Speech and Hearing Research, 20,* 303–318.

Gallagher, T.M. (1981). Contingent query sequences within adult–child discourse. *Journal of Child Language, 8,* 51–62.

Gallagher, T., & Darnton, B. (1978). Conversational aspects of the speech of language disordered children: Revision behaviors. *Journal of Speech and Hearing Research, 21,* 118–125.

Gobbi, L., Cipani, E., Hudson, C., & Lapenta-Neudeck, R. (1986). Developing spontaneous requesting among children with severe mental retardation. *Mental Retardation, 24,* 357–363.

Goldstein, H., & Kaczmarek, L. (1992). Promoting communicative interaction among children in integrated intervention settings. In S.F. Warren & J. Reichle (Eds.), *Communication and language intervention: Vol. 1. Causes and effects in communication and language intervention* (pp. 81–111). Baltimore: Paul H. Brookes Publishing Co.

Guess, D., Sailor, W., & Baer, D. (1974). To teach language to retarded children. In R.L. Schiefelbusch & L.L. Lloyd (Eds.), *Language perspectives: Acquisition, retardation, and intervention.* Baltimore: University Park Press.

Guevremont, D., Osnes, P., & Stokes, T. (1986a). Preparation for effective self-regulation: The development of generalized verbal control. *Journal of Applied Behavior Analysis, 19,* 99–104.

Guevremont, D., Osnes, P., & Stokes, T. (1986b). Programming maintenance after correspondence training interventions with children. *Journal of Applied Behavior Analysis, 19,* 215–219.

Guevremont, D., Osnes, P., & Stokes, T. (1988a). The functional role of preschoolers' verbalizations in the generalization of self-instructional training. *Journal of Applied Behavior Analysis, 21,* 45–55.

Guevremont, D., Osnes, P., & Stokes, T. (1988b). Preschoolers' goal setting with contracting to facilitate maintenance. *Behavior Modification, 12,* 404–423.

Halle, J., Baer, D., & Spradlin, J. (1981). An analysis of teachers' generalized use of delay in helping children: A stimulus control procedure to increase language use in handicapped children. *Journal of Applied Behavior Analysis, 14,* 389–409.

Hemmeter, M. L. (1991). *The effects of parent-implemented language intervention on the language skills of young children with developmental delays.* Unpublished doctoral dissertation. Vanderbilt University, Nashville.

Israel, A. (1973). Developing correspondence between verbal and nonverbal behavior: Switching sequences. *Psychological Reports, 32,* 1111–1117.

Israel, A. (1978). Some thoughts on correspondence between saying and doing. *Journal of Applied Behavior Analysis, 11,* 271–276.

Israel, A., & Brown, M. (1977). Correspondence training, prior verbal training, and control of nonverbal behavior via control of verbal behavior. *Journal of Applied Behavior Analysis, 10,* 333–338.

Israel, A., & O'Leary, K.D. (1973). Developing correspondence between children's words and deeds. *Child Development, 44,* 575–581.

Kaiser, A., & Alpert, K. (in preparation). *Milieu teaching.*

Karlan, G., & Rusch. F. (1982). Correspondence between saying and doing: Some thoughts on defining correspondence and future directions for application. *Journal of Applied Behavior Analysis, 15,* 151–162.

Karoly, P., & Dirks, M. (1977). Developing self-control in preschool children through correspondence training. *Behavior Therapy, 8,* 398–405.

Kent, L. (1974). *Language acquisition program for the retarded or multiply impaired.* Champaign, IL: Research Press.

Lamarre, J., & Holland, J.G. (1985). The functional independence of mands and tacts. *Journal of the Experimental Analysis of Behavior, 43,* 5–19.

MacDonald, J. (1989). *Becoming partners with children.* Tucson, AZ: Communication Skill Builders.

Mahoney, G., & Powell, A. (1986). *Transactional intervention program: Teacher's guide.* Farmington, CT: Pediatric Research and Training Center, University of Connecticut Health Center.

McLean, J., McLean, L., Brady, N., & Etter, R. (1991). Communication profiles of two types of gesture using nonverbal persons with severe to profound mental retardation. *Journal of Speech and Hearing Disorders, 34,* 294–308.

McLean, J., & Snyder-Mclean, L. (1988). Application of pragmatics to severely mentally retarded children and youth. In R. Schiefelbusch & L.L. Lloyd (Eds.), *Language perspectives: Acquisition, retardation, and intervention* (2nd ed., pp. 343–366). Austin, TX: PRO-ED.

Miller, J., MacKenzie, H., & Chapman, R. (1981). Unpublished manuscript, University of Wisconsin-Madison.

Mittler, P., & Berry, P. (1977). Demanding language. In P. Mitter (Ed.). *Research to practice in mental retardation: Education and training* (Vol. II, pp. 245–251). Baltimore: University Park Press.

Paniagua, F.A. (1989). Lying by children: Why children say one thing, do another? *Psychological Reports, 64,* 971–984.

Paniagua, F., & Baer, D. (1988). Luria's regularity concept and its replacement in verbal–nonverbal correspondence training. *Psychological Reports, 62,* 371–378.

Random House Dictionary (1988). New York: Random House.

Reichle, J. (1991). *Establishing conditional requests among learners with severe developmental disabilities.* Unpublished manuscript. University of Minnesota, Minneapolis.

Reichle, J. (1990a). *Developing communication intervention strategies for persons with developmental disabilities: Case studies.* Unpublished manuscript, University of Minnesota, Minneapolis.

Reichle, J. (1990b). *The influence of object preference on the use of generalized requesting and rejecting skills.* Unpublished manuscript, University of Minnesota, Minneapolis.

Reichle, J., & Keogh, W. (1986). Communication instruction for learners with severe handicaps: Some unresolved issues. In R. Horner, L. Meyer, & H.D. Fredericks, (Eds.), *Education of learners with severe handicaps: Exemplary service strategies* (pp. 189–219). Baltimore: Paul H. Brookes Publishing Co.

Reichle, J., Schermer, E., & Anderson, H. (1990). *Teaching requesting assistance using a general case approach.* Unpublished manuscript, University of Minnesota, Minneapolis.

Reichle, J., & Wacker, D. (Eds.). (in preparation). *Communicative approaches to the management of challenging behavior.* Baltimore: Paul H. Brookes Publishing Co.

Reichle, J., York, J., & Eynon, D. (1989). Influence of indicating preferences for initiating, maintaining, and terminating interactions. In F. Brown & D.H. Lehr (Eds.), *Persons with profound disabilities: Issues and practices* (pp. 191–211). Baltimore: Paul H. Brookes Publishing Co.

Reichle, J., York, J., & Sigafoos, J. (1991). *Implementing augmentative and alternative communication: Strategies for learners with severe disabilities.* Baltimore: Paul H. Brookes Publishing Co.

Risley, T.R., & Hart, B. (1968). Developing correspondence between the non-verbal and verbal behavior of preschool children. *Journal of Applied Behavior Analysis, 1,* 267–281.

Rogers-Warren, A., & Baer, D. (1976). Correspondence between saying and doing: Teaching children to share and praise. *Journal of Applied Behavior Analysis, 9,* 335–354.

Shalz, M., & O'Reilly, A.W. (1990). Conversational or communicative skill? A reassessment of two-year-olds' behavior in miscommunication episodes. *Journal of Child Language, 17,* 131–146.

Simic, J., & Bucher, B. (1980). Development of spontaneous manding in language deficient children. *Journal of Applied Behavior Analysis, 13,* 523–528.

Tannock, R., & Girolametto, L. (1992). Reassessing parent-focused language intervention programs. In S.F. Warren & J. Reichle (Eds.), *Communication and language intervention: Vol. 1. Causes and effects in communication and language intervention* (pp. 49–79). Baltimore: Paul H. Brookes Publishing Co.

Tetlie, R., & Reichle, J. (1986). *The match between signed request and object selection in four learners with severe handicaps.* Unpublished master's thesis, University of Minnesota, Minneapolis.

Warren, S.F., & Rogers-Warren, A.K. (Eds.). (1985). *Teaching functional language.* Austin, TX: PRO-ED.

Weistuch, L., & Lewis, M. (1986, April). *Effect of maternal language intervention strategies on the language of delayed two- to four-year-olds*. Paper presented at the Eastern Psychological Association Conference, New York.

Wetherby, A. M., & Prizant, B. M. (1989). The expression of communicative intent: Assessment guidelines. *Seminars in Speech and Language, 10,* 77–91.

Wetherby, A.M., & Prizant, B.M. (1992). Profiling young children's communicative competence. In S.F. Warren & J. Reichle (Eds.), *Communication and language intervention: Vol. 1. Causes and effects in communication and language intervention* (pp. 217–253). Baltimore: Paul H. Brookes Publishing Co.

Wilcox, M.J., & Webster, E. (1980). Early discourse behaviors: Children's response to listener feedback. *Child Development, 51,* 1120–1125.

Yoder, P., & Davies, B. (1990). Do parental questions and topic continuations elicit replies from developmentally delayed children?: A sequential analysis. *Journal of Speech and Hearing Research, 33,* 563–573.

Yoder, P., Davies, B., & Bishop, K. (1992). Getting children with developmental disabilities to talk to adults. In S.F. Warren & J. Reichle (Eds.), *Communication and language intervention: Vol. 1. Causes and effects in communication and language intervention* (pp. 255–275). Baltimore: Paul H. Brookes Publishing Co.

PART III

Shared Meanings and Important Partnerships in Communication

7

"Don't Talk to Him; He's Weird"
A Social Consequences Account
of Language and Social Interactions

Mabel L. Rice

THE TITLE OF THIS CHAPTER includes a direct quote from a preschooler, "Don't talk to him; he's weird!" The comment occurred during a visit to the Language Acquisition Preschool. It was play-center time, when the children can choose their own activities and interact freely, with a minimum of adult interference. The dramatic play area included a toy cash register, which was a very popular item. Whoever ran the cash register was the "boss" in the store scenario. A 4-year-old normally developing boy, John (all names are fictitious), was operating the cash register, seated at a little table with another normally developing boy, Bill, of the same age. They were pretending to buy and sell toy food items, John as cashier and Bill as customer. They were engaged in verbal dialogue appropriate to the imagined setting, something along the lines of "How much is this?" "Ok, I'll buy it." "Here is your change." A third boy, Gary, a youngster with limited language skills, but otherwise normally developing social and intellectual abilities, approached John and Bill to show them the toy truck he was carrying. Gary said to Bill, "See my truck." Bill looked at him, then turned back to John, without responding to Gary's initiation. Gary tried again, the same outcome. He then made a third attempt, at which time John told Bill, in a rather forceful voice, "Don't talk to him; he's weird!" With that advice, Gary turned and ran toward another group of children.

This scene reminds us of the stark frankness of young children in their interactions with each other. It also captures some of the realities of adult

Preparation of this chapter was supported by Grant No. HD24U80001 from the U.S. Department of Education to the Kansas Early Childhood Research Institute. Appreciation is expressed to my present and former colleagues in research conducted in the Language Acquisition Preschool, whose work has contributed substantively to the content of this chapter: Betty Bunce, Pamela Hadley, Marie Sell, Ruth Watkins, and Kim Wilcox.

interactions, where there are many parallels in adults' social categorizing of individuals who seem to be somewhat different. Therefore, we take notice of such early manifestation of social judgments and their consequences.

This example is typical of what we have observed over the past several years in a series of studies documenting the social interactions of preschool children with speech-language impairments. Our observations are of children whose only problem is the development of speech and/or language; their general intellectual abilities are within normal limits, and their social interactions are generally appropriate (they are not children with autism or emotional disturbances or "behavioral disturbances"); they have normal hearing and no other signs of neurologic differences. In a real sense, they have a "hidden handicap," one that is not visible and may not become apparent until they are 3 years of age or older. It is, nevertheless, a handicap with pervasive implications for social and academic development.

Our work with these children has led us to consider our assumptions about the relationship between children's language skills and social interactions, and the formulation of a Social Consequences Account of language impairment. In the following discussion, socialization as a source of language is distinguished from language as a tool of socialization, and a brief review of each perspective is included. Then, language intervention in natural social contexts is considered, with description of one such intervention setting, that of the Language Acquisition Preschool (LAP). Next is a report of evidence of social consequences of language impairment, followed by a brief summary of other reports of social interactions of children with disabilities with normal peers. A brief reprise of the Social Consequences Account is then provided, in which it is argued that children with limited language are vulnerable in two ways: They are unable to fully capitalize on socialization as a source of language, and they are at risk for participation in social interactions as a consequence of their limited language. The final section presents some implications for language intervention with young children.

SOCIALIZATION AS A SOURCE OF LANGUAGE DEVELOPMENT

Since the early 1970s much has been written about the social underpinnings of language development (cf. Gleason, Hay, & Cain, 1989). The bulk of the studies focus on the transition from the prelinguistic period to the emergence of language. It is widely recognized that early language skills emerge in the context of interactions between babies and adults. Numerous studies document the existence of a special input register, in which adults speak "parentese" to their children, who in turn are especially responsive to this register. Gleason et al. (1989) differentiate between the infant's "predisposition for social interaction" as a motivational source of language and the early communication behaviors of adults as models for language. They argue that the infants' need for social attachment leads to their imitation of input language, the give-and-take of early discourse-like communicative interactions with babies, and other rudimentary patterns of early communication.

Toddlers use their early linguistic skills to express their social intentions, as described by researchers studying the pragmatic aspects of language (e.g., Bates, 1976; Greenfield & Smith, 1976; Halliday, 1975). Language is a means of commenting on objects and events of interest, of drawing attention to themselves and their needs, of requesting objects and activities, and of engaging in social routines, such as "bye-bye" and "hi."

As children become skilled language users, they engage in dialogues and conversations, which in turn become a basis for their further mastery of language. For example, children participate in book-reading routines, which provide a context well suited to furthering their understanding of the lexicon and grammatical structures (e.g., Snow & Goldfield, 1983). They interact with a variety of speakers, thereby gaining access to differing patterns of input. They engage in disputes with their peers, they report on their activities, they ask questions, and so on. In so doing, they begin to influence their conversational partners, who are sources of verbal input, and who, in turn, respond to the children. In a very real sense, children who demonstrate strong linguistic and interactive skills help create their own natural laboratory to facilitate language acquisition.

In short, children's early socialization needs and experiences form an important foundation for subsequent language development. Even the most ardent advocates for the social bases of language, however, do not argue that socialization alone, in and of itself, fully accounts for children's language development. Instead, they acknowledge the role of inborn neurologic factors, as well as the cognitive prerequisites that underlie and accompany language development (cf. Gleason et al., 1989). The perspective in this chapter is that language-specific acquisition mechanisms are also involved, mechanisms that are less robust in some children than others. In this multidimensional model of language development, then, socialization serves as an enhancement for language development, a facilitator that can create a situation optimally suitable for the nurturance of emerging linguistic competencies. The creation of such situations is the business of those professionals who attempt to teach language to youngsters with limited skills.

LANGUAGE AS A TOOL OF SOCIALIZATION

Social Status

Early on, children use their language and verbal interactive skills as a way of furthering their social development. By elementary school, children's conversational competencies are associated with their social status. Low-status children are less likely to initiate conversations with their peers (Garnica, 1981) and are less sought after as conversational partners (Cooper, Marquis, & Ayers-Lopez, 1982; Tabors, 1987).

The relationship between peer status and communication ability is formed during the preschool years. This is well-documented in two recent studies. Hazen and Black (1989) first determined the popularity of their preschool subjects by asking which children a particular child would like to play with and which children he or she would not like to play with. They then sorted the children into groups, based on their liked and disliked scores. They found that well-liked children were more inclined to clearly direct their initiations to specific listeners, to speak to more than one interaction partner, to respond contingently to others, and to acknowledge others. In a follow-up study, Black and Hazen (1990) extended the liked/disliked distinction to explore the effect of familiarity. They observed the interactions of acquainted and unacquainted preschoolers. They reported that when entering the play of children they did not know, disliked children were less responsive to peers and more likely to make irrelevant comments than were liked children. With acquainted peers, disliked children not only were less responsive and produced more irrelevant statements than liked children, they also were less likely to clearly direct their communication to specific peers. The authors concluded that the findings allow for differentiating between communication skills related to the emergence of social status and those related to the maintenance of social status. Apparently, responsiveness and contribution to coherent conversation are important to both the establishment and maintenance of social status, whereas failure to socially direct communications may be more related to the maintenance of social status.

To the extent that social acceptance is facilitated by conversational skills, preschool children with limited communication ability would be at risk for full integration into their peer social groups. If they are unable to initiate conversational turns, or to respond appropriately to initiations by their peers, they are less likely to move into the mainstream groupings of their playmates.

Cultural Status

Theorists who regard the child as a member of a cultural group have long recognized the role of language in children's socialization. Foremost among these theorists is Vygotsky (1978), who viewed language as a conventionalized, socially determined interactive system. Within his model of child development, the association of language and culture is very intimate:Cultural knowledge determines the course of language development, and, conversely, communicative interactions enculturate a child. Hymes (1972) bridged the disciplines of anthropology and linguistics with his definition of the full range of linguistic competencies as "communicative competence." This concept emphasizes the wide scope of underlying knowledge needed for the use of linguistic roles in social contexts. Hymes's interest in culturally situated language use inspired a number of cross-cultural studies of children's language acquisition.

Observations of children learning language in diverse settings show that children become sensitive to cultural conventions revealed in language, including such basics as relative status (e.g., whom one can talk to and how to do so), how to resolve disputes, gender roles, expressions of affection, indications of respect, and even attitudes about children's ability to learn to talk (cf. Ervin-Tripp & Gordon, 1986; Heath, 1989; Saville-Troike, 1982; Schieffelin & Ochs, 1986). Language acts as a signal for cultural distinctions that children "pick up." In turn, language users reveal their social position by virtue of their choice of linguistic forms and interactive styles. For example, preschool children are sensitive to registers indicative of relative status. They know that doctors can be bossy to nurses, delivering many directives, but nurses must be more polite in their requests of doctors (Anderson, 1977).

In short, children absorb social and cultural distinctions as they learn to use language appropriately. They are sensitive to differences in how other children communicate, as well as to the style of interactions appropriate for different settings. Intrinsic to this enculturation is awareness of culturally defined ways of grouping people. Children form clusters of liked and less-liked peers, and they recognize individual differences in behavior and demeanor. Their verbal interactions are played out in the web of these culturally absorbed expectations about the behavior of others.

Language Intervention in Natural Social Contexts

Disorders of language development constitute the single largest handicapping condition in early childhood. Of the preschool children who received special education services in school year 1986, 69%, or 184,727 of the 265,814 children served, were categorized as speech-language impaired (Office of Special Education, 1988). These children, then, comprise a primary group for early intervention.

During the 1970s and 1980s, interventionists recognized that the conclusions coming from the normative literature emphasized that language acquisition was largely child-driven, with young children talking about what they were interested in to accomplish their own social needs. There was recognition that the traditional adult-directed, one-to-one therapy model was not optimally suited to young children's language needs or for the teaching of discourse skills. New teaching methods appeared, such as incidental teaching strategies (Hart & Risley, 1975; Hart & Rogers-Warren, 1978). Johnston (1985) summarized the intervention principles to be derived from the normative literature as those of fit, focus, and functionality: Language activities should *fit* a child's available meanings, provide *focused linguistic input,* and teach *functionally* relevant language. Thus, language intervention shifted its emphasis toward the social context of language learning. The advantages of naturalistic language environments were espoused (Norris & Hoffman, 1990).

At the same time, there was growing recognition of the primacy of the preschool years for intervention. With the passage of the Education of the Handicapped Act Amendments of 1986 (PL 99-457), there was a mandate for states to provide early intervention services to all eligible children from birth to 5 years of age (Thiele & Hamilton, 1991). Across the country, there now is widespread consideration of how best to meet the needs of young children with handicaps. One specification of services to young children is that they be offered in a least restrictive environment, that is, one with a maximal opportunity for enhancing a child's development, preferably in the context of normally developing peers.

Language Acquisition Preschool (LAP)

LAP is one of the preschool intervention settings at the University of Kansas designed to teach language in a naturalistic, mainstreamed setting. Three approximately equal groups of children are enrolled: normally developing children, children learning English as a second language (ESL), and children with specific language impairment (SLI). The children are all between 3–5 years of age.

The SLI children meet several criteria, which can be summarized as speech and/or language skills significantly below the expectations for their chronological age, combined with normal or above performance on a nonverbal test of intelligence, normal social functioning, and no evidence of perceptual or neurologic problems. These children are ones with a "hidden handicap." To a casual observer of the group, they cannot be identified on the basis of how they look or how they behave. They come from all socioeconomic groups. With these youngsters, we have an opportunity to investigate the effects of speech and/or language impairment without the complications introduced by social, intellectual, or sensory deficits, racial differences, or major socioeconomic differentiation.

The ESL children meet the following criteria: They are recent arrivals to the U.S. who demonstrate normal language development in their native language, who are just being introduced to English, and who are as close to 3 years of age as possible. Most of these children are from the families of middle-class graduate students or faculty at the university. Therefore, the ESL children are less proficient than the SLI children at the outset, although they often catch up with and sometimes exceed the SLI children. They also differ from the SLI children in that they have a history of successful communication development.

Several features of LAP are relevant for the following discussion. The curriculum is a modification of the High Scope cognitive-social approach (Hohmann, Bonet, & Weikart, 1978). Throughout the daily activities, there is encouragement of child-directed learning, with many opportunities for children to interact verbally with each other and the teachers. Language development is emphasized throughout the curriculum. There is no special "language time," nor is individual therapy provided for the SLI or ESL children (although each SLI child has an Individualized Education Program with explicit remediation goals). All special instruction is tailored to a child's moment-to-moment interests in the context of the classroom activities.

One activity of each day is play-center time, which is a 40-minute period when children can choose their own activity from among four options: art activities, books and puzzles, blocks and toy vehicles, or dramatic play. The theme for dramatic play changes from day to day. Some of the children's favorites are: visit to a fast-food restaurant, visit to the veterinarian (when they take their stuffed animals for a check-up), bathe the babies (dollies), and outdoor camping. During the play-center time, children can wander from activity to activity, talk to whomever they choose, or play quietly by themselves. It is during this time that individual therapy activities are negotiated with the SLI children, and any other children who choose to participate in the interactions.

Summative evaluations over 3 years document the effectiveness of the curriculum (Bunce, Rice, & Wilcox, 1990). A sample of 14 SLI children who were enrolled in the program during that time, for an average of three semesters, demonstrated significant gains in vocabulary, receptive and expressive language, and articulation. Their mean scores on standardized tests increased from an initial level of one or more standard deviations below the normative mean to performance within the normal range. In comparison, the normal models' scores improved somewhat, but not at a level of statistical significance. Thus, the rate of improvement was actually higher for the SLI children than for the normal children who served as controls. Improvement was also evident in the SLI children's mean length of utterance, which increased from an entry level average within Brown's (1973) Stage II (2.25) to an exit level of late Stage V ($>$ 4.0). These improvements are thought to be related to the children's therapy goals, 88% of which were achieved or showing improvement.

SOCIAL CONSEQUENCES OF LANGUAGE IMPAIRMENT

Peer Relationships

In the naturalistic mix of young children with varying levels of communicative competence assembled in LAP, it soon became apparent that there were interesting things happening in the patterns of social interactions. We devised a means of measuring social interactions, with an on-line data recording system, the Social Interactive Coding System (SICS; Rice, Sell, &

Hadley, 1990), that did not require videotaping and the consequent time consuming transcript analysis procedures. We were interested in obtaining clinically relevant information in a timely fashion. The targeted interactive skills were initiations and responses, cross-coded according to the person with whom the child was interacting. Initiation was defined as a verbal attempt to begin an interaction with another person. Responses could be verbal or non-verbal. In effect, the coding captured who was talking to whom and who initiated the interaction.

Initiations and responses are conversational moves that are sensitive to the interface of verbal and social abilities (cf. Black & Hazen, 1990; Fey, 1986; Hazen & Black, 1989). In order to initiate successfully, a child must have a good sense of when to approach another child, be able to negotiate joint attention, and find an appropriate way to talk about something. Successful initiations are associated with social success, whereas a disproportionately high number of responses are associated with a passive social role.

Children's social interactions were observed during play-center time, when the children have relatively free choice of activities and interactants. These observations revealed that the social interactions of the LAP children were significantly influenced by the children's facility with communication. Normally developing children were the preferred partners for all children's social interactions (Rice, Sell, & Hadley, 1991), suggesting that the children were sensitive to the relative communicative competence of their peers at an early age. Conversely, children with limited communication skills were ignored more often by their peers (28% of their initiations, compared to 12% for normally developing children's initiations [Hadley & Rice, 1991]) and were, in turn, less responsive to initiations directed to them (they did not respond to 30% of the initiations to them; normally developing children failed to respond to only 7% of initiations to them [Hadley & Rice, 1991]). Children with speech articulation problems and limited intelligibility shortened their responses (40%–60% of communicatively limited children's responses were one-word or nonverbal responses, compared to 34% of the responses by the control group of children [Rice et al., 1991]). Children with communication limitations were more likely to initiate interactions with adults (63% compared to 49% for the normally developing children) and less likely to initiate interactions with their normally developing peers (37% compared to 51% [Rice et al., 1991]).

The general impression is that as young as 3 years of age, children are sensitive to relative differences in verbal facility and begin to make adjustments in their social interactions. Children with less skill have difficulty negotiating the interpersonal communicative space. Thus, they develop compensatory strategies, such as reliance on adults for mediation of social interactions and to meet their needs. It is particularly striking that these social consequences seem to result primarily from differences in communication skill. That inference is drawn from two observations. One is that the ESL and

SLI groups of children, both of which have limited communicative competencies, demonstrate similar patterns of discourse adjustments, although they differ in ethnic or cultural identity. The second observation is that the SLI children are not differentiated from the control group of children on the basis of general developmental status, ethnic identity, or general socioeconomic status (as indexed by mothers' level of educational attainment and employment). The average educational level for mothers of children in both groups is some college without a degree. The most frequent employment status category for both groups of mothers is that of full-time mother (44% for controls, 67% for SLI [Weinberg, 1991]). Thus, the social consequences of limited speech and language skill in these observations is not readily explained by other child attributes such as ethnic or cultural differences or other handicapping conditions.

This is not to suggest that within or across the groups of ESL and SLI children there is a uniform profile of speech and language problems, to which the discourse adjustments can be linked. As with other clinical populations in service settings, the observed children vary in their particular psycholinguistic competencies. Some have receptive and expressive limitations, while others have reasonably good receptive skills but restricted expressive repertoires (cf. Hadley & Rice, 1991; Rice et al., 1991). The group differences in SICS findings, then, can best be interpreted in very general terms of relative competencies, of children with "adequate" communicative skills versus those with "less adequate" skills. The many possible ways in which "less adequate" skills can influence patterns of initiation and response to peers remain to be determined.

Our premise is that youngsters with communication limitations are vulnerable to a negative social spiral, starting in the preschool years. This spiral would play out this way: To begin with, some children lack the flexibility in using language or the intelligibility in using speech that is essential for easy entry into and maintenance of social discourse with their peers. Because they lack the expected, conventionalized, and socially adjusted uses of language, they are more likely to be ignored, rebuffed, or excluded from peer interactions. Furthermore, they recognize this problem, although probably not on a conscious level, and develop compensatory strategies, such as a greater reliance on adults, if adults are available and receptive to their overtures, or a shortening of responses, if their speech is unintelligible.

Adult Judgments

How do children arrive at such intuitions, if this is the case, about social competencies? How do they come to judgments of "weirdness" on the basis of interpersonal communication strategies? Is this a developmental phase or part of a broader cultural bias that children are capable of incorporating into their perspectives about each other?

The possibility of a general social bias was raised by new evidence about the school promotion policies of kindergarten teachers. Catts (1990) is conducting a longitudinal study in which preschool and kindergarten SLI children are being followed into the elementary grades. He reports that 33% of kindergarten children *suspected* of speech and language problems (i.e., those children referred for evaluation) repeated kindergarten or were placed in developmental first-grade programs. (Developmental first grades are an "in-between" transitional year to provide further preparation for entry into the regular first-grade curriculum [cf. Walsh, 1989].) Of the 35 children with *significant* language impairments, 17, or 49%, did not advance to regular first-grade classrooms. Discussions with the teachers indicate that many of these placement decisions were based on perceived social immaturity.

We hypothesized that these placements were influenced by the teachers' social judgments based on the child's use of verbal interactive skills in the classroom (Rice, Alexander, & Hadley, in preparation). The reasoning is this: Teachers associate high verbal success with bright, popular children, in much the same way that people make assumptions about dialect speakers; those who speak a standard dialect are perceived as being brighter and more socially responsible than are speakers of nonstandard dialects (Grosjean, 1982; Lambert, Hodgson, Gardner, & Fillenbaum, 1960).

To test this hypothesis, 1½-minute audiotape samples of preschool children's speech were played for adult judges, who were asked to judge the children's intelligence, social maturity, likelihood of success in kindergarten, leadership status, and popularity, as well as the parents' educational levels and social status. The children were drawn from three groups, with one boy and one girl from each group. One group was composed of children with speech problems only, the second was composed of children with language problems as well as with speech unintelligibility, and the third was composed of children with age-appropriate speech and language skills. The judges were not informed of the child's communicative status, and the samples were presented in a mixed order. Four groups of adult judges rated the children: kindergarten teachers, women with college educations the same age as the teachers, undergraduate college students, and practicing speech-language pathologists.

The findings provide strong support for our hypothesis that adult judges, including teachers, may bring a social bias to their evaluations of children with speech and language problems. On a 5-point rating scale, where 1 was low and 5 was high, SLI children were perceived to be less intelligent than their normally developing peers (mean SLI = 2.4, controls = 3.62, on a scale where 2 was "below average," 3 was "average," and 4 was "above average") and less likely to succeed in kindergarten (mean SLI = 2.37, controls = 4.22, on a scale where 1 was "definitely not succeed," 3 was "maybe," and 5 was "definitely succeed"). The negative bias was also evident in judgments of the children's parents. The raters judged the parents of SLI children to have less education than the comparison group (mean SLI = 2.40, controls = 3.63, on a scale where 2 was "high school," 3 was "some college," and 4 was "completed 4-year degree") and to have lower socioeconomic status (SLI = 2.35, controls = 3.34, on a scale where 2 was "blue collar," 3 was "middle class," and 4 was "upper middle class"). For each of the items on the questionnaire, the same relative orderings of groups applied: speech and language impairments < speech impairments < normal competency.

The four groups of adult judges did not differ in their ratings of the children. Thus, kindergarten teachers are not a special group in this regard, but instead reflect a more pervasive tendency to associate verbal competence with intelligence, probable success in school, parental education, and socioeconomic success.

It is as if adults, in making these judgments of children's speech, call upon a naive causal model of specific language impairment, in which discernible speech-language problems are attributable to more general child deficits (e.g., limited intelligence, delayed social maturity) and/or a lack of adequate resources in the home (e.g., limited parental education or socioeconomic resources). There are several problems with such a naive causal model. One is that it seriously underestimates the complexity of factors contributing to SLI, including the possibility of impaired language-specific acquisition mechanisms (that would operate somewhat independently of other areas of children's intellectual development or parental socioeducational status [cf. Rice et al., 1991]). A second problem is that this model could contribute to serious misinterpretations of a particular child's academic aptitude, a possibility discussed below.

OTHER REPORTS OF SOCIAL INTERACTIONS
OF CHILDREN WITH DISABILITIES WITH NORMAL PEERS

There are parallel reports of limited social interactions in the case of children with other disabling conditions. The best documentation comes from Guralnick's (1990) studies of the peer relations of preschool children with mental retardation and nonhandicapped preschool children in mainstreamed playgroups. He concludes that "handicapped children form a socially separate subgroup in preschool settings. In general, nonhandicapped children tend to interact far less frequently with handicapped children than they do with other nonhandicapped children. . . . Moreover, greater degrees of social separation are found for children with more severe disabilities" (p. 287). He then goes on to state that "handicapped children are perceived as being of lower social status and are treated accordingly as reflected in speech style analyses. As noted, this latter pattern is also found when delayed children interact with other delayed children" (p. 294).

As Guralnick points out, in the case of children with mental retardation, it is not easy to identify a single source of their social difficulties. The social interaction differences may be related to these children's cognitive or social skills deficits, or to an interaction between the two, as well as to the children's particular limitations with interactive speech and language skills. In addition, for some children, physical differences may serve as visual cues for an individual's handicapped status.

Hemphill and Siperstein (1990) established a link between the low social status of children with mental retardation in elementary school and their limited conversational skills. They asked nonretarded students to view one of two 3-minute videotapes. In one version, a child with mild retardation displayed competent conversational skills with a nonretarded peer; in the other, the same child showed conversational deficits characteristic of many children with mental retardation. Students rated the child differently in the two scenes. When conversation was skillful, the child was viewed as likeable by other peers; when it was unskillful, the child was regarded as likely to be rejected or isolated by peers.

Similar problems with social interactions have been documented for children with hearing impairments. Vandell and George (1981) report that although preschoolers with hearing impairments were persistent initiators in interactions with normal peers, they encountered interaction difficulties. Their initiation attempts were more likely than those of normal peers to be actively refused. Vandell and George question an account that places social immaturity as the reason for the communicative failures of children with hearing impairments. Instead, they argue that "the social climate in which deaf children exist may ultimately depress their attempts to interact and hence hinder subsequent development of their social skills" (p. 634). They argue that an increased likelihood of failure with hearing peers has a negative effect on children with hearing impairments, such that they eventually adjust their communication strategies, and thereby appear to be socially immature at older ages.

THE SOCIAL CONSEQUENCES ACCOUNT OF LIMITED LANGUAGE SKILL: REPRISE, PREDICTIONS, AND CAVEATS

Reprise

A Social Consequences Account of limited language skill argues that social and language development intertwine in the following ways. Socialization can serve to motivate young children's use of language. At the same time, early on, language becomes a tool of socialization and a means of enculturation. Children with limited language seem to be vulnerable from both perspectives. To begin with, they are less able to parlay their early social experiences into linguistic skills, or at least they are much slower in doing so. As a consequence of less-than-expected language skills, they are at risk for participation in the social interactions that drive further language development and social status. They become the victims of an assumed association of verbal skills and social sensitivity, cognitive ability, and social status. Preschool children are evidently able to make some social assumptions based on verbal skill, and adults, including teachers and speech-language pathologists, do so as well.

Predictions

The Social Consequences Account predicts that part of the risk for school achievement of SLI children could be attributable to a combination of low teacher expectations and low self-esteem on the part of the child. It is well established that children with language impairments (but less so children with speech impairments) are at risk for academic achievement and social acceptance (cf. Weiner, 1985). In particular, a finding replicated across a number of studies is that SLI children encounter problems with reading (Catts, 1989, 1990). In addition, as described earlier, children with speech and language impairments are more likely to be retained in kindergarten or placed in developmental first grades, a practice with dubious educational outcomes and a negative effect on children's self-esteem (Peterson, DeGracie, & Ayabe, 1987).

If an SLI child is perceived initially as socially immature, or less cognitively capable than his or her peers, those judgments could play out in ways that limit educational opportunities, as well as impair the development of healthy self-esteem. Walsh (1989) reports that the decision not to promote a child to regular first grade can depend upon the child's perceived social maturity. Teachers' most common explanation of why children were not promoted was as follows: Children who are academically advanced, but socially immature, are promoted to transitional first grades, whereas children who are academically slow are retained in kindergarten. Suspected difficulties with cognitive abilities can be quickly ruled out by appropriate evaluation with nonverbal intelligence measures. The determination of social maturity, however, seems to rest heavily with the judgment of the classroom teacher.

Thus, to the extent that social immaturity is inferred from children's conversational interactions, the SLI child could be grievously misrepresented. There are two ways in which their behavior could be misinterpreted. One is if their interactive skills are limited, such that they show less initiative in the classroom or less success in their interactions with other children or teachers. Another is if they develop inappropriate compensatory behaviors for coping with their interactive limitations, such as calling out or hitting other children. In either case, a teacher may misinterpret the secondary limitations associated with a communication problem, and the accompanying history of limited success in social interactions, as indicative of a child's social acumen. The irony is that such a pattern of social adjustment would be expected if a child were fully aware of his or her conversational limitations (i.e., if a child were socially astute). So the SLI child who withdraws or lingers on the edge of peer interactions because of an awareness of limited verbal interactive skills would be at risk for designation as socially immature and, hence, in need of accommodation in the academic curriculum, although many of these children test within the normal range on nonverbal achievement tests. It may turn out that from the very outset the academic achievement of SLI children is jeopardized by a social corollary of their language limitations.

Caveats

Much more information about the details of a Social Consequences Account is needed before its full value can be ascertained. Of primary importance is identification of the ways that the children's particular sociolinguistic deficits impair their ability to initiate turns and maintain conversations. How do the children's limitations play out in interpersonal exchanges? Where are the deviations from the expected competencies of young children? Of equal and related significance is the need to identify the features that account for the judgments of social and cognitive maturity. Is it something particular to verbal competence, or something in the nonverbal domain, such as latency of response, eye gaze, or some breakdown in the intricate coordination of these two dimensions? Finally, more information is needed to determine the nature of the disparity between these children's verbal competencies and those expected in classrooms. What rules for talking apply in kindergarten classrooms? Are kindergarten settings different from those of preschools in regard to the ways in which children interact with each other? And do the interactive expectations for institutional settings differ significantly from those of the children's homes? Answers to these questions will inform accounts of children's emerging communicative competencies, their social development, cultural biases toward individuals with communicative differences, educational policy, and intervention for children with communication problems.

IMPLICATIONS FOR INTERVENTION

The Social Consequences Account suggests intervention at several levels: the teachers and adults with whom a child interacts, the intervention setting, and interactions with individual children. These three levels constitute a nested set: if the first two cannot be established, the effectiveness of the third is jeopardized.

Teachers and Adults

If it is the lot of a child with communication limitations to encounter some strongly ingrained social biases, then it is the responsibility of the interventionist to attempt to redress these biases as they might most directly affect a given individual. Although it is not likely that one can change the judgments of society at large, it may be possible to defuse some of the most egregious misconceptions in the case of a particular child. A variety of strategies could be applied. One would be to *provide information* to professionals working with the child, to explain the dissociation between language skills on the one hand and social and cognitive abilities on the other hand. Another would be to *counsel family members,* if needed, about the possible frustrations encountered by children with social insights and motivations and limited verbal means by which to accomplish them. A third would be to *provide transition planning* from one service setting to another, or from one class placement to another, to ensure that professionals are not misled by initial impressions. This is especially critical when children move from the preschool setting to the kindergarten classroom, where they will be judged for their ability to stay in the "main track" with their peers. Finally, the provision of *inservice presentations* on the topic of social consequences of language impairment may help prevent similar misconceptions from being applied to other children and adults.

The Intervention Setting

In order to maximize the probability that a child will improve his or her ability to interact with other children, there must be opportunities for such interactions to occur spontaneously as children go about the give-and-take of their play. Furthermore, such interactions play out differently with normally developing peers compared to interactions between children with similar limitations. It is in the mainstreamed contexts that children with language impairments are able to observe and interact with normal language models, to get the full flavor of the discourse styles of verbal children. Without such contexts, it is virtually assured that they will lack the opportunities to develop the competencies that will allow them to move from the social periphery into the thick of the discourse negotiations. And if they are not able to participate in verbal negotiations, they are very unlikely to learn how to win them.

These observations lead to the conclusion that the preferred setting for speech-language intervention with preschool SLI children is a mainstreamed classroom, in which SLI children interact with their age-mates, their social and intellectual peers. There are many possible ways to configure such settings. One example is that of the Language Acquisition Preschool. Other approaches may work equally well, depending upon the local resources and the needs of particular children. Mainstreamed settings could include preschools, daycare centers, Head Start programs, or specially designed language facilitation classrooms.

The essential feature is that there be at least some designated portion of the curriculum that allows children free choice in activities and playmates and encouragement to interact with other children. Role-playing activities seem to be especially effective ways to establish meaningful interactions, as are joint construction projects or activities with favorite toys (cf. Watkins & Bunce, 1990). Within these activities and throughout the curriculum, the teacher's role is to facilitate language learning and encourage children's interactions with peers.

Interactions with Individual Children

Placement in a mainstreamed setting, while necessary, is not sufficient for the development of interactive skills. Instead, children with communication limitations tend to remain on the edge of peer interactions, as discussed above. Thus, it is necessary to target explicit social interaction intervention goals for individual children. Within the mainstreamed setting, it is possible to observe a child's social interactions and to compile baseline information from which to plan intervention. The Social Interactive Coding System (Rice et al., 1990) is one possible scheme, and others could be devised. What is important is to capture who is talking to whom and how the interactions play out.

Intervention can then focus on implementation of interactive techniques designed to increase the probability of a child with language impairments initiating and carrying out interactions with children without language impairments. While it is possible, in principle, to devise such interactions in individual child pairs, it is impossible to simulate fully the dynamics of a naturally occurring interaction among children in a group. Thus, it is preferable to carry out intervention in the ongoing context of meaningful interactions among children. Although our documentation is not complete, we have field tested some intervention techniques in LAP that may have general utility. They are offered here as suggestions for others to try. They could be implemented by specialists working in the classroom, or by the classroom teacher in consultation with specialists. In LAP they are carried out by student speech-language pathologists and the assistant teacher, an early childhood educator, as well as by the teacher, who is a speech-language pathologist.

Our techniques focus on ways to increase the number of initiations toward peers as a way of manipulating the participation of the child with a language impairment in conversations, which in turn serve as natural laboratories for further discourse learning. These techniques are similar to those developed to increase children's social interactions (which are not defined exclusively as verbal interaction [cf. Strain & Odom, 1986]). In these studies, nonhandicapped peers are trained to direct social overtures to exceptional children, or teachers are trained to prompt children's initiations. There is strong empirical evidence that such techniques lead to an increase in social interactions. What has proven problematic, however, is generalization to other peers in other settings (cf. Odom, Hoyson, Jamieson, & Strain, 1985).

Our techniques differ in some important ways from the social interaction prompting studies. First, we focus on conversational (verbal) interactions.

Second, we begin with the child's initiation toward the adult. Given our findings with the SICS data, we wish to reduce the proportion of verbal initiations directed toward adults in the classroom and increase the proportion directed toward peers. Focusing on the child's spontaneous initiation toward a teacher may contribute to the effectiveness of the technique, in that it maximizes the likelihood that the child will be attentive to the interactions and find the subsequent interactions to be meaningful. It also presents a naturalistic way to incorporate the peers into an interaction with a targeted child.

When a child initiates toward an adult, such as when a child tells the teacher to "See this!" the adult can then do one of two things, each of which increases the likelihood of the child initiating toward a peer. One is to *redirect* the initiation. This consists of the adult suggesting to the child that he or she direct that request or comment toward a nearby child: "Why don't you ask Susan to look at your picture? I am sure she would like to." The adult then can monitor the subsequent interaction to facilitate further interaction, if it is appropriate within the context to do so. It is virtually impossible to force children to do these things, so it is crucial that the adult maintain a low profile. Sometimes the best thing to do if an initiation doesn't succeed is to ignore the failure and just move on and wait for the next opportunity.

The second possible response is to *model the form of an initiation,* such as "Go say, 'Susan, see my picture'." A model provides more assistance to a child who may lack the ability to formulate the appropriate entry. Again, the teacher can unobtrusively monitor what happens, to determine if another attempt can be worked into the interaction if the first one fails, or to provide further encouragement if it succeeds.

Another technique, not dependent on a child's initial overture, is to *prompt initiations* toward other children. If a teacher notices that a child is uninvolved and an interaction could be established, he or she can suggest to the child, "Ask Mary if she wants to make pictures." As with the other techniques, the timing of this one depends upon the context and the child's probable interest in doing so.

CONCLUSION

At present, our understanding of the ways in which language limitations play out in children's social interactions is still quite limited, as is our knowledge of how sociocultural biases affect youngsters with atypical communication skills. Future research may well reveal new dimensions and provide new directions for intervention. As the knowledge base accumulates, interventionists can collect their own observations and field test the adequacy of models such as the Social Consequences Account. It is hoped that this combination of research and intervention will lead to intervention that is maximally effective for children and prepares them for lives as full participants in the social interactions that form the fabric of an individual's role in society.

REFERENCES

Anderson, E. (1977). *Learning to speak with style.* Unpublished doctoral dissertation, Stanford University, Stanford.

Bates, E. (1976). *Language and context: Studies in the acquisition of pragmatics.* New York: Academic Press.

Berko Gleason, J.B., Hay, D., & Cain, L. (1989). Social and affective determinants of language acquisition. In M.L. Rice & R.L. Schiefelbusch (Eds.), *The teachability of language* (pp. 171–186). Baltimore: Paul H. Brookes Publishing Co.

Black, B., & Hazen, N.L. (1990). Social status and patterns of communication in acquainted and unacquainted preschool children. *Developmental Psychology, 26,* 379–387.

Brown, R. (1973). *A first language.* Cambridge, MA: Harvard University Press.

Bunce, B.H., Rice, M.L., & Wilcox, K.A. (1990, November). *LAP update: The effectiveness of language intervention within a classroom setting.* Paper presented at the annual convention of the American Speech-Language-Hearing Association, Seattle.

Catts, H. (1989). Defining dyslexia as a developmental language disorder. *Annals of Dyslexia, 39,* 50–64.

Catts, H. (1990). Promoting successful transition to the primary grades: Prediction of reading problems in speech and language handicapped children. *Kansas Early Childhood Research Institute annual report.* Lawrence: University of Kansas, Life Span Institute.

Cooper, C.R., Marquis, A., & Ayers-Lopez, L. (1982). Peer learning in the classroom: Tracing developmental patterns and consequences of children's spontaneous interactions. In L.C. Wilkinson (Ed.), *Communication in the classroom* (pp. 69–84). New York: Academic Press.

Ervin-Tripp, S., & Gordon, D. (1986). The development of requests. In R.L. Schiefelbusch (Ed.), *Language competence: Assessment and intervention* (pp. 61–96). San Diego: College-Hill Press.

Fey, M.E. (1986). *Language intervention with young children.* San Diego: College-Hill Press.

Garnica, O.K. (1981). Social dominance and conversational interaction: The omega child in the classroom. In J.L. Green & C. Wallat (Eds.), *Ethnography and language in educational settings* (pp. 229–250). Norwood, NJ: Ablex.

Gleason, J. B., Hay, D., & Cain, L. (1989). Social and affective determinants of language acquisition. In M. L. Rice & R. L. Schiefelbusch (Eds.), *The teachability of language* (pp. 171–186). Baltimore: Paul H. Brookes Publishing Co.

Greenfield, P., & Smith, J. (1976). *The structure of communication in early language development.* New York: Academic Press.

Grosjean, F. (1982). *Life with two languages: An introduction to bilingualism.* Cambridge, MA: Harvard University Press.

Guralnick, M.J. (1990). Peer interactions and the development of handicapped children's social and communicative competence. In H.C. Foot, M.J. Morgan, & R.H. Shute (Eds.), *Children helping children* (pp. 275–305). New York: John Wiley & Sons.

Hadley, P.A., & Rice, M.L. (1991). Conversational responsiveness of speech- and language-impaired preschoolers. *Journal of Speech and Hearing Research, 34*(6), 1308–1317.

Halliday, M.A.K. (1975). *Learning how to mean: Explorations in the development of language.* New York: Elsevier/North Holland.

Hart, B., & Risley, T. (1975). Incidental teaching of language in the preschool. *Journal of Applied Behavior Analysis, 8,* 411–420.

Hart, B., & Rogers-Warren, A. (1978). A milieu approach to teaching language. In R.L. Schiefelbusch (Ed.), *Language intervention strategies* (pp. 193–235). Baltimore: University Park Press.

Hazen, N.L., & Black, B. (1989). Preschool peer communication skills: The role of social status and interaction context. *Child Development, 60,* 867–876.

Heath, S.B. (1989). The learner as cultural member. In M.L. Rice & R.L. Schiefelbusch (Eds.), *The teachability of language* (pp. 333–350). Baltimore: Paul H. Brookes Publishing Co.

Hemphill, L., & Siperstein, G.N. (1990). Conversational competence and peer response to mildly retarded children. *Journal of Educational Psychology, 82*(1), 128–134.

Hohmann, M., Bonet, B., & Weikart, D.P. (1978). *Young children in action.* Ypsilanti, MI: High Scope Press.

Hymes, D. (1972). On communicative competence. In J.B. Pride & J. Holmes (Eds.), *Sociolinguistics* (pp. 269–293). Harmondsworth, England: Penguin.

Johnston, J.R. (1985). Fit, focus, and functionality: An essay on early language intervention. *Child Language Teaching and Therapy, 1,* 125–134.

Lambert, W., Hodgson, R., Gardner, R., & Fillenbaum, R. (1960). Evaluational reactions to spoken languages. *Journal of Abnormal and Social Psychology, 60,* 44–51.

Norris, J.A., & Hoffman, P.R. (1990). Language intervention within naturalistic environments. *Language, Speech and Hearing Sciences in Schools, 21,* 72–84.

Odom, S., Hoyson, M., Jamieson, B., & Strain, P. (1985). Increasing handicapped preschoolers' peer interactions: Cross-setting and component analysis. *Journal of Applied Behavior Analysis, 18,* 3–16.

Office of Special Education Programs (1988). *Report to Congress.* Washington, DC: Author.

Peterson, S.E., DeGracie, J.S., & Ayabe, C.R. (1987). A longitudinal study of the effects of retention/promotion on academic achievement. *American Educational Research Journal, 24,* 107–118.

Rice, M.L. (1990). Children with specific language impairment: Toward a model of teachability. In N.A. Krasnegor, D.M. Rumbaugh, R.L. Schiefelbusch, & M. Studdert-Kennedy (Eds.), *Biological and behavioral determinants of language development* (pp. 447–480). Hillsdale, NJ: Lawrence Erlbaum Associates.

Rice, M.L., Alexander, A.L., & Hadley, P.A. (in preparation). *Adult judgments of children with speech and language impairment.*

Rice, M.L., Sell, M.A., & Hadley, P.A. (1990). The Social Interactive Coding System (SICS): An on-line, clinically relevant descriptive tool. *Language, Speech, and Hearing Services in Schools, 21,* 2–14.

Rice, M.L., Sell, M.A., & Hadley, P.A. (1991). Social interactions of speech- and language-impaired children. *Journal of Speech and Hearing Research, 34*(6), 1299–1307.

Saville-Troike, M. (1982). *The ethnography of communication.* Baltimore: University Park Press.

Schieffelin, B.B., & Ochs, E. (Eds.). (1986). *Language and socialization across cultures*. Cambridge: Cambridge University Press.

Snow, C.E., & Goldfield, B.A. (1983). Turn the page please: Situation-specific language acquisition. *Journal of Child Language, 10,* 551–569.

Strain, P., & Odom, S. (1986). Peer social interactions: Effective intervention for social skills development of exceptional children. *Exceptional Children, 52,* 543–551.

Tabors, P.O. (1987). *The development of communicative competence by second language learners in a nursery school classroom: An ethnolinguistic study*. Unpublished doctoral dissertation, Harvard University, Cambridge.

Thiele, J.E., & Hamilton, J.L. (1991). Implementing the early childhood formula: Programs under PL 99-457. *Journal of Early Intervention, 15,* 5–12.

Vandell, D.L., & George, L.B. (1981). Social interaction in hearing and deaf preschoolers: Successes and failures in initiations. *Child Development, 52,* 627–635.

Vygotsky, L.S. (1978). *Mind in society: The development of higher psychological processes*. (M. Cole, V. John-Steiner, S. Scribner, & E. Souberman, Eds. and Trans.), Cambridge, MA: Harvard University Press.

Walsh, D.J. (1989). Changes in kindergarten. Why here? Why now? *Early Childhood Research Quarterly, 4,* 377–391.

Watkins, R.V., & Bunce, B.H. (1990). *Language intervention in a preschool classroom: The LAP model*. Unpublished manuscript, University of Kansas, Lawrence.

Weinberg, A. (1991). *Construct validity of the speech and language assessment scale: A tool for recording parent judgments*. Unpublished master's thesis, University of Kansas, Lawrence.

Weiner, P. (1985). The value of follow-up studies. *Topics in Language Disorders, 5,* 78–92.

8

Facilitating Children's Social-Communicative Interactions Through the Use of Peer-Mediated Interventions

Michaelene M. Ostrosky, Ann P. Kaiser, and Samuel L. Odom

THE DEVELOPMENT OF MEANINGFUL AND productive social relationships with one's peers is a primary task of early childhood. Developing peer relationships has important benefits for language, communication, and social and cognitive development, as well as for the socialization of aggressive tendencies (Garvey, 1986; Goldstein & Ferrell, 1987; Goldstein & Wickstrom, 1986; Guralnick, 1981; Jenkins, Speltz, & Odom, 1985; Rubin & Lollis, 1988). Positive peer relations contribute to the acquisition of basic skills in unique and significant ways that interactions with adults either cannot or will not produce (Hartup, 1979). Furthermore, later adjustment problems appear to be associated with difficulties in establishing appropriate peer relations in early childhood (Parker & Asher, 1987).

Interacting socially with peers in a positive manner is a skill learned incidentally by most children during their early years. However, for some children, acquiring the prerequisite social communication skills necessary for successful peer interactions is difficult. It may be necessary to teach peer-directed social communication to children lacking these important skills. Teaching nondisabled children strategies to facilitate the occurrence of positive social-communicative interactions with partners who have special needs appears to be a promising intervention for a number of reasons.

POTENTIAL ADVANTAGES OF PEERS
AS SOCIAL COMMUNICATION FACILITATORS

First, the coequal nature of peer interactions provides an appropriate situation for children to learn essential communicative and social interaction skills (Guralnick, 1981; Hartup, 1978). The reciprocity displayed in peer interactions supports give-and-take learning, where interactions are characterized by a joint frame of reference with partners communicating about an activity or object they have experienced. Child–child exchanges rely on participation and balanced contributions by both partners. As communication skills develop and children begin to engage in more frequent interactions with their peers, they typically emerge as active and equal members of communication exchanges. *Both* parties receive enrichment from peer relationships, for they are reciprocal (Perske, 1988).

The role of nondisabled peers as social communication facilitators for their peers with disabilities is supported by the developmental literature describing children's abilities to initiate, maintain, and modify verbal behaviors during interactions with their peers (Garvey & Hogan, 1973; Keenan, 1977; Mueller, Bleier, Krakow, Hegedus, & Cournoyer, 1977). Children are able to initiate, respond to, and maintain social-communicative "conversations" as early as 9 months of age, when they can be observed playing social games such as "peek-a-boo."

Second, young children have been observed to make verbal adaptations when necessary during interactions with less skilled peers (Gelman & Shatz, 1977; Guralnick & Paul-Brown, 1984). These observed natural adaptations in language use are theoretically consistent with the communicative purposes of peer interactions. According to sociolinguistic theory, the predominant motivation for language use and language acquisition is effective communication (Owens, 1984). The speaker selects the form and content that best fulfills his or her intentions, based on perceptions about the communicative environment. The form of the speaker's utterance is controlled by an awareness of, and assumptions about, the listener's knowledge of the referent. Children's abilities to make adaptations when interacting with peers at lower developmental levels increase the likelihood of successful interactions.

Finally, children learn language during dynamic social interactions with experienced language users in their environments (Light, 1988). Participants influence each other during the course of these interactions, as each participant enters the interaction with a set of behaviors that potentially allow him or her to benefit from his or her partner's social-communicative actions (McNaughton & Light, 1989). While the importance of the partner in an interaction has not always been recognized, this variable is a major factor in the success or failure of many communicative interactions. Often communicative interactions are successful only because the partners understand and interpret the intent of each other's actions. Thus, when communication is considered as a transactional process, the importance of instructing non-disabled peers in social communication facilitation techniques, and the importance of providing conversational instruction to children with special needs to enable them to successfully interact with one another, becomes evident.

This chapter discusses the importance of peer interactions in the development of young children and the role that social communication skills play in these interactions. The results of peer-mediated intervention studies designed to improve social-communicative interactions between children with and children without special needs are also described. Principal components of an effective model of intervention to improve peer-directed social-communicative skills based on current research findings and developmental theory are presented, and, finally, future research questions related to the proposed model of intervention are discussed.

THE ROLE OF SOCIAL
COMMUNICATION IN PEER INTERACTIONS

The ability to engage in positive peer relationships is central to children's development (Hartup, 1978; Strain, Guralnick, & Walker, 1986). Most children naturally learn strategies that enable them to initiate and maintain interactions with their age-mates. As children develop, interactions become more sophisticated, with social communication skills playing an increasingly important role in sustaining peer-to-peer interactions.

Typical social-communicative interactions are characterized by joint attention, establishing eye contact, turn-taking, topic maintenance, and responsiveness (Berninger & Garvey, 1980; Charlesworth & Hartup, 1967; Leiter, 1977; Nelson, 1985). For young children, interacting socially involves verbal and nonverbal communication, with gestures often complementing verbalizations (Finkelstein, Dent, Gallagher, & Ramey, 1978; Guralnick, 1986; Rubenstein & Howes, 1976).

The quality and quantity of children's social-communicative interactions are the result of their linguistic and conversational skills, as well as of the social support provided by the communication partner (Hart & Risley, 1980; Kaiser, 1990; Thomasello & Farrar, 1986). Peer social-communicative exchanges are also affected by the familiarity of the interaction setting and its routine, developmental- and chronological-age matches between children, the interaction style of partners, and the quality and quantity of interaction opportunities available in a given environment (Peck, 1989).

Four social purposes are accomplished in peer-to-peer communicative interactions: 1) the expression of needs and wants, 2) information transfer, 3) social closeness, and 4) social etiquette (Light, 1988). When communicating needs and wants, the initiator's goal is to control the behavior of a partner so that he or she provides a desired object or performs a desired action. When sharing information, the focus of the social-communicative interaction is to develop a structure to support the exchange of ideas, thoughts, and experiences. Communicative interactions aimed at promoting social closeness seek to establish, maintain, and develop interpersonal relationships. Finally, interactions focusing on social etiquette tend to be highly predictable, with the speaker's goal to take his or her designated conversational turns in a socially acceptable manner.

According to Guralnick (1976), the achievement of positive social-communicative exchanges with peers is influenced by three additional variables. First, the status attributed to a child may influence the quality and quantity of interactions in which that child is involved. Children of presumed higher status typically control the direction of peer interactions. Second, the intended function of a social-communicative exchange exerts a strong influence on a child's ability to interact positively. An interaction focusing on providing information to a partner may be more likely to end positively than one aimed at controlling a partner's behavior. The third variable that Guralnick believes is important in achieving positive social-communicative interactions is establishing a joint frame of reference. The importance of joint attention in communicative interactions is evident as early as the toddler stage when language is not yet well developed (Owens, 1984). Research has shown that peer interactions based on shared meanings are associated with longer episodes of interaction than those exchanges without a common focus of attention (Brenner & Mueller, 1982). Failure to agree on a theme frequently results in short and often abrupt social exchanges between peers.

Social communication skills play an important role in establishing and maintaining peer interactions. Successful peer-to-peer exchanges are influenced by the social and physical context, the social support provided by individuals in the environment, and children's abilities to use social-communicative strategies effectively during interactions.

SOCIAL-COMMUNICATIVE INTERACTIONS WHEN ONE PARTNER HAS SPECIAL NEEDS

Children with special needs often exhibit difficulty in acquiring the social, communication, and play skills that are characteristic of, and develop from, interactions with their peers (Guralnick, 1981). They may not acquire these skills through observational learning. Furthermore, they may have relatively fewer opportunities to engage in positive social-communicative interactions with age-mates compared with their nondisabled peers. The majority of young children with special needs engage infrequently in sustained social-communicative exchanges with age-mates, and, thus, their peer-related social behavior often lags substantially behind their cognitive development (Guralnick,

1986). As children with special needs mature, delays in social, language, and cognitive abilities become proportionately more severe (Gaylord-Ross, Haring, Breen, & Pitts-Conway, 1984).

Expressive language deficits are common to many children with special needs and can significantly contribute to peer interaction deficits (Mahoney, Glover, & Finger, 1981). Because language plays such an important role in regulating social-communicative interactions, an inability to engage in dialogue can undermine the development of positive peer relationships. A child's lack of language skills may be a primary barrier to everyday play interactions and the formation of friendships (Rice, chap. 7, this volume).

Research suggests that improvements can be made in peer-to-peer social-communicative interactions that involve a partner with special needs. For some children with communication delays, reducing peer direction and increasing responsiveness to their initiations may increase the quantity and quality of their communication behavior (Peck, 1989). Successful interventions utilizing nondisabled peers as social interaction interventionists (Chandler, Ostrosky, Odom, & Rainey, 1990) support the assumption that peers can be taught to function as facilitators of social-communicative interactions with children with special needs. Although there are some important differences, many features of the communication input of nondisabled children to children with special needs are similar to the adjustments in communication input made by parents to their children with special needs. These commonalities suggest that peers can be taught to alter their behavior to facilitate social communication of children with special needs (Goldstein & Ferrell, 1987; Goldstein & Wickstrom, 1986; Hunt, Alwell, & Goetz, 1988; Hunt, Alwell, Goetz, & Sailor, 1990).

Typically, when nondisabled children converse with children with special needs, their speech is syntactically simpler, less diverse, and contains a variety of devices such as repetition, prompting, rephrasing, questioning, and demonstrating (Peck, 1989). Guralnick and Paul-Brown (1980) observed that during interactions with children with special needs, nondisabled children tend to adapt their verbalizations as a function of the children's developmental levels. Furthermore, nondisabled children have been observed to be extremely persistent and creative during these interactions. They often use multiple strategies simultaneously, particularly combining nonverbal cues with verbalizations in an effort to maximize communication effectiveness when addressing peers with special needs (Guralnick & Paul-Brown, 1984).

The extent to which nondisabled partners are able to adapt their behavior to repair and maintain social-communicative interactions with children with special needs is important. While many children with special needs are unable to maintain interactions with their peers for an extended period of time, nondisabled children are typically able to repair communication breakdowns and often do so during interactions with peers with special needs. Thus, the presence of a nondisabled peer who can repair communication breakdowns is likely to increase the duration of peer-to-peer communications involving children with special needs. In addition, these interactions model strategies for repair for less skilled children.

Although such interactions with peers with special needs are characterized by many positive adaptive qualities, differences are evident when comparing the interactions of nondisabled children with peers with and without special needs. Herink and Lee (1985) compared the behavior in integrated classrooms of 20 preschoolers with mild and moderate cognitive disabilities to 20 children without special needs. They found that the children with disabilities appeared integrated into the social and emotional aspects of their peer groups, but not into the verbal life of these groups. Children with special needs had more extensive interactions with adults than they did with peers, while the reverse held true for nondisabled children. Children with special needs received more verbal input from adults, while nondisabled children's experiences were characterized as more peer oriented. These findings could indicate that adults compensated for the limited interactions between children with and children without special needs by assuming the role of playmate, or that the adults preempted the disabled children's "social time," or some combination of these or other factors.

Although there is inconclusive evidence pinpointing the factors that contribute to increased interactions with adults on the part of children with special needs, these data suggest that children with and children without disabilities may be exposed to rather different verbal experiences in integrated preschool settings. Researchers have also observed that in comparison to interactions with their nondisabled peers, normally developing children justify requests less when interacting with children with special needs. They tend to adopt highly directive and controlling interaction styles and appear less responsive to children whose communication development is significantly delayed in form or rate. They tend to use strong, unmitigated directives such as "Do this," especially when interacting with children with moderate and severe delays (Guralnick & Paul-Brown, 1989).

The severity of a child's disability and the amount of interaction he or she experiences with nondisabled children appear to be inversely related. Children with moderate and severe disabilities typically receive very little social and communicative attention from nondisabled peers, in comparison to children with mild delays (Guralnick, 1980). It appears that when addressing children with more severe handicaps, nondisabled children adopt an instructional strategy that focuses more on prompting compliance to behavioral requests than on engaging in conversation or making requests for information. While the potential for facilitating social communication still exists, this pattern of behavior suggests that the severity of a child's disability determines whether "peer-like" or "adult-like" interaction patterns will develop (Lefebvre & Strain, 1989).

The low frequency of interactions between nondisabled children and children with severe intellectual disabilities may be a result of inferior status attributed to these children (Ervin-Tripp, 1977; Guralnick & Paul-Brown, 1980), or that communicative attempts made by individuals with severe delays are often difficult to interpret (McNaughton & Light, 1989). Unclear communicative attempts may result in missed opportunities for interaction. Because others tend to anticipate their needs and wants, individuals with severe intellectual disabilities are often provided few opportunities in their natural environments to communicate. Developing or discovering a response that can function as a reliable communicative signal to a peer is critical for individuals with severe disabilities who must learn that they can effect change upon an environment that includes responsive communication partners.

PEER-MEDIATED INTERVENTIONS

Training peers to interact positively with children with special needs can enhance the efforts of professionals by expanding the resources and instructional opportunities available to children with special needs. Peer-mediated interventions reduce the amount of one-to-one teacher instruction needed, and they provide exposure to peer modeling under informal conditions. Additionally, interactions with peers encourage independence as children learn to interact with age-mates rather than depend on the classroom teacher to fulfill the role of playmate.

Positive interactions with age-mates can benefit both children with and children without special needs, for peer attention often functions as a powerful reinforcer for developing and maintaining interactions (Johnston & Johnston, 1972). As the reinforcing value of peer interaction is enhanced through programmed intervention, patterns of limited or negative interactions can be altered, with positive interactions replacing negative ones (Paul, 1985). By providing positive feedback to children for engaging in appropriate interactions, adults can increase the probability that these behaviors will continue (Lefebvre & Strain, 1989; Odom, Ostrosky, McEvoy, Peterson, & McConnell, 1990; Paul, 1985).

Including nondisabled age-mates in intervention efforts for children with special needs also has the potential benefit of facilitating children's generalization of skills across settings and people. Including multiple exemplars is an important strategy when programming for generalization and maintenance (Brady, Shores, Gunter, McEvoy, Fox, & White, 1984; Stokes & Baer, 1977). Peers who serve as intervention agents in one setting or activity may also participate in other activities with their age-mates with special needs. Thus, these peers may function as discriminative stimuli for positive interactive behaviors, and they may support generalization to other environments (Goldstein & Wickstrom, 1986; Johnston & Johnston, 1972; Paul, 1985).

The results of social interaction research support the utilization of nondisabled peers to facilitate the development of social competence by young children with special needs. Nondisabled children have been taught to use strategies such as sharing, share requests, affection, comments, play organizers, answering, giving assistance, and requesting assistance to engage children with special needs in positive social interactions (Chandler et al., 1990; Odom et al., 1990; Strain, Odom, & McConnell, 1984). Increases in the frequency of initiations by nondisabled peers and in the percentage of play time that children with and children without special needs engaged in social interaction have been observed (Chandler et al., 1990).

Interventions To Increase Peer Social-Communicative Interactions

Research that examines the effects of peer-mediated interventions to facilitate social-communicative interactions between individuals with and individuals without special needs is limited. Studies describing peer communicative behaviors and intervention studies focusing on teaching social interaction skills are more prevalent, and these have served as the foundation for designing programs to facilitate children's acquisition and use of social-communicative strategies.

Two studies of peer-mediated conversation training were conducted by Hunt and her colleagues (Hunt et al., 1988; Hunt et al., 1990). In the first experiment, three high school–age students with severe disabilities, who evidenced inappropriate behaviors, and five nondisabled peers participated in a conversation training program using communication books as the medium for conversation. Conversation training was implemented during the first 5 minutes of daily 10-minute sessions, while during the second 5 minutes no instruction was provided but measurement continued. Students with severe disabilities were taught to initiate conversation by presenting their communication books as they greeted their partners and to pair spoken words and phrases by pointing to pictures. Nondisabled peers were taught to comment and ask questions in reference to the pictures and then to wait for the students with special needs to respond or comment. The effects of conversation training were evaluated using a multiple baseline design across the three subjects. Changes in frequency or duration of inappropriate social behavior and frequency of conversational turns were documented in order to test the hypothesis that conversation training is functionally related to the reduction of inappropriate behaviors. When training was introduced, two students showed immediate and pronounced effects, as evidenced by an increase in the frequency of conversational turns and a decrease in the frequency or duration of inappropriate behaviors during the first 5 minutes. The third subject displayed less dramatic changes, with improvements in conversational turns and a reduction in inappropriate behaviors occurring more slowly. A comparison of the first 5 minutes with the second 5 minutes of the session indicated that a reduction in frequency or duration of inappropriate interaction was maintained without teacher support during the second 5 minutes.

In a second study, Hunt and her colleagues (1990) attempted to determine if newly acquired conversational skills and a reduction of inappropriate behaviors would generalize to noninstructional contexts and partners. In a multiple baseline design across three high school students with severe disabilities who evidenced inappropriate behaviors, conversation training was implemented, and interactions with 18 trained and 15 untrained peers were examined. For all three students, training resulted in substantial increases in frequency of conversational turns, which remained at a fairly constant level as teacher prompting was faded across sessions. Additionally, during generalization settings with trained but novel partners, the three subjects demonstrated increased turn-taking, which remained high throughout the study. During 15-minute unstructured generalization periods with trained and untrained partners, increases in communication behaviors by the three students with special needs were observed and remained stable, while the frequency of inappropriate behaviors decreased during these periods.

Goldstein and his colleagues (Goldstein & Ferrell, 1987; Goldstein & Wickstrom, 1986) have successfully trained nondisabled peers to promote social-communicative interactions with children with behavioral, social, and communicative deficits. Using a direct instruction approach, Goldstein and Wickstrom (1986) trained two nondisabled preschoolers to use six strategies thought to facilitate interaction: 1) establishing eye contact; 2) establishing joint focus of attention; 3) descriptive talk; 4) prompting requests; 5) responding to others by repeating, expanding, or requesting clarification; and 6) redirecting play activities. In a multiple baseline design across three children with special needs, posters were introduced to prompt peers to engage in communicative interactions, and teacher prompting and reinforcement were provided. The use of the six strategies resulted in increased rates of communicative interaction for each of the three target children. The intervention had immediate effects on the number of communicative responses per session for the target children, probably due to the increased opportunities to respond to peer initiations. Increases in two of the target children's initiation rates were evident after approximately 20 sessions of intervention. When peers were no longer prompted to use the strategies, all three subjects maintained frequencies of initiations and responses above baseline levels, although the rates were variable.

In a systematic replication of the previous study, Goldstein and Ferrell (1987) extended this work by: 1) determining the efficacy of teaching all nondisabled classmates to serve as peer confederates, 2) examining the relationship between target children's rates of initiations and responses and the behaviors displayed by peers and the teacher, 3) determining if teacher reinforcement of the target children would augment the effects of the peer-mediated intervention, and 4) assessing the extent of generalization with trained peers during other play times. All six nondisabled classmates of three preschoolers with special needs were trained to use the four most effective strategies identified in the previous study (Goldstein & Wickstrom, 1986). Results showed that peers could learn social communication facilitation strategies, and increases in communicative interaction occurred when the peers were prompted to use the strategies with the target children. However, variability was a factor in evaluating changes in target children's rates of initiations. Increases in two target children's response rates were observed during free play sessions, and generalization was demonstrated by one subject.

These four studies support the feasibility of utilizing peers as facilitators of social communication for children with special needs. Positive changes were documented by increased frequency of interactions, target children's responses, initiation rates (Goldstein & Ferrell, 1987; Goldstein & Wickstrom, 1986), and conversational turns (Hunt et al., 1988), maintenance of gains when teacher support was withdrawn (Goldstein & Ferrell, 1987; Hunt et al., 1988; Hunt et al., 1990), generalization of effects (Goldstein & Ferrell, 1987; Hunt et al., 1990), and decreased frequency or duration of inappropriate social behavior (Hunt et al., 1988; Hunt et al., 1990). However, several limitations are apparent when evaluating these intervention studies.

All four studies involved small sample sizes and results can be generalized only to learners with characteristics similar to those of the subjects involved in the studies. The three children in Goldstein and Ferrell's study (1987) were diagnosed as behavior disordered and entered the preschool program with a variety of maladaptive behaviors, including inappropriate play skills, lack of social responsiveness, and noncompliance. These three children demonstrated receptive language scores within the 40- to 48-month range, expressive scores within the 36- to 48-month range, and mean utterance lengths of 1.7–3.8 morphemes. One subject's developmental functioning was within normal limits on the Learning Accomplishment Profile (LeMay, Griffin, & Sanford, 1977). Goldstein and Wickstrom's (1986) subjects were three preschool children with behavior disorders and language delays who demonstrated a variety of autistic-like behaviors, including inappropriate play, lack of social responsiveness, stereotypy, and limited language. Mean utterance lengths ranged from single words to 3.6 morphemes per utterance, with receptive language levels ranging from 32–44 months. Peers in both studies by Goldstein and colleagues were nondisabled preschoolers enrolled in the model demonstration classroom.

Subjects in the interventions described by Hunt and colleagues (Hunt et al., 1988; Hunt et al., 1990) were high school students with severe disabilities. Nondisabled partners were also high-school students, with the exception of one university practicum student. The students in Hunt's investigations (Hunt et al., 1988; Hunt et al., 1990) were older and more sophisticated language users than the preschool children in the studies by Goldstein (Goldstein & Ferrell, 1987; Goldstein & Wickstrom, 1986), a factor that may be related to the designs of the intervention programs. Instructing nondisabled high school students always to end their conversational turn with a question and always to begin their turn by commenting on something said by their partners is a much more sophisticated intervention than instructing preschoolers to establish eye contact, offer choices, or say something about what their peers with special needs are doing. The nondisabled peers in the studies by Hunt (Hunt et al., 1988; Hunt et al., 1990) were expected to maintain conversations with their partners and to repair breakdowns in communication, whereas the nondisabled preschoolers in Goldstein's studies (Goldstein & Ferrell, 1987; Goldstein & Wickstrom, 1986) were taught individual strategies known to facilitate interaction but were not taught a specific conversational turn-taking structure.

In addition to the already-mentioned weaknesses, design issues including situational and temporal similarities of the two conversation periods (Hunt et al., 1988), incomplete experimental analysis due to the end of the school year (Goldstein & Ferrell, 1987), and order effects (Goldstein & Ferrell, 1987) limit the interpretation of the findings and suggest the need for further investigations. Two studies failed to assess generalization effects to nontraining settings or with naive classmates (Goldstein & Wickstrom, 1986; Hunt et al., 1988), and the need for qualitative analysis was mentioned by Hunt and colleagues (Hunt et al., 1988; Hunt et al., 1990). While quantitative measurement systems enabled researchers to assess discrete social-communicative behaviors, changes in the affect of participants and the development of friendships were not analyzed, although they were observed and reported anecdotally by teachers. Further investigation is needed in this important area, and studies need to be designed based on those components that have proven successful in facilitating social-communicative interactions between children with and children without special needs.

A MODEL OF INTERVENTION TO FACILITATE
POSITIVE SOCIAL-COMMUNICATIVE INTERACTIONS

Nondisabled children naturally make adaptations when interacting with less skilled communication partners. Through the provision of structured training and support, positive changes can occur in the social-communicative interactions between children with and children without special needs. The studies by Hunt and her colleagues (Hunt et al., 1988; Hunt et al., 1990) and Goldstein and his colleagues (Goldstein & Ferrell, 1987; Goldstein & Wickstrom,

1986) offer a foundation for a model of intervention designed to facilitate peer social-communicative interactions. Based upon these researchers' findings and suggestions, social interaction research, and normal developmental literature, seven principles are proposed to guide the development of an effective intervention (Table 1). These principles are elaborated in the sections that follow.

Promote Peer Interaction and Facilitate Communication Between Children With and Children Without Special Needs

The primary goals of peer-mediated social communication intervention are to promote peer interaction and to facilitate communication between children with and children without special needs. The most appropriate role for peers is that of facilitator, not primary interventionist. While nondisabled peers can provide support for adult-implemented interventions that teach specific interaction or communication strategies to children with special needs, peers should not be primary communication interventionists. Adult-implemented interventions may include a multifaceted language assessment of the target children's strengths and needs to focus on teaching new or emerging communication skills. Peer-mediated interventions should support child acquisition of social-communicative strategies by providing appropriate behavioral models, providing opportunities for successful communication, and facilitating generalization across environments and individuals. Nondisabled peers should not be expected to "teach" language targets or specific social-communicative behaviors. In addition, such teaching may not be necessary when adult-implemented training and facilitated peer interactions are included in the target children's communication program. Positive changes in the social-communicative interactions of children with special needs may result from their observational learning during their interactions with peers, from adult-

Table 1.   Principles to guide the development of an effective intervention

1.   Promote peer interaction and facilitate communication between children with and children without special needs.

2.   Teach *all* children social-communicative strategies to maximize the effects of an intervention.

3.   As initial participants, choose children who are likely to be successful.

4.   Provide individualized instruction to children with special needs, focusing on initiation and response strategies.

5.   Provide instruction to nondisabled children in conversational strategies known to elicit verbal and nonverbal behaviors from children with special needs.

6.   A direct instruction approach should be used to teach desired social-communicative behaviors to all children.

7.   Maintenance and generalization must be programmed for.

implemented direct instructional programs designed to teach specific social communication skills, from nondisabled peers' increased responsiveness and positive interactions, or as a result of a combination of these factors.

Teach All Children Social-Communicative Strategies To Maximize the Effects of an Intervention

Nondisabled peers *and* target children with special needs must be taught social-communicative strategies to maximize the effects of an intervention to foster positive peer interactions. Data support the importance of teaching all children social communication strategies in order to facilitate extended conversational interactions (Haring, Breen, & Laitinen, 1989). Providing instruction to nondisabled peers alone will not necessarily produce changes in the social-communicative behaviors of children with special needs. Although increases in responsiveness by children with special needs in interventions when only nondisabled peers were trained have been observed, increased rates of initiation by children with special needs rarely occurred (Goldstein & Ferrell, 1987; Goldstein & Wickstrom, 1986). Observed gains in responsiveness may be the result of increased opportunities for interaction, whereas changes in rate of initiation may be dependent on teaching specific interactional techniques to children with social communication deficits.

Interventions to teach children with special needs social-communicative strategies should focus on conversational skills that are characteristic of peer interactions. Age-appropriate conversational topics and typical activities should be included so that discourse training is functional for children with special needs. Age-appropriate materials should be used during structured play, and toy-play skills needed for participation in an activity should be taught to the children with special needs, if necessary.

Conversational skills should be taught during naturally occurring interactions between children with and children without special needs. Adults should take advantage of these interactions to teach appropriate social-communicative skills, concentrating on skills that are desirable in these settings, that arise in response to natural cues, and that evoke natural consequences from the environment (Calculator, 1988). Communication skills targeted for intervention should be those that help children participate more actively and independently in current and future environments (Calculator, 1988).

Providing training to children with special needs only and placing them in settings with untrained peers will not automatically result in positive peer–peer exchanges (Strain, Odom, & McConnell, 1984). Responsive peers must be available to interact with children with special needs in order to sustain their newly learned behaviors. Typically, children with and children without special needs require different levels of training, with nondisabled peers providing most of the support for maintaining social-communicative interactions. It is important that instruction in social communication strategies is provided to *all* children in order to maximize the effects of an intervention aimed at promoting positive peer interactions.

As Initial Participants, Choose
Children Who Are Likely To Be Successful

Children with and children without special needs most likely to succeed in acquiring and using social communication skills should be chosen as initial intervention participants. While an intervention aimed at facilitating the social communication skills of children with special needs eventually should include *all* classmates and potential peers, it is best to begin skill training with a subgroup who are likely to experience success in learning the strategies. Research on implementing classwide communication strategies has shown that initially training a small number of children enables the adult to become comfortable in prompting procedures and in making adaptations in training based on children's performance (Kaiser & Ostrosky, 1990).

Several criteria should be considered to select children. Nondisabled children chosen as facilitators should exhibit age-appropriate language and play skills, be highly interactive with peers during unstructured free-play periods, and be responsive to adult direction. These guidelines have proven useful for selecting peers to participate in social interaction interventions, and it seems appropriate that peers involved in social communication interventions should possess similar characteristics (Odom et al., 1988).

Children with special needs should exhibit some basic toy-play skills such as the ability to construct simple objects and engage in rudimentary fine motor activities (Odom et al., 1988). Nondisabled peers may have difficulty interacting with children with special needs for sustained periods of time if the target children are unable to play with toys appropriately. Additionally, target children who have limited toy-play skills may experience frustration in play groups designed to promote social communication if they are unable to participate in play activities. Children with special needs who are not skilled players should be taught basic toy-play skills before engaging in peer-mediated social communication play groups. Strategies for facilitating peer interaction, along with learning toy-play skills, include having children with and children without special needs participate in large-group activities together (i.e., circle time, music time, snack time). Adults can use these periods to encourage positive interactions between children.

Children with special needs chosen to participate in a social communication intervention should be able to communicate consistently using gestures, words, or signs. Initially it may be necessary to help nondisabled peers interpret the communicative signals of the children with whom they are interacting. To ensure success for all participants, it is important that target children communicate consistently and intelligibly so that initiations and responses are not overlooked and opportunities for interaction not missed.

Several additional factors should be considered when selecting potential conversation partners. Children should be paired with peers who share common interests, enjoy being with each other, approach one another regularly and naturally, and are within natural proximity to one another due to participation in the same activities or classes. Children who exhibit a dislike for or disinterest in one another should not be assigned to the same structured play group. Regularity of approach, rather than behavioral characteristics during interactions, may be an important measure for determining peer preference, since some children with special needs display inappropriate behaviors as a means of communicating during interactions with peers (Donnellan, Mirenda, Mesaros, & Fassbender, 1984). Because a wide range of atypical or socially inappropriate behaviors can perform communicative functions, caution should be exercised when evaluating specific behaviors as indicative of negative or positive interactions. For example, a child who invariably hits an age-mate on the head whenever he or she approaches might actually be expressing a desire to interact; however, the child lacks appropriate initiation skills. Children displaying high rates of negative behaviors toward peers may require individualized instruction in appropriate approach behaviors before including them as participants in a peer-mediated intervention, and peers may need instruction about individual children's strategies for communication. If necessary, behavior management programs to reduce aggressive behaviors should be conducted in conjunction with programs to increase or teach approach behaviors.

Provide Individualized Instruction to Children with Special Needs

Children with special needs should be taught developmentally appropriate initiation and response skills, with consideration given to an individual child's strengths and needs. Although participation in structured play groups may be sufficient to promote peer social-communicative development for nondisabled children, this is often not true for children with special needs (Guralnick, 1981). A three-step model of intervention that includes direct instruction to children with social communication deficits, training peer facilitators, and providing support during peer interactions appears necessary. Preliminary intervention with children with special needs increases the likelihood that effective interactions will result from the peer-mediated portion of the intervention. Training nondisabled peers as responsive partners and appropriate models of positive social-communicative interaction sets the stage for successful interactions. The third step, bringing target children and peers together to practice their newly learned conversational interaction skills, enables all children to use the social communication strategies at high rates in a supportive setting.

Individualized instruction to children with special needs should focus on both initiation and response strategies. Productive social communication skills, which allow individuals to control their environment, and receptive skills, which are an essential component in the development of a person's role as a listener, are important areas to target for the development of positive social-communicative exchanges. It may be necessary to teach children with special needs to initiate topics of joint interest, because topic initiation is a critical communication skill that promotes conversational control (Light, 1988). Children who have learned appropriate initiation strategies need not rely on their peers to begin interactions if they are able to use gestures, words, pictures, or signs to begin a conversation (Hunt et al., 1988; Hunt et al., 1990). While it is true that individuals who are unable to initiate effectively exhibit difficulties during peer interactions, high rates of initiation are not the only indication of communicative competence (Light, 1988).

Children with special needs should also receive instruction in responding appropriately to peer initiations and in maintaining interactions, if these skills are lacking. Since successful interaction depends on a joint focus of attention, communicative competence may depend, in part, on demonstrating respon-siveness to a partner and topic (Light, 1988). Children with special needs may need training in responding appropriately to their peers, with adults providing individualized instruction that builds upon children's existing strengths. As children become skilled at interacting with their nondisabled peers, increases in the frequency of social-communicative interactions, as well as positive changes in the quality of these exchanges, should be evident.

To maximize the effectiveness of an intervention, conversation training with target children should begin before the peer-mediated intervention is implemented. Children with special needs should receive some instruction in social communication strategies before participating in play groups in which their nondisabled peers assume the role of facilitators. Conversational skill training should be a part of the daily classroom routine for children with special needs, with peer-mediated interventions secondary to these adult-implemented procedures. Target children should participate in structured play groups with their trained peers once individualized instruction in basic initia-tion and response strategies has begun.

Provide Instruction to Nondisabled Children
in Conversational Strategies Known To Elicit Verbal
and Nonverbal Behaviors from Children with Special Needs

Skill training for nondisabled peers should focus on conversation strategies known to elicit verbal and nonverbal behaviors from target children. Several skills are important for facilitating social-communicative interactions between children with and children without special needs, as mentioned previously: joint attention, establishing eye contact, commenting, responding, requesting information, mands for compliance, and turn-taking (Goldstein & Ferrell, 1987; Goldstein & Wickstrom, 1986; Hunt et al., 1988; Hunt et al., 1990). These skills, which nondisabled children typically exhibit during interactions with their peers, are likely to result in improved interactions when used in interactions with children with disabilities. These skills are optimal starting points for an intervention utilizing peers as facilitators of social communication for children with special needs, because nondisabled peers may need only adult support and feedback to increase their use of these skills during peer interactions.

Joint attention (attending to materials, activities, or ideas that are of immediate interest to another individual) is a basic component of most successful conversations. Nondisabled peers must learn to engage in conversations that focus on topics of interest to their age-mates with special needs. By attending to the materials target children are playing with and the way they are playing with them, nondisabled peers can enter into and potentially extend this play behavior through social-communicative interaction. Nondisabled children must be taught to observe the play behavior of children with special needs before commenting on their actions or becoming involved in the play theme. Establishing eye contact serves as a signal to indicate a readiness and intention to engage in an interaction, and its importance should not be understated in social communication skill training. Nondisabled peers should be taught to look at their partners during social-communicative interactions.

Nondisabled peers should also receive instruction in using descriptive talk during interactions with children with special needs. This strategy involves providing a verbal commentary about the child's presumed interests, feelings, or thoughts regarding his or her focus of attention (Mahoney & Powell, 1988). Descriptive talk requires peers to attend to the target children's behavior, provide a brief verbal description of the ongoing play theme, and allow the target children an opportunity to respond. Use of this strategy has been associated with increased engagement between children with and without special needs (Dunst, McWilliam, & Holbert, 1986). As communication partners begin to initiate to children with special needs at higher frequencies, increased opportunities are available for social-communicative interactions.

Teaching nondisabled peers strategies that prompt children with special needs to become involved in play activities and conversation is another way to facilitate social-communicative interaction. Requesting information and organizing target children's play behavior are strategies that require that children with special needs respond in order to maintain an interaction. For example, asking a partner what he or she is building, or assigning him or her the role of doctor during a sociodramatic sequence, is likely to result in a response from the target child. When a nondisabled peer asks a question or instructs a target child to assume a role or comply with a request, an increased potential for turn-taking arises.

A final conversational skill important to include in training nondisabled peers to be facilitators of social communication is responsiveness. Peer-mediated interventions must be evaluated not only in terms of changes in the frequency of initiations, but also in terms of changes in the responsiveness of peers to children with special needs. Results of a molecular analysis by Haring et al. (1989) demonstrated that when nondisabled students' responses correctly corresponded to target children's initiations, 67% of the conversations contained one or more additional turns. However, when the response did not correspond to an initiation, very few interactions progressed beyond the original initiation–response sequence.

Increased responsiveness by conversational partners has the potential for producing dramatic effects on children's language production (Haring, Roger, Lee, Breen, & Gaylord-Ross, 1986). Peer responsiveness to social initiations is especially important as a reinforcer for an individual's initial attempts at social interaction. As nondisabled peers begin to respond at higher frequencies to children with special needs, these children become more motivated to interact. In turn, target children may begin to initiate more frequently, resulting in positive changes in social-communicative interactions. Nondisabled children should receive instruction in social communication facilitation strategies prior to the start of play groups. Beginning instruction before regular play groups are assembled minimizes the establishment of poor interaction patterns.

When nondisabled peers are taught strategies to support the social-communicative interactions of children with special needs during play, benefits can potentially occur for *both* partners. Nondisabled children learn techniques that emphasize establishing joint attention, turn-taking, and responsiveness and may become more proficient in their interactions with other children, including their nondisabled peers (Greenwood, 1981). For children with special needs, intervention may result in increases in interaction and communication directed to their peers, as initiation and responding skills are developed (Goldstein & Wickstrom, 1986).

A Direct Instruction Approach Should Be Used To
Teach Desired Social-Communicative Behaviors to All Children

A direct instruction approach should be used to teach peers and target children desired social-communicative behaviors. Children should receive instruction in social communication skills, using procedures most likely to result in rapid learning. For nondisabled peers, instruction may occur in group training prior to structured play groups; however, it may be necessary to design individualized programs for children with special needs, once skills have been targeted for intervention based on behavioral needs. Procedures that have proven successful in teaching peer interaction skills include: 1) discussion of the strategies to be taught, 2) demonstration of the skills by an adult, 3) critiquing examples and non-examples, 4) role-playing, and 5) adult feedback regarding the correctness of strategy use (Chandler et al., 1990; Goldstein & Ferrell, 1987; Goldstein & Wickstrom, 1986; Ladd & Mize, 1983). Reinforcement procedures may also prove useful in shaping interactions of children with and children without special needs; however, adult support must be systematically faded in order to maintain results without continued training (Lefebvre & Strain, 1989). Regardless of the methods of instruction, teaching should be tailored to the individual needs of children, with additional practice provided as necessary and the length of training contingent on skill acquisition. For example, some children may require supplementary practice with an adult to become proficient with a particular strategy, while other children may already have the strategy in their repertoire and may need only an occasional reminder to use it. Booster sessions should occur periodically to review strategies and to assist in the maintenance of satisfactory levels of social-communicative interaction between children with and children without special needs, as well as to train new social communication skills.

To facilitate the acquisition of social communication strategies, adults should verbally and/or nonverbally prompt children to interact with one another when opportunities arise. Children's play themes should be observed before suggestions for interaction are offered, and verbal or nonverbal feedback should be provided to support correct strategy use. Adult support, through prompting and providing feedback, assists in children's acquisition of social communication strategies. However, adults must be careful not to interrupt ongoing social-communicative interactions when providing feedback. As children become more skilled at engaging age-mates, adults should fade their level of support, with the natural contingencies of positive interaction maintaining the exchanges.

Program for Maintenance and Generalization

Strategies that promote maintenance and generalization must be an integral part of instructional programming. Training methods that support the maintenance and generalization of newly learned skills must be an integral part of peer-mediated interventions. Eight strategies known to support maintenance and generalization of social communication skills should be included in an intervention program.

First, before peers can be expected to use social-communicative strategies during interactions with children with special needs, they should consistently demonstrate mastery of the targeted behaviors during training sessions (Goldstein & Ferrell, 1987; Goldstein & Wickstrom, 1986). Allowing adequate practice time for peers to become proficient at using one social-communicative skill before providing instruction in additional skills supports the independent use of skills in interactions with children with special needs and the maintenance of skill use over time. Additional skills should be introduced when children consistently demonstrate mastery of a strategy. Monitoring peer behavior during practice sessions and play groups will assist in making programming changes if individual children are experiencing difficulty with strategies, as well as enable adults to evaluate the maintenance of skills over time.

Second, due to the long acquisition period necessary for communication changes to occur for children with limited conversational skills, adults must carefully monitor changes in behavior and the effects of various strategies on acquisition. It may take 30–40 training sessions before effects are observed for target child behaviors in peer-implemented interventions (Goldstein & Ferrell, 1987; Goldstein & Wickstrom, 1986; Hunt et al., 1988; Hunt et al., 1990). Therefore, skill training and opportunities for peer interaction should become a regular part of the classroom routine to ensure opportunities for conversational skill building and maintaining peer interactions.

Third, when peers are consistently facilitating social-communicative interactions with their age-mates with special needs, the adult should begin decreasing the level of support provided to them. Systematically fading adult support helps ensure that positive changes in social-communicative interaction are maintained. For example, Lefebvre and Strain (1989) implemented a group oriented reinforcement contingency and were effective in reducing levels of teacher prompts without compromising rates of appropriate interaction between socially withdrawn children and their nondisabled peers. The use of a poster and group contingency allowed the teacher to be less obtrusive in prompting interactions and to focus more closely on the specific needs of the target children. Goldstein and colleagues used posters to assist in withdrawing teacher support from their interventions (Goldstein & Ferrell, 1987; Goldstein & Wickstrom, 1986). Chandler and colleagues (1990) were also able to systematically withdraw teacher verbal and visual support, while maintaining high rates of peer initiations and engagement in social interaction between young children with and without special needs. In these four studies, environmental cues such as posters and visual feedback sheets served as prompts to engage in interactions, without reliance on intrusive verbal prompts from an adult. While it may be initially necessary for adults to verbally prompt children with and children without special needs to communicate and interact with one another on a frequent basis, it is presumed that over time peer interactions will become reinforcing and adult support will no longer be necessary.

Fourth, to facilitate the maintenance of skills, adults should make structured play groups a part of the classroom routine (Falvey, Bishop, Grenot-Scheyer, & Coots, 1988). By having responsive partners present during play groups, the adult can continue to encourage children with and children without special needs to engage in positive social-communicative interactions when skill training has ended. The adult should continue to introduce the play groups, provide suggestions of play themes if necessary, and review the children's social-communicative interactions at the end of the play period in order to maintain strategy use by all children. The adult should also introduce new social-communicative strategies as children with and children without special needs master those initially trained.

Fifth, it is important that adults refrain from interrupting ongoing peer interactions in order to praise children for their social-communicative behaviors. Instead, adults should draw attention to positive instances of interaction during the review portion of the play periods. Reinforcing peer-to-peer interactions as they occur has the potential for terminating positive interactions, because children redirect their attention to the adult.

Sixth, some evidence suggests that maintenance of program effects may decrease several months after fading. Periodic instruction should be given to facilitate the maintenance of positive social communication between children (Halle, Baer, & Spradlin, 1981). Booster sessions are useful for reviewing social-communicative strategies learned during the training component of the intervention and as a medium for introducing new conversational strategies. As target children become more skillful interactors, it may be necessary to teach additional strategies to nondisabled peers in order to facilitate the generalization of new skills by target children.

Seventh, researchers have cited the lack of socially responsive partners in generalization settings as a key factor contributing to the lack of generalization effects (Strain et al., 1984). Stokes and Baer (1977) suggest that to support the generalization of skills learned in structured environments, sufficient exemplars should be trained to facilitate generalization to untrained stimulus conditions and to untrained responses. Providing classwide instruction should facilitate generalization as all children acquire initiation and responding skills and are able to interact successfully with one another. Providing multiple trained peers may also strengthen natural maintenance contingencies for children with special needs, because interactions with peers become reinforcing in and of themselves. Consistently providing children with structured and unstructured opportunities to interact with peers will facilitate generalization as children learn that there are expectations for positive social-communicative interaction between age-mates.

Finally, a social-communicative intervention with an emphasis on peer interaction in natural settings must concentrate on functional skills in order to promote generalization (Falvey et al., 1988; Guess & Helmstetter, 1986). Social-communicative skills, such as initiating to age-mates, establishing eye contact, and responding, are functional skills that can positively affect the development of peer relationships.

These eight principles for effective intervention provide a structure on which to build comprehensive peer-implemented intervention to improve the social-communicative interactions of children with and children without special needs. These principles describe characteristics of peer interactions that are found in the developmental literature. They encompass the major elements deemed important by researchers who have investigated peer-implemented social communication interventions, as well as by those researchers who have investigated peer social interaction.

RECOMMENDATIONS FOR FUTURE RESEARCH

Current research on peer-mediated interventions to facilitate the social communication of children with special needs suggests many questions related to the content, procedures, and outcomes of these interventions. In general, researchers need to begin to evaluate factors that affect the *relationships* between children with and children without special needs, rather than simply continuing to focus on teaching discrete behaviors. Descriptive studies that assist in specifying behaviors that lead to the development of peer relationships, and studies assessing the impact of these variables, the efficiency of skill training, and differential effects resulting from interventions are necessary to advance peer-mediated social communication research.

Training issues that require further systematic study include a closer analysis of the key social communication strategies necessary to optimize interactions between peers with and peers without special needs, which lead to the development of positive peer relationships. Strategies that enable children to develop positive relationships with age-mates must be investigated, as well as outcome measures that accurately assess these relationships.

Because children with disabilities have diverse needs, it is necessary for nondisabled peers to be proficient in a variety of strategies. Training must focus on the individual strengths and needs of children with *and* children without disabilities. Strategies that promote successful interactions with individuals with severe disabilities are particularly important and necessary. Research efforts should focus on developing strategies for nondisabled peers that enable them to communicate with individuals who use alternative and augmentative communication systems (i.e., sign language, communication books, voice synthesizers). The integration of behavioral strategies and technology provides an ideal starting point for developing instructional procedures to facilitate social communication between children with severe communication disabilities and their nondisabled peers. As researchers begin to explore methods for individualizing social communication training, the effectiveness of specific techniques must be evaluated in order to develop training procedures that result in positive changes in peer interactions.

An additional area to explore is evaluation of the impact of facilitator variables on the success of instructional approaches. The effect of peer characteristics on the acquisition and use of trained strategies may provide answers to why certain peer facilitators acquire and use social communication strategies at higher frequencies or with greater success than others. Facilitator characteristics worthy of exploration include age, education, experiences with individuals at different developmental levels, and play skills. These characteristics may prove especially important for developing intervention programs for individuals with severe disabilities.

The establishment of self-sustaining relationships between children with and children without special needs requires knowledge of characteristics in existing positive peer relationships. Children with disabilities may need to be taught functional social-communicative skills in order to engage in interactions such as those that naturally occur between nondisabled age-mates. Determining the conversational topics of nondisabled age-mates may assist in selecting age-appropriate materials and activities when designing interventions. Researchers also need to investigate if interactions between children with and children without special needs are sufficiently reinforcing to nondisabled children so that the relationship is maintained when adult support is faded.

Evaluating the effectiveness of different formats for providing instruction is another area in need of further investigation. Approaches for structuring training efforts may include large-group sessions, small-group instruction, individual sessions, or some combination of these. Training children with and children without special needs together in social-communicative strategies should also be evaluated in terms of cost-effectiveness and acquisition of strategies.

Generalization and maintenance issues requiring further investigation include instructional programming so that children can sustain interactions in generalization settings without external reinforcers or adult support. Skill training that gradually requires children to self-monitor peer social-communicative behaviors, or that includes a correspondence training component may result in increased generalization and maintenance effects. Attitudinal changes, the development of friendships between children with and children without special needs, and factors that inhibit or support the formation of friendships must also be evaluated as factors in the maintenance of skills.

Finally, future research should consider the settings in which social-communicative interactions are to occur in an effort to evaluate generalization in these environments. Assessing necessary social communication skills in community, home, and school settings will assist in the design of interventions as researchers plan instructional programming based on these needed skills.

REFERENCES

Berninger, G., & Garvey, C. (1980). Complementary balance in the use of the interrogative form by nursery school dyads. *Journal of Child Language, 8,* 297–311.

Brady, M.P., Shores, R.E., Gunter, P., McEvoy, M.A., Fox, J.J., & White, C.

(1984). Generalization of an adolescent's social interaction behavior via multiple peers in a classroom setting. *Journal of The Association for Persons with Severe Handicaps, 9*(4), 278–286.

Brenner, J., & Mueller, E. (1982). Shared meaning in boy toddlers' peer relations. *Child Development, 53,* 380–391.

Calculator, S. (1988). Promoting the acquisition and generalization of conversational skills by individuals with severe disabilities. *Augmentative and Alternative Communication, 4,* 94–103.

Chandler, L.K., Ostrosky, M.M., Odom, S.L., & Rainey, S. (1990, May). *Removing the teacher from peer-mediated interventions: Cross-site effects.* Paper presented at the annual convention of the Association for Behavior Analysis, Nashville.

Charlesworth, R., & Hartup, W.W. (1967). Positive social reinforcement in the nursery school peer group. *Child Development, 18,* 993–1002.

Donnellan, A., Mirenda, P., Mesaros, R., & Fassbender, L. (1984). Analyzing the communicative functions of aberrant behaviors. *Journal of The Association for Persons with Severe Handicaps, 9,* 201–212.

Dunst, C.J., McWilliam, R., & Holbert, K. (1986). Assessment of preschool classroom environments. *Diagnostique, 11*(3/4) 212–232.

Ervin-Tripp, S. (1977). Wait for me, roller skate! In S. Ervin-Tripp & C. Mitchell-Kernan (Eds.), *Child discourse* (pp. 165–168). New York: Academic Press.

Falvey, M., Bishop, K., Grenot-Scheyer, M., & Coots, J. (1988). Issues and trends in mental retardation. In S. Calculator & J. Bedrosian (Eds.), *Communication assessment and intervention for adults with mental retardation* (pp. 45–66). San Diego: College-Hill Press.

Finkelstein, N.W., Dent, C., Gallagher, K., & Ramey, C.T. (1978). Social behavior of infants and toddlers in a day-care environment. *Developmental Psychology, 14*(3), 257–262.

Garvey, C. (1986). Peer relations and the growth of communication. In E.C. Mueller & C.R. Cooper (Eds.), *Process and outcome in peer relationships* (pp. 329–345). Orlando, FL: Academic Press.

Garvey, C., & Hogan, R. (1973). Social speech and social interaction: Egocentrism revisited. *Child Development, 44,* 562–568.

Gaylord-Ross, R.J., Haring, T.G., Breen, C., & Pitts-Conway, V. (1984). The training and generalization of social interaction skills with autistic youth. *Journal of Applied Behavior Analysis, 17,* 229–247.

Gelman, R., & Shatz, M. (1977). Appropriate speech adjustments: The operation of conversational constraints on talk to two-year-olds. In M. Lewis & L.A. Rosenblum (Eds.), *Interaction, conversation, and the development of language* (pp. 27–62). New York: Gardner Press.

Goldstein, H., & Ferrell, D.R. (1987). Augmenting communicative interaction between handicapped and nonhandicapped preschool children. *Journal of Speech and Hearing Disorders, 52,* 200–211.

Goldstein, H., & Wickstrom, S. (1986). Peer intervention effects on communicative interaction among handicapped and nonhandicapped preschoolers. *Journal of Applied Behavior Analysis, 19,* 209–214.

Greenwood, C. (1981). Peer-oriented behavioral technology and ethical issues. In P.S. Strain (Ed.), *The utilization of peers as behavior change agents* (pp. 327–360). New York: Plenum Press.

Guess, D., & Helmstetter, E. (1986). Skill cluster instruction and the individualized sequencing model. In R. Horner, L. Meyer, & H.D. Fredericks (Eds.), *Education of learners with severe handicaps: Exemplary service strategies* (pp. 221–248). Baltimore: Paul H. Brookes Publishing Co.

Guralnick, M.J. (1976). The value of integrating handicapped and nonhandicapped preschool children. *American Journal of Orthopsychiatry, 45*(2), 236–245.

Guralnick, M.J. (1980). Social interactions among preschool children. *Exceptional Children, 46*(4), 248–253.

Guralnick, M.J. (1981). Peer influences on development of communicative competence. In P. Strain (Ed.), *The utilization of peers as behavior change agents* (pp. 31–68). New York: Plenum Press.

Guralnick, M.J. (1986). The peer relations of young handicapped and nonhandicapped children. In P.S. Strain, M.J. Guralnick, & H.M. Walker (Eds.), *Children's social behavior: Development, assessment, and modification* (pp. 93–140). New York: Academic Press.

Guralnick, M.J., & Paul-Brown, D. (1980). Functional and discourse analyses of nonhandicapped preschool children's speech to handicapped children. *American Journal of Mental Deficiency, 84*, 444–454.

Guralnick, M.J., & Paul-Brown, D. (1984). Communicative adjustments during behavior request episodes among children at different developmental levels. *Child Development, 55*, 911–919.

Guralnick, M.J., & Paul-Brown, D. (1989). Peer-related communicative competence of preschool children: Developmental and adaptive characteristics. *Journal of Speech and Hearing Research, 32*(4), 930–943.

Halle, J., Baer, D., & Spradlin, J. (1981). Teachers' generalized use of delay as a stimulus control procedure to increase language use in handicapped children. *Journal of Applied Behavior Analysis, 14*(4), 389–409.

Haring, T.G., Breen, C., & Laitinen, R. (1989, May). *Molecular characteristics of social conversation skills among handicapped and nonhandicapped elementary students*. Paper presented at the annual convention of the Association for Behavior Analysis, Milwaukee.

Haring, T.G., Roger, B., Lee, M., Breen, C., & Gaylord-Ross, R. (1986). Teaching social language to moderately handicapped students. *Journal of Applied Behavior Analysis, 19*(2), 159–172.

Hart, B.M., & Risley, T.R. (1980). In vivo language intervention: Unanticipated general effects. *Journal of Applied Behavior Analysis, 13*, 407–432.

Hartup, W.W. (1978). Peer interaction and the processes of socialization. In M.J. Guralnick (Ed.), *Early intervention and the integration of handicapped and nonhandicapped children* (pp. 27–52). Baltimore: University Park Press.

Hartup, W.W. (1979). Peer relations and the growth of social competence. In M.W. Kent & J.E. Rolf (Eds.), *Primary prevention of psychopathology* (Vol. III, pp. 150–170). Hanover, NH: University Press of New England.

Herink, N., & Lee, P.C. (1985). Patterns of social interaction of mainstreamed preschool children: Hopeful news from the field. *Exceptional Child, 32*(3), 191–199.

Hunt, P., Alwell, M., & Goetz, L. (1988). Acquisition of conversation skills and the reduction of inappropriate social interaction behaviors. *Journal of The Association for Persons with Severe Handicaps, 13*(1), 20–27.

Hunt, P., Alwell, M., Goetz, L., & Sailor, W. (1990). Generalized effects of conversation skill training. *Journal of The Association for Persons with Severe Handicaps, 15*(4), 250–260.

Jenkins, J.R., Speltz, M.L., & Odom, S.L. (1985). Integrating normal and handicapped preschoolers: Effects on child development and social interaction. *Exceptional Children, 52*(1), 7–17.

Johnston, J.M., & Johnston, G.T. (1972). Modifications of consonant speech-sound articulation in young children. *Journal of Applied Behavior Analysis, 5*(3), 233–246.

Kaiser, A.P. (1990). A two-fold model of environment: Implications for early language learning. In S.R. Shroeder (Ed.), *Ecobehavior analysis and developmental disabilities: The twenty-first century* (pp. 141–153). New York: Springer-Verlag.

Kaiser, A.P., & Ostrosky, M.M. (1990, June). *Incidental teaching: Language instruction in the natural milieu.* Workshop presented at the Early Childhood Special Education Summer Institute II. Cedar Rapids, IA.

Keenan, E.O. (1977). Making it last: Repetition in children's discourse. In S. Ervin-Tripp & C. Mitchell-Kernan (Eds.), *Child discourse.* New York: Academic Press.

Ladd, G.W., & Mize, J. (1983). A cognitive-social learning model of social-skill training. *Psychological Review, 90*(2), 127–157.

Lefebvre, D., & Strain, P.S. (1989). Effects of a group contingency on the frequency of social interactions among autistic and nonhandicapped preschool children: Making LRE efficacious. *Journal of Early Intervention, 13*(4), 329–341.

Leiter, M.P. (1977). A study of reciprocity in preschool play groups. *Child Development, 48,* 1288–1295.

LeMay, D., Griffin, P., & Sanford, A. (1977). *Learning Accomplishment Profile— Diagnostic Edition.* Winston-Salem: Kaplan Press.

Light, J. (1988). Interaction involving individuals using augmentative and alternative communication systems: State of the art and future. *Augmentative and Alternative Communication, 4,* 66–82.

Mahoney, G., Glover, A., & Finger, I. (1981). Relationship between language and sensorimotor development of Down syndrome and nonretarded children. *Journal of Mental Deficiency, 86*(1), 21–27.

Mahoney, G., & Powell, A. (1988). Modifying parent–child interaction: Enhancing the development of handicapped children. *Journal of Special Education, 22,* 82–96.

McNaughton, D., & Light, J. (1989). Teaching facilitators to support the communicative skills of an adult with severe cognitive disabilities: A case study. *Augmentative and Alternative Communication, 4,* 35–41.

Mueller, E., Bleier, M., Krakow, J., Hegedus, K., & Cournoyer, P. (1977). The development of peer verbal interaction among two-year-old boys. *Child Development, 48,* 284–287.

Nelson, K. (1985). *Making sense: The acquisition of shared meaning.* Orlando: Academic Press.

Odom, S.L., Bender, M.K., Stein, M.L., Doran, L. P., Houden, P.M., McInnes, M., Gilbert, M.M., DeKlyen, M., Speltz, M.L., & Jenkins, J.R. (1988). *The integrated preschool curriculum.* Seattle: University of Washington Press.

Odom, S.L., Ostrosky, M., McEvoy, M., Peterson, C., & McConnell, S. (1990, April). *The effects of three strategies for promoting peer social interaction of preschool children with disabilities.* Presentation at the annual convention of the International Council for Exceptional Children, Toronto.

Owens, R.E. (1984). *Language development.* Columbus, OH: Charles E. Merrill.

Parker, J.G., & Asher, S.R. (1987). Peer relations and later personal adjustment: Are low-accepted children at risk? *Psychological Bulletin, 102,* 357–389.

Paul, L. (1985). Programming peer support for functional language. In S.F. Warren & A.K. Rogers-Warren (Eds.), *Teaching functional language* (pp. 289–307). Austin, TX: PRO-ED.

Peck, C.A. (1989). Assessment of social communicative competence: Evaluating environments. *Seminars in Speech and Language, 10*(1), 1–15.

Perske, R. (1988). *Circles of friends.* Nashville: Abingdon Press.

Rubenstein, J., & Howes, C. (1976). The effects of peers on toddler interaction with mother and toys. *Child Development, 47,* 597–605.

Rubin, K.H., & Lollis, S.P. (1988). Origins and consequences of social withdrawal. In J. Belsky & T. Nezworsky (Eds.), *Clinical implications of attachment* (pp. 219–252). Hillsdale, NJ: Lawrence Erlbaum Associates.

Stokes, T.F., & Baer, D.M. (1977). An implicit technology of generalization. *Journal of Applied Behavior Analysis, 10,* 349–367.

Strain, P.S., Odom, S.L., & McConnell, S.R. (1984). Promoting social reciprocity of exceptional children: Identification, target behavior selection, and intervention. *Remedial and Special Education, 5,* 21–28.

Strain, P.S., Guralnick, M.J., & Walker, H.M. (1986). *Children's social behavior: Development, assessment, and modification.* New York: Academic Press.

Thomasello, M., & Farrar, M.F. (1986). Joint attention in early language. *Child Development, 57,* 1454–1463.

9

Communicating the Meaning
of Events
Through Social Referencing

Tedra A. Walden

THERE ARE MANY WAYS OF COMMUNICATING and many kinds of things that may be communicated about. One kind of verbal and nonverbal communication occurs in social referencing, when one person influences another in a situation where there is some uncertainty about what is going on and what should be done. When one person bases his or her personal interpretation of an event partly or wholly on the behavior of another person, we say that social referencing has occurred. Thus, social referencing involves communication in the form of an individual's reactions to events. People communicate by expressing emotions and by behaving in certain ways. These reactions are taken as indicators of their interpretations of events. Sometimes these reactions are communicated intentionally and sometimes unintentionally; sometimes they are genuine and sometimes feigned. Because the onset of social referencing is believed to be in the second half of the first year of life (Walden & Ogan, 1988), it is certainly one of the earliest forms of intentional communication that the infant engages in with other individuals.

COMMUNICATING THE MEANING
OF EVENTS THROUGH SOCIAL REFERENCING

People of all ages use social referencing as a means of communicating about events. Adults have been reported to engage in social referencing (e.g., Kerber & Coles, 1978) and in similar processes, such as social comparison,

The research presented in this chapter was supported by Grant No. P01-15051 from the National Institute for Child Health and Human Development.

attitude change, and conformity. Normally developing children as young as 1 year of age engage in social referencing in situations that include the approach of an unfamiliar person (Feinman & Lewis, 1983), going over an apparent drop-off (Sorce, Emde, Campos, & Klinnert, 1985), interacting with unfamiliar toys (Walden & Ogan, 1988), and responding to unusual noises (Hirshberg & Svejda, 1990). In these situations, when caregivers display fear toward the event, infants are less friendly to the unfamiliar person, less likely to cross the apparent drop-off, and less likely to play with the unusual toys than when their caregivers show positive reactions toward the event. Infants are also likely to display negative affect when caregivers respond negatively and positive affect when caregivers respond positively. Children with cognitive delays do not show the same proclivity to rely on social referencing. That is, in situations in which it is appropriate and pertinent to notice the reactions of others and to respond similarly, children with intellectual delays are less likely to do so than are normally developing children (Walden, Knieps, & Baxter, 1991).

Social referencing is a powerful strategy for a child who is just learning how to behave and to regulate his or her affect. In its basic form, social referencing can be a fairly simple information gathering strategy that can be applied in almost any situation where there are other people. Because young children are often in new situations, there are obviously many occasions when social referencing can be useful. As Brown and DeLoache (1978) argued, young children are in a sense universal novices in that "children find themselves in [novel] situations more often than do adults and very young children may be neophytes in almost all problem situations" (p. 13). Similarly, Siegler and Jenkins (1989) noted that children "constantly need to discover strategies to cope with situations that adults find quite routine. They also need to find out where newly discovered strategies apply" (pp. 2–3). Referencing another person is a strategy that is used by prelinguistic infants, who rely on emotional expressions, vocal tone, and gestures (Caron, Caron, & MacLean, 1988; Fernald, 1989). Later in infancy, children consider linguistic content along with nonlinguistic sources of information in dealing with events.

Affect and Behavior Regulation

Social referencing can be observed in several domains of behavior: affective expressions; behavior directed at target objects or events; and children's behavior directed toward parents, especially looks at parents. When behavior toward targets of parental messages is influenced in the direction of the messages, we say that behavior regulation has occurred. It is often useful to contrast the child's behavior toward the target of parents' positive reactions with that child's behavior toward the target of parents' negative reactions. In our work, we include two series of trials, in which one target is paired with positive affective messages and one with fearful affective messages, and we include a subsequent free-play period during which both targets become simultaneously available to the child for play. During the free-play period, the crucial test of social referencing occurs. Does the child respond differentially to the targets of positive and of fearful messages? In order to respond differentially to each target, the child must make the referential link between what was communicated and the target to which each communication referred. In this way, social referencing is communication in which two people communicate information about a third person or external object.

Even if children do not make the appropriate referential link between a caregiver's message and the target to which it refers, affective communications might still influence children's behavior. That is, a caregiver's affective expressions might be interpreted by a young child as referring to the child him- or herself or to the current interaction. Children may "match" the caregiver's affect through processes of affect sharing (Tronick, 1982), affect matching (Malatesta & Haviland, 1982), attunement (Stern, Hofer, Haft, & Dore, 1985), or contagion (Sagi & Hoffman, 1976). All these similar processes can be thought of as types of affect regulation, because a child's affect changes in the direction of the parent's affect during the trials in which affect is displayed. Thus, children could match parental affect, although they have no understanding of the circumstances that elicited that affect. Children who are normally developing tend to regulate their affect in the direction of parents' affective messages by the end of their second year (Baxter, Knieps, & Walden, 1991) and possibly much sooner (Malatesta & Haviland, 1982; Tronick, 1982). We have no evidence that children with developmental delays match the affect of their caregivers, and some evidence suggests that children with delays do not show affect regulation (Baxter et al., 1991).

Children look longer and more often at their parents' expressions of fear than at their expressions of happiness (Walden & Ogan, 1988, Zarbatany & Lamb, 1985). This is also true when infants are presented with photographs of facial expressions of unfamiliar persons (Nelson & Dolgin, 1985). The behavior of normally developing children in social referencing procedures appears to be more influenced by their parents' fearful expressions than by their positive ones (Hornik, Risenhoover, & Gunnar, 1987). This may reflect greater signal value of fearful expressions to young children (Lanzetta & Orr, 1980; Walden & Ogan, 1988); that is, children may have a bias toward responding to potentially threatening events. Ellsworth and Smith (1988) suggested that this "conservative" strategy protects against misclassifying potentially dangerous situations as safe, which is a higher risk outcome than misclassifying benign situations. Thus, the more significant value of the negative expressions may produce the asymmetry found in looking at positive and negative expressions. Because fearful messages may contain critical information that is important for well-being, they may be attended to more closely than the less critical positive messages.

Social Referencing Skills

There are several skills that facilitate social referencing. One is the ability and propensity to inhibit behavior until referential information is obtained. Some children behave warily in general and are likely to inhibit behavior toward unusual stimuli until receiving information from others present. Other children behave more boldly and are likely to approach or even touch unfamiliar stimuli without referencing others. A number of scientists have suggested that wariness in the face of the unfamiliar represents an important individual difference in behavior (Bronson & Pankey, 1977; Kagan, Reznick, Snidman, Gibbons, & Johnson, 1988). Individual differences in the tendency to inhibit behavior without social input would be expected to influence the likelihood of social referencing and the behavior and affect regulation that may result. Walden and Ogan (1988) reported a developmental trend in wariness, when wariness was defined in terms of the temporal relation between looking at caregivers and touching novel toys in a social referencing procedure. Children who touched the novel toys before looking at caregivers were said to behave boldly, and children who delayed touching the toys until referencing their caregivers were said to behave warily. Older children were significantly more likely to behave warily than were younger children. Cross-sectional studies of infants at different ages suggest that a trend toward increased wariness appears to occur around 18 months of age. Walden et al. (1991) found that children who were intellectually delayed were less likely to behave warily than children with the same mental age who were normally developing. Among delayed children, there was no increase in wary behavior with advanced chronological or mental age from infancy through 4 years. Thus, children who are delayed might be expected to be less influenced by the emotional signals of their caregivers when interpreting and responding to novel situations. It is a matter for future research to discover if developing increased abilities in children with intellectual delays to inhibit behavior when faced with uncertainty may promote the effectiveness of social referential information in regulating their behavior and affect in new or unusual situations.

Infant attentional characteristics are important contributors to social referencing. Attention is thought to be an integral part of learning situations, since it partly determines what an individual learns from any given collection of stimulus cues. The abilities to sustain and to move attentional focus are both critical to social referencing (Bretherton, 1985). Joint and coordinated attention, in which a child learns to coordinate and distribute attention to objects and persons in the environment, may be an important precursor to the ability to learn from social interactions in general (Tomasello & Farrar, 1986) and from social referencing specifically (Walden et al., 1991). That is, in order to link a person's reaction to the appropriate eliciting stimulus, a child must be able to hold both in mind simultaneously, or at least to focus on the two sequentially (alternating from one to the other), linking them together.

Children who are normally developing show evidence of the ability to coordinate attention in the second year of life. There is some evidence that caregivers play an active role in scaffolding or supporting the development of coordinated attention by using interaction strategies that facilitate joint attention to people and objects (Smith, Adamson, & Bakeman, 1986). Furby (1974) suggested that lower mental functioning is associated with difficulty in inhibiting a response to one stimulus in order to shift attention to another stimulus. Our data on wariness were in line with this hypothesis, in that younger children and children who were developmentally delayed at any age were less likely to behave warily and inhibit behavior until the caregiver was referenced. We have only preliminary evidence linking attentional capacities to social referencing or to its effects of behavior and affect regulation (Walden & Johnson, 1990). Future work in this area should investigate the relation between infant attention and social referencing, as well as questions regarding whether attentional capabilities can be improved or increased with practice or training.

Attention to people and objects in the environment contributes to the ability to make the referential link between the affective communications contained in the social environment and the external objects to which they refer. However, actually making the appropriate referential link requires more than just attention to both factors. It also requires what Terrace (1985) called the principle of reference, the idea that words (or in this case, expressions) can map onto objects. By the age of roughly 4 months, a parent can direct an infant's attention to an object simply by looking at it (Bruner, 1983), and by the second half of the first year, pointing can direct an infant's attention to a target (Murphy & Messer, 1977). By the eighth month, there is a tendency for an infant to follow an adult's direction of gaze (Collis & Schaffer, 1975; Scaife & Bruner, 1975). Thus, by the end of the first year of life, infants who develop normally have notions of reference, as well as the ability to follow another's focus of attention when the referent is clear. A deficit in this area would be expected to create aberrations in social referencing outcomes.

Active social referencing involves an awareness that one's own mental state and that of another can be related, or of "intersubjectivity" (Bretherton, 1985). In order to seek social referential information, one must understand that another's interpretation can be inferred from his or her behavior and that the information is relevant to one's own interpretation. Thus, a distinction between the active search for information and the passive receipt of information has been proposed to be theoretically significant in the early development of social referencing (Campos, 1983).

Children can actively solicit communications from their caregivers or others, or they can be passive recipients of the messages of others. When children actively solicit information, they may do so with gaze or by means of other nonverbal requests such as pointing. Children may also use verbal requests, which may be combined with nonverbal strategies. The limited comprehension of verbal communications by infants implies that early affective social referencing must rely heavily on nonverbal expressions, such as facial expressions, vocal tone, or paralinguistic cues. This reliance changes with development, as children become more verbal and add linguistic strategies to their repertoire. Infants' performances when they have limited verbal skills also suggest that nonverbal gestures and cues or paralinguistic features of communications (Caron et al., 1988; Fernald, 1989) may be the primary sources of information that infants use to understand the content of messages and identify the referents of the communications.

We do not know yet if differences in search activities of the learner affect social referencing. That is, do children who obtain social referential information through an active search differ in their use of the information from children who simply passively receive the messages? The answer to this question may have implications for the functioning of children who are intellectually delayed when compared to children who are normally developing. Walden et al. (1991) reported that although children with developmental delays initiate looks at their parents as often, and their parents give them as many messages as parents of children who are normally developing, the timing of the parents in giving messages that *coincided* with their children's looks was less accurate for dyads with a child who was intellectually delayed. Parents of children with delays often timed their messages to occur when their children were not looking at them. Thus, they may have been in states of attentional engagement that were not optimal for making the referential link between parents' messages and the eliciting stimuli. Because these children with developmental delays gave a higher proportion of looks that were considered ambiguous, Walden et al. (1991) speculated that poorer quality signals produced by the children with delays contributed to the parents' difficulty in responding contingently. Although the children with delays received many social referential messages from their parents, they showed no evidence of behavior regulation toward the targets of their parents' messages. Thus, it is possible that the timing of parents' messages may facilitate or interfere with children's use of social information to regulate their behavior appropriately.

The Medium or the Message?

Scientists have grappled very little with questions of exactly *what* is communicated in instances of social referencing (cf. Hornik & Gunnar, 1988). Is affect communicated? Or is instrumental information communicated? Perhaps a general sense of security is communicated by the presence or responsiveness of another individual. This is related to the idea that social referencing is hypothesized to be partly a function of uncertainty (Feinman, 1982), but uncertainty about what? Is the child uncertain about what to do? How to feel? How to interpret the event? Are all these decisions made in concert or are they dependent on different factors? Differences in such processes make these distinctions important.

Most studies of social referencing to date have confounded the different aspects of messages. Parents are instructed to produce specific, designated, affective expressions, but within this task, they deviate in their expressive communications. Some parents include both affective expressions and instrumental information ("Ooo, scary! Don't touch it!") in their messages. In a study of the messages produced by mothers instructed to encourage their children to play with a particular toy, Hornik and Gunnar (1988) reported that mothers smiled when their infants looked at them 95% of the time, and 96% of all messages had positive hedonic tone. However, 79% of the messages contained instrumental information (what to do), whereas 7% contained affective information (how to feel), and 8% contained both instrumental and affective information. They concluded that, "Mothers best help the child to like a new, ambiguous event by telling the toddler how to act and what to do while providing information about how to feel largely through facial expressions" (p. 629).

Furthermore, studies of social referencing have thus far confounded the medium with the message. Parents or other caregivers are usually the providers of social referential messages to children, and it is possible that a valuable message would be worthless if delivered by an unfamiliar person. For example, the message "Don't worry. I'm here and I'll take care of you," communicated by a stranger may transmit less actual information about how to respond than when it is communicated by the infant's parent. One study, in which information was provided by strangers to year-old infants, did report behavior regulation based on social referencing (Klinnert, Emde, & Butterfield, 1983), and Hirshberg and Svejda (1990) reported no differences in social referencing of mothers compared to fathers.

Parents vary in the type and quality of the social referential messages that they give their children. Some parents give clear and informative messages. Others give ambiguous messages or more neutral messages. Some parents emphasize instrumental information, and others focus more directly on affective messages. These variations undoubtedly influence children's behavior and affect, and the influence may change with age (Knieps & Walden, 1991). Part of the message is communicated through linguistic content (although in our studies we inhibit parents from using what is probably the most effective linguistic form, "No!"), and part of the message is communicated through facial expressions, vocal tone, gestures, and other body movements.

Social Referencing as an Interaction

Data from our project suggest that social referencing may build upon behaviors that have served other functions earlier (Walden & Ogan, 1988). Behaviors that have been taken as indices of attachment—looking at parents in the presence of an arousing stimulus, for example—may take on referential and intentionally communicative functions when social referencing begins. Younger infants' looks tend to be quicker glances and are less likely to focus exclusively on the parents' faces than the looks of older children. The topology of young infants' looks suggests that they function to check on the continuing presence of the caregiver, rather than to seek information about interpreting an external stimulus. The behavior of these younger children toward external arousing stimuli is not influenced by the communicative messages they receive from their parents; however, parents provide these messages to their young infants anyway. The messages are effective in influencing young infants' affect (in that young infants tend to match their parent's affect, showing positive expressions when their parents are positive and negative expressions when their parents are negative). There is no evidence that these young infants understand the referential nature of the communication. Later, toward the end of the first year, children begin to use conventional means of communicating (e.g., gestures, referential looks) and come to understand that their parents can be useful sources of information, because the parents have often displayed this kind of information (affective reactions) in the past. At this point, children use their parents' communications to regulate their behavior toward the eliciting stimuli. Thus, parents may contribute to the development of social referencing by having been reliable providers of information and affect in past interactions.

Infant attention is thought to be an integral part of learning situations, significantly determining what children learn. The abilities to sustain and to shift attentional focus, mentioned previously, are critical to this process. Coordinated joint attention, in which a child learns to coordinate attention to objects and persons in the environment, is an important precursor to the ability to learn from interpersonal interactions via social referencing.

Children probably do not develop these abilities without help from those around them. Learning about the environment is a problem to be solved, and early problem-solving activities are best accomplished with collaboration and support from more expert persons. The child's learning during joint attention may be dependent, in part, on a caregiver's sensitivity to the child's attentional, motor, and cognitive abilities. The parent's use of attention-directing strategies that are concordant with the child's abilities can provide a scaffold for learning experiences. Parents control certain components of the task so that within their capabilities children can attend to and learn from those components (Heckhausen, 1987; Hodapp, Goldfield, & Boyatzis, 1984;

Smith et al., 1986). The caregiver modifies input in relation to his or her perception of the child's need for assistance. Specialized assistance is tailored to the child and to the situation. Specialized assistance may be even more critical to a child with developmental disabilities.

There are several ways in which parents can assist their infants with attentional tasks early in their development. One very early task of the infant is to sustain attention to an object or person. The infant can be assisted in this task by an expert who provides a scaffold to support this behavior. For example, a parent can help an infant to sustain attention by appropriately timing interactions to occur at the infant's best times, that is, during periods of calm alertness. The caregiver also controls the length and pace of interactions. Attention is best sustained through the use of compelling stimuli in a setting free from other distractions. With development, the infant acquires the ability to sustain attention to a physical or social stimulus. At this point, the parent may be able to follow the infant's attention and join in, without redirecting the focus of attention. Toward the end of the first year, parents may be able to redirect the infant's focus of attention. Redirecting attention has gradations, also. For example, an 8- or 9-month-old infant will follow the direction of another person's gaze, but only if the other person's face is within his or her field of vision. Only later will an infant follow another's gaze if he or she has to look to see the other person. A similar developmental trend is true of following the direction of gestural pointing.

For some children, controlling attention and behavior is a difficult task. Parents of these children may help or attempt to help the child succeed in this task by the sensitive use of strategies that make it more likely that the child will control his or her attention and behavior. Studies of the relation between parental scaffolding and infant performance have yet to clearly demonstrate the predicted facilitation of infant performance with appropriate-level mediation compared to infant performance with inappropriate-level scaffolding (Heckhausen, 1987; Hodapp et al., 1984).

In our study of the importance of the timing of messages, we found data consistent with the hypothesis that parents of children with developmental delays are more directive than parents of normally developing children (Walden et al., 1991). Consistent with other studies that have suggested that parents of children with developmental delays are more directive (Buckhalt, Rutherford, & Goldberg, 1978; Cardoso-Martins & Mervis, 1985; Field, 1980) in a social referencing situation, parents of children with delays sometimes bombarded their children with messages that showed no evidence of being solicited by the children. Nearly one third of the communications of parents who had children with delays were unsolicited, compared with one tenth in the normally developing group. The reason for this parent behavior was not addressed in this study. Providing unsolicited messages might be a good strategy if it helped children to use information appropriately; for example, it might be helpful if children used the information to regulate their behavior toward the referent of the parent's message. However, the children with developmental delays did not show evidence that they regulated their behavior in this manner. Nor did the parents who were more directive have children who showed enhanced behavior regulation relative to children of less directive parents.

Walden et al. (1991) speculated that the unsolicited social referential messages may have represented attempts to redirect the child's attention toward the parent and thus encourage social referencing or social interaction in general. This may be an example of a "lower-limit" reaction described by Bell (1979), in which an interaction partner attempts to stimulate or prime insufficient or nonexistent behavior of the other. Although this parental behavior may not have facilitated behavior regulation, perhaps it facilitated social interaction in general or other aspects of social referencing (e.g., referential looks, which were found to be at least as frequent for children who had developmental delays as for normally developing children with equivalent mental ages). Thus, unsolicited messages may have served to scaffold referential looks for the children with delays but not to facilitate behavior regulation. These speculations are consistent with the meager data pertinent to this issue, but they have not been tested by any studies with sufficiently strong research designs.

CONCLUSIONS

This chapter is not the first published paper to suggest that emotional communications are among the earliest forms of communication between the infant and other persons (Malatesta & Haviland, 1982; Stern, 1985; Tronick, 1982). Certainly, other forms of affective communication occur before the onset of social referencing. Affective communication may be the primary channel of communication for the young infant; however, it is supplemented by other forms of communication as the infant develops. Early affective communications may set the stage for social referencing to develop when the child begins to gain intersubjectivity and to master the principle of reference.

The work discussed in this chapter highlights the fact that a great deal of learning occurs in the context of social-affective relationships. This may be a particularly potent form of learning for the young child who is a novice in many situations and who must figure out how to feel and behave with respect to the many new events encountered every day.

Familiar caregivers who are sensitive to the growing child's developmental level may provide a scaffold for the child's responses so that the child can perform more competently in the context of the interaction than outside the interaction. In the early development of referential communication, the young child may require this type of scaffold to engage at all in joint referencing. The type and timing of social referential information should be varied to facilitate the child's understanding of the information and the ability to effectively use that information. No special conditions are needed for adequate performance when the necessary skills have developed. It is possible that social referencing may become an automatized strategy used in regulating the distribution of attention to various aspects of the environment and in information processing.

There are many skills requisite to social referencing, and infants vary in their competence to master all those skills. Deficits in any part of the process—from information search, to behavior inhibition, to regulation—could result in aberrant outcomes. During the last half of the first year of life, infants acquire and consolidate social referencing skills, and over the next year or two, social referencing becomes more refined and complex. We would expect that children with intellectual delays might have a protracted period of development during which deficits in at least one area might prevent smooth social referencing and behavior, as well as affect regulation.

Although social referencing can be reasonably reliably induced under experimental conditions, it occurs under a limited set of conditions (Sorce et al., 1985). Little is known about the aspects of situations that induce relatively more or less social referencing (Walden & Baxter, 1989). In this respect and in many others, we have a lot to learn about the influence of social referencing on behavior in naturally occurring situations of stress or uncertainty.

REFERENCES

Baxter, A., Knieps, L., & Walden, T. (1991). *Affective expressions of Down syndrome and normally developing infants in a social referencing situation.* Unpublished manuscript, Vanderbilt University, Nashville.

Bell, R.Q. (1979). Parent, child, and reciprocal influences. *American Psychologist, 34,* 821–826.

Bretherton, I. (1985). Social referencing and the interfacing of minds: A commentary on the views of Feinman and Campos. *Merrill-Palmer Quarterly, 30,* 419–427.

Bronson, G.W., & Pankey, W.B. (1977). On the distinction between fear and wariness. *Child Development, 48,* 1167–1183.

Brown, A., & DeLoache, J. (1978). Skills, plans, & self-regulation. In R.S. Siegler (Ed.), *Children's thinking: What develops?* (pp. 3–35). Hillsdale, NJ: Lawrence Erlbaum Associates.

Bruner, J. (1983). *Child's talk.* New York: Norton.

Buckhalt, J.A., Rutherford, R.B., & Goldberg, K.E. (1978). Verbal and nonverbal interaction of mothers with their Down's syndrome and nonretarded infants. *American Journal of Mental Deficiency, 82,* 337–343.

Campos, J. (1983). The importance of affective communication in social referencing: A commentary on Feinman. *Merrill-Palmer Quarterly, 29,* 83–87.

Cardoso-Martins, C., & Mervis, C. (1985). Maternal speech to prelinguistic children with Down syndrome. *American Journal of Mental Deficiency, 89,* 451–458.

Caron, A.J., Caron, R.F., & MacLean, D.J. (1988). Infant discrimination of naturalistic emotional expressions: The role of face and voice. *Child Development, 59,* 604–616.

Collis, G.M., & Schaffer, H.R. (1975). Synchronization of visual attention in mother-infant pairs. *Journal of Child Psychology and Psychiatry, 16,* 315–320.

Ellsworth, P., & Smith, C.A. (1988). Shades of joy: Patterns of appraisal differentiating pleasant emotions. *Cognition and Emotion, 2,* 301–331.

Feinman, S. (1982). Social referencing in infancy. *Merrill-Palmer Quarterly, 28,* 445–470.

Feinman, S., & Lewis, M. (1983). Social referencing at 10 months: A second order effect on infants' responses to strangers. *Child Development, 54,* 878–887.

Fernald, A. (1989). Intonation and communicative intent in mothers' speech to infants: Is the melody the message? *Child Development, 60,* 1497–1510.

Field, T.M. (1980). Interaction of high-risk infants: Quantitative and qualitative differences. In D. Savin, R. Hawkins, A. Walker, & J. Penticuff (Eds.), *Exceptional infant* (Vol. 4, pp. 120–143). New York: Brunner/Mazel.

Furby, L. (1974). Attentional habituation and mental retardation: A theoretical interpretation of MA and IQ differences in problem solving. *Human Development, 17,* 118–138.

Heckhausen, J. (1987). Balancing for weakness and challenging developmental potential: A longitudinal study of mother–infant dyads in apprenticeship interactions. *Developmental Psychology, 23,* 762–770.

Hirshberg, L., & Svejda, M. (1990). When infants look to their parents: I. Infants' social referencing of mothers compared to fathers. *Child Development, 61,* 1175–1186.

Hodapp, R., Goldfield, E., & Boyatzis, C. (1984). The use and effectiveness of maternal scaffolding in mother-infant games. *Child Development, 55,* 772–781.

Hornik, R., & Gunnar, M. (1988). A descriptive analysis of infant social referencing. *Child Development, 59,* 626–634.

Hornik, R., Risenhoover, N., & Gunnar, M. (1987). The effects of maternal positive, neutral and negative affective communications on infant responses to new toys. *Child Development, 58,* 937–944.

Kagan, J., Reznick, J.S., Snidman, N., Gibbons, J., & Johnson, M.O. (1988). Childhood derivatives of inhibition and lack of inhibition to the unfamiliar. *Child Development, 59,* 1580–1589.

Kerber, K., & Coles, M. (1978). The role of perceived physiological activity in affective judgments. *Journal of Experimental Social Psychology, 14,* 419–433.

Klinnert, M., Emde, R., & Butterfield, P. (1983). *Social referencing: The infant's use of emotional signals from a friendly adult with mother present.* Paper presented at the biennial meeting of the Society for Research in Child Development, Detroit.

Knieps, L., & Walden, T. (1991). *Characteristics of parental messages and infant social referencing.* Unpublished manuscript, Vanderbilt University, Nashville.

Lanzetta, J., & Orr, S. (1980). Influence of facial expressions on the classical conditioning of fear. *Journal of Personality and Social Psychology, 33,* 354–370.

Malatesta, C.Z., & Haviland, J. (1982). Learning display rules: The socialization of emotion and expression in infancy. *Child Development, 53,* 991–1003.

Murphy, D., & Messer, D. (1977). Mothers, infants, and pointing: A study of a gesture. In R.H. Schaffer (Ed.), *Studies in mother–infant instruction* (pp. 323–354). New York: Academic Press.

Nelson, C., & Dolgin, K. (1985). The generalized discrimination of facial expressions by seven-month-old infants. *Child Development, 56,* 58–61.

Sagi, A., & Hoffman, M.L. (1976). Empathic distress in newborns. *Developmental Psychology, 12,* 175–176.

Scaife, M., & Bruner, J. (1975). The capacity for joint visual attention in the infant. *Nature, 253,* 265–266.

Siegler, R.S., & Jenkins, E. (1989). *How children discover new strategies*. Hillsdale, NJ: Lawrence Erlbaum Associates.

Smith, C., Adamson, L., & Bakeman, R. (1986, April). *Interactional predictors of early language*. Paper presented at the fifth biennial International Conference on Infant Studies, Los Angeles.

Sorce, J., Emde, R., Campos, J., & Klinnert, M. (1985). Maternal emotional signaling: Its effect on the visual cliff behavior of 1-year-olds. *Developmental Psychology, 21,* 195–200.

Stern, D. (1985). *The interpersonal world of the human infant*. New York: Basic Books.

Stern, D.N., Hofer, L., Haft, W., & Dore, J. (1985). Affect attunement: The sharing of feeling states between mother and infant by means of intermodal fluency. In T. Field & N. Fox (Eds.), *Social perception in infants* (pp. 249–268). Norwood, NJ: Ablex.

Terrace, H.S. (1985). In the beginning was the "name." *American Psychologist, 40,* 1011–1028.

Tomasello, M., & Farrar, J. (1986). Joint attention and early language. *Child Development, 57,* 1454–1463.

Tronick, E. (1982). Affectivity and sharing. In E. Tronick (Ed.), *Social interchange in infancy* (pp. 1–6). Baltimore: University Park Press.

Walden, T., & Baxter, A. (1989). The effect of age and context on infant social referencing. *Child Development, 60,* 1511–1518.

Walden, T., & Johnson, K. (1990, April). *Infant attention and social referencing*. Paper presented at the seventh biennial International Conference on Infant Studies, Montreal.

Walden, T., Knieps, L., & Baxter, A. (1991). Contingent provision of social referential information by parents of normally developing and delayed children. *American Journal on Mental Retardation, 96,* 177–187.

Walden, T.A., & Ogan, T.A. (1988). The development of social referencing. *Child Development, 59,* 1230–1240.

Zarbatany, L., & Lamb, M. (1985). Social referencing as a function of information source: Mothers versus strangers. *Infant Behavior and Development, 8,* 25–33.

10

Affective Development and Communication in Young Children with Autism

Connie Kasari, Marian Sigman,
Nurit Yirmiya, and Peter Mundy

COMMUNICATION IS LARGELY A SOCIAL phenomenon. From the infant's earliest interactions of sharing affect and attention with the caregiver to later sophisticated discourse, the process of communication presumes a merging of attention and topic, an intersubjectivity. Intersubjectivity, defined as a "shared understanding that is based on a common focus of attention" (Rogoff, 1990, p. 71), can be assumed whether an interaction is verbal or nonverbal in nature.

The focus of this chapter is on the affective and communication development of young children with autism. In providing a theoretical framework for considering these abilities in children, we rely primarily on the concept of intersubjectivity from the Vygotskian school of psychology (Rogoff, 1990; Vygotsky, 1978; Wertsch, 1985). Interpretations of Vygotsky's theory have focused on developmental aspects of the infant's ability to establish intersubjectivity and on the role of the caregiver in guiding the process. In order for the process of communication and, in particular, intersubjectivity to progress, the theory presupposes that both adult and child are intact, normally developing organisms. In the case of autism, children exhibit significant social deficiencies that inhibit their ability to achieve intersubjectivity. In this chapter, we begin by examining the normal process of intersubjectivity in infancy and then focus on the child with autism. We examine the skill of the child with autism in achieving intersubjectivity by a focus on the child's abilities to share emotions and to achieve mutual engagement with others in several different

This research was supported by NIMH postdoctoral fellowship MH 16381 and NINCDS Grant No. 30526. Appreciation is extended to Angie Pena, Larry Epstein, Alma Lopez, Allison Anson, Alisa Hoffman, and Lisa Capps for their contributions to this work.

contexts. We consider the effect that an inability to engage in intersubjectivity—whether sharing affective states or attending to a partner vis-à-vis other events—has on other developing skills, including cognitive, language, and emotional abilities.

INTERSUBJECTIVITY IN INFANCY:
THE SHARING OF ATTENTION AND AFFECT

Intersubjectivity has much to do with shared meanings between individuals. Initially, infants and caregivers share emotional states. Later, they share attention to each other while incorporating objects or events into this shared focus. Therefore, intersubjectivity undergoes developmental change with respect to the topic being shared. Models of communication and emotional development have been devised that incorporate these developmental changes in intersubjectivity (Adamson & Bakeman, 1982; Klinnert, Campos, Sorce, Emde, & Svejda, 1983). The model of communication described by Adamson and Bakeman (1982) is particularly useful in organizing the developmental change in intersubjectivity.

In the first phase of communication, infants and caregivers engage in face-to-face interactions that involve sharing and regulation of mutual attention and affective expression. This phase of "affective reciprocity" (Adamson & Bakeman, 1982) or "primary intersubjectivity" (Trevarthen, 1979) is characterized by the sharing of affective information without any obvious indication that the infant is aware of the differentiation between self and other. While very young infants are capable of expressing affect patterns that represent the emotions of surprise, happiness, fear, sadness, anger, disgust, and pain (Emde, Gaensbauer, & Harmon, 1976; Izard, Huebner, Risser, McGinnes, & Dougherty, 1980), they are unable to discriminate the expressions of others (Klinnert et al., 1983). Consequently, at this stage they smile in response to both frowns and smiles of the caregiver. More importantly, during this period, the infant's facial expressions become important regulators of social interaction. For example, a smile may signal the caregiver to continue an interaction and a frown to change something about the interaction (Sorce & Emde, 1982).

Halfway through the first year of life, infants expand their attention from a primary focus on face-to-face interactions to include interest in objects or events external to the dyad. This change in behavior marks the beginning of the second phase of communicative development, sometimes referred to as "secondary intersubjectivity" (Trevarthen & Hubley, 1978). In this phase, the topic shifts from a two-person communication centered on self to a two-person communication regarding a third event (Klinnert et al., 1983). During the course of the next 12 months, infants develop the ability to react to the affective quality of a facial expression, share attention with another regarding some event or object (joint attention), and seek affective information from the caregiver (social referencing). These developments reflect the infant's changing awareness that others can see and are interested in what they see (Rheingold, Hay, & West, 1976). Joint attention and social referencing have a common characteristic in that both are three-way communications. In joint attention the child and caregiver are sharing a point of view about an event, while in social referencing the child is seeking emotional information from another regarding an event. These abilities differ to the extent that the event being shared is seen as ambiguous. An ambiguous event might be meeting a stranger or seeing a particular animal for the first time. Consequently, the child may look to the adult to obtain instrumental information (i.e., how to act toward the event) or emotional guidance (i.e., how to feel about the event) (Hornik & Gunnar, 1988). If the event being shared is viewed as clearly positive (e.g., seeing a favorite toy), the child may look to the adult in the context of positive affect for the sole purpose of sharing affect. These changes to three-way communication during the second phase of communication development are particularly important to the child's growing awareness of the differentiation between self and other (Bretherton, 1984).

This ability is expanded as children begin to use language and symbolic play, and this constitutes the third phase of communicative development. Children become increasingly able to label the emotional states and intentions of themselves and others and to project their own behaviors and feelings onto other recipients, such as dolls. Therefore, language and symbolic play, generally considered as cognitive skills, are also heavily dependent on social interest and social interaction.

SHARING OF ATTENTION AND AFFECT IN AUTISM

The foregoing literature cited on normal development provides a theoretically useful framework for exploring the early social development of children with autism. Because of the presumed relationship between language and earlier nonverbal behaviors (Bruner, 1975), several autism researchers have focused on nonverbal behaviors that occur prior to the development of language. Furthermore, there is a general belief that the social deficits characteristic of autism first appear in children's earliest interactions. Since children are diagnosed with autism after infancy, this belief is primarily founded in retrospective data. One study of autistic behavior in infancy has been reported. In this study, 16-week old fraternal twins, both assumed to be normal, were filmed separately in face-to-face interactions with their mother (Kubicek, 1980). Results of microanalytic coding revealed that compared to his brother, the twin later diagnosed with autism was characterized by a neutral facial expression, lack of eye contact, and rigid posturing. The reciprocity of affective sharing that was characteristic of the twin who was normal was lacking in the twin later diagnosed as autistic. This report gives credence to the belief of many parents that something is amiss early on in the social behavior of the child with autism.

In the following sections, we review studies on the establishment of intersubjectivity in the child with autism by focusing on the sharing of attention and affect with both familiar and unfamiliar people. We also explore how skill in intersubjectivity may be related to the child's understanding of emotion in others, as well as to his or her development of more advanced cognitive emotions.

Sharing of Attention

Intersubjectivity by definition requires joint patterns of attention between people. Children with autism have been noted for their tendency to avert their gaze from people (Kanner, 1943), their preoccupation with objects to the exclusion of faces (Hermelin & O'Connor, 1970), and their lack of differentiation between people (Kanner, 1943). Therefore, exploring the contexts in which children with autism are able to share attention with others is important in understanding their capacity for intersubjectivity.

Several early studies indicated that children with autism tended not to establish secondary intersubjectivity when interacting with others. They rarely pointed to external events, followed points, or alternated looking between objects and people when compared to normal children of similar mental levels (Curcio, 1978; Wetherby & Prutting, 1984). Because the majority of children with autism are also mentally retarded, and mentally retarded children tend to show fewer of these behaviors than mental age-matched normal controls (Greenwald & Leonard, 1979), it was unclear whether this deficit in sharing attention was related to autism or to developmental immaturity.

Studies of the ability of children with autism to share attention with both familiar and unfamiliar people, compared with children with mental retardation and children who are developing normally, have been carried out in our laboratory. The children's display of joint attention behaviors while interacting with an unfamiliar experimenter was assessed using an experimenter–child interaction that is commonly used with children with mental retardation and with children who are normally developing (Mundy, Seibert, & Hogan, 1984). Using this paradigm, we were able to assess three nonverbal functions: social interaction skills (behaviors used to engage in turn-taking with another), indicating or joint attention skills (behaviors used to direct or share the attention of the adult to an object or event), and requesting skills (behaviors used to elicit aid in obtaining objects or events).

Results of this study revealed that children with autism performed similarly to children with mental retardation and to children who were developing normally in their abilities to initiate and respond to social overtures and to initiate and respond to object requests of the experimenter (Mundy, Sigman,

Ungerer, & Sherman, 1986). However, children with autism were considerably impaired in their ability to direct or share attention with the experimenter. This deficit in indicating or joint attention skills appeared to be specific to autism because the children without autism did not show this inability.

Using two different paradigms, we have examined the use of mutual and joint attention in interactions with their caregivers by children with autism. In the first paradigm, children were observed with their parents during episodes of free play (with both caregiver and a stranger present), separation (with a stranger present and caregiver absent), and reunion (with a stranger and caregiver present). The behaviors of the children with autism were compared with those of children who were normally developing (Sigman & Ungerer, 1984) and with those of children with mental retardation, matched on mental age (Sigman & Mundy, 1989). Results of these studies indicated that episodes of mutual looking between caregivers and their children were comparable for all three groups. Furthermore, the children with autism were clearly able to differentiate between the caregiver and a stranger as assessed by the differences in the amount of social behavior (e.g., smiles, looks, touches) directed toward the adults. However, the play behavior of these children was quite different from the children who were developing normally. Compared with their peers, the children with autism showed little evidence of symbolic play with objects, particularly directed toward dolls. More importantly, in this situation, the children with autism were content to play with the toys alone. They rarely established intersubjectivity with the adult by showing objects or bringing objects to the parent to view. This failure to share interest in toys with the parent was quite unlike the behavior of the other children, who appeared eager to share their attention to and experiences with the toys.

In the situation described above, caregivers were asked not to interact with their children so that the children's attempts to initiate interactions could be examined. Using a different paradigm, we specifically asked caregivers to engage their children in interaction. The results yielded some similarities and differences in both child (Sigman, Mundy, Sherman, & Ungerer, 1986) and caregiver (Kasari, Sigman, Mundy, & Yirmiya, 1988) behaviors. The children with autism engaged in similar amounts of looking, smiling, and vocalizing with their caregivers compared with children without autism. However, a major difference in their behavior was that they tended not to show objects or point to objects or events with their caregivers. This finding was similar to their play behavior in the unstructured situation above and appeared to be unaltered by the active engagement of the caregiver. It seemed that the children with autism failed to understand that the parent might be interested in sharing their attention to or interest in a toy. In terms of caregiver behavior, parents of children with autism tended to hold their children on task more than other caregivers, perhaps in an attempt to achieve intersubjectivity. There was no difference in the amount of mutually sustained play that caregivers engaged in or in their responsiveness to their children's nonverbal signals. Moreover, all caregivers used similar strategies to direct their children's attention to and engagement with objects. Consequently, the difference in child behavior could not be attributed merely to differences in caregiver behavior.

Summary

In summary, it appears that in interactions with both familiar and unfamiliar people, children with autism clearly show an interest in social interaction and an awareness that another person can aid in obtaining objects or in performing acts. However, these children did display a specific pattern of social deficits. They appeared to lack intersubjectivity, which requires an appreciation that another person has a point of view, and an interest in objects or events that can be mutually shared. This lack of appreciation is evident especially in their failure to show toys to people and share attention of events or objects in structured and unstructured social interactions. Consequently, it appears that the social behavior of children with autism does not so much reflect social disinterest as a lack of social understanding. The lack of social understanding reflected in the failure to share attention with another person may be a precursor to the lack of understanding of another person's mental state that has been observed in older individuals with autism (Leslie & Happe, 1989). Studies investigating this possibility are needed.

These studies also raised questions concerning the sharing of affect by children with autism. In the model of communication proposed by Adamson and Bakeman (1982), sharing of affective states precedes the sharing of attention vis-à-vis other events. Affect, however, is presumed to be integrated into attentional states. Recent studies on affect expression and on the coordination of affect with other behaviors of children with autism are reviewed in the following sections.

Sharing of Affect

Investigating affect expression in children with autism poses unique problems for the researcher. One problem is that autism is not reliably diagnosed until late in the second or third year of life. By this time, children who are normally developing have often learned some cultural and personal rules for the display of emotional expressions (Malatesta, 1982; Saarni, 1978). In other words, they may be able to mask socially undesirable feelings with a facial expression. The majority of children diagnosed with autism are functioning in the mentally retarded range (Rutter, 1985). Because a concordance between level of cognitive functioning and affective behavior has been found (Decarie, 1978), the expression of affect is probably influenced by both experience and developmental level. Therefore, the researcher must take care in matching samples of children according to chronological and mental age. To answer some questions, mental age may need to be determined by a nonverbal measure, while in other cases, a verbal mental age measure is more appropriate (Sigman, 1989). Another problem is that children with autism are generally deficient in their understanding and expression of language. Consequently, researchers are constrained in their attempts to use self-report measures with these children. Instead, they must rely on observations of nonverbal behaviors. Even so, caution must be exercised in interpreting these affective nonverbal behaviors as directly reflecting inner experiences. If children with autism show different affect expressions, one cannot be certain if it is because they lack social interest or motivation or if they are unable to show conventional expressions although they experience emotional feeling. Regardless, caregivers routinely use a number of nonverbal behaviors to interpret what their children may be experiencing. These behaviors include vocal, gestural, and facial displays commonly attributed to particular emotional or feeling states. Studies of the affect of children with autism have generally focused on these categories of nonverbal behavior.

Initial Studies

In one of the earliest studies on emotional expression, Ricks (1979) examined the vocal expressions of children with autism under four situations designed to elicit particular emotions (e.g., frustration, surprise). Parents of the children with autism could identify their own child and the feeling conveyed by their child. However, parents of children with mental retardation and parents of children who were normally developing could not identify the emotional states of the children with autism, but they could identify the feelings of all of the other children. These results suggest that children without autism have a common nonverbal language to express feeling states, whereas the children with autism, although understood by their parents, expressed idiosyncratic vocalizations to signify a particular feeling.

In a study that examined gestural expressivity, Attwood, Frith, and Hermelin (1988) documented spontaneous use of gestures in social interactions in a variety of children (i.e., children with autism, mental retardation, or typical developmental patterns). The children were observed in two different situations: on the playground, where social interactions could be easily avoided, and during mealtime, where interactions were more difficult to avoid. The gestures used by the children were classified as deictic (i.e., pointing), instrumental (i.e., gestures used to regulate the behavior of another), and expressive (i.e., gestures used to express feelings). Results indicated that while the control groups engaged in all three types of gestures, the gestural behavior of the children with autism was conspicuous for the complete absence of expressive gestures. Furthermore, children with autism displayed very few deictic gestures. It appears, then, that the use of social gestures by children with autism was largely confined to instrumental gestures that require little appreciation of another person.

While gestures and vocalizations are important signals of affective behavior, facial expression is probably the most salient. Clinical reports vary as to the characteristics of facial expression of children with autism. In a survey of teachers and houseparents, children with autism were reported to show a range of affective responses, including smiling, laughing, and weeping expressions (Langdell, 1978). However, these were not common; most children's behavior was characterized by flatness in affect. The affective expression of surprise was reported as completely absent. Furthermore, when affect was expressed, it was reported to be fairly extreme, lacking the gradations or shading of expression typical of children who are normally developing. In addition, the affect expressions of children with autism generally did not appear contingent to the situation. Underlying these descriptions of the affective expression of the child with autism is the general sense that it is difficult to interpret the child's face according to conventional expressions indicating emotions.

Whether children with autism were capable of displaying facial expressions that could be recognized and interpreted by others was the focus of another study by Langdell (1981). In this study, children with autism, mental retardation, and who were normally developing of the same mental age were asked to assume a happy or sad face. These attempts were photographed, and judges independently rated if the attempt was well, adequately, or badly recognizable as the intended emotion. While judges had little difficulty recognizing the emotion that the children in the control group were attempting to display, they frequently found it difficult to interpret the attempts of the children with autism. Because it is not known from these results whether the children with autism had difficulty in expressing a certain emotion or had difficulty understanding the verbal instructions, Langdell (1981) repeated the study, this time with the children imitating an experimenter's facial expression. The results of this follow-up study yielded similar findings. Judges had much greater difficulty recognizing the expressions of the children with autism. However, the fact that other studies have found that children with autism show deficits in their ability to imitate (Dawson & Adams, 1984; Wing, 1976) makes the interpretation of these results as an indication solely of an expressive deficit less tenable.

The results of initial studies examining the affective expressiveness of children with autism suggested that there were idiosyncratic differences, or a paucity of gestural, vocal, and facial expressions of the children. Studies were lacking that directly observed facial expressions of children with autism while they were engaged in social interactions with others. With the advent of reliable and valid methodologies for examining facial expressions of children, recent studies have attempted to fill this void.

Facial Expression

Clinical observations of the facial expressions of individuals with autism have ranged from "apparent absence of emotional reaction" (American Psychiatric Association, 1987, p. 35) to "extremes of emotion in a way which is quite inappropriate for their age and the social situation" (Ricks & Wing, 1975, p. 201). Although for many years clinical reports had documented the unusual features of individual children, not until recently had researchers attempted to characterize empirically the affective characteristics of children with autism compared with appropriate control groups. In addressing this issue, the Langdell studies were problematic because of their reliance on verbal comprehension and imitation skill. At least two recent studies, using different methodologies, have examined the spontaneous facial expressions of children with autism without relying directly on cognitive processing abilities.

In a study by Snow, Hertzog, and Shapiro (1987), facial expressions of emotion were examined in children with autism. Children with autism, 2- to 4-years-old, were matched with children with mental retardation on mental age. Observations of spontaneous facial expressions were rated as positive, negative, or neutral using an interval coding system applied to videotaped play segments. The expressions were further classified as directed toward a social partner (teacher, psychiatrist, parent), directed toward objects, or random and unrelated. Results indicated that the children with autism displayed fewer intervals of affect (either positive or negative) and that they displayed significantly less positive affect than children with mental retardation who served as the comparison group. Furthermore, when they did display affect, they were less likely to direct expressions toward the social partner and more likely to show solitary-play or random, unrelated affect.

Children with autism may indeed exhibit patterns of facial expression that are syndrome-specific. Studies have found that children with mental retardation, particularly infants with Down syndrome, show patterns of facial expression that are different from infants who are normally developing (Brooks-Gunn & Lewis, 1982; Cicchetti & Sroufe, 1978). In fact, in two recent studies, children with Down syndrome were found to display positive affect significantly more often than mental age-matched children who were normally developing (Kasari, Mundy, Yirmiya, & Sigman, 1990; Loveland, 1987). Therefore, the observation that children with autism show less positive affect than children with mental retardation may not be that surprising if recent data on the affect expressiveness of these children is considered. Because the Snow et al. (1987) study did not employ a control group of children who were developing normally, it is not known if the difference in the display of positive affect is specific to autism or to mental retardation.

This issue has been addressed directly in a study from our laboratory (Yirmiya, Kasari, Sigman, & Mundy, 1989). The study was unique in several ways. First, it compared the expressions of children with autism to those of children with mental retardation (half diagnosed with Down syndrome and half with unknown etiologies) matched on mental and chronological age and to expressions of children who were normally developing matched on mental age. This is important because only by employing these control groups can one determine if a particular affective characteristic of the children with autism is specific to autism or is a general deficit associated with mental retardation. Second, the study utilized methodology that involves the micro-analytic coding of affect expressions. This type of methodology has been extensively used with children who are developing normally (Izard, Kagan, & Zajonc, 1984) and has been found to be reliable and valid (Matias, Cohn, & Ross, 1989). The approach to coding facial expression uses an anatomically based system that observes discrete changes in facial musculature to determine reliable facial expressions (Izard, 1979). Codes assigned to muscle changes are then translated into a priori formulas that are interpreted as representing a specific feeling state (i.e., emotion). Third, observations of children were conducted in a standard interaction situation. The paradigm used was the child–experimenter interaction designed to assess prelinguistic communication skills that was described previously (see Mundy et al., 1986).

Two questions regarding the facial expressions of children with autism were investigated. These questions were derived directly from clinical reports. The first question focused on whether children with autism would display expressions of affect less often than other children. That is, would they show more neutral affect, as had been observed clinically? A second question was concerned with the issue of clarity. We were particularly interested in whether these children would show more blends of expression that potentially would compromise the interpretation of expressed emotion.

Results indicated that all three groups of children displayed expressions of affect for comparable periods of time. In this analysis, the amount of time children showed a flat or neutral expression was subtracted from periods of time when they showed any affect expression. These data indicated that the children with autism were not more neutral or flat in their facial expressions than the other children. In fact, quite the opposite was found. Children with autism displayed significantly more of the coded affect expressions compared with the children without autism.

Discrete expressions indicating positive, negative, neutral, and interest emotions were also examined. The groups differed only in the amount of time they showed expressions of negative affect. Children with autism displayed negative expressions for a significantly greater percentage of time than the other groups. However, the percentage of time that all children showed negative expressions was very low overall (1.27% of the session for children with autism and less than 1% for each of the other two groups). More importantly, in this study, no difference was found in the percentage of time that each group displayed positive, neutral, or interest expressions, although there was a nonsignificant trend for the children with autism to show less positive affect.

In an attempt to examine the issue of clarity of expression, blends of affect expressions were compared. A blend is the simultaneous combination of two or more expressions. That is, the face does not exhibit the complete muscle configurations that would reliably indicate one particular emotion. Blends in this study were grouped into three categories: positive blends (e.g., a combination of joy and surprise), negative blends (e.g., a combination of fear and anger), and incongruous blends (e.g., a combination of joy and anger). Overall, blends of emotional expressions accounted for only a small percentage of total time. The number of children displaying positive blends did not differ for the three groups; however, the number showing negative and incongruous blends did. A greater number of children with autism expressed negative and incongruous blends than did other children.

Based on the results of this study, the facial expressions displayed by the children with autism showed a pattern of affect that was both similar to and different from children who were mentally retarded and children who were normally developing of comparable mental age. These results are interesting from a number of perspectives. First, the children with autism, as the other children, spent the majority of the interaction displaying positive, neutral, or interest expressions. The clinical impression that the affect of children with autism is more flat or that children with autism are lacking in facial expressiveness compared with other children was not borne out by these data. Instead, the children with autism displayed a greater variety of expressions, including more blends of expressions.

The difference in the presence of blends probably contributes to the impression that children with autism are less clear in their displays of facial expression. Blends undoubtedly compromise clarity, because the face is giving a mixed message about what the child is feeling (at least based on the conventional appearance of the expression). It must be noted, however, that the overall display of expression blends was a very small percentage of the total affect display. On the one hand, it is possible that relatively brief and infrequent displays of expression blends may not be perceived by the receiver and, therefore, have little impact on the affective sharing of the interactive experience, or interpretation of affective meaning, between the experimenter and child. This would seem especially likely if blends were expressed that "fit" the interaction. For example, blends of positive affects (e.g., joy and interest) expressed during a positively toned interaction would not raise much speculation as to the intent of the sender's affective state. On the other hand, it is unclear what impact even relatively brief and infrequent displays of affect blends have on an interaction when they do not fit the interaction. Blends of negative (e.g., sadness and fear) and incongruous (e.g., joy and anger) affect that occur in the context of a positive interaction are likely to raise the receiver's suspicions as to the sender's affective state or intent. Overall, it is unclear what effect the pattern of affective blends displayed by the children with autism might have on others, but this pattern was clearly different from that displayed by the other children.

Another difference was that the children with autism showed negative affect in a situation that typically elicited positive affect in the other children. This would suggest that children with autism enjoyed the experience less or were less interested in it than the other children. However, evidence from our previous research suggests that this is not the case. In this same situation, the assessment of nonverbal communication skills indicated that the children with autism did not differ from the children without autism in their initiation and response to social interaction behaviors or in their attempts to elicit behaviors from the adult. For example, they reached out to the adult to have a song and a tickle repeated, and they gave toys to the adult to wind or otherwise activate as much as other children did. In fact the only difference found was in their limited use of behaviors to direct or share attention with the adult. As stated previously, this difference was not attributed to children with autism being less interested in the interaction. Rather, it was hypothesized as reflecting a lack of understanding that others have a point of view that can be shared.

The results of our study on the facial expressions of children with autism might also suggest that the difference in affect display reflects a lack of social understanding more than social disinterest. The children with autism showed as many expressions of interest and positive affect as the other children. Although they displayed more negative and incongruous blends than other children, these were a relatively small percentage overall. Furthermore, the presence of blends might indicate that the children with autism were less clear about the adult's social intent and had less understanding of the social situation.

In the affect studies we have reviewed, differences were found in expressivity in the vocal, gestural, and facial channels separately. Typically, we observe and interpret several channels of communication at once. It may be that it is the lack of coherence of social behavior that is most peculiar to autism (Lord, 1984; Rutter, 1985). Two recent studies have documented discrepancies in the coherence of affect and attention among young children with autism (Dawson, Hill, Spencer, & Galpert, 1990; Kasari, Sigman, Mundy, & Yirmiya, 1990). In both studies, the children with autism and the control children showed comparable amounts of positive affect. Differences emerged when the coordination of attention and affect were examined. In the Dawson et al. (1990) study, the children with autism coordinated positive affect with looking at their mothers significantly less often than the control group children who were normally developing. In other words, the children with autism appeared less able to use affect as a communicative signal. In the Kasari et al. (1990) study, the focus of the study was on children's integration of affect with nonverbal communication gestures. Positive affect was expected to be differentially expressed according to the function of nonverbal communication gestures, which was implied by Bruner (1981) when he wrote that there must be some "mood marking procedure to distinguish indicating from commanding or requesting" (p. 67). Therefore, in this study, children's affect expressions, attention to people and objects, and nonverbal communication gestures of requesting and joint attention were coded second-by-second during the prelinguistic communication procedure described earlier (Mundy et al., 1986). As hypothesized, the children who were normally developing expressed positive affect differentially with requesting and joint attention acts. They were more likely to share positive affect with an adult when they were indicating interest in or sharing the experience of an event or toy than when requesting assistance with toys. In contrast, the children with autism differed significantly from the children without autism in their failure to display high levels of positive affect during joint attention interactions. That is, even when they did share attention with another person for the sole purpose of sharing the event, they rarely did so with positive affect. As in the Dawson et al. (1990) study, the children with autism seemed less able to use affect to communicate with another person.

Summary

These results suggest that children with autism appear different from other children in that their facial expressions do not always match the social context. They tend not to use attentional patterns or gestures to achieve intersubjectivity, and they also appear less likely to use positive affect to give meaning to joint patterns of attention. A related question is whether their responses to the emotions or feelings of other persons are also different from those of other children.

RECOGNITION AND RESPONSE TO EMOTION IN OTHERS

The difficulties that children with autism experience in intersubjectivity, specifically in sharing affect and attention, are with abilities that develop in the first 2 years of life in normally developing infants. During this period, infants also learn to recognize and differentiate specific emotions in others, such as the difference between anger and joy. Later in early childhood, children begin to respond to complex social emotions that require a certain degree of cognitive ability. For example, children learn to evaluate their performance by comparing it with some standard and begin to feel pride when their performance matches or exceeds the standard.

The extent to which difficulties in sharing and expressing affect and attention influence a child's responsiveness to the emotions of another and to his or her development of more advanced emotions has not been investigated.

However, there is evidence that the reactions of children with autism to the emotions of others, the understanding of these emotions, and the development of certain complex emotions is impaired relative to children without autism. Emotion recognition studies have generally been conducted with older individuals with autism. In a series of studies by Hobson (1983, 1986), children with autism and nonverbal mental age-matched children without autism were tested to determine their ability to match various components of feeling states with facial expressions. In these studies, the children were asked to match videotaped segments or pictures of gestures, vocalizations, or contexts to drawn or photographed pictures of objects and facial expressions of emotion. Results showed that all of the children could appropriately match the gestures, sounds, and situations to nonpersonal objects (e.g., bird, train). In contrast, the children with autism were markedly deficient in their ability to match the various components with facial expressions. In another matching task, children with pervasive developmental disorders (PDD) and children who were normally developing and matched for mental age were tested for their ability to match objects, faces, and affects (Braverman, Fein, Lucci, & Waterhouse, 1989). These tasks were designed to be comparable in level of difficulty. Results indicated that the PDD children were more impaired on face and affect matching than on object matching, but the effects were quite small. Similar findings were reported by Ozonoff, Pennington, and Rogers (1990). However, in the latter study, the effects disappeared when children were matched on a verbal measure of mental age.

The inability of children with autism to recognize expressions of emotions may reflect a general insensitivity to faces. In two related studies, Jennings (1973) and Weeks and Hobson (1987) found that children with autism showed a preference in matching photographs based on accessories (i.e., hats) rather than facial expression. In these experiments, a correct response could match the photographs on the basis of similarity in hats or match on the basis of similarity in facial expression. Results indicated that the children without autism of similar mental age sorted the pictures by facial expressions, whereas nearly all of the children with autism sorted by hats. Langdell (1978) examined the abilities of three groups of children (children with autism, children with mental retardation, and children who were normally developing) to recognize their classmates from partially covered or inverted photographs. He found that the children with autism tended to be better at recognizing their classmates using the lower portion of the face in contrast to the other groups of children who tended to use the upper portion of the face. The children with autism did equally well at recognizing faces whether upright or inverted, unlike the children without autism, who experienced great difficulty in recognizing inverted faces. He concluded that for the child with autism, a face represented merely a visual pattern of single details that were easy to recognize regardless of orientation, as opposed to a meaningful social pattern of integrated features.

Hobson, Ouston, and Lee (1989) extended this investigation through a study of the ability of children with autism to recognize identity and emotions in faces, compared with children with mental retardation matched on chronological age and verbal ability. Using this matching procedure, they found that the children with autism were as able as children with mental retardation to match emotions and identity when a full face was shown. However, when specific features were covered, as in the Langdell (1981) study, children with autism had much greater difficulty matching emotions than matching identity. The children with autism were also more proficient in recognizing identity and emotion in upside-down faces than were the children with mental retardation. The results of this study corroborated Langdell's earlier findings; however, the differences were smaller when children were matched for verbal abilities.

In general, knowledge of the ability of younger children with autism to recognize and respond to the emotions of others is limited. However, in a recent study, the responses of young children with autism to various negative emotions in other people and their ability to reference others for information regarding ambiguous events was investigated (Sigman, Kasari, Kwon, & Yirmiya, in press). Children were observed as an adult feigned distress (after pretending to hurt her finger), discomfort (fell ill while playing with child), and fear (in response to a mechanical toy that suddenly entered the room). The results indicated that the greatest difference between the children with autism and other children was in the nearly complete lack of attention by the children with autism to the person displaying the emotion, whether distress, discomfort, or fear. Unlike the other children, who showed a great deal of interest in or concern for the adult, the children with autism often turned away from or ignored the emotional display of the adult. It is unclear from these results whether the children with autism ignored the adult because they did not recognize or understand the emotion, or if they avoided contact for other reasons. Other studies are needed to address this issue.

DEVELOPMENT OF COMPLEX SOCIAL EMOTIONS

The majority of studies conducted on emotion in children with autism have focused on the expression or recognition of simple or primary emotions, such as sadness, joy, and anger. Few studies have examined the development of higher level emotional abilities in children with autism, such as pride, embarrassment, and empathy. Development of complex emotions requires certain cognitive advances and greater understanding of social situations. For example, the development of pride depends on an understanding of self as a distinct entity (Lewis, in press) and an awareness of the implications of one's accomplishments according to normative standards (Stipek, 1983). Young children are in some degree dependent upon others to provide feedback as to whether their accomplishments are "pride worthy," so the role of an audience is also important. Because children with autism have difficulty making inferences about another person's mental state and appreciating the beliefs, emotions, and desires of others (Baron-Cohen, 1991; Baron-Cohen, Leslie, & Frith, 1985; Leslie & Frith, 1988; Ozonoff, Pennington, & Rogers, 1989), their ability to experience complex emotions may be particularly impaired.

We recently observed young children with autism in an achievement context that commonly elicits pride-like responses in children who are normally developing (Kasari, Sigman, Baumgartner, & Stipek, in press). Three groups of children (children with autism, children with mental retardation, and children who were normally developing) were given developmentally appropriate puzzles to complete and were praised for completing the second, but not the first, puzzle. Results indicated that children with autism were just as likely as other children to smile when they completed the puzzles. That is, children with autism appeared to take as much pleasure in their achievements as children without autism. However, children with autism were less likely to seek another's attention for their achievement, either by explicitly calling attention to the completed puzzle or by looking at the person. In fact, one third of the children with autism actually looked away from the adult. Stipek, Recchia, and McClintic (1992) have proposed that attention seeking in toddlers is evidence of self-reflective processes that are presumed to be associated with pride. Our results, therefore, failed to provide evidence for pride— in the sense of a self-reflective and socially mediated emotion—in children with autism. The most consistent differences between the children with and children without autism were found in the praise condition. Children with autism were less likely to respond positively to praise, and less likely to attempt to make contact with the praising adult by looking up or turning toward him or her. Based on the results of this study, we cannot say that children with autism do not experience pride. However, the nature of pride (e.g., the degree to which it is socially mediated) and the situations in which it is experienced (e.g., social versus independent) may be different for children with and children without autism.

Studies are needed that examine the emotional responses of children with autism in other situations, for example, their empathic responses to peers in distress. Studies are also needed that explore these children's feelings or experiences in situations that commonly elicit complex social emotions in other children.

Recently, we examined empathy in a sample of children with autism who tested within the normal range of intelligence and who were between the ages of 9–16 (Yirmiya, Sigman, Kasari, & Mundy, 1992). Children were asked to identify the emotion experienced by the protagonist in videotaped vignettes and to report their own emotional response. Although the children with autism did better than expected, they did worse than the normally developing children in the control group in assuming the perspective of another person and responding affectively. Children were also asked to give examples of a personal experience of certain emotions, such as happiness, sadness, anger, pride, and embarrassment. The children with autism had the greatest difficulty recounting appropriate examples of pride and embarrassment (Capps, Yirmiya, & Sigman, in press). Their responses tended to be more labored (requiring more prompts to complete their response and the use of more "I think" phrases), and they gave more scripted or stereotyped examples. They also rarely gave examples of embarrassment that suggested the presence of an audience. These results suggest that the behavioral responses of children with autism in situations designed to elicit complex social emotions, and their feelings and experiences with these emotions, may be limited.

SUMMARY AND FUTURE DIRECTIONS

Although clinical reports portray a picture of autistic behavior that shows little social awareness, we have presented data that take issue with some of these commonly held notions. Rather than a pervasive lack of responsiveness to other people, recent data suggest that there are specific areas in which children with autism have social difficulty (Mundy & Sigman, 1989). These areas appear to share an underlying theme. That is, the social deficits seem to be based on a common inability of children with autism to share or regulate affective meaning with others. This lack of affective sharing is particularly apparent in the abilities of young children with autism to use attention-regulating gestures and affective expressions. Children who are normally developing learn these abilities during the period of infancy. Therefore, the inability to share affect and attention may reflect one of the earliest deficit areas of autism and may be partly responsible for the observed deficits in the later developing abilities of symbolic play, language, theory of mind, and complex social emotions, such as empathy. These later developing abilities are dependent on a certain level of social understanding and social interaction skills. The studies we have reviewed show that children with autism are very much interested in interacting with others who are both familiar and unfamiliar to them. Therefore, it seems that the social interaction deficits of children with autism result from a lack of social understanding and not from social disinterest. Their particular difficulties in relating to others may stem from a failure to understand the subtleties of social interactions, which typically involve a complex integration of affective and attentional behaviors.

Future research investigations need to focus on the links between abilities in affective sharing and later developing abilities. Longitudinal studies would be useful in investigating how an inability in achieving intersubjectivity with another person may be related to later observed difficulties in complex emotions and theory of mind. Studies are also needed that examine the responses of children with autism in other emotion eliciting situations. How do children respond to distress observed in their peers? What is the relation between the children who respond most empathically and their cognitive and communicative abilities? Can interventions that facilitate empathic responding increase the frequency with which it occurs? Do children in such interventions report or appear to have more satisfying relationships with others?

Intervention efforts have rarely focused on facilitating change in the affect or emotion of children with autism. There is some recent evidence, however, that facilitating moderate levels of shared positive affect may have beneficial effects. In a study of young children with autism, Rogers and Lewis (1989) found that their intervention strategy resulted in the development of closer interpersonal relationships and greater gains in cognitive, language, and social abilities. These abilities were maintained or increased over a year-long treatment period. Their treatment strategy recognized the important role of positive affect by facilitating moderately strong, positive affect during learning activities in order to increase the interpersonal relationship of the child and the adult. Moreover, it was believed that the positively oriented intervention approach increased the child's attention and motivation, resulting in more opportunities to learn through imitation and social interactions. Other intervention studies are needed that examine the important role positive affect may play in facilitating social-communicative and cognitive change in children with autism. In addition, interventions focused on teaching children the "language of emotion" (i.e., the ability to talk about emotional experiences) might facilitate richer communication and social interaction experiences. In achieving this difficult task, an intervention approach that incorporates aspects of Vygotskian theory, such as learning in the zone of proximal development and the achievement of intersubjectivity, may be beneficial.

REFERENCES

Adamson, L., & Bakeman, R. (1982). Affectivity and reference: Concepts, methods, and techniques in the study of communication development of 6-to-18-month-old infants. In T. Field & A. Fogel (Eds.), *Emotion and early interaction* (pp. 213–236). Hillsdale, NJ: Lawrence Erlbaum Associates.

American Psychiatric Association (APA). (1987). *Diagnostic and statistical manual of mental disorders* (3rd ed., rev.). Washington, DC: Author.

Attwood, A.J., Frith, U., & Hermelin, B. (1988). The understanding and use of interpersonal gestures by autistic and Down's syndrome children. *Journal of Autism and Developmental Disorders, 18,* 241–257.

Baron-Cohen, S. (1991). Do people with autism understand what causes emotion? *Child Development, 62,* 385–395.

Baron-Cohen, S., Leslie, A.M., & Frith, U. (1985). Does the autistic child have a "theory of mind"? *Cognition, 21*, 37–46.

Braverman, M., Fein, D., Lucci, D., & Waterhouse, L. (1989). Affect comprehension in children with pervasive developmental disorders. *Journal of Autism and Developmental Disorders, 19*, 301–316.

Bretherton, I. (1984). *Symbolic play: The development of social understanding*. Orlando, FL: Academic Press.

Brooks-Gunn, J., & Lewis, M. (1982). Affective exchanges between normal and handicapped infants and their mothers. In T. Field & A. Fogel (Eds.), *Emotion and early interaction* (pp. 161–188). Hillsdale, NJ: Lawrence Erlbaum Associates.

Bruner, J. (1975). The ontogenesis of speech acts. *Journal of Child Language, 2*, 1–19.

Bruner, J. (1981). Learning how to do things with words. In J. Bruner & A. Garton (Eds.), *Human growth and development* (pp. 62–84). London: Oxford University Press.

Capps, L., Yirmiya, N., & Sigman, M. (in press). Understanding of simple and complex emotions in non-retarded children with autism. *Journal of Child Psychology and Psychiatry*.

Cicchetti, D., & Sroufe, L. A. (1978). An organizational view of affect: Illustration from the study of Down's syndrome infants. In M. Lewis & L. A. Rosenblum (Eds.), *The development of affect* (pp. 309–350). New York: Plenum.

Curcio, F. (1978). Sensorimotor functioning and communication in mute children with autism. *Journal of Autism and Childhood Schizophrenia, 2*, 264–287.

Dawson, G., & Adams, A. (1984). Imitation and social responsiveness in children with autism. *Journal of Abnormal Child Psychology, 12*, 209–225.

Dawson, G., Hill, D., Spencer, A., Galpert, L., & Watson, L. (1990). Affective exchanges between young autistic children and their mothers. *Journal of Abnormal Child Psychology, 18*, 335–345.

Decarie, T.G. (1978). Affect development and cognition in a Piagetian context. In M. Lewis & L. Rosenblum (Eds.), *The development of affect* (pp. 183–204). New York: Plenum.

Ekman, P. (1982). *Emotion in the human face* (2nd ed.). New York: Cambridge University Press.

Emde, R.N., Gaensbauer, T.J., & Harmon, R.J. (1976). *Emotional expression in infancy*. New York: International Universities Press.

Greenwald, C., & Leonard, L. (1979). Communicative and sensorimotor development of Down's syndrome children. *American Journal of Mental Deficiency, 84*, 296–303.

Hermelin, B., & O'Connor, N. (1970). *Psychological experiments with children with autism*. Elmsford, NY: Pergamon.

Hobson, R.P. (1983). The autistic child's recognition of age-related features of people, animals and things. *British Journal of Developmental Psychology, 1*, 343–352.

Hobson, R.P. (1986). The autistic child's appraisal of expressions of emotion. *Journal of Child Psychology and Psychiatry, 27*, 321–342.

Hobson, R.P., Ouston, J., & Lee, A. (1989). Naming emotions in faces and voices: Abilities and disabilities in autism and mental retardation. *British Journal of Developmental Psychology, 7*, 237–250.

Hornik, R., & Gunnar, M. (1988). A descriptive analysis of infant social referencing. *Child Development, 59*, 626–634.

Izard, C.E. (1979). *The maximally discriminative facial movement coding system (MAX)*. Newark: University of Delaware.

Izard, C.E., Huebner, R.R., Risser, D., McGinnes, G., & Dougherty, L. (1980). The young infant's ability to produce discrete emotion expressions. *Developmental Psychology, 16*, 132–140.

Izard, C.E., Kagan, J., & Zajonc, R.B. (1984). *Emotions, cognition and behavior*. New York: Cambridge University Press.

Jennings, W.B. (1973). *A study of the preference for affective cues in children with autism*. Unpublished doctoral dissertation, Memphis State University.

Kanner, L. (1943). Autistic disturbance of affective contact. *Nervous Child, 2*, 217–250.

Kasari, C., Mundy, P., Yirmiya, N., & Sigman, M. (1990). Affect and attention in children with Down syndrome. *American Journal on Mental Retardation, 95*, 55–67.

Kasari, C., Sigman, M., Baumgartner, P., & Stipek, D. J. (in press). Pride and mastery in children with autism. *Journal of Child Psychology and Psychiatry*.

Kasari, C., Sigman, M., Mundy, P., & Yirmiya, N. (1988). Caregiver interactions with children with autism. *Journal of Abnormal Child Psychology, 16*, 45–56.

Kasari, C., Sigman, M., Mundy, P., & Yirmiya, N. (1990). Affective sharing in the context of joint attention interactions of normal, autistic, and mentally retarded children. *Journal of Autism and Developmental Disorders, 20*, 87–100.

Klinnert, M.D., Campos, J.J., Sorce, J.F., Emde, R.N., & Svejda, M. (1983). Emotions as behavior regulators: Social referencing in infancy. In R. Plutchnik & H. Kellerman (Eds.), *Emotion: Theory, research and experience* (Vol. 2, pp. 57–86). New York: Academic Press.

Kubicek, L.F. (1980). Organization in two mother–infant interactions involving a normal infant and his fraternal twin brother who was later diagnosed as autistic. In T.M. Field, S. Goldberg, D. Stern, & A.M. Sostek (Eds.), *High-risk infants and children: Adult and peer interactions* (pp. 99–110). New York: Academic Press.

Langdell, T. (1978). Recognition of faces: An approach to the study of autism. *Journal of Child Psychology and Psychiatry, 19*, 255–268.

Langdell, T. (1981). *Face perception: An approach to the study of autism*. Unpublished doctoral dissertation, University of London.

Leslie, A., & Firth, U. (1988). Autistic children's understanding of seeing, knowing and believing. *Briatish Journal of Developmental Psychology, 6*, 315–324.

Leslie, A., & Happé, F. (1989). Autism and ostensive communication: The relevance of metarepresentation. *Development and Psychopathology, 1*, 205–212.

Lewis, M. (in press). Thinking and feeling: The elephant's tail. In C. Maher, M. Schwebel, & N. Fagley (Eds.), *Thinking and problem solving in the developmental process: International perspectives*. New Brunswick, NJ: Rutgers University Press.

Lord, C. (1984). The development of peer relations in children with autism. In F.J. Morrison, C. Lord, & D.P. Keating (Eds.), *Applied developmental psychology* (pp. 166–230). New York: Academic Press.

Loveland, K.A. (1987). Behavior of young children with Down syndrome before the mirror: Finding things reflected. *Child Development, 58*, 928–936.

Malatesta, C.Z. (1982). The expression and regulation of emotion: A lifespan perspective. In T. Field & A. Fogel (Eds.), *Emotion and early interaction* (pp. 1–24). Hillsdale, NJ: Lawrence Erlbaum Associates.

Matias, R., Cohn, J.F., & Ross, S. (1989). A comparison of two systems that code infant affective expression. *Developmental Psychology, 25*, 483–489.

Mundy, P., Seibert, J., & Hogan, A. (1984). Relationships between sensorimotor and early communication abilities in developmentally delayed children. *Merrill-Palmer Quarterly, 30*, 33–48.

Mundy, P., & Sigman, M. (1989). Specifying the nature of the social impairment in autism. In G. Dawson (Ed.), *Autism: New perspectives on diagnosis, nature, and treatment* (pp. 3–21). New York: Guilford.

Mundy, P., Sigman, M., Ungerer, J.A., & Sherman, T. (1986). Defining the social deficits in autism: The contribution of nonverbal communication measures. *Journal of Child Psychology and Psychiatry, 27,* 657–669.

Ozonoff, S., Pennington, B.F., & Rogers, S.J. (1990). Are there emotion perception deficits in young children with autism? *Journal of Child Psychology and Psychiatry, 51,* 343–361.

Rheingold, H.L., Hay, D.F., & West, M.J. (1976). Sharing in the second year of life. *Child Development, 47,* 1148–1158.

Ricks, D.M. (1979). Making sense of experience to make sensible sounds. In M. Bullowa (Ed.), *Before speech: The beginning of interpersonal communication* (pp. 245–268). New York: Cambridge University Press.

Ricks, D.M., & Wing, L. (1975). Language, communication, and the use of symbols in normal and autistic children. *Journal of Autism and Childhood Schizophrenia, 5,* 191–221.

Rogers, S.J., & Lewis, H. (1989). An effective day treatment model for young children with pervasive developmental disorders. *Journal of the American Academy of Child and Adolescent Psychiatry, 28,* 207–214.

Rogoff, B. (1990). *Apprenticeship in thinking: Cognitive development in social context.* New York: Oxford University Press.

Rutter, M. (1985). Infantile autism and other pervasive developmental disorders. In M. Rutter & L. Hersov (Eds.), *Child and adolescent psychiatry: Modern approaches* (pp. 545–566). Oxford: Blackwell Scientific Publications.

Saarni, C. (1978). Cognitive and communicative features of emotional experience, or do you show what you think you feel? In M. Lewis & L. Rosenblum (Eds.), *The development of affect* (pp. 361–375). New York: Plenum.

Sigman, M. (1989). The application of developmental knowledge to a clinical problem: The study of childhood autism. In D. Cicchetti (Ed.), *The emergence of a discipline: Rochester symposium on developmental psychopathology.* Hillsdale, NJ: Lawrence Erlbaum Associates.

Sigman, M., Kasari, C., Kwon, J.H., & Yirmiya, N. (in press). Response to negative emotion in others in children with autism. *Child Development.*

Sigman, M., & Mundy, P. (1989). The development of social attachments in children with autism. *Journal of the American Academy of Child and Adolescent Psychiatry, 28,* 74–81.

Sigman, M., Mundy, P., Sherman, T., & Ungerer, J.A. (1986). Social interactions of autistic, mentally retarded, and normal children with their caregivers. *Journal of Child Psychology and Psychiatry, 27,* 647–655.

Sigman, M., & Ungerer, J.A. (1984). Attachment behaviors in autistic children. *Journal of Autism and Developmental Disorders, 14,* 231–244.

Snow, M.E., Hertzog, M.E., & Shapiro, T. (1987). Expressions of emotion in young children with autism. *Journal of the American Academy of Child and Adolescent Psychiatry, 26,* 836–838.

Sorce, J.F., & Emde, R.N. (1982). The meaning of infant emotional expressions: Regularities in caregiving responses in normal and Down's syndrome infants. *Journal of Child Psychology and Psychiatry, 23,* 145–158.

Stipek, D. (1983). A developmental analysis of pride and shame. *Human Development, 26,* 42–54.

Stipek, D., Recchia, S., & McClintic, S. (1992). Self-evaluation in young children. *SRCD Monographs, 57* (1, Serial No. 226).

Trevarthen, C. (1979). Communication and cooperation in early infancy: A description of primary subjectivity. In M. Bullowa (Ed.), *Before speech: The beginning of interpersonal communication* (pp. 321–347). New York: Cambridge University Press.

Trevarthen, C., & Hubley, P. (1978). Secondary intersubjectivity: Confidence, confiding and acts of meaning in the first year. In A. Lock (Ed.), *Action, gesture, and symbol* (pp. 183–229). London: Academic Press.

Vygotsky, L.S. (1978). *Mind in society: The development of higher psychological processes*. Cambridge, MA: Harvard University Press.

Weeks, S.J., & Hobson, R.P. (1987). The salience of facial expression for children with autism. *Journal of Child Psychology and Psychiatry, 28*, 137–151.

Wertsch, J.V. (1985). *Vygotsky and the social formation of mind*. Cambridge, MA: Harvard University Press.

Wetherby, A.M., & Prutting, C.A. (1984). Profiles of communicative and cognitive-social abilities in children with autism. *Journal of Speech and Hearing Research, 27*, 367–377.

Wing, L. (1976). Epidemiology and theories of aetiology. In L. Wing (Ed.), *Early childhood autism* (2nd ed., pp. 65–92). Oxford: Pergamon.

Yirmiya, N., Kasari, C., Sigman, M., & Mundy, P. (1989). Facial expression of affect in autistic, mentally retarded, and normal children. *Journal of Child Psychology and Psychiatry, 30*, 725–735.

Yirmiya, N., Sigman, M., Kasari, C., & Mundy, P. (1992). Empathy and cognition in high-functioning children with autism. *Child Development, 63*, 150–160.

11

Speech Intelligibility and Communicative Competence in Children

Raymond D. Kent

T HE SOCIAL USE OF LANGUAGE implies interaction. Indeed, language itself is predicated on interaction, specifically, the exchange of verbal information between two or more persons. An essential aspect of verbal interaction is mutual intelligibility. Unfortunately, mutual intelligibility cannot be assumed for many children with language impairment. In addition to other difficulties they may have, these children often rely on a spoken language that is understood with difficulty, if at all, by their listeners. Imagine, for example, a clinician who attempts a language analysis for the following exchange:

Clinician:	"Tell me what you did today."
Child:	[unintelligible]
Clinician:	"Could you say that again?"
Child:	[unintelligible]
Clinician:	[trying another tack] "What's your favorite toy?"
Child:	[unintelligible]

Certainly, communication isn't always as difficult as in this example, but unintelligible utterances, whether words, phrases, or whole sentences, appear with considerable frequency in language transcripts. Their appearance reminds us that children are not always easily understood. Children become aware of their failures to communicate, and they may react in various ways. One child may become reticent to speak, and another may rely on simple (predictable) language structures.

This work was supported in part by P.H.S. Research Grant No. DC00319 from the National Institute on Deafness and Other Communication Disorders.

ROLE OF INTELLIGIBILITY IN THE SOCIAL USE OF LANGUAGE

This chapter considers the role of intelligibility as a critical factor in determining how children use language in social situations. Speech intelligibility can facilitate or inhibit a child's social use of language. The child with a severe intelligibility deficit enters communicative settings with an immediate obstacle that must be overcome. The means of overcoming this obstacle are various, including avoidance of talking, simplification of vocal utterances, reliance on nonverbal gestures, increasing redundancy or contextual support, and, finally, simply expecting communication to be difficult. Intelligibility is critical to communicative success and is, therefore, a fundamental concern in the assessment of children's social use of language. In fact, intelligibility can figure critically in any assessment of spoken language.

DEFINITION OF INTELLIGIBILITY

One way of defining intelligibility is in terms of discrimination (Connolly, 1986; Kent, Weismer, Kent, & Rosenbek, 1989). Usually, the discrimination occurs among words in a lexicon shared by speaker and listener. The listener discriminates the words actually or potentially produced by the speaker. As words are identified, the listener can parse sentences (assign syntactic functions to words as they are heard) and infer the meaning of the speaker's utterance. Less commonly, the word spoken is not in the listener's lexicon, in which case the listener relies almost entirely on contextual factors to infer the speaker's meaning or communicative intent. In this definition of intelligibility, speaker and listener are engaged in a cooperative process. The speaker's responsibility is to provide sufficient information in the acoustic signal of speech so that the listener can determine, or at least hypothesize, the speaker's linguistic message. The listener's responsibility is to attend to the speech signal and apply the various types of knowledge needed to decode that signal. The knowledge to be applied varies with the speaker and the circumstances of the communication. Types of knowledge include knowledge of phonetic structure of the language, communicative context, speaker attributes, social setting, and constraints on message formulation or transmission.

A narrower conceptualization of intelligibility is specific to the speaker and emphasizes the capability of the speaker to produce an understandable spoken message. In this view, intelligibility is an attribute of an individual speaker, rather than an attribute of a communicative situation involving at least one speaker and one listener. This narrow definition of intelligibility is often assumed explicitly or implicitly in applied tasks, such as clinical assessment of communicative function. For example, the objective of clinical appraisal may be to offer conclusions such as "Tommy's speech is 50% intelligible."

Although the narrow conceptualization just discussed is often used in practice, it is always *incorrect*. The seriousness of the error stems from the same factors that make this narrow definition untenable in general applications. An intelligibility score is not an absolute quantity but is rather a function of factors such as test material, personnel, training, and test procedures (Flanagan, 1972). Clinical research shows that different intelligibility scores may result when the same speakers are rated with different materials (Frearson, 1985; Monsen, 1983). The intelligibility score is not an attribute of the speaker alone but rather an attribute of, at the very least, the speaker–listener dyad, the speech content or materials, and the speaking situation. This interactive aspect of intelligibility has long been recognized in evaluating transmission systems in communication engineering, but perhaps it has been underestimated in the clinical evaluation of children's speech.

COMMUNICATIVE COMPETENCE

Intelligibility is an important dimension of a larger construct, which might be called *communicative competence* or *determinability* (Connolly, 1986). Communication can fail for many reasons, including an unintelligible utterance, a lexical confusion between speaker and listener, a parsing error committed by the listener, a linguistic selection error on the part of the speaker, a pragmatically inappropriate verbal response, or a lapse of attention on the part of the listener. The overall process is subject to a number of frailties. Fortunately, general communication fares quite well in the face of inefficiencies and mistakes, partly because of offsetting factors that enhance the robustness of spoken language. For example, natural languages have a redundancy rate of about 50%, so that listeners do not need to hear the complete and unadulterated speech signal to derive an interpretation of it. Indeed, experiments on speech perception have shown that listeners can be totally unaware that selected sounds in a sentence have been replaced by a noise (Warren, 1984). In addition, the shared knowledge between listener and speaker helps to define the linguistic boundaries of communication by narrowing the realm of lexical and syntactic possibilities. Communication can be more difficult when speaker and listener have a common ground that is limited or uncertain. Spoken language is aided also by the adaptive nature of speech perception and word recognition. A speaker who is nearly unintelligible on first hearing often becomes more intelligible as the listener gains experience with the speaker's dialectical and idiolectal patterns.

Figure 1 shows three major approaches to the study of communicative competence (Politzer & McGroarty, 1983). The first approach emphasizes the

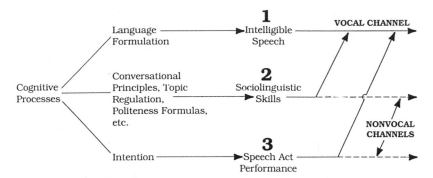

Figure 1. Three major approaches that have been taken to study communicative competence: 1) evaluation of intelligibility, 2) analysis of sociolinguistic skills, and 3) considerations of speech act performance.

intelligibility of the signal, that is, the degree to which information is conveyed or received. Work in this area has been strongly influenced by research in psychology and communication engineering (Wang, Rose, & Maxwell, 1973). The second approach is based on sociolinguistic research (Hymes, 1972a, 1972b) and focuses on the appropriateness of communication with respect to factors such as conversational principles, politeness conventions, topic regulation, and other sociolinguistic parameters. The third approach concentrates on speech act analyses of language (Austin, 1962; Searle, 1969) and seeks to define communicative competence in terms of successful performance of speech acts. Intelligibility is typically evaluated in terms of a vocal channel only, but communication has both vocal and nonvocal channels, the latter including visible characteristics such as gestures, facial expressions, and manipulation of the physical environment. The channels for each of the three approaches are shown on the right side of Figure 1. Allowance has been made for nonvocal channels of communication that may supplement or substitute for the vocal channel.

This chapter is concerned with intelligibility, but, as Figure 1 indicates, intelligibility is only one means of examining communicative competence. If we take a closer look at speech intelligibility itself, we find that several factors contribute to an intelligible speech sample.

Figure 2 is a heuristic model that is suggested for the investigation of intelligibility. Cognitive processes and language formulation give rise to a phonological representation of an utterance and a parallel set of affective reactions. The accompanying affective reactions constitute a paralinguistic component of spoken language. The phonological message and the affective reactions are motorically expressed as vocal behavior through the regulation of the three major subsystems of speaking—the respiratory, laryngeal, and

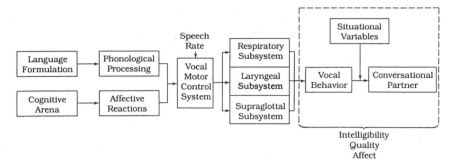

Figure 2.   Heuristic model for the study and assessment of intelligibility in a general framework leading from language formulation to vocal communication with a conversational partner.

supraglottal (or articulatory) subsystems. The output of the motor subsystems of speech is vocal behavior, which, subject to the influences of environmental and contextual factors, is apprehended by a listener (typically an interlocutor).

Each block in the diagram in Figure 2 contributes to the eventual spoken message, and each block is associated with a large research literature and a host of yet unanswered questions. Language formulation, a key element in this model, remains poorly understood, despite many valiant attempts to explain it (Levelt, 1989, offers a comprehensive overview). Furthermore, little is known about the ways in which the linguistic and emotional aspects of communication interact, particularly in the young child. Speech motor control is a difficult area of study, all the more so in the child's developing motor system. Without motor expression, there is no language modality. As Sperry (1952) observed, "The entire output of our thinking machine consists of nothing but patterns of motor coordination" (p. 297). Speech is the means by which thought, expressed as language, gains motor expression. Nonvocal channels, such as gestures, also can be used, whether to supplement the vocal channel or to substitute for it. The communicative event, then, is defined by vocal signals and accompanying behaviors such as eye contact, gestures, and environmental manipulation.

The intelligibility of a message is seriously challenged by deficiencies in speech production (e.g., by the limited speech and language abilities of a young child), by degradation of the speech signal (e.g., by ambient noise), and by inefficiencies or uncertainties in the processing of the speech message by the listener. All too often, the deleterious effects of these three factors are compounded, as when a young child with limited abilities in spoken language communicates with an unfamiliar person in a noisy setting.

ASSESSING THE INTELLIGIBILITY OF CHILDREN'S SPEECH

Interestingly, there is no commonly accepted test of intelligibility for children's speech. Tests abound for speech articulation proficiency, phonology, receptive vocabulary, receptive and productive syntax, and even pragmatics. When intelligibility is assessed, it is often evaluated impressionistically (Kent et al., 1989). On the one hand, this approach is understandable, given the difficulty of defining a measure appropriate to the task. On the other hand, the impressionistic judgment has questionable reliability and validity (Kent, 1992; Schiavetti, 1992). When quantitative methods are used, they often result in a perceptual rating scale, especially an equal interval scale. However, recent research (Schiavetti, 1992) demonstrates that this kind of scale may be psychometrically unsuited to intelligibility, which, being a prothetic dimension, is more appropriately scaled with direct magnitude estimation.

In addition, impressionistic verbal descriptions and rating-scale judgments suffice only as estimates of overall intelligibility. Their application yields only an index of communicative failure, and they offer little or no *analytic* potential. Such descriptions do not explain why the failure occurred and therefore do not substantially inform either the diagnostic process or the intervention process. Indeed, these procedures may even fail to distinguish among intelligibility, sociolinguistic, and speech act failures, as described in connection with Figure 1. These procedures also have shortcomings in yielding an overall index of intelligibility, for they are notorious for midscale insensitivity (Kent, 1992). Slight or severe impairments can be fairly reliably assessed, but variations within the midrange are often intolerably unreliable. Finally, impressionistic descriptions and rating-scale judgments are not easily related to other important domains of communication, such as articulatory proficiency.

The need, then, is for an assessment tool that: 1) permits an overall measure of intelligibility (i.e., an index of communicative dysfunction), 2) has analytic potential to disclose the reasons for reduced intelligibility, 3) can be applied over the entire range of intelligibility with acceptable sensitivity, and 4) can be interpreted within other relevant measures of speech and language function to gain an overall understanding of communicative competence.

Intelligibility based on word recognition seems most suited to these criteria. The word is a good candidate because it is easily elicited from pictures, conversation, or imitation. Words may be selected from age-appropriate vocabularies. The percent of words recognized is a useful overall measure of intelligibility. If the tested words are carefully chosen, errors in recognition may be analyzed to determine error patterns, such as phonetic features. Word recognition tests can be used over the full range of intelligibility. Finally, when words are used as the focus of intelligibility, the results can be related to a number of other speech-language processes, including vocabulary, phonology, and aspects of syntax. This is not to say that word recognition tests are the only way, or even the best way, to evaluate intelligibility. Ultimately, the best way to assess a speaker's intelligibility is with a word recognition test *and* a sentence (or conversational) test, at minimum.

To give a clearer picture of what is meant by a word-recognition intelligibility test, a short description is given of such a test that is under development. The test, tentatively called the Children's Phonologically Structured Intelligibility Test (CPSIT), is a word-identification test in which the stimuli are grouped into phonological subsets identified with developmental levels of vowel and consonant mastery (Dinnsen, Chin, Elbert, & Powell, 1990; Haelsig & Madison, 1986; Hodson & Paden, 1990; Sander, 1972). The construction of the test with respect to developmental phonological categories offers several advantages for both research and clinical application. First, because the phonological construction reflects normal development (the general pattern of which also applies to many children with speech-language disorders [Tallal, 1988]), the structure of the test is keyed to the expected developmental pattern. The advantage is that a 3-year-old child with an immature phonological system need not be tested on phonetic contrasts that typically are mastered much later in childhood. The combined phonological-developmental construction also gives the examiner an immediate opportunity to judge the child's performance relative to the normal pattern.

A second advantage to this test construction is that a number of word candidates can be used to evaluate a given phonological contrast. For example, evaluation of a child's ability to produce the syllable-initial voicing contrast (that distinguishes word pairs such as "pig-big") can be performed with a variety of word pairs that contrast phonetically only in this feature. This aspect of the test is particularly important in assessing management, since a contrast can be trained with some word pairs and tested with other (untrained) pairs.

A third advantage of the phonological structuring is that it enables an analytic interpretation of an intelligibility deficit. Two individuals with the same overall intelligibility score do not necessarily have the same speech difficulties (Kent et al., 1989; Ziegler, Hartmann & von Cramon, 1988). Ideally, an intelligibility test should do more than provide a relative estimate of impairment; it should also give some insight into the basis of that impairment.

The basic structure of the CPSIT is described in Table 1. The word pairs given in the table are illustrative and do not constitute a complete list of words. (Generally, words within the vocabulary of young children are preferred.) The listeners' responses can be analyzed to yield both an overall score (percent of words correctly transmitted), several phonological contrast scores (based on the error rates for each subset), and a composite contrast score (the

Table 1. Phonetic contrasts and sample word pairs for the Children's Phonologically Structured Intelligibility Test (CPSIT)

Subset (phonetic contrast)	Sample word pairs
1. corner vowels /i u a/	she-shoe, me-ma, hoop-hop
2. diphthongs /aɪ/, /ɔɪ/ and /aʊ/	bye-boy, boy-bow, hi-how
3. additional vowel contrasts	hit-hate, hate-hat, fit-foot
4. stop-nasal	my-bye, do-new, pan-pad
5. stop-glide	ball-wall, yell-dell, bye-why
6. syllable-initial voicing	bye-pie, bat-pat, down-town, game-came
7. anterior-nonanterior	see-she, so-show, take-cake
8. fricative-affricate	shoe-chew, wash-watch, share-chair
9. liquid-nonliquid	lawn-yawn, run-done
10. strident-nonstrident	sing-thing, bash-bath
11. lateral-rhotic	lake-rake, light-right
12. syllable structure CV-CVC	tie-tight, my-might
13. syllable structure CVC-CCVC	pot-spot, sick-stick, tough-stuff
14. syllable structure CVC-CVCC	sick-six, kid-kids

means of the error rates for a group of subset scores, for example, subsets 4, 5, 8, 9, and 11 constitute a composite subset for manner of consonant articulation; and subsets 12, 13, and 14 constitute a composite subset for syllable structure). This approach has been informative in research on children with hearing impairments (Boothroyd, 1985) and dysarthria in adults (Kent et al., 1989; Kent et al., 1990).

This type of intelligibility assessment seems to hold promise for the study of early spoken language development in children with Down syndrome. Miolo, Kent, and Miller (1991) used a version of the CPSIT to evaluate the speech intelligibility of eight children with Down syndrome (mean age of 62 months; range of 55–72 months). The scores on the intelligibility test were highly correlated (Spearman rank correlation coefficient) with three other measures of expressive language. The correlations and measures were: 0.88 with the percentage intelligibility computed from the Systematic Analysis of Language Transcripts (SALT [Miller & Chapman, 1986]), 0.86 with the Early Language Inventory (Bates et al., 1986), and 0.81 with mean length of utterance in morphemes obtained from SALT. The analytic potential of the intelligibility test was demonstrated by its ability to differentiate children in terms of their difficulties with particular phonetic contrasts.

The intelligibility of a speaker's message is determined by several factors, and the interaction of these factors complicates the analysis of intelligibility deficits. However, a child's intelligibility can be evaluated to achieve at least a first-level separation of the major factors represented in Figure 2. Of particular importance are language formulation, phonological processing, and vocal motor control system. Language formulation is discussed following a consideration of phonology and vocal motor control. The cognitive and affective components are not treated at any length in this chapter, except as they directly relate to issues of language formulation.

Phonology, defined as the sound patterning of language, is immediately relevant, because phonological patterns that deviate from the adult standard of a language can greatly impair intelligibility. Indeed, studies of children with phonological disorders implicitly define highly unintelligible children as those with severe phonological disorders. However, it should be noted that phonological disorders can cover a broad range of etiologies, including neurologic dysfunction, craniofacial anomalies, hearing impairment, specific learning problems, in addition to a large group of disorders of unknown etiology (Shriberg, Kwiatkowski, Best, Hengst, & Terselic-Weber, 1986). The patterning of sounds in language is not synonymous with intelligibility, but some degree of conformance to adult phonological patterns is a common denominator of intelligible speech. Phonology (at least phonology of the segmental variety) consists at the least of an inventory of sounds and a regulatory system that governs the contextual use of these sounds.

As might be expected, intelligibility is inversely correlated with the number of phonological errors in a child's speech (Billman, 1986; Hodson & Paden, 1990; Vihman & Greenlee, 1987). Billman (1986) reported a significant correlation between the average score for percentage of occurrence of phonological processes and the average intelligibility score (the latter based on the average number of words correctly identified by four adult listeners from a total of 100 words produced). However, the phonological processes that were most highly correlated with reduced intelligibility were prevocalic singleton omissions (e.g., [æ t] for "cat") and backing (e.g., [k ɔ I] for "toy"). These two processes occur *infrequently.* This result indicates that certain less frequently occurring processes may have special diagnostic value. In addition, whereas children with moderate phonological impairment tend to have phonological patterns in which substitution processes dominate, children with severe phonological disorders tend to use a combination of substitution and sequential processes (Hodson, 1982; Hodson & Paden, 1983; Nettelbladt, 1983; Yavas & Lamprecht, 1988). Examples of substitution processes are backing ([k u] for "two"), palatal fronting ([s i] for "she"), and liquid gliding ([w ɛ d] for "red"). Examples of sequential processes are cluster reduction ([g i n] for "green"), weak syllable deletion ([p ɑ k] for "pocket"), final fricative deletion ([k I] for "kiss"), and labial assimilation ([s p u m] for "spoon").

Phonology is also concerned with sound sequences and combinations. The child learning to speak gradually masters the production of an element in a variety of linguistic and phonetic contexts. Speech is a motor skill, but a special motor skill, in which motor processes are coordinated with linguistic propositions and formulations. Vocal motor control can be assessed with a number of published or unpublished procedures. Hodge (in press) describes a thorough and clinically useful assessment of speech motor control in children. The assessment of motor control can be combined with the results of conventional articulation tests or a test such as CPSIT to create an integrated picture of a child's speech production capabilities.

The issue of variability in children's speech behavior should be underscored. Speech, in both its phonological and motoric aspects, is more variable in children than in adults (Kent & Forner, 1980). As a result, the acoustic pattern of a given utterance is less repeatable in a child's speech than in an adult's speech. The greater variability of a child's productions may make the listener's task more difficult. Some aspects of the pattern of speech are largely predictable, as long as the speaker conforms to the adult standard of language and speaking skill. However, predictability may be diminished in a child's production. Consequently, listeners are less able to make use of top-down (predictive) processes in speech perception. This possibility is one aspect of the concept of intelligibility that involves, at minimum, a talker, a communicative setting, and a listener. The speaker and listener both bring knowledge to the communicative act, but in some cases, the utility of the listener's knowledge depends on the capabilities of the speaker.

A THREEFOLD NESTING FOR ASSESSMENT

Figure 1 portrays the components that need to be addressed in research on communicative competence. This illustration also represents basic processes that are involved in the task of speaking and, therefore, processes relevant in the assessment of children's communicative competence. These processes are mutually limiting and facilitating. The child who has a severe intelligibility impairment often has limited communicative resources. The intention to communicate must be linked with sufficiently intelligible speech and appropriate sociolinguistic parameters. Deficiencies in any one area can limit flexibility in the others. Intelligibility difficulties, in particular, can impair the development of communication. Abbeduto (personal communication, June, 1990) has suggested that children with limited intelligibility may circumvent these limitations by using strategies that allow them to minimize talking. They might, for example, utter brief rather than informative descriptions in referential tasks, or use simple linguistic forms rather than contextually appropriate forms when making requests. The consequence of these strategies is that the children lose valuable opportunities and experiences in the social use of language. The development of sociolinguistic skills might be hampered by the child's reluctance to engage in a variety of communicative functions. Limitations in intelligibility also could impair a child's adaptability to various speaking situations, such as unfamiliar listeners, noisy or distracting environments, and new communicative settings.

A threefold concept for assessment is represented as: (Language use (Communicative competence (intelligibility))). That is, the social use of language subsumes communicative competence, which in turn subsumes intelligibility. Assessment procedures should recognize the nesting or interdependency of these components. Fortunately, some recent approaches place intelligibility in the larger communicative framework. Osberger (1992) proposes a Meaningful Use of Speech Scale (MUSS) that seeks to describe three basic features of the use of speech by a child with a hearing impairment in relation to general functions of communication. The first feature is the degree to which the child uses speech independently of supportive communicative functions such as gestures, signs, or other nonvocal methods. The second feature pertains to the degree to which the child's use of speech changes with familiarity of the listener. The third feature addresses the child's use of clarification and repair strategies. MUSS was developed for children with hearing impairments, but its principles should apply to many populations, particularly to children with reduced intelligibility of any kind. Indeed, clarification request sequences have been studied in children with language impairments (Brinton & Fujiki, 1982; Brinton, Fujiki, & Sonnenberg, 1988; Gallagher & Darnton, 1978; Garvey, 1977).

Osberger (1992) also conceptualized two primary factors that influence intelligibility in the form of a simple diagram composed of the two dimensions, Context (that varies from highly unpredictable to highly predictable) and Listener Experience (that varies from highly nonexperienced to highly experienced). Figure 3 elaborates on Osberger's idea by adding a third dimension, Complexity of Utterance (that varies from low to high). The resulting cube may be taken as a general scheme for expressing the conditions of intelligible speech. The easiest situation is the corner labeled 1, which corresponds to high context (therefore high predictability of message components), highly experienced listener, and low complexity of utterance. The most difficult situation is corner 7, which combines low context, highly inexperienced listener, and high utterance complexity. The cube diagram can be thought of as the space for the design of intervention. The clinician or teacher can select corners of the cube, that is, communicative situations, depending on the child's communicative status. A highly unintelligible child with impaired language formulation would be most successful in corner 1. As the child gains communicative facility, more demanding situations can be structured by moving along one or more of the cube dimensions. For example, once a child has developed a satisfactory degree of communicative competence in corner 1, the next intervention might work toward corner 2 (reducing contextual support), corner 4 (introducing a nonfamiliar listener), or corner 8 (increasing utterance

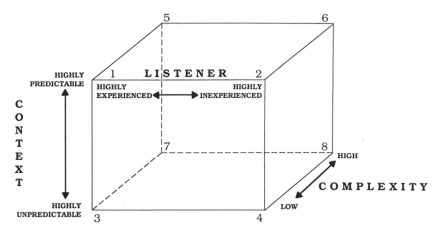

Figure 3. Three-dimensional diagram showing the primary dimensions that affect a child's speech intelligibility: listener familiarity or experience, context, and complexity of communication.

complexity). An example of moving from corner 1 to corner 2 is to remove toys or other visible objects from the communicative environment while retaining them as topics of communication.

Finally, Figure 4 is an alternative diagram of four dimensions of the child's social use of speech and language. The four dimensions are intelligibility, reliance on speech, appropriateness of communication, and use of clarification and repair strategies. Although these are not necessarily orthogonal elements of behavior, they are sufficiently independent that registration on each dimension has a useful descriptive or characterizing value. These elements also serve as basic dimensions in intervention planning.

This diagram illustrates that intelligibility is strongly related to the social use of language and may often be a limiting factor in a child's success in social communication. At the same time, intelligibility deficits should be understood in the larger context of a child's social use of language. The management of reduced intelligibility should take this context into account.

One implication of this discussion is that the most useful assessment of intelligibility might be accomplished through *triangulation*. This term is used in ethnography in a manner similar to its application in surveying, where triangulation means that a location is fixed by reference to other points. The ethnographer uses triangulation to study cultural phenomena that are not easily or validly measured by any single instrument. Perhaps the most useful way to measure a child's intelligibility is through triangulation involving a word intelligibility test, a sentence intelligibility test, and an assessment of conversational speech. This combination yields an assessment of a child's overall communicative ability. Modifications can be introduced in each pro-

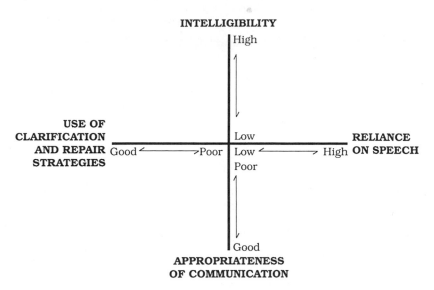

Figure 4.   The four principal dimensions of the child's orientation to the social use of language: intelligibility, reliance on speech, appropriateness of communication, and use of clarification and repair strategies.

cedure to assess the individual components illustrated in Figure 2. For example, conversation can be assessed with variations in situation and partner.

RESEARCH DIRECTIONS

A primary need for research is the development of reliable and informative tests of speech intelligibility for children. The rating-scale approaches commonly in use are of questionable reliability and usually provide little in the way of prognostic or management information. It seems unlikely that any one form of intelligibility test will suffice. Rather, assessment needs probably require at least two or three complementary tests, including one based on single-word recognition and another based on phrase, sentence, or conversational speech. Intelligibility is not a monolithic faculty but rather a multidimensional accomplishment that subsumes motor-phonetic skills, phonological knowledge, language formulation abilities, and sociolinguistic operations. Appropriate assessment tools are sorely needed for each of these areas and for their integration, which occurs in the act of speaking.

A challenging but important area of research is the exploration of how speech intelligibility interacts with social language usage. Obviously, intelligibility is an important dimension of language usage, but research is needed to determine how intelligibility deficits are related to various communication behaviors, including language formulation and conversational tactics. Research might also address the ways in which intelligibility interacts with other aspects of communication during interventions. The interventionist should be able to know when an intelligibility deficit interferes with language use to the extent that intelligibility itself is a necessary focus of intervention. It is also important to develop ways to distinguish a child's speech intelligibility from the other components of social language usage.

Hymes (1972a) proposed that speech events be analyzed in terms of the relations among 16 components mnemonically abbreviated as SPEAKING. The same idea can be applied to the analysis of speech intelligibility with the mnemonic device expanded as follows:

Setting: physical situation, ambient noise and lighting, visibility of conversational partners, and social context

Participants: familiarity, roles, and other characteristics of the persons involved in the communicative act

Energy: vocal effort or overall intensity level (Children do not always adjust their effort levels to account effectively for distance and noise variables.)

Adaptation: adjustment, in time, to situation, language function, and participants (requires monitoring, adaptation to perceived communication failure, and repair strategies)

Keys: emotion, tone or manner of the individual speech event

Inference: hypothecation based on information conveyed (Speech as a source of information is in some sense nearly always incomplete, so that the communicative partners must infer one another's communicative intents and messages.)

Norms: acoustic, phonetic, phonological, prosodic, and sociolinguistic norms apply to the communicative event (These norms can be specified both statistically and procedurally.)

Genre: formality, purpose, and other features that distinguish among speaking events (Speech has style registers that relate to intelligibility and shared knowledge.)

These components should be considered in plans for research or clinical management of children with communicative impairments. Although it may not be necessary to include each component in every research design or every management plan, the various components represent a menu from which the appropriate components can be selected. Few of these components have been sufficiently investigated. Frequently, research is designed to control for some of these factors, but not to explore their significance in socially functional language. Consider, for example, setting. Investigations of children's spoken language often place the research subject in a quiet environment with relatively few distracting stimuli. However, children typically contend with noisy, highly distracting environments. They may experience interruptions, simultaneous speech from others, and variable levels of background noise. How do children with language disorders cope with these environmental disturbances? Research also tends to examine spoken language under circumstances in which subjects communicate with a small set of partners (often one other person), in a particular situation, discussing a narrow range of topics. Accompanying behaviors such as emotion or accommodation may be ignored in the research design. How do children with language disorders handle predictable or unpredictable variations in audience, situation, or topic? Granted, it may be too much to ask that any one research project consider all the factors in SPEAKING, but it does seem appropriate to examine them in a long-term research effort.

Intelligibility has been the center of this chapter, partly because intelligibility has been a rather neglected aspect in studies of the social use of language, but also because intelligibility does play a central role in spoken language. In particular, intelligibility places overall limits on spoken language, and social language is usually spoken language. A fundamental question to be addressed is therefore: How well can the child be understood? Sadly, there is little agreement on the means to answer this question. Nevertheless, we can at least agree that the question is important and that there are reasonable steps to take in seeking an answer.

REFERENCES

Austin, L.J. (1962). *How to do things with words.* London: Oxford University Press.
Bates, E., Beeghley, M., Bretherton, I., McNew, S., O'Connell, B., Reznick, S., Shore, C., Snyder, L., & Volterra, V. (1986). *Early language inventory.* (A revised form of this inventory has been published as *The MacArthur Communicative Development: Infants.* (Available from Center for Research in Language, University of California at San Diego, UCSD C-008, San Diego, CA 92093.)
Billman, K.S. (1986). *Phonological processes and intelligibility of spontaneous utterances in young children.* Unpublished master's thesis, San Diego State University.
Boothroyd, A. (1985). Evaluation of speech production of the hearing impaired: Some benefits of forced-choice testing. *Journal of Speech and Hearing Research, 28,* 185–196.
Brinton, B., & Fujiki, M. (1982). A comparison of request-response sequences in the discourse of normal and language-disordered children. *Journal of Speech and Hearing Disorders, 47,* 57–62.
Brinton, B., Fujiki, M., & Sonnenberg, E.A. (1988). Responses to requests for clarification by linguistically normal and language-impaired children in conversation. *Journal of Speech and Hearing Disorders, 53,* 383–391.
Connolly, J.H. (1986). Intelligibility: A linguistic view. *British Journal of Disorders of Communication, 21,* 371–376.
Dinnsen, D., Chin, S.B., Elbert, M., & Powell, T. (1990). Some constraints on functionally disordered phonologies: Phonetic inventories and phonotactics. *Journal of Speech and Hearing Research, 33,* 28–37.
Flanagan, J.L. (1972). *Speech analysis, synthesis and perception.* New York: Springer-Verlag.

Frearson, B. (1985). A comparison of the AIDS sentence list and spontaneous speech intelligibility scores for dysarthric speech. *Australian Journal of Human Communication Disorders, 13,* 5–21.

Gallagher, T., & Darnton, B.A. (1978). Conversational aspects of the speech of language-impaired children: Revision behaviors. *Journal of Speech and Hearing Research, 21,* 118–133.

Garvey, C. (1977). The contingent query: A dependent act in conversation. In M. Lewis & L.A. Rosenblum (Eds.), *Interaction, conversation and the development of language* (pp. 63–93). New York: John Wiley & Sons.

Haelsig, P.C., & Madison, C.L. (1986). A study of phonological processes exhibited by 3-, 4- and 5-year-old children. *Language, Speech, and Hearing Services in Schools, 17,* 107–114.

Hodge, M.M. (in press). Assessing early speech motor function. *Clinics in Communication Disorders.*

Hodson, B.W. (1982). Remediation of speech patterns associated with low levels of phonological performance. In M. Crary (Ed.), *Phonological intervention: Concepts and procedures* (pp. 97–115). San Diego, CA: College-Hill Press.

Hodson, B.W., & Paden, E. (1983). *Targeting intelligible speech.* San Diego, CA: College-Hill Press.

Hodson, B.W., & Paden, E. (1990). *Targeting intelligible speech* (2nd ed.). San Diego, CA: College-Hill Press.

Hymes, D. (1972a). On communicative competence. In J.B. Pride & J. Holmes (Eds.), *Sociolinguistics* (pp. 269–285). Harmondsworth, England: Penguin.

Hymes, D. (1972b). Models of interaction of language and social life. In J.J. Gumperz & D. Hymes (Eds.), *Directions in sociolinguistics* (pp. 181–224). New York: Holt, Rinehart and Winston.

Kent, R.D. (1992). Research needs in the assessment of speech motor disorders. In *Proceedings of the NINCDS conference, Assessment of Speech and Voice Production: Research and Clinical Applications* (pp. 17–29). Bethesda, MD: National Institute on Deafness and Other Communication Disorders.

Kent, R.D., & Forner, L.L. (1980). Speech segment durations in sentence recitations by children and adults. *Journal of Phonetics, 8,* 157–168.

Kent, R.D., Kent, J.F., Weismer, G., Sufit, R.L., Rosenbek, J.C., Martin, R.E., & Brooks, B.R. (1990). Impairment of speech intelligibility in men with amyotrophic lateral sclerosis. *Journal of Speech and Hearing Research, 55,* 721–728.

Kent, R.D., Weismer, G., Kent, J.F., & Rosenbek, J.C. (1989). Toward phonetic intelligibility testing in dysarthria. *Journal of Speech and Hearing Research, 54,* 482–499.

Levelt, W.J.M. (1989). *Speaking.* Cambridge, MA: MIT Press.

Miller, J., & Chapman, R. (1986). *SALT: Systematic analysis of language transcripts* [Computer program]. Madison: Waisman Center on Mental Retardation and Human Development, University of Wisconsin-Madison.

Miolo, G., Kent, R., & Miller, J. (1991, May). *Predicting speech intelligibility and phonological development in children with Down syndrome.* Paper presented at the Gatlinburg Conference on Research and Theory in Mental Retardation and Developmental Disabilities, Key Biscayne, FL.

Monsen, R.B. (1983). The oral speech intelligibility of hearing-impaired talkers. *Journal of Speech and Hearing Disorders, 43,* 286–296.

Nettelbladt, U. (1983). *Developmental studies of dysphonology in children.* Lund, Sweden: CWK Gleerup.

Osberger, M.J. (1992). Speech intelligibility in the hearing impaired: Research and clinical implications. In R.D. Kent (Ed.), *Intelligibility in speech disorders: Theory, measurement and management* (pp. 233–264). Philadelphia: John Benjamins.

Politzer, R.L., & McGroarty, M. (1983). A discrete point test of communicative competence. *International Review of Applied Linguistics in Language Teaching, 21,* 179–191.

Sander, E. (1972). When are speech sounds learned? *Journal of Speech and Hearing Disorders, 37,* 55–63.

Schiavetti, N. (1992). Scaling procedures for the measurement of speech intelligibility. In R.D. Kent (Ed.), *Intelligibility in speech disorders: Theory, measurement and management* (pp. 11–34). Philadelphia: John Benjamins.

Searle, J. (1969). *Speech acts.* London: Cambridge University Press.

Shriberg, L.D., Kwiatkowski, J., Best, S., Hengst, J., & Terselie-Weber, B. (1988). Characteristics of children with speech delays of unknown origin. *Journal of Speech and Hearing Disorders, 51,* 140–161.

Sperry, R.W. (1952). Neurology and the mind–brain problem. *American Scientist, 40,* 291–312.

Tallal, P. (1988). Developmental language disorders. In J. Kavanagh & T. Truss (Eds.), *Learning disabilities: proceedings of the national conference* (pp. 181–272). Parkton, MD: York Press.

Vihman, M.M., & Greenlee, M. (1987). Individual differences in phonological development: Ages one and three years. *Journal of Speech and Hearing Research, 30,* 503–521.

Wang, M., Rose, S., & Maxwell, J. (1973). *The development of language communication skills tasks.* Pittsburgh, PA: University of Pittsburgh, Learning Research and Development Center.

Warren, R.M. (1984). Perceptual restoration of obliterated sounds. *Psychological Bulletin, 96,* 371–383.

Yavas, M., & Lamprecht, R. (1988). Processes and intelligibility in disordered phonology. *Clinical Linguistics and Phonetics, 2,* 329–345.

Ziegler, W., Hartmann, E., & von Cramon, D. (1988). Word identification testing in the diagnostic evaluation of dysarthric speech. *Clinical Linguistics and Phonetics, 2,* 291–308.

PART IV

Foundations for Enhancing
the Effectiveness of Intervention

12

Programming Conceptual and Communication Skill Development
A Methodological Stimulus-Class Analysis

William J. McIlvane, William V. Dube,
Gina Green, and Richard W. Serna

A CHILD'S CONCEPTUAL AND COMMUNICATION skills normally develop with little formal teaching through naturally occurring interchanges with the social environment. Opportunities for informal learning abound as adults, older children, and peers seek to engage the child in mutually reinforcing social interactions. In addition, the child seems to learn a great deal merely by listening to what others say, watching what they do, and observing the effects of those behaviors on the environment. For some children, however, development does not follow a normal course. This chapter concerns issues relevant to establishing conceptual and communication skills in children who do not acquire them through informal social teaching.

When a child displays severe intellectual impairments, one cannot assume that learning will occur by observation, even in relatively structured teaching settings (MacDonald, Dixon, & LeBlanc, 1986). Direct individual instruction may prove necessary. Also, a child with such impairments may require alternatives to the complex response requirements imposed by communication systems that are based on spoken words or manual signs. For many children with severe mental handicaps, particularly those with motor difficulties, it may be appropriate to consider a selection-based communication system. In selection-based systems, arrays of potentially meaningful stimuli are presented. The child is required only to learn the meanings of these

Data collection and manuscript preparation were supported in part by NICHD Grant Nos. HD 22218, HD 25995, and HD 28141. We also acknowledge support from the Department of Mental Retardation of the Commonwealth of Massachusetts (Contract 3403-8403-306). We thank Joanne Kledaras, Fay Iennaco, and Steve McDonald for help in preparing the manuscript.

stimuli and to respond to them with a simple motor response (e.g., touching). Examples of such systems include those that use Blissymbols (e.g., Harris-Vanderheiden, Brown, MacKensie, Reinen, & Scheibel, 1975), lexigrams (e.g., Romski, Sevcik, & Rumbaugh, 1985), pictorial representations of events (e.g., Mirenda, 1985), and speech synthesizers (e.g., Goossens' & Kraat, 1985). None of these systems imposes the complex motor requirements of speech or sign. Ample research literature provides guidance on designing procedures for teaching the necessary discrimination skills.

Selection-based communication systems have been studied since the 1970s. Their major precedent was the ambitious research that sought to demonstrate the capacity for language and conceptual development in chimpanzees (e.g., Premack, 1976; Rumbaugh, 1977). Efforts to apply similar methods to ameliorate problems resulting from human developmental disabilities logically followed.

RATIONALE FOR
SELECTION-BASED SYSTEMS IN A SOCIAL CONTEXT

On the surface, efforts to teach a child with disabilities to operate a selection-based communication system may seem difficult to justify. Clearly, it is preferable that the child acquire the language spoken by his or her verbal community. Despite considerable research, however, there are many children who are beyond the reach of even highly structured spoken language intervention programs (Guess, Sailor, & Baer, 1978). For these children, selection-based systems may help bring them into contact with the social environment in several useful ways.

The child who fails to acquire spoken language may at least learn some communication skills in a selection-based system. Unlike systems based on manual signs, selection-based systems can be useful in a very wide range of social situations by making use of broadly communicative pictures and symbols (e.g., printed words). Even modest achievements extend the child's ability to express needs and wants, thereby establishing the potential for positive social interactions. Lacking a formal communication system, the child may have no alternative to primitive and, perhaps, disruptive communicative behavior that may be only intermittently effective (Carr & Durand, 1985). It seems reasonable to suggest that a reliable way to communicate makes adequate social adjustment more likely.

Selection-based systems also provide a structured medium for teaching. A related advantage is the potential of these systems to evaluate the cognitive abilities of a child with severe handicaps. Evaluation can be based on mastery and generalization of performances that are directly taught (Sidman, 1986). In addition, that same training may establish the behaviors required to use formal testing instruments (e.g., Leiter scales).

There is a third rationale for selection-based systems that applies to children who demonstrate at least some capability for speech. A few studies have shown that attaining some competency with these systems may be followed by improvements in a child's spoken language abilities (e.g., Romski, White, Millen, & Rumbaugh, 1984). Thus, establishing some means for communicating with the social environment—even an atypical one—may enable the child to be more receptive to both formal and informal communication learning opportunities.

RATIONALE FOR THE PRESENT ANALYSIS

This chapter addresses three interrelated purposes: 1) to summarize, review, and evaluate aspects of basic research on discrimination learning that are relevant to selection-based communication systems; 2) to describe relevant findings from our laboratory studies, in particular novel programming methods that may help teach children who have exceptional difficulties in learning the prerequisite discrimination skills; and 3) to initiate a formal integration of basic discrimination learning research findings with those of previous research on selection-based communication. More generally, we propose to begin to relate those findings to descriptive analyses of the development of children's language and categorization skills. Although these topics are clearly relevant to each other, past efforts to relate them have been circumscribed and largely informal. We believe that selection-based communication systems provide a natural bridge between these areas. Accordingly, we consider topics that might otherwise receive little attention in a discussion of communication system development.

The three sections of this chapter outline a methodological stimulus-class analysis of aspects of conceptual and communication skill development. First, we present concepts and procedures that are fundamental to the analytical approach. Next, we describe methodologies for teaching and evaluating learners with severe disabilities. Finally, we consider the relevance of the preceding material in the analysis of selection-based communication and conceptual development.

STIMULUS CLASSES: BASIC CONSIDERATIONS

Extensive research conducted with humans and nonhumans has shown that discrimination training typically establishes control by stimulus classes rather than merely by specific stimuli (Skinner, 1935). Historically, stimulus classes have been defined in a variety of ways, but all definitions make some reference to a commonality among the members of the class. That commonality may or may not involve physical characteristics, but it always entails some form of functional equivalence in the control of behavior (Goldiamond, 1966).

Two further characteristics of stimulus-class membership are often not made fully explicit. The first is that stimulus-class membership depends critically on context. Two stimuli that are members of a stimulus class under one set of conditions may not be class members under different conditions. The second aspect is that stimulus classes can be seen as the directly observable behavioral product of training and test procedures. They need not be viewed as theoretical entities or intervening variables that "cause" behavior (McIlvane & Dube, 1990).

In considering stimulus classes, it is critical to distinguish class membership based on common physical features from that based on other common properties. The following sections discuss this distinction and illustrate the contextual dependency of stimulus-class membership.

Class Membership Based on Physical Features (Feature Classes)

We use the term "feature class" to refer to a stimulus class in which membership is defined by common physical features. Feature-class membership can be explained and discussed by reference to the well-known "identity matching-to-sample" procedure. Figure 1 shows an example. In this particular identity matching procedure, the sample and comparison stimuli are food items: a pear slice, some grapes, and a small piece of cake; each item is a verified reinforcer. Although all three items are displayed simultaneously as comparison stimuli on each matching-to-sample trial, only one item is correct on any given trial. The positive comparison is indicated by a sample stimulus that is physically identical to it. When the sample is the pear slice, for example, selection of the pear comparison is followed by delivery of that food. Other behaviors in the presence of the pear sample, such as selecting the cake, the grapes, or doing anything else, are not followed by reinforcers.

There is always some variation among so-called "identical" stimuli when the sample and comparison stimuli are food items. For example, each of the sample and comparison pear slices, grapes, and pieces of cake may differ slightly in color, shape, size, or orientation. Considerable research with individuals with severe mental retardation and autism has shown that these slight variations may have no effect on the accuracy of matching-to-sample performance (e.g., McIlvane & Stoddard, 1981; McIlvane, Withstandley, & Stoddard, 1984). These empirical findings demonstrate that food items are members of feature classes. With reference to Figure 1, while any given pear slice may differ slightly from any other one, each slice retains certain distinctive features that allow the learner to discriminate those stimuli as different from the cake, the grapes, and other stimuli displayed in the food matching procedure.

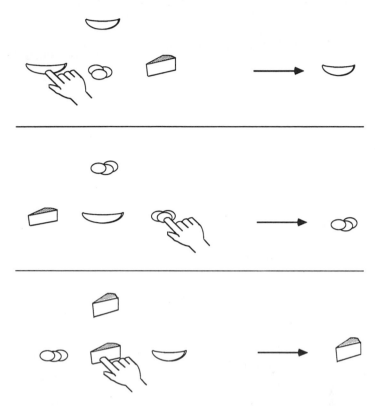

Figure 1. Identity matching-to-sample displays with food items. Arrows and foods on the right illustrate outcome-specific consequences for correct selections.

Contextual Dependency of Feature-Class Membership

Identity-matching contingencies could be arranged, however, to produce feature-class membership different from that indicated by Figure 1. Given the same identity-matching baseline, one might introduce new trials that presented, for example, only pear slices as sample and comparison stimuli. The slices might differ from one another in certain respects (e.g., shape, size, presence or absence of peel). If the subject is able to discriminate one pear slice from another on one of these bases, it would show further feature-class development in the context of the new matching-to-sample trials. That membership, however, need not interfere with the feature classes that were evident in the context of the original identity-matching baseline trials.

Class Membership Based on
Other Commonalities (Arbitrary Classes)

Stimulus classes not based on common physical features are termed "arbitrary classes." The commonality that produces arbitrary-class membership often

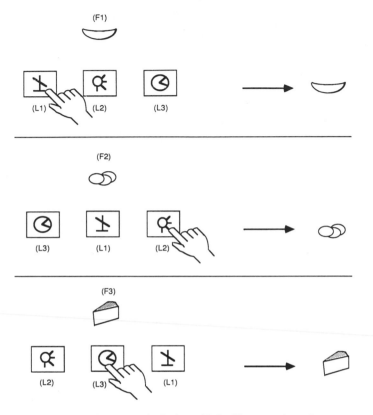

Figure 2. Arbitrary matching-to-sample displays with food item samples and nonrepresentative form comparisons. Arrows and foods on the right illustrate outcome-specific consequences for correct selections.

depends on a relationship with reinforcing stimuli in a given context. Figure 2 shows examples in the context of an arbitrary matching-to-sample procedure that resembles one used by Romski and Sevcik (1988) to initiate selection-based communication training with learners who had severe mental disabilities. As in the preceding identity matching procedure, the sample stimuli are three different food items. The simultaneously displayed comparison stimuli, however, are nonrepresentative forms that might be used as symbols or lexigrams in a selection-based communication system. Different forms are selected in the presence of each food item. When the pear slice (designated F1) is the sample, selection of its corresponding form (designated L1) is followed by the delivery of a pear-slice reinforcer. In that context, no other behavior results in reinforcement. Thus, F1 and L1 are potentially members of an arbitrary stimulus class on the basis of a conditional relation involving the pear-slice reinforcer.

These illustrative matching-to-sample procedures typically arrange outcome-specific contingencies in which correct selections in the presence of each sample are followed by a reinforcer that is only available in the presence of that sample. Procedures of this type are routinely used in the early stages of establishing a selection-based communication system (Romski & Sevcik, 1988).

The arbitrary-matching performances shown in Figure 2 establish conditions under which each sample and its corresponding positive comparison could be members of an arbitrary stimulus class (F1L1, F2L2, and F3L3). All of these sample/positive comparison stimulus pairs have something in common: Deliveries of reinforcers (specific foods in this case) are contingent upon certain behavior with respect to those stimulus pairs. Stimulus-class formation, however, should not be assumed without evidence that the members of the putative classes are functionally equivalent in their control of behavior. Figure 3 illustrates test procedures that might be used to evaluate possible functional equivalence.

The left portion of Figure 3 shows the arbitrary-matching baseline (TRAIN), and the right portion shows one test for functional equivalence (TEST), which is a test for functional sample–comparison reversibility. On test trials, the forms are samples and the food items are comparisons, reversing the training relationship. If the test performance is that illustrated in Figure 3, then both the food items and the forms can serve equally well as samples or comparison stimuli. Positive test results of this type have been obtained in a number of studies with children and adults with and without mental disabilities (e.g., Dube, McIlvane, Mackay, & Stoddard, 1987; Sidman et al., 1982).

Figure 4 shows another type of functional equivalence test. The test is for transfer of discriminative (*S*+ versus *S*−) functions among members of a putative stimulus class. Either before or after the arbitrary-matching baseline is established (upper left portion of Figure 4), food-item samples appear additionally on simple, simultaneous discrimination trials (upper right portion). One food item, F1 perhaps, is designated as the invariant positive stimulus (*S*+), and F2 and F3 are the negative stimuli (*S*−). Arbitrary-matching and simple-discrimination trials are then intermixed in the same baseline. Finally, test trials, shown in the lower portion of Figure 4, display the forms in the simple-discrimination format (i.e., without a sample). The question is whether the forms will exhibit the same discriminative (i.e., *S*+ and *S*−) functions as the food items in the simple-discrimination context. In other words, do the food items and the forms prove functionally equivalent in that context? Functional equivalence of this type has been shown in people with mental retardation and also in children and adults with normal capabilities (e.g., de Rose, McIlvane, Dube, Galpin, & Stoddard, 1988; Sidman, Wynne, Maguire, & Barnes, 1989).

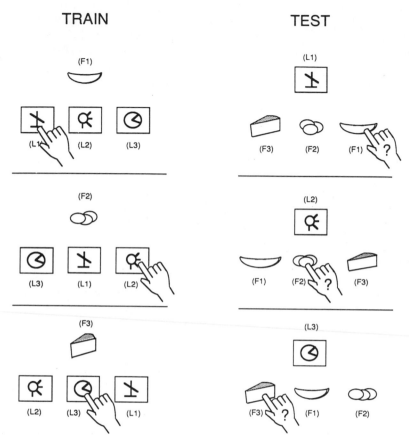

Figure 3. Matching-to-sample displays for tests of sample–comparison reversibility. Left: trained arbitrary-matching baseline with food samples and form comparisons; right: test trials with form samples and food comparisons.

Contextual Dependency of Arbitrary-Class Membership

The contextual dependency of the functional equivalence (and thus the arbitrary stimulus-class membership) becomes obvious when behavior toward the food items and forms outside the context of the discrimination procedures is considered. The learner would be likely to consume only the food, for example. Lack of functional equivalence in this context, however, would not change the status of the previously demonstrated arbitrary stimulus classes.

Additional evidence for the contextual dependency of arbitrary-class membership can be found in recent demonstrations that passing one kind of test for class membership does not necessarily mean that other kinds of tests will be passed. For example, recent work has shown that positive findings on a functional sample–comparison reversibility test need not be accompanied by positive findings on a discriminative function transfer test (de Rose et al.,

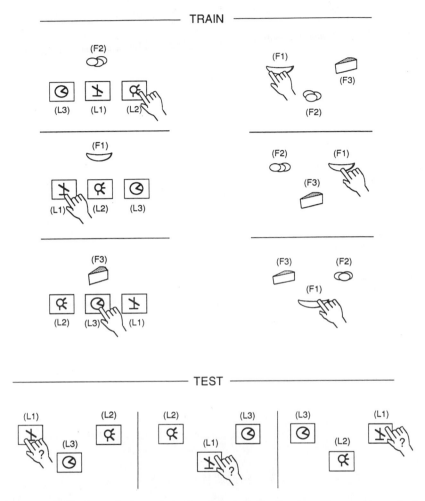

Figure 4. Trial displays for tests of transfer of discriminative functions. Upper portion: trained baseline of arbitrary matching (left) and simple discrimination (right); lower portion: simple-discrimination test trials.

1988) and vice versa (Sidman et al., 1989). For example, matching pictures with printed words and vice versa need not assure that a name applied to a picture will also be applied to the printed word (cf. Lazar, Davis-Lang, & Sanchez, 1984). The reasons for these findings are not clear at present.

METHODOLOGICAL BACKGROUND

Conditional Discrimination
Although stimulus classes can be established in a variety of ways, selection-based communication systems typically use a conditional-discrimination pro-

cedure. In such procedures, the discriminative functions of simultaneously or successively displayed stimuli are not invariant, but instead depend upon the presence of other stimuli. The matching-to-sample procedures described previously are good examples, because the $S+$ and $S-$ functions of comparison stimuli depend upon the sample stimulus.

Teaching Conditional Discrimination: Some Potential Problems

Conditional-discrimination procedures such as matching-to-sample have been used for at least two centuries to teach people with disabilities (cf. Itard, 1801/1962). Impressive case studies notwithstanding, the fact remains that many learners with developmental disabilities have problems learning conditional discrimination (e.g., Saunders & Spradlin, 1989, 1990). The following discussion highlights the need for improvements in conditional discrimination teaching methodology.

Differential Reinforcement (Trial-and-Error) Training

Simple differential reinforcement—the traditional method for establishing discrimination—can create a number of problems when used with learners with developmental limitations. The first is that the procedures are often ineffective, and many individuals make little or no progress despite protracted training (e.g., Zeaman & House, 1963). One reason for this appears to be that trial-and-error responding may establish and maintain control by irrelevant stimulus differences ("error patterns," e.g., McIlvane, Kledaras, Dube, & Stoddard, 1989). Another problem is that the many errors generated by trial-and-error methods can be aversive and may produce emotional responses that interfere with learning (Stoddard & Sidman, 1967; Terrace, 1971). Therefore, we have sought methodology that will teach conditional discrimination with few or no errors.

Errorless Learning Procedures and Matching-to-Sample

A number of potentially errorless programming techniques have been developed in stimulus-control research since the 1960s (e.g., Hively, 1962; Sidman & Stoddard, 1966). The central and defining goal of these techniques is effective, potentially errorless transfer of stimulus control. These techniques begin with reliable control by some "prompt" stimulus difference and no control by a "target" stimulus difference. The prompt is at first superimposed on the target. Then, a series of graduated stimulus changes encourages transfer from the prompt to the target.

While stimulus-control transfer procedures are generally useful in teaching simple form discriminations, they have not been shown to be equally successful in teaching the conditional discriminations required by identity-matching and arbitrary-matching procedures. This is not to say that such methods are never effective in teaching conditional discrimination. To the contrary, when they are effective, they tend to teach conditional discrimination extremely rapidly and efficiently. These procedures, however, can produce highly idiosyncratic and uneven results within and across subjects. Many individuals do not learn even after exposure to a number of different prompting techniques.

Our recent work has examined ways to apply programming techniques more effectively to the task of teaching learners with severe disabilities. Individuals who are lower functioning—those most in need of language training—may have difficulty acquiring conditional discrimination via typical programming methods (Soraci et al., 1987; cf. McIlvane, Kledaras, Killory-Andersen, & Sheiber, 1989). A description follows of our efforts to analyze these problems and to devise procedures to overcome them.

We have examined both identity-matching and arbitrary-matching procedures. Arbitrary-matching procedures are, of course, essential to teach symbol-to-referent matching relations. Identity-matching baselines are also useful to the language trainer because they permit him or her to verify prerequisite visual discriminations among teaching stimuli. In studies of selection-based systems, however, these prerequisites are often assumed and not verified explicitly. Hence, when initial training goes very slowly or fails entirely, the reason may not be clear. Did the failure occur merely because the learner did not discriminate visually among the symbols? The identity-matching baseline allows this possibility to be evaluated in a format that does not simultaneously require learning the symbol-to-referent matching relations.

A New Method for Programming Identity Matching-to-Sample

Program Overview

Recently, we reported a new method for teaching identity matching-to-sample (Dube, Iennaco, Rocco, Kledaras, & McIlvane, 1992; McIlvane, Dube, Kledaras, Iennaco, & Stoddard, 1990). The design takes into account the fact that matching-to-sample has behavioral prerequisites in addition to, and different from, those of simple discrimination. We start, however, with simple form discriminations that can be taught reliably with existing prompting techniques. Given this secure entry point, we then elaborate the baseline systematically, progressing from simple discrimination to the more complex performance of identity matching-to-sample.

Phase 1: Reliable Simple Discrimination

The program begins by establishing discrimination of the presence versus the absence of a form (e.g., a printed letter). The learner must scan a stimulus display, respond by touching the form, ignore irrelevant cues (e.g., position), and refrain from touching when no form is displayed. These modest entry requirements are easily established by modeling and shaping. Reliable form versus no form discrimination is typically established within a session or two, and most individuals with severe mental retardation learn this form of discrimination within four sessions.

The form versus no form discrimination is then elaborated. The learner must discriminate between forms displayed simultaneously. For example, the letters "A" and "B" are displayed, and touching "A" is reinforced while touching "B" is not. Simultaneous discrimination establishes further prerequisites for more complex learning, such as to compare alternative forms and to respond to only one of them. Virtually all of our subjects have learned such form discriminations within a session or two using stimulus fading (Sidman & Stoddard, 1966) or delayed prompting (Touchette, 1971) procedures. Before going on, we teach several different form discriminations to verify that the procedures teach reliably and with few errors.

Phase 2: One-Trial Simple Discrimination Learning

Accurate identity matching can occur only if the sample stimulus exerts instantaneous (i.e., within-trial) control over responding. On a trial with sample "A," for example, a learner is reinforced for selecting comparison "A" and not "B." On the very next trial, if the sample is "B," then the learner's behavior must immediately come under control of sample "B"; the stimulus that controlled most recently (i.e., "A" on the preceding trial) must not interfere. Because samples must immediately become effective controlling stimuli as each matching trial is presented, one-trial discrimination learning would seem to be a prerequisite step toward matching-to-sample.

To establish one-trial simple discrimination learning, we continue to teach simple discriminations with errorless programming procedures. Stimuli are drawn without replacement from a large pool of different forms (currently 120) so that the learner is continually acquiring new discriminations. When the pool is exhausted, the stimuli are reused, but the same stimuli are never displayed together twice. A stimulus that appears as a correct choice will eventually reappear as an incorrect choice, but only after two or three sessions.

The essential feature of our teaching procedure is that it gradually and systematically eliminates the programmed prompts (cf. Herman & Arbeit, 1973). Early in training, as many as 48 prompting trials might be provided to teach a given discrimination; at intermediate steps, less than half that number suffices. Eventually, the programmed instruction for each new discrimination is reduced to one trial—a reinforced "demonstration" trial that displays the correct stimulus alone. For example, on the demonstration trial, "Y" is displayed alone, and its selection is reinforced. On the next discrimination trial, "Y" is displayed with "Z," and, again, selection of "Y" is reinforced.

To date, four subjects with severe mental retardation (who had earlier failed to learn identity matching with standard teaching procedures) have completed prompt-elimination programs such as the one described above (Dube et al., 1992; McIlvane et al., 1990). Although all subjects made some errors, all ultimately achieved highly accurate one-trial learning.

Phase 3: Nonconditional Identity Matching

When one-trial learning has been established, we introduce the matching-to-sample procedure. In two major procedural changes, the demonstration trial becomes the sample, and the discrimination trial becomes the comparison display. First, responses on demonstration trials (on which the correct stimulus is displayed alone) are followed only by discrimination trials and not by tangible reinforcers. Second, the demonstration-trial stimulus is moved to the center key, and it remains present after the learner touches it. These seemingly small procedural changes have not proven trivial. Temporary difficulties were encountered with two of the four who passed through the Phase 3 program (Dube et al., 1992).

At the end of Phase 3, the trial procedure becomes one of nonconditional identity matching: Because new stimuli continue to appear on every trial within a session, the correct/incorrect functions of the choice stimuli are not conditional (Dube, McIlvane, & Green, 1992; Mishkin & Delacour, 1975; Wright, Cook, Rivera, Sands, & Delius, 1988).

Phase 4: Conditional Identity Matching

Conditional identity matching requires reversals (typically repeated) of stimulus functions: When "A" is the sample, comparison "A" is correct ($S+$) and "B" is incorrect ($S-$); on a following trial, if "B" is the sample, then "A" becomes $S-$ and "B" becomes $S+$. Phase 2 and 3 results showed that reversing the $S+/S-$ functions of specific stimuli was not disruptive, provided that two or three sessions intervened between function reversals. To establish more frequent reversals, we gradually reduce the number of intervening trials. At first, a few stimuli that appear on early trials of a session reappear near the end of the session with a changed function. For example, suppose that the first trial displays comparisons "A" versus "B," with "A" as the sample. After perhaps 20 intervening trials, the display might be "Y" versus "A," with "Y" as the sample. Over successive sessions: 1) the number of stimuli that reappear increases, 2) the number of reappearances of each stimulus increases, and 3) the number of different stimuli in each session decreases. Ultimately, only two stimuli appear in each session, and their $S+/S-$ functions reverse irregularly from trial to trial. All four of our subjects completed Phase 4 with very few errors. Further, generalized conditional identity matching was displayed immediately on tests with novel stimuli.

New Methods for Programming Arbitrary Matching-to-Sample

Problems encountered in teaching arbitrary matching-to-sample resemble those with identity matching. Problems are further compounded by the fact that the sample and positive comparison stimuli do not resemble each other. The method used to teach identity matching, therefore, is not directly applicable, and other methods must be employed. Several methods that are currently being studied are described below.

Sample Stimulus Control Shaping Methods

One program for teaching the first instances of arbitrary matching-to-sample uses a stimulus control shaping procedure (McIlvane & Dube, 1992). The starting point is identity matching-to-sample. The essential feature of the program is that the physical characteristics of the sample stimuli are altered until they no longer resemble the comparisons. Recent studies have demonstrated the efficacy of these sample-shaping methods. Individuals with mental retardation and preschoolers with normal capabilities rapidly learned arbitrary matching of nonrepresentative forms after failing to learn with standard training procedures (McIlvane, 1992; Zygmont, Lazar, Dube, & McIlvane, 1992). Ongoing studies are replicating these findings with educationally relevant stimuli. In one study, for example, we are teaching learners who have severe mental retardation to match pictures to initial letters ("A" matched with "apple," "B" with "boat").

The sample-shaping method has proven to be a straightforward and effective method for establishing arbitrary-matching baselines. It may not be appropriate for all applications, however. We briefly describe two other teaching methods under study.

Yoked Reversal (Contingency Class) Procedure

We have used a yoked reversal method successfully with individuals with severe mental retardation who had previously failed to learn arbitrary matching after training with a number of prompting methods. This procedure establishes arbitrary stimulus classes by making two physically dissimilar stimuli jointly discriminative for the same consequences (reinforcement or extinction).

For example, suppose one wants to establish arbitrary-matching relations in which the learner matches "A" with "apple" and "B" with "boat." Training begins by teaching simple, simultaneous discriminations with a potentially errorless teaching method such as stimulus fading. Two stimuli, "B" and "boat" for example, serve as $S+$ on interspersed trials. "A" and "apple," respectively, serve as $S-$ on those same trials. When the "B" versus "A" and the "boat" versus "apple" discriminations are made reliably, there is a programmed reversal of the discriminative functions of all stimuli. "A" and "apple" become $S+$, and "B" and "boat" become $S-$; training continues until the reversed discriminations are made with high accuracy. From this point on, the contingencies are reversed again and again, until reversing one discrimination leads to an immediate, emergent reversal of the other without the need for explicit training. This phenomenon has been termed contingency-class formation (Sidman et al., 1989; cf. Vaughan, 1988). For example, suppose "A" and "apple" jointly exhibit $S+$ functions, and "B" and "boat" jointly exhibit $S-$ functions. Contingency-class formation is shown when a programmed reversal of the "A" versus "B" discrimination (i.e., making "A" the $S-$ and "B" the $S+$) is followed immediately by an unprogrammed reversal of the "apple" versus "boat" discrimination (i.e., "apple" now functions as $S-$ and "boat" as $S+$). The unprogrammed reversal can occur if "A" and "apple" are members of one arbitrary stimulus class, and "B" and "boat" are members of another class. When contingency-class formation is achieved, the arbitrary matching-to-sample procedure is introduced with methods such as those in Phase 3 of our identity-matching program (see McIlvane et al., 1990, for details).

Differential Sample–Response Procedure

This procedure has been used in a number of studies with individuals with mental retardation (Saunders & Spradlin, 1989, 1990) and with nonhumans (Sidman et al., 1982; cf. Cohen, Brady, & Lowry, 1981) after typical training methods had not succeeded. Differential responses have included patterns of responding generated by different reinforcement schedules (e.g., rapid responding generated by fixed-ratio [FR] schedules versus slower responding resulting from differential reinforcement of low rates [DRL]) and sample imitation. Differential responses to the sample stimuli ensure that the subject makes successive discriminations among them. The recent work with individuals with mental retardation also features programmed introduction of discrimination reversal to establish and maintain simultaneous discrimination of the comparison stimuli.

Potential Disadvantages of the Yoked
Reversal and Differential Sample–Response Procedures

Both procedures share two undesirable features. First, both appear to require a relatively large number of training sessions. Second, the early introduction of discrimination reversals may lead to many errors, even when gradual programming is employed. The sample stimulus-control shaping method, however, seems to work far more rapidly. This favorable outcome is probably because successive discrimination of the samples, simultaneous discrimination of the comparisons, and instructional control of comparison discrimination reversal are all verified by the identity-matching entry requirements. Thus, the sample-shaping procedure seems to be the procedure of choice at the current time.

Summary

Research described in this section presents the foundation for an effective methodology for teaching the behavioral prerequisites for selection-based communication systems. Two aspects appear to be especially significant. The first is the well-validated set of procedures for establishing the simple discrimination entry requirements (e.g., Richmond & Bell, 1986; Sidman & Stoddard, 1966). The second aspect is the conceptually straightforward and coherent transition from simple discrimination through identity matching to increasingly complex forms of arbitrary matching-to-sample. Although further research is needed to determine whether this transition can be accomplished routinely with learners who have the most severe disabilities, the present methods do seem to represent a significant improvement over those used in the past.

STIMULUS CLASSES IN COMMUNICATION SKILL AND CONCEPTUAL DEVELOPMENT

Many questions about intellectual development can be cast more parsimoniously as questions about the stimulus classes that control behavior (cf. Sidman, 1986). In this final section, we discuss feature and arbitrary stimulus classes in relation to aspects of cognitive functioning that are conceptually and/or procedurally central in establishing and elaborating a selection-based communication system.

Rapid Stimulus-Class Development

Although rapid acquisition of discrimination is not a conceptual necessity in stimulus-class development, it may prove necessary practically before a sufficiently extensive and flexible selection-based communication repertoire can be developed. The general picture that emerges from studies of discrimination learning in subjects with developmental disabilities may lead to a pessimistic view. It might be concluded that such subjects characteristically learn discriminations slowly, with considerable training effort, and with many failures (e.g., House, Hanley, & Magid, 1979). This picture, however, may be biased by the methodologies applied to the study of discrimination learning.

Discrimination learning studies typically examine "experimentally naive" subjects who are presumed to have little extra-experimental experience relevant to the particular aspect of learning under study. By minimizing extra-experimental influence, the goal is to minimize problems in isolating the variables that determine whether or not learning occurs. Results of such studies, however, only answer questions about the learning ability of inexperienced subjects; they do not tell us how learning ability changes as training continues. Our successes in producing one-trial discrimination learning, however, make it evident that rapid versus slow discrimination acquisition need not differentiate individuals with developmental limitations from individuals with more highly developed repertoires.

Our findings make some additional points that seem relevant to the definition of behavioral objectives in teaching the basics of a selection-based communication system. The first point concerns the role of prompting procedures (e.g., stimulus fading, stimulus shaping, delayed prompting) in teaching. In the past, such methods were seen as sufficient and probably necessary to overcome the characteristic learning problems inherent in individuals with mental retardation and other developmental disabilities. Viewed in that light, extensive (and expensive) development and validation of programs for teaching highly specific skills were justifiable, based on their ability to reach those with even severe learning problems (cf. Sidman & Stoddard, 1966). However, few were willing to invest the time and labor necessary to develop programs to teach functional skills using these procedures.

Our work suggests a new role for errorless teaching methods. Rather than using them routinely to teach discrimination of specific stimuli, instead, the focus could be on producing discrimination learning skills that can be applied readily to new stimulus sets. Current efforts to develop ever more elaborate and intricate prompting techniques (e.g., Lancioni, Hoogeveen, Smeets, Boelens, & Leonard, 1989) might be supplemented or perhaps even supplanted by efforts to teach those with developmental limitations without elaborate prompting.

Also at issue is how best to teach the visual discriminations that are required in selection-based systems. Acquisition of early elements of the system (i.e., the initial word units) often requires protracted training. Later elements are often acquired more rapidly (e.g., Romski & Sevcik, 1988), a finding predicted by the results of research on so-called "learning set" phenomena (Harlow, 1949; Kaufman & Prehm, 1966). As we implied earlier, it is logical to ask: 1) how much of the later improvement reflects only improvements in visual discrimination skills, and 2) whether those skills might be taught more rapidly and efficiently using procedures that did not seek to establish the prerequisite visual discriminations and the arbitrary-class membership at the same time.

Stimulus Control by Relational Properties

It is a virtual axiom of developmental psychology that very young children and comparably functioning individuals with developmental disabilities tend to respond to "absolute" rather than to "relational" stimulus properties. Control by absolute properties is shown when discriminative control depends upon the presence of the specific stimulus features that were present during training. Control by relational properties is evident when discriminative control is maintained in the absence of the specific stimuli that were present during training, providing that critical relational information is preserved (cf. Premack, 1989). Research on transposition (Reese, 1968) may be the best known example. Also well-known is the research on stimulus control by the property of identity or "sameness."

Control by the Relational Property of Identity in Matching-to-Sample

Tests for generalized identity matching are a common means for evaluating control by this relational property with both human and nonhuman subjects (Weinstein, 1941). Such tests can be illustrated with reference to the identity matching-to-sample task that was described in Figure 1. Appropriate tests would replace the original three food items with three new, physically dissimilar items. How will the child respond? If he or she continues to select comparison stimuli that are identical to the sample, then one can infer that identity-matching training had established stimulus control by the general property of identity. If not, however, then the inference is that identity-matching performances with the original food items reflected only control by specific physical characteristics.

If the child does display generalized identity matching, one might then go on to ask further questions. For example, one might ask about the degree to which identity matching was truly generalized. Would the child perform similarly with photographs or other representations of the food items? Would feature classes be evident with these two-dimensional stimuli?

Studies of children with mental retardation and of children with normal capabilities suggest that control by the relational property of identity develops relatively late (e.g., House, Brown, & Scott, 1974; cf. Greenfield, 1985), after substantial language skill is evident. In a broader view, however, the generalized ability to determine whether two stimuli are the same or different would seem to be a critical prerequisite for all but the most primitive conceptual development. Findings that the relational property of identity is late developing may depend on the methods employed to assess the skill. For example, studies described previously in the section on methodological background show that stimulus control by the relational property of identity can be developed in individuals who have severe mental retardation. Moreover, studies in our laboratory have demonstrated generalized identity matching in even less capable subjects without elaborate training regimens (e.g., McIlvane, Withstandley, & Stoddard, 1984). Studies of oddity learning have also shown that procedural refinements can establish identity relations in children functioning at a level lower than that suggested by developmental studies (e.g., Soraci et al., 1987).

Generalized Arbitrary Matching-to-Sample

On the face of it, generalized learning in arbitrary-matching procedures would not seem possible; arbitrary stimulus–stimulus relations require explicit training. This fact notwithstanding, aspects of arbitrary-matching performance do seem to generalize. Perhaps the best example is the "exclusion" phenomenon that has been studied in subjects with mental retardation ranging from mild (Dixon, 1977) to profound (McIlvane, Bass, O'Brien, Gerovac, & Stoddard, 1984) and also in children who are developing normally (McIlvane, Munson, & Stoddard, 1988; cf. Vincent-Smith, Bricker, & Bricker, 1974).

Exclusion is demonstrable after arbitrary matching-to-sample training defines a baseline set of relations involving, for example, spoken word (W) samples and object (O) comparison stimuli (W1:O1, W2:O2, W3:O3). On exclusion trials, a defined comparison object (e.g., O1) is displayed with a comparison object not yet defined (O4); the spoken sample word (W4) is also undefined and novel. Under these conditions, subjects typically demonstrate an emergent W4:O4 relation, immediately selecting the undefined comparison in response to the undefined sample. The emergent matching relation has been attributed to "responding away from" or "excluding" the defined object (i.e., rejecting O1 in the presence of W4). Recent data, however, suggest that shared novelty of undefined samples and comparisons might also be an important variable in some studies (McIlvane, Kledaras, Lowry, & Stoddard, in press).

Exclusion can be the basis of a powerful but as yet incompletely understood teaching strategy. For example, in research using procedures such as the ones just described, subjects with profound mental retardation demonstrated emergent object naming (i.e., producing W4 when shown O4) following as few as two exclusion trials (McIlvane et al., 1984).

While it remains to be determined if and how these results relate to normal language acquisition, we note some interesting and possibly important parallels. For example, these results seem to have features in common with the "fast mapping" of words that seems to occur in the early stages of normal language acquisition (e.g., Rice, Buhr, & Nemeth, 1990). An even closer relationship seems apparent between exclusion and the N3C (novel name–novel category) vocabulary learning strategies described by Mervis and Bertrand (chap. 13, this volume).

The "arbitrary assignment" phenomenon reported by Stromer (1986) and Saunders, Saunders, Kirby, and Spradlin (1988) also merits discussion in this context. These studies showed that subjects with mental retardation and extensive arbitrary-matching histories spontaneously exhibited conditional discrimination on problems that presented entirely new stimuli. The arbitrary assignment phenomenon seems to indicate that subjects learn the general rule that each comparison stimulus of a given comparison display is to be related to one and only one sample stimulus. A question for future research is if and how such learning might relate to Mervis and Bertrand's observation that children seem to learn *that* words refer to objects before they learn specific word–object relations.

Stimulus Equivalence

The problem of stimulus equivalence has a long history in comparative, experimental, and developmental psychology. The fundamental question is how two nonidentical stimuli can have the same effects on behavior. Stimulus equivalence follows directly from a stimulus-class analysis. We now differentiate "feature equivalence" based on common physical features from "arbitrary equivalence" having other bases.

Feature Equivalence

In an earlier example, we defined feature-class membership in terms of overlapping physical features among similar but nonidentical stimuli (e.g. two pear slices, two grapes). When two stimuli that share some features also have more or less obvious differences, it is logical to ask about the equivalence of those stimuli in the control of behavior. For example, in early research with learners who were severely retarded, Sidman and Stoddard (1966) used fading methods to establish discrimination of a circle $(S+)$ from a relatively flat ellipse $(S-)$. Subsequent tests showed that some forms but not others could be substituted for the circle without disrupting discrimination (i.e., without occasioning ellipse selections). Maintenance of discrimination with some of the substituted forms apparently resulted because those forms were comparable to the circle in terms of size, area, and other physical features.

Outside the laboratory, feature equivalence is a fundamental concern of those who study language acquisition and conceptual development. It is common, for example, to ask questions about how a young child recognizes that a given item belongs or does not belong to a given conceptual class (e.g., Mervis & Bertrand, chap. 13, this volume). In our present analytical terms, under what circumstances do stimuli that have physical differences control the same behavior? Although questions of this type have been central in developmental studies, they have been neglected by those interested in basic analyses of stimulus control. One likely factor in this neglect is that studies of primary stimulus generalization (Bickel & Etzel, 1985) have established bases for predicting the outcomes. Nonetheless, research to confirm or disconfirm such predictions appears necessary, and some reports are beginning to appear (Fields, Reeve, Adams, & Verhave, 1991).

Feature equivalence is a topic of particular importance in the design of selection-based communication systems. Certain very simple picture-based systems (cf. Mirenda, 1985) require only that the learner respond to photographs of objects or events. The logic behind such systems, of course, is to reduce the teaching burden by allowing the learner to respond to stimuli that physically resemble the actual objects or events. Feature equivalence development has another advantage for teachers interested in establishing selection-based communication. For purely practical reasons, these teachers may want to conduct training with pictures of objects or other events, particularly if computer-assisted instructional techniques are employed (Dube & McIlvane, 1989).

Developing Feature Equivalence

With children who are normally developing, functional equivalence between objects and corresponding pictorial stimuli (i.e., photographs, line drawings) can often be assumed. However, a growing number of studies with learners who were very young or learners with severe retardation have shown that such equivalence cannot be assumed (e.g., Lignugaris/Kraft, McCullar, Exum, & Salzberg, 1988). Learners who have severe retardation, for example, may not accurately match objects with photographs even though they can match identical objects and identical photographs (Sevcik & Romski, 1986; cf. Dixon, 1981).

The discrimination learning literature provides surprisingly few direct, easily translatable procedures for developing feature equivalences in special populations. Most of the available information comes from applied efforts to document the effectiveness of combining verbal and/or physical prompts with differential reinforcement techniques (Lignugaris/Kraft et al., 1988). As noted earlier, these techniques prove effective with some learners, but many learners are likely to require more sophisticated programming. However, there is a notable lack of research on errorless teaching methods for establishing feature equivalence. The problem may be technical rather than conceptual. Transforming the stimulus features of three-dimensional objects into two-dimensional representations is a difficult (but probably not insurmountable) problem. We are examining the feasibility of applying computer graphics and videodisc technologies to the problem.

Contextual Control of Feature Equivalence

As an instance of feature-class membership, feature equivalence depends on context and training history. In some contexts, for example, it might be appropriate to classify humans and other mammals together on physical bases (e.g., the presence of hair). In other contexts, such equivalence would be obviously inappropriate. Again, however, empirical analysis of the contextual dependency of feature-class membership is a problem that has rarely been addressed in formal experimental studies.

Arbitrary Equivalence

Stimulus equivalence not based on common physical features is critically important in the analysis of language and other behavioral repertoires with generative characteristics. The effects of spoken, signed, or written words depend upon equivalence relations involving, for example, corresponding objects, actions, and stimulus properties. Selection-based communication systems, of course, also depend upon such relations.

Arbitrary stimulus equivalence has been defined in a number of ways since the mid-1960s, and a consensus definition has yet to emerge. Examples of the proposed definitions and a brief explanation of each follow.

Functional Equivalence ("Mutual Substitutability")

This definition is essentially the same as the definition of an arbitrary stimulus class. It was proposed by Goldiamond (1966), subsequently developed further by Spradlin, Cotter, and Baxley (1973), and Sidman (1977), and ultimately formalized by Vaughan (1988). Goldiamond cited the example of three physically dissimilar stimuli that were all functionally equivalent in controlling the behaviors involved in stopping one's car (a red light, a stop sign, and a traffic officer's upraised hand). An important feature of the definition of the functional equivalence class was that a variable applied to one member of the class should have similar effects upon other members (cf. Goldiamond, 1962). For example, a variable that might lead one to ignore the officer's upraised hand (e.g., a medical emergency) would have similar effects with respect to a red light and a stop sign.

Sidman's Equivalence Tests

This proposal, offered by Sidman (Sidman & Tailby, 1982; Sidman et al., 1982), applies primarily to the evaluation of stimulus equivalence in arbitrary matching-to-sample procedures. He proposed equivalence tests derived from elementary mathematics texts. Briefly, the tests require subjects to acquire conditional relations involving stimulus sets A, B, and C. For example, the subject might learn to select comparison stimuli B1 and B2 conditionally upon sample stimuli A1 and A2, respectively (AB matching). The subject might additionally learn to select comparisons C1 and C2 conditionally upon samples B1 and B2, respectively (BC matching). Having learned a baseline of AB and BC, the tests are for *reflexivity* (AA, BB, CC), *symmetry* (BA, CB), and *transitivity* (AC). The reflexivity and symmetry tests correspond directly to the tests for generalized identity matching and functional sample–comparison reversibility that were described previously. Another test (CA) was termed the *equivalence* test, because it simultaneously evaluated symmetry and transitivity, and could by itself serve to document equivalence-class formation in a subject capable of generalized identity matching.

In Sidman's view, positive outcomes on equivalence tests may reflect a basic behavioral process that may not be explainable in terms of other processes (cf. Catania, 1984). Moreover, citing the apparent failures of nonhumans to pass all of the necessary tests, Sidman suggests that only humans may be capable of stimulus equivalence (Sidman, 1990). This capability, he suggests, may provide the basis for language and other behavioral repertoires with generative properties.

Relational Frames ("Arbitrarily Applicable Relational Responding")

This proposal, offered by Hayes (1990), views Sidman's form of stimulus equivalence as only one instance of a general tendency of humans to respond to arbitrary relations among stimuli. In Hayes's theory, the term "stimulus equivalence" is redefined in a manner that goes far beyond functional substitutability or equivalence in the control of behavior; stimulus equivalence encompasses virtually all arbitrary relations that could logically hold among stimuli (relational frames). In Hayes's view, relational frames do not require new processes. Rather, they emerge as a product of one's social experience, particularly in relation to language training. The example often given is that of the child who is learning that the male parent is called "Daddy." The child may be taught directly not only to say "Daddy" in the presence of this parent but also to search for the parent when "Where's Daddy?" is spoken and the parent is not in sight. Hayes thus suggests a naturalistic model of how the child learns bidirectional relationships such as those evident on tests for sample–comparison reversibility. With respect to selection-based communication systems, Hayes's proposal implies that emergent behavior reflecting equivalence relations should not be demonstrable very early in training, but it could develop as training progressed.

Implications of Equivalence Definitions

The differences in the definition of arbitrary-stimulus equivalence may be of relatively little concern to the designer of a selection-based communication system. The fundamental concern may be merely that the performances are not rote conditional discriminations. This concern is largely resolved if the learner routinely demonstrates the emergence of new behavior without explicit training, a feature that is common to all definitions. If the interest is delineation or evaluation of cognitive functioning, however, it may be important to define precisely the nature of the conditional relations that are acquired. For example, if learners are classified according to their capacity for demonstrating arbitrary-stimulus equivalence, it is critical to differentiate among the various definitions (cf. Hayes, 1989; McIntyre, Cleary, & Thompson, 1989; Saunders, 1989; Vaughan, 1989).

Development of Arbitrary Equivalence

Arbitrary-stimulus equivalence can be developed via straightforward application of well-defined teaching methodologies. Errorless teaching methodologies have been employed to establish baseline performances in a number of studies with learners who are young and have severe mental retardation (e.g., Dube et al., 1987; Sidman & Tailby, 1982).

Several options are available for students who do not demonstrate immediate emergent matching on initial test trials. One option is simply to continue testing while reviewing the baseline performances. Spradlin and colleagues (1973) first reported the now common finding that new performances may emerge gradually in the course of repeated tests, even though test trials were not followed by feedback. If gradual emergence is not observed, one alternative is to teach one or more of the potentially emergent performances directly, while continuing to test the remainder (cf. Sidman, Willson-Morris, & Kirk, 1986).

Arbitrary-Stimulus Equivalence and the Analysis of Meaning

When arbitrary equivalence is established, a likely conclusion is that one stimulus acquires the same meaning as another. Although there are difficulties in defining "meaning" precisely, the outcomes of the stimulus-equivalence tests outlined above provide useful information for the designers of selection-based communication systems. If novel behavior routinely emerges without explicit training, it need not be a concern that the learner's conditional-discrimination performances are merely the same type of "rote" behavior that one could routinely generate in laboratory animals like rats or pigeons. Recent research from our laboratory offers further potentially useful tests. These can be illustrated with reference to Figure 5 and Figure 6.

Figure 5 shows identity-matching contingencies involving printed words. The words correspond to the food items and lexigrams that were sample and comparison stimuli in the arbitrary-matching procedure shown in Figure 2. As before, outcome-specific reinforcement contingencies are employed; each correct selection of "pear," "cake," and "grape" is followed by the appropriate food items. Given the matching-to-sample training procedures described in Figures 2 and 5, it is reasonable to investigate the status of the lexigrams and food items in relation to the printed words. This relation can be evaluated with the tests shown in Figure 6.

One test would present the lexigrams as samples and the printed words as comparisons; another would reverse the sample–comparison arrangement. If the learner did match the lexigrams and printed words as illustrated in Figure 6, the results would demonstrate that the subject does in fact relate the lexigrams and printed words by virtue of their common relations with the food-item reinforcers. We may take the positive test outcome as clear evidence that the learner does in fact know the meanings of the lexigrams and printed words. Findings of this type have been reported in a series of studies with learners with mental retardation (Dube et al., 1987; Dube, McIlvane, Maguire, Mackay, & Stoddard, 1989; McIlvane et al., 1990).

Functional Communication Using a Selection-Based System

Previous sections have outlined a methodological approach for establishing and elaborating a selection repertoire. Given appropriate training, the student may become proficient at matching stimulus class members such as objects,

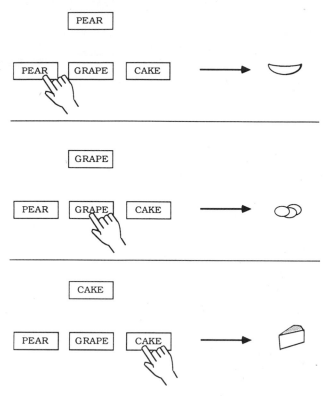

Figure 5. Identity matching-to-sample displays with printed food names. Arrows and foods on the right illustrate outcome-specific consequences for correct selections.

pictures, lexigrams, and printed or dictated words. Although such a repertoire is an essential prerequisite for a selection-based communication system, functional use of the system requires more. In matching-to-sample, if a teacher displays a sample stimulus and asks, "What is this?" there is a clearly specified correct answer (i.e., the matching comparison stimulus). In functional communication, however, the teacher's questions may not have "correct" answers (e.g., "What do you want?"). Moreover, functional communication must allow the learner to assume the role of questioner by initiating communication in appropriate circumstances (e.g., "May I have this?" "What is this?").

Sometimes, learners may demonstrate a rudimentary form of requesting without explicit training. For example, Romski, Sevcik, and Pate (1988) taught students with severe retardation to label food items by selecting lexigrams. If the student selected a lexigram between labeling trials, the teacher interpreted this as a request for the corresponding food item and delivered it to the student. Three students began to display such responses after they had

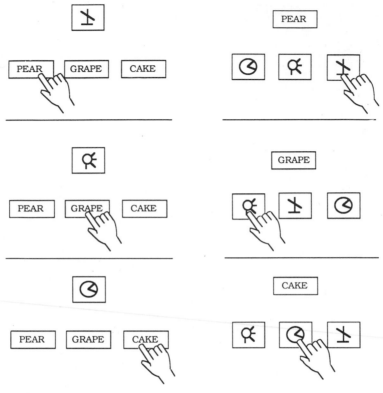

Figure 6. Matching-to-sample displays for equivalence tests with printed food names and forms.

learned to label several (4–12) lexigrams. However, transfer from labeling to requesting repertoires does not always occur (e.g., Carr & Kologinsky, 1983; Hall & Sundberg, 1987; Lamarre & Holland, 1985; Sigafoos, Doss, & Reichle, 1989). How might training contingencies to promote such a transfer be set up?

One approach derives from functional analyses of the independence and interdependence of labeling and requesting (tact versus mand distinction [Skinner, 1957]). Although both types of performances may be physically identical (e.g., pointing to a "pear" lexigram), functional analysis differentiates them on the basis of the situations in which they are displayed. The learner labels in response to the teacher's question (i.e., "What is that?") with reference to a stimulus that is directly observable. The variables that determine requests (e.g., establishing operations and their corresponding motivational states), however, may not be immediately obvious. In studies that investigate the relationship between these two types of behavior, the situation is often arranged to encourage the development of control by motivational variables. For example, a learner may be taught to use a bottle opener and also to match the opener to a lexigram. The learner is then given an unopened bottle of cola; will he or she then, in the absence of the opener, select the opener lexigram? The results of such studies provide support for analysis of labeling and requesting as functionally separate behaviors. Learners did not request items, such as the opener, on initial opportunities to do so. Generalized transfer from labeling to requesting was observed only after explicit training in requesting for one or more examples (Sigafoos et al., 1989; cf. Carr & Kologinsky, 1983; Hall & Sundberg, 1987). Transfer was also observed when labeling training followed teaching that had established a generalized form of request, "Want," in appropriate motivational situations (Sigafoos, Reichle, Doss, Hall, & Pettitt, 1990).

There seems to be a clear need to formalize procedures for teaching functional use of selection-based communication systems. Fortunately, guidance can be taken from the extensive research on procedures to encourage generalization of spoken language skills. On the face of it, there appears to be no conceptual barrier to adapting aspects of strategies such as milieu teaching (Kaiser, Yoder, & Keetz, 1992), perhaps with initial emphasis on some of its constituent tactics (e.g., mand-model [Warren, McQuarter, & Rogers-Warren, 1984]). Given the typically severe behavioral limitations of candidates for selection-based communication systems, additional consideration might be given to implementing the supported routines approach that has been described by Spradlin, Saunders, and Saunders (1992).

More Complex Stimulus Classes and Class Interactions

Functional communication via a selection-based communication system may require that the teacher initially establish only one-to-one correspondence between system elements and environmental events. For children who are relatively higher functioning, however, the selection-based system might correspond more closely to the language of his or her social environment. Natural languages are, of course, inherently complex. For example, elements are used in sequence to describe multiple attributes of a given stimulus, or temporal or spatial relations between stimuli. In addition, natural languages feature countless and varied stimulus classes, the complexity of which goes well beyond the elementary examples considered in preceding sections. Studies of stimulus classes have sometimes addressed more complex stimulus situations and response requirements, however. The following section considers illustrative examples that are potentially relevant to the design of a selection-based communication system. Topics include research on stimulus combinations and sequences, stimulus classes based on ordinal relations in sequential responding, and contextual control of stimulus-class membership.

Element Combinations

A selection-based communication system potentially can use elements in combination to permit more precise labeling and requesting. A good conceptual model for designing training procedures is the "miniature linguistic system" that can be established via "matrix training" procedures (e.g., Goldstein, chap. 14, this volume; Wetherby & Striefel, 1978). Figure 7 presents a

	SECOND			
---	SOCKS	BALL	HAT	CUP
RED	T	T	E	E
GREEN	E	T	T	E
YELLOW	E	E	T	T
BLUE	T	E	E	T

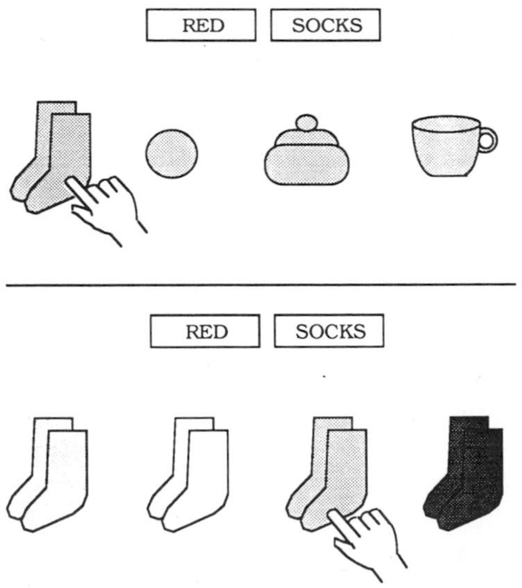

Figure 7. Upper portion: matrix training and testing paradigm. Rows and columns = nominal adjectives (colors) and nouns (objects), respectively. T = trained combinations (e.g., red socks, green ball); E = potential emergent combinations (e.g., green socks, yellow ball). Lower portion: arbitrary matching-to-sample displays for trials that display four different objects of the same color (top) and four of the same object in different colors (bottom).

simple example, a 4 x 4 matrix of performances that might be established in the initial stages of selection-based communication training.

The matrix includes four colors (nominally adjectives) and four objects (nominally nouns). For convenience of exposition, the stimuli in this example are printed words and objects. The learner is taught to select the object indicated by "T." For example, the printed words "red socks" are displayed, and the learner is to touch the red socks; if "green hat" is displayed, the learner is to touch the green hat. Training contingencies are arranged to prevent control by only one of the simultaneously displayed elements, and an example is shown in Figure 7. The learner is required to make selections from displays with: 1) four objects that are all the same color (e.g., red socks, red ball, red hat, red cup) or 2) each object displayed in all four colors (e.g., red socks, green socks, yellow socks, blue socks). Given such training, the question is whether the learner will respond appropriately to the novel adjective-noun combinations indicated by "*E*" (for emergent responses) in Figure 7. A number of studies using varied stimuli have produced positive findings (see Goldstein, chap. 14, this volume).

Emergent behavior engendered by matrix training has been termed "recombinative generalization." This descriptive term expresses the major finding of matrix training research—generalized (i.e., emergent) performances that are apparent recombinations of elements of previously learned performances. As with other emergent performances, recombinative generalization appears to be amenable to a stimulus-class analysis. Analysis at several levels may ultimately prove necessary to provide a full account of the phenomenon.

At a very basic level, we see the potential for feature classes involving both colors and objects. With respect to colors, all red, green, yellow, and blue items are potentially members of natural feature classes. When arbitrary-matching relations are established involving one or more feature-class members (e.g., red objects) and a printed color name (e.g., "red"), the remaining class members may also be matched to that color name. With respect to the objects, all socks, all balls, all hats, and all cups are potential feature-class members on the basis of multiple overlapping physical features. Again, when arbitrary-matching relations are established involving one or more class members (e.g., socks) and a printed object name (e.g., "socks"), the remaining class members may prove substitutable.

Recombinative generalization in this analysis can be seen merely as arbitrary matching-to-compound samples. The learner must attend to both elements (e.g., "red" and "socks") and select the item that is a member of both feature classes. Matrix training procedures, in fact, have this characteristic in common with the discrimination training procedures used to teach "overselective" children with mental retardation and autism to attend to both elements of compound samples (Schreibman, Charlop, & Koegel, 1982).

Element Sequences

Natural languages have a major syntactic component. Words are to be spoken in specified sequences, and the meaning of a given word often depends on the position of that word in a longer sequence of words. Furthermore, the sequential position of words relative to other words may be an important determiner of grammatical-class membership (cf. Braine, 1986). In English, for example, modifiers typically precede and actions typically follow agents. The matrix training procedure shown in Figure 7 follows this ordering convention. When the full matrix of performances is displayed, it is natural to ask whether the order is important in the stimulus control of performance (and in recombinative generalization more broadly). For example, would the learner's behavior be affected if the printed words were displayed "socks red" rather than "red socks"? If behavior were disrupted, the results would show at the least that word position was critical to control of performance (Iverson, Sidman, & Carrigan, 1986). Such results would raise the question of whether the sequential position of the words (i.e., color first, object second) was a variable that influenced the observed recombinative generalization.

If element order is to be made explicitly relevant in a selection-based system, the teacher must arrange training contingencies that require control by ordinal stimulus properties. The learner could be required to label items by selecting elements in sequence. Such training procedures can also be described with reference to Figure 7 and Figure 8.

In this case, "T" in the upper portion of Figure 7 represents sequential selections that are established directly (e.g., "red" → "socks," "green" → "ball"); "E" represents sequential performances that might emerge without explicit training. Figure 8 illustrates a trial in which the student learns to select a color name first and an object name second. The emergence of new sequential performances would reflect stimulus classes based on several stimulus properties. As in the earlier matrix training example, appropriate arbitrary and feature classes would be required. In addition, the nominal adjectives and nouns would have to be members of "sequence" classes based on their ordinal positions in the sequences that were established directly. According to this analysis, the adjectives and nouns would be members of "first" and "second" classes, respectively.

At another level of analysis, classes of stimuli that do not have common physical features could also be used in matrix training procedures to produce emergent sequential performances. In fact, matrix training typically involves sets of elements that are assumed to make up arbitrary linguistic classes rather than feature classes. For example, in addition to participating in feature and arbitrary classes, the sets of words in our matrix (Figure 7) could be members of superordinate classes that might be labeled "colors" (or "adjectives") and "objects" (cf. Rosch & Mervis, 1975). Similarly, a group of spoken action

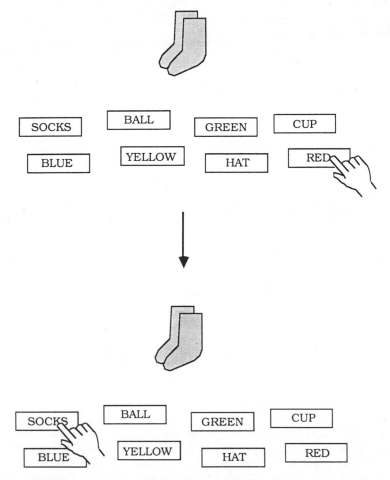

Figure 8.   Sequential arbitrary matching-to-sample displays. Students select the printed color name first (top) and a printed object name second (bottom).

words that bear little physical resemblance to one another may constitute a stimulus class, as may groups of words representing objects, locations, or prepositions (cf. Goldstein & Mousetis, 1989; Striefel & Wetherby, 1973). Such classes are based on arbitrary, learned relations among elements within each class. Sequential performances involving elements of arbitrary classes, such as prepositions and locations, could be taught the same way as the color-object sequences in our previous illustration. For instance, the learner might learn to make "on" → "chair," "under" → "bed," and other sequential selections of printed words in response to pictures. The emergence of new sequential performances representing untrained recombinations of elements from the arbitrary classes would suggest that sequence training established relative ordinal relations between members of the prepositions class and members of the locations class.

Developing Control by Element Combinations and Sequences

Matrix training with prompting and differential reinforcement has successfully taught performances analogous to those illustrated in the lower part of Figure 7 to a number of learners with severe mental retardation (e.g., Goldstein, Angelo, & Mousetis, 1987). Procedures for establishing responding of the type shown in Figure 8 have not been investigated widely with populations with developmental limitations. In particular, there has been little study of methods for establishing ordinal-class membership.

Useful strategies for teaching sequential responding have been suggested by recent research conducted in our laboratories. This exploratory research sought to teach learners who were developmentally young or with severe mental retardation to respond sequentially to four- and five-element arrays of simultaneously displayed arbitrary forms (Mackay, Stoddard, & Spencer, 1989; Stromer & Mackay, 1990). Sequential responding was first established with two or more arrays (e.g., A1-A2-A3-A4 and B1-B2-B3-B4) by combining forward chaining and stimulus fading methods (Sidman & Rosenberger, 1967). Subsequent tests presented mixed sequences (e.g., A1-B2-A3-B4 and B1-A2-B3-A4). Typically, functional equivalence was shown; the elements proved mutually substitutable according to their established ordinal position in the original sequences.

A potentially important aspect of the work was the development of a novel procedure for teaching new sequential behavior with few or no errors. The procedure resembles the exclusion methods that were described earlier. Exclusion in the sequencing task was evaluated by replacing elements of previously established sequences with novel (N) elements (e.g., A1-A2-N3-A4 and N1-B2-B3-B4). Subjects typically responded to a novel element in the ordinal position of the stimulus that it replaced in the sequence, apparently by excluding the other elements based on their membership in different sequence classes. Moreover, when four different novel elements were substituted in four different positions in various sequences, the novel elements subsequently became members of the sequence classes. For example, when formerly novel elements were displayed together for the first time, they were responded to in a sequence consistent with their exclusion-training history (i.e., N1-N2-N3-N4). Entirely new sequential performances could be generated virtually errorlessly.

Constraints on Recombinative
Generalization Based on Sequence-Class Membership

Studies of sequence-class formation and recombinative generalization establish the basis for generating reasonably elaborate behavioral repertoires with relatively little direct training. However, further research appears necessary before these procedures can begin to model the complexity of naturally occurring language repertoires. For example, recombinative generalization is not always appropriate. This point was made in early work by Bruner (1975). He taught children who were normally capable what he termed "language frames." In these, words of a common type were displayed in an order that was consistent with the children's natural language:

1	2	3	4	5
The	man	ate	his	lunch
A	lady	wore	my	hat
The	doctor	broke	a	bottle
My	son	drove	our	car

The children were then asked to provide examples that matched the frames. Bruner reports that children quickly recombined words to make meaningful sentences (e.g., "My doctor broke his hat"). The children also produced recombinations that seemed "sensible" but "silly" (e.g., "A lady ate a bottle"). Notably, the children did not produce recombinations that violated the frames (e.g., Man the lunch his ate). In the context Bruner established, the words in the language frames were members of arbitrary-sequence classes; every word was substitutable for every other word that shared the same ordinal position. However, the children discriminated that: 1) certain "legal" recombinations were meaningless, and 2) recombinative generalization outside the context of the exercise was inappropriate.

The children in Bruner's study apparently had already learned through interactions with their verbal community that recombinations of words are controlled by variables in addition to, and perhaps interacting with, ordinal relations among sequence elements. The specific semantic classes to which words belong and the general context in which words are uttered determine which sequential recombinations will be reinforced in natural language situations. Effects of these variables have not yet been examined carefully in matrix training and stimulus-class research with learners with mental retardation.

Contextual Control of Arbitrary-Class Membership

In highly complex selection-based communication systems, the designer may begin to consider modeling aspects of natural languages in which the same element has different meanings under different circumstances (e.g., "fly" as a noun versus "fly" as a verb). He or she may also have to consider whether or not to emulate another aspect of natural language, that elements may be members of more than one stimulus class (or conceptual category). Either case entails establishing contextual control of arbitrary-class membership (Sidman, 1986). Such contextual control has been demonstrated in a number of studies with adults and children who have normal capabilities (e.g., Bush, Sidman, & de Rose, 1989; Lazar & Kotlarchyk, 1986; Lynch & Green, 1991). Although there have been no reports of comparable successes with individuals who are very young or with severe mental retardation, other results suggest that contextual control of class membership is not necessarily beyond their capacity (e.g., Silverman, Anderson, Marshall, & Baer, 1986; cf. Stoddard & McIlvane, 1986). Nonetheless, developing contextual control of arbitrary stimulus-class membership requires venturing beyond the current secure database. Given that selection-based systems are designed rather than naturally evolving, where possible, potential teaching problems may be bypassed by avoiding unnecessary contextual dependencies.

Stimulus-Class Analysis in Current Selection-Based Communication Training

A reasonable question at this point is how the detailed analytical approach described in this chapter can benefit the special education or communication specialist who wants to establish selection-based communication. For such individuals, the scientific interests that inspire formal experimental studies and theoretical analyses, such as those considered here, are clearly secondary to the main interest—teaching the child to communicate.

Now and in the immediate future, the major contribution of stimulus-control analysis is likely to be in helping to diagnose and overcome problems that are frequently encountered in learners who have the most severe intellectual handicaps. In our experience, communication trainers working with this population have at best only intermittent success in reaching their students. Inspiring, positive outcomes with some students are offset by puzzling and frustrating failures with others. Properly applied, the stimulus-control shaping procedures and other methods described in this chapter will help to reach more children, thereby increasing the frequency of positive teaching outcomes. Moreover, once an initial foothold has been established, application of systematic procedures for programming more rapid and flexible discrimination learning is likely to encourage more rapid expansion of the selection-based communication repertoire.

In time, the analysis presented here may lead to more precise and detailed protocols for teaching selection-based communication skills and for assessing what has been learned. In typical communication training settings described in other chapters in this volume, instruction is delivered under fluid and constantly changing circumstances. By necessity, teaching strategies must be expressed in fairly general and abstract terms that must then be translated "on the fly" by the trainer into actual teaching interactions. Selection-based communication systems, by contrast, are inherently more structured, thereby more suited to advanced planning of the details (as opposed to the manner) of teaching, that is, for example, what stimuli are to be presented, in what order, what response alternatives are permitted, and what teaching sequence modifications are made contingent on performance.

We think it likely that highly structured teaching interventions of the type suggested may make it possible eventually, for example, to teach many learners with severe mental retardation to recognize, respond to, and learn the meanings of printed words and word sequences. Unfortunately, there has been little research on this possibility (e.g., Singh & Singh, 1986). However, there have recently been promising reports that some members of this population can learn to recognize printed words when they are paired with lexigrams (Sevcik, Romski, & Robinson, 1991). Some of the earliest research on stimulus equivalence in individuals with mental retardation sought to teach skills prerequisite for reading (e.g., Sidman, 1971), and more recent studies are beginning to confirm those promising initial results (McIlvane, in press). Selection-based communication via a "written" medium, such as constructing printed words from a pool of letters (analogous to typing [Dube, McDonald, McIlvane, & Mackay, 1991; Mackay & Sidman, 1984]), does not impose the initial distance from the social environment that is inherent in several other approaches. A written medium, however, may impose a greater initial learning burden on the individual with a mental handicap, because printed words are likely to be more difficult to discriminate (and thus to construct) than single stimuli such as lexigrams or Blissymbols. Thus, selection-based communication via printed words may prove to be an attractive alternative only to the extent that teaching can overcome these difficulties.

There remains, of course, the problem of how to bring individuals with mental handicaps into contact with teaching that can meet their needs. In an ideal world, every effort to establish and elaborate a selection-based communication repertoire would entail the careful analysis of the learner's entry skills, routine implementation of the most generally effective teaching procedures, ongoing modification of teaching procedures to meet individual needs, full evaluation and documentation of what has been learned—in short, all of the trademarks of good laboratory research. Unfortunately, instruction at this level is highly complex, difficult, costly, and probably impractical without more support than that readily available in most training settings. We think it unlikely that the full potential of the framework and methods presented in this chapter can be realized without computer assistance and/or computer management to handle the complexities of the instructional process (see Ager, 1989, for a discussion of relevant issues).

CONCLUSIONS AND RECOMMENDATIONS FOR FURTHER RESEARCH

Research in discrimination learning has brought us to the point where we can realistically anticipate an effective technology for teaching selection-based communication skills to learners who have severe intellectual and/or motor disabilities. Several opportunities for further research are apparent.

First, we need to know the limits of the current technology. The performances that we have considered so far have been relatively primitive, corresponding roughly to the single words and word combinations that characterize the initial stages of language learning (Bloom, 1974). It is an open question whether we will be able to elaborate these simple performances into more complex communication systems. It is an open question, for example, whether research on sequence classes has the potential to contribute to the scientific analysis and teaching of true syntactic relations. Research that attempts to develop contextual control of arbitrary-class membership in learners with severe retardation might help to define the range of possible performances. A conceptually related issue is if and how stimulus-class analysis applies to even more complex aspects of language. A possible role for stimulus-class analysis may be in describing the interaction of semantic classes in mastery of the verb lexicon (cf. Pinker, 1986). As yet, however, there have been no formal attempts to develop such possibilities.

Second, we need to know if current approaches in selection-based communication can be improved to expand the potential of the individual with intellectual disabilities for communicating in the social environment. Procedures that use pictures or other representations of objects have the potential for communicating broadly. Unfortunately, many events of significance in an individual's life are not amenable to expression in this way. When symbolic (i.e., arbitrary) stimuli must be employed by necessity, what are the optimal types? Printed words corresponding to the language spoken in the individual's community would seem to have the greatest potential for broad communication.

A related question is if it is possible to adapt the approach taken in our laboratory studies to the social environment of the language learner. Initially, it might seem difficult to reconcile the rigorous procedures and attention to detail that characterize laboratory studies with the informal and apparently less structured circumstances of the social environment. For us, however, "structure" need not be synonymous with the fixed-trial approach that characterizes discrimination research. It seems likely that similarly rigorous methods could be developed for application under more naturalistic circumstances. One can imagine, for example, procedures in which "trials" to establish and evaluate a given target performance are systematically arranged in the course of naturally occurring activities. There appear to be some appropriate models in developmental language research (e.g., Mervis, Mervis, Johnson, & Bertrand, in press) to provide both conceptual and technical guidance.

Finally, we need to know more about the degree to which establishing selection-based communication encourages the development of other communication and social skills. There have been several encouraging reports (e.g.,

Romski et al., 1984), but the efforts so far have been largely informal and unsystematic. Research to obtain more than anecdotal evidence is needed.

REFERENCES

Ager, A.K.S. (1989). Applications of microcomputer technology in the field of mental retardation. In J.A. Mulick & R.F. Antonak (Eds.), *Transitions in mental retardation* (Vol. 4, pp. 1–14). Norwood, NJ: Ablex.

Bickel, W.K., & Etzel, B.C. (1985). The quantal nature of controlling stimulus–response relations as measured in tests of stimulus generalization. *Journal of the Experimental Analysis of Behavior, 44*, 247–270.

Bloom, L. (1974). Talking, understanding, and thinking. In R.L. Schiefelbusch & L. Lloyd (Eds.), *Language perspectives: Acquisition, retardation, and intervention* (pp. 283–311). Baltimore: University Park Press.

Braine, M.D.S. (1986). What is learned in acquiring word classes—A step toward acquisition theory. In B. MacWhinney (Ed.), *Mechanisms of language acquisition* (pp. 65–87). Hillsdale, NJ: Lawrence Erlbaum Associates.

Bruner, J.S. (1975). *Toward a theory of instruction.* Cambridge, MA: Harvard University Press.

Bush, K.M., Sidman, M., & de Rose, T. (1989). Contextual control of emergent equivalence relations. *Journal of the Experimental Analysis of Behavior, 51*, 29–45.

Carr, E.G., & Durand, V.M. (1985). Reducing behavior problems through functional communication training. *Journal of Applied Behavior Analysis, 18*, 111–126.

Carr, E.G., & Kologinsky, E. (1983). Acquisition of sign language by autistic children II: Spontaneity and generalization effects. *Journal of Applied Behavior Analysis, 16*, 297–314.

Catania, A.C. (1984). *Learning* (2nd ed.). Englewood Cliffs, NJ: Prentice Hall.

Cohen, L.R., Brady, J., & Lowry, M. (1981). The role of differential responding in matching-to-sample and delayed matching performance. In M.L. Commons & J.A. Nevin (Eds.), *Quantitative analysis of behavior: Vol. 1. Discriminative properties of reinforcement schedules* (pp. 345–364). Cambridge, MA: Ballinger.

de Rose, J.C., McIlvane, W.J., Dube, W.V., Galpin, V., & Stoddard, L.T. (1988). Emergent simple discrimination established by indirect relation to differential consequences. *Journal of the Experimental Analysis of Behavior, 50*, 1–20.

Dixon, L.S. (1977). The nature of control by spoken words over visual stimulus selection. *Journal of the Experimental Analysis of Behavior, 27*, 433–442.

Dixon, L.S. (1981). A functional analysis of photo–object matching skills of severely retarded adolescents. *Journal of Applied Behavior Analysis, 14*, 465–478.

Dube, W.V., Iennaco, F.M., Rocco, F.J., Kledaras, J.B., & McIlvane, W.J. (1992). Generalized identity matching to sample: An analysis and new programming techniques. *Journal of Behavioral Education, 2*, 29–51.

Dube, W.V., McDonald, S.J., McIlvane, W.J., & Mackay, H.A. (1991). Constructed-response matching to sample and spelling instruction. *Journal of Applied Behavior Analysis, 24*, 305–317.

Dube, W.V., & McIlvane, W.J. (1989). Adapting a microcomputer for behavioral evaluation of mentally retarded individuals. In J.A. Mulick & R.F. Antonack (Eds.), *Transitions in mental retardation* (Vol. 4, pp. 104–127). Norwood, NJ: Ablex.

Dube, W.V., McIlvane, W.J., & Green, G. (1992). An analysis of generalized identity matching-to-sample test procedures. *Psychological Record, 42,* 17–28.

Dube, W.V., McIlvane, W.J., Mackay, H.A., & Stoddard, L.T. (1987). Stimulus class membership established via stimulus–reinforcer relations. *Journal of the Experimental Analysis of Behavior, 47,* 159–175.

Dube, W.V., McIlvane, W.J., Maguire, R.A., Mackay, H.A., & Stoddard, L.T. (1989). Stimulus class formation and stimulus–reinforcer relations. *Journal of the Experimental Analysis of Behavior, 51,* 65–76.

Fields, L., Reeve, K.F., Adams, B.J., & Verhave, T. (1991). Stimulus generalization and equivalence classes: A model for natural categories. *Journal of the Experimental Analysis of Behavior, 55,* 305–312.

Goldiamond, I. (1962). Perception. In A.J. Bachrach (Ed.), *Experimental foundations of clinical psychology.* New York: Basic Books.

Goldiamond, I. (1966). Perception, language, and conceptualization rules. In B. Kleinmuntz (Ed.), *Problem solving* (pp. 183–224). New York: John Wiley & Sons.

Goldstein, H., Angelo, D., & Mousetis, L. (1987). Acquisition and extension of syntactic repertoires by severely mentally retarded youth. *Research in Developmental Disabilities, 8,* 549–574.

Goldstein, H., & Mousetis, L. (1989). Generalized language learning by children with severe mental retardation: Effects of peers' expressive modeling. *Journal of Applied Behavior Analysis, 22,* 245–259.

Goossens', C., & Kraat, A. (1985). Technology as a tool for conversation and language learning for the physically disabled. *Topics in Language Disorders, 6,* 56–70.

Greenfield, D.B. (1985). Facilitating mentally retarded children's relational learning through novelty–familiarity training. *American Journal of Mental Deficiency, 90,* 342–348.

Guess, D., Sailor, W., & Baer, D.M. (1978). Children with limited language. In R.L. Schiefelbusch (Ed.), *Language intervention strategies* (pp. 101–143). Baltimore: University Park Press.

Hall, G., & Sundberg, M.L. (1987). Teaching mands by manipulating conditioned establishing operations. *Analysis of Verbal Behavior, 5,* 41–53.

Harlow, H.F. (1949). The formation of learning sets. *Psychological Review, 56,* 51–65.

Harris-Vanderheiden, D., Brown, W.P., MacKensie, P., Reinen, S., & Scheibel, C. (1975). Symbol communication for the mentally handicapped. *Mental Retardation, 13,* 34–37.

Hayes, S.C. (1989). Nonhumans have not yet shown stimulus equivalence. *Journal of the Experimental Analysis of Behavior, 51,* 385–392.

Hayes, S.C. (1990). A relational control theory of stimulus equivalence. In L.J. Hayes & P.N. Chase (Eds.), *Dialogues on verbal behavior: Proceedings of the First International Institute on Verbal Relations* (pp. 19–46). Reno, NV: Context Press.

Herman, L.M., & Arbeit, W.R., (1973). Stimulus control and auditory discrimination learning sets in the bottlenosed dolphin. *Journal of the Experimental Analysis of Behavior, 19,* 379–394.

Hively, W. (1962). Programming stimuli in matching to sample. *Journal of the Experimental Analysis of Behavior, 5,* 279–298.

House, B.J., Brown, A.L., & Scott, M.S. (1974). Children's discrimination learning based on identity or difference. In H.W. Reese (Ed.), *Advances in child development and behavior* (Vol. 9, pp. 1–45). New York: Academic Press.

House, B.J., Hanley, M.J., & Magid, D.F. (1979). A limitation on the law of effect. *American Journal of Mental Deficiency, 84*, 132–136.

Itard, J.M.G. (1801/1962). *The wild boy of Aveyron* (G. Humphries & M. Humphries, Trans.). New York: Appleton-Century-Crofts.

Iverson, I.H., Sidman, M., & Carrigan, P. (1986). Stimulus definition in conditional discriminations. *Journal of the Experimental Analysis of Behavior, 45*, 297–304.

Kaiser, A.P., Yoder, P.J., & Keetz, A. (1992). Evaluating milieu teaching. In S. F. Warren & J. Reichle (Eds.), *Communication and language intervention series: Vol. 1. Causes and effects in communication and language intervention* (pp. 9–47). Baltimore: Paul H. Brookes Publishing Co.

Kaufman, M.E., & Prehm, H.J. (1966). A review of research on learning sets and transfer of training in mental defectives. In N.R. Ellis (Ed.), *International review of research in mental retardation* (Vol. 2, pp. 123–149). New York: Academic Press.

Lamarre, J., & Holland, J.G. (1985). The functional independence of mands and tacts. *Journal of the Experimental Analysis of Behavior, 43*, 5–19.

Lancioni, G.E., Hoogeveen, F.R., Smeets, P.M., Boelens, H.H., & Leonard, S.N. (1989). Errorless discrimination of reversible letters: Superimposition and fading combined with an intervening response. *Psychological Record, 39*, 373–385.

Lazar, R., Davis-Lang, D., & Sanchez, L. (1984). The formation of visual stimulus equivalence in children. *Journal of the Experimental Analysis of Behavior, 41*, 251–266.

Lazar, R.M., & Kotlarchyk, B.J. (1986). Second-order control of sequence-class equivalences in children. *Behavioural Processes, 13*, 205–213.

Lignugaris/Kraft, B., McCullar, G.L., Exum, M., & Salzberg, C.L. (1988). A review of research on picture reading skills of developmentally disabled individuals. *Journal of Special Education, 22*, 297–329.

Lynch, D.C., & Green, G. (1991). Development and crossmodal transfer of fifth-term control of emergent relations. *Journal of the Experimental Analysis of Behavior, 56*, 139–154.

MacDonald, R.P.F., Dixon, L.S., & LeBlanc, J.M. (1986). Stimulus class formation following observational learning. *Analysis and Intervention in Developmental Disabilities, 6*, 73–87.

Mackay, H.A., & Sidman, M. (1984). Teaching new behavior via equivalence relations. In P.H. Brooks, R. Sperber, & C. MacCauley (Eds.), *Learning and cognition in the mentally retarded* (pp. 493–513). Hillsdale, NJ: Lawrence Erlbaum Associates.

Mackay, H.A., Stoddard, L.T., & Spencer, T.J. (1989). Symbols and meaning classes: Multiple sequence production and the emergence of ordinal stimulus classes. *Experimental Analysis of Human Behavior Bulletin, 7*, 16–17.

McIlvane, W.J. (in press). Stimulus control analysis and nonverbal instructional technology for people with mental handicaps. In N.R. Bray (Ed.), *International review of research in mental retardation*.

McIlvane, W.J., Bass, R.W., O'Brien, J.M., Gerovac, B.J., & Stoddard, L.T. (1984). Spoken and signed naming of foods after receptive exclusion training in severe retardation. *Applied Research in Mental Retardation, 5*, 1–27.

McIlvane, W.J., & Dube, W.V. (1992). Stimulus control shaping and stimulus control topographies. *Behavior Analyst, 15*, 89–94.

McIlvane, W.J., & Dube, W.V. (1990). Do stimulus classes form before they are tested? *Analysis of Verbal Behavior, 8*, 13–18.

McIlvane, W.J., Dube, W.V., Kledaras, J.B., Iennaco, F.M., & Stoddard, L.T. (1990). Teaching relational discrimination to mentally retarded individuals: Some problems and possible solutions. *American Journal on Mental Retardation, 95,* 283–286.

McIlvane, W.J., Kledaras, J.B., Dube, W.V., & Stoddard, L.T. (1989). Automated instruction of severely and profoundly retarded individuals. In J.A. Mulick & R.F. Antonak (Eds.), *Transitions in mental retardation* (Vol. 4, pp. 15–76). Norwood, NJ: Ablex.

McIlvane, W.J., Kledaras, J.B., Killory-Anderson, R., & Sheiber, F. (1989). Teaching with noncriterion-related prompts: A possible subject variable. *Psychological Record, 39,* 131–142.

McIlvane, W.J., Kledaras, J.B., Lowry, M.W., & Stoddard, L.T. (in press). Studies of exclusion in individuals with severe mental retardation. *Research in Developmental Disabilities.*

McIlvane, W.J., Munson, L.C., & Stoddard, L.T. (1988). Some observations on control by spoken words in children's conditional discrimination and matching by exclusion. *Journal of Experimental Child Psychology, 45,* 472–495.

McIlvane, W.J., & Stoddard, L.T. (1981). Acquisition of matching-to-sample performances in severe mental retardation: Learning by exclusion. *Journal of Mental Deficiency Research, 25,* 33–48.

McIlvane, W.J., Withstandley, J.K., & Stoddard, L.T. (1984). Positive and negative stimulus relations in severely retarded persons' conditional discriminations. *Analysis and Intervention in Developmental Disabilities, 4,* 235–251.

McIntyre, K.D., Cleary, J., & Thompson, T. (1989). Reply to Saunders and Hayes. *Journal of the Experimental Analysis of Behavior, 51,* 393–396.

Mervis, C.B., Mervis, C.A., Johnson, K.E., & Bertrand, J. (in press). Studying early lexical development: The value of the systematic diary method. In C. Rovee-Collier & L. Lipsett (Eds.), *Advances in infancy research* (Vol. 7). Norwood, NJ: Ablex.

Mirenda, P. (1985). Designing pictorial communication systems for physically able-bodied students with severe handicaps. *Augmentative and Alternative Communication, 1,* 58–64.

Mishkin, M., & Delacour, J. (1975). An analysis of short-term visual memory in the monkey. *Journal of Experimental Psychology: Animal Behavior Processes, 1,* 326–334.

Pinker, S. (1986). Resolving a learnability paradox in the acquisition of the verb lexicon. In M.L. Rice & R.L. Schiefelbusch (Eds.), *The teachability of language* (pp. 13–61). Baltimore: Paul H. Brookes Publishing Co.

Premack, D. (1976). *Intelligence in the ape and man.* Hillsdale, NJ: Lawrence Erlbaum Associates.

Premack, D. (1989). Some thoughts about transfer. In M.L. Rice & R.L. Schiefelbusch (Eds.), *The teachability of language* (pp. 239–262). Baltimore: Paul H. Brookes Publishing Co.

Reese, H.W. (1968). *The perception of stimulus relations: Discrimination learning and transposition.* New York: Academic Press.

Rice, M.L., Buhr, J.C., & Nemeth, M. (1990). Fast mapping word-learning abilities of language-delayed preschoolers. *Journal of Speech and Hearing Disorders, 55,* 33–42.

Richmond, G., & Bell, J. (1986). Comparison of trial-and-error and graduated stimulus change procedures across tasks. *Analysis and Intervention in Developmental Disabilities, 6,* 127–136.

Romski, M.A., & Sevcik, R.A. (1988). Augmentative and alternative communication: Considerations for individuals with severe intellectual disabilities. *Augmentative and Alternative Communication, 4,* 83–93.

Romski, M.A., Sevcik, R.A., & Pate, J.L. (1988). The establishment of symbolic communication in persons with severe retardation. *Journal of Speech and Hearing Disorders, 53,* 94–107.

Romski, M.A., Sevcik, R.A., & Rumbaugh, D.M. (1985). Retention of symbolic communication skills in five severely retarded persons. *American Journal on Mental Deficiency, 89,* 441–444.

Romski, M.A., White, R.A., Millen, C.E., & Rumbaugh, D.M. (1984). Effects of computer-keyboard teaching on the symbolic communication of severely retarded persons: Five case studies. *Psychological Record, 34,* 39–54.

Rosch, E., & Mervis, C.B. (1975). Family resemblances: Studies in the internal structure of categories. *Cognitive Psychology, 7,* 573–605.

Rumbaugh, D.M. (Ed.). (1977). *Language learning by a chimpanzee: The Lana Project.* New York: Academic Press.

Saunders, K.J. (1989). Naming in conditional discrimination and stimulus equivalence. *Journal of the Experimental Analysis of Behavior, 51,* 379–384.

Saunders, K.J., & Spradlin, J.E. (1989). Conditional discrimination in mentally retarded adults: The effects of training the component simple discriminations. *Journal of the Experimental Analysis of Behavior, 52,* 1–12.

Saunders, K.J., & Spradlin, J.E. (1990). Conditional discrimination in mentally retarded adults: The development of generalized skills. *Journal of the Experimental Analysis of Behavior, 54,* 239–250.

Saunders, R.R., Saunders, K.J., Kirby, K.C., & Spradlin, J.E. (1988). The merger and development of equivalence classes by unreinforced conditional selection of comparison stimuli. *Journal of the Experimental Analysis of Behavior, 50,* 145–162.

Schreibman, L., Charlop, M.H., & Koegel, R.L. (1982). Teaching autistic children to use extra-stimulus prompts. *Journal of Experimental Child Psychology, 33,* 475–491.

Sevcik, R.A., & Romski, M.A. (1986). Representational matching skills of persons with severe retardation. *Augmentative and Alternative Communication, 2,* 160–164.

Sevcik, R.A., Romski, M.A., & Robinson, B.R.. (1991, November). *Printed English word recognition by nonspeaking children with mental retardation.* Paper presented at the annual meeting of the American Speech-Language-Hearing Association, Atlanta.

Sidman, M. (1971). Reading and auditory-visual equivalences. *Journal of Speech and Reading Research, 14,* 5–13.

Sidman, M. (1977). Teaching some basic prerequisites for reading. In P. Mittler (Ed.), *Research to practice in mental retardation* (Vol. II, pp. 353–360). Baltimore: University Park Press.

Sidman, M. (1986). The measurement of behavioral development. In N.A. Krasnegor, D.B. Gray, & T. Thompson (Eds.), *Advances in behavioral pharmacology: Vol. 5. Developmental behavioral pharmacology* (pp. 43–52). Hillsdale, NJ: Lawrence Erlbaum Associates.

Sidman, M. (1990). Equivalence relations: Where do they come from? In D.E. Blackman & H. Lejeune (Eds.), *Behavior analysis in theory and practice: Contributions and controversies* (pp. 93–114). Hillsdale, NJ: Lawrence Erlbaum Associates.

Sidman, M., Rauzin, R., Lazar, R., Cunningham, S., Tailby, W., & Carrigan, P. (1982). A search for symmetry in the conditional discriminations of rhesus monkeys, baboons, and children. *Journal of the Experimental Analysis of Behavior, 37,* 23–44.

Sidman, M., & Rosenberger, P.B. (1967). Several methods for teaching serial position to monkeys. *Journal of the Experimental Analysis of Behavior, 10,* 467–478.

Sidman, M., & Stoddard, L.T. (1966). Programming perception and learning for retarded children. In N.R. Ellis (Ed.), *International review of research in mental retardation* (Vol. 2, pp. 151–208). New York: Academic Press.

Sidman, M., & Tailby, W. (1982). Conditional discrimination vs. matching-to-sample: An expansion of the testing paradigm. *Journal of the Experimental Analysis of Behavior, 37,* 5–22.

Sidman, M., Willson-Morris, M., & Kirk, B. (1986). Matching-to-sample procedures and the development of equivalence relations: The role of naming. *Analysis and Intervention in Developmental Disabilities, 6,* 1–19.

Sidman, M., Wynne, C.K., Maguire, R.W., & Barnes, T. (1989). Functional classes and equivalence relations. *Journal of the Experimental Analysis of Behavior, 52,* 261–274.

Sigafoos, J., Doss, S., & Reichle, J. (1989). Developing mand and tact repertoires in persons with severe developmental disabilities using graphic symbols. *Research in Developmental Disabilities, 10,* 183–200.

Sigafoos, J., Reichle, J., Doss, S., Hall, C., & Pettitt, L. (1990). "Spontaneous" transfer of stimulus control from tact to mand contingencies. *Research in Developmental Disabilities, 11,* 165–176.

Silverman, K., Anderson, S.R., Marshall, A.M., & Baer, D.M. (1986). Establishing and generalizing audience control of new language repertoires. *Analysis and Intervention in Developmental Disabilities, 6,* 21–40.

Singh, N.N., & Singh, J. (1986). Reading acquisition and remediation in the mentally retarded. In N.R. Ellis & N.W. Bray (Eds.), *International review of research in mental retardation* (Vol. 14, pp. 165–199). New York: Academic Press.

Skinner, B.F. (1935). The generic nature of the concepts of stimulus and response. *Journal of General Psychology, 12,* 40–65.

Skinner, B.F. (1957). *Verbal behavior.* New York: Appleton-Century-Crofts.

Soraci, S.A., Jr., Deckner, C.W., Haenlein, M., Baumeister, A.A., Murata-Soraci, K., & Blanton, R.L. (1987). Oddity performance in preschool children at risk for mental retardation: Transfer and maintenance. *Research in Developmental Disabilities, 8,* 137–151.

Spradlin, J.E., Cotter, V.W., & Baxley, N. (1973). Establishing a conditional discrimination without direct training: A study of transfer with retarded adolescents. *American Journal of Mental Deficiency, 77,* 556–566.

Spradlin, J.E., Saunders, R.R., & Saunders, K.J. (1992). The use of routines in teaching language skills to people with severe disabilities. In L.R. Hayes & S.C. Hayes (Eds.), *Understanding verbal relations* (pp. 29–42). Reno, NV: Context Press.

Stoddard, L.T., & McIlvane, W.J. (1986). Stimulus control research and developmentally disabled individuals. *Analysis and Intervention in Developmental Disabilities, 6,* 155–178.

Stoddard, L.T., & Sidman, M. (1967). The effects of errors on children's performance on a circle–ellipse discrimination. *Journal of the Experimental Analysis of Behavior, 10,* 261–270.

Striefel, S., & Wetherby, B. (1973). Instruction-following behavior of a retarded child and its controlling stimuli. *Journal of Applied Behavior Analysis, 6,* 663–670.

Stromer, R. (1986). Control by exclusion in arbitrary matching-to-sample. *Analysis and Intervention in Developmental Disabilities, 6,* 59–72.

Stromer, R., & Mackay, H.A. (1990). A note on the study of transitive relations in stimulus sequences. *Experimental Analysis of Human Behavior Bulletin, 8,* 2–5.

Terrace, H.S. (1971). Escape from S−. *Learning and Motivation, 2,* 148–163.

Touchette, P.E. (1971). Transfer of stimulus control: Measuring the moment of transfer. *Journal of the Experimental Analysis of Behavior, 15,* 347–354.

Vaughan, W. (1988). Formation of equivalence sets in pigeons. *Journal of Experimental Psychology: Animal Behavior Processes, 14,* 36–42.

Vaughan, W. (1989). Reply to Hayes. *Journal of the Experimental Analysis of Behavior, 51,* 397.

Vincent-Smith, L., Bricker, D., & Bricker, W. (1974). Acquisition of receptive vocabulary in the toddler-age child. *Child Development, 45,* 189–193.

Warren, S.F., McQuarter, R.J., & Rogers-Warren, A.K. (1984). The effects of teacher mands and models on the speech of unresponsive language-delayed children. *Journal of Speech and Hearing Research, 49,* 43–52.

Weinstein, B. (1941). Matching-from-sample by rhesus monkeys and by children. *Journal of Comparative Psychology, 31,* 195–213.

Wetherby, B., & Striefel, S. (1978). Application of miniature linguistic system of matrix-training procedures. In R.L. Schiefelbusch (Ed.), *Language intervention strategies* (pp. 317–356). Baltimore: University Park Press.

Wright, A.A., Cook, R.G., Rivera, J.J., Sands, S.F., & Delius, J.D. (1988). Concept learning by pigeons: Matching-to-sample with trial-unique video picture stimuli. *Animal Learning and Behavior, 16,* 436–444.

Zeaman, D., & House, B.J. (1963). The role of attention in retardate discrimination learning. In N.R. Ellis (Ed.), *Handbook of mental deficiency, psychological theory, and research* (pp. 159–223). New York: McGraw-Hill.

Zygmont, D., Lazar, R., Dube, W.V., & McIlvane, W.J. (1992). Teaching arbitrary matching via stimulus shaping to children and mentally retarded adults. *Journal of the Experimental Analysis of Behavior, 57,* 109–117.

13

Acquisition of
Early Object Labels

The Roles of
Operating Principles and Input

Carolyn B. Mervis and Jacquelyn Bertrand

IMAGINE THE FOLLOWING SCENARIO: SIXTEEN-month-old Daniel and his mother are at a pond. Suddenly, his mother notices a beaver gnawing on a small tree. She knows that Daniel has never seen a beaver before, not even in a picture. Excitedly, she points in the direction of the beaver and says, "Look, Daniel! Beaver!" What is Daniel to decide that "beaver" means? If this question is asked of a group of preschoolers, the uniform answer is that Daniel will decide that "beaver" refers to beavers. The children's attitude is, "What else could Daniel possibly think?" But why are the children so confident?

The supportive nonlinguistic input provided by Daniel's mother is an important reason for the children's confidence. In this case, Daniel's mother was pointing to the intended referent as she said "beaver." This action would serve to focus Daniel's attention in the location of the beaver. Thus—assuming that Daniel believed that when someone focused his attention on a particular location, any accompanying speech should refer to something relevant to that location—the pointing gesture would greatly narrow the field of possible referents for "beaver." On this basis, Daniel would not even consider the

The research and theory development described in this chapter were supported by Grant Nos. HD26892 and HD27042 from the National Institute of Child Health and Human Development and by Grant No. BNS 84-19036 from the National Science Foundation, awarded to Carolyn Mervis. We would like to thank the many parents and children who have participated so enthusiastically in our studies. In particular, we would like to acknowledge the generous assistance of The Early Years School, The Elaine Clark Variety Center, and the Down Syndrome Association of Atlanta. We appreciate the contributions of the members of our research group, especially Sharon Forshee, Kathy Johnson, and Cindy Mervis. Les Cohen, Roberta Golinkoff, Ann Kaiser, and Mike Tomasello provided thoughtful comments on an earlier draft of this chapter.

possibility that "beaver" could refer to such things as a boat tied to a tree in the opposite direction from that indicated by his mother or to the soaring of a hawk overhead, behind his mother.

Thus, the pointing gesture plays an important role in helping to delineate the possible referents of "beaver." However, pointing alone cannot identify the referent conclusively. For example, in addition to the beaver, the pointing gesture would permit such referents as "creature gnawing on something," "beaver standing on its hind legs," "creature with a flat tail," "brown things," "gnawing," or "things that beavers do." A priori, all of these, as well as a number of others, are reasonable possibilities, given the focus of the pointing gesture. Even if Daniel were to hear "beaver" several more times, in a variety of ostensive situations, he would not be able to identify the intended referent conclusively, given only the focus provided by the pointing gesture.

In fact, if a child were to consider all the possibilities of what a particular word might mean, even given ostensive input, he or she would have great difficulty determining the meaning of a single word. Yet, Templin (1957) has estimated that 6-year-olds who are developing normally have about 14,000 words (including derived forms) in their vocabularies. By this age, the majority of children with mental retardation have acquired at least several hundred words. Most children, with or without developmental disabilities, acquire a basic vocabulary relatively rapidly.

Recently, several researchers (e.g., Clark, 1983; Golinkoff, Hirsh-Pasek, Bailey, & Wenger, in press; Golinkoff, Mervis, & Hirsh-Pasek, 1992; Markman, 1989; Mervis, 1988, 1990a, 1990b; Mervis & Bertrand, 1990) have argued that lexical acquisition proceeds as rapidly as it does because the child has a set of operating principles that guide the task of word learning. The term "operating principle" originated in the psycholinguistics literature (Slobin, 1973, 1985) to describe the implicit and explicit strategies that children use to determine how to go about acquiring language. Lexical operating principles are like heuristics in problem solving. That is, these principles are intelligent strategies that increase the likelihood that certain hypotheses will be entertained when determining the referent for a word. These principles are acquired in a developmental order (Golinkoff et al., 1992; Mervis, 1990b; Mervis & Bertrand, 1990). As new principles are acquired, the inferences that young children make concerning the reference of a particular word are likely to change. We argue that lexical principles are necessary, even given supportive nonlinguistic (e.g., pointing to the intended referent) and linguistic input. At the same time, these principles are not sufficient; adequate supportive linguistic and nonlinguistic input also are necessary for lexical acquisition to proceed.

The purpose of this chapter is to consider early lexical development from a principles perspective. We will focus on early lexical development by children who are developing normally and by children who have mental retardation. We emphasize object words, for several reasons. First, a review of the early lexical acquisition literature indicates that almost all of the available data for children with mental retardation are concerned with object words (Barrett & Diniz, 1989). The majority of the data regarding the early lexical development of children who are developing normally are also concerned with object words (e.g., Mervis, 1983, 1990b). Second, examination of early productive vocabulary lists of individual children who are developing normally indicates that object words are consistently the most frequent class of words. This is true not only for children whose acquisition strategy is analytic (cf. Nelson, 1973, referential strategy); even children whose acquisition strategy is holistic (cf. Nelson, 1973, expressive style) have more object words than any other single type of word in their vocabularies (Bates, Thal, & Janowsky, 1992).[1] The difference between the early lexicons of children with analytic styles and children with holistic styles is reflected in the degree to which object words predominate, rather than whether or not object words predominate. Third, the principles perspective has been worked out best for object words. Our focus on object words is not meant to underestimate the importance of social-regulative words (e.g., uh-oh, allgone, hi, please) in many children's early vocabularies. Children's earliest words tend to be either object words or social-regulative words. Unfortunately, not enough is known about the acquisition of social-regulative words for us to address their development here.

Four of the earliest lexical operating principles evidenced by very young children are described in this chapter (see Table 1), and the data supporting these principles and implications of these principles are examined. Because most of the available data involve language production, our consideration of language comprehension is necessarily limited. It is important to remember, however, that many children will acquire some of these principles during the preverbal period. The roles of the child's cognitive abilities and of linguistic input in the use of lexical principles are discussed. We also consider possible links between some of these lexical principles and early cognitive principles concerned with categorization. We conclude the chapter with a consideration

---

[1]Researchers who study early language development have identified two contrasting learning styles that young children may adopt for the task of language acquisition. According to Bates, Thal, and Janowsky (1992), a child's learning style is manifested across the various aspects of early language development: babbling, first words, and first word combinations. Children who use an analytic style approach language acquisition by breaking the input into small units and working out the organization of these units before attempting to synthesize them. In babbling, analytic children focus on short and consistent consonant-vowel segments. The first words of these children are primarily object names, and early word combinations are telegraphic. In contrast, children who use an holistic style start by producing relatively large chunks of speech in familiar contexts. Early on, the speech of these children sounds more like adult speech than does the speech of analytic children. Holistic children gradually break these larger units down into their component parts. In babbling, holistic children produce long streams of vowels with an occasional consonant, using sentence intonation. The first words of these children are more varied than those of analytic children and often include formulaic expressions such as "gimme." Early word combinations include large numbers of frozen expressions or formulae with very limited productivity.

Table 1. Early lexical operating principles

Principle	Description
Object Scope	Words refer to whole objects.
Extendibility	Words may be used to label objects related to the original referent.
Categorical Scope	Words are extended to objects that share shape (and function) with the original referent.
Novel Name–Nameless Category	A new word maps to an object that belongs to a category for which the child does not yet have a name.

of the implications of the principles approach for early language intervention and a discussion of the importance of studies with special populations for determination of the universality (or non-universality) of the proposed lexical operating principles.

THE PRINCIPLE OF OBJECT SCOPE

One of the first lexical principles evidenced by young children is the principle of Object Scope. According to this principle, *words refer to whole objects* (cf. Golinkoff et al., 1992; Macnamara, 1982; Markman, 1989; Mervis, 1987; Mervis & Long, 1987). Below, we address two major implications of this principle for very early lexical development. (For a more detailed discussion, see Mervis, 1990b.) We then consider aspects of the child's cognitive abilities and of the linguistic input that aid the child in his or her use of the principle of Object Scope.

Implications of the Principle of Object Scope

Treatment of Non-nouns as Object Labels

The first implication of Object Scope is that early in the process of language acquisition, children should sometimes treat words that are not nouns as if they were object labels. A number of such cases have been reported for children who were developing normally, involving the use of adjectives, verbs, or interjections as object labels. For example, Hoffman's son initially assumed that "hot" was the label for stoves (Hoffman, 1968; cited in Macnamara, 1982). Both of Mervis's sons initially assumed that "hot" was the label for cups (including coffee mugs; Mervis, 1987). Both children used "hot" to refer to cups, mugs, glasses, and bowls, regardless of whether there was anything in them that could be considered hot (and even when they were empty). During this period, "hot" was never used in reference to other items that were hot (e.g., fire, stove, hot water in bathtub). The diary data for Mervis's children also documented several other instances of misconstruals.

For example, Ari initially assumed that "more" was the label for juice and that "tickle tickle" was the label for fishes. Velleman, Mangipudi, and Locke (1989) described a child who considered "hi" to be the label for telephones. Recent longitudinal studies of the early language development of children with developmental delays have also documented these types of misconstruals. For example, Velleman et al. (1989) reported that one of the children with Down syndrome who participated in their study also misconstrued "hi" to refer to telephones. One child with Williams syndrome who is participating in our ongoing longitudinal study treated "bang" as the label for hammers, and another child treated "two" as the label for coins. This child used "two" in reference to coins of all types, regardless of how many (e.g., one, two, several, a large pile) were present. "Two" was never used in relation to other objects, even when exactly two items were present.

Referents for Children's Earliest Words

The second implication of Object Scope is that children's earliest referential words should refer to whole objects, rather than to parts, attributes, or actions of the objects. Examination of lists of children's first 10 words indicates that virtually all of these words are either names of whole objects (including people's names) or are nonreferential (e.g., hi, uh-oh). The early word lists Nelson (1973) reported for 18 children who were developing normally did not include any labels for parts of objects and included only one attribute word, which was used by only one child. Gillham (1979), in a study of four children with Down syndrome and 14 children who were developing normally, found a few names for body parts among both groups of children's earliest words. However, these words were produced by only a few of the children.

The data just described are observational. One experimental study (Mervis & Long, 1987), using specially designed artificial stimuli, has been conducted to test the implication that words refer to whole objects, rather than to parts of objects. In this study, the experimenter pointed directly at a part of an object at the same time as she provided a nonsense syllable label. She then removed the object and placed three additional objects in front of the child. One of these objects had the same overall shape as the original object, but did not have the part that was labeled; another object had a different overall shape, but did have the labeled part in the same position as on the original object; the third object had still another overall shape and did not have the labeled part. The child was asked to show the experimenter the [nonsense syllable]. Results indicated that 18-month-olds who were developing normally almost always responded by indicating the object with the same overall shape as the original, even though this choice did not have the labeled part. These results provide strong support for the hypothesis that early language learners believe that a word used in reference to a novel type of object refers to the whole object, rather than to a part of the object, even when the ostensive gesture is directed to the part.

Facilitators of the Principle of Object Scope

Comprehension and Production of Ostensive Gestures

Ostensive definition is a common form of introduction of a new word to a young child. As we indicated, ostensive definition does not uniquely indicate the intended referent. Nevertheless, this form of definition greatly restricts the range of possible referents—assuming that the child knows how to take advantage of ostensive input. Examples of ostensive input include pointing, eye gaze, and showing something. Ostensive definition, combined with the principle of Object Scope, usually will correctly delimit the intended referent. For example, in play with young children, when adults point to a particular location and say something, there often is only one object in that location. Given the principle of Object Scope, the child should treat the object in that location as the referent of the word.

Pointing is a particularly frequent form of ostensive input. During the first several months of life, infants do not benefit from the pointing gesture; their response is to look at the tip of the extended finger. At about 9 or 10 months of age, infants who are developing normally begin to follow a pointed finger in the intended distal direction (Lock, 1978; Murphy & Messer, 1977). Thus, the pointed finger serves as a method of gaze regulation. The results of Mundy, Seibert, and Hogan's (1984) cross-sectional study of infants with developmental delays (a mixed group including children with delays due to Down syndrome, other organic problems, or unknown etiology) indicated that these children also were able to follow a pointing gesture by a mental age of about 10 months. At about 9 or 10 months of age, infants who are developing normally also are able to follow an adult's eye gaze to the intended distal location (Schaife & Bruner, 1975). Published data are not available for this second measure for children with developmental delays.

Also at age 9 or 10 months, infants who are developing normally begin to produce these same gestures; they initiate gaze regulation by pointing to an object, and they look back and forth between the object and the adult to ensure that the adult is looking in the indicated direction (Bates, Camaioni, & Volterra, 1975; Franco & Butterworth, 1991). Mundy et al. (1984) found that children with developmental delays developed similar abilities at a mental age of about 10 months. In summary, by a mental age of 9 or 10 months, infants are able to take advantage of ostensive input both by comprehending such input when it is provided by an adult and by producing such input to indicate to an adult the entity of interest (see Adamson & Bakeman, in press). It appears that at this age infants realize that gestures can be used to indicate something in the environment. This is the same mental age at which infants begin to be able to use the principle of Object Scope (as evidenced by comprehension of object names [Benedict, 1979]).

Facilitative Linguistic Input

Bridges (1986) argued that adult speech to a young child reflects what the adult considers to be the child's immediate interest. Bridges argued further that parents interpret much of the behavior of children between the ages of 9–18 months as indicating a special interest in objects. Examples of behaviors that are consistent with this parental interpretation include close visual examination and manipulative exploration of toys by the child. Thus, parents would be expected to produce a large number of object names. It would be helpful to the child if these object names were highlighted linguistically. Although adult-directed speech does not make object labels salient (Gentner, 1982), child-directed speech (at least in American English) does highlight these labels. In a comparison of nouns and verbs in child-directed speech, Goldfield (1990) found that nouns are produced more frequently, with greater stress, with fewer inflections, and more often in final position. These characteristics, particularly increased stress and sentence-final position, fit well with operating principles for segmenting the speech stream (Peters, 1985; Slobin, 1985). Thus, these characteristics serve to emphasize exactly those words that are most important for the principle of Object Scope—names for objects. Examination of our videotapes of mother–child interaction, in which the child is developmentally delayed (due to Down syndrome, Williams syndrome, or severe delays of unknown etiology), indicates that maternal speech to these children displayed these same characteristics. All the descriptive studies to date have involved American English-speaking mothers. An important question remains: Does maternal speech in languages that permit noun deletion (the strongest test would involve Japanese or Korean) also have these characteristics? That is, is the highlighting of object labels a universal characteristic of maternal speech, or is this form of facilitation of the principle of Object Scope restricted to particular languages?

Thus, the child-directed speech of English-speaking mothers fits well with the first implication of Object Scope (words refer primarily to objects). There also is evidence that child-directed speech fits well with the second implication that words refer to whole objects, rather than to object parts. Ninio (1980; Ninio & Bruner, 1978), in separate studies of English-speaking mothers and Hebrew-speaking mothers, found that in bookreading situations, about 95% of maternal deictic utterances referred to whole objects. In the few exceptions, utterances usually were marked explicitly to indicate the relation between the whole object and the singled-out attribute (e.g., "That's the kitty's ear," rather than "That's an ear"). Once again, the study of child-directed speech in languages such as Japanese or Korean is critical; these studies have yet to be conducted.

As noted above, the principle of Object Scope sometimes leads children to make incorrect inferences about the referent of a particular word. For example, children sometimes decide that verbs or attributes presented alone or in deictic utterances are in fact labels for objects. Ninio (1980) found that when mothers asked, "What's this?" at the same time making clear from an adult perspective that the intended referent was a part (e.g., by touching or tapping a specific part), the children almost always answered with the name of the whole object, although they knew the name of the part. Gillham (1979) reported that in the past, early language training programs for children with developmental delays often focused initially on color words, with the consequence that children did not learn any words. (If children tried to treat the color word as the name of an object, they would become confused almost immediately, because the adult would be applying the same "name" to extremely diverse objects. Furthermore, adults would appear to be calling the same type of object [e.g., blocks] by a variety of names.) When the focus of these programs was changed to object labels, however, the children were more successful.

Limitation of the Principle of Object Scope: Restriction of Range of Referents

In the earliest phases of language acquisition, some children may take object names to refer only to the specific objects that someone previously labeled with that name. The principle of Object Scope does not include a mechanism for the extension of words to previously unlabeled objects. The next principle discussed, Extendibility, provides a mechanism to achieve this. For many children, the principles of Object Scope and Extendibility are acquired at about the same time. For such children, extension of object labels is not problematic. However, if a child began to comprehend or produce language prior to acquisition of the principle of Extendibility, his or her use of earliest words would initially be restricted to objects that previously had been labeled by someone else. One possible consequence is that common nouns would be treated as proper names (cf. Dromi, 1987). Bloom (1973) reports two such instances for her daughter, involving the words "bird" and "record player." Allison initially behaved as if "bird" referred only to a particular bird mobile and "record player" referred only to a particular phonograph. Barrett (1986), in a diary study of his older son's early lexical development, noted that Adam initially used "dog" to refer only to an appliqued dog on one of his bibs—the primary referent for "dog" in adult speech addressed to the child. The evidence from a longitudinal study of the first 10 words of four children (Harris, Barrett, Jones, & Brookes, 1988) also provides support for the implication that in the earliest stages of language production a child may use a word only in reference to objects that someone else previously labeled with that word. In this study, there were several cases in which a mother used a particular word only in reference to a single object. In all such cases, her child was found to use the word only to refer to that same exemplar.

THE PRINCIPLE OF EXTENDIBILITY

Children who have only the principle of Object Scope are limited to treating words that they consider referential as labels for exemplars that have already been named for them. This restriction leads to underextension of object words, and these underextensions may be so severe as to result in a common noun being treated as a proper name. To tap into the power of words to label categories, however, the child must realize that most object labels operate as common nouns. The principle of Extendibility states that *a word may be used to label objects related to the original referent* (Golinkoff et al., 1992). Below, we discuss the major implications of this principle and then consider one important way that input may influence the type of extension the child evidences for a particular word.

Implications of the Principle of Extendibility

Spontaneous Extension of a Word to New Referents

The first implication of the principle of Extendibility is that children should extend the words that they know (understand or produce) to other related objects, even if a child has never heard a label for these objects. That is, children should no longer severely restrict the extension of the words they know. This implication is strongly supported by the results of recent diary studies (e.g., Barrett, 1986; Bloom, 1973; Dromi, 1987; Mervis, Mervis, Johnson, & Bertrand, 1992) and diary studies from the early 1900s (e.g., see review in Clark, 1973). In all of these studies, instances of restriction of word extension to a single object or a very small set of previously named objects are limited to the child's first few words. The same results were obtained in a longitudinal study of young children with Down syndrome (Mervis, 1984). As noted above, some children never evidence this type of extreme restriction. For these children, the principle of Extendibility presumably was acquired either at the same time as, or very soon after, the principle of Object Scope.

Once the child acquires the principle of Extendibility, extreme restriction of extension should occur only in cases in which the child believes that there are no related referents. For example, if the child chooses a categorical basis for extension, and the original referent was a very atypical exemplar of the adult category labeled by the word, the child may not extend the word to other objects because he or she does not consider any of the available objects to be categorically related to the original exemplar. Two examples of this type of restriction were found in Ari's early vocabulary. In both cases, the object that usually was labeled for him with the relevant word was an extremely atypical exemplar of the adult-appropriate category (Mervis, 1987). These exemplars were so atypical that it was not unusual for other adults to indicate that they did not know what the objects were. For instance, Ari first produced the word "horsie" in reference to his stuffed rocking horse. The rocking horse's head and face were clearly that of an animal, but did not fit well with any particular type of animal. Similarly, the overall shape of the object did not match that of any particular type of animal. From an adult perspective, identity of the object as a horse had to be inferred from the presence of a mane down the back of the head and a saddle on the animal's back. For a long period, this particular rocking horse was the only referent Ari labeled "horsie," although adults labeled other horses "horsie" when talking with him. Ari's restriction of the extension of "horsie" to this one object made sense, given that he was using a categorical basis for the extension of "horsie." None of the other objects that Ari saw were similar in overall shape to this rocking horse.

Variety of Bases for Extension

The principle of Extendibility specifies only that the new exemplars should be somehow related to the previously labeled exemplars. Thus, the principle allows for a wide variety of bases for extension. For example, new referents may be related to the original referent because of any of a number of different types of similarity (e.g., similarity of shape, similarity in size, similarity in texture, similarity in taste). As another possibility, new referents may be related to the original referent by use in concert with that referent (e.g., by being included in the same event schema). As a third possibility, a new referent may be related to the original referent by a chain of attributes connecting the original referent to the new one through a series of previously identified referents.

Studies of children's first 50 words provide evidence for all of these types of extension, although extensions based on similarity are by far the most frequent. Clark (1973) documented instances of overextensions based on similarity of form (overall shape), size, or taste in early diary studies. For example, with regard to similarity of shape, Imedadze (1960, cited in Clark, 1973) found that his child used "ball" to refer to spherical objects, including radishes and stone spheres at the entrance to a park. With regard to similarity of size, Moore (1896) reported that his child used "fly" to refer to all small insects, specks of dust, crumbs, and his own toes. With regard to similarity of taste, Taine (1877) reported that the child he studied used "chocolate" to refer to chocolate, sugar, tarts, grapes, figs, and peaches.

Most of the diary examples of similarity-based extension involved similarity of form. This type of basis has been extensively documented in longitudinal studies of children who were developing normally (e.g., Chapman, Leonard, & Mervis, 1986; Mervis, 1984; Mervis et al., 1992; Rescorla, 1980) and of children with Down syndrome (Mervis, 1984). Mervis (1984, 1987, 1990a) studied the extensions of three words: "ball," "car," and "kitty," on the first day that these words were comprehended. Twelve children participated in the study: six children who were developing normally and six children with Down syndrome. Extension was determined by comprehension tests for the category name. On each comprehension trial, four objects were placed in a row in front of the child, and the child was asked to give the experimenter the object she named ("ball," "car," or "kitty"). In general, objects for a trial were determined as follows: one object that adults would consider a member of the category labeled by the target word; one object that was similar in shape to members of the target category but that adults would not consider a member of the target category; one object that was not very similar in shape to members of the target category but was a member of the same superordinate category as the target category; and one unrelated object. For example, a trial for comprehension of "kitty" might include a Siamese cat, a tiger, a rabbit, and a cup. Several trials were included for each of the three target words. Results indicated that in all but a few instances (see Mervis, 1984) all of the children extended each of the words beyond the exemplars that their mothers had labeled during the play session. In all cases, the additional exemplars were similar in form to the previously labeled exemplars. For example, if a mother labeled a toy calico cat "kitty," her child was likely to comprehend "kitty" in reference to toy Siamese cats, leopards, tigers, and lions. We have obtained parallel data for the children with Williams syndrome in our ongoing longitudinal study, and also for a boy with Noonan syndrome whom we are following longitudinally. The use of a form-based metric of similarity is consistent with the cognitive Form-Function principle of categorization, discussed below in conjunction with the next lexical operating principle, Categorical Scope.

Recent diary studies, in addition to providing further evidence of shape-based extensions, have documented that extension may occur on the basis of use in concert with the original (or other previous) referents. The strongest evidence for this type of extension was provided by Dromi (1987; Dromi & Fishelzon, 1986) in her diary study of her daughter Keren's early lexicon. Dromi found that for a significant proportion of Keren's first 50 words, relatedness by similarity of shape was not the basis for extension. Dromi labeled the basis for extension of these words "indeterminate," to indicate that it did not correspond to an obvious adult-used basis. The most striking of these extensions were based on use in concert with the original referent—by inclusion in the same event schema. Consider the example of "niyar" ("[a] piece of paper," in Hebrew). The initial referent of "niyar" indeed was a piece of paper. However, Keren extended this word to refer to the elements of her writing/drawing schema. Thus, she used "niyar" to indicate pencils, pens, pieces of paper, typed pages, or drawings (even if they were not on paper). In this case, as well as in cases discussed below, the word was used both during the relevant event and outside the event to label entities often included in the event. Gillis (1987) also documented this type of extension by a boy learning Dutch as his native language. Mervis et al. (1992) found that the extensions of two of Ethan's early words fit this pattern. This type of extension also has been demonstrated by children with developmental delays. One child (Shelly) in our ongoing longitudinal study of the early development of children with Williams syndrome used the word "na-na" (derived from "night-night") to label the elements of her going to bed schema. This was Shelly's first word. She most often used "na-na" to indicate bottles. However, she also used the word to indicate such things as cribs or other types of beds, or as a request to be put in her crib.

Finally, a small number of cases have been documented in which new referents were related to the original referent by a chain of attributes connecting the original referent to the new one through a series of previously identified referents. A frequently cited example was reported by Darwin (cited in Romanes, 1889). The child studied initially used "duck" to refer to live ducks. The word then was overextended to refer to water (presumably because ducks often are found in water), to other birds and insects (presumably because of their wings or flying), to other liquids (presumably because of their similarity to water), to an eagle on a coin (presumably because of the similarity in shape between eagles and ducks), and finally to other coins (presumably because of their similarity in shape to the eagle coin). This type of extension is a combination of extension based on similarity and extension based on inclusion in the same event schema.

Potential Impact of Input on Bases for Extension

At the onset of language acquisition, children have available both pre-linguistic object concepts and prelinguistic event concepts (Mervis, 1990b). As indicated above, extension patterns of the majority of early words are form based (based on object concepts). For at least some children, however, many early words are situationally based (based on inclusion in the same event schema). The principle of Extendibility does not indicate what the basis for extension should be.

Effect of Transparency or Nontransparency of Input on Basis for Extension

How, then, does the child determine the basis for extension of a particular word? An important possibility is that the input provided to the child for a particular word plays a major role in determining the basis on which the child extends that word (Mervis et al., 1992). In particular, when the input is transparent, the child is likely to treat the word as a label for an object category. In general, transparent input involves ostensive reference to the object to which the child is attending at the time input is given. For example, the adult might point to an object and, when the child looks in the direction of the point, provide a label for the object. In contrast, when the input is not transparent, the child is likely to treat the word as a label for the components of an event schema. Non-ostensive input often is not transparent to the child just beginning to acquire language. For example, when a label is provided in a non-ostensive manner, the child is likely to have difficulty determining the word-referent mapping. Another form of nontransparent input from the perspective of a child beginning to acquire language involves using the label in the absence of any obvious visible referent. (Of course, rather than assign any referents to a particular word, children who are beginning to acquire language often simply ignore the word.)

A particularly strong demonstration of how dramatically input may affect the extension that different children assign to the same word is provided by a comparison of the acquisition of "bubble" by Mervis's two sons (for an expanded discussion, see Mervis et al., 1992). The diary data for Ari and Ethan provide documentation of the input they received regarding "bubble" and the objects that they considered to be referents of "bubble." The input situations in which Ari heard the word "bubble" were referentially very clear. In most cases, the referent was bubbles that formed while washing dishes or bathing Ari. The intended referent was indicated by pointing or by the direction of Ari's eye gaze. Ari's use of "bubble" indicated that it referred to an object concept. He most frequently used "bubble" to refer to actual bubbles. In addition, as were most of his early object words, "bubble" was overextended on the basis of form. Examples of overextensions included foam formed on the top of boiling soup stock, a raw egg yolk projecting up above the egg white, and circles forming in a puddle during a light drizzle.

In contrast, the input situations in which Ethan heard the word "bubble" were more ambiguous. Ethan often heard Ari use the word to request that someone blow bubbles for him. Generally, this request occurred in the absence of bubbles or the materials needed to blow bubbles. In other cases, Ari or an adult would talk about blowing bubbles while holding the bottle of bubble soap or the bubble wand. The proportion of times that "bubble" was used when the referent clearly was a bubble was relatively small. In turn, Ethan's use of "bubble" indicated that it referred to an event concept. "Bubble" was used to refer to the bubble-blowing event in general and to specific components of the event, including, for example, bubble soap, bubble soap bottle, bubble wand, and bubbles. That is, Ethan treated "bubble" as a word to be used in the context of various important elements of the bubble-blowing event.

If the child receives non-ostensive input, he or she may be able to use prior lexical, syntactic, or pragmatic knowledge to disambiguate the word. However, because the principle of Extendibility is available close to the onset of language acquisition, these types of prior knowledge will be extremely limited at first. As the child's linguistic knowledge increases, the input necessary to enable the child to choose an object-concept basis for a new word need not be as precise. For example, the child eventually becomes capable of using syntactic cues to disambiguate the input. As vocabulary size increases, the child becomes increasingly capable of using knowledge about the referents of other words in an utterance to help determine the intended referent of an unknown word. Thus, using situational bases to determine the referents of words should most likely occur at the onset of language acquisition (when the child has the fewest resources for disambiguating input that is not transparent from the start), and should become less frequent as language knowledge increases. This argument is consistent with the finding that situationally based words occur only early in lexical development (e.g., Dromi, 1987; Dromi & Fishelzon, 1986; Nelson, 1985, 1988). If the argument is correct, then the importance of input as a determinant of the type of extension a child chooses for a particular word should be greatest at the onset of language acquisition.

Few studies have collected sufficient information about the input provided for an individual child's early words and the child's extension of these words to provide a measure of the impact of input style on the extension of early words. However, this information is available from the diary studies of Dromi's daughter (1987) and Mervis's sons (Mervis et al., 1992). Data from these studies suggest a strong relation between transparency of input and choice of an object concept as the basis for extension. For both Ari and Ethan, the input for unknown object words was almost always transparent regarding the referent of the object label. For two object words, however, the input for Ari was transparent, whereas the input for Ethan was not. For these words, Ari evidenced an object-concept (shape) basis for extension, whereas Ethan evidenced a situation-concept (event) basis. All of the children's other words were based on object concepts. In contrast, Keren was given nontransparent input for many more words (Dromi, in press). In particular, this input did not involve ostensive definition. In turn, Keren treated many more of her early words as situationally based (Dromi, 1987, in press). As predicted, across the three children, all words that were situationally based were acquired early in the one-word period.

Limitations on the Impact of Input

We have argued that provision of transparent input should facilitate use of an object-concept basis for extension. This is not equivalent to arguing that the child's extension is totally determined by the extension for the word demonstrated by the adult. That is, once the child chooses an object-concept basis, he or she will extend the word based on the child's object category, rather than on the adult's category. Thus, the child's extension of the word does not necessarily correspond to the extension modeled by the adults. Mervis (1984) found that mothers of children with Down syndrome usually labeled objects with their correct names (e.g., referring to a tiger as "tiger") when talking to their children. In contrast, mothers of children who were developing normally often labeled objects with the name they thought the child would consider appropriate (e.g., referring to the tiger as "kitty"). Despite these differences in input, both groups of children formed the same category, as measured by comprehension tests. Objects such as tigers were considered to be kitties, whether or not this contradicted the maternal input.

In a detailed study of the extension of Ari's first word ("duckie"), Mervis (1987; Mervis et al., 1992) found that most of the objects for which Ari comprehended "duckie" were objects that his parents previously had labeled "duckie" for him, or at least were objects that his parents would consider to be ducks. Interestingly, some objects that Ari considered to be ducks either had been explicitly labeled as something else for him (e.g., "chicken," referring to a stylized wind-up chicken) or had not been labeled for him and would not be considered ducks by his parents (e.g., geese). Furthermore, Ari did not include in his duck category several stylized objects that his parents often had labeled "duck" for him (e.g., Donald Duck head rattle, flat duck rattle with an open center). The data from the group study of children who were developing normally and children with Down syndrome (Mervis, 1984), and from the diary study of Ari (Mervis et al., 1992), provide strong evidence that input alone does not determine category extensions of young children.

THE PRINCIPLE OF CATEGORICAL SCOPE

Children's use of a situation basis for word extension is limited to the very early period of lexical development (e.g., the first 50–60 words). The child's choice of a situation basis is a dead end lexically; languages do not use the same word to indicate each separate component of an event schema. Thus, the child eventually must give up this basis for extension in favor of an object-concept basis. Advances in the child's syntactic knowledge and increases in vocabulary size make it easier for the child to determine the referent of an utterance, even when the input is not transparent from the start. Although these advances result in an increase in the proportion of early words that are based on object concepts rather than situationally based, these advances alone are never sufficient to allow the child to unambiguously interpret all of the speech that he or she hears. Nevertheless, at some point, children categorically abandon the possibility of word extension being situationally based. The realization that the extension of object words *must* be based on object categories results from the onset of the availability of the principle of Categorical Scope. According to this principle, *words that label objects should be extended to exemplars that share shape (and function) with the original referent* (cf. Golinkoff et al., 1992; Mervis 1990b, Object Category as Referent principle). Thus, the principle of Categorical Scope refines the principle of Extendibility with regard to object words: Rather than based on any type of relation, extension is based on shared form (and function). Prior to the availability of the lexical principle of Categorical Scope, children have a similar, and crucial, cognitive operating principle concerned with category formation. Below, we discuss this cognitive principle and then consider the impact of the principle of Categorical Scope.

The Form-Function Principle

The most basic cognitive operating principle concerned with category formation is the Form-Function principle. This principle states that the form and function of objects generally are noticeably correlated, and this correlation should be used as the basis for category formation (Mervis, 1988, 1990b). Thus, objects in the same category should have similar clusters of form attributes (overall shape, salient parts) and similar functions or characteristic actions, predictable from their forms. Object categories are based on shared form and function, rather than on such factors as shared size, texture, or inclusion in the same event schema.

The Form-Function principle becomes available to infants early in the fifth stage of the sensorimotor period, when infants begin to explore objects for the purpose of learning about their properties (Piaget, 1954). One result of these explorations is that infants begin to discover particular functions, or characteristic actions, of specific types of objects along with the form attributes that are correlated with (or afford) these activities. For example, infants discover that objects that are spherical generally can roll. Infants also may learn about form-function correlations by watching an adult interact with an object or by watching an object move on its own. Younger and Cohen (1985, 1986) have shown that 10-month-olds who are developing normally take correlations involving form attributes into account when making categorization decisions. The ability of 10-month-olds to take into account a correlation between a form attribute and a function attribute when making categorization decisions has not been addressed experimentally. The youngest children for whom experimental data are available are 14-month-olds. Madole (1992), using a paradigm similar to Younger and Cohen, demonstrated that infants of this age took correlations between form attributes and function attributes (correlations between the form of a specific part of an object and the function related to that part) into account when making categorization decisions. Thus, the Form-Function principle is available by the age of 14 months for children who are developing normally. However, children do not immediately realize that the cognitive Form-Function principle should be the basis for a lexical principle.

Form-function correlations are more obvious for basic level categories (e.g., ball) than for higher level categories (superordinate categories, e.g., toy) or lower level categories (subordinate categories, e.g., baseball). This is because basic level categories are the most general categories for which large clusters of correlated form and function attributes are present (Rosch, Mervis,

Gray, Johnson, & Boyes-Braem, 1976). Given that form-function correlations are most obvious for basic level categories, one would expect that basic level categories are established before either superordinate or subordinate categories. This prediction has been strongly supported for both children who are developing normally (Mervis, 1983) and children with Down syndrome (Mervis, 1990a).

It is important to note that objects often afford more than one set of form-function correlations, even at the basic level. Therefore, everyone does not necessarily attend to the same set of form-function correlations for a given object. The actual basic-level categories that people form on the basis of the Form-Function principle may vary since different groups notice or emphasize different attributes of the same object because of different experiences or different degrees of expertise. Differences between very young children and adults often occur because children do not share adult knowledge of culturally appropriate functions of objects and correlated form attributes. This lack of knowledge may lead children to deemphasize attributes of an object that are important from an adult perspective. At the same time, children often focus on a form-function correlation that adults ignore for that object (Mervis, 1984, 1987, 1988).

The effect of differences between the attributes to which very young children and adults attend may be made clearer by an example. Consider the case of a spherical bank. Very young children do not have a concept of money or of saving money. Therefore, when confronted with a spherical bank, they will ignore the slot and keyhole, which are attributes important to the adult classification of the object as a bank. At the same time, these children will notice that the object is spherical and rolls. Accordingly, very young children will classify the spherical bank as a ball. In this way, the extension of child-basic categories often is expected to differ from corresponding adult-basic categories.

Substantial evidence has been offered in support of the expected differences between child-basic and adult-basic categories (e.g., Chapman et al., 1986; Mervis, 1984, 1987, 1988, 1990a). At present, however, evidence for use of the Form-Function principle as the basis for spontaneously formed categories (as opposed to categories induced in the child by experimental procedures, e.g., during the familiarization phase of studies using a habituation-dishabituation paradigm) is derived from studies of category extension as determined by comprehension or production of the category name. Because this evidence involves linguistic data, it also is relevant to the principle of Categorical Scope and is discussed below.

Impact of the Principle of Categorical Scope

Use of the cognitive Form-Function principle is consistent with the lexical principle of Categorical Scope. However, evidence that category-name extension for *some* of a child's words fits with the Form-Function principle is not evidence that the lexical principle of Categorical Scope is available to the child. Why not? Because use of the cognitive Form-Function principle also is consistent with the lexical principle of Extendibility, that is, words should be extended to other referents that are related in some way to the original referent. One possible basis for "relatedness" is similarity of form (and function, due to the correlation of form and function). As long as the child continues to use other bases (e.g., similarity of taste or size, or inclusion in the same event schema) in addition to similarity of form for the extension of some of his or her newly acquired object words, the child is considered to be using the more general principle of Extendibility, rather than the more specific principle of Categorical Scope.

Once the principle of Categorical Scope is available, children should extend words that label objects only to other objects in the same child-basic category. Thus, support for the attainment of the principle of Categorical Scope must be obtained from data indicating that the child no longer uses other possible bases for the extension of object words. Once again, data must be obtained from longitudinal studies, and the most convincing data would come from diary studies in which the extension of every word in the child's early vocabulary was recorded. Published accounts of the early vocabulary of four children who were developing normally fit this requirement (Barrett, 1986; Dromi, 1987; Mervis et al., in press). Consideration of the evidence from these studies suggests that by the time the child has attained a productive vocabulary of about 50–60 words, the principle of Categorical Scope is in use. At this point, the only object words not extended based on basic level category membership were the few words that named categories at either the superordinate or subordinate level. Note that for individual children, the principle may become available well before the attainment of 60 words. Similarly, for children who show an holistic style of language learning, the Categorical Scope principle may not become available until well after attainment of 60 words. Determination of when individual children first begin to honor the principle of Categorical Scope is best obtained experimentally. For example, when the child extends a newly learned word on the basis of basic level category membership, even though the input provided for the word was not initially transparent, the child is honoring the principle of Categorical Scope. If only the principle of Extendibility were available, this type of input should lead to extension based on participation in the same event schema. Such experiments have yet to be conducted.

THE NOVEL NAME–NAMELESS CATEGORY (N3C) PRINCIPLE

For the first several months after the onset of language production, children who are developing normally acquire new words very slowly, beginning with one or two words per month, and gradually increasing to one or two words per week. During this period, vocabulary acquisition has a distinctly deliberate look. Children begin to produce a new object word only after they have heard the new word multiple times. Furthermore, the child does not learn all, or even many, of the new object words that he or she hears multiple times. Object-word learning generally is restricted to names for objects that the child finds particularly interesting. This same type of learning process is followed by children with developmental disabilities. For some of these children, however, the initial period of slow, deliberate acquisition may extend for years or the entire lifespan (cf. Romski & Sevcik, 1991).

The principles that have been discussed so far provide a solid basis for the acquisition of object words during this first period of vocabulary acquisition. For most children, this period encompasses the production of their first 50–75 words. These principles are not adequate, however, to account for the rate of vocabulary acquisition after this period. Carey (1978) has argued that children must acquire 6–9 new words per day if their vocabulary size at age 6 years is to be consistent with Templin's (1957) estimate of 14,000 words in a typical 6-year-old's vocabulary. The basis for this dramatically increased rate of word learning is provided by an additional principle, the Novel Name–Nameless Category (N3C) principle. According to this principle, *new words map to categories for which the child does not yet have a name*. Below, we consider the impact of the N3C principle on vocabulary learning.

Implications of the N3C Principle

Fast-Mapping

Suppose a child is in a situation in which he or she knows the basic level name for all but one of the objects that could be a referent for a new word (given the previously discussed principles and roles of input). The major implication of the N3C principle is that in this situation the child maps a new label to the object for which he or she did not have a name. For example, suppose that an 18-month-old who is developing normally is given a toy toolbox including a hammer, a screwdriver, a saw, and a wrench. The child already knows the names for the hammer, screwdriver, and saw. If the parent said, "I see a wrench," as parent and child looked into the toolbox, a child who had the N3C principle should map the word "wrench" to the correct referent, given that the child already knew the names of all objects except the wrench. This phenomenon has generally been referred to as "fast-mapping" (Carey, 1978). Evidence of the ability to fast-map new object labels has been provided for 2-year-olds who were developing normally (Golinkoff et al., 1992), preschool children with specific language impairment (Dollaghan, 1987; Rice, 1991), and children and adolescents with Down syndrome (Chapman, Kay-Raining Bird, & Schwartz, 1990).

In these studies, the relation between vocabulary size and the ability to fast-map object words was not considered. In two recently completed studies (Mervis & Bertrand, 1991), we targeted children at the age at which we expected the vocabulary spurt to be attained to begin to determine the relation between ability to use the N3C principle and the presence of a vocabulary spurt. The participants in the first study were children who were developing normally; children were between the ages of 16–19 months at the time of the first visit. Of the 32 children who participated, 16 were able to use the N3C principle, as measured by the ability to fast-map new object labels. These children correctly fast-mapped an average of 3.60 out of 4 possible new labels. The chance rate of correct performance would have been less than 1 label out of 4. The mean productive vocabulary size of these children, as measured by the MacArthur Communicative Development Inventory (CDI) (Fenson et al., 1991), was 95 words, and mean comprehension vocabulary was 244 words. The remaining 16 children were unable to fast-map new labels, correctly mapping only 0.50 out of 4 possible labels. The mean productive vocabulary size of these children was 45 words; mean comprehension vocabulary was 164 words. Thus, the children who could fast-map had larger productive and comprehension vocabularies than the children who could not. These differences in vocabulary size and ability to fast-map were not due to differences in age; the mean age of the children who could fast-map was the same as that of the children who could not: 1; 5.12 (1 year, 5 months, and 12 days).

To obtain a more direct measure of the relation of the attainment of a vocabulary spurt and the ability to use the N3C principle, we followed the 16 children who had not been able to fast-map on the first visit. The mothers of these children were given a copy of the vocabulary list for the Toddler version of the CDI and were asked to record new words and date of first use as their child produced them. We then contacted these mothers once a week by telephone to find out the new words learned that week. When a child demonstrated a vocabulary spurt (defined as 10 or more new words in a 14-day period), we immediately scheduled a second visit. The procedure for this visit was the same as for the first, except that a different set of objects was used for the fast-mapping task. The mean age of the children at the time of the second visit was 1;7.15. At this visit, all of the children were able to use the N3C principle. The mean number of new words correctly fast-mapped was 3.10 out of 4 possible. The mean productive vocabulary size of these children was 94 words, and the mean comprehension vocabulary size was 256 words.

In a second study, 20 children with Down syndrome, ranging in age from 29 to 42 months, participated. The same procedure was followed as for the first visit of the previous study. Eight of the children were able to use the N3C principle, fast-mapping correctly a mean of 3.13 new words out of 4 possible. The mean productive vocabulary size of these children was 156 words, and mean comprehension vocabulary size was 300 words. The remaining 12 children were not able to use the N3C principle, fast-mapping only a mean of 0.66 new words correctly out of 4 possible. The mean productive vocabulary size of these children was 27 words; mean comprehension vocabulary size was 150 words. Once again, the two groups did not differ in mean age: 2;10.11 for the children who could fast-map, and 2;10.09 for the children who could not. Unfortunately, we were unable to conduct a longitudinal follow-up of the children who had been unable to fast-map at the first visit.

The results of these two studies indicate a strong relation between the ability to use the N3C principle (as measured by fast-mapping of new object names) and the attainment of the vocabulary spurt. Children who had attained a vocabulary spurt were able to fast-map, whereas children who had not attained a vocabulary spurt were not able to fast-map. This finding held for children who were developing normally and for children with Down syndrome. Related results have been obtained in studies of older individuals with severe mental retardation. In these studies, the presence or absence of a vocabulary spurt was not measured directly. However, results indicated that the individuals with greater language ability were able to fast-map, whereas the individuals with less language ability could not. In a study that used a similar procedure to that of the two studies reported in Mervis and Bertrand (1991), Romski and Sevcik (1991) found that adolescents with severe mental retardation who demonstrated an "advanced learning style" were able to fast-map new object names. In contrast, adolescents with severe mental retardation who demonstrated a "beginning learning style" were unable to fast-map successfully. McIlvane (1991), in summarizing his studies of adults with severe mental retardation, reported that some, but not all, could successfully complete his fast-mapping task. In general, the language abilities of the individuals who could complete the task were more advanced than those of the individuals who could not.

Similar Onset of N3C and a Related Cognitive Principle

An underlying assumption of the N3C principle is that all objects have a name. According to the principle of Categorical Scope, the name for any object should be extended to other members of the same basic-level category. Thus, combination of the principles of N3C and Categorical Scope yields the prediction that all objects have a basic level name. A cognitive principle related to N3C is that all objects belong to some category. When this principle is combined with the Form-Function principle, the resulting prediction is that all objects belong to some basic-level category. To determine the relation between the acquisition of the lexical principle and the related cognitive principle, we included a measure of the cognitive principle in the two studies described above (Mervis & Bertrand, 1991). This measure originally was used by Gopnik and Meltzoff (1987).

According to Gopnik and Meltzoff (1987), performance on a spontaneous object sorting task can be used as a measure of whether the child considers that all objects belong to some category. In this task, the child is presented with eight objects: four identical objects from one category (e.g., plastic boxes) and four identical objects from a second category (e.g., balls). The child is asked to fix the objects up, to put them where they go. If the child separates out the objects from one category only while ignoring the objects from the other category, he or she is assumed to believe that *some* objects belong to a category. This behavior is referred to as Level 1 categorization. In contrast, if the child deliberately divides the objects into two groups based on category membership (or forms a one-to-one correspondence between the objects from the two categories), it is assumed that he or she believes that *all* objects belong to some category. These behaviors are referred to as Level 3 categorization. More recently, Gopnik and Meltzoff (in press) have shown that the results of this categorization task are the same, regardless of whether the objects in a category are identical to one another or show basic-level variation. The results of Gopnik and Meltzoff's (1987) longitudinal study of 12 children who were developing normally indicated that Level 3 categorization first was demonstrated slightly before or at the time of the vocabulary spurt.

The design of our studies (Mervis & Bertrand, 1991) allowed for comparisons of attainment of the vocabulary spurt, ability to fast-map, and Level 3 categorization. Overall, the findings indicated a strong relation between the three measures. The results of our first study indicated that at the initial visit 13 of the 16 children who could fast-map demonstrated Level 3 categorization skills. Six of the 16 children who could not fast-map demonstrated Level 3 categorization skills. These differences between the two groups in vocabulary size, ability to fast-map, and categorization skills were not due simply to general differences in cognitive development; the number of children in each group who had attained advanced Stage 6 of object permanence (as measured by Uzgiris & Hunt, 1975) was virtually identical. Of greater importance are the data from the second visit. Recall that for this visit, children were seen as soon as they had demonstrated a vocabulary spurt. All 16 children were able to fast-map, and 14 demonstrated Level 3 categorization. Once again, a general increase in cognitive development cannot explain these results; there was no change in the number of children who attained advanced Stage 6 of object permanence at the time of the first visit and the number of children who attained this ability at the time of the second visit. The results of our second study indicated an even stronger relation between manifestations of the related lexical and cognitive principles. In this study, all 8 of the children with Down syndrome who could fast-map demonstrated Level 3 categorization skills. In contrast, only 1 of the 12 children with Down syndrome who could not fast-map showed Level 3 categorization skills. It is important to point out that the N3C principle is based on a fundamental insight about objects, rather than simply a "process of elimination" strategy. Thus, intervention attempts should focus on facilitating the cognitive insight rather than on training the surface strategy.

SUMMARY AND DISCUSSION

In this chapter, we have considered the acquisition of early object labels. We have described four lexical operating principles acquired relatively early in language development. These principles are acquired in a developmental order. As new principles are added, development proceeds on two fronts. First, changes occur in the referents (extension) that a child posits for a newly learned word. Second, the amount of linguistic and nonlinguistic scaffolding that is needed for a child to acquire a new word changes dramatically. Below, we briefly review the four principles and the types of changes that each brings to word learning.

According to the principle of Object Scope, words refer to whole objects (e.g., as opposed to actions, attributes, or object parts). The child who has available only the principle of Object Scope will treat the new word as the label for the object in reference to which he or she believes the word was used by the adult. Nonlinguistic input (e.g., referential pointing) plays an important role in determining which object the child decides was intended as the referent. The word will be applied to additional objects only if someone else does so first. That is, the child does not extend his or her use of the word beyond uses already modeled.

The second principle, Extendibility, appears to be acquired at about the same time as, or shortly after, the principle of Object Scope. According to the principle of Extendibility, words may be used to label referents related to the original referent. This principle provides a basis for the child to extend the use of a word to related objects that no one has labeled for the child. The basis for extension is left open; the new objects simply must somehow be related to the original object. Children may use a variety of bases for extension, among these, extension based on similarity of form and extension based on participation in the same event schema (situation). The transparency of the input provided about the word plays a major role in determining the type of basis chosen by the child. Thus, in many cases, the basis for the child's extension of a word is not the same type as that used by adults for that word.

Children's use of a situational basis for word extension is a dead end lexically, because, as we pointed out earlier, languages do not use the same word to indicate each separate component in an event schema. The child eventually must abandon this type of basis in favor of an object-concept basis. The third principle, Categorical Scope, permits the child to do so. According to this principle, a word that labels an object should be extended to other objects that share shape (and function) with the original referent. That is, a word should be extended to members of the basic-level category to which the original exemplar belongs. This is the basis on which adults extend basic object names. Once this principle becomes available, the basis for object word extension should be the same for children as for adults. Note, however, that this does not mean that the extension of a given word will be identical for young children and adults; in many cases, their basic level categories differ, because of attention to different form-function correlations for the same object. Attainment of Categorical Scope provides the child with a solid basis for acquisition of object words, although acquisition will be slow and deliberate.

The final principle, Novel Name–Nameless Category (N3C), provides the insight for use of an important strategy for relatively rapid vocabulary acquisition. According to this principle, new object words should be applied to objects for which the child does not yet have a name. Combined with the principle of Categorical Scope, the N3C principle implies that every object has a name, and that name should be extended to exemplars of the basic level category to which the original referent belongs. Once the N3C principle is available, there is a dramatic change in the type of input the child takes advantage of for acquisition of a new word. Because the child believes that new words should map to basic-level categories for which he or she does not yet have a name, the adult no longer needs to indicate explicitly which object is the intended referent of a new word. If there is an object available for which the child does not have a label, he or she will treat the new word as the name of that object and other members of its child-basic category. At this point, the child is able to fast-map the new object word to its appropriate category.

Implications for Intervention

The principles framework offers a solid basis for the design of intervention programs concerned with facilitating early language development. First, the framework provides suggestions regarding the type of input language to be used by adults interacting with young children. For example, it is crucial, particularly when children have not yet acquired the Categorical Scope or N3C principles and have limited syntactic knowledge, that input be transparent, both linguistically and nonlinguistically. Thus, adults should follow the focus of the child (cf. Tomasello & Farrar, 1986), or at least make sure that the child has followed the adult's focus, before labeling an object for the child. The label should be provided at the end of the utterance and should be stressed.

The principles framework also offers suggestions for selecting intervention activities for young children. For instance, because the principles are acquired in a developmental order, interventionists can determine the principles already available to a child and use this information to choose play activities (and the type of structure for these activities) to facilitate the acquisition of the next principle in the sequence. Additional research is needed to establish empirically what activities are most likely to be helpful.

It is important to keep in mind that the goal is to promote the cognitive or linguistic insights underlying a particular principle, rather than to teach the child the surface strategy that appears to mimic the principle. For example, with regard to the N3C principle, it is important to facilitate the realizations that all objects belong to some category, and that all categories have a name, rather than simply teaching the child to choose the object for which he or she doesn't have a name when an array of objects is presented. This lesson will not generalize to naturalistic (real life) situations, whereas the knowledge gained from the cognitive and linguistic insights will.

Knowledge of the principles the child has available allows for realistic expectations concerning the type of category extension a child is likely to choose for a particular word. For example, if the child has only the principle of Object Scope, the child can be expected to use a word he or she "knows" only in reference to objects that someone has previously labeled for the child. If the child also has available the principle of Extendibility, he or she can be expected to extend a word to novel instances, but the basis for extension is quite dependent on the input, and may differ dramatically from the basis an adult would use. Only when the child has acquired the principle of Categorical Scope does it become reasonable to expect him or her to choose consistently the same type of category basis (similarity based on form-function correlations) as an adult would. And even at this point, the child's extension often is not exactly the same as the adult's; children often attend to different form-function correlations for a given object than do adults, because of differences in knowledge about or prior experience with the object. Attention to different form-function correlations often results in different category assignments for the same object.

Directions for Future Research

The proposed principles offer a coherent framework for early acquisition of object words for children who are developing normally and, to the extent this framework has been tested, for children with mental retardation. However, much work remains. The viability of the principles approach for the acquisition of other types of words (e.g., action words, attributes) needs to be addressed. Important issues remain even with regard to object words. The question of the universality (or nonuniversality) of the proposed operating principles for lexical acquisition across a range of language types and ability types is critical. The special population for which the most data are available is young children who have Down syndrome. In this chapter, we presented evidence suggesting that the limited data available for these children were compatible with these principles. It is necessary not only to gather more data on children with Down syndrome, but to study other populations as well. In choosing target populations, it is important to consider the general relations between language abilities and cognitive abilities that individuals within that population are expected to manifest. Ideally, target populations would contrast with regard to these general relations, and use of contrasting populations offers the strongest test of universality. Individuals with Down syndrome generally have cognitive abilities that exceed their language abilities (e.g., Fowler, 1990; Gibson, 1978). An ideal contrast population would be one in which individuals generally have language abilities that exceed their cognitive abilities. Individuals with Williams syndrome appear to constitute such a population (Bellugi, Bihrle, Neville, Jernigan, & Doherty, 1992; Bellugi, Marks, Bihrle, & Sabo, 1988). Thus, data from young children with Williams syndrome are crucial. At present, the available data for these children consist of the few observations reported earlier in this chapter. A high priority for our research program is to obtain additional data, both observational and experimental, from young children with Williams syndrome. To the extent that children with Down syndrome and children with Williams syndrome appear to be using the same lexical operating principles as children who are developing normally, confidence in the generality (or, potentially, universality) of these principles will be greatly increased. With this knowledge will come even greater confidence in the use of these principles as the basis for interventions designed to facilitate early language development.

REFERENCES

Adamson, L.B., & Bakeman, R. (1992). The development of shared attention during infancy. In R. Vasta (Ed.), *Annals of Child Development* (Vol. 8, pp. 1–41). London: Jessica Kingsley Publishers.

Barrett, M.D. (1986). Early semantic representation and early word-usage. In S.A. Kuczaj, II & M.D. Barrett (Eds.), *The development of word meaning: Progress in cognitive development research* (pp. 39–67). New York: Springer-Verlag.

Barrett, M.D., & Diniz, F. (1989). Lexical development in mentally handicapped children. In M. Beveridge, G. Conti-Ramsden, & I. Leudar (Eds.), *Language and communication in mentally handicapped people* (pp. 3–32). New York: Chapman and Hall.

Bates, E., Camaioni, L., & Volterra, V. (1975). The acquisition of performatives prior to speech. *Merrill-Palmer Quarterly, 21,* 205–226.

Bates, E., Thal, D., & Janowsky, J. (1992). Early language development and its neural correlates. In I. Rapin & S. Segalowitz (Eds.), *Handbook of neuropsychology: Vol. 6. Child neurology.* Amsterdam: Elsevier.

Bellugi, U., Bihrle, A., Neville, H., Jernigan, T., & Doherty, S. (1992). Language, cognition, and brain organization in a neurodevelopmental disorder. In M. Gunnar & C. Nelson (Eds.), *Developmental behavioral neuroscience: The Minnesota Symposium* (pp. 201–232). Hillsdale, NJ: Lawrence Erlbaum Associates.

Bellugi, U., Marks, S., Bihrle, A., & Sabo, H. (1988). Dissociation between language and cognitive functions in Williams syndrome. In K. Mogford & D. Bishop (Eds.), *Language development in exceptional circumstances* (pp. 177–189). London: Churchill Livingstone.

Benedict, H. (1979). Early lexical development: Comprehension and production. *Journal of Child Language, 6,* 183–200.

Bloom, L. (1973). *One word at a time: The use of single word utterances before syntax*. The Hague, The Netherlands: Mouton.

Bridges, A. (1986). Actions and things: What adults talk about to 1-year-olds. In S.A. Kuczaj, II & M.D. Barrett (Eds.), *The development of word meaning: Progress in cognitive development research* (pp. 225–255). New York: Springer-Verlag.

Carey, S. (1978). The child as word learner. In M. Halle, J. Bresnan, & G.A. Miller (Eds.), *Linguistic theory and psychological reality* (pp. 264–293). Cambridge, MA: MIT Press.

Chapman, R.S., Kay-Raining Bird, E., & Schwartz, S.E. (1990). Fast mapping of words in event contexts by children with Down syndrome. *Journal of Speech and Hearing Disorders, 55*, 761–770.

Chapman, K.L., Leonard, L.B., & Mervis, C.B. (1986). The effects of feedback on young children's inappropriate word usage. *Journal of Child Language, 13*, 101–117.

Clark, E.V. (1973). What's in a word? On the child's acquisition of semantics in his first language. In T.E. Moore (Ed.), *Cognitive development and the acquisition of language* (pp. 65–110). New York: Academic Press.

Clark, E.V. (1983). Meaning and concepts. In J.H. Flavell, & E.M. Markman (Eds.), *Handbook of child psychology: Vol. 3. Cognitive development* (pp. 787–840). New York: John Wiley & Sons.

Dollaghan, C. (1987). Fast mapping in normal and language-impaired children. *Journal of Speech and Hearing Disorders, 52*, 218–222.

Dromi, E. (1987). *Early lexical development*. New York: Cambridge University Press.

Dromi, E. (in press). The mysteries of early lexical development: Underlying cognitive and linguistic processes in meaning acquisition. In E. Dromi (Ed.), *Language and cognition: A developmental perspective*. Norwood, NJ: Ablex.

Dromi, E., & Fishelzon, G. (1986). Similarity, specificity and contrast: A study of early semantic categories. *Papers and Reports in Child Language Development, 25*, 25–32.

Fenson, L., Dale, P.S., Reznick, J.S., Thal, D., Bates, D., Hartung, J.P., Pethick, S., & Reilly, J.S. (1991). *Technical manual for the MacArthur Communicative Development Inventories*. San Diego, CA: San Diego State University.

Fowler, A.E. (1990). Language abilities in children with Down syndrome: Evidence for a specific syntactic delay. In D. Cicchetti & M. Beeghly (Eds.), *Children with Down syndrome: A developmental perspective* (pp. 302–328). Cambridge: Cambridge University Press.

Franco, F., & Butterworth, G. (1991, April). *Infant pointing: prelinguistic reference and co-reference*. Paper presented at the conference of the Society for Research in Child Development, Seattle.

Gentner, D. (1982). Why nouns are learned before verbs: Linguistic relativity versus natural partitioning. In S. Kuczaj, II (Ed.), *Language development Vol. 2: Language, thought and culture* (pp. 301–334). Hillsdale, NJ: Lawrence Erlbaum Associates.

Gibson, D. (1978). *Down's syndrome: The psychology of mongolism*. Cambridge: Cambridge University Press.

Gillham, B. (1979). *The first words language programme: A basic language programme for mentally handicapped children*. London: Allen and Unwin.

Gillis, S. (1987). Words and categories at the onset of language acquisition: Product versus process. *Belgian Journal of Linguistics, 2*, 37–53.

Goldfield, B.A. (1990, April). *Maternal input and the child's acquisition of nouns and verbs.* Paper presented at the seventh International Conference on Infant Studies, Montreal.

Golinkoff, R.M., Hirsh-Pasek, K., Bailey, L.M., & Wenger, D. (in press). Young children and adults use lexical principles to learn new nouns. *Developmental Psychology.*

Golinkoff, R.M., Mervis, C.B., & Hirsh-Pasek, K. (1992). *Early object labels: The case for lexical principles.* Manuscript submitted for review.

Gopnik, A., & Meltzoff, A.N. (1987). The development of categorization in the second year and its relation to other cognitive and linguistic developments. *Child Development, 58,* 1523–1531.

Gopnik, A., & Meltzoff, A.N. (in press). Categorization and naming: Basic-level sorting in 18-month-olds and its relation to language. *Child Development.*

Harris, M.B., Barrett, M., Jones, D., & Brookes, S. (1988). Linguistic input and early word meanings. *Journal of Child Language, 15,* 77–94.

Lock, A. (1978). The emergence of language. In A. Lock (Ed.), *Action, gesture and symbol: The emergence of language* (pp. 3–18). New York: Academic Press.

Macnamara, J. (1982). *Names for things: A study of human learning.* Cambridge, MA: MIT Press.

Madole, K.L. (1992). *Infants' categorization of objects: The role of part structure and functional properties.* Unpublished doctoral dissertation, University of Texas, Austin.

Markman, E.M. (1989). *Categorization and naming in children: Problems of induction.* Cambridge, MA: Bradford/MIT Press.

McIlvane, W. (1991, May). *Acquisition of spoken words: Object relations in people with severe mental retardation: The role of novelty in learning by exclusion.* Gatlinburg Conference on Research and Theory in Mental Retardation and Developmental Disabilities, Key Biscayne, FL.

Mervis, C.B. (1983). Acquisition of a lexicon. *Contemporary Educational Psychology, 8,* 210–236.

Mervis, C.B. (1984). Early lexical development: The contributions of mother and child. In C. Sophian (Ed.), *Origins of cognitive skills* (pp. 339–370). Hillsdale, NJ: Lawrence Erlbaum Associates.

Mervis, C.B. (1987). Child-basic object categories and early lexical development. In U. Neisser (Ed.), *Concepts and conceptual development: Ecological and intellectual factors in categorization* (pp. 201–233). Cambridge: Cambridge University Press.

Mervis, C.B. (1988). Early lexical development: Theory and application. In L. Nadel (Ed.), *The psychobiology of Down syndrome* (pp. 101–145). Cambridge, MA: Bradford/MIT Press.

Mervis, C.B. (1990a). Early conceptual development by children with Down syndrome. In D. Cicchetti & M. Beeghly (Eds.), *Children with Down syndrome: A developmental perspective* (pp. 252–301). Cambridge: Cambridge University Press.

Mervis, C.B. (1990b). Operating principles, input and early lexical development. *Communicazioni Scientifiche di Psicologia Generala, 4,* 7–25.

Mervis, C.B., & Bertrand, J. (1990, June). *Acquisition of early object labels: The role of operating principles.* Paper presented at NICHD conference on The Social Use of Language: Pathways to Success, Nashville.

Mervis, C.B., & Bertrand, J. (1991, May). *Acquisition of new words by children with Down syndrome.* Gatlinburg Conference on Research and Theory in Mental Retardation and Developmental Disabilities, Key Biscayne, FL.

Mervis, C.B., & Long, L.M. (1987, April). *Words refer to whole objects: Young children's interpretation of the referent of a novel word.* Paper presented at the conference of the Society for Research in Child Development, Baltimore.

Mervis, C.B., Mervis, C.A., Johnson, K.E., & Bertrand, J. (1992). Studying early lexical development: The value of the systematic diary method. In C. Rovee-Collier & L. Lipsitt (Eds.), *Advances in infancy research* (Vol. 7, pp. 291–378). Norwood, NJ: Ablex.

Moore, K.C. (1896). The mental development of a child. *Psychological Review, Monograph Supplement,* 1(3).

Mundy, P., Seibert, J., & Hogan, A. (1984). Relationship between sensorimotor and early communication abilities in developmentally delayed children. *Merrill-Palmer Quarterly, 30,* 33–48.

Murphy, C.M., & Messer, D.J. (1977). Mothers, infants, and pointing: A study of gesture. In H. Schaffer (Ed.), *Studies in mother-infant interaction* (pp. 325–354). New York: Academic Press.

Nelson, K. (1973). Structure and strategy in learning to talk. *Monographs of the Society for Research in Child Development, 38,* (1–2, serial No. 149).

Nelson, K. (1985). *Making sense: The acquisition of shared meaning.* Orlando, FL: Academic Press.

Nelson, K. (1988). Constraints on word learning? *Cognitive Development, 3,* 221–246.

Ninio, A. (1980). Ostensive definition in vocabulary teaching. *Journal of Child Language, 7,* 565–573.

Ninio, A., & Bruner, J. (1978). The achievement and antecedents of labelling. *Journal of Child Language, 5,* 1–15.

Peters, A.M. (1985). Language segmentation: Operating principles for the perception and analysis of language. In D.I. Slobin (Ed.), *The crosslinguistic study of language acquisition: Vol. 2. Theoretical issues* (pp. 1029–1067). Hillsdale, NJ: Lawrence Erlbaum Associates.

Piaget, J. (1954). *The construction of reality in the child.* New York: Basic Books.

Rescorla, L.A. (1980). Overextension in early language development. *Journal of Child Language, 7,* 321–335.

Rice, M. (1991). Children with specific language impairment: Toward a model of teachability. In N. Krasnegor, D. Rumbaugh, R. Schiefelbusch, & M. Studdart-Kennedy (Eds.), *Biological and behavioral determinants of language development* (pp. 447–480). Hillsdale, NJ: Lawrence Erlbaum Associates.

Romanes, G.J. (1889). *Mental evolution in man: Origin of the human faculty.* New York: Appleton and Co.

Romski, M.A., & Sevcik, R.A. (1991, May). *Visual symbol mapping in children with mental retardation: Role of extant comprehension skills.* Gatlinburg Conference on Research and Theory in Mental Retardation and Developmental Disabilities; Key Biscayne, FL.

Rosch, E., Mervis, C.B., Gray, W.D., Johnson, D.M., & Boyes-Braem, P. (1976). Basic objects in natural categories. *Cognitive Psychology, 8,* 382–439.

Schaife, B.K., & Bruner, J.S. (1975). The capacity for joint visual attention in the infant. *Nature, 253,* 265–266.

Slobin, D.I. (1973). Cognitive prerequisites for the development of grammar. In C.A. Ferguson & D.I. Slobin (Eds.), *Studies of child language development* (pp. 175–208). New York: Holt, Rinehart & Winston.

Slobin, D.I. (1985). Crosslinguistic evidence for the language making capacity. In D.I. Slobin (Ed.), *The crosslinguistic study of language acquisition: Vol. 2.*

Theoretical issues (pp. 1157–1256). Hillsdale, NJ: Lawrence Erlbaum Associates.

Taine, H. (1877). Acquisition of language by children, *Mind, 2,* 252–259.

Templin, M. (1957). *Certain language skills in children: Their development and interrelationship.* Minneapolis: University of Minnesota Press.

Tomasello, M., & Farrar, M.J. (1986). Joint attention and early language. *Child Development, 57,* 1454–1463.

Uzgiris, I., & Hunt, J. McV. (1975). *Assessment in infancy: Ordinal scales of psychological development.* Urbana: University of Illinois Press.

Velleman, S., Mangipudi, L., & Locke, J. (1989). Prelinguistic phonetic contingency: Data from Down syndrome. *First Language, 9,* 159–174.

Younger, B.A., & Cohen, L.B. (1985). How infants form categories. In G.H. Bower (Ed.), *The psychology of learning and motivation: Advances in research and theory* (Vol. 19, pp. 211–247). Orlando, FL: Academic Press.

Younger, B.A., & Cohen, L.B. (1986). Developmental change in infants' perception of correlations among attributes. *Child Development, 57,* 803–815.

14

Structuring Environmental Input To Facilitate Generalized Language Learning by Children with Mental Retardation

Howard Goldstein

Most LANGUAGE INTERVENTIONISTS LONG AGO realized that children with mental retardation need to learn how to comprehend sentences they had never heard before and how to produce sentences they had not been taught. This chief characteristic of language, which Hockett (1958) referred to as *productivity,* seems critical to whether children with mental retardation can be viable communicative participants in typical social environments. The thought of teaching children a myriad of individual responses and trying to predict what would comprise a suitably functional repertoire is overwhelming. Conceding that one need not teach each and every response begs the question of how to teach most efficiently. Although some progress has been made with the enormous task of *what* to teach (see Haney, Wilson, & Halle, 1988; Reichle & Keogh, 1985), it is progress concerning *how* to teach that is addressed in this chapter. Learning processes that have the potential to minimize the effort involved in direct teaching of individual responses is discussed. This chapter highlights research on three such processes that have been shown to contribute to language learning in children with mental retardation: recombinative generalization, observational learning, and crossmodal transfer.

Preparation of this chapter was supported by Grant No. HD-17850 from the National Institute of Child Health and Human Development and Grant No. G00-87-30528 from the U.S. Department of Education. I am especially grateful for the enlightening discussions with the following colleagues, who helped shape many of the ideas presented in this chapter: Bruce Wetherby, William Brown, Charles Salzberg, and Benjamin Lignugaris/Kraft.

SHAPE

	1	2	3	4
A	nasling	nascaw	nasdeg	naskop
B	wecling	weccaw	wecdeg	weckop
C	sownling	sowncaw	sowndeg	sownkop
D	rowling	rowcaw	rowdeg	rowkop

COLOR

Figure 1. An example of a 4 x 4 color-shape matrix, based on Esper (1925). The shaded cells represent color-shape combinations that were not trained.

RECOMBINATIVE GENERALIZATION

Wetherby (1978) drew upon work by the psycholinguist Irwin Esper, dating back to 1925, to offer an explanation of generalization during language learning. Esper organized artificial linguistic systems in matrices, such as the adjective-noun matrix shown in Figure 1. Two-word nonsense combinations that were assigned to colored shapes were taught to adults. Esper (1925, 1973) proposed that through the process of analogy, adults could learn to respond to untrained color-shape combinations. Much research has built, sometimes unknowingly, on Esper's idea of representing the sequencing of constituent linguistic units within matrices.[1] Through research on matrix-training strategies, much has been learned about how structuring the environment can explain, predict, and control the learning of language comprehension and production among children with mental retardation.

---

[1]It should be clear that in referring to matrix training, there is no intention to relate matrices to cognitive structures. On the contrary, language matrices are used to describe the organization of language in the environment, not in the child.

Wetherby and his colleagues (Wetherby, 1978; Wetherby & Striefel, 1978) noted that the generalization demonstrated in many behavior analysis studies in the late 1960s and in the 1970s conducted primarily with individuals with mental retardation could be explained by applying a language matrix conceptualization. The types of generalization that could be explained include the ability of children to affix morphemes, such as the regular plural, -s, to nouns, to produce words that had not been directly taught, and the ability to understand instructions comprised of words not previously combined in training tasks. Production or comprehension of novel combinations of morphemes, words, or phrases has been referred to as *recombinative generalization* (Goldstein, 1983, 1985). The term describes generalization across novel recombinations of linguistic constituents. As is discussed below, the term is a bit of a misnomer because the emergence of untrained behavior is actually a product of discrimination, not generalization. First, it is important to consider why a matrix-training conceptualization was advanced as an alternative to other common explanations of generalization derived from learning theory.

Several early investigations of generative language among individuals with mental retardation focused on the plural morpheme (Guess, 1969; Guess, Sailor, Rutherford, & Baer, 1968; Sailor, 1971). Early in language development, children begin to acquire grammatical morphemes to mark more subtle meanings of their utterances; one of the first morphemes learned marks numerosity by forming plural nouns. The basic rule is to append -s to the end of a noun to form a plural. In fact, three phonological rules specify the permissible ways of doing this. When the work of Guess and colleagues established generalized production of plural morphemes in children with mental retardation, their account of this development was based on the notion of *response class*.

Response classes exist when responses covary as a function of *similarities* in controlling stimulus conditions. Usually the responses in a class are topographically similar or they have similar effects on the environment. A group of responses covary with each other as a function of a reinforcement contingency placed on a subset of the total group of responses. So, for example, if the addition of the -s suffix is reinforced in the context of more than one subject, then the plural suffix might be expected to be appended similarly when other objects are present (Guess et al., 1968).

The response-class notion does not seem to offer a completely satisfying explanation of generative language behavior. This explanation stresses how *similarities* in stimulus conditions determine responding and, certainly, understates the importance of *differences* in antecedent stimuli. It is the differences in antecedent stimuli that may hold the key to understanding generalization. Figure 2 uses a matrix to illustrate how responses are evoked based on two stimulus dimensions: 1) horizontally, by the different discriminative stimuli

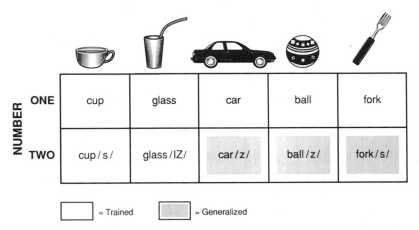

Figure 2. An example of a matrix representing singular and plural nouns, based on Guess Sailor, Rutherford, and Baer (1968).

that determine the appropriate nouns; and 2) vertically, by the different *relative* stimulus contexts (e.g., one versus more than one) that determine whether the plural morpheme should be appended.

Recombinative generalization has been proposed to stress how differences rather than similarities in stimulus conditions determine responding (Goldstein, 1983). Recombinative generalization is defined as "differential responding to novel combinations of stimulus components that have been included previously in other stimulus contexts" (Goldstein, 1983, p. 281). In the plural morpheme example, the stimulus components consisted of individual objects and the presence or absence of numerosity (one versus more than one object). The associated linguistic responses consisted of nouns and the plural suffixes.

When familiar stimuli are recombined in novel ways, stimulus components continue to exert precise control over corresponding responses that are sequenced in a rule-governed manner. Thus, although novel or untrained responses are derived, discriminative responding (e.g., to the presence or absence of numerosity) is responsible. Whereas generalization is traditionally viewed as the absence of discrimination, the notion of recombinative generalization actually emphasizes the determinants of *discriminative* responding.

Generative use of comparative and superlative adjective morphemes presents a more complex problem (Baer & Guess, 1973). Stimulus components include referents for polar adjectives (e.g., big and little, happy and sad) and morphological markers (*-er* and *-est*). In this case, the discriminations required of children are more complex, because the adjectives refer to more abstract concepts than numerosity, and comparative and superlative suffixes refer to relative distinctions in the stimulus context. A recombinative generalization-based account of appropriate generalized use of these adjectives emphasizes multiple controlling stimuli in the environment, be they concrete or abstract referents, obvious or subtle relations among these referents, differences in speaker or listener perspectives, or other factors.

Matrix Training

We have concluded several studies examining the combination of words with concrete referents. Figure 3 presents an example of an object-location matrix from a study by Goldstein and Mousetis (1989). This matrix combines seven objects and seven locations (with a single preposition, "on"), yielding 49 two-term utterances. Children were required to describe an event modeled by a trainer with a complete and correct two-term or three-term utterance (e.g., "penny [on] rug"). Alternatively, the trainer presented an instruction, such as

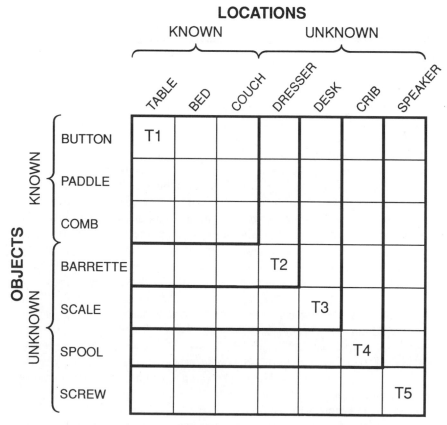

Figure 3. An example of a 7 x 7 object location matrix, based on Goldstein and Mousetis (1989). Training items (T) are designated within each of the five submatrices.

"Put the comb on the couch," and the subject responded receptively by placing an object in a specific location.

In Figure 3, the upper left corner represents a submatrix comprised of individual words that children with severe mental retardation were able to label accurately during pretraining assessments. Although they could correctly label objects and locations using individual words, they did not produce two-word utterances to describe object-location events. Teaching each child to produce a single object-location utterance using known words from this submatrix was sufficient to result in correct production of the other eight object-location combinations within the submatrix. However, because the children remained unfamiliar with the other individual object and location words, they were unable to describe the other 40 object-location relations.

Next, training items were selected that combined a new object (e.g., barrette) with a new location (e.g., dresser). As each item was introduced, recombinative generalization was demonstrated in a predictable manner. The subjects produced accurate responses that included newly learned words combined with previously known words. This process was replicated within each of these four submatrices (outlined in Figure 3) in succession. New object and location words did not need to be taught individually; subjects responded correctly if one of the two words were known. This pattern of responding indicates that the subjects must have been utilizing a rule for relating word order to word classes. The reasoning must go something like this: The first word refers to the object-word class, so *barrette* must refer to the *thing that is being moved.* The second word refers to the location-word class so *dresser* must refer to the *thing on which the object is being placed.* Knowledge of these word-referent associations (i.e., appropriate stimulus control) was demonstrated when the words were used correctly in novel, untrained utterances. It would be useful to devise a direct test for the emergence of this expanded word class. Do subjects categorize new stimuli appropriately into object and location classes? Although subjects need not have the metalinguistic skills necessary to label these word classes, existence of these skills is virtually guaranteed by the impressive demonstration of recombinative generalization.

Matrix-training procedures also were used to teach the three-dimensional language matrix shown in Figure 4 (Goldstein & Mousetis, 1989). Three object labels were combined with five prepositions and with six locations, yielding 90 three-term utterances. Training began with a single item selected from a submatrix that combined three known object words (button, penny, and comb), two known preposition words (on and under), and three location words (rug, bed, and couch). Three unknown prepositions and three unknown locations subsequently were introduced within three additional submatrices, represented in Figure 4 by the dotted grey cells, the speckled grey cells, and the white cells. The results were similar to those obtained in the two-dimensional matrix study: Training of one item from the submatrix of known words

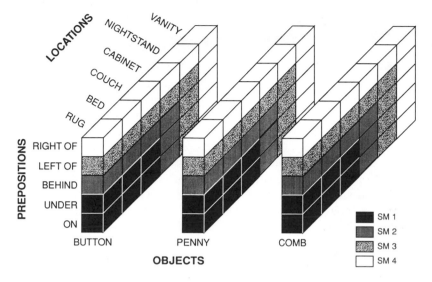

Figure 4. An example of a 3 x 5 x 6 object-preposition-location matrix, based on Goldstein and Mousetis (1989). Submatrix 1 (SM 1) comprises known object, preposition, and location words. SM 2, SM 3, and SM 4 each represent the introduction of an unknown preposition and an unknown location.

resulted in generalized responding to the remaining 17 cells in that submatrix. Then, recombinative generalization progressed systematically as a single item was introduced from the remaining three submatrices. Training of one item from submatrices 2, 3, and 4 resulted sequentially in generalization to the remaining 17, 23, and 24 cells in those submatrices, respectively. Thus, with the introduction of a training item from submatrix 2, it appeared that the children were applying a somewhat more complicated three-part rule to determine word-referent associations, for example: 1) the first word, *comb* (a known word), refers to a member of the object class, things that are moved; 2) the last word, *cabinet,* refers to a member of the location class, where the object is placed; and 3) the middle stressed word, *behind,* is a member of a word class that indicates the spatial relation between the object and location. The entry of *behind* and *cabinet* into their respective word classes was apparent when children correctly recombined these words into utterances comprised of previously learned objects, prepositions, and locations.

In summary, Goldstein and Mousetis (1989) used matrix-training strategies to teach six children with severe mental retardation to combine known words into two- or three-word utterances consistent with relatively simple syntactic rules. In three or four training phases, the children learned two unknown words concurrently and induced word-referent relations consistent with an object-preposition-location word order rule. By using a multiple baseline design across submatrices, we were able to show that generalization progressed in a predictable fashion. The general result was impressive: Recombinative generalization and generalization across modalities (or crossmodal transfer) accounted for 95%–98% of the responses learned. Only 5 expressive responses were modeled from two-dimensional matrices representing 49 receptive and 49 expressive object-location responses. Likewise, only 4 expressive responses were modeled from three-dimensional matrices representing 90 receptive and 90 expressive object-preposition-location responses.

It is surprising that little experimental research has sought to systematically investigate how differences in individual linguistic repertoires might relate to the prediction and control of developing language skills. This line of research (Goldstein, 1983, 1985; Goldstein, Angelo, & Mousetis, 1987; Goldstein & Mousetis, 1989) has allowed us to account for differences in generalization based on the relationship between children's linguistic repertoires and what is being taught. The examples given illustrate the effect of the child's knowledge of words and word classes included in a language matrix on the selection and quantity of items that must be trained to produce recombinative generalization (see Goldstein, 1985).

OBSERVATIONAL LEARNING

Observational learning is another process that is crucial to the learning of language in natural environments. Indeed, it is easy to argue that it has been underutilized in intervention efforts (cf. Baer, Peterson, & Sherman, 1967; Browder, Schoen, & Lentz, 1986–1987; Cullinan, Kauffman, & LaFleur, 1975; Glidden & Warner, 1982). The critical issue is not whether individuals with developmental disabilities demonstrate observational learning. It is more important to understand when observational learning is more and less likely to occur and, if initially absent, how it can be facilitated. That is, the issue is not who will learn observationally, but when individuals will and will not learn new modeled responses.

Observational learning was a second learning process investigated by Goldstein and Mousetis (1989). In this study, "trained" responses were actually *modeled* by peers of the subjects, peers also with mental retardation. Generalization processes have been shown to be just as robust when training was accomplished via peer modeling (Goldstein & Brown, 1989; Goldstein & Mousetis, 1989) as when direct matrix-training procedures were used (Ezell & Goldstein, 1989; Goldstein et al., 1987; Karlan et al., 1982; Mineo & Goldstein, 1990; Romski & Ruder, 1984; Striefel, Wetherby, & Karlan, 1976, 1978). The demonstration of observational learning by children with mental retardation is not an "all or none" phenomenon (Goldstein & Brown, 1989). Assuming that observational learning is a basic learning process even for individuals with profound mental retardation, our understanding of the process revolves around questions of what can be learned observationally and under what circumstances. Factors that might predict outcomes include the extent to which modeled behaviors differ from those in the subjects' repertoires and the extent to which additional distracting stimuli are present in the modeling environment. For example, one might predict that modeled responses that are consonant with the learner's language repertoire are likely to be learned observationally in structured settings (Egel, Richman, & Koegel, 1981; Goldstein & Mousetis, 1989; McCuller, 1980) and responses that are discrepant are most likely not to be learned.

There is preliminary evidence that the ability of individuals with mental retardation to profit from modeling experiences can be increased (Goldstein & Brown, 1989; Goldstein & Mousetis, 1989; McCuller, 1980), but investigating this issue remains elusive. Determining *how* to increase observational learning abilities effectively presents two problems. First, modeling of language responses has often been so successful that opportunities for studying the acquisition of observational learning abilities have been severely limited. Second, and more importantly, it is easy to confuse lack of observational learning with discrimination problems. That is, on some occasions when it appeared that observational learning had not occurred, we found that it had occurred, but not accurately or completely. The difference between failure to learn observationally and discrimination problems can be determined only by carefully analyzing error patterns. For example, a child who seemed not to learn "scale on nightstand" persisted in confusing "scale" and "bean," which was a component of a previously trained response. In the context of our object-preposition-location task, this subject found the discrimination between two objects similar in size and in color to be difficult. Another subject had difficulty in learning the discrimination between "right of" and "left of," which, as it turned out, had little to do with his ability to profit from modeling. By examining error patterns, it may be possible to design individual interventions to ameliorate specific discrimination problems.

In a related study (Goldstein & Mousetis, 1990), six subjects with severe mental retardation were exposed to peers who modeled receptive object-preposition-location responses rather than expressive responses. Results nearly identical to those in the expressive modeling study described above (Goldstein & Mousetis, 1989) were obtained. Again, the children quickly began demonstrating generalized learning subsequent to the modeling of responses that combined known words before introducing unknown object, location, and preposition words. Together, these studies show the potential of organizing modeling experiences according to matrix-training principles in order to obtain widespread recombinative generalization.

Although miniature furniture and dollhouses were used in these experiments with children with severe mental retardation, generalization to more naturalistic stimuli with new examiners has been consistently impressive

(Goldstein et al., 1987; Goldstein & Brown, 1989; Goldstein & Mousetis, 1989, 1990). The results of these studies suggest that it might be possible to shift the context for observational language learning from these experimental materials into more natural environments, such as the classroom, and therein teach functional language repertoires with great efficiency. In summary, the efficiency of language training for children with mental retardation can be enhanced by coupling observational learning and matrix-training strategies.

CROSSMODAL TRANSFER

Crossmodal transfer is a third process that we believe contributes to learning efficiency. Crossmodal transfer between comprehension and production, although often demonstrated, is not well understood (cf. Bloom, 1974; Goldstein et al., 1987; Ingram, 1974; Lee, 1981). Language interventionists continue to struggle with the question of whether to teach in one modality before another. Expressive learning usually results in transfer to comprehension, but not always (Connell, 1986; Keller & Bucher, 1979; Miller, Cuvo, & Borakove, 1977). Receptive learning is not likely to transfer to verbal production, but sometimes it does (Cuvo & Riva, 1980; Lee, 1981; McIlvane, Bass, O'Brien, Gerovac, & Stoddard, 1984). In our expressive modeling experiment (Goldstein & Mousetis, 1989), there was no consistent learning in one modality before the other, and, most often, performance was similar in both modalities at any point in time. It was notable that receptive responding did not always precede expressive responding, particularly because developmental theory predicts that this is unlikely. In fact, we have found this to be true repeatedly in several studies, even when training was being conducted in the receptive modality (Goldstein & Brown, 1989; Goldstein et al., 1987; Goldstein & Mousetis, 1989). That is, subjects sometimes produced untrained responses in the expressive modality before the associated responses were demonstrated in the receptive modality. The fact that these responses were attributable to recombinative generalization diminishes the argument that rote responding was responsible for these unexpected results. It may be that the traditional hypothesis that comprehension precedes production needs to be reexamined in light of complex tasks of approximately equal difficulty.

A task analysis of comprehension and production tasks that scrutinizes carefully both the antecedent stimuli and the responses involved in various linguistic performances may be revealing. Complex discriminative responding based on at least two or three relevant components is required in both receptive and expressive tasks involving object-preposition-location responses. In our experiments, there is basically one type of receptive response and one type of expressive response required. It might be argued that the object manipulation response topographies for receptive tasks are easier than the verbal production topographies for the expressive tasks.

Perhaps more relevant than the different response topographies, however, are the differences in antecedent stimuli. Memory demands may be less for the expressive task. In our studies, in the expressive task, the trainer places an object in a particular place, and the object and location remain visible while the subject describes their orientation in the expressive task. In contrast, for the receptive task, object, preposition, and location words must be remembered after the trainer presents an instruction (e.g., "Put the shoe under the dresser"). When the instruction has been delivered, the subject must select the object, find the location, and place the object in the appropriate orientation to the location. The transience of antecedent stimuli may be of little importance when comparing receptive and expressive tasks that are simple (e.g., when learning single word-referent associations), but may affect performance more when the tasks are more complex. Judgments about the relative complexity of tasks cannot be made, however, without taking into account the relevant learning history of the individuals. In fact, the example discussed below illustrates how results obtained with children learning single words were not replicated with adults when they were presented appropriately challenging receptive and expressive language tasks.

Although we have provided some evidence of transfer from comprehension to production, such transfer is not the typical result. Thus, one longstanding question about the relationship between receptive and expressive language concerns how best to facilitate transfer between modalities, especially from comprehension to production. Other investigators (Ruder, Hermann, & Schiefelbusch, 1977; Ruder, Smith, & Hermann, 1974) found that the addition of verbal imitation training after comprehension training facilitated verbal label production when teaching single words to children. A modest extension of the stimulus-equivalence paradigm would predict the same result. This prediction is illustrated in Table 1. If individuals are able to imitate words and match pictures (two reflexive relationships), and if they are taught to identify pictures associated with those words, then they might be expected to demonstrate the symmetrical relationship by saying the words corresponding to the appropriate pictures without explicit training.

Research using the stimulus-equivalence paradigm has begun to identify the conditions that yield untrained relationships between substitutable mem-

Table 1. Application of stimulus-equivalence paradigm to transfer from comprehension to production

	Stimuli	Responses
Verbal imitation	(A) dictated words	(A') spoken words
Picture matching	(B) pictures	(B) pictures
Auditory comprehension	(A) dictated words	(B) pictures
Verbal production	(B) pictures	(A') spoken words

bers of a stimulus class (e.g., McIlvane, Dube, Green, & Serna, chap. 12, this volume; Sidman, 1971; Sidman & Cresson, 1973; Sidman & Tailby, 1982; Spradlin, Cotter, & Baxley, 1973; Wulz & Hollis, 1979). For example, a myriad of substitutable stimuli might represent the stimulus class "car" (e.g., different referents: coupes, sedans, sport cars; different symbols: printed words, pictures, photographs, emblems, trademarks; different linguistic responses: hearing or saying "car"), but only a few of the possible equivalent relationships among them need to be taught directly. For our example, we are interested in a stimulus-equivalence application in which: 1) pictures, 2) words that are heard, and 3) words that are spoken form stimulus classes.

In a series of studies with typical adults, associations between colored shapes and two-word Russian utterances organized according to 4 x 4 language matrices were taught. Matrix-training procedures were sufficient to establish generalized receptive performance, but, as shown in Table 2, transfer to production after comprehension training was not very good (31% and 25% of words produced correctly). Imitation training on the eight words subsequent to comprehension training resulted in somewhat better transfer (54% and 61%). But nearly complete transfer occurred only when limited verbal labeling production training (on 4 of 16 utterances) followed comprehension training. In Experiment 2, syllables were combined from several words, so that subjects had to attend to each syllable in order to accurately respond receptively. The words comprising a 4 x 4 submatrix for Experiment 2 are shown at the bottom of Table 2. Transfer to production improved under these conditions (49% and 34%), but was still far from complete. Finally, it was hypothesized that perhaps we had misconstrued our application of the stimulus-equivalence paradigm. The verbal imitation component, although sufficient to facilitate receptive-expressive transfer for children learning single words, seemed suspect. We believed that verbal imitation alone did not establish a repertoire of verbal responses that could be retrieved during the verbal production component. Thus, to establish a more permanent relationship be-

Table 2. Mean percentage of transfer to production (words correct) following various training conditions

Training conditions	Experiment 1	Experiment 2	Experiment 3
Comprehension	31%, 25%	49%, 34%	
Comprehension + imitation	54%		61%
Comprehension + production	89%	87%	
Imitation + comprehension			56%
Comprehension + memorization			88%
Memorization + comprehension			86%

Examples of words constituting 4 x 4 submatrices in Experiment 2 included the following nouns: *kawspaetia, rawpobia, kawpobka,* and *rawspaetka*; adjectives: *zelany, zegraty, zezavy,* and *bawlany*.

tween dictated words and spoken words, subjects were required to memorize the eight words. Memorization before or after comprehension training resulted in near complete transfer to production (86% and 88%). This finding recalls an argument made by Lee (1981): Crossmodal transfer may be attributable to shifting of stimulus control, but only if the receptive and expressive response topographies are already in individuals' behavioral repertoires.

Our understanding of the relationship between comprehension and production remains incomplete. We cannot reliably predict when receptive and expressive repertoires develop independently and when crossmodal transfer occurs. The results of our analog studies with adults indicate that the role of existing repertoires and their relationship to what is being taught must not be overlooked. It is not practical to have children with mental retardation memorize lists of new words, but our findings that memorization facilitated production may help explain why extensive crossmodal transfer was demonstrated when semantic relations were taught in previous studies (Goldstein et al., 1987; Goldstein & Brown, 1989; Goldstein & Mousetis, 1989). At the outset of these studies, some words were known and some were unknown. Both receptive and expressive modeling experiences were concentrated on carefully selected training items, and these procedures seemed sufficient to establish previously unknown words in individuals' expressive repertoires. As substitutable members of stimulus classes, their appearance in untrained sequences of words appeared to result from the coupling of recombinative generalization and crossmodal transfer. Thus, although individuals were exposed to receptive modeling only, they produced expressive responses and did so in a productive fashion, demonstrating recombinative generalization as well.

Employing strategies for promoting crossmodal transfer should add to the efficiency of language training for children with mental retardation. We have proposed that careful analyses of comprehension and production tasks may help predict when the development of expressive skills is likely to precede the development of receptive skills. It may be that we have been misguided in believing that imitation training will facilitate transfer from comprehension to production. Rather, it appears that transfer to production depends on whether verbal responses have been previously established in an individual's verbal repertoire.

CLINICAL IMPLICATIONS

The research summarized in this chapter only begins to investigate the combined potential of the three learning processes as each contributes to the acquisition of linguistic behavior not trained directly. The studies by Goldstein and Mousetis (1989, 1990) seem good illustrations of how children with mental retardation demonstrate observational learning, recombinative generalization, and crossmodal transfer together. In these studies, 12 children with mental retardation observationally learned responses modeled by their peers. On those few occasions when it appeared that subjects were not able to learn observationally, relatively brief interventions were implemented to help the children learn relevant discriminations. Subsequent to these interventions, children were able to observationally learn additional responses that were equally complex.

By organizing the modeled responses according to matrix-training strategies, children were able to recombine words to generate untrained responses. An analysis of recombinative generalization that stresses the determinants of discriminative responding was offered as an explanation for the learning of relatively simple linguistic rules. Structuring the experiences for training new semantic relations so that utterances are composed initially of previously learned words simplifies the learning task for children (see Goldstein, 1985) and results in more rapid generalization. Recombinative generalization has been shown to be responsible for a vast majority of the learning of new structures. For example, just 4 out of 90 object-preposition-location utterances needed to be taught (Goldstein & Mousetis, 1989).

Finally, the process of crossmodal transfer has the potential to double the learning efficiency, if linguistic responses learned receptively can be produced expressively, and vice versa. Acknowledging that this learning process is not well understood, we have proposed some tactics that might guide the process of promoting more widespread crossmodal transfer. It has been suggested that we analyze more closely the demands inherent in receptive and expressive tasks and how these vary as linguistic structures become more complex. Further complicating our ability to predict and control crossmodal transfer is analysis of the relationship between task requirements and the learners' behavioral repertoires. Nevertheless, it appears that transfer from comprehension to production can be facilitated if opportunities can be provided for individuals to learn to produce new words included in those structures, and if that production is not limited simply to immediate imitation of modeled utterances.

FUTURE RESEARCH

Although much of the research reviewed in this chapter has involved children with mental retardation, the focus has been on elucidating basic learning processes. Consequently, the studies have been conducted in relatively controlled settings. On one hand, much of the contextual support, such as extralinguistic cuing, that aids the development of language has been eliminated in order to investigate the role of specified environmental conditions on language development. On the other hand, distracting stimuli that may interfere with learning also have been minimized.

A number of avenues for *basic* research on these generative learning processes are evident, such as:

1. Investigations of the application of matrix-training strategies for promoting generative learning of a larger repertoire of linguistic structures, leading to more complex syntactic development
2. Investigations of how the selection of target behaviors and control over irrelevant stimuli in the modeling situation interact with the learning of new linguistic skills observationally
3. Investigations of how manipulating the task demands inherent in varying receptive and expressive performances affect the development of receptive and expressive language skills as they progress in concert.

Likewise, there are a number of avenues for *applied* research that are warranted, such as:

1. Investigations of strategies for incorporating matrix-training strategies into language intervention in more naturalistic contexts
2. Investigations of strategies for optimizing the observational learning that results from group instruction
3. Investigations of the application of stimulus-equivalence procedures within naturalistic contexts to maximize functional language comprehension and production, reading, and writing performances that are learned without direct training
4. Investigations of treatment packages that incorporate strategies for promoting recombinative generalization, observational learning, and crossmodal transfer to maximize the efficiency of language instruction in naturalistic contexts
5. Investigations of the far-reaching effects of teaching specific linguistic structures on general communication development.

Clearly, more research is needed to develop these procedures for application in language intervention programs in more naturalistic settings. Nevertheless, there is reason to believe that the systematic and collective application of such procedures can enhance recombinative generalization, observational learning, and crossmodal transfer and may have a profound impact on the efficiency of our language intervention efforts. There is much work to be done, but there is reason to feel optimistic that empirically derived language intervention procedures can be integrated in ways to improve the quality of life of individuals with mental retardation by enhancing their ability to communicate effectively in a variety of social, educational, and community contexts.

REFERENCES

Baer, D.M., & Guess, D. (1973). Teaching productive noun suffixes to severely retarded children. *American Journal of Mental Deficiency, 77,* 498–505.

Baer, D.M., Peterson, R.F., & Sherman, J. (1967). The development of imitation by reinforcing behavior similarity to a model. *Journal of the Experimental Analysis of Behavior, 10,* 405–416.

Bloom, L. (1974). Talking, understanding, and thinking. In R.L. Schiefelbusch & L.L. Lloyd (Eds.), *Language perspectives: Acquisition, retardation, and intervention* (pp. 285–311). Baltimore: University Park Press.

Browder, D., Schoen, S., & Lentz, F. (1986–1987). Learning to learn through observation. *Journal of Special Education, 20,* 447–461.

Connell, P.J. (1986). Acquisition of semantic role by language-disordered children: Differences between production and comprehension. *Journal of Speech and Hearing Research, 29,* 366–374.

Cullinan, D., Kauffman, J., & LaFleur, N. (1975). Modeling: Research with implications for special education. *Journal of Special Education, 9,* 209–221.

Cuvo, A., & Riva, M. (1980). Generalization and transfer between comprehension and production: A comparison of retarded and nonretarded persons. *Journal of Applied Behavior Analysis, 11,* 474–477.

Egel, A.L., Richman, G., & Koegel, R.L. (1981). Normal peer models and autistic children's learning. *Journal of Applied Behavior Analysis, 14,* 3–12.

Esper, E. (1925). A technique for the experimental investigation of associative interference in artificial linguistic material. *Language Monographs, 1.*

Esper, E. (1973). *Analogy and association in linguistics and psychology.* Athens: University of Georgia Press.

Ezell, H., & Goldstein, H. (1989). Effects of imitation on language comprehension and transfer to production in children with mental retardation. *Journal of Speech and Hearing Disorders, 54,* 49–56.

Glidden, L.M., & Warner, D.A. (1982). Research on imitation in mentally retarded persons: Theory-bound or ecological validity run amuck? *Applied Research in Mental Retardation, 3,* 383–395.

Goldstein, H. (1983). Recombinative generalization: Relationships between environmental conditions and the linguistic repertoires of language learners. *Analysis and Intervention in Developmental Disabilities, 3,* 279–293.

Goldstein, H. (1985). Enhancing language generalization using matrix and stimulus equivalence training. In S. Warren & A. Rogers-Warren (Eds.), *Teaching functional language* (pp. 225–249). Baltimore: University Park Press.

Goldstein, H., Angelo, D., & Mousetis, L. (1987). Acquisition and extension of syntactic repertoires by severely mentally retarded youth. *Research in Developmental Disabilities, 8,* 549–574.

Goldstein, H., & Brown, W. (1989). Observational learning of receptive and expressive language by preschool children. *Education and Treatment of Children, 12,* 5–37.

Goldstein, H., & Mousetis, L. (1989). Generalized language learning by children with severe mental retardation: Effects of peers' expressive modeling. *Journal of Applied Behavior Analysis, 22,* 245–259.

Goldstein, H., & Mousetis, L. (1990). *Generalized language learning by children with severe mental retardation: Effects of peers' receptive modeling.* Unpublished manuscript.

Guess, D. (1969). A functional analysis of receptive language and productive speech: Acquisition of the plural morpheme. *Journal of Applied Behavior Analysis, 2,* 55–64.

Guess, D., Sailor, W., Rutherford, G., & Baer, D.M. (1968). An experimental analysis of linguistic development: The productive use of the plural morpheme. *Journal of Applied Behavior Analysis, 1,* 297–306.

Haney, J.I., Wilson, J.W., & Halle, J. (1988). Adults with mental retardation: Who they are, where they are, and how their communicative needs can be met. In S.N.

Calculator & J.L. Bedrosian (Eds.), *Communication assessment and intervention for adults with mental retardation* (pp. 69–94). Boston: Little, Brown.

Hockett, C.F. (1958). *A course in modern linguistics.* New York: Macmillan.

Ingram, D. (1974). The relationship between comprehension and production. In R.L. Schiefelbusch & L.L. Lloyd (Eds.), *Language perspectives: Acquisition, retardation, and intervention* (pp. 313–334). Baltimore: University Park Press.

Karlan, G., Brenn-White, B., Lentz, A., Hodur, P., Egger, D., & Frankoff, D. (1982). Establishing generalized, productive verb-noun phrase usage in a manual language system with moderately handicapped children. *Journal of Speech and Hearing Disorders, 47,* 31–42.

Keller, M.F., & Bucher, B.D. (1979). Transfer between receptive and productive language in developmentally disabled children. *Journal of Applied Behavior Analysis, 12,* 311.

Lee, V. (1981). Prepositional phrases spoken and heard. *Journal of the Experimental Analysis of Behavior, 35,* 227–242.

McCuller, W.R. (1980). *Acquisition of generalized verb-noun instruction following in profoundly retarded adults.* Unpublished doctoral dissertation, Peabody College of Vanderbilt University, Nashville.

McIlvane, W.J,. Bass, R.W., O'Brien, J.M., Gerovac, B.J., & Stoddard, L.T. (1984). Spoken and signed naming of foods after receptive exclusion training in severe retardation. *Applied Research in Mental Retardation, 5,* 1–28.

Miller, M.A., Cuvo, A.J., & Borakove, L.S. (1977). Teaching naming of coin values comprehension before production versus production alone. *Journal of Applied Behavior Analysis, 10,* 735–736.

Mineo, B., & Goldstein, H. (1990). Generative learning of receptive and expressive action-object responses by language-delayed preschoolers. *Journal of Speech and Hearing Disorders, 55,* 665–678.

Reichle, J., & Keogh, W.J. (1985). Communication intervention: A selective review of what, when, and how to teach. In S. Warren & A. Rogers-Warren (Eds.), *Teaching functional language* (pp. 25–59). Baltimore: University Park Press.

Romski, M.A., & Ruder, K.F. (1984). Effects of speech and speech and sign instruction on oral language learning and generalization of action + object combinations by Down's Syndrome children. *Journal of Speech and Hearing Disorders, 49,* 292–302.

Ruder, K., Hermann, P., & Schiefelbusch, R. (1977). Effects of verbal imitation and comprehension training on verbal production. *Journal of Psycholinguistic Research, 6,* 59–72.

Ruder, K., Smith, M., & Hermann, P. (1974). Effects of verbal imitation and comprehension on verbal production of lexical items. In L.V. McReynolds (Ed.), *Developing systematic procedures for training children's language. Asha Monographs, 18,* 15–29.

Sailor, W. (1971). Reinforcement and generalization of productive plural allomorphs in two retarded children. *Journal of Applied Behavior Analysis, 4,* 305–310.

Sidman, M. (1971). Reading and auditory-visual equivalences. *Journal of Speech and Hearing Research, 14,* 5–13.

Sidman, M., & Cresson, O., Jr. (1973). Reading and crossmodal transfer of stimulus equivalences in severe retardation. *American Journal of Mental Deficiency, 77,* 515–523.

Sidman, M., & Tailby, W. (1982). Conditional discriminations vs. matching to sample: An expansion of the testing paradigm. *Journal of the Experimental Analysis of Behavior, 37,* 5–22.

Spradlin, J.E., Cotter, V.W., & Baxley, N. (1973). Establishing a conditional discrimination without direct training: A study of transfer with retarded adolescents. *American Journal of Mental Deficiency, 77,* 556–566.

Striefel, S., Wetherby, B., & Karlan, G. (1976). Establishing generalized verb-noun instruction-following skills in retarded children. *Journal of Experimental Child Psychology, 22,* 247–260.

Striefel, S., Wetherby, B., & Karlan, G. (1978). Developing generalized instruction-following behavior in the severely retarded. In C. Meyers (Ed.), *Quality of life in severely and profoundly mentally retarded people: Research foundations for improvement* (pp. 267–326). Washington, DC: American Association on Mental Deficiency.

Wetherby, B. (1978). Miniature language and functional analysis of verbal behavior. In R. Schiefelbusch (Ed.), *Bases of language intervention* (pp. 397–448). Baltimore: University Park Press.

Wetherby, B., & Striefel, S. (1978). Application of miniature linguistic system or matrix training procedures. In R. Schiefelbusch (Ed.), *Bases of language intervention* (pp. 318–356). Baltimore: University Park Press.

Wulz, S.V., & Hollis, J. (1979). Application of manual signing to the development of reading skills. In R.L. Schiefelbusch & J. Hollis (Eds.), *Language intervention from ape to child* (pp. 465–489). Baltimore: University Park Press.

15

Speech and Language Abilities of Children with Down Syndrome

A Parent's Perspective

Siegfried M. Pueschel and Marita R. Hopmann

THE PROFESSIONAL LITERATURE IS REPLETE with articles concerning speech and language development, communication disorders, language comprehension processes, linguistic environments, oral speech mechanisms, and hearing impairments in children with Down syndrome (Dahle & McCollister, 1986; Downs & Balkany, 1988; Fowler, 1990; Miller, 1987; Parsons, Iacono, & Rozner, 1987; Rondal, 1988; Whiteman, Simpson, & Compton, 1986). Although professionals have studied various aspects of speech and language in persons with this chromosome disorder, there are only a few anecdotal reports that focus on parental perspectives on the communication skills of children with Down syndrome.

Buckley and Sacks's (1987) survey, carried out in England, seems to stand alone as a direct treatment of the topic of parental views of language concerns of children with Down syndrome. Buckley and Sacks asked 90 families who had a teenager with Down syndrome to complete a questionnaire pertaining to the language development of their children and to their abilities to communicate effectively in everyday situations. Analyses of parent responses to the questionnaires revealed that of the 40 girls in this study, 70% of those under the age of 14 and 77% over the age of 14 used sentences of five or more words. Of the 50 boys enrolled in this study, 46% of those under the age of 14 and 70% over the age of 14 used sentences of five or more words. In general, the older group were perceived to have more advanced language and communication skills than the younger group, and the boys showed greater

The authors thank Alex Hopmann for his assistance in preparing the data for analysis.

delays than the girls. The authors conclude by recommending language intervention that starts in infancy and continues through the teenage years.

In this country, current priorities to place children with Down syndrome
in integrated settings bring new attention to the importance of adequate communication skills for these youngsters. As federal regulations for children
with disabilities (e.g., Individuals with Disabilities Education Act) point out,
parents play a central role in both influencing their children's current skill
levels and in setting goals for their children's therapeutic interventions. Although parents are seen as essential partners in this process, little systematic
information is available about parents' views of their children's communication skills and needs.

Our investigations were designed to obtain information from parents of
children with Down syndrome on a variety of topics concerning their youngsters' communication and language skills. We were interested in gaining information about parents' assessment of their children's current language skill
levels and in probing the parents' evaluation of important contributions to
their children's attainment of language.

SUBJECTS AND METHODS

The children recruited for this study are part of a group of over 400 persons
with Down syndrome followed by the senior author at the Child Development
Center of Rhode Island Hospital, a University Affiliated Program. The Child
Development Center provides comprehensive services to individuals with developmental disabilities and has a close relationship with the two local cytoge-
netic laboratories.

We sent questionnaires to 273 parents of individuals with Down syndrome between the ages of 1–21 years. On a two-page form (see appendix),
parents were asked questions relating to their son's or daughter's communication skills. The questionnaire focused on expressive and receptive language,
articulation, sign language, reading skills, middle ear infections, hearing
impairment, and other language related experiences. Although a total of 78
statements were listed on the questionnaire, in the present analysis of the
responses 55 selected statements were used.

In the first part of the questionnaire (questions 1–30), parents were asked
to check the most appropriate answer using a key with the choices "always,"
"mostly," "sometimes," "never," and "does not apply." For example, parents responded to the statement "My child says just single words" with "does
not apply" if their child spoke in phrases or sentences. In order to simplify the
presentation of the data, the first three responses were summarized as "yes"
responses in the section on results and in Tables 2 and 3.[1] In the second part of

---

[1]We are aware of the constraints and potential difficulties in interpretation that this reduction
of the responses may bring about; however, we felt it would be important to present the data in a
clear and simplified way.

the questionnaire (questions 31–70), statements were phrased to elicit "yes," "no," or "does not apply" responses (see Tables 4–8). The final series of questions (71–78) inquired about the importance of various persons and experiences on the child's language development. For these questions, parents were asked to indicate whether a specific experience was "very helpful," "somewhat helpful," or "not helpful" (Table 10). In addition, there were two open-ended questions: "Please let us know your main concern regarding your child's language and communication," and "Please make further comments if you wish with regard to any aspect of speech and language concerns in your child or regarding children with Down syndrome in general."

Of the 273 questionnaires sent to parents, 44 were returned due to wrong addresses. One hundred and sixty one completed questionnaires were returned to us by the participating parents, producing a response rate of 70%. Seven questionnaires were excluded: two individuals were over 21 years of age, and five others have mosaicism Down syndrome. Thus, a total of 154 questionnaires were available for final analysis.

RESULTS

As expected, the vast majority of children (92%) had trisomy 21, 4% had translocation, 3% had mosaicism Down syndrome, and the karyotype of two children was unknown. As mentioned above, the children with mosaicism Down syndrome were excluded from further analysis.

As shown in Table 1, there was a fairly even distribution of youngsters with Down syndrome in the different age groups: 25 children were in Group I (1–3 years), 33 in Group II (4–6 years), 31 in Group III (7–10 years), 34 in Group IV (11–16 years), and 31 in Group V (17–21 years). There were comparable numbers of males and females in each group, with a total of 83 males and 71 females included in this study.

Most of the children were spoken to in English (94%). Three children were spoken to in both English and Spanish, two children in English and Portuguese, another two in English and French, and two were spoken to in Cambodian.

Many parents of the children in the study were well educated: 88% of mothers and 84% of fathers graduated from high school, 20% of both mothers

Table 1. Age groups of children in communication and language skills study

Age range	Male	Female	Total
1–3	12	13	25
4–6	17	16	33
7–10	18	13	31
11–16	19	15	34
17–21	17	14	31

and fathers graduated from college, and 6% of mothers and 18% of fathers had engaged in graduate studies.

Analyzing the parental responses about their children's expressive language skills, we found that 88% of the 1- to 3-year-old children with Down syndrome are reported to say single words. Although there is a steady decrease across age groups in the number of children reported to say just one word, this characterization was given for a substantial number (39%) of the 17- to 21-year-olds. As shown in Table 2, children in the older age groups are reported to communicate often in short phrases or in sentences. In the three oldest age groups, 77%–91% of individuals with Down syndrome speak in sentences.

Further clarification on the children's expressive language skills comes from analyses of statements about the use of syntax such as: "My child talks about past events," "My child talks about future events," and "My child uses articles." Only a few of the toddlers (12%) were reported to talk about past or future events, and 16% were reported to use articles in their speech. These three aspects of syntax are reported as present in the vast majority of the children 7 years and older, with the use of articles showing the least change across ages (Table 2).

Overall, the parents view their children as active conversationalists: The majority of even the youngest children are reported to be starting and participating in conversations. The ability to start and to participate in conversations as well as ask questions increases with age, up to 16 years. The most active conversationalists, according to these indicators, are children in the 7- to 10-year-old and 11- to 16-year-old age groups, with over 90% of the youngsters reported as starting and participating in conversations and asking questions.

The impact of the children's difficulties with articulation was assessed by general questions about intelligibility, distinguishing between interlocutors who are very familiar with the child and those who lack any familiarity, as shown in Table 3. The parents in our study were very positive about their children's abilities to be understood. The vast majority of children, even the youngest group, were described as being effective in getting others to understand them. Parents reported that 91%–100% of their children are effective in getting others to understand them, and 84%–100% are understood by family members but less often by strangers (64%–94%).

The children's feelings of frustration were assessed by asking their parents questions that distinguished between the child's frustration with the inability to express him- or herself and frustration when his or her efforts were not effective. As shown in Table 3, children in all age groups were reported to become frustrated when they were unable to express themselves (74%–91%). This frustration is noted even among the toddlers, a group that was also characterized as being effective in getting others to understand them.

Table 2. Parents' evaluation of their children's expressive language abilities

My child	1- to 3-year-olds			4- to 6-year-olds			7- to 10-year-olds			11- to 16-year-olds			17- to 21-year-olds		
	Yes	No	NA	Yes	No	NA	Yes	No	NA	Yes	No	NA	Yes	No	NA
says just single words	88	0	12	79	0	21	52	19	29	41	21	38	39	16	45
talks in 2- to 3-word phrases	44	36	20	82	6	12	77	3	20	67	9	24	52	13	35
talks in sentences	20	52	28	64	30	6	87	10	3	91	3	6	77	10	13
talks about past events	12	44	44	58	36	6	80	13	7	91	3	6	83	7	10
talks about future events	12	48	40	45	43	12	80	13	7	84	10	6	86	7	7
uses articles	16	48	36	26	71	3	80	10	10	84	10	6	77	13	10
starts conversations	60	24	16	76	24	0	94	6	0	91	3	6	84	10	6
participates in conversations	52	24	24	76	21	3	91	6	3	91	3	6	81	13	6
asks questions	40	40	20	73	24	3	94	3	3	88	6	6	81	16	3

Numbers = percent of children as indicated by parent responses.

Table 3. Parents' evaluation of their children's ability to make themselves understood

My child	1- to 3-year-olds			4- to 6-year-olds			7- to 10-year-olds			11- to 16-year-olds			17- to 21-year-olds		
	Yes	No	NA	Yes	No	NA	Yes	No	NA	Yes	No	NA	Yes	No	NA
is effective in getting others to understand him or her	92	4	4	100	0	0	97	3	0	91	0	9	91	6	3
is understood by family members	84	0	16	97	3	0	100	0	0	97	0	3	87	0	13
is understood by strangers	64	20	16	85	12	3	94	3	3	88	6	6	91	3	6
is frustrated when unable to express him- or herself	76	16	8	84	13	3	81	19	0	91	9	0	74	16	10
is frustrated when not understood	72	16	12	85	12	3	90	10	0	88	9	3	74	16	10

Numbers = percent of children as indicated by parent responses.

Evaluation of parental responses of receptive language skills indicates that 92%–100% of the children studied "understand what others say to him or her," and 88%–97% "understand words that he or she does not say." There were no appreciable age-group differences concerning these categories in Table 4. Thus, the vast majority of children, even in the youngest age group, were reported to have good comprehension abilities.

The parents' views of their children's speech were assessed by a series of questions addressing issues of speech production and a general question about articulation. As shown in Table 5, the speech problem identified most by parents for the two youngest groups (1- to 3- and 4- to 6-year-olds) is "speaks too loudly." Speaking too softly is reported to be a problem in all but the youngest group. Few toddlers are identified with the characteristic hoarse or deep voice (12% and 16% respectively), but about one third of the children in the older groups are reported to have this speech quality.

Excessively rapid speech is rare among the toddlers but is evident in all other groups, characterizing three fourths of the 7- to 10-year-old children. Overall, stuttering appears to be far less common than excessively rapid speech; nevertheless, 56% of parents of 11- to 16-year-old children reported stuttering. Less than half of the 1- to 3-year-olds were described as having problems with articulation, whereas the vast majority of the older children (71%–94%) were reported to have articulation difficulties.

Children's experiences with sign language were examined by asking parents if their children were learning sign language, how many signs they (currently) used, and if the experiences with signing helped make the child less frustrated and facilitated talking. As noted in Table 6, more children in the younger age groups are learning sign language (56% of 1- to 3-year-olds and 43% of 4- to 6-year-olds) than in the older age groups (13%–22%). The largest number of children (16%) who use more than 50 signs are 4- to 6-year-olds.

Many parents of children in the younger age groups indicated that signing is helpful (48% of 1- to 3-year-olds and 78% of the 4- to 6-year-olds) and makes the child less frustrated (36% of the 1- to 3-year-olds and 68% of the 4- to 6-year-olds) (Table 7). In particular, more than two thirds of the parents with children 4–6 years of age report that signing helps their children to say words.

Another set of questions dealt with the child's ability to read. As shown in Table 8, the analysis by age found that the number of children reported to read sentences and books increased with the age of the children. In particular, in the two later age groups (11–16 and 17–21 years) more than half of the individuals were reported to demonstrate these skills. Most children between 7–10 and 11–16 years of age were reported to enjoy reading (47% and 58%, respectively). More children in the older age groups, specifically in the 17- to 21-year-old group (53%), were reported to use a phonetic approach when reading.

Table 4. Parent's evaluation of their children's receptive language abilities

My child	1- to 3-year-olds			4- to 6-year-olds			7- to 10-year-olds			11- to 16-year-olds			17- to 21-year-olds		
	Yes	No	NA	Yes	No	NA	Yes	No	NA	Yes	No	NA	Yes	No	NA
understands what others say to him or her	92	4	4	100	0	0	97	0	3	97	0	3	97	3	0
understands words that he or she does not say	88	8	4	97	0	3	97	3	0	94	0	6	91	3	6
listens when talked to	100	0	0	100	0	0	97	3	0	100	0	0	97	3	0

Numbers = percent of children as indicated by parent responses.

Table 5. Parents' evaluation of selected speech problems in their children

My child	1- to 3-year-olds			4- to 6-year-olds			7- to 10-year-olds			11- to 16-year-olds			17- to 21-year-olds		
	Yes	No	NA	Yes	No	NA	Yes	No	NA	Yes	No	NA	Yes	No	NA
speaks too loudly	60	24	16	61	33	6	64	26	10	70	24	6	39	42	19
speaks too softly	16	60	24	45	49	6	52	42	6	49	42	9	42	39	19
speaks with a hoarse voice	12	56	32	33	55	12	32	45	23	30	52	18	20	70	10
speaks with a deep voice	16	56	28	33	58	9	42	39	19	43	39	18	33	48	19
speaks too rapidly	8	56	36	36	61	3	74	26	0	59	35	6	46	35	19
stutters	0	52	48	9	78	13	38	52	10	56	35	9	23	57	20
has problems with articulation	44	8	48	85	6	9	94	0	6	91	3	6	71	16	13

Numbers = percent of children as indicated by parent responses.

Table 6. Parents' evaluation of their children's abilities to use signs

My child	1- to 3-year-olds			4- to 6-year-olds			7- to 10-year-olds			11- to 16-year-olds			17- to 21-year-olds		
	Yes	No	NA	Yes	No	NA	Yes	No	NA	Yes	No	NA	Yes	No	NA
is learning sign language	56	12	32	43	30	27	13	23	64	15	12	73	22	13	65
uses fewer than 10 signs	52	12	36	32	32	36	10	10	80	12	9	79	13	13	74
uses between 10 and 50 signs	16	48	36	16	39	45	0	19	81	3	15	82	10	16	74
uses more than 50 signs	4	56	40	16	39	45	3	16	81	0	15	85	3	23	74

Numbers = percent of children as indicated by parent responses.

Table 7. Parents' evaluation of usefulness of signing by their children

Parents find	1- to 3-year-olds			4- to 6-year-olds			7- to 10-year-olds			11- to 16-year-olds			17- to 21-year-olds		
	Yes	No	NA	Yes	No	NA	Yes	No	NA	Yes	No	NA	Yes	No	NA
signing helpful	48	16	36	78	3	19	23	3	74	12	12	76	17	3	80
signing makes child less frustrated	36	24	40	68	3	29	21	3	76	12	6	82	17	4	79
signing helps child to say words	20	36	44	71	3	26	21	10	69	9	9	82	11	3	86

Numbers = percent of children as indicated by parent responses.

Table 8. Parents' evaluation of their children's reading skills

My child	1- to 3-year-olds			4- to 6-year-olds			7- to 10-year-olds			11- to 16-year-olds			17- to 21-year-olds		
	Yes	No	NA	Yes	No	NA	Yes	No	NA	Yes	No	NA	Yes	No	NA
reads more than 50 words	0	8	92	0	18	82	20	33	47	47	27	26	50	20	30
reads sentences	0	8	92	3	9	88	47	13	40	61	15	24	67	10	23
reads books	0	8	92	3	9	88	27	33	40	56	19	25	50	27	23
enjoys reading	0	8	92	3	6	91	47	10	43	58	21	21	45	19	36
speaks more clearly when he or she reads aloud	0	8	92	6	6	88	37	13	50	50	18	32	28	21	51
can sound out new words (uses phonics)	0	8	92	6	12	82	21	38	41	44	29	27	53	17	30

Numbers = percent of children as indicated by parent responses.

Most parents reported that their children received speech therapy in school or in early intervention programs (see Table 9). It is noteworthy, however, that 48% of parents reported that their children in the 1–3 age group received speech therapy in school or early intervention programs, whereas 97% of children in 4–6 and 7–10 age groups received such intervention as part of their school programs. According to the parents' responses, speech therapy was often provided in a one-on-one or small group basis, in particular for children 4–6 and 7–10 years old (91% and 77%, respectively). Most parents found speech therapy to be helpful (52%–88%). Some parents indicated that the speech therapy provided to their children "is inadequate," in particular for children in the 1–3 age group.

The parents' evaluations of their children's progress was assessed both through a direct question (number 69) and by asking about the loss of language skills, something not frequently observed in the language development of nonhandicapped children but sometimes mentioned by parents of children with Down syndrome. The periods of most impressive language progress seem to be in the 4–6 and 7–10 age groups. The vast majority of the parents of children in these two groups reported that their children were making adequate progress. In contrast, fewer than half of the parents of the 1–3 age group reported adequate progress, reflecting the slow development of early language. Surprisingly, almost half of the parents of the 16- to 21-year-olds reported that their children were making good progress. Whereas a few parents of children in each age group reported that their children seemed to lose language skills, almost one fifth of the parents of the 16- to 21-year-olds reported that this was true for their children.

Table 10 provides a summary of parental responses to the question, "How important have the following persons been in helping your child develop language?" As noted in this table, parents, brothers and sisters, as well as teachers and speech therapists were reported to have helped the child in his or her language acquisition. Parents reported themselves to be most important in assisting their children to develop language, followed by speech therapists, siblings, nonhandicapped classmates, television, and, lastly, classmates with special needs. At every age level, television was seen as at least as helpful for language development as were nonhandicapped classmates. About one half of the parents judged television to be helpful in language development for children over 3 years of age. A number of parents volunteered that music has been important in their child's language development.

DISCUSSION

This study was exploratory in nature; nevertheless, we have valuable information to share with professionals and families who have a child with Down syndrome. For the professional, directions for further investigation are brought

Table 9. Parents' evaluation of speech therapy for their children

My child receives speech therapy	1- to 3-year-olds			4- to 6-year-olds			7- to 10-year-olds			11- to 16-year-olds			17- to 21-year-olds		
	Yes	No	NA	Yes	No	NA	Yes	No	NA	Yes	No	NA	Yes	No	NA
in school or early intervention program	48	36	16	97	3	0	97	3	0	85	12	3	71	16	13
privately	8	64	28	18	67	15	13	61	26	18	65	17	6	52	42
one-on-one or in a small group	36	40	24	91	6	3	77	13	10	76	15	9	61	10	29
in the general classroom	24	44	32	76	18	6	42	32	26	47	41	12	35	29	36
and it is adequate	28	40	32	70	18	12	52	29	19	47	38	15	39	13	48
and it is helpful	52	16	32	88	6	6	80	10	10	79	12	9	65	3	32
and is at a standstill	0	56	44	21	64	15	10	58	32	15	59	26	16	32	52

Numbers = percent of children as indicated by parent responses.

Table 10. Parents' evaluation of who and what has helped their children with language development

How important has the following been in helping your child develop language?	1- to 3-year-olds			4- to 6-year-olds			7- to 10-year-olds			11- to 16-year-olds			17- to 21-year-olds		
	Very helpful	Somewhat helpful	Not helpful	Very helpful	Somewhat helpful	Not helpful	Very helpful	Somewhat helpful	Not helpful	Very helpful	Somewhat helpful	Not helpful	Very helpful	Somewhat helpful	Not helpful
parents	72	20	8	76	21	3	77	23	0	85	15	0	74	19	7
siblings	44	16	40	64	21	15	77	16	7	73	18	9	55	23	22
speech therapists	48	20	32	76	21	3	77	13	10	79	15	6	65	22	13
nondisabled classmates	24	12	64	49	30	21	35	23	42	44	29	27	52	35	13
classmates with special needs	4	28	68	9	39	52	10	42	48	9	38	53	19	42	39
television	24	24	52	52	30	18	52	32	16	53	35	12	52	22	26

Numbers = percent of children as indicated by parent responses.

into focus. For parents, we provided some information concerning parents' views of typical and atypical communication and language behaviors and patterns where so little has been available.

In the absence of normative data about the communication and language development of persons with Down syndrome, parents and professionals wonder about reasonable expectations and typical achievements. Published clinical reports only rarely give information about the sampling procedures; thus, the reader is left with the impression that the research participants are somehow "representative" of all people with Down syndrome of their age. These reports are seldom written for general audiences, and thus the problem of interpretation lies with the professional, who may or may not have had sufficient experience with individuals with Down syndrome to respond to a parent's questions about normative behavior. A careful reading of the published work would not help one interpret our finding that about 40% of parents of the teenagers surveyed report that their sons and daughters are communicating in single words. Just focusing on the two more extreme response categories, 13% of the parents of the younger teenagers and 24% of the older group reported that their sons and daughters "always" or "mostly" said just single words. In contrast, only 6% of the parents in Buckley and Sacks's(1987) study of adolescents with Down syndrome stated that single words were the "usual length of the utterances."

Although there were occasional poignant comments about the complete absence of a systematic communication system with a teenage son or daughter, most of the parents' responses were very positive and enthusiastic about their children's skills. Yet, the parents' general optimism should not be confused with the accuracy of their reports. A direct assessment of the views of parents of children with Down syndrome about specific language skills of their sons and daughters (Hopmann, 1991) revealed results that were comparable with the results of parents of nonhandicapped youngsters.[2] Without a great degree of specificity, the items in the questionnaire permit a broad interpretation. Many parents wrote about how pleased they are with their son's or daughter's accomplishments, compared with their worst fears. In addition, we assume that there was a selection bias of our respondents: Although we did receive questionnaires from a few parents whose older teenagers were nonverbal, we imagine that parents whose children are perceived as doing well were more likely to return the completed form.

Finally, the apparently high parental estimations revealed in the responses help focus our attention on a common source of irritation between

---

[2]Mothers of children with Down syndrome who were regularly producing multiword utterances were asked to predict the choices that children would make on the PPVT-R and the TACL-R. After the parents completed the tests as they anticipated their child would, the children were administered the same test.

professionals and parents in the assessment process of a child with Down syndrome. Parents complain about their child being evaluated unfairly, and having school personnel set behavioral goals for their child that the child has already achieved. Although it is readily acknowledged that young nonhandicapped children demonstrate more advanced communication skills with family members than in school, this same point is sometimes disregarded when considering youngsters with disabilities of similar developmental levels. It is possible that persons with Down syndrome exhibit large setting-related variability in their communication skills. Future research will have to explore this fascinating possibility.

A broad view of the developmental trends from the parents' responses shows modest achievements during the first 3 years of life, when the majority of the toddlers are described as saying just single words. It is important for parents to know that language development is often very delayed for youngsters with Down syndrome.

The professional needs to consider the implications of a young person spending the first few years of his or her life without a systematic means of communication. Two somewhat separate issues present themselves. First, either formal (regulations about availability of speech/language/audiology early intervention services) or informal guidelines, which mandate that parents seek professional assistance for the child's communication skills only when the child begins to talk, must be examined in the context of the apparent age at which this event takes place. To be more specific, all families with a son or daughter with Down syndrome need the direct services of a speech pathologist or other professional trained in facilitation of early communication. Often, other aspects of the child's development are more noticeable to parents (e.g., motor development); when parents are given a "menu of services" from which to make a selection, in infancy, communication may be seen as less pressing. Second, speech therapists and program directors who view intervention as directed toward "training speech habits" are not likely to see the infant as an appropriate candidate. Up-to-date education and training for speech and language therapists in the nature of early communication and how to facilitate its development is required, as well as the opportunity for the therapist to work on a regular basis with the child's caregivers to instruct and model facilitative techniques. Clinicians may feel support for recommending the use of total communication (i.e., signs accompanying oral communication) as routine in the care of an infant with Down syndrome, rather than waiting to see if the child has particular difficulty with oral expression.

The relatively high evaluations by the parents of their children's ability to communicate effectively is consistent with the treatment of the topic by Dodd and Leahy (1989). Rather than viewing this as a source of reassurance, these authors suggest that the acceptance by parents of young children with Down syndrome of poorly pronounced phonological forms contributes to the distinctive deficit associated with the syndrome. They argue that family members and those who are very familiar with the young person with Down syndrome may learn unusual substitutions and other distinctive patterns, thus decreasing the child's incentive to learn the phonological patterns of the larger speech community.

Regarding the issue of intelligibility, we see that the adolescents Buckley and Sacks (1987) studied were reported to be understood by their parents at approximately the same rates as the teenagers in our group. However, in the British sample, there is a considerable discrepancy between the levels given for comprehension by family members versus strangers (the ratio being greater than 3:1). By contrast, the parents in our study indicated only a 9% difference for the younger teenagers, and, in fact, a slight superiority for the strangers with the older group.

The use of signs reveals quite a bit about the educational practice of the era and society. There appears to be a striking difference in the use of signs between adolescents in England and those we studied. About half of Buckley and Sacks's (1987) sample used signs, while a much smaller proportion of our teenagers do (15% of the younger adolescents and 25% of the older group). Although the number of people in this age group who are using signs is small by comparison with the British sample, the adolescents in our study group seem to be using signs as a dynamic element in their communication systems, as reflected by the fact that their parents indicate that they are still learning sign language.

The picture is dramatically different when we examine the use of signs by the younger children in our study. The majority of parents of children in the youngest group reported that their children were learning signs, although it is reported that only some of these children show evidence that their oral communication is facilitated by the signing. It is not until the children are older than 3 years of age that the majority of parents see evidence of facilitative effects of signing, reducing their child's frustration, and assisting the child to say words. The number of children learning sign language drops in the 7- to 10-year-old group. This may be a time when parents and therapists are less committed to the benefits of total communication, having seen evidence of the child using some verbal communication.

Most of the parents in Buckley and Sacks's (1987) study reported that their teenagers' response to communication breakdowns was to give up. We wonder if that helps explain what looks like an inverted U-shaped distribution in our data: The parents of the youngest group and those of the oldest group reported less frustration from their sons and daughters than the three middle age groups. No doubt, by the time an individual is 17 years old, the person with Down syndrome has developed a personal coping style to adapt to communication dysfunction. Quite possibly, the modal style is based on expectations of being neither understood nor understanding, contributing to the "happy and easy-to-please" stereotype associated with Down syndrome. This would be consistent with Dodd and Leahy's (1989) view that many individuals with Down syndrome are so overwhelmed by auditory stimulation that they learn to not attend to auditory events.

Inspection of the pragmatic items suggests that successful communication may be taking place in the absence of multiword language development. Nevertheless, only half of the parents of the youngest children report that their children are participating in conversations, and, although the percentage rises over the age span that we examined, 80% of the parents of the oldest teenagers endorsed this item. We are left to conclude that 1 out of 5 of these individuals were reported to be not able to participate in this most fundamental aspect of human interaction. We wonder if a contributing factor to this problem could be the common assumption by parents (and presumably others) that the person with Down syndrome understands what others are saying. In fact, the majority of parents of all the children except the youngest group reported that their sons and daughters understand what others say to them.

Our study revealed that about half of the teenagers are reported to be reading, sounding out new words, and enjoying the activity. This information is of special importance as there are few accounts in widely available sources of reading among persons with Down syndrome (Buckley, 1985; Irwin, 1989; LaVeck & Brehm, 1978; Lorenz, Sloper, & Cunningham, 1985; Oelwein, 1988; Rynders & Horrobin, 1990). Parents and caregivers of younger children need to be encouraged to read to them and with them, behaviors that are likely to assist the children in learning to read and to enjoy reading. Written material and videotapes are available to assist parents and teachers in making (minimal) adaptations to facilitate reading development for those with Down syndrome (Buckley, Emslie, Haslegrave, & Le Prevost, 1986).

The parents' views about sources of influence on their child's language development brought into focus two controversial and sensitive topics: peers and television. Interactions with children without special needs are viewed much more positively than those with special needs. This leads one to wonder how many parents of children with Down syndrome imagine that an ideal environment is populated exclusively by "normal" children, except for their child. It is clear that the specific nature of the facilitating effect of nonhandicapped peers for communication skills needs to be understood better so that parents and professionals can create educational environments that can be endorsed with enthusiasm.

Those who have made frequent home visits or spoken candidly with parents of children with Down syndrome will not be surprised by the high endorsement of television in our data. Even greater enthusiasm expressed for the benefits of television might have resulted had we explicitly included videos in the category with television. Many of the young people with Down syndrome at the Child Development Center seem to be easily and consistently entertained at home by watching television or videos. We suspect that the facilitative effect that parents attend to involves the children's occasional mimicking of introductory jingles or frequently repeated phrases that they have come to associate with the program or central character. In our educational programs for parents, we have strongly and frequently advocated the importance of dynamic, contingently responsive environments to facilitate language development, and we repeatedly evaluate television and videos according to these criteria. We question how many of the parents might have given an even more enthusiastic endorsement of television if the question had not been associated with the Child Development Center.

The information presented in this chapter speaks strongly for the need of two types of data about the communication and language skills of young people with Down syndrome. First, we need to acquire good normative studies of the communication and language skills associated with Down syndrome, as helpful guidelines for both parents and professionals. These data must include both thorough standardized assessments using instruments with strong psychometric properties, and also evaluations of communication skills demonstrated in play settings with a family member. Second, complementing these cross-sectional data are longitudinal data, describing various developmental paths associated with Down syndrome.

We hope that our study of the views of parents has contributed to the argument for the need for this information, and that subsequent studies of language and communication skills of persons with Down syndrome will explore in more depth some of the topics we have described.

REFERENCES

Buckley, S. (1985). Attaining basic educational skills: Reading, writing, and number. In D. Lane & B. Stratford (Eds.), *Current approaches to Down's syndrome* (pp. 315–343). London: Holt, Rinehart & Winston.

Buckley, S., Emslie, M., Haslegrave, G., & Le Prevost, P. (1986). *The development of language and reading skills in children with Down's syndrome*. Portsmouth, England: Portsmouth Polytechnic.

Buckley, S., & Sacks, B. (1987). *The adolescent with Down's syndrome: Life for the teenager and for the family*. Portsmouth, England: Portsmouth Down's Syndrome Trust.

Dahle, A.J., & McCollister, F.P. (1986). Hearing and otologic disorders in children with Down syndrome. *American Journal of Mental Deficiency, 90,* 636–642.

Dodd, B., & Leahy, J. (1989). Phonological disorders and mental handicap. In M. Beveridge, G. Conti-Ramsden, & I. Leuder (Eds.), *Language and communication in mentally handicapped people* (pp. 33–56). New York: Routledge, Chapman & Hall.

Downs, M.P., & Balkany, T.J. (1988). Otologic problems and hearing impairment in Down syndrome. In V. Dmitriev & P.L. Oelwein (Eds.), *Advances in Down syndrome* (pp. 19–34). Seattle: Special Child Publications.

Fowler, A.E. (1990). Language abilities in children with Down syndrome: Evidence for a specific syntactic delay. In D. Cicchetti & M. Beeghly (Eds.), *Children with Down syndrome: A developmental perspective* (pp. 302–328). Cambridge: Cambridge University Press.

Hopmann, M.R. (1991). *Parent perceptions of their children's language skills.* Unpublished manuscript.

Individuals with Disabilities Education Act of 1990 (PL 101-476). (October 30, 1990). Title 20, U. S. C. 1400 et seq.: *U.S. Statutes at Large, 104*, 1103–1151.

Irwin, K.C. (1989). The school achievement of children with Down's syndrome. *New Zealand Medical Journal, 102*, 11–13.

LaVeck, B., & Brehm, S. (1978). Individual variability among children with Down syndrome. *Mental Retardation, 2*, 135–137.

Lorenz, S., Sloper, T., & Cummingham, C. (1985). Reading and Down's syndrome. *British Journal of Special Education, 12*, 65–67.

Miller, J.F. (1987). Language and communication characteristics of children with Down syndrome. In S. Pueschel, C. Tingey, J. Rynders, A. Crocker, & D.M. Crutcher (Eds.), *New perspectives on Down syndrome* (pp. 233–262). Baltimore: Paul H. Brookes Publishing Co.

Oelwein, P.L. (1988). Preschool and kindergarten programs: Strategies for meeting objectives. In V. Dmitriev & P.L. Oelwein (Eds.), *Advances in Down syndrome* (pp. 131–157). Seattle: Special Child Publications.

Parsons, C.L., Iacono, T.A., & Rozner, L. (1987). Effect of tongue reduction on articulation in children with Down's syndrome. *American Journal of Mental Deficiency, 91*, 328–332.

Rondal, J.A. (1988). Language development in Down syndrome: A life-span perspective. *International Journal of Behavior Development, 11*, 21–36.

Rondal, J.A., & Lambert, J.L. (1983). The speech of mentally retarded adults in a dyadic communication situation: Some formal and informal aspects. *Psychologica Belgica, 23*, 49–56.

Rynders, J.E., & Horrobin, J.M. (1990). Always trainable? Never educable? Updating educational expectations concerning children with Down syndrome. *American Journal on Mental Retardation, 95*, 77–83.

Whiteman, B.C., Simpson, G.B., & Compton, W.C. (1986). Relationship of otitis media and language impairment in adolescents with Down syndrome. *Mental Retardation, 24*, 353–356.

Appendix

Parent Questionnaire

Name of child: _____ Birth date: _____
Address: _____ Telephone: _____
Type of Down syndrome: Trisomy 21 ☐ Translocation ☐ Mosaicism ☐
                Don't know ☐
Languages spoken to the child: English ☐ Spanish ☐ Portuguese ☐
                Other (please specify) ☐ _____
Highest grade completed by father _____
Highest grade completed by mother _____

Please mark with an X the appropriate answer below:

My child	Always	Mostly	Some-times	Never	Does not apply	Comments
1. says just single words*	☐	☐	☐	☐	☐	_____
2. talks in 2- to 3-word phrases*	☐	☐	☐	☐	☐	_____
3. talks in sentences*	☐	☐	☐	☐	☐	_____
4. starts conver-sations*	☐	☐	☐	☐	☐	_____
5. participates in conver-sations*	☐	☐	☐	☐	☐	_____
6. talks about past events*	☐	☐	☐	☐	☐	_____
7. talks about future events*	☐	☐	☐	☐	☐	_____

(continued)

Parent Questionnaire
(*continued*)

My child	Always	Mostly	Some-times	Never	Does not apply	Comments
8. uses articles (a, an, the)*	☐	☐	☐	☐	☐	_____
9. talks on the telephone	☐	☐	☐	☐	☐	_____
10. uses a computer to write words	☐	☐	☐	☐	☐	_____
11. talks to him-/her-self	☐	☐	☐	☐	☐	_____
12. asks questions*	☐	☐	☐	☐	☐	_____
13. understands what others say to him/her*	☐	☐	☐	☐	☐	_____
14. understands words that he/she does not say*	☐	☐	☐	☐	☐	_____
15. is effective in getting others to understand him/her*	☐	☐	☐	☐	☐	_____
16. listens when talked to*	☐	☐	☐	☐	☐	_____
17. looks at the person with whom he/she is talking	☐	☐	☐	☐	☐	_____

(*continued*)

Parent Questionnaire
(*continued*)

My child	Always	Mostly	Some-times	Never	Does not apply	Comments
18. is frustrated when unable to express him- or herself*	☐	☐	☐	☐	☐	_____
19. is frustrated when he/she is not being understood*	☐	☐	☐	☐	☐	_____
20. speaks too loudly*	☐	☐	☐	☐	☐	_____
21. speaks too softly*	☐	☐	☐	☐	☐	_____
22. speaks clearly enough	☐	☐	☐	☐	☐	_____
23. speaks with a hoarse voice*	☐	☐	☐	☐	☐	_____
24. speaks with a deep voice*	☐	☐	☐	☐	☐	_____
25. speaks too rapidly*	☐	☐	☐	☐	☐	_____
26. stutters*	☐	☐	☐	☐	☐	_____
27. is understood by family members*	☐	☐	☐	☐	☐	_____
28. is understood by strangers*	☐	☐	☐	☐	☐	_____

(*continued*)

Parent Questionnaire
(*continued*)

My child	Always	Mostly	Some-times	Never	Does not apply	Comments
29. has a "large" tongue that causes speech problems*	☐	☐	☐	☐	☐	_____
30. has problems with articu-lation*	☐	☐	☐	☐	☐	_____

Please let us know your main concern regarding your child's language and communication:

_____

_____

_____

My child	Yes	No	Does not apply	Comments
31. has not had an opportunity to learn signs	☐	☐	☐	_____
32. is learning sign language*	☐	☐	☐	_____
33. uses fewer than 10 signs*	☐	☐	☐	_____
34. uses between 10–50 signs*	☐	☐	☐	_____
35. uses more than 50 signs*	☐	☐	☐	_____
36. learns signs easily	☐	☐	☐	_____
37. learns the sign for a word first and then learns to say the word	☐	☐	☐	_____
38. learned signs but no longer uses signs	☐	☐	☐	_____

(*continued*)

Parent Questionnaire
(*continued*)

Parents find	Yes	No	Does not apply	Comments
39. signing helpful*	☐	☐	☐	_____
40. signing makes child less frustrated*	☐	☐	☐	_____
41. signing helps child to say words*	☐	☐	☐	_____

My child

	Yes	No	Does not apply	Comments
42. does not read	☐	☐	☐	_____
43. reads fewer than 10 words	☐	☐	☐	_____
44. reads between 10–50 words	☐	☐	☐	_____
45. reads more than 50 words	☐	☐	☐	_____
46. reads sentences*	☐	☐	☐	_____
47. reads books*	☐	☐	☐	_____
48. enjoys reading*	☐	☐	☐	_____
49. speaks more clearly when he/she reads aloud*	☐	☐	☐	_____
50. can sound out new words (uses phonics)*	☐	☐	☐	_____

My child

	Yes	No	Does not apply	Comments
51. hears well*	☐	☐	☐	_____
52. has a mild hearing impairment*	☐	☐	☐	_____
53. has a moderate/severe hearing impairment*	☐	☐	☐	_____
54. has had ear infections*	☐	☐	☐	_____
55. has fluid in the middle ear*	☐	☐	☐	_____
56. has tubes in the middle ear*	☐	☐	☐	_____
57. wears a hearing aid*	☐	☐	☐	_____

(*continued*)

Parent Questionnaire
(*continued*)

	Yes	No	Does not apply	Comments
My child's speech and language skills				
58. are more advanced than we had expected	☐	☐	☐	_____
59. are less advanced than we had expected	☐	☐	☐	_____
60. are about as advanced as we had expected	☐	☐	☐	_____
61. I/we did not know what to expect	☐	☐	☐	_____
My child receives speech therapy				
62. in school or early intervention*	☐	☐	☐	_____
63. privately*	☐	☐	☐	_____
64. in one-on-one or a small group*	☐	☐	☐	_____
65. in the general classroom*	☐	☐	☐	_____
66. and it is adequate*	☐	☐	☐	_____
67. and it is helpful*	☐	☐	☐	_____
68. and is at a standstill*	☐	☐	☐	_____
69. and seems to loose language skills	☐	☐	☐	_____
70. and seems to make good progress	☐	☐	☐	_____

How important has the following been in helping your child develop language?

	Very helpful	Somewhat helpful	Not helpful	
71. parent(s)*	☐	☐	☐	_____
72. brothers and sisters*	☐	☐	☐	_____
73. teachers*	☐	☐	☐	_____
74. speech therapist(s)*	☐	☐	☐	_____
75. nondisabled classmates*	☐	☐	☐	_____

(*continued*)

Parent Questionnaire
(*continued*)

	Very helpful	Somewhat helpful	Not helpful	Comments
76. classmates with special needs*	☐	☐	☐	_____
77. television*	☐	☐	☐	_____
78. other (specify)	☐	☐	☐	_____

Please make further comments if you wish with regard to any aspect of speech and language concerns in your child or regarding children with Down syndrome in general:

_____

_____

_____

_____

_____

* = items used in tables.

PART V

Perspectives on the Future

16

Parent Perspectives
Best Practice and
Recommendations for Research

Diane M. Crutcher

As THE PARENT OF A child with Down syndrome who is nearly 18 years of age, I have come to understand personally the importance of the social use of language as a pathway to success. The aspects of our daughter's life that were easier (amazingly enough) to affect and mediate—such as behavior, appearance, and academic achievements—paved the way for opportunities and successes, but these aspects were incomplete without the knowledge and techniques to use language appropriately in a social situation.

For many years, I had the privilege of being a national leader in the disability arena, interacting with some of the finest researchers in the area of speech and language in this country. I learned of their commitment to those they serve and to their peers "back home" who are the day-to-day clinicians making a difference in lives of individual children. It is clear to me that the best friends our children with speech and language delays will ever have are those clinicians and researchers. This chapter is intended to offer those professionals, as well as the children and families who need and receive such services, further insights into how communication intervention might better be accomplished. The pathway to best practice and policies is through research, its dissemination, and practical application. From my personal and professional experiences, I have formulated what I believe represents a consensus regarding parents' perspectives on best practice in speech and language therapy.

This chapter is dedicated to my friend, Kristen.

PARENTS' PERCEIVED LIMITATIONS
OF SPEECH-LANGUAGE INTERVENTION

These opinions derive from three major limitations that parents perceive exist in the service delivery of speech and language intervention. The first perceived limitation is a lack of time and, perhaps, a lack of awareness or willingness to explore therapeutic techniques specifically for the *individual* child. The second limitation is a lack of time and, perhaps, a lack of awareness, willingness, or ability to modify formal therapeutic techniques into strategies that fit a family's natural lifestyle.

The time constraints under which most therapists work are extraordinary. The tendency far too often is to resort to a "one-size-fits-all" strategy for intervention, which is defensible when therapists have very large caseloads. Nonetheless, the goal must always be *individualized* programming. Also, in the typical school setting where teachers and clinicians stay in one building and have restricted work hours, it is possible that a therapist has minimal contact with a student's family—perhaps only once each year. Under these conditions, establishing the consultative relationship between family members and the speech-language professional, which is necessary in order to adapt therapeutic techniques for use at home, is very difficult. It is, however, well worth the effort required of those clinicians.

The third perceived limitation is an unwillingness or inability by speech-language professionals to realize that families with children with speech and language needs also have other aspects of their lives that need attention daily (e.g., financial challenges, job-related issues, health concerns, emotional events concerning the child with the disability and other family members).

What may be perceived by the professional as a lack of family interest in the child's therapy could in reality be a need for attention by the family to another member or important event. In relatively stable and functional families, the family should decide how language teaching and reinforcement is accomplished, regardless of the preference of the speech-language professional regarding specific techniques. Therapy individualized for a particular child and designed for ease of family implementation allows for natural integration of language teaching into the lifestyle of the family unit, even when the child with a disability is not the exclusive focus of attention.

SPECIFIC PARENTAL CONCERNS

In searching for answers to questions from families regarding the quality, individuality, and long-term effects of their children's speech and language programs, I have had the opportunity to interact with thousands of families of children who have speech and language needs, as well as with the professionals who serve them. Table 1 summarizes the most frequently expressed paren-

Table 1. Parental concerns regarding speech and language intervention

1. Overemphasis on perfect articulation
2. Lack of carryover to promote generalization
3. Rate and volume of speaking, eye contact, and appropriate spatial distance under-emphasized in therapy
4. Techniques and strategies to promote generalization
5. Little attention to turn-taking and listening skills
6. Private and public therapy: continuity and confusion
7. "Dysfunctional" versus functional families
8. Lack of options for therapies, techniques, and individual programs
9. Short-term versus long-term objectives
10. Lack of established protocols concerning:
    a. age range for benefit
    b. hearing problems
    c. auditory/visual problems
    d. transition
    e. surgical interventions
11. Dissemination of research findings
12. Use of computer technology
13. Consideration of anatomic issues
14. Third-party payments
15. Use of phonics
16. Sensitivity to families and children

tal concerns regarding speech and language intervention for children with disabilities.

Overemphasis on Articulation

There seems to be an overemphasis by clinicians (particularly those within school systems) on the need to perfect articulation at the expense of training to ensure generalization of skills for use in natural language environments. A case in point is one family's report of the last few years of high school-based speech therapy for their child, where the emphasis was on accomplishing the "zth" sound rather than on what seemed to her parents to be a more productive pursuit, the social use of language. A balance should be achieved between teaching a skill *and* ensuring global application in everyday conversation.

Lack of Carryover

A lack of carryover from the therapy program to the classroom and to the home is a consistent concern of parents. Consultation with families is not regularly scheduled. Therapists rarely relay treatment methods and progress to other therapists, teachers, or family members, because there are few planned occasions to do so. It is imperative that service personnel build into their schedules frequent opportunities to meet with "significant others" in the child's life to share methods, discuss attitudes, provide follow-up information, and to review the child's general progress and continuing needs.

Aspects of Speech Intelligibility Underemphasized

Aspects of speech intelligibility related to rate, volume, and eye contact may be perceived to be *underemphasized* because of a perceived overemphasis on articulation skills. Perfect articulation is ineffective if the rate of speech is too fast or too slow, if the volume too soft or loud, if eye contact is inappropriate or nonexistent, or if appropriate conversational distance is not maintained. Practical skills, such as ascertaining and maintaining a proper distance between conversants, and speaking at an appropriate rate and volume, are too often not being taught. Again, a balance should be achieved between basic skills acquisition and application of those skills in conversational language.

Approaches To Promote Generalization

Systematic strategies for significant others in the child's life to help in generalizing skills gained from language intervention techniques are needed. Ensuring the child's use of newly learned skills in everyday family interactions assures successful intervention. Approaches to promote generalization and maintenance should be analyzed, with the family's input, to ascertain if and how a particular approach fits its lifestyle. The more natural a technique is for the family, the more likely it will be implemented successfully, leading to improved communication by the child.

Neglect of Social Language Behaviors

Overemphasis on articulation may also lead to neglect of social language behaviors, such as turn-taking and listening skills. A child *cannot* be a good conversant nor optimally learn without developing the skill of listening. Turn-taking emphasizes listening and social courtesy in conversation. The primary goal of language intervention should be to teach those interactional skills that form the basis of socially acceptable language usage.

Effective Supplemental Therapy

The effects of supplementing school-provided speech therapy with private programs can be counterproductive unless coordination between therapists occurs. Coordination ends up most often as the responsibility of family members who are, quite likely, ill-equipped to provide meaningful feedback and interface between the speech professionals. Parents prefer that service providers frequently and directly talk to one another and always seek to include the family in planning and evaluating therapy. Regular allocation of time for coordination and sharing information between professionals leads to a more united effort on the child's behalf.

Dysfunctional versus Functional Families

Professional judgment of a family as "dysfunctional" or "functional" does not appear to allow for individual differences in the characteristics of family relationships, the roles of family members as interventionists, stress management, empowerment, decision making, coping skills, and enhancement of the family unit. Families should be viewed as functional unless specifically proven to be dysfunctional. Functional should not be defined as two-parent, middle-class, white, college-educated families. Rather, functional families may be any combination of members of any socioeconomic status, race, educational level, profession, or religion. The key to a functional family is a loving and caring attitude.

Range of Therapeutic Options

Clinicians too often tend to offer families a single strategy for facilitating their children's development rather than a range of therapeutic options. Individualization of programming and inclusion of the family in choosing a specific approach and targets for intervention are more likely to improve carryover of the *right* techniques and, therefore, successful intervention.

Short-Term versus Long-Term Objectives

Some short-term objectives in speech and language intervention do not necessarily seem to lead to skills needed by a fully functioning and capable adult. Although they may appear immediately functional, unless they are a step in meeting long-range goals, their applicability may be questionable. The development of a capable adult should always be the ultimate consideration in choosing intervention techniques and establishing goals. Assuring the social use of language should be a goal throughout intervention.

Lack of Established Protocols

Optimal Age for Benefit

There seems to be a lack of established and published protocols for identifying the age at which therapy can be beneficial. Can infants who are at risk for speech and language deficits benefit from beginning therapy within the first few months of life? Also, is there an upper-age limit to benefit from therapy? Parents of older children are too often faced with the problem of obtaining support for continued intervention—as if any of us ever stop learning and growing. Perhaps professional concerns are related to a slow rate of progress, which seems unfounded to families. Definitive information, including data about the age at which communication intervention should be initiated for maximum effectiveness, is needed so that clinicians and other service providers can allocate appropriate resources to all children in need.

Children At Risk for Hearing Problems

Established protocols are needed for assessment, diagnosis, and intervention of hearing problems in children who are at risk for hearing impairments. Some disabilities are more likely to be accompanied by hearing loss than others. It is important to screen all children for potential hearing loss, and it is particularly important to screen children with a greater likelihood of hearing loss so that appropriate approaches to ameliorate the condition can be provided early enough to prevent secondary learning problems. Families should be assisted in the early identification of hearing-related problems in order to prevent hearing loss in their children if at all possible.

Children At Risk for Auditory or Visual Processing Problems

There is a lack of protocols to identify and treat auditory and visual processing problems related to speech and language acquisition and use. In some children with disabilities, there is a greater likelihood that auditory and/or visual processing problems may be present. The possibility of related perceptual processing difficulties should be actively pursued by the speech-language professional in evaluating the child's language skills and addressed, if necessary, along with speech and language intervention. Information about the nature and impact of perceptual processing difficulties should be communicated to the family and the child's teachers and therapists in order to provide appropriate and coordinated interventions.

Facilitating Transitions

Established protocols are lacking to facilitate transitions from one program, therapist, or setting to another. The family should not be expected to determine what is relevant information that should be communicated to other care providers and therapists when the child enters a new program or changes therapists. Rather, professionals should be responsible for transferring clear and accurate information in a timely fashion to their counterparts. Transferring information about the child's language skills should extend beyond speech clinicians to teachers, other therapists, and family members.

Surgical Interventions

Protocols need to be established in order to modify interventions to include surgical alterations in facial structure, especially tongue reduction. Surgical alterations of children's facial structures is a relatively new treatment, primarily for children with Down syndrome. Because one desirable outcome of this surgery is improved speech, therapeutic speech intervention should be adjusted to the new physical characteristics of the child. The surgery should be discussed beforehand with the family and the professionals who know and work with the child. Planning and sharing information before and after surgery ensures more effective therapeutic intervention by clinicians who are focused on optimizing the child's altered physical structure.

Dissemination of Research Findings

The dissemination of research findings regarding new techniques for intervention and information about general and specific disabilities seems disorganized and incomplete. Dissemination should include not only the typical books and journals, but also public service announcements (audio and video), television programming (including PBS), electronic bulletin boards, parent-group newsletters, monographs, conferences for parents and professionals, and formal training sessions. If all of these outlets for dissemination were fully utilized, more research outcomes could be brought to the attention of clinicians as well as families. Overall, improving the timely provision of research-based knowledge is a key to ensuring the success of individual children.

Use of Computer Technology

The use of computer technology to improve speech and language for children who are nonverbal is increasing, but its use for children with speech and language impairments is not frequently an option. Because computer-assisted technology is expensive, it is often not accessible or accessible only to children with very specific characteristics. Computer-assisted communication may be a viable option for many children with disabilities, and even short-term use might help the development of functional language. More research is needed on using computer technology with the full range of children with communication disorders.

Anatomic Issues

Too often, interventionists do not seem to consider individual anatomic issues related to speech production (e.g., hypotonia of tongue and jaw musculature). Again, a one-size-fits-all approach to therapy seems to be applied, regardless of a child's particular physical characteristics that might affect therapeutic outcomes. Therapy must be individualized with particular attention to *all* characteristcs of the child that affect speech production and the social use of speech and language skills.

Third-Party Payments

The relationship between physical problems (e.g., delayed motor development) and delayed speech and language development does not appear well documented. Public documentation of this critical relationship is needed to gain support for third-party payments for physical and speech therapy. Families of children with disabilities, who are often already overwhelmed by financial responsibilities, may not be able to obtain related services supported by insurance without specific documentation. Again, publication and synthesis of clinical outcomes in a form that would be useful in such circumstances would be invaluable to families trying to provide their children with optimal services despite limited economic resources.

Use of Phonics

The use of phonics seems to be underemphasized. A more global approach to speech and language acquisition could better ensure enhanced skills in other areas. Fully promoting phonics as a base of speech and language training requires coordination with instruction in related academic domains but also leads to carryover in other areas, including reading. Team interventions that address a full range of language-related skills are needed to support adequate language use by older students.

Sensitivity to Children and Families

Sensitivity to children and families too often appears forgotten in the process of delivering services. Regardless of the extent of the child's needs and disability, age, functional level, socioeconomic status, race, nationality, or creed, families deserve respect, support, and encouragement at all times. There seems to be a predisposition among professionals to stereotype families who have members with disabilities. Problems in families are viewed as unimportant, inconsequential, or even unreal. Families with children with disabilities have the same positive and negative experiences and the same characteristics as families with normally developing children. Issues facing families must be seriously considered and accepted as a part of family–professional interactions and the child's program. It is essential that professionals treat families with dignity and respect.

These needs reflect continuing family concerns. Most families sincerely desire that their children with speech and language delays will have opportunities to become fully functioning, socially capable adults who are able to communicate at work, at home, and in a full range of community activities. Children with speech and language deficits should have an opportunity to participate in all types of relationships as a result of learning social language use. They should have speech that is as clear as possible and be able to speak with appropriate rate and volume, while making eye contact, maintaining an appropriate distance, taking conversational turns, and listening. Most importantly, these children and their families deserve respect and support throughout the intervention process.

There are two keys to ensuring success for communicative interactions of adults with disabilities: 1) individualized therapeutic programming to optimize participation in integrated employment, living, and recreation; and 2) communication between parents and all professionals responsible for the child's development. Continuing communication is integral to every aspect of therapy and to the goal of functional language use. Everyone involved in the therapeutic process must participate in a partnership based on unified intent of purpose and mutual respect, in order that the individual may have a full repertoire of useful communication skills.

The tendency of professionals to categorically view the parent's perspective as unrealistic must change. If a concern is perceived and expressed by parents, it is real and should be dealt with immediately and appropriately. The issues presented in this chapter *have been perceived* over and over by families whose children have speech and language deficits. The concerns of these families are real. It is hoped that this chapter will focus attention on familial concerns. Attention to family concerns will, in turn, ensure that the child has greater success in acquiring the language skills that will support him or her as a fully functioning, social capable adult.

17

Early Communication
and Language Intervention
Challenges for
the 1990s and Beyond

Steven F. Warren

THE FIELD OF EARLY COMMUNICATION and language intervention has developed in significant ways since the 1970s. Scores of studies have been conducted in that time, the vast majority aimed at testing various procedures or intervention packages with small numbers of children for limited time periods. This "technology building" period is continuing. However, if early communication and language intervention is to achieve preventive and remedial potential, it must move well beyond this initial research and development phase. The question is, in what directions will it be most profitable for this field to proceed? This chapter proposes some possible answers to this question.

It is clearly unwise to speculate about profitable future directions without some appreciation for the past and present. Thus, in the first part of this chapter, I present a brief, selective, and admittedly biased perspective on the history and present status of the field of communication and language intervention research. The remainder of the chapter discusses two general directions in which the field must proceed if it is to continue to develop efficacious intervention procedures and treatment packages.

A BRIEF, SELECTIVE, AND PERSONAL PERSPECTIVE
ON THE HISTORY OF LANGUAGE INTERVENTION

The first concerted efforts to address the communication and language problems of children with mental retardation and developmental disabilities were

---

I would like to acknowledge the insightful comments and feedback of Ann Kaiser, Paul Yoder, and Keith Nelson in response to earlier drafts of this manuscript.

initiated in the 1960s—an era that was, in retrospect, filled with both heady idealism and stifling insularity. In those days, the views of most investigators were heavily influenced either by the nativists or radical behaviorists. The nativists posited that the important elements of the language acquisition process could be explained as a hard-wired, predetermined system (Chomsky, 1965). The radical behaviorists assumed that the environment had such massive effects on development that even moderate levels of mental retardation could be "cured," given the right environmental manipulations (J. E. Spradlin, personal communication, March, 1976).

The insularity of this era was aptly captured in the introductory paragraph of Bricker and Bricker's 1974 chapter on early language training strategies published in the Schiefelbusch and Lloyd language perspective book (Schiefelbusch & Lloyd, 1974). "Within the context of current psycholinguistic conceptions of language development, a discussion of intervention approaches to the language learning of young children is not greatly different from arguing for birth control and abortion in a convent" (Bricker & Bricker, 1974, p. 431). They went on to chronicle several compelling examples of the virtually complete isolation of work by nativists (read "muddle-headed mentalists") and behaviorists (read "mindless mechanics") from each other. The insularity of the times was such that Menyuk (1971) could write a book about language acquisition and training that included an impressive number of citations (225), virtually none of which came from either the operant or cognitive literature of that period. At the same time, Risley and his colleagues (Risley, Hart, & Doke, 1972) published a discussion chapter on the operant approach to language that did not include a single citation of linguistic, psycholinguistic, or cognitive material.

Despite the heated paradigm wars of this period, some researchers designed early language intervention approaches that borrowed freely from divergent theoretical perspectives. Communication training curricula developed by Bricker and Bricker (1970) and Miller and Yoder (1972) utilized information from psycholinguistic literature to devise the content of instruction and to target certain processes for intervention, but used instructional procedures adapted from applied behavior analysis literature.

The heightened interest in and influence of pragmatics (the study of how language is used and functions in context) that emerged in the 1970s created substantial common ground for language intervention researchers previously isolated by divergent theoretical perspectives (see Kaiser & Warren, 1988, for a discussion). The notion that "form follows function" (Nelson, 1973; Ratner & Bruner, 1978) and an expanded emphasis on "communication" and the social bases of language (cf. Bruner, 1975; Snow & Ferguson, 1977) led to new intervention approaches that tried to embed instruction into conversation and that emphasized effective communication irrespective of form (Fey, 1986; MacDonald, 1985). These approaches were further buttressed by theoretical inquiries into the normal process of language acquisition (e.g., Bates, Benigni, Bretherton, Camaioni, & Volterra, 1979; Bloom, Lightbown, & Hood, 1975; Braine, 1976). Investigators working from this perspective (often referred to as social interactionists) have found little evidence of Chomsky's (1965) proposed "language acquisition device" (Bates & MacWhinney, 1989; Nelson, 1991). The results of many of these investigations led to the "functionalist" approach to language development and intervention (Bates, Thal, & Marchman, 1991). Functionalism, in this case, is defined as the belief that "the forms of natural language are created, governed, constrained, acquired, and used in the service of communication function" (Bates & MacWhinney, 1982, p. 78).

Concurrent with the development of contemporary intervention approaches based on social interactionist theories, changes also were occurring in intervention approaches being developed by investigators working in the methodological traditions of applied behavior analysis. These changes were primarily the result of inductive efforts by these investigators to achieve meaningful generalization from their intervention efforts. Much of the language intervention research before and during the 1970s was notable for either not measuring generalization in a meaningful way or for failing to achieve it (Warren & Rogers-Warren, 1980). These failures influenced researchers to experiment with new intervention methods such as incidental language teaching (e.g., Hart & Risley, 1980). The effects of these efforts are evident in a variety of ways (Goldstein & Hockenberger, 1991). The development of the milieu language intervention model (Warren & Kaiser, 1988) represents an excellent example. Over 20 empirical studies have been published on the effects of this approach (see Kaiser, Yoder, & Keetz, 1992, for a review). Most of the specific features that comprise the milieu approach were initially developed and studied within an applied behavior analysis framework. However, these techniques are typically analogous to important features of early adult–child interactions that have been posited by development researchers as potentially contributing to the social and language development of children (Warren & Kaiser, 1986).

The convergence of inductively and deductively driven work has resulted in something approaching general agreement about the most effective contexts for early communication and language intervention. While arguments continue about specific procedures and terminology, there is broad agreement that the most effective intervention context is an emotionally rich, engaging environment with specific "challenges" matched to the child's learning problems and abilities. Furthermore, certain enabling conditions (e.g., high quality attentional engagement, a developmental match between the child's level of performance and the new skills to be taught in intervention, and minimal separation between form and function) are necessary for optimal learning (Nelson, 1989).

CURRENT APPROACHES TO LANGUAGE INTERVENTION

At present, there is a surprising degree of agreement about basic approaches to intervention among the scientists investigating this topic. This concurrence is widely acknowledged in the field. For example, Carrow-Woolfolk (1988), in her book on theory, assessment, and intervention in language disorders, noted that, "an encouraging sign of professional maturity is the respect for other positions that is discernible in recent literature" (p. vi). Furthermore, Donahue and Watson (1990), in their review of the second edition of the Schiefelbusch and Lloyd (1988) book, note the relative consensus among authors from historically divergent approaches to language. In the larger context of developmental psycholinguistics, Golinkoff and Hirsh-Pasek observed that the general field of child language seems to be experiencing a theoretical migration to some common middle ground, "with nativistic theories leaving room for learning, and non-nativistic theories leaving room for initial biases in the system" (Golinkoff & Hirsh-Pasek, 1990, p. 82). Finally, the current literature on early communication and language intervention exhibits nothing remotely approaching the conceptual, methodological, or procedural insularity that existed even 10 years ago.

The current conceptual and methodological congruence is qualified in several ways. The basic issues on which theories continue to diverge are "the relationship among language, cognitive, and social roles in development and . . . the location of control in shaping the direction that development takes in the child" (Carrow-Woolfolk, 1988, p. 184). These divergences leave a lot of open territory. These differences may be considered either major or minor, depending on the perspective of the observer. Furthermore, they may be logically unresolvable due to the fundamentally divergent assumptions of the theoretical perspectives upon which they rest (Chapman, 1990). The extent to which further integration is necessary, desirable, or even possible is debatable. Such integration may be necessary and desirable, but only possible within a larger systems-level framework of human development and behavior.

At the same time that a modest level of congruence has been obtained in the field, a modest degree of effectiveness of interventions has been demonstrated. A number of comprehensive analyses of various language intervention procedures and approaches (e.g., Fey, 1986; Goldstein & Hockenberger, 1991; Kaiser, Yoder, & Keetz, 1992; Nelson, 1989; Tannock & Girolametto, 1992; Warren & Kaiser, 1986) have indicated that state-of-the-art remediation procedures can have substantial effects on the use of already acquired language. In at least some cases, current remediation procedures appear to facilitate acquisition of new language (e.g., Camarata & Nelson, in press; Warren & Bambara, 1989; Wilcox, Kouri, & Caswell, 1991). However, there is little evidence that early communication and language intervention effects maintain longitudinally or that training enhances a child's general ability to acquire language independent of intervention. In short, after some 2 decades of work, we have achieved a level of conceptual congruence concerning some of the specific procedures that might be employed in early language intervention, and a modest but promising level of intervention technology.

The move toward a generally accepted model of language development and remediation and further work on developing and testing the effects of specific intervention procedures continue. The remainder of this chapter considers two questions: First, what should inform or guide further conceptual development of the field of language intervention? Second, how can the technology of language intervention be enhanced in ways that will make this endeavor maximally effective?

MOVING TOWARD A MEANINGFUL SYSTEMS APPROACH

Language does not develop or operate independently of other domains of human functioning. Nevertheless, the impact of Chomsky's theory of syntax (Chomsky, 1959, 1965) resulted in language being treated as a special case of human functioning, both behaviorally and biologically (Andresen, 1991). With the ascendancy of the functionalist perspective, it has become increasingly clear that further conceptual development in the fields of language acquisition and intervention will depend largely on the extent to which language is reintegrated with behavior and biology (Bates et al., 1991). That is, further conceptual development and improved intervention will depend on the extent to which the study of language places development and intervention within a larger systems approach to human behavior.

Many researchers in the field of child development began urging the development of "systems thinking, approaches, and theories" in the 1970s (e.g., Bronfenbrenner, 1977; Rogers-Warren & Warren, 1977; Sameroff & Chandler, 1975). These recommendations have had some effect. For example, Sameroff's transactional model (Sameroff & Chandler, 1975) spurred substantial research on reciprocal influences within the parent–child relationship. In the 1970s, by expanding the study of language acquisition to communication acquisition, the field of child language experienced what has been called the "pragmatics" revolution. There is little evidence that researchers in language intervention have embraced anything approaching a *general systems theory* (i.e., Boulding, 1956) in any formal or dynamic sense (Sameroff, 1983). It is true that perspectives have broadened, some independent and dependent variables have been reconceptualized, and some important but limited concepts, such as bidirectional effects, insularity, and connectionist nets, have been added. A systems view of individual development as hierarchically organized in multiple levels (e.g., genes, cells, organs, behavior, context) that influence each other bidirectionally has been largely accepted. Nevertheless, there is a lack, for the most part, of general explanatory mechanisms that would lead to full theory development (Gottlieb, 1991).

Indications of Change

There are some indications that we are moving toward the development of systems theory in the dynamic sense. First, some early versions of more sophisticated systems theories are appearing. An excellent example is Gottlieb's (1991) theory on the canalization of behavioral development, which has yet to be fully explicated. Gottlieb's theory is notable because of the extent to which it proposes bidirectional influences among the environment, behavior, neural activity, and genetic activity. Genes, for example, are seen as part of the developmental systems and are not "inviolate or immune to influences from other levels of the system" (Gottlieb, 1991, p. 10). Instead, genes are viewed as a set of instructions, the expression of which is altered and ultimately determined by influences at environmental, behavioral, and neural levels of the developmental system. Development from this perspective is seen as multidetermined, probabilistic, and nonlinear. The model of these bidirectional influences is displayed in Figure 1.

A second indication of movement toward a systems approach is enhanced interest in the processes that enable and guide development, as opposed to the products of development. Two good examples of this are the emergence of dynamical systems theory (Thelen & Ulrich, 1991) and connectionist models of neural activity and development (Rummelhart & McClelland, 1986).

Dynamical systems theory is an attempt to answer this question: How do organisms induce qualitatively new behavioral forms during ontogenesis, the novel structures and functional properties of which cannot be deduced from or reduced to the characteristics of the organism's antecedent conditions (Wolff,

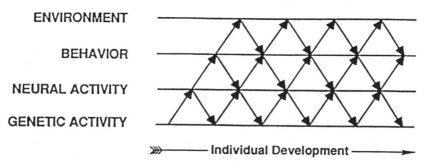

BIDIRECTIONAL INFLUENCES

ENVIRONMENT

BEHAVIOR

NEURAL ACTIVITY

GENETIC ACTIVITY

≫ —— Individual Development ——▶

Figure 1.   A simplified scheme of the developmental systems view, showing a hierarchy of four mutually interacting components in which there are "top-down" as well as "bottom-up" bidirectional influences. (From Gottlieb, G. [1991]. Experiential canalization of behavioral development: Theory. *Developmental Psychology, 27,* 6; reprinted by permission.)

1991). Instead of describing development, dynamical systems theory attempts to explain what makes development happen—what leads to nonlinear leaps in performance, which arise from processes that appear to be continuous? The intellectual heritage of dynamical systems theory includes general systems theory (Sameroff, 1983) and Piagetian theory, from which it differs by positing no hard-wired structures for motor behavior or cognition (Fogel & Thelen, 1987).

> This approach replaces the static language of codes, schemas, and programs with the dynamic concepts of stability change, phase shifts, and attractors and repellors. This is a world where clouds and vortices and oscillating chemicals and fractals and chaos replace boxes connected by little arrows as the dominant metaphors. Dynamics promise a science of behavior that is truly nonreductionist. Just as the behavior of clouds or of a mountain stream cannot in principle be understood by the behavior of a water molecule, so also the behavior of a human is not knowable from the activity of the neuron or the gene. Finally, dynamical principles have the potential of uniting under a common language an understanding of complex systems of a great variety of material substrates and time scales. (Thelen, 1989, p. 91)

Dynamical systems theory is far from being fully elaborated, and its ultimate value and relevance remain to be determined empirically (Wolff, 1991). However, by positing a set of general mechanisms for change and growth, the theory holds promise for refocusing the field on how infants and children actually acquire new behaviors, irrespective of domain.

A second example of increased focus on the processes that guide development and behavior is the recent multidisciplinary research conducted by those interested in connectionist or distributed systems of knowledge acquisition and use at the neural level (e.g., Elman, 1991a; Rummelhart & McClelland, 1986). Instead of a mechanistic, hard-wired, deterministic view of the brain and its activity, the connectionist view is that of "a connection machine, a massive, fluid system of densely interconnected units that converge parallel on one or more dynamical solutions to any given input problem" (Bates et al., 1991, p. 14). In this system, knowledge is not contained in individual symbolic units somehow stored in a state of suspended animation within the brain until called upon, but in patterns of weighted connections among many different units. Like dynamical systems theory, connectionism focuses on process, not product.

As abstract as the connectionist metaphor may seem, some simulation studies using parallel-processing-network computer models have already produced results relevant to theories of language development, with possible implications for intervention. An excellent example is Elman's (1991b) demonstration in which a network model was unable to learn a complex grammar when both the network and the input were unchanging. However, when the input was presented incrementally (as it is in human language acquisition), or when the network began with a limited memory that gradually increased (like a child's memory over time), the network was able to learn the grammar. As Elman points out, these results suggest that the early memory limitations of a human learner may play a critical, positive role in language acquisition, making it possible to master a body of knowledge that could not be learned by a mature system.

Dynamical systems theory and connectionist models of distributed intelligence remain more potential than reality. What is important about these approaches for this discussion is that they represent real efforts to understand the basic processes guiding development, and they appear to be far less mechanistic and far more dynamic, probabilistic, and "life-like" than most of their predecessors.

A third indication of progress toward a systems approach can be found in the recent research literature on communication disorders. There are an increasing number of studies in which the independent variable represents one traditional domain of behavior (e.g., motor development) and at least one of the dependent variables represents another domain (e.g., communication). In these cross-domain studies, the analysis occurs at the same level of the system—actual behavior. There is also a smaller, but increasing number of analyses that span levels of the system; for example, the analysis of observable, overt social behavior via specific, measurable neural activity. Both types of analyses are needed to develop a systems level understanding of communication and language. Two recent examples of cross-domain work and one example of cross-level work are highlighted below.

A highly relevant example of cross-domain analysis comes from the work of Miller and his colleagues (Miller, Miolo, Sedey, Pierce, & Rosin, 1989) on the causes of expressive delay in children with Down syndrome. In a study of 92 young children, 46 of whom had Down syndrome, Miller found a strong correlation between the development of speech motor function and productive vocabulary. Specifically, Miller found that functional movement of the oral motor structure predicted the number of words a child produced better than either measures of language comprehension or mental age. This finding has potential implications for very early communication intervention in the form of motor intervention.

A second example of cross-domain work is the recent research on the communicative functions of aberrant behavior. This research has demonstrated that such severely aberrant behaviors as scratching, head-banging, and screaming can be rapidly decreased and even eliminated by identifying their communicative functions (e.g., to escape an undesirable activity), and then replacing them with more conventional communication signs or gestures. An excellent example of this is presented in a study by Durand and Carr (1991). In this study, assessment indicated that escape from academic demands was involved in the maintenance of three students' severely challenging behaviors (e.g., head-hitting, head-banging, pinching others). Intervention involved teaching alternative assistance-seeking and attention-getting phrases to these students (e.g., "Help me," "Am I doing good work?") in an effort to replace challenging behaviors with these verbal equivalents. This intervention substantially reduced the challenging behaviors. The effects transferred across new tasks, environments, and teachers, and were observed to maintain up to 2 years later.

An example of cross-systems research is Dawson's investigations of the development of early social and communication behavior in children with autism. She and her colleagues have shown through studies of cortical-event related potentials (Dawson, Finley, Phillips, Galpert, & Lewy, 1988; Dawson & Lewy, 1989b) that deficiencies in the arousal modulation of children with autism may selectively affect attention to and processing of social information at the neural level. These neurologic processing difficulties are hypothesized to lead to the low aversion threshold of children with autism for social novelty and unpredictability, which may in turn distort socioemotional development in terms of the early formation of attachments to people, in the expression of emotions, and in the interpersonal coordination of affective expression (Dawson & Lewy, 1989a).

Working from this base, Dawson also has produced recent empirical evidence that attention to others by children with autism can be increased by sensitive interactive strategies (e.g., contingent imitation of the child's behavior by the adult) that provide simplified, predictable, and highly contingent responses and allow the children to control and regulate the amount of stimulation (Dawson & Galpert, 1990).

These examples of cross-domain and cross-level research demonstrate the interrelationship of communication and other domains of behavior and levels of systemic interaction. They are evidence of how language and communication function as parts of horizontal systems of behavior (e.g., motor to language) and hierarchical systems (e.g., neural to language).

Research across systems levels should be stimulated greatly by developments and breakthroughs at neural and genetic levels of the human system. For example, technologies for more directly assessing the activity and behavior of the brain itself are proliferating rapidly. Relatively new methods such as magnetic resonance imaging, positron emission tomography, and magnetoencephalography will doubtlessly be enhanced by future advancements, making the "window into the brain" larger and clearer. The relatively noninvasive nature of most new brain-imaging techniques allows investigators to monitor and observe deep brain structures and their functional activities. As more noninvasive and cost-effective techniques are developed, researchers will be encouraged to link specific neural activity with overt behavior in more and more ways. These techniques and the scientific opportunities they provide should revolutionize the behavioral sciences in ways that have yet to be imagined. Work in genetics (i.e., the Human Genome Project) also promises to radically affect our knowledge of influences on human behavior, by identifying genetic contributions to a range of diseases and disorders.

Breakthroughs in knowledge about the genetic and neurologic levels of the human system will increase the necessity for a formal systems theory, if we are ultimately to understand how activity at these levels influence operations of the whole system. As understanding of these levels of the human system increases, interest in the contributions of behavior itself, and of the environment in the development and expression of behavior, will correspondingly increase. Precision in specifying the roles of these elements should also increase. Cross-domain and cross-level research studies, such as those described above, are preliminary but crucial to the actual development and explication of a systems approach to communication, as well as to human behavior in general. Such studies form the empirical building blocks of systems theory. Without empirical studies, a systems theory remains an abstract and even irrelevant idea. With such studies, a theory can be shaped toward greater accuracy and validity (Lerner, 1991).

Impact on Intervention

How will a systems-level understanding of human development and behavior affect early language and communication intervention research and practice? First, this understanding is important to communication intervention because as we come to understand the causal mechanisms behind typical and atypical development from this perspective, we should be more able to refine and optimize our interventions. For example, if an underlying influence on expressive language delay in children with Down syndrome is delayed oral motor development, as suggested by Miller's data (Miller et al., 1989), a two-part early intervention approach might be chosen. First, we might somehow stimulate oral motor development. Concurrently, we might provide the child with a gesture/sign system to use until oral motor abilities improve, then switch to an oral approach as the child achieves the necessary motor development. That is, we may decide to intervene on motor behavior to stimulate later language development, because our knowledge of how these systems interlock horizontally tells us that this should be the best way to proceed.

A second way that a systems level approach may influence early language intervention is by helping to determine if and when to begin intervention. In the majority of cases, language intervention does not begin until we have very clear evidence of a substantial delay in productive language. Because many children who eventually develop language skills do not normally begin speaking until they are 2 years of age, and because many children show initial productive language problems due to otitis media, from which they eventually recover fully (Whitehurst, Fischel, Arnold, & Lonigan, 1992), most practitioners take a conservative approach to early intervention. For many children, this approach results in intervention delayed for years after basic problems have occurred. However, as our knowledge of neurologic development increases, we may be able to more reliably determine when crucial processes in early brain development have failed to occur, been delayed, or occurred only partially.

For example, between 9–24 months of age, the density of short-range synaptic connections within and across the cerebral cortex reaches approximately 150% of levels observed in human adults. This growth, which is termed synaptogenesis, corresponds closely to the primary milestones of early language development. Synaptogenesis appears to peak at two points that correspond closely with two well-known bursts in normal language development—the so-called vocabulary burst between 16–20 months and the passage from single to multiword speech between 18–20 months (Bates, Thal, & Janowsky, in press). These neural correlates of language development are intriguing. If they do not occur on schedule, does the vocabulary burst also fail to occur? Can synaptogenesis be triggered or enhanced by environmental events? Can synaptogenesis be discerned reliably and inexpensively? These and other questions will take years to answer. However, the answers might open a new era of early intervention, perhaps at the prelinguistic level, and very possibly using methods yet to be conceived.

Third, as breakthroughs at the gene and neural levels occur, efforts to prevent or remediate behavioral problems by interventions at these levels will also occur. These interventions may take many forms (e.g., genetic engineering, gene therapy). A primary question will be the extent to which interventions at this level can compensate for deficiencies at other levels of the system (e.g., a depriving environment). Our present state of systems knowledge suggests that the effectiveness of interventions at these levels will be determined by how "receptive" and "effective" the system can be made at other levels. Thus, multidisciplinary collaboration between interventionists at different levels of the system (e.g., genetists, pediatricians, neurologists, educators, family therapists, speech-language pathologists) is likely to increase as their interdependence in efforts to prevent or remediate problems of development and behavior become more obvious.

Summary

Early communication and language development is probably both a cause and effect of processes that occur in other domains of behavior and across levels of human development. We truly cannot understand the process of language acquisition, or optimize our intervention approaches, until we understand how these domains and levels interlock and function in parallel and overlapping ways as a system.

CHILD-BASED ELICITATION STRATEGIES

Developments in systems theory, and the findings from the genetics and neurologic sciences, may eventually have a major impact on language intervention practices. In the meantime, what research directions are most likely to enhance practice and improve outcomes for children? Systematic research on an old idea, that of enhancing the child's own learning strategies (instead of directly teaching the child specific skills), constitutes at least one answer to this question.

By the use of the term "strategy," I do not mean to imply an operation that is either necessarily "cognitive" or one that requires a level of meta-linguistic awareness to execute. For the present discussion, a child-based elicitation strategy can be defined as the child's propensity to engage in a class of behavior that reliably elicits useful new information (e.g., models of how to do things, answers to questions) that might then be incorporated into the child's repertoire of skills. By use of the term strategy, I imply a general skill, useful over the long term to learn a variety of skills. This definition is admittedly narrow in that it excludes any reference to how new information might be memorized, encoded, and so forth. I do not wish to deny the existence and important functions of these types of cognitive operations. However, because these operations are not likely to be *direct* candidates for intervention, their role in learning is not central to the current discussion.

Both behavioristic and cognitive approaches to language acquisition have tended to neglect the issue of whether and to what extent a child can be taught generalized strategies that should be useful in acquiring language and other skills across multiple contexts. This is true, although the potential value of attempting to teach or enhance child-based strategies has been recognized almost since the inception of the field (e.g., Bricker & Bricker, 1974; Guess, Sailor, & Baer, 1974; Miller & Yoder, 1974). Behavioristic approaches have, for the most part, focused on designing optimal learning environments intended to make the child's learning task easier. Cognitive approaches have tended to focus more on internalized abilities (e.g., encoding operations, short-term memory) that at best can be indirectly facilitated. Exceptions to these generalizations can be found among cognitive (i.e., Nelson, 1989) and behavioral (e.g., Goldstein & Mousetis, 1989) researchers. Still, taken as a whole, emphasis on the identification of powerful and teachable child-based elicitation strategies has been neglected too often.

Why Teach Elicitation Strategies?

Shatz (1987) reintroduced the concept of "bootstrapping operations" as a way to conceptualize the child's active role in the language acquisition process. According to Shatz (1987):

> Children must engage in the unfamiliar world of conversational communication from a very early age, and they have a variety of behaviors that help them get by on the little they know while at the same time assisting in the construction of a more adequate knowledge base. That is, children use what they know to learn more, thereby achieving their own success. In idiomatic language, they pull themselves up by their bootstraps. (p. 1)

Shatz goes on to describe a fluid system of bootstrapping operations that operate as mechanisms for acquisition of all sorts of knowledge about communication. These include one set of operations, termed elicitation operations, that allow learners to gain information from the environment. Elicitation operations include use of early gestures, action responding, imitation, and direct questions. Two other kinds of bootstrapping operations, entry operations and expansions operations, are conceptualized as more directly motivated by the processing capacities of the learner. Elicitation operations, however, include several general strategies that a child might be directly taught to use. (However, Shatz does not speculate whether these strategies might be taught directly.)

Whether one agrees with Shatz's approach or not, her arguments have helped to refocus on the issue of the child's contribution to the acquisition process. The potential of teaching elicitation strategies to children also deserves another look by intervention researchers, because current approaches to intervention that rely on the design of optimal learning environments are unlikely to be sufficient. Even if optimally effective learning environments can be devised, how likely is the average child to spend a meaningful amount of time in these environments?

The real world for many children is one of impoverished environments— of public school systems faced with limited funds and overwhelming problems, of segregated special education systems that may retard social and communicative development, of environments that respond most positively to children who are quiet and stay in their seats, of speech-language pathologists who may be inadequately trained to devise effective in-classroom intervention programs, and of policies that ensure that children with developmental delays only receive speech-language services if their language development is significantly delayed relative to measures of their general cognitive development. In short, the chances of spending more than a small amount of time in an optimal learning environment are not very good for many children. On one hand, this is a depressing and perhaps overgeneralized portrait of the real world. On the other hand, this view offers challenges that could move the field forward in practical *and* scientific ways. If we cannot count on the child's environment to be "optimal" for very much of the time, then we should determine how to assist the child, assuming we may only be able to influence a small portion of his or her environment, for a limited time. Probably, this assumption has always been valid, but it has had limited influence on our approaches to language intervention. Instead we have often (naively) operated on the assumption that we should be able to permanently optimize a significant portion of the child's environment.

Even if a child were to spend several hours a day in an optimal learning environment, which has been designed to enhance his or her language development, only a fraction of the child's available learning time is being optimized. Typically, children learn language and other skills all day, every day.

It has been estimated that by the age of 4, the typical child will have uttered 10–20 million words and will have listened to 20–40 million words (Chapman et al., 1992). This is a very substantial database! Even if formal language intervention were conducted daily, the majority of a child's language acquisition would likely be accounted for by the rest of his or her environment. It makes intuitive sense to try to equip children who have difficulty in learning language with a few powerful strategies that will help them more effectively learn in everyday contexts.

Typical children acquire language successfully in environments that are far from optimal. The acquisition of language appears to be a buffered and overdetermined process. Children can compensate for severe disabilities, such as deafness and blindness, and still acquire a functional language system. Normal acquisition can proceed even when input varies quantitatively and qualitatively. Children's natural learning strategies are robust and varied. Apparently, children learn a variety of ways that allow them to overcome either a poor environment or major input limitations.

Some Major Challenges

Despite the potential of intervention approaches that enhance child-based elicitation strategies, there are at least two major challenges involved in realizing the potential of such strategies. First, language acquisition is a transactional process. Consequently, for the child's elicitation strategies to work effectively, they must be scaffolded or supported by adult behaviors. For example, we have been investigating the possible role of spontaneous imitation as a strategy for young children with mild mental retardation in early productive language acquisition (Warren, Kim, & Yoder, 1991). We have some indication that spontaneous imitation may be a particularly useful strategy for these children when they are learning to express basic semantic relationships such as action–object and agent–action. As children begin to acquire these target structures through conversationally based intervention, they also begin to spontaneously imitate exemplars that are provided by the adults in their environment (cf. Warren & Bambara, 1989; Warren & Gazdag, 1990). For instance, upon observing an adult pushing a toy car and uttering "push car" as a comment, the child pushes his or her own toy car, commenting "push car, push car" (an action–object construction). The adult responded to this imitation with a confirmatory comment, "Yea, you're pushing your car too," and then a follow-up question, "Can you push your car at mine?" Spontaneous imitations embedded in conversation such as this may function as bridging mechanisms, helping the child to incorporate the form being learned into his or her everyday usage repertoire (Snow, Perlmann, & Nathan, 1987). Spontaneous imitation may help a child to explore and acquire the multiple functions that a particular form may serve. However, spontaneous imitation as a learning strategy may be of little value if adults do not use the target form frequently and provide the child with opportunities to use it functionally, as the adult did in the above example. In sum, the usefulness of child-based elicitation strategies across various contexts is an open question.

The second challenge is to determine the extent to which child-based elicitation strategies can be taught, as well as the effects that these strategies have on children's language use and development. Several child-based elicitation strategies are good candidates for study:

Asking questions about objects and events
Responding to the questions and comments of others
Imitating the actions, words, and behavior of others
Gesturing toward objects and events of interest
Saying nice, positive comments to others
Seeking assistance and help from others

To serve as effective strategies, children probably need to engage in these behaviors *frequently,* across a wide range of contexts. There is correlational evidence that the more children talk, the more progress they make in acquiring language (Hart & Risley, 1980; Landon & Sommers, 1979; Nelson, 1973; Schachter, 1979). Apparently, as children participate actively in the language milieu that surrounds them, the more practice they get, and the more the language milieu shapes their subsequent behavior in a wide variety of ways.

Each of the strategies listed above may have limits of usefulness at certain points in development. For example, imitation strategies appear to be most useful in acquiring the forms and functions of basic vocabulary and semantic relationships. Longitudinal research suggests that continued reliance on imitation may not be efficacious past the early periods of language learning (Nelson, Baker, Denninger, Bonvillian, & Kaplan, 1985). However, a question-asking strategy (i.e., "What's that?") may become increasingly useful as development advances.

A careful review of the language intervention literature reveals studies in which one or more of the strategies described above have been taught. For example, Ezell and Goldstein (1991) taught children to ask clarification questions. Commenting has been reported as a dependent variable in two studies of milieu language teaching (Warren & Bambara, 1989; Warren & Gazdag, 1990). Imitation of peer behaviors was utilized by Goldstein and Mousetis (1989) to facilitate generalization. Several investigators have also reported increases in the frequency of talking (measured in various ways [see Kaiser, Yoder, & Keetz, 1992; Warren & Kaiser, 1986, for reviews]). However, no studies that we are aware of have determined if the child learned a generalized strategy, or how conversational partners responded to the child's use of that strategy. In order to fully understand the usefulness of a strategy, it is critical to determine if the elicitation behavior prompts potential teaching responses from conversational partners.

A Research Agenda

These challenges can be reformulated into a long-term research agenda. Seven general questions might be posed:

1. To what extent can we teach broadly generalized elicitation strategies?
2. To what extent is it necessary to utilize different instructional procedures to teach various elicitation strategies to children at the same "developmental levels" but with different etiologies (i.e., mental retardation, autism, hearing impairments)?
3. To what extent do these strategies actually elicit "teaching responses" from various conversational partners?
4. If elicitation strategies elicit teaching responses, to what extent do these responses, in turn, actually enhance the child's language acquisition?
5. To what extent do other processes or abilities enable or impede the use and effects of elicitation strategies by the child (e.g., ability to change and alter strategies based on context and feedback)?
6. To what extent can the child's elicitation strategies compensate for adverse environmental conditions?
7. To what extent can child-based elicitation strategies overcome or minimize the effects of underlying cognitive or neurologic deficiencies that cannot be directly manipulated?

Efforts to answer the questions 6 and 7 necessarily depend on our success in answering the first five questions. Some groundwork for an answer to the first question was established as we developed a basic intervention technology. That is, what we already know about teaching communication and language skills to young children is an excellent starting point for teaching these children broader generalized strategies.

Summary

In some respects, the idea of incorporating child-based elicitation strategies into intervention represents the logical conclusion of the efforts since the 1980s to develop child-responsive (as opposed to adult-directed) intervention strategies. Now, instead of attempting to teach to the child's attentional lead and embed instruction in meaningful activities, we could attempt to give the child a set of strategies to help the child be his or her own teacher. Certainly, many limitations to this approach may be discovered. For the present, these limitations are largely unknown, and the effects of teaching strategies for learning remains an empirical question.

CONCLUSION

The field of early language intervention has been engaged primarily in developing and testing basic technology for almost 3 decades. This era remains far from over. Some fundamental problems have not yet been investigated (e.g., prelinguistic intervention), others have been reformulated (e.g., the treatment of aberrant behavior), and meaningful examination of generalization and long-term longitudinal effects of language intervention have not received substantial attention. Nevertheless, the field has made substantial progress in delineating basic intervention principles, based on convergent theoretical and empirical evidence.

The field of early language intervention arguably has achieved its initial success by being primarily problem-driven. Theory has been used as a tool by some leading contributors to the field, but not, in most cases, as an end (e.g., promoting behaviorism) in itself. This has facilitated continued advancement amidst the rapidly shifting theories of human behavior and child language acquisition.

The field also has been inter- and even transdisciplinary, in a narrow sense, throughout its brief history (Warren & Reichle, 1992). Leading researchers publish in a variety of journals and have primary affiliations with several disciplines, including developmental psychology, speech and hearing sciences, and special education. However, for the field to take full advantage of the expected advances in genetic and neurologic sciences, it will have to achieve a truly remarkable degree of interdisciplinary integration and collaboration. Many behavioral scientists will find it necessary to acquire, or at least achieve, some appreciation and understanding of, methods and techniques utilized to study and manipulate different levels of the human developmental system. Lerner (1991) has argued that the same daunting challenge faces the behavioral sciences in general.

What should our goal be in early communication and language intervention? To teach specific skills to children, or to teach them strategies for learning more effectively outside of formal intervention efforts? Both of these are important and legitimate intervention goals from my perspective. However, so far the field has virtually ignored the implications of the second part of this question. A broad-based systematic effort to explore the potential of child-based elicitation strategies may focus the field on this issue with productive and perhaps unpredicted consequences.

Being problem-driven and transdisciplinary are obviously critical qualities for scientists interested in developing optimally effective intervention approaches. These qualities should assist investigators in their continuing efforts to conduct relevant, important research, even as our understanding of human development and behavior rapidly evolves. They are also qualities that should support participation in a true systems approach to intervention. Finally, these qualities should be equally valuable in determining the role that child-based elicitation strategies might play in remediation efforts.

REFERENCES

Andresen, J.T. (1991). Skinner and Chomsky thirty years later or: The return of the repressed. *The Behavior Analyst, 14,* 49–60.

Bates, E., Benigni, L., Bretherton, I., Camaioni, L., & Volterra, V. (1979). *The emergence of symbols: Cognition and communication in infancy.* New York: Academic Press.

Bates, E., & MacWhinney, B. (1982). Functionalist approaches to grammar. In E. Wanner & L. Gleitman (Eds.), *Language acquisition: The state of the art* (pp. 24–42). Cambridge: Cambridge University Press.

Bates, E., & MacWhinney, B. (1989). Functionalism and the competition model. In B. MacWhinney & E. Bates (Eds.), *The crosslinguistic study of sentence processing* (pp. 108–147). New York: Cambridge University Press.

Bates, E., Thal, D., & Janowsky, J.S. (in press). Early language development and its neural correlates. In I. Rapin & S. Segalowitz (Eds.), *Handbook of neuropsychology: Vol. 6. Child neurology.* Amsterdam: Elsevier.

Bates, E., Thal, D., & Marchman, V. (1991). From symbols to syntax. In N. Krasnegor, D. Rumbaugh, & R. Schiefelbusch (Eds.), *Language acquisition: Biological and behavioral determinants* (pp. 244–283). Hillsdale, NJ: Lawrence Erlbaum Associates.

Bloom, L., Lightbown, P., & Hood, L. (1975). Structure and variation in child language. *Monographs of the Society for Research in Child Development, 40*(Serial No. 160).

Boulding, K. (1956). General systems theory: The skeleton of science. *Management Science, 2,* 197–208.

Braine, M. (1976). Children's first word combinations. *Monographs of the Society for Research in Child Development, 41.*

Bricker, W.A., & Bricker, D.D. (1970). A program of language training for the severely language handicapped child. *Exceptional Children, 37,* 101–111.

Bricker, W.A., & Bricker, D.D. (1974). An early language training strategy. In R.L. Schiefelbusch & L.L. Lloyd (Eds.), *Language perspectives: Acquisition, retardation, and intervention* (pp. 431–468). Baltimore: University Park Press.

Bronfenbrenner, U. (1977). Toward an experimental ecology of human development. *American Psychologist, 32,* 513–531.

Bruner, J.S. (1975). The ontogenesis of speech acts. *Journal of Child Language, 2,* 1–19.

Camarata, S.M., & Nelson, K.E. (in press). Treatment efficacy as a function of target selection in the remediation of child language disorders. *Clinical Linguistics and Phonetics.*

Carrow-Woolfolk, E. (1988). *Theory, assessment, and intervention in language disorders: An integrative approach.* Philadelphia: Grune & Stratton.

Chapman, R.S. (1990). Models of language disorder. In J.F. Miller (Ed.), *New directions in research on child language disorders* (pp. 287–298). San Diego, CA: College-Hill Press.

Chapman, R.S., Streim, N., Crais, E., Salmon, D., Strand, E., & Negri-Shoultz, N. (1992). Child talk: Assumptions of a development process model for early language learning. In R.S. Chapman (Ed.), *Child talk: Processes in language acquisition and disorders.* Chicago: Mosby-Year Book.

Chomsky, N. (1959). Verbal behavior by B.F. Skinner. *Language, 35,* 26–58.

Chomsky, N. (1965). *Aspects of the theory of syntax.* Cambridge, MA: MIT Press.

Dawson, G., Finley, C., Phillips, S., Galpert, L., & Lewy, A. (1988). Reduced P3 amplitude of the event-related brain potential: Its relationship to language ability in autism. *Journal of Autism and Developmental Disorders, 18,* 493–504.

Dawson, G., & Galpert, L. (1990). Mothers' use of imitative play for facilitating social responsiveness and toy play in young autistic children. *Development and Psychopathology, 2,* 151–162.

Dawson, G., & Lewy, A. (1989a). Arousal, attention, and the socioemotional impairments of individuals with autism. In G. Dawson (Ed.), *Autism: Nature, diagnosis, and treatment* (pp. 49–74). New York: Guilford.

Dawson, G., & Lewy, A. (1989b). Reciprocal subcortical-cortical influences in autism: The role of attentional mechanisms. In G. Dawson (Ed.), *Autism: Nature, diagnosis, and treatment* (pp. 144–173). New York: Guilford.

Donahue, M., & Watson, L. (1990). [Review of *Language perspectives: Acquisition, retardation, and intervention*]. *American Journal on Mental Retardation, 94,* 567–574.

Durand, V.M., & Carr, E.G. (1991). Functional communication training to reduce challenging behavior: Maintenance and application in new settings. *Journal of Applied Behavior Analysis, 24,* 251–264.

Elman, J.L. (1991a). Distributed representations, simple recurrent networks, and grammatical structure. *Machine Learning, 7,* 195–225.

Elman, J.L. (1991b). *Incremental learning, or the importance of starting small* (CRL Technical Report No. 9101). La Jolla, CA: University of California-San Diego, Center for Research in Language.

Ezell, J.K., & Goldstein, H. (1991). Observational learning of comprehension monitoring skills in children who exhibit mental retardation. *Journal of Speech and Hearing Research, 34,* 141–154.

Fey, M.E. (1986). *Language intervention with young children.* San Diego, CA: College-Hill Press.

Fogel, A., & Thelen, E. (1987). The development of expressive and communicative action in the first year: Reinterpreting the evidence from a dynamic systems perspective. *Developmental Psychology, 23,* 747–761.

Goldstein, H., & Hockenberger, E.H. (1991). Significant progress in child language intervention: An 11-year retrospective. *Research in Developmental Disabilities, 12,* 401–425.

Goldstein, H., & Mousetis, L. (1989). Generalized language learning by children with severe mental retardation: Effects of peers' expressive modeling. *Journal of Applied Behavior Analysis, 22,* 245–259.

Golinkoff, R.M., & Hirsh-Pasek, K. (1990). Let the mute speak: What infants can tell us about language acquisition. *Merrill-Palmer Quarterly, 36,* 67–92.

Gottlieb, G. (1991). Experiential canalization of behavioral development: Theory. *Developmental Psychology, 27,* 4–13.

Guess, D., Sailor, W., & Baer, D.M. (1974). To teach language to retarded children. In R.L. Schiefelbusch & L.L. Lloyd (Eds.), *Language perspectives: Acquisition, retardation, and intervention* (pp. 431–468). Baltimore: University Park Press.

Hart, B., & Risley, T. (1980). In vivo language intervention: Unanticipated general effects. *Journal of Applied Behavior Analysis, 13,* 407–432.

Kaiser, A., & Warren, S.F. (1988). Pragmatics and generalization. In R.L. Schiefelbusch & L.L. Lloyd (Eds.), *Language perspectives II: Acquisition, assessment, and intervention* (pp. 397–442). Austin, TX: PRO-ED.

Kaiser, A., Yoder, P., & Keetz, A. (1992). Evaluating milieu teaching. In S. Warren & J. Reichle (Eds.), *Communication and language intervention: Vol. 1. Causes and effects in communication and language intervention* (pp. 9–47). Baltimore: Paul H. Brookes Publishing Co.

Landon, S.J., & Sommers, R.K. (1979). Talkativeness and children's linguistic abilities. *Language and Speech, 22,* 269–275.

Lerner, R.M. (1991). Changing organism-context relations as the basic process of development: A developmental contextual perspective. *Developmental Psychology, 27,* 27–32.

MacDonald, J. (1985). Language through conversation: A model for intervention with language-delayed persons. In S. Warren & A. Rogers-Warren (Eds.), *Teaching functional language: Generalization and maintenance of language skills* (pp. 89–122). Baltimore: University Park Press.

Menyuk, P. (1971). *The acquisition and development of language.* Englewood Cliffs, NJ: Prentice Hall.

Miller, J., Miolo, G., Sedey, A., Pierce, K., & Rosin, M. (1989, November). *Predicting lexical growth in children with Down syndrome.* Paper presented at the annual convention of the American Speech-Language-Hearing Association, St. Louis.

Miller, J.F., & Yoder, D.E. (1972). A syntax teaching program. In J.E. McLean, D.E. Yoder, & R.L. Schiefelbusch (Eds.), *Language intervention with the retarded.* Baltimore: University Park Press.

Miller, J.F., & Yoder, D.E. (1974). An ontogenetic language teaching strategy for retarded children. In R.L. Schiefelbusch & L.L. Lloyd (Eds.), *Language perspectives: Acquisition, retardation, and intervention* (pp. 505–528). Baltimore: University Park Press.

Nelson, K. (1973). Structure and strategy in learning to talk. *Monographs of the Society for Research in Child Development, 38.*

Nelson, K.E. (1989). Strategies for first language teaching. In M.L. Rice & R.L. Schiefelbusch (Eds.), *The teachability of language* (pp. 263–310). Baltimore: Paul H. Brookes Publishing Co.

Nelson, K.E. (1991). On differentiated language-learning models and differentiated interventions. In N. Krasnegor, D. Rumbaugh, & R. Schiefelbusch (Eds.), *Language acqusition: Biological and behavioral determinants* (pp. 399–428). Hillsdale, NJ: Lawrence Erlbaum Associates.

Nelson, K.E., Baker, N.D., Denninger, M., Bonvillian, J.D., & Kaplan, B.J. (1985). Cookie versus do-it-again: Imitative-referential and personal-syntactic-initiating language styles in young children. *Linguistics, 23,* 433–454.

Ratner, M., & Bruner, J.S. (1978). Games, social exchanges, and the acquisition of language. *Journal of Child Language, 5,* 391–402.

Risley, T.R., Hart, B.M., & Doke, L. (1972). Operant language development: The outline of a therapeutic technology. In R.L. Schiefelbusch (Ed.), *Language of the mentally retarded* (pp. 177–198). Baltimore: University Park Press.

Rogers-Warren, A.K., & Warren, S.F. (1977). *Ecological perspectives in behavior analysis.* Baltimore: University Park Press.

Rummelhart, D.E., McClelland, J.L., & the PDP Research Group.(1986). *Parallel distributed processing: Explorations in the microstructure of cognition* (Vol. 1). Cambridge, MA: Bradford Books.

Sameroff, A.J. (1983). Developmental systems: Contexts and evolution. In W. Kessen (Ed.), *Handbook of child psychology: Vol. 1. History, theory and methods* (pp. 237–294). New York: John Wiley & Sons.

Sameroff, A.J., & Chandler, J.M. (1975). Reproductive risk and the continuum of caretaking casualty. In F.D. Horowitz, M. Hetherington, S. Scarr-Salapatek, & G. Siegel (Eds.), *Review of child development research* (Vol. 4, pp. 187–244). Chicago: University of Chicago Press.

Schachter, F.F. (1979). *Everyday mother talk to toddlers.* New York: Academic Press.

Schiefelbusch, R.L., & Lloyd, L.L. (Eds.). (1974). *Language perspectives: Acquisition, retardation, and intervention.* Baltimore: University Park Press.

Schiefelbusch, R.L., & Lloyd, L.L. (Eds.). (1988). *Language perspectives: Acquisition, retardation, and intervention* (2nd ed.). Austin, TX: PRO-ED.

Shatz, M. (1987). Bootstrapping operations in child language. In K. Nelson, & A. van Kleeck (Eds.), *Children's language* (Vol. VI, pp. 1–22). Hillsdale, NJ: Lawrence Erlbaum Associates.

Snow, C., & Ferguson, C. (Eds.). (1977). *Talking to children: Language input and acquisition*. New York: Cambridge University Press.

Snow, C., Perlmann, R., & Nathan, D. (1987). Why routines are different: Toward a multiple factors model of the relation between input and language acquisition. In K. Nelson & A. van Kleeck (Eds.), *Child language* (Vol. 6, pp. 65–97). Hillsdale, NJ: Lawrence Erlbaum Associates.

Tannock, R., & Girolametto, L. (1992). Reassessing parent-focused language intervention programs. In S. Warren & J. Reichle (Eds.), *Communication and language intervention: Vol. 1. Causes and effects in communication and language intervention* (pp. 49–79). Baltimore: Paul H. Brookes Publishing Co.

Thelen, E. (1989). Self-organization in developmental processes: Can systems approaches work? In M. Gunnar & E. Thelen (Eds.), *Systems and development: The Minnesota symposium on child psychology* (Vol. 22, pp. 77–117). Hillsdale, NJ: Lawrence Erlbaum Associates.

Thelen, E., & Ulrich, B.D. (1991). Hidden skills. *Monographs of the Society for Research in Child Development, 56*(1, Serial No. 223).

Warren, S.F., & Bambara, L.M. (1989). An experimental analysis of milieu language intervention: Teaching the action–object form. *Journal of Speech and Hearing Disorders, 54,* 448–461.

Warren, S.F., & Gazdag, G.A. (1990). Facilitating early language development with milieu intervention procedures. *Journal of Early Intervention, 14,* 62–86.

Warren, S.F., & Kaiser, A. (1986). Incidental language teaching: A critical review. *Journal of Speech and Hearing Disorders, 51,* 291–299.

Warren, S.F., & Kaiser, A. (1988). Research in early language intervention. In S.L. Odom & M.B. Karnes (Eds.), *Early intervention for infants and children with handicaps: An empirical base* (pp. 89–108). Baltimore: Paul H. Brookes Publishing Co.

Warren, S.F., Kim, K., & Yoder, P.J. (May, 1991). *The role of spontaneous imitation in early language intervention*. Presentation at the Gatlinburg Conference on Research and Theory in Mental Retardation and Developmental Disabilities, Key Biscayne, FL.

Warren, S.F., & Reichle, J. (1992). The emerging field of communication and language intervention. In S. Warren & J. Reichle (Eds.), *Communication and language intervention: Vol. 1. Causes and effects in communication and language intervention* (pp. 1–8). Baltimore: Paul H. Brookes Publishing Co.

Warren, S.F., & Rogers-Warren, A. (1980). Current perspectives in language remediation: A special monograph. *Education and Treatment of Children, 3,* 133–152.

Whitehurst, G.J., Fischel, J.E., Arnold, D.S., & Lonigan, C. (1992). Evaluating outcomes with children with expressive language delay. In S. Warren & J. Reichle (Eds.), *Communication and language intervention: Vol. 1. Causes and effects in communication and language intervention* (pp. 277–313). Baltimore: Paul H. Brookes Publishing Co.

Wilcox, M.J., Kouri, T.A., & Caswell, S.B. (1991). Early language intervention: A comparison of classroom and individual treatment. *American Journal of Speech-Language Pathology, 1,* 49–62.

Wolff, P.H. (1991). How are new behavioral forms and functions introduced during ontogenesis? *Monographs of the Society for Research in Child Development, 56*(1, Serial No. 223), 99–103.

Author Index

Acunzo, M., 124
Adamdson, L., 48
Adams, A., 44, 208
Adams, B.J., 262
Adamson, L., 45, 50, 98, 191, 195,
  202, 206, 292
Ager, A.K.S., 277
Akhtar, N., 48
Alexander, A., 99, 148
Alpert, C.L., 55, 65, 66, 69, 77
Alpert, K., 21, 97, 106
Alwell, M., 81, 163, 166, 167, 168,
  169, 174, 175, 178
Anderson, E., 143
Anderson, H., 108
Anderson, S., 46
Anderson, S.R., 276
Andresen, J.T., 379
Angelo, D., 274, 324, 326, 329
Anselmi, D., 124
Appolloni, T., 63
Arbeit, W.R., 254
Arnold, D.S., 384
Arpan, R., 20
Asher, S.R., 159
Attwood, A.J., 207
Austin, L.J., 226
Ayabe, C.R., 151
Ayers-Lopez, L., 142

Baer, D.M., 11, 14, 46, 106, 117, 120,
  124, 129, 165, 179, 244, 276, 319,
  320, 324, 386
Baer, R., 129
Bailey, L.M., 288
Bakeman, R., 45, 48, 50, 90, 191,
  195, 202, 206, 292
Baker, B., 15, 86
Baker, N.D., 389

Balkany, T.J., 335
Bambara, L.M., 46, 378, 388
Barnes, S., 48
Barnes, T., 249, 251, 257
Barnett, J.R., 41
Baron-Cohen, S., 216
Barrett, M.D., 289, 294, 295, 304
Bass, R.W., 261, 326
Bates, E., 37, 38, 42, 44, 49, 50, 53,
  72, 141, 289, 292, 377, 379, 381,
  385
Baumeister, A.A., 253, 260
Baumgartner, P., 216
Baxley, N., 264, 266, 328
Baxter, A., 188, 189, 190, 192, 195,
  196
Baxter, D., 46
Bayles, K., 72
Bell, J., 258
Bell, R.Q., 196
Bellugi, U., 312
Bender, M.K., 172
Benedict, H., 38, 40, 48, 292
Benigni, L., 38, 42, 44, 53, 377
Berko Gleason, J.B., 85, 140, 141
Berninger, G., 161
Berry, P., 127
Bertrand, J., 261, 262, 278, 288, 295,
  296, 298, 299, 300, 301, 306, 307,
  308
Best, S., 231
Beukelman, D., 98
Bickel, W.K., 262
Bihrle, A., 312
Billman, K.S., 231
Bishop, K., 24, 48, 124, 178, 179
Black, B., 142, 146
Blair, G., 73
Blank, M., 20
Blanton, R.L., 253, 260

Bleier, M., 160
Bloom, L., 278, 294, 295, 326, 377
Blott, J., 14
Blount, R., 129
Boelens, H.H., 259
Bonet, B., 144
Bonvillian, J.D., 86, 389
Boothroyd, A., 230
Borakove, L.S., 326
Boulding, K., 379
Bowerman, M., 14
Boyatzis, C., 194, 195
Boyes-Braem, P., 303
Brady, J., 257
Brady, M.P., 165
Braine, M., 272, 377
Brakke, K., 97
Braverman, M., 214
Breen, C., 163, 171, 176
Brehm, S., 353
Brenner, J., 162
Brenn-White, B., 324
Bretherton, I., 38, 42, 44, 53, 190,
   191, 203, 377
Bricker, D., 13, 14, 15, 16, 17, 21, 23,
   24, 26, 117, 120, 261, 376, 386
Bricker, W., 13, 14, 117, 120, 261,
   376, 386
Bridges, A., 293
Brinton, B., 124, 125, 233
Bronfenbrenner, U., 379
Bronson, G.W., 190
Brookes, S., 294
Brooks, B.R., 230
Brooks-Gunn, J., 46, 47, 209
Browder, D., 324
Brown, A., 188, 260
Brown, J., 23
Brown, K., 86
Brown, M., 129
Brown, R., 145
Brown, W., 244, 324, 325, 326, 329
Bruner, J.S., 38, 45, 47, 50, 51, 73,
   85, 191, 203, 213, 275, 292, 293,
   376
Bryan, A.A., 54
Bucher, B., 123, 326
Buckhalt, J.A., 195
Buckley, S., 335, 350, 352, 353
Budd, C., 81
Buhr, J.C., 261
Bunce, B.H., 145

Bush, K.M., 276
Butterfield, P., 193
Butterworth, G., 292

Cain, D.H., 35, 49, 54
Cain, L., 85, 140, 141
Calculator, S., 171
Camaioni, L., 38, 42, 44, 53, 292, 377
Camarata, S.M., 378
Campbell, D.T., 53
Campos, J., 188, 191, 197, 202
Capps, L., 217
Cardoso-Martins, C., 195
Carey, S., 305
Carlson, L., 23
Caron, A.J., 188, 192
Caron, R.F., 188, 192
Carpenter, R., 110–114
Carr, E.G., 81, 109, 123, 244, 268,
   269, 382
Carrier, J., 14
Carrigan, P., 249, 264, 272
Carrow-Woolfolk, E., 378
Carta, J., 24
Caswell, S.B., 378
Catania, A.C., 264
Catts, H., 147, 151
Chadsey-Rusch, J., 48
Chandler, J.M., 379
Chandler, L.K., 163, 166, 177, 178
Chandler, M.J., 54
Chapman, K.L., 296
Chapman, R., 54, 89, 107, 230, 305,
   378, 388
Charlesworth, R., 161
Charlop, M., 123, 124, 270
Cheseldine, S., 65
Chin, S.B., 229
Chomsky, N., 36, 376, 377, 379
Cicchetti, D., 209
Cipani, E., 123, 124
Cirrin, F., 86, 109, 110–114
Clark, E.V., 288, 295, 296
Clarke, R., 51
Cleary, J., 265
Coggins, T.E., 54, 110–114, 125
Cohen, L.B., 302
Cohen, L.R., 257
Cohn, J.F., 210
Cole, K., 23, 55
Coles, M., 187

Collet-Klingenberg, L., 48
Collins, A., 23
Collis, G.M., 191
Compton, W.C., 335
Connell, P.J., 326
Connolly, J.H., 224, 225
Conti-Ramsden, G., 45
Cook, R.G., 255
Cook, T.D., 53
Cooke, S.K., 63
Cooke, T.B., 63
Cooper, C.R., 142
Coots, J., 178, 179
Cotter, V.W., 264, 266, 328
Cournoyer, P., 160
Crais, E., 388
Crawley, S., 41
Cresson, O., 328
Cripe, J., 21, 24
Cromer, R., 14
Cross, T., 72
Crouch, K., 129
Cullinan, D., 324
Cunningham, C., 353
Cunningham, S., 249, 264
Curcio, F., 204
Cuvo, A.J., 326

Dahle, A.J., 335
Dale, P., 23, 55
Darnton, B., 124, 233
Daurelle, L.A., 63
Davies, B., 24, 45, 48, 106, 124
Davis-Lang, D., 251
Dawson, G., 22, 44, 208, 212, 213, 383
Deacon, J., 129
Deal, A.G., 54
Decarie, T.G., 206
Deckner, C.W., 253, 260
Deffebach, K., 98
de Freitas Ribiero, A., 129
DeGracie, J.S., 151
DeKlyen, M., 172
Delacour, J., 255
Delius, J.D., 255
DeLoache, J., 188
Denninger, M., 389
Dent, C., 161
de Rose, J.C., 249, 250
de Rose, T., 276

Detrich, R., 129
Devieux, J., 41
Diniz, F., 289
Dinnsen, D., 229
Dirks, M., 129
Dixon, L.S., 243, 261
Dodd, B., 351, 353
Doherty, S., 312
Doke, L., 376
Dolgin, K., 189
Dollaghan, C., 305
Donahue, M., 378
Donnellan, A., 173
Doran, L.P., 172
Dore, J., 109, 110–114, 189
Doss, L.S., 121, 268, 269
Dougherty, L., 202
Downs, M.P., 335
Drake, D., 41
Dromi, E., 294, 295, 297, 300, 304
Dube, W.V., 246, 249, 250, 252, 253, 255, 256, 257, 263, 265, 266, 277
Duchan, J., 21
Duguid, P., 23
Dunham, F., 48
Dunham, P., 48
Dunn, L.M., 87, 95
Dunst, C., 16, 17, 54, 175
Durand, V.M., 81, 109, 244, 382

Egel, A.L., 325
Egger, D., 324
Elbert, M., 229
Ellsworth, P., 189
Elman, J.L., 381
Embry, L.H., 81
Emde, R., 188, 193, 197, 202
Emslie, M., 353
Ervin-Tripp, S., 143, 165
Esper, E., 318
Etzel, B.C., 262
Exum, M., 263
Eynon, D., 107
Ezell, H.K., 47, 324, 389

Falk, A., 13
Falvey, M., 178, 179
Farran, D.C., 43, 50, 56
Farrar, J., 190
Farrar, M.F., 45, 47, 161

Farrar, M.J., 310
Fassbender, L., 173
Feagans, L., 46, 50, 56
Fein, D., 214
Feinman, S., 188, 193
Ferguson, C., 47, 376
Fernald, A., 188, 192
Ferrell, D.R., 159, 163, 167, 168, 169, 171, 175, 177, 178
Fey, M.E., 17, 146, 376, 378
Field, T., 44
Fields, L., 262
Fillenbaum, R., 148
Finger, I., 163
Finkelstein, N.W., 161
Finley, C., 383
Fischel, J.E., 384
Fishelzon, G., 297, 300
Flanagan, J.L., 225
Fogel, A., 381
Forner, L.L., 232
Fowler, A.E., 312, 335
Fox, J.J., 63, 165
Franco, F., 292
Frankoff, D., 324
Frearson, B., 225
Friedman, K.A., 55
Friedman, P., 55
Friedman, S., 41
Friel-Patti, S., 45
Fristoe, M., 96, 98
Frith, U., 207, 216
Fujiki, M., 124, 125, 233
Furby, L., 191
Furrow, D., 40, 48
Fygetakis, L., 13

Gaensbauer, T.J., 202
Gallagher, K., 161
Gallagher, T.M., 124, 125, 233
Galpert, L., 212, 213, 383
Galpin, V., 249, 250
Gardner, R., 148
Garnica, O.K., 142
Garvey, C., 159, 160, 161, 233
Gaylord-Ross, R., 163, 176
Gazdag, G., 50, 51, 53, 388
Gelman, R., 160
Gentner, D., 293
George, L.B., 150
Germond, J., 50

Gerovac, B.J., 261, 326
Gibbons, J., 190
Gibson, D., 312
Gilbert, M.M., 172
Gilbreath, B.J., 39, 47, 52
Gillham, B., 291, 294
Gillis, S., 298
Girolametto, L., 65, 67, 68, 105, 107, 122, 378
Giumento, A., 22, 23
Gleitman, H., 48
Gleitman, L., 48
Glidden, L.M., 324
Glover, A., 163
Gobbi, L., 123, 124
Goetz, L., 56, 81, 163, 166, 167, 168, 169, 174, 175, 178
Goldberg, K.E., 195
Goldberg, S., 40, 41, 44, 47
Goldfield, B.A., 141, 293
Goldfield, E., 194, 195
Goldiamond, I., 246, 264
Goldstein, H., 20, 22, 24, 47, 107, 159, 163, 166, 167, 168, 169, 171, 175, 176, 177, 178, 270, 273, 274, 319, 320, 321, 322, 323, 324, 325, 326, 329, 330, 377, 378, 386, 389
Goldstein, S.B., 64
Golinkoff, R.M., 38, 50, 95, 288, 290, 295, 301, 305, 378
Goossens', C., 244
Gopnik, A., 307, 308
Gordon, D., 143
Gorenflo, C., 99
Gorenflo, D., 99
Gottlieb, G., 379, 380
Graham, L., 14
Gray, B., 13
Gray, W.D., 303
Green, G., 255, 276
Green, J.A., 51
Greenfield, D.B., 260
Greenfield, P., 97, 141
Greenlee, M., 231
Greenwald, C., 204
Greenwood, C., 24, 176
Grenot-Scheyer, M., 178, 179
Grosjean, F., 148
Guaralnick, M.J., 159
Guenther, H., 13
Guess, D., 11, 14, 19, 106, 117, 120, 179, 244, 319, 320, 386

Guevremont, D., 129
Guida, J., 19
Gunnar, M., 189, 192, 193, 203
Gunter, P., 165
Guralnick, L., 163, 164, 165, 173
Guralnick, M.J., 22, 85, 149, 160, 161, 162
Gustafson, G.E., 51
Gutfreund, M., 48
Guthrie, J., 54

Hadley, P.A., 85, 146, 147, 148, 149, 154
Haelsig, P.C., 229
Haenlein, M., 253, 260
Haft, W., 189
Hall, C., 269
Hall, G., 268, 269
Halle, J., 48, 97, 124, 179, 317
Halliday, M.A.K., 141
Hamilton, J.L., 144
Hancock, T.B., 66
Haney, J.I., 317
Hanley, M.J., 258
Happé, F., 206
Harding, C.G., 44, 50
Haring, T.G., 19, 163, 171, 176
Harlow, H.F., 259
Harmon, R.J., 202
Harris, M.B., 294
Harris, S.L., 64
Harris-Vanderheiden, D., 15, 244
Hart, B., 17, 72, 129, 143, 161, 376, 377, 389
Hartmann, E., 229
Hartup, W.W., 159, 160, 161
Haslegrave, G., 353
Haviland, J., 189, 196
Hay, D., 85, 140, 141, 203
Hayes, S.C., 265
Hazen, N.L., 142, 146
Heath, S.B., 143
Heckhausen, J., 194, 195
Hegedus, K., 160
Helmstetter, E., 179
Hemmeter, M.L., 66, 78, 122
Hemphill, L., 150
Hendrickson, J., 21, 77
Hengst, J., 231
Herink, N., 164
Herman, L.M., 254

Hermann, P., 327
Hermelin, B., 204, 207
Hertzog, M.E., 209
Hill, D., 212, 213
Hirshberg, L., 188, 193
Hirsh-Pasek, K., 95, 288, 290, 295, 301, 378
Hively, W., 252
Hobson, R.P., 214, 215
Hockenberger, E.H., 377, 378
Hockett, C.F., 317
Hodapp, R., 86, 194, 195
Hodge, M.M., 232
Hodgson, R., 148
Hodson, B.W., 229, 231
Hodur, P., 324
Hofer, L., 189
Hoffman, M.L., 189
Hogan, A., 204, 292
Hogan, R., 160
Hohmann, M., 144
Holbert, K., 175
Holland, J.G., 108, 268
Hollis, J., 328
Hood, L., 377
Hoogeveen, F.R., 259
Hopkins, W., 88
Hopmann, M.R., 350
Horner, R., 81
Hornik, R., 189, 192, 193, 203
Horrobin, J.M., 353
Horstmeier, D., 15
Horton, K., 14, 18
Houden, P.M., 172
House, B.J., 252, 258, 260
Howes, C., 161
Hoyson, M., 154
Hubley, P., 202
Hudson, C., 123, 124
Huebner, R.R., 202
Hunt, J.McV., 308
Hunt, P., 81, 163, 166, 167, 168, 169, 174, 175, 178
Huttenlocher, J., 95
Hymes, D., 142, 226, 237

Iacono, T., 86, 335
Iennaco, F.M., 253, 255, 257, 266
Ingram, D., 326
Inhelder, I., 45
Irwin, K.C., 353

Israel, A., 129
Itard, J.M.G., 252
Iverson, I.H., 272
Izard, C.E., 202, 210

Jamieson, B., 154
Janowsky, J., 289, 385
Jenkins, E., 188
Jenkins, J.R., 159, 172
Jennings, W.B., 214
Jernigan, T., 312
Johnson, D.M., 303
Johnson, J., 20, 40, 41
Johnson, K.E., 191, 278, 295, 296,
    298, 299, 300, 301
Johnson, M.O., 190
Johnson-Dorn, N., 19
Johnston, G.T., 165, 166
Johnston, J.M., 143, 165, 166
Jones, D., 294

Kaczmarek, L., 20, 22, 24, 107
Kagan, J., 190, 210
Kahn, J., 39
Kaiser, A.P., 21, 23, 45, 46, 55, 63,
    65, 66, 67, 69, 73, 77, 78, 81, 97,
    105, 106, 161, 172, 269, 376, 377,
    378, 389
Kanner, L., 204
Kaplan, B., 50
Kaplan, B.J., 389
Kaplan, S., 81
Kaplan, T., 81
Karlan, G., 129, 324
Karoly, P., 129
Kasari, C., 37, 42, 53, 205, 209, 212,
    215, 216
Kauffman, J., 324
Kaufman, M.E., 259
Kay-Raining Bird, E., 305
Keenan, E.O., 160
Keetz, A., 23, 67, 269, 377, 378
Keller, M.F., 326
Kemper, S., 39
Kennedy, N., 20
Kent, J.F., 224, 228, 229, 230
Kent, L., 13, 14, 106, 117, 120
Kent, R.D., 224, 228, 229, 230, 232

Keogh, W., 18, 19, 121, 317
Kerber, K., 187
Kerr, N., 11
Kettz, A., 389
Killory-Anderson, R., 253
Kim, K., 50, 51, 53, 388
Kirby, K.C., 261
Kirk, B., 266
Kledaras, J.B., 252, 253, 255, 257,
    261, 266
Klein, D., 13
Klinger, L., 22
Klinnert, M., 188, 193, 197, 202
Knieps, L., 188, 189, 190, 192, 193,
    195, 196
Knopp, C., 86
Koegel, R.L., 20, 270, 325
Kologinsky, E., 123, 268, 269
Konarski, E., Jr., 129
Kotlarchyk, B.J., 276
Kouri, T.A., 378
Kraat, A., 244
Krakow, J., 160
Kristal, J., 81
Kubicek, L.F., 203
Kwiatkowski, J., 231
Kwon, J.H., 215

Ladd, G.W., 177
LaFleur, N., 324
Laitinen, R., 171, 176
Lamarre, J., 108, 268
Lamb, M., 189
Lamberg, W., 148
Lamprecht, R., 231
Lancioni, G.E., 259
Landesman, S., 99
Landon, S.J., 389
Langdell, T., 208, 214, 215
Lanyon, R.I., 64
Lanzetta, J., 189
Lapenta-Neudeck, R., 123, 124
LaVeck, B., 353
Layton, T., 51
Lazar, R., 249, 251, 256, 264, 276
Leahy, J., 351, 353
LeBlanc, J.M., 243
Lee, A., 215
Lee, M., 176
Lee, P.C., 164

Lee, V., 326, 329
Lefebvre, D., 165, 177, 178
Leiter, M.P., 161
Lenneberg, E.H., 37
Lentz, F., 324
Leonard, L., 204, 296
Leonard, S.N., 259
Le Prevost, P., 353
Lerner, R.M., 384, 391
Leslie, A., 206, 216
Levelt, W.J.M., 227
Lewis, H., 218
Lewis, M., 46, 47, 65, 106, 188, 209, 216
Lewy, A., 44, 383
Light, J., 160, 161, 165, 174
Lightbown, P., 377
Lignugaris/Kraft, B., 263
Lloyd, L., 14, 93, 96, 98, 376, 378
Lock, A., 292
Locke, J., 38, 291
Locke, P., 96
Lojkasek, M., 41
Lollis, S.P., 159
Long, L.M., 290, 291
Lonigan, C., 384
Lord, C., 212
Lorenz, S., 353
Lovaas, O., 13
Lowry, M., 257, 261
Lucci, D., 214
Lynch, D.C., 276

MacAulay, B., 13
MacDonald, J., 14, 15, 17, 19, 20, 39, 47, 52, 106, 107, 376
MacDonald, R.P.F., 243
MacGregor, D., 41
MacKain, K., 41
Mackay, H.A., 249, 265, 266, 274, 277
MacKensie, P., 244
MacKenzie, H., 107
MacLean, D.J., 188, 192
MacLean, W.M., 63
Macnamara, J., 290
MacWhinney, B., 377
Madison, C.L., 229
Madole, K.L., 302
Magid, D.F., 258

Maguire, R.A., 266
Maguire, R.W., 249, 251, 257
Mahoney, G., 15, 17, 18, 20, 43, 47–48, 65, 67, 106, 163, 175
Malatesta, C.Z., 189, 196, 206
Mangipudi, L., 291
Manolson, A., 17, 20, 47
Marchman, V., 377, 379, 381
Marcovitch, S., 41
Markman, E.M., 288, 290
Marks, S., 312
Marquis, A., 142
Marshall, A., 46, 276
Martin, R.E., 230
Matias, R., 210
Maurer, H., 73
Maxwell, J., 226
McClelland, J.L., 380, 381
McClintic, S., 216
McCollister, F.P., 335
McCollum, J., 43
McConkey, R., 65
McConnell, S., 165, 166, 171, 179
McCormick, L., 19
McCullar, G.L., 263
McCuller, W.R., 325
McDonald, K., 88
McDonald, S.J., 277
McEvoy, M., 165, 166
McGinnes, G., 202
McGinnis, J., 98
McGroarty, M., 225
McIlvane, W.J., 246, 249, 250, 252, 253, 255, 256, 257, 260, 261, 263, 265, 266, 276, 277, 307, 326
McInnes, M., 172
McIntyre, K.D., 265
McLean, J., 13, 15, 19, 20, 110–114, 119, 120
McNaughton, D., 160, 165
McQuarter, R.J., 269
McWilliams, R.A., 47, 175
Meltzoff, A.N., 307, 308
Melum, A., 20
Menyuk, P., 14, 376
Mervis, C.A., 278, 295, 296, 298, 299, 300, 301
Mervis, C.B., 195, 261, 262, 272, 278, 288, 289, 290, 291, 295, 296, 297, 298, 299, 300, 301, 302, 303, 304, 306, 307, 308

Mesaros, R., 173
Messer, D., 191, 292
Meyerson, L., 11
Michael, J., 11
Milch, R.E., 64
Millen, C.E., 96, 245, 279
Miller, J.F., 13, 14, 37, 89, 107, 230,
    335, 376, 382, 384, 386
Miller, M.A., 326
Miller, S.J., 64
Mills, P., 23, 55
Mineo, B., 324
Miolo, G., 230, 382, 384
Mirenda, P., 86, 96, 173, 244, 262
Mishkin, M., 255
Mistry, J., 50
Mittler, P., 127
Mize, J., 177
Monsen, R.B., 225
Moore, K.C., 296
Morrow, D., 98
Mousetis, L., 273, 274, 321, 322, 323,
    324, 325, 326, 329, 330, 386, 389
Mueller, E., 160, 162
Mundy, P., 37, 42, 53, 204, 205, 209,
    210, 212, 213, 216, 217, 292
Munson, L., 40, 41, 47, 261
Murata-Soraci, K., 253, 260
Murphy, C.M., 292
Murphy, D., 191
Murray, A.D., 40, 41
Musselwhite, C., 19

Nathan, D.C., 38, 40, 45, 47, 51, 388
Negri-Shoultz, N., 388
Nelson, C., 189
Nelson, K., 40, 45, 48, 86, 95, 161,
    289, 291, 300, 376, 377, 378, 386,
    389
Nemeth, M., 261
Nettelbladt, U., 231
Neville, H., 312
Newport, E., 48
Ninio, A., 293, 294
Noonan, M., 19

O'Brien, J.M., 261, 326
Ochs, E., 143
O'Connell, B., 37, 38, 49, 50

O'Connell, J.C., 43, 50
O'Connor, M., 65
O'Connor, N., 204
Odom, S.L., 154, 159, 163, 165, 166,
    171, 172, 177, 178, 179
Oelwein, P.L., 353
Ogan, T.A., 187, 188, 189, 190, 194
O'Leary, K.D., 129
Oliver, C., 97
Olson, S.L., 72
Olswang, L.B., 54
O'Reilly, A.W., 125
Orr, S., 189
Osberger, M.J., 233
Osnes, P., 129
Ostrosky, M.M., 163, 165, 166, 172,
    177, 178
Ouston, J., 215
Owens, R.E., 160, 162
Ozonoff, S., 214, 216

Paden, E., 229, 231
Paniagua, F.A., 129
Pankey, W.B., 190
Parker, J.G., 159
Parsons, C.L., 335
Pate, J.L., 86, 96, 267
Paul, L., 165, 166
Paul-Brown, D., 160, 163, 164, 165
Peck, C., 19, 25, 161, 163
Pennington, B.F., 214, 216
Perlmann, R., 38, 40, 45, 47, 51, 388
Perske, R., 160
Peters, A.M., 293
Peters, J., 40, 41
Peterson, C., 165, 166
Peterson, R.F., 324
Peterson, S.E., 151
Pettitt, L., 269
Phillips, S., 383
Piaget, J., 45, 302
Pierce, K., 382, 384
Pinker, S., 278
Pitts-Conway, V., 163
Politzer, R.L., 225
Powell, A., 15, 17, 18, 20, 43, 47, 48,
    65, 106, 175
Powell, T., 229
Prehm, H.J., 259
Premack, A., 15

Premack, D., 15, 244, 260
Price, P., 65
Primavera, L., 44
Prizant, B.M., 54, 109, 110–114
Prutting, C.A., 204

Radziszewska, B., 50
Rainey, S., 163, 166, 177, 178
Ramey, C., 99, 161
Ratner, N., 45, 47, 73, 376
Rauzin, R., 249, 264
Recchia, S., 86, 216
Reese, H.W., 260
Reeve, K.F., 262
Reichle, J., 18, 19, 25, 97, 107, 108, 115, 116, 118, 121, 123, 126, 129, 268, 269, 317, 391
Reinen, S., 244
Rescorla, L.A., 296
Reumann, R., 86
Reznick, J.S., 190
Rheingold, H.L., 203
Rice, M.L., 39, 85, 145, 146, 147, 148, 149, 154, 163, 261, 305
Richardson, S., 13
Richman, G., 325
Richmond, G., 258
Ricks, D.M., 207, 209
Riksen-Walraven, J.M., 45, 55
Risenhoover, N., 189
Risley, T., 17, 64, 129, 143, 161, 376, 377, 389
Risser, D., 202
Riva, M., 326
Rivera, J.J., 255
Robenalt, K., 48
Robinson, B., 90, 93
Robinson, B.R., 277
Robinson, C., 43
Rocco, F.J., 253, 255
Roger, B., 176
Rogers, S.J., 214, 216, 218
Rogers-Warren, A.K., 17, 72, 80, 107, 129, 143, 269, 377, 379
Rogoff, B., 50, 201
Romski, M.A., 22, 86, 89, 90, 91, 92, 93, 94, 95, 96, 98, 244, 245, 248, 249, 259, 263, 267, 277, 279, 305, 307, 324
Rondal, J.A., 335

Rosch, E., 272, 302
Rose, S., 226
Rosenbek, J.C., 224, 228, 229, 230
Rosenberg, S., 43
Rosenberger, P.B., 274
Rosin, M., 382, 384
Ross, S., 210
Rowland, C., 86, 109, 110–114
Roy, C., 45, 47, 73
Rozner, L., 335
Rubenstein, J., 161
Rubert, E., 88
Rubin, K.H., 159
Ruder, K., 324, 327
Rumbaugh, D.M., 87, 96, 97, 244, 245, 279
Rummelhart, D.E., 380, 381
Rusch, F., 129
Rushmer, N., 20
Rutherford, G., 11, 319, 320
Rutherford, R.B., 195
Rutter, M., 206, 212
Ryan, B., 13
Rynders, J.E., 353

Saarni, C., 206
Sabo, H., 312
Sachs, J., 18
Sack, S., 20
Sacks, B., 335, 350
Sacks, S., 352
Sagi, A., 189
Sailor, W., 11, 14, 19, 56, 81, 106, 117, 120, 163, 166, 167, 168, 169, 174, 175, 178, 244, 319, 320, 386
Sainato, D., 24
Salmon, D., 388
Salzberg, C.C., 65
Salzberg, C.L., 263
Salzinger, S., 81
Sameroff, A.J., 39, 54, 379
Sanchez, L., 251
Sander, E., 229
Sands, S.F., 255
Satterly, D., 48
Saunders, K.J., 252, 257, 261, 265, 269
Saunders, R.R., 261, 269
Savage-Rumbaugh, E.S., 88, 95, 97
Savalle-Boyajian, S., 81

Saville-Troike, M., 143
Scaife, M., 191
Schachter, F.F., 389
Schaffer, H., 15, 191
Schaife, B.K., 292
Scheibel, C., 244
Schermer, E., 108
Schiavetti, N., 228
Schiefelbusch, R.L., 14, 15, 16, 17, 18, 19, 86, 327, 376, 378
Schieffelin, B.B., 143
Schlesinger, I., 14
Schoen, S., 324
Schreibman, L., 123, 124, 270
Schuler, A., 19
Schuyler, V., 20
Schwartz, R., 38
Schwartz, S.E., 305
Scott, M.S., 260
Searle, J., 226
Sedey, A., 382, 384
Seibert, J., 204, 292
Seitz, S., 65
Sell, M.A., 85, 145, 146, 147, 149, 154
Sevcik, R.A., 22, 86, 88, 89, 90, 91, 92, 93, 94, 95, 96, 97, 98, 244, 248, 249, 259, 263, 267, 277, 305, 307
Shalz, M., 125
Shane, H., 19
Shapiro, T., 209
Shatz, M., 42, 43, 79, 160, 386, 387
Sheiber, F., 253
Sherman, J., 324
Sherman, T., 204, 205, 210, 213
Sherrod, K., 41, 73
Shore, C., 37, 38, 49, 50
Shores, R.E., 165
Shriberg, L.D., 231
Sidman, M., 244, 249, 251, 252, 254, 257, 258, 259, 262, 264, 265, 266, 272, 274, 275, 276, 277, 328
Siegel, L., 65
Siegel-Causey, E., 19
Siegler, R.S., 188
Sigafoos, J., 25, 97, 116, 118, 123, 126, 268, 269
Sigman, M., 37, 42, 204, 205, 207, 209, 210, 212, 213, 215, 216, 217
Silverman, K., 276

Simic, J., 123
Simpson, G.B., 335
Singh, J., 277
Singh, N.N., 277
Siperstein, G.N., 150
Skinner, B.F., 245, 268
Sloane, H.N., 64
Slobin, D.I., 288, 293
Sloper, T., 353
Smeets, P.M., 259
Smith, C.A., 189, 191, 195
Smith, J., 141
Smith, L., 37, 42, 53
Smith, M., 327
Snidman, N., 190
Snow, C., 38, 39, 40, 44, 45, 47, 51, 52, 72, 141, 376, 388
Snow, M.E., 209
Snyder-McLean, L., 15, 19, 20, 110–114, 119
Solomonson, B., 20
Sommers, R.K., 389
Sonnenberg, E., 124, 233
Soraci, S.A., Jr., 253, 260
Sorce, J., 188, 197, 202
Sowers, J., 20
Speltz, M.L., 159, 172
Spencer, A., 212, 213
Spencer, T.J., 274
Sperry, R.W., 227
Spiker, S., 41
Spradlin, J.E., 124, 179, 252, 257, 261, 264, 266, 269, 328, 376
Sroufe, L.A., 209
St. Louis, K., 19
Stark, R., 17
Stayton, V., 43
Stein, M.L., 172
Stern, D., 41, 189, 196
Stipek, D.J., 216
Stoddard, L.T., 246, 249, 250, 252, 253, 254, 255, 257, 258, 259, 260, 261, 262, 265, 266, 274, 276, 326
Stoel-Gammon, C., 49, 125
Stokes, T., 46, 129, 165, 179
Strain, P.S., 22, 154, 161, 165, 166, 171, 177, 178, 179
Strand, E., 388
Streim, N., 388
Stremel, K., 13, 14

Stremel-Campbell, K., 19
Striefel, S., 270, 273, 319, 324
Stromer, R., 261, 274
Sufit, R.L., 230
Sundberg, M.L., 268, 269
Svejda, M., 188, 193, 202

Tabors, P.O., 142
Tailby, W., 249, 264, 265, 328
Taine, H., 296
Tallal, P., 229
Tannock, R., 65, 67, 105, 107, 122, 378
Templin, M., 305
Terrace, H.S., 191, 252
Terselie-Weber, B., 231
Tetlie, R., 129
Thal, D., 289, 377, 379, 381, 385
Theimer, R., 19
Thelen, E., 380, 381
Thibodeau, M., 123, 124
Thiele, J.E., 144
Thompson, T., 265
Tiegerman, E., 44
Tomasello, M., 45, 47, 85, 124, 161, 190, 310
Tomlinson, C., 19
Touchette, P.E., 254
Trevarthen, C., 202
Trivette, C.M., 54
Tronick, E., 189, 196
Turner, G., 96

Udell, T., 19
Ulrich, B.D., 380
Ungerer, J.A., 204, 205, 210, 213
Uzgiris, I., 308

Valdez-Menchaca, M.C., 45
Vandell, D.L., 150
Vanderheiden, G., 15
Vaughan, W., 257, 265
Velleman, S., 291
Verhave, T., 262
Viallani, T.V., 65
Vihman, M.M., 231
Vincent-Smith, L., 261
Volterra, V., 38, 42, 44, 53, 292, 377

von Cramon, D., 229
von Tetzchner, S., 37, 42, 53
Vygotsky, L.S., 142, 201

Wacker, D., 121
Wahler, R., 81
Walden, T., 187, 188, 189, 190, 191, 192, 193, 194, 195, 196
Walker, H.M., 161
Walker, V.G., 35, 49, 54
Walsh, D.J., 148, 151
Wang, M., 226
Warner, D.A., 324
Warren, R.M., 225
Warren, S.F., 45, 46, 50, 51, 53, 80, 107, 269, 376, 377, 378, 379, 388, 391
Waryas, C., 14
Waterhouse, L., 214
Watson, L., 212, 213, 378
Webster, E., 124, 125
Weeks, S.J., 214
Weikart, D.P., 144
Weinberg, A., 147
Weiner, P., 151
Weinstein, B., 260
Weismer, G., 224, 228, 229, 230
Weiss, R., 47
Weistuch, L., 65, 106
Weitzner-Linn, B., 21
Wells, G., 48
Wenger, D., 288
Weninger, J., 129
Werner, H., 50
Wertsch, J.V., 201
West, M., 51, 203
Wetherby, A., 35, 49, 54, 109, 110–114, 204
Wetherby, B., 270, 273, 318, 319, 324
White, C., 165
White, R.A., 96, 245, 279
Whitehurst, G.J., 45, 73, 384
Whiteman, B.C., 335
Wickstrom, S., 159, 163, 166, 167, 168, 169, 171, 175, 176, 177, 178
Wilcox, J., 43, 44, 47, 54, 55
Wilcox, K.A., 145
Wilcox, M.J., 124, 125, 378
Wilkinson, K., 92, 93, 94, 98

Williams, J., 129
Willson-Morris, M., 266
Wilson, J.W., 317
Wing, L., 208, 209
Withstandley, J.K., 246, 260
Wolchick, S.A., 64
Wolf, M.M., 64
Wolff, P.H., 381
Wondolowski, K., 81
Wright, A.A., 255
Wulz, S.V., 328
Wynne, C.K., 249, 251, 257

Yavas, M., 231
Yirmiya, N., 37, 42, 205, 209, 212, 215, 216, 217

Yoder, D., 13, 14, 19, 376, 386
Yoder, P.J., 23, 24, 40, 41, 45, 46, 47, 48, 50, 51, 53, 55, 67, 69, 97, 106, 124, 269, 377, 378, 388, 389
Yonclas, D.G., 35, 49, 54
York, J., 25, 97, 107, 116, 118, 123, 126
Younger, B.A., 302

Zajonc, R.B., 210
Zarbatny, L., 189
Zeaman, D., 252
Ziegler, W., 229
Zigler, E., 86
Zimmerman, B.J., 73
Zygmont, D., 256

Subject Index

Aberrant behavior, communicative functions of, cross-domain research on, 382–383

Acceptable forms of behavior, for expression of communicative functions, 120

Achievement, SAL, measurement of, 89–90

Actions, utterances and, correspondence of, 128–130

Activity-based intervention, 21–22, 23

Adults, *see* Caregivers; Parent *entries*; Teachers

Advanced learning pattern, SAL and, 91

Affect
behavior regulation and, social referencing and, 188–189
sharing of
in autism, 203–204, 206–213
intersubjectivity and, 202–203

Affective development, autism and, 201–218
see also Autism

Affective environment, parent-implemented intervention and, 76

Alternative modes of communication, development of, trend toward, 18–19

Analytic learning style, holistic learning style versus, 289n

Appropriate language, models of, in parent-implemented intervention, 76–77

Arbitrary classes, 247–249
membership in
contextual control of, 275–276
contextual dependency of, 250–251

Arbitrary equivalence, 263–264
analysis of meaning and, 266
definitions of, implications of, 265
development of, 265–266

Arbitrary matching-to-sample
generalized, stimulus control and, 260–261
new method for programming, 256–257
recombinative generalization as, 271

Articulation, *see* Speech intelligibility

Attention
sharing of
in autism, 203–206
intersubjectivity and, 202–203
social referencing and, 190–191, 194–195

Auditory processing problems, children at risk for, protocols and, 370

Augmentative systems, 85–101
advent of, language intervention goals and, 15
development of, 18–19
instructional approaches using, 86–87
language learning through, 87–89
learner's environment and, 25
research on
future agenda for, 100–101
implications for practice, 99–100
see also System for Augmenting Language (SAL)

Autism
affect and, 203–204, 206–213
development of complex social emotions, 215–217
facial expression and, 208, 209–213
future research on, 217–218
initial studies of, 207–208

Autism—*continued*
affective development and communication in, 201–218
attention and, 203–206
cross-systems research on, 383
responses in, to emotion in others, 213–215

Babbling, prelinguistic–linguistic relationship and, 38
Beginning learning pattern, SAL and, 91
Behavior(s)
aberrant, communicative functions of, 382–383
communicative, use in all phases of social interaction, 122–127
emergent, engendered by matrix training, 271
forms of, used to express initial communicative functions, 119–120
inhibition of, social referencing and, 190
parent-implemented intervention effects on, 81
regulation of, affect and, 188–189
sequential, teaching of, 274
social
parent concerns about, 368
see also Social *entries*
Bootstrapping operations, elicitation strategies and, 386–387
Brain imaging, 383–384

Caregivers
choices of, child responsiveness influencing, 73
involvement of
history of, 15, 19–20
importance of, 22
as part of environment, 24–25, 73–74
see also Parent *entries*
Categorical Scope, principle of, 301–304
Form-Function principle and, 302–303
impact of, 303–304

Child
behavior of, parent-implemented intervention effects on, 81
contributions of, to environment, 72–73
cues of, parental behaviors responding to, 40–41
engagement of, *see* Engagement
parents and, *see* Parent *entries*
responsiveness of, effects on environment, 73
sensitivity to, 372–373
Child-based elicitation strategies, 385–390
challenges in, 388–389
research agenda and, 390
rationale for, 386–388
Child-driven models, of relationship between prelinguistic and linguistic communication, 37–39
Children's Phonologically Structured Intelligibility Test (CPSIT), 229–230
Clarification, partner's requests for, 124–125
Classroom environment, home environment versus, milieu teaching in, 66
Cognitive disabilities
language instructional approaches and, 86–87
social interactions and, 85–86
Commenting episodes, prelinguistic intervention and, 50–51
Communication, alternative modes of, trend toward development of, 18–19
Communication partners
generalization to, SAL and, 93–94
perceptions of, SAL and, 99
role of, in SAL, 88–89
see also Parent *entries*
Communication skills, conceptual skills and, programming of, *see* Stimulus-class analysis
Communicative competence, speech intelligibility and, 225–228
see also Speech intelligibility
Communicative functions, 109–117
of aberrant behavior, cross-domain research on, 382–383

initial, forms of behavior used for expression of, 119–120
repair strategy and, 125
repertoire of, establishment of, 117–119
Communicative interaction, see Interaction
Communicative repertoire, initial, see Initial communicative repertoire
Communicative use probes (CUPs), in SAL achievement measurement, 89–90
Competence
communicative, see Communicative competence
social, see Social competence
Comprehension
learning through augmented means and, 95–96
of ostensive gestures, 292
production and, relationship between, 326–329
Computer-based speech output device, see Speech output device
Conceptual skills, communication skills and, programming of, see Stimulus-class analysis
Conditional discrimination, stimulus-class analysis and, 251–252
potential problems with, 252–253
see also Stimulus-class analysis
Connectionism, 381–382
Context
conversational, learners who may benefit from, 106–108
feature classes and, 247
feature equivalence and, 263
social, see Social context(s)
Contextual control, of arbitrary-class membership, 275–276
Contextual dependency, of arbitrary-class membership, 250–251
Contingencies, in environment, 72
Contingency class procedure, in arbitrary matching-to-sample, 256–57
Contingent imitation, in prelinguistic intervention, 44, 48–49
Contingent responsivity
in prelinguistic intervention, 44–45
social aspects of environment and, 72

Conventional acts, for expression of initial communicative functions, 119, 120
Conventionality, requesting and, 49
Conversation
Down syndrome and, 338
initiation of, see Initiations
maintenance of, 124–126
shared meanings in, 7–8
Conversational facilitation strategies, parent-implemented, 67–68
see also Parent-implemented intervention
Conversational intervention context, learners who may benefit from, identification of, 106–108
Conversational repair, 124–126
Correlational studies, of prelinguistic–linguistic communication relationship, 40–41, 42
CPSIT, see Children's Phonologically Structured Intelligibility Test
Cross-domain research, cross-level research and, 382–384
Crossmodal transfer, 326–329
Cues
of child, parental behaviors responding to, 40–41
see also Prompts
Cultural status, language and, 142–143
CUPs, see Communicative use probes

Daily activities, objectives embedded in, 21–22, 23
Daycare, commenting frequency and, 50–51
Definition, ostensive, 292
Development, influence of language skills on, 86
Developmental disabilities, see Disabilities
Developmental perspective, milieu teaching and, prelinguistic, 46–47
Dialogue format, approaches based on, 20
Didactic language intervention models, parent-implemented interventions based on, 64–65

Differential reinforcement training
conditional discrimination and, 252
see also Matrix training
Differential responses, *see* Recombinative generalization
Differential sample–response procedure, in arbitrary matching-to-sample, 257
Direct instruction, for teaching desired social-communicative behaviors, 176–177
Disabilities
augmentative systems and, *see* Augmentative systems
children with, social interactions with normal peers, 149–150
communicative repair and, 125
prelinguistic intervention and, 46
severe, *see* Severe disabilities
see also specific type
Discrimination
conditional
potential problems with teaching of, 252–253
stimulus-class analysis and, 251–252
see also Stimulus-class analysis
intelligibility and, 224
Discriminative responding, 320
Down syndrome
cross-domain analysis of, 382
parent perspectives and, 335–354, 365–373
parent questionnaire about children with, 356–362
speech and language abilities of children with
parental expectations of, 350
parents' perspective on, 335–354
research results on, 337–347
research subjects and methods on, 336–337
see also Mental retardation
Dynamical systems theory, 380–381

Early intervention
development of, 17–18
present and future challenges in, 375–391

see also Language intervention; *specific aspect or type of intervention*
Early object labels
acquisition of, 287–312
future research on, 311–312
Categorical Scope principle and, 301–304
Extendibility principle and, 295–301
non-nouns as, 290–291
N3C principle and, 304–309
Object Scope principle and, 290–294
principles framework for, 287–312
intervention implications of, 310–311
referents and, 291
Ecological perspective, 19–20
Education for All Handicapped Children Act (PL 94-142), legislative-legalistic shift with, 18
Education of the Handicapped Act Amendments of 1986 (PL 99-457)
early intervention and, 17
interdisciplinary approaches and, 16
language intervention in natural social contexts and, 144
Part H of, prelinguistic intervention and, 35
Element combinations, in selection-based system, 270–271, 274
Element sequences, in selection-based system, 272–274
Elicitation, child-based, 385–390
Emergent behavior, engendered by matrix training, 271
Emergent sequential performances, 272–274
Emotion
in others, recognition and response in autism, 213–215
see also Affect
Engagement
environment and, 71
increasing, prelinguistic intervention and, 47
English as a second language (ESL) students, LAP and, 144
peer relationships and, 145–147
Environment
affective, 76

augmented language learning and, 101
caregiver's contributions to, 72–73
child's contributions to, 72–73
home versus classroom, milieu teaching in, 66
for intervention, social interactions and, 153–154
learning, 24–25
  components of, 70–72
  as system, 74–75
  mediation of, 71–72
  physical components of, 71
  relational aspects of, 70, 71–72
  social components of, 71–72
  in transactional model of parent–child interaction, 39
Environmental arrangement, in parent-implemented intervention, 75–76
Environmental input, structuring of, 317–331
  clinical implications of research on, 329–330
  crossmodal transfer and, 326–329
  future research on, 330–331
  observational learning and, 324–326
  recombinative generalization and, 318–324
Environmental system, parent-implemented intervention and, 70–75
  impact on environment, 80
  see also Parent-implemented intervention
Equivalence
  definitions of, implications of, 265
  stimulus, 262–266
Equivalence tests, Sidman's, 264
Errorless learning procedures, conditional discrimination and, 252–253
ESL students, see English as a second language students
Expectations, parental, Down syndrome and, 350
Explicit prompts, 47–48
Expressive language skills, Down syndrome and, 338, 339
Extendibility, principle of, 295–301
  implications of, 295–298

  limitations on impact of input, 300–301
  potential impact of input on bases for extension, 298–300

Facial expression
  affect and, autism and, 208, 209–213
  of others, autism and, 214–215
Facilitating Augmentative Communication Through Technology (FACTT), 100
Facilitative linguistic input, Object Scope and, 293–294
FACTT, see Facilitating Augmentative Communication Through Technology
Family, see Caregivers; Parent entries
  dysfunctional versus functional, parent concerns about judgment as, 369
  relationships within, parent-implemented intervention effects on, 81
  sensitivity to, 372–373
Family-systems approach, prelinguistic intervention and, 54
Fast-mapping, 305–307
Feature classes, 246
  element combination in, 271
  membership in, contextual dependency of, 247
Feature equivalence, 262–263
  contextual control of, 263
  development of, 263
Fidelity of treatment, parent-implemented intervention and, research on, 68–69
Focused linguistic input, 143
Form-Function principle, Categorical Scope and, 302–303
Functional equivalence, 264

Generalization
  approaches to promotion of, parent concerns about, 368
  facilitation of, environmental input and, see Environmental input, structuring of

Generalization—*continued*
observational learning and, 325–326
parent-implemented intervention and,
80–81
pragmatic form versus social function
and, 115–117
program for, peer-mediated intervention and, 177–180
recombinative, *see* Recombinative
generalization
Generalized arbitrary matching-to-
sample, stimulus control and,
260–261
Genetics, research in, 383–384
Gestures
affect and, autism and, 207–208
ostensive, comprehension and production of, 292
see also Sign language

Handicaps, *see* Disabilities
Hearing problems, children at risk for,
protocols and, 370
Holistic learning style, analytic learning
style versus, 289n
Home environment, milieu teaching in,
66
see also Parent-implemented intervention
Hybrid model, for parent-implemented
intervention, 75–78

Identity matching-to-sample
new method for programming,
253–255
relational property of, stimulus control by, 260
IEP, *see* Individualized education program
Imaging technology, 383–384
Imitation
contingent, in prelinguistic intervention, 44, 48–49
as goal of prelinguistic intervention,
51
Incidental teaching, 17
in parent-implemented intervention,
77
in prelinguistic intervention, 47, 48

Individualization, parent perspectives
on, 366
Individualized education program (IEP),
alternative modes of communication and, 18
Individualized instruction, for children
with special needs, 173–174
Infants
attention of, social referencing and,
190–191, 194–195
cues of, parental behaviors responding to, 40–41
Form-Function principle and, 302
intersubjectivity and, 202–203
language intervention for, development of, 17–18
Initial communicative repertoire
communicative functions and
behavior used for expression of,
119–120
descriptions of, 109–117
procedures for establishment of,
117–119
conversational intervention and,
learners who may benefit from,
106–108
development of, severe disabilities
and, 105–132
existing, instructional strategies that
consider, 120–122
pragmatic form versus social function
and, 108–109
social interaction and, 122–127
spontaneity and, 127–128
utterance correspondence with actions
and, 128–130
Initiations, 123–124
learner, importance of, 23–24
ostensive gestures in, 292
spontaneity and, 127–128
Input, *see* Environmental input;
Linguistic input
Instruction
direct, for teaching desired social-
communicative behaviors,
176–177
individualized, for children with special needs, 173–174
Instructional approaches, 86–87
considering existing communicative
repertoire, 120–122

Instrumental communication
  intents of, 109–117
    see also Communicative functions
  prelinguistic intervention and, 49–50
Integration
  Down syndrome and, 336
  SAL and, 99
  social communication skills and, 4
Intelligible speech, see Speech intelligibility
Intentionality, requesting and, 49
Intents, instrumental, 109–117
  see also Communicative functions
Interaction
  components of, delineation of,
    122–123
  generalization to range of partners,
    SAL and, 93–94
  initiation of, see Initiations
  maintenance of, 124–126
    spontaneity and, 127–128
  parent–child, see Parent–child interaction
  social, see Social interactions
  social referencing as, 194–196
  termination of, 126–127
    maintenance of, 127–128
  when one partner has special needs,
    162–165
  peer-mediated intervention and,
    170–171
  see also Conversation
Interdisciplinary approaches, development of, 16
Intersubjectivity
  in infancy, 202–203
  social referencing and, 191
  see also Affect; Attention
IQ, constancy of, former belief in, 12

Judgments, adult, language impairment
  effects on, 147–149, 152–153

Labels, object, early, see Early object
  labels
Language
  social uses of, 21–23
    intelligibility and, 224
  as tool of socialization, 141–145

Language Acquisition Preschool (LAP),
  144–145
  peer relationships and, 145–147
  interactions with individual children, 154
Language development
  facilitation of, parental linguistic input and, 40–41, 45
  measures of, parent-implemented intervention and, 68, 79–80
  parent-implemented intervention impact on, longitudinal assessments
    of, 79–80
  socialization as source of, 140–141
Language impairments
  social consequences of, 145–149,
    150–152
  specific, see Specific language impairments (SLI)
Language intervention
  caregiver involvement in, 15
  changing approach to, indications of,
    380–384
  child-based elicitation strategies in,
    385–390
  current strategies in, 378–379
  future and, 20–25
  history of, 11–26
  perspective on, 375–377
  for infants, development of, 17–18
  instructional approaches to, 86–87
  in natural social contexts, 143–144
  nondevelopmental approaches to, 14
  parent-implemented, see Parent-implemented intervention
  present and future challenges in,
    375–391
  primary, parent-implemented intervention impact on, 80–81
  research-application interface in, enhancement of, 26
  systems-level approach affecting,
    384–385
Language learning
  through augmented means, 85–101
    see also Augmentative systems;
      System for Augmenting Language (SAL)
  generalized, see Generalization
Language-learning environment
  components of, 70–72

Language-learning environment—
    continued
    see also Environment
Language programs, formal, develop-
    ment of, 13
Language systems, nonvocal, develop-
    ment of, 14–15
LAP, *see* Language Acquisition Pre-
    school
Learner, environment of, 24–25, 70–72
    see also Environment
Learner-oriented approaches, 23–24
Learning, observational, 324–326
Learning pattern, SAL and, 91–92
    see also System for Augmenting Lan-
    guage (SAL)
Learning processes, communication
    basis in, 7
Learning strategies, parent-implemented
    intervention impact on, longitu-
    dinal assessments of, 79–80
Learning styles, object labels and, 289
Lexical development, principles per-
    spective of, 287–312
    see also Early object labels; Operat-
    ing principles
Lexicon, *see* Vocabulary
Linguistic communication
    prelinguistic communication and
    relationship between, 36–43
        see also Prelinguistic communication
    prelinguistic intervention affecting, 53
Linguistic input
    facilitative, Object Scope and, 293–294
    focused, 143
    impact of, limitations on, 300–301
    of parents, language development fa-
        cilitation through, 40–41
    transparency or nontransparency of,
        effect on basis for extension,
        298–300
Linguistic mapping
    language development and, 40
    in prelinguistic intervention, 45
Longitudinal assessments, of impact of
    parent-implemented intervention,
    79–80

Maintenance, program for, peer-mediated
    intervention and, 177–180

Mand-model technique, in prelinguistic
    intervention, 47, 48
Mapping, linguistic
    language development and, 40
    in prelinguistic intervention, 45
Matching-to-sample
    conditional discrimination and,
        252–253
        see also Arbitrary matching-to-
        sample; Identity matching-to-
        sample
Maternal responsiveness, language de-
    velopment and, 40
Matrix training
    element combinations and, 270–271,
        274
    element sequences and, 272–274
    recombinative generalization and
        in children with mental retardation,
        318–324
        see also Environmental input
Meaning(s)
    analysis of, arbitrary stimulus equiva-
        lence and, 266
    of events, communication through so-
        cial referencing, *see* Social refer-
        encing
    shared, 7–8
Meaningful Use of Speech Scale
    (MUSS), 233
Mental retardation
    generalized language learning in chil-
        dren with, structuring environ-
        mental input for facilitation of,
        see Environmental input, struc-
        turing of
    prelinguistic intervention and, re-
        questing and, 50
    prelinguistic–linguistic relationship
        and, 42
        see also Down syndrome
Milieu teaching
    development of, 17
    in parent-implemented intervention,
        65–67, 77
        see also Parent-implemented inter-
        vention
    in prelinguistic intervention, 46–49
    social context and, 21
Modeling, in observational learning,
    mental retardation and, 324–326

Morphemes, plural, mental retardation and, 319
MUSS, see Meaningful Use of Speech Scale
"Mutual substitutability," 264

Natural languages, syntactic component of, 272
Natural social contexts, language intervention in, 143–144
Naturalistic approaches
  development of, 17
  learning through augmented means and, 97, 100
  social context and, 21
  see also Milieu teaching
Neurologic research, 383–384
Nonsymbolic communication skills, extant, influence on learning through augmented means, 96
Nonverbal message, linguistic mapping of, language development and, 40
Nonvocal language systems, development of, 14–15
Novel Name–Nameless Category (N3C) principle, 304–309
  fast-mapping and, 305–307
  implications of, 305–309
  similar onset of related cognitive principle and, 307–309
N3C principle, see Novel Name–Nameless Category principle

Object labels
  early, see Early object labels
  non-nouns treated as, 290–291
Object Scope, principle of, 290–294
  facilitators of, 292–294
  implications of, 290–291
  limitation of, 294
Object sorting task, spontaneous, 308
Objectives
  embedded in daily activities, 21–22, 23
Observational learning, 324–326
Operating principles
  early object labels and, 288
  see also Early object labels

Novel Name–Nameless Category (N3C) principle, 304–309
principle of Categorical Scope, 301–304
principle of Extendibility, 295–301
principle of Object Scope, 290–294
Ostensive gestures, comprehension and production of, 292
Outcome measurement, SAL and, 89–90

Parent(s)
  behaviors of, changes resulting from prelinguistic intervention, 52–53
  of children with Down syndrome
    perspective on speech and language abilities, 335–354
    questionnaire for, 356–362
  concerns of
    anatomic issues, 371
    about computer technology, 371
    dissemination of research findings, 371
    generalization promotion approaches, 368
    judgment as dysfunctional versus functional family, 368–369
    lack of carryover, 367–368
    lack of established protocols, 369–370
    neglect of social language behaviors, 368
    overemphasis on articulation, 367
    about phonics, 372
    sensitivity to, 372–373
    short-term versus long-term objectives, 369
    supplemental therapy, 368–369
    therapeutic options, 369
    third-party payments, 371–372
    underemphasis on aspects of speech intelligibility, 368
  interaction style of
    prelinguistic intervention and, 52–53
    see also Parent–child interaction
  involvement of
    ecological perspective and, 19–20
    history of, 15
    importance of, 22

Parent(s)—*continued*
 see also Parent-implemented intervention
 linguistic input of, language development facilitation through, 40–41
 perspectives of, 365–373
  children with Down syndrome and, 335–354, 365–373
  perceived limitations of speech-language intervention, 366
 responsiveness of, social aspects of environment and, 72
 see also Communication partners; Family
Parent–child interaction
 responsive, 76–77
 transactional model of, 39–42, 54
Parent-implemented intervention, 63–82
 corollary changes resulting from, 81
 effectiveness of, 67–68
 environmental system implications for, 70–75
 hybrid model for, 75–78
 rationale for, 63–64
 research on, 64–70
  conceptual limitations of, 69
  empirical limitations of, 67–68
  future directions in, 78–82
  methodological limitations of, 67–69
Part H of PL 99-457, prelinguistic intervention and, 35
Participation
 social routines and, prelinguistic intervention and, 51–52
 see also Interaction
Partners, *see* Communication partners; Parent(s)
Peer(s)
 inclusion of, 20
  social environment and, 24
 see also Social *entries*
Peer interactions
 children with handicaps and, 149–150
 effects of language impairment on, 145–147
 peer-mediated interventions to increase, 166–169
 social communication in, 161–162
Peer-mediated interventions, 159–181
 benefits of, 165–168

direct instruction approach to teaching desired behaviors and, 176–177
 future research on, recommendations for, 180–181
 to increase peer social-communicative interactions, 166–169, 171–172
 individualized instruction and, 173–174
 initial participants in, selection of, 172–173
 instruction for nondisabled children in, 174–176
 maintenance and generalization program with, 177–180
 model of, 169–180
 modeling, children with mental retardation and, 324–326
Phonology
 components of, 231–232
 CPSIT and, 229–230
 defined, 231
Physical features, stimulus-class membership based on, 246–247
PL 94-142, legislative-legalistic shift with, 18
PL 99-457, *see* Education of the Handicapped Act Amendments of 1986
Play, importance of, development of concept of, 17–18
Plural morphemes, mental retardation and, 319
Pointing, Object Scope and, 292
Practitioners
 parent perceptions of, 366
 researchers and, dialogue between, 26
 sensitivity of, 372–373
 see also Teachers
Pragmatic form, social function versus, 108–109
Prelinguistic communication, 49–52
 defined, 35–36
 intervention in, *see* Prelinguistic intervention
 linguistic communication and
  child-driven models of, 37–39
  relationship between, 36–43
  transition from, to linguistic communication, 36–37
Prelinguistic intervention, 35–56

current studies of, 43–44
evaluation of, 49–53
linguistic variables targeted by,
   49–52
milieu teaching in, 46–49
practical implications of, 54–55
research implications of, 53–54
specific techniques for, 44–46
Primary interventions, enhancement of,
   parent-implemented intervention
   and, 80–81
Primitive acts, for expression of initial
   communicative functions, 119,
   120
Printed words, recognition of, SAL
   and, 93
Project FACTT, 100
Prompts
   fading of, time-delay, 124
   in matrix training, see Matrix training
   in milieu teaching, 47–48
      for prelinguistic intervention, 48
   see also Cues

QUEST, see Teacher/Parent Questionnaire
Questionnaire, for parents of children
   with Down syndrome, 356–362

Reading ability, Down syndrome and,
   341, 346
Receptive language skills
   Down syndrome and, 341, 342
   influences of, on language learning
      through augmented means,
      95–96
Recombinative generalization, 271,
   318–324
   constraints on, 274–275
Referencing, commenting episodes and,
   50
Referential acts, for expression of initial
   communicative functions,
   119–120
Referential symbols, social regulative
   symbols and, 98
Referents, 128–129
   for children's earliest words, 291
      facilitative linguistic input and,
      293–294

new, spontaneous extension of word
   to, 295–296
range of, restriction of, 294
Reflexivity, tests for, 264
Reinforcement, differential
   conditional discrimination and, 252
   see also Matrix training
Relational frames, stimulus equivalence
   and, 265
Relational properties, stimulus control
   by, 259–261
Repair strategy, in interaction maintenance, 124–125
Requesting
   defined, 49–50
   prelinguistic intervention and, 49–50
   social referencing and, 192
Research
   on affect and autism, recommenda-
      tions for future, 217–218
   agenda for, child-based strategies
      and, 390
   application and, enhancement of in-
      terface between, 26
   on augmentative systems
      future agenda, 100–101
      implications for practice, 99–100
      see also System for Augmenting
         Language (SAL)
   cross-domain and cross-level studies
      in, 382–384
   dissemination of findings, parent con-
      cerns about, 371
   on early object label acquisition, fu-
      ture directions in, 311–312
   on parent-implemented intervention,
      64–70
      future directions in, 78–82
   on peer-mediated interventions,
      recommendations for future,
      180–181
   on prelinguistic communication inter-
      vention, 43–44, 53–54
   on prelinguistic–linguistic communi-
      cation relationship, 40–41,
      42
   on selection-based communication
      systems, recommendations for
      future, 277–279
   on speech and language abilities of
      children with Down syndrome,
      337–347

Research—*continued*
on speech intelligibility tests, future directions in, 235–237
on structuring of environmental input
clinical implications of, 329–330
future directions in, 330–331
Responding
discriminative, 320
relational, arbitrarily applicable, 265
sequential, teaching strategies for, 274
Response class, 319–320
see also Stimulus-class analysis
Responsive interaction, in parent-implemented intervention, 76–77
Responsiveness
adult
language development and, 40, 45
social aspects of environment and, 72
child, effects on environment, 73
to emotion in others, autism and, 213–215
Responsivity, contingent, 72
in prelinguistic intervention, 44–45
Routines
interactive, learners who may benefit from, 106–108
social, in prelinguistic intervention, 45, 51–52

SAL, *see* System for Augmenting Language
SALT, *see* Systematic Analysis of Language Transcripts
Scaffolded modeling, in prelinguistic intervention, 45
Selection-based communication systems, 244, 276–277
element combinations in, 270–271
element sequences in, 272–274
functional communication using, 266–269
rationale for, in social context, 244–245
see also Stimulus-class analysis
Sentences, length of, language development and, 40
Sequence-class membership, recombinative generalization based on, constraints on, 274–275

Sequential responding, teaching strategies for, 274
Sequential selections, stimulus class and, 272–274
Severe disabilities
initial communicative repertoire and, 105–132
see also Initial communicative repertoire
language instructional approaches and, 86–87
naturalistic approaches and, 22–23
SAL and
integration into society and, 99
potential for achievement with, 100
see also Disabilities; *specific type*
Shared meanings, 7–8
Siblings
in milieu teaching, 65–66
see also Family
SICS, *see* Social Interactive Coding System
Sidman's equivalence tests, 264
Sign language
Down syndrome and, 341, 344–345, 352
see also Gestures
SLI, *see* Specific language impairments
Social acceptability, forms of communication and, 120
Social bias, language impairment and, 147–149
Social communication
bases of, 7
effective, requirements for, 3–4
enhancement of, 3–9
peer-mediated interventions and, 159–181
see also Peer-mediated interventions
role of, in peer interactions, 161–162
Social competence
development of, trend toward emphasis on, 16–17
partners' perceptions of, SAL and, 99
Social components of environment, 71–72
Social consequences, of language impairment, 145–149, 150–152
intervention implications of, 152–155
Social context(s), 21
natural, language intervention in, 143–144

selection-based systems in, rationale
for, 244–245
Social emotions, complex, autism and,
215–217
Social function
pragmatic form versus, 108–109
see also Communicative functions
Social interactions, 139–156
all phases of, use of communicative
behavior in, 122–127
cognitive disabilities and, 85–86
with individual children, 154–155
intervention setting and, 153–154
see also Interaction; Peer entries
Social Interactive Coding System
(SICS), 145–147
Social referencing, 187–197
affect and, behavior regulation and,
188–189
as interaction, 194–196
medium versus message and,
192–193
skills for facilitation of, 190–192
Social regulative symbols, 98
Social routines, in prelinguistic intervention, 45, 51–52
Social status, language and, 141–142
Social uses of language, 21–23
intelligibility and, 224
Socialization
language as tool of, 141–145
as source of language development,
140–141
Sociolinguistics, communicative competence and, 226
SPEAKING method, in speech intelligibility analysis, 236, 237
Specific language impairments (SLI)
developmental difficulties with, 85
LAP and, 144–145
peer relationships and, 145–147
social consequences of, 151–152
Speech
rapidity of, Down syndrome and, 341
see also Utterances
Speech act analyses, communicative
competence and, 226
Speech comprehension, learning
through augmented means and,
95–96
Speech intelligibility
assessment of, 228–232

research directions for, 235–237
threefold nesting for, 232–235
communicative competence and,
223–237
defined, 224–225
Down syndrome and, 338, 340, 352
role of, in social use of language,
224
SAL achievement and, 93
study of, heuristic model for,
226–227
Speech output device, in SAL, 87,
96–97
see also System for Augmenting Language (SAL)
Speech therapy
Down syndrome and, 347
see also Language intervention
Spontaneity, role of, in conversation initiation, maintenance, and termination, 127–128
Stimulus-class analysis, 243–279
arbitrary classes in, 247–251
basic considerations in, 245–251
communication skill and conceptual
development and, 258–277
rapid stimulus-class development,
258–259
stimulus control by relational properties, 259–261
stimulus equivalence, 262–266
complex stimulus classes and class
interactions in, 269–276
constraints on recombinative generalization and, 274–275
contextual control of arbitrary-class
membership, 275–276
element combinations, 270–271,
274
element sequences, 272–274
in current selection-based communication training, 276–277
feature classes in, 246–247
methodological background of,
251–258
arbitrary matching-to-sample and,
256–257
conditional discrimination in,
251–253
identity matching-to-sample and,
253–255
rationale for, 245

Stimulus-class analysis—*continued*
  research on, recommendations for,
    277–279
  see also Selection-based communica-
    tion systems
Stimulus-class development, rapid,
    258–259
Stimulus control
  by relational properties, 259–261
  response classes and, 319
Stimulus equivalence, 262–266
  crossmodal transfer and, 327–328
Symbol(s)
  acquisition of, augmentative systems
    and, *see* Augmentative systems;
    System for Augmenting Lan-
    guage (SAL)
  first, learning with SAL, 90–92
  use of, available vocabulary and, 98
Symbol combinations, emergence of,
    SAL and, 92
Symbol-system language programs, de-
    velopment of, 14–15
Syntax, natural languages and, 272
Synthetic speech, *see* Speech output de-
    vice
System for Augmenting Language
    (SAL), 87–89
  achievement with
    influences on, 95–99
    in learning first symbols, 90–92
    measurement of, 89–90
    products of, 92–95
  see also Augmentative systems
Systematic Analysis of Language Tran-
    scripts (SALT), 89–90
  CPSIT and, 230
Systems approach, movement toward,
    379–385
  impact on intervention, 384–385

Taxonomies, for describing instrumental
    communicative intents, 109–117
Teachability, assumptions about, in
    1960s, 12
Teacher/Parent Questionnaire (QUEST),
    in SAL, 89
Teachers
  judgments of, language impairment
    effects on, 147–149, 152–153
  see also Practitioners

Time delay, in prelinguistic interven-
    tion, 47, 48
Time-delay prompt fading procedure,
    initiations and, 124
Transactional model, of parent–child in-
    teraction, 39–42, 54
Transfer, crossmodal, 326–329
Transitions, facilitation of, 370
Transitivity, tests for, 264
Transparent input, nontransparent input
    versus, basis for extension and,
    298–300
Trisomy 21, *see* Down syndrome
Turn-taking
  parent-implemented intervention and,
    76
  prelinguistic intervention and, 51–52

Utterances
  actions and, correspondence of,
    128–130
  functions of, 109–117
  parental, length of, 40

VAMs, *see* Vocabulary assessment mea-
    sures
Visual-graphic symbols, in SAL,
    87–88
Visual modalities, speech output de-
    vices versus, 96–97
Visual processing problems, children at
    risk for, protocols and, 370
Vocabulary
  acquisition of, N3C principle and,
    304–309
  available, influence on learning
    through augmented means, 98
  prelinguistic intervention and, 53
  of visual-graphic symbols, in SAL,
    87–88
Vocabulary assessment measures
    (VAMs), in SAL achievement
    measurement, 90
  recognition of printed English words
    and, 93
Vocal imitation
  prelinguistic intervention and, 51
  see also Imitation

Word(s)
  earliest, referents for, 291, 293–294
  printed, recognition of, SAL and, 93
  spontaneous extension of, to new ref-
      erents, 295–296
  see also Vocabulary

Word-recognition intelligibility test,
  228–230

Yoked reversal procedure, in arbitrary
  matching-to-sample, 256–57